Cover: Look into the eyes. You could be looking at your ancestor or ancient relative. Regardless of whether a blood of kinship treks through your veins, at least some of your ancestors probably bore a similar demeanor. A firmness of gaze. Eyes that, because of primitive conditions of the time, had seen ample death at a young age and ample work. Except for the train, no transportation then moved faster than the horse – a horse, which often enough you fed, saddled, and cleaned up after. Sufficient income to be well dressed when required, never a dandy. A vest, suit, and a deliberately displayed pocket watch chain. In a studio chair of suitable style, a tasseled one at that, getting one of the few photographs ever taken of you. Properly speaking, not a photograph at all – it was printed on metal and called a tintype. A photographer could prepare and deliver the finished item to the customer in a few minutes. From about 1865 to 1910, the most popular sizes were in the neighborhood of 2.5" x 3.8," as was the one which was enlarged for this cover. Surely an expert can read the clothing and chair to better date the picture and status of the man, but let's pull 1880 out of thin air and out of equally thin air say this man was at the 80th income and wealth percentile. With the spreadsheets and data used in this book, an estimated inflation adjusted annual income for this fellow would have been about $7,300, and his net worth may well have been about $45,700. Whether you wish to look to history or to the present, we wish you the very best in your journey through the following pages. By the way, this fellow is believed to have lived in the Appalachian Mountains of Southwest Virginia – a fortunate person to live in such a nice place.

And on the rear cover there is a couple about whom you may conjecture on your own. Their image too came from a tintype.

The cover shows real people of the kind that have existed throughout time. From this starting point we go on to see how income and wealth distribution now influence us common folk and the economies we live in.

Distribution of Lives

The Income Maldistribution Plague 2012
The Complete Unabridged Edition

Ike Jeanes

DiLives
Publishing

Published in the USA by
Dilives Inc.
Dilives Publishing
Dilives.com

ISBN-10: 0985665602 (pbk.)
ISBN-13: 978-0-9856656-0-9 (pbk.)

ISBN-10: 0985665610 (hbk.)
ISBN-13: 978-0-9856656-1-6 (hbk.)

Library of Congress Control Number: 2012945929
Library of Congress Subject Headings, Cataloging Data:

1. United States -- Economic conditions -- 21st century.
2. Income distribution.
3. Income distribution -- United States.
4. Equality – United States.
5. Income distribution -- History -- 20th century.
6. Income distribution -- United States -- History.
7. Wealth -- United States.

Summary: This work reveals a new method for viewing and understanding income distribution from bottom to top. It illustrates the profound adverse impact of maldistribution on individuals and the economy as a whole.
Suggested Cataloging: HC110.I5 J43 2012.

In Memory of

Frances Jeanes

Contents

Handy Tips Concerning the Ebook Edition

The ebook and pbook are designed to work together. Each graph has an identification number that corresponds with the print version's page number. For example, graph-15 will occur on page 15 of the printed book. Since graph numbers correspond with the printed book's page numbers, you often can easily identify where corresponding passages occur. The object is to be able to use the two together and to be able to cite passages without great difficulty. Similarly you can maintain continuity among users having a variety of e-Readers.

If you are new to ebooks and have read primarily fiction, you may not have noticed that you can ZOOM into a full page view of a graph to see its details. Move the cursor to a point within the graph and select it (or employ the particular zoom technique that your e-Reader uses).

Endnotes are at end of the text. You can jump to an endnote by clicking on its reference number. Footnotes are placed roughly where they would have occurred in the printed copy.

If you have a color ebook reader, you will be pleased to see that all graphs use colored graph lines.

To have the work on ebook is nice. But turning the pages at your library or on your own hardcopy is the deluxe way to thumb through the graphs and quickly get the full picture.

The version you have in hand is *The Complete Unabridged Edition*. The short *Condensed Edition* does not contain Chapters 4, 5, 7, 8 and 9.

Hopefully you will find the printed book, the ebook, and the Dilives website (which has downloadable income-distribution spreadsheets and various addenda) to be useful.

CH. 1

GETTING STARTED

How am I doing?
How are we doing?
How are they doing?

Whether you are at the highest reaches of society or at the lowest, you will see how income and wealth distributions alter your life. They form the vital meeting point between personal and national economics. Once we see their shape, we can see how people at all times have fared, whether it be in 1776 or in the present. On this topic, the following pages deliver greater precision than has been previously available.

Over coffee, tea, or your liquor of choice, you can speak with greater confidence. Notwithstanding more than a passing interest in this area, I could not fathom the story until the data took form. A form far clearer than I have seen before. A worldview forever changed.

Income-distribution numbers are such a disappointing collection of dubious, obscure, and insufficient data that the high-powered computer that I hear humming in the background has been grinding along for four days and nights without pause just to deliver a basic printout. Such slugging along calls out that the subject matter is not obvious.

The economic language commonly used to describe income distribution has prevented us from arriving at solutions that can be easily calculated. This book shows how you can arrive at solutions. It quickly becomes clear that the first need is to dispense with technical language. The most reliable gauge for income distribution in your nation or in your workplace is highly democratic: the percentage of total income that the bottom 60% (the clear majority) receives, abbreviated as the MAJ. This reference point shows how well corporations and nations treat the majority.

At its extremes, the MAJ *(to repeat it: the percentage of income received by 60% of the population)* can range from about 48% on the high end to about 9% on the low end. Yes, nations have existed under such widely different schemes. The worldwide historical median settles down to about 33% for the MAJ.

MAJ33, 33%MAJ, and 1/3MAJ all mean the same (pronounced $\text{MAJ}_{\text{ority}}$).*

At the time of the American Revolutionary War, the MAJ stood at about 30% in the United States and exceeded 35% in the New England States. In Europe it was stuck in the 18% to 21% range. The greater degree of fairness and liberty in the USA was a potent motivator, intellectually and economically. However, initial U.S. income equality slowly eroded until the era preceding the Great Depression when the MAJ hovered in the neighborhood of 25% in the U.S. and many other nations. The great story is that many nations, including the United States, completely reversed maldistribution by the 1950s and continued to progress toward even greater equality until the 1970s, when a few nations, including the United States, slowly moved back to pre-Great Depression levels.[1]

To change an income distribution is to change the distribution of incentives. When you reduce incentives at the MAJ in order to provide disproportional compensation at the top, the character and culture of 60% of the population changes. This book argues that maldistribution diminishes incentives for more than half of the population. It does the stockholder no good. It does the customer no good. It does the company no good. It does the nation no good.

The data is uncomplicated and straightforward. Using MAJ data is easy enough that you need not wait for governments or economists. On your own, you can easily see how changes in income and wealth distributions influence you, your family, your nation, and your world. Without information at the level of specificity provided in the spreadsheets that come with this book, it would be impossible to competently manage an economy

---

* On a few occasions, when the context implies, the expression MAJ alone without a number refers to the people in the 60% majority rather than the distribution. In this book "the majority" refers to the 60% majority.

for a democracy or to comprehend your economic place within the democracy.

Income distribution is a cultural decision. In all of recent history, highly successful nations, including the United States, have performed well when income distribution was equitable. The market economy does not necessitate maldistribution. The vast majority of high per capita income nations now have distributions roughly equal to or higher than MAJ33. Just as an equitable distribution was attractive to our forefathers, it is attractive for us. However, a 25% MAJ is a threat, and a practice.

There is a cautionary tale here that leftist revolutionaries and rightwing politicians should be well schooled in. Extreme income distributions, left or right, do not work. *The unambiguous position in this book, as will be shown in the data, is that a MAJ significantly exceeding 36% does reduce incentives for highly capable people to such an extent that the wellbeing of 60% of the population is imperiled because of a failure to adequately remunerate some of its most productive citizens. A 25% or lower MAJ is catastrophic. A MAJ in the neighborhood of 33% is reliable and appropriate.*

Albeit the cry "1/3 for the MAJ" or to state it in workaday language – "1/3 of the income for 60% of the population" – may strike you (as it did me) as being grossly unfair, revolutionaries at the right and left would find themselves to be of greatest benefit to their constituents by marching under that single uncompromising and consistent banner. The problem is a dicey one. In either a democracy or an effective market economy, an uncertain balance must be struck between sufficient compensation for the 60% majority (so that they can live productive and fulfilling lives and be rewarded for their essential work), and adequate income for those of exceptionally high ability who need to be compensated for their education, conscientiousness, responsibility, inventiveness, value to society, and sometimes difficult and hard work. Your view may be different. Examine the data. See what you think.

It is inappropriate to focus on redistribution. The focus is on giving people a realistic and honest chance, from birth to death. The primary wrong is that, at all levels, maldistribution distorts the vital relationships between people necessary for an economy to thrive. That is where the damage is done.

The USA does not now suffer from being a "mature economy." It suffers from being a maldistributed one. The market economy suffers greatly at the hands of maldistribution. Maldistribution in any nation has broadly reaching adverse tentacles – the bigger the nation, the more adverse the global impact. More positively, the long throw of United States and global history shows that prudent distributions in market economies cause nations to thrive. Maldistribution anywhere requires sensible attention and correction.

Income distribution fundamentally influences how economies perform. For too long, serious thinkers have viewed the objective of changing income distribution as allowing compassion to interfere with economic process. It has been viewed as a laudable objective to keep the topic confined to malcontents, agitators, and other undesirables outside of mainstream thinking. That view is wrong. Every citizen, every economist, and every businessperson needs to know how income distribution works.

Structure.

This work is in two parts: the words you have in your hands and separate data in spreadsheet form, which you can download and use as you see fit.[2] The spreadsheet data show outcomes produced for individuals across the spectrum: 1) at different rates of economic growth; and 2) under various conditions of income and wealth distribution. To disproportionately emphasize any of these components without taking all of them into consideration is a monstrous wrong and reliably leads to unfortunate outcomes.

When you look closely at real world income distributions, you will see variations about the trend lines. They plainly exist. The variations do not tell the story of maldistribution. The small disputatious points along the way are of little importance. The story is about enormous influences that occur because of changes in the central tendencies as maldistribution progresses or is reversed. Characteristic shapes of the curves, when implemented as they are in the real world, deliver the damages coming from maldistribution. That is the story told here.

Five years ago, I began writing the basic computer program that made this book possible. Time since then has been spent repeatedly improving programs and bringing the work to a point where maldistribution could be adequately discussed.

The spreadsheets include a USA distribution of income and wealth analysis from 1776 to the present. To the extent possible, they also include most nations of the world as far back as there was sufficient data. For nations other than the USA, the spreadsheets mainly include data going back to about 1950. The 235 years of analysis for the USA and the often 60 years for other nations are intended to provide a long-term worldwide scope of the general condition of income distribution and, at a less reliable level, wealth distribution.

It was a great, but not insurmountable, impediment that in many instances important data were unavailable. It was still possible to make inferences and interpolate between known points or mathematically combine data from several sources. I attempted to do this to the best of my ability, honestly, and without bias. There were many judgment calls. In an unknown few I will have been wrong. Those instances can be corrected when new and more complete information becomes available. But, overall, the outcome seems to give a reasonable, broad view of how we and our ancestors fared from the distant reaches of history to the present.

A key spreadsheet accompanying this book contains a sorted lookup table of 400 representative distribution curves based on thousands of income-distribution reports worldwide compiled over the past 50 years. When you hear someone mention a MAJ25 or MAJ33 (or any other specified distribution), attempt to picture in your mind the shape of the distribution curve. You can plot these curves using the lookup-table spreadsheet to see their precise shape. And you will often see these curves throughout this book. From them you can get a clear view of income distribution from bottom to top.

The lookup table shows income distributions for people along the complete percentile-scarcity scale from lowest to highest income earners (as soon will be shown). This is the go-to list for viewing central tendencies throughout all possible income distributions. Graphs in the upcoming chapter were developed from this lookup table. You too can use the table to make graphs and to answer your own questions. In most instances, the table is sufficient to describe principal features of most distribution scenarios. It is especially useful for illustrating the influence of changes in income distribution over time for people of the same ability at high scarcity levels. An abbreviated lookup table is duplicated in the Appendix.

A motivated few may want to use the data to reverse-engineer the income-distribution programs. That's fine and presumably advantageous. If you like, you may copy and publish graphs used in this book. A citation would be appreciated.[3]

A few clarifying remarks and calculations are included within reduced-sized square brackets. When you see square brackets, you can safely ignore them, unless you want to delve deeper than customarily necessary.

Kinds of distribution.

Distributions come in three distinct forms: the static case, the transitional case, and the wealth case.

The Static Case:

The static case shows how a nation is distributing income now. As long as income distribution remains unchanged, the saying "A rising tide floats all boats" applies. This is to say that at all points on the income-distribution curve, people at all strata tend to receive an equal income increase when average per capita income grows, no matter how equitable or adverse the distribution may be. For example, at a real per capita income growth rate of 1.5% (after inflation) substantially everyone's standard of living doubles each 46.6 years [2= (1+1.5%)^46.6].

The Transitional Case:

The transitional income-distribution case (such as going from a 33% to a 25% MAJ), which has been in progress in the USA since the 1970s, presents entirely different conditions. In the USA, it is now the most damaging of the three forms. For the MAJ, the transitional case adds to the insult of receiving less income, the pestilence of reducing or negating income growth. With the maldistribution transition, even when average per capita income grows, "the boats don't float evenly." People at the bottom find their incomes decrease or grow at a slow rate. Those at the high end of the curve often find their incomes growing three or more times faster than the average per capita income. Because of this great range of influence, average economic growth rates reported in the news usually have little to do with how individual families fare, whether they are at the high or low end of the spectrum.

The Wealth Case:

Lastly, there is distribution of wealth. Only when necessary will this book discuss it. The focus of this book is on INCOME distribution, not WEALTH distribution. They are vastly different. Income distribution is about getting out of the starting gate. The wealth data I have developed is not quite ready for prime time, so it is relegated primarily to spreadsheets.

Notwithstanding, a great deal of effort was spent to develop USA wealth curves that approximated known conditions during the past three decades. For earlier dates, the data is as accurate as I am now able to provide. With time, better data is apt to become available.

The Percentile-Scarcity Scale and the X$.

Within income-distribution analysis, there is a subtle and surprising point of transformative impact. There is no zero percentile. There is no 100th percentile. Conventional percentiles are limited to 99 points: 1 to 99. This is perfectly satisfactory in most instances for discussing ranking. But in all income distributions, the total of the parts must sum to 100%. Thus the conventional 99-point percentile system has an unintended adverse consequence. It does not cover the full 100 points (100%).

By using a 100-point system for income distribution instead of a 99 point system, there is a fortunate convergence. Each of the 100 points simultaneously tells two things: First, and most obviously, it tells the percentage of total income received at each point. Second, and presumably more important for most readers, the same number tells the X$ (pronounced "X" "Dollar"), which is the income multiple relative to average income.

For example, if the 95th percentile received **2.7** percent of total income, a person within the 95th percentile would also receive **2.7** times the average income (the X$). That makes the business of understanding incomes and distribution simple – the numbers are the same for the first 100 points. The majority of the data in the spreadsheets are shown in an X$ configuration. Let's look at the first and second features of the X$ in greater detail.

First feature:

With the 100-point method, the income multiples for any size group of interest up to the Top1% can be summed to determine the percentage of income earned in any subsection you want to investigate.* And you can precisely see how anyone's income stands relative to any other person. It becomes abundantly clear that the 100-point system delivers the message: *Income distribution and your income position relative to the average income are precisely the same thing.*

---

* A technical point: Observe that points numbered 100 and higher are ranks within the Top1%, as are the Lower½% and the Upper½%, and cannot be summed. Their sum is already contained within the Top1%.

In conversation, the difference between the 99 and 100-point ranking systems is slight. So, for simplicity, when using the word "percentile," this book will always refer to the 100-point system unless it explicitly states "conventional percentile" (the 99-point system).

You will notice that the 100-point ranking system is a simple percentage system where, for example, the numbers 1, 50, 95 refer respectively to the person at the 1%, 50% and 95% points.

Second feature:

The X$ is similar to the way high income is described in the media, where a CEO may be described, for example, as earning 200 times the income of the average citizen (a 200X$). The principal difference in the spreadsheets and here is that you have X$ for everyone from bottom to top, not just your CEO.

The X$ always indicates the multiple, which when multiplied by the average income, gives the income at that point. This applies whether your income is high or low. Like a balloon, you narrow it in one place, it becomes larger in another. The X$ indicates your relative standing in the economy. When your standing is unjustifiably reduced, you have good reason to be concerned.

To give hypothetical examples: In a country where $50,000 was the average income, an X$ of 10 would indicate that the annual income at this level would be $500,000 [$500,000= $50,000x10]; a 20X$ would be $1,000,000 [$1,000,000= $50,000x20]. A fractional X$ of 0.5 would denote a $25,000 income [$25,000= $50,000x0.5].*

The X$ method makes it easy to convert any currency into whatever currency you are comfortable using, whether it be dollars, yuan, yen, euros, pounds, pesos, et cetera. It also accommodates for changes in income over time. Whether the data is 50 years old or resides 50 years in the future, the same technique applies.

Or, to say it another way: The X$ is just a different form of currency. It cuts across nations and classes. It expresses how many average incomes you are earning a year. Some of those at the top might crudely argue, pay

---

* The hypothetical $50,000 average income will be used for purposes of example when dollar amounts are used in the upcoming chapter.

me a 1,000 people* a year (1,000X$) and I'll be perfectly happy. Such sentiments are not as remote as you might imagine. In the modern USA, about one-in-4-million people are at this income level.[4]

Combining the two:

Throughout this book, the Percentile-Scarcity Scale is used on the horizontal graph axis to show income from lowest to highest rank. It starts with percentages and then at the 100th position, switches to scarcity. To reiterate its construction, the scale shows percentile rankings when the number is less than 100. But when it reaches 100 or higher, it denotes scarcity. To see the Percentile-Scarcity Scale in action, glance at graph-12 (page 12; observe that graph and page numbers will always be the same). In graph-12 a low number like 95 indicates the 95th percentile, but a high number like 125 denotes the income for a person at the one-in-125-income level. Similarly 2,000 indicates a person at the one-in-2,000-scarcity level; and 1,000,000 (had it been on the graph) would have shown a person at the one-in-a-million level.

To differentiate the Top1% from one-in-a-hundred, which is a single point within the Top1% (as are all other numbers greater than 100), this book and its spreadsheets will always state "Top1%," and the simple number "100" will always refer to one-in-a-hundred.

Using MAJ income to evaluate nations.

Knowing these simple relationships illustrates the irrelevancy of average per capita GDP data, as generally reported. When evaluating nations, per capita GDP is reported as if it were the gold standard for measuring the wellbeing of an economy. If your interests are democratic, that would be far from the truth. You need to look at how each individual fares from bottom to top. The X$ puts this information in your hands.

Using MAJ designations to measure income-distribution characteristics makes it easy to perform back-of-the-napkin calculations for how the economic wellbeing of the majority changes when income distribution changes. You do not need reams of data.

Once the MAJ is known, the average income for the 60% majority can be easily calculated. Just use this formula: The average X$ for the majority = MAJ/60. The "60" refers to the 60 points represented by the majority.

---

* Or, "average incomes" if you prefer.

For example, a $45,000 average income at a MAJ25 distribution means an average $18,750 income for the majority [At a MAJ25, $18,750= $45,000*25/60]. And, in case it should cross your mind, at MAJ33 it would have been $25,000 instead of $18,750 [$25,000= $45,000 * 33.333/60].[5]

For evaluating nations, this method is far more useful than GDP per capita for telling how the majority is doing because it takes into account income distribution [Average MAJ income = GDP per capita * MAJ/60]. *Average MAJ income simultaneously measures economic vigor and income distribution.*

This formula plainly drives home the point that when economists and commentators freely talk about average income without adjusting for maldistribution, they are ignoring the wellbeing of the majority of the population. Many governments also do not seem to care much either. They often ambiguously, infrequently, and wrongly report income distribution, even in major nations.

CH. 2

A WORLD OF DIFFERENCE: one third or one fourth

Basic graphs of the 1/3 to 1/4 transition.

Many of us know about the Forbes 400, which gives a focused view of the wealth of individuals at the top in the USA. What is provided in this book and its spreadsheets is a broad estimate of income and wealth for everyone. At current population levels worldwide, I am unable to resist the temptation to glibly say the "MAJ 4 billion" [4.2= 7*60%]. To carry it to the next level, why be more attentive to the Forbes 400 than a MAJ 4 billion?

In this light, the work departs from a history told for and by the victors. Instead it finds its heart in a deliberately balanced view of everyone's position on the income scale. Regardless of the distribution curve or the transition between distribution curves, there are discernible threads. We can see their influence as we move from equitable MAJ distributions to maldistributed MAJs.

To draw focus to the influence of the downward transition toward maldistribution, the move from a 33% to a 25% MAJ over 30 years will be the case illustrated in this chapter. As seen in the next two graphs (#12 & #14), income levels are expressed as a multiple of the average income using an X$ designation.

The differences between MAJ33 and MAJ25 income distributions are so great that they cannot be easily represented on a single graph. In the following graph-12, we start with the upper 5% of income earners comparing earnings on the MAJ25 and MAJ33 distribution curves. The MAJ of 33%

income remains in approximately the same range as at a MAJ of 25% at the low end of this graph.

#12

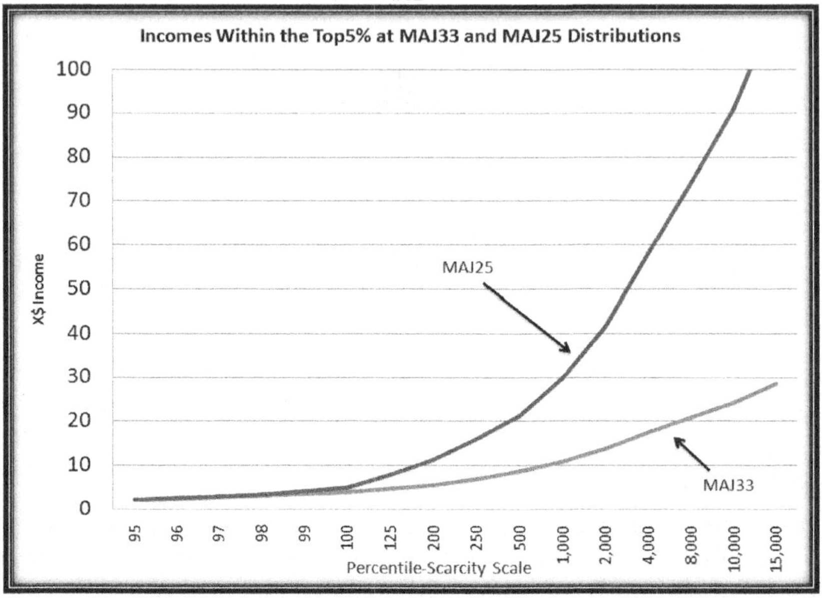

But as scarcity increases, the incomes on the two curves diverge widely. By the time a person reaches the one-in-10,000-income-scarcity level, the income at MAJ33 is a 24.3X$ and the income at MAJ25 is a 90.7X$. To familiarize you with the process, this would mean that a person classified at an ability equivalent to a one-in-a-thousand-scarcity level would tend to earn $1,213,000 at MAJ33 versus $4,537,000 at MAJ25 [$1,213,000= $50,000 x 24.3 and $4,537,000= $50,000 x 90.7]. In short, a person of the same ability earns vastly different amounts based on the prevailing income-distribution culture.*

Keeping the MAJ share of income low has substantial advantages for those at the top. Those advantages progressively increase as scarcity increases. Keep in mind that a person who truly possesses economically desirable abilities that are so rare as to be present in only in one in 10,000 people – presumably by his or her merit – is contributing greatly to how

---

* Using this same method as in the first graph-11 but looking explicitly at U.S. history in the spreadsheets (not in the graphs here), a person at the one-in-a-million level of income ability in the USA would have tended to earn roughly 128 times as much as the "average income person" in 1977, but in 2007, would have tended to earn about 661 times as much.

the economy and society operates. The objective is not to begrudge that person high compensation. However, maldistribution results in overcompensating all of those high scarcity levels, whether they possess economically desirable characteristics or not. This is seen in the above graph-12 by the difference between the lower and upper curve.

Maldistribution gains accrue primarily to the Top1%, most particularly the upper half percent. To continually say "upper half percent" and "lower half of the Top1%" exercises the tongue excessively. To get around it, the two halves of the Top1% are referred to as the "Lower½%" and the "Upper½%," notwithstanding that those in the "Lower½%" usually do quite well.

Whenever you think of the Top1%, keep in mind that the dividing point between the Lower½%, and Upper½% is the one-in-200-scarcity level [scarcity= 1/(1-percent probability); 200= 1/(1-95.5%); Upper½%= 100%-95.5%]. The same number of people within the Top1% exist on each side of this point. The numerous points within the Upper½% displayed in the graphs serve to show the range of income within the Upper½%.

The teeter point.

Now that we have looked at the upper portion of the curves, we will turn our attention to the lower portion. But before doing so let's consider how analyzing income-distribution curves differs from most forms of economic analysis where you need to control for various factors and you usually need to qualify your analysis with a variety of hedging statements.

In a pleasant contrast to ambiguity, the nice point with income-distribution curves is that you do not need to control for other components because the data is already isolated to reflect income distribution alone. Whether you are a labor union member, a CEO, an economist, or an interested citizen, you can easily reference the spreadsheet lookup table and compare different MAJ-defined income-distribution curves.* With simple access to the curves, you can speak with great authority, even when you don't have economic training. Often you can make broad categorical statements when discussing income distribution that are not possible in other forms of economic analysis, as you will see from time to time in the following pages. Graph-14, for example, gives a definitive picture.

---

*My curves and curves based on other studies are included in the spreadsheets. The Congressional Budget Office data (first released in Oct. 2011), in my view, presents the most credible full-range U.S. 1979-2006 data now available, as discussed in greater detail in the Appendix.

In it, the wedge-like separation between the curves at all points lower than the 92nd percentile shows the loss sustained as a direct result of going from a MAJ33 to a MAJ25. The bottom 92% lose so that the top 8% can gain.

#14

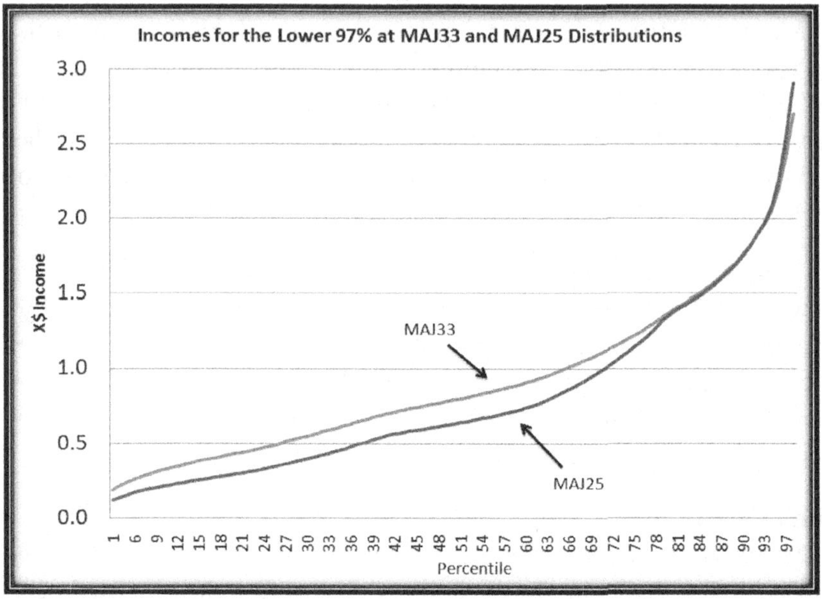

Think of the old seesaw. In income distribution, the teeter point is like a seesaw fulcrum. On one side you have the rich and near-rich. On the other side you have everyone else. The teeter point can occur anywhere between the 82nd and 92nd percentile. Because of its centrality we will often refer to the teeter point when discussing income distributions. The invariant rule is that those beneath the prevailing teeter point are harmed by maldistribution. Those above it benefit.

There is a zone of indifference where income-distribution changes have slight influence. If we take a 6% income change as an arbitrary threshold sufficient to be significant, then those from about the 76th to 96th percentile (1/5th of the population) would be indifferent to changes produced by transitions in income distribution. As you can see in the above graph-14, the two curves are practically indistinguishable within this range. The sum of the incomes for this 1/5th of the nation would remain approximately constant at 34.8% during a move from MAJ33 to MAJ25.

Given that the 34.8% income share for this 1/5th of the population is greater than the income share (33% or 25%) for the 60% majority (either at

MAJ33 or MAJ25), this mid-region can be a political status quo deadweight that can readily align with the highest earners who receive the huge bounty from maldistribution. This midrange mainly comprises highly responsible people. If they extrapolate from their own income conditions, they are apt to be disinclined to take great interest in income-distribution issues.

Notwithstanding that the damage becomes increasingly intense beneath the 72nd percentile, the 60% majority is apt to face daunting opposition at MAJ25 because the zone of indifference is so large (graph-14 and 16). The slim hope for the 60% majority resides in those people within the zone of indifference being concerned about the problem, and those at the top also seeing the impropriety of receiving a disproportionately large share.

A change in income distribution is a society-wide decision to increase incentives for one sector and reduce incentives for another. Explicitly, you cannot increase incentives at any point on the scale without reducing incentives elsewhere because a total income pie must be divided. And it must mathematically sum to 100%.

A maldistribution transition subverts the normally beneficial influence of Adam Smith's "invisible hand" for the narrow purpose of providing advantages for the wealthy alone.*

The following graph-16 shows a large range from those at the bottom up to the one in 200 scarcity point. The MAJ are the first 60 points on the Percentile-Scarcity Scale. As seen in the graph-16, all points in the MAJ (points beneath 61) are having their status reduced at least 18% by moving to MAJ25, and in some instances more than 40%. The influence is not abstract.

Once the MAJ income share plummets to 25 or there about, the 60% majority is no longer a player in the economic system to the degree it once was. The opportunities that allowed it to contribute to the vitality of the nation have been removed. This observation is not overlooked by families. They can see that their parents and grandparents walked with their heads higher and with greater pride – a sense of accomplishment and wellbeing for having been able to contribute a greater share to the nation.

---

* By way of introduction for those of you who are not economists, Adam Smith was one of the great broad-minded figures of the Enlightenment who wrote an influential book, *The Wealth of Nations* (1776). His work illustrated how the market economy, by free interactions of people to buy and sell goods, tended to be of widespread benefit to all. Much economic theory can be traced back to him.

Your income reflects the degree to which you contribute to the economy (GDP), and often by extension to society as a whole – what you build and what you leave behind. The majority in former generations (particularly in the 1950s-1970s in the U.S.) contributed relatively more to society and to the nation than their descendants have had the opportunity to do. The 60% majority experiences it today, as do their children. They have been crushed by a process so tortuously slow that it was barely perceptible, until the damage was done. It was an exercise of poorly performed Bonsai economics – small changes over long periods of time that radically changed the ultimate configuration; an exercise that needs to be reversed.

#16

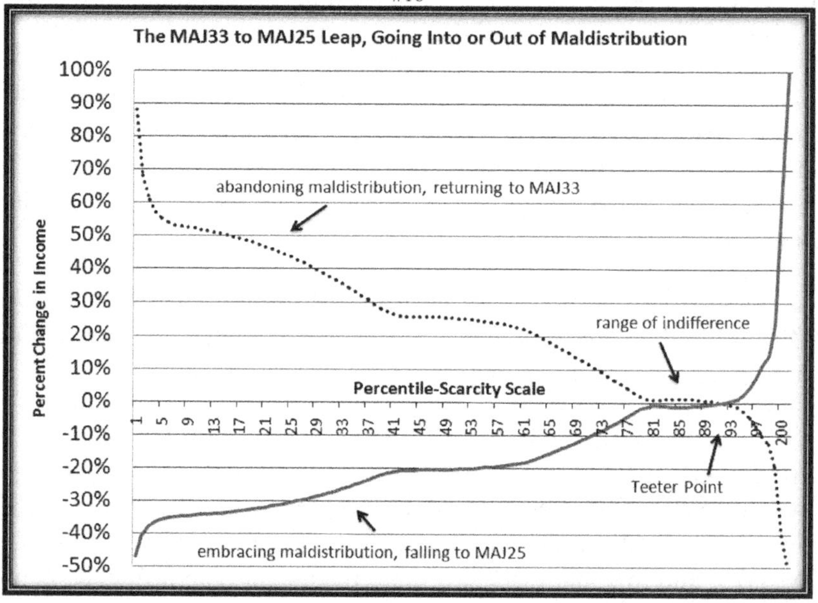

As shown in the graph-16 at all points beneath 60 on the Percentile-Scarcity Scale, abandoning maldistribution would increase the majority's income at least 22%, and for most people in this region, the increase would be considerably greater.

The point should not be lost on the 92% of the population that their income, too, would increase as the conditions at the MAJ improve. The focus on the MAJ carries with it the implicit changes throughout the continuum along the income-distribution curve.

You can DIY (Do It Yourself). To address scenarios of your own, you can develop graphs similar to the above by using the spreadsheet lookup table. The first curve was produced by dividing the MAJ33 curve by the

MAJ25 curve; the second, by dividing the MAJ25 curve by the MAJ33 curve. It's quite easy. No need to wait for governments or economists to do it for you.

Above and beneath the teeter point.

#17

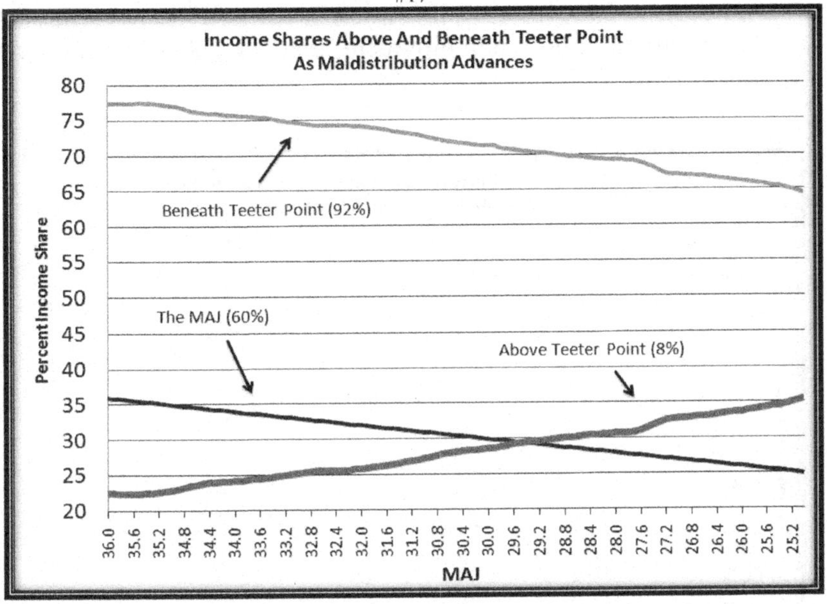

In graph-17, we can see how income shares change above and beneath the teeter point as maldistribution advances. Ninety-two percent of the population lose 10.6% of their income share by going from MAJ33 to MAJ25. At a MAJ 29.5, the upper 8% of the population get the same income share as the bottom 60%. By MAJ25, the upper 8% receive 10.5% more of the income than all of the bottom 60% together.

Unemployment trumped by maldistribution.

There is important work to be done at all levels. The degree to which income is reduced by virtue of moves toward maldistribution results in a loss of status for the 60% majority and all others beneath the teeter point. It reduces the degree to which they are afforded the opportunity to contribute to the economy. Assuming a generation to be about 26 years, the 30-year transition discussed here is slightly longer than a single generation.[6]

Many people living today have never seen a fair distribution. Instead, they are now living with an income distribution that has resulted in their incomes being a fraction of what they should be, as the following graph-18 zooms in to show.

Let's pause and consider the following graph-18 from a different angle. In the news, we hear repeated reports about employment rates. In the 1990s, U.S. unemployment rates looked fine. Yet this era created an economy based on low wages for most workers that sharply contrasted with their formerly better and steadier blue-collar jobs.[7] Often in economic theory and policy, full employment is a guiding mantra; but for the majority, it was maldistribution, not unemployment, that sucked out the lion's share of income.

#18

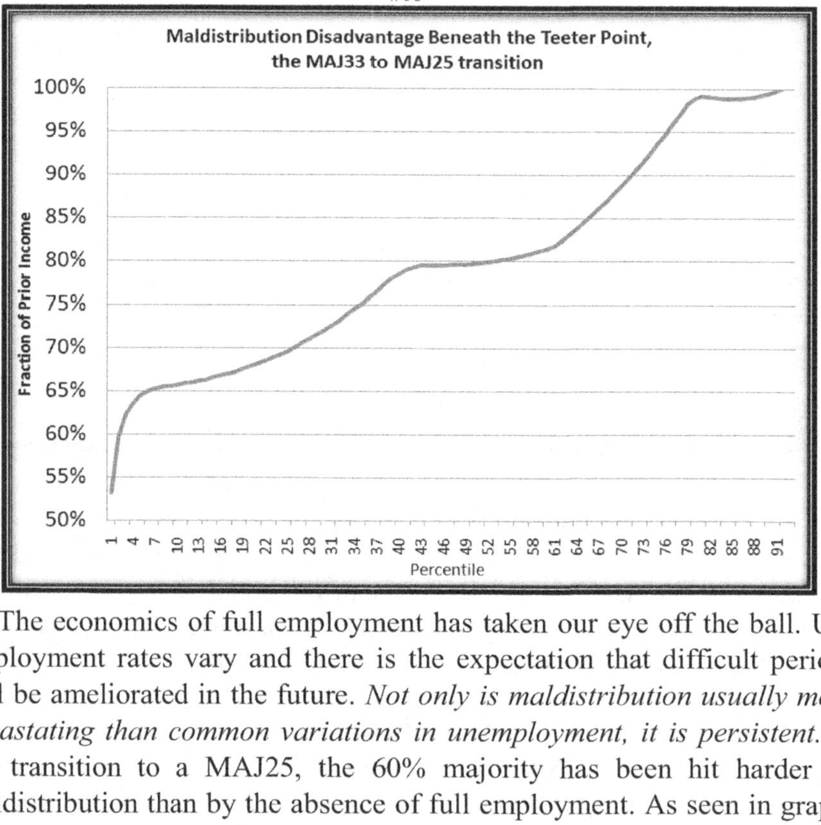

The economics of full employment has taken our eye off the ball. Unemployment rates vary and there is the expectation that difficult periods will be ameliorated in the future. *Not only is maldistribution usually more devastating than common variations in unemployment, it is persistent.* In the transition to a MAJ25, the 60% majority has been hit harder by maldistribution than by the absence of full employment. As seen in graph-18, some members of this class have been trampled.

If we ask ourselves, "Is unemployment the key issue?", perhaps numbers tell a story. A 10% unemployment rate represents a 5.5% increase over customary unemployment [at a structural unemployment* of 4.5%, 10=

* Structural unemployment in the formal sense refers to a mismatch between labor demand and worker skills or location. Frictional unemployment relates a normal time lag between a worker searching for a job and finding one. However, for purposes of this book, I refer to structural unemployment

4.5+5.5]. Using back-of-the-napkin techniques, a 5.5% increased unemployment for the MAJ translates into about a 5.5% loss of income for the MAJ. A MAJ25 *unremittingly and in every year and in every future year* takes away 25% of the income they would have received at MAJ33 [-25%= 25/ 33.333-1]. Which do you prefer – a 5.5% transitory loss in income or a 25% permanent loss in income?

If the economy had stayed at a MAJ33, the 60% majority would have had an income, on average, one third higher than it now is (note the gain of ⅓ is greater than the loss of ¼ because the base was reduced to such a small number). In many instances, the ⅓ gain would have been sufficient to have avoided going heavily into debt, or to raise children so that they had greater advantages, and ____ well, you fill in the blank yourself. A one third higher income would have spelled vast advantages for this class. Just think how an instant one third income raise for the rest of your life would influence you [⅓= 33.3%= 33.333/25-1; -¼= (25/33.3333)-1].

#19

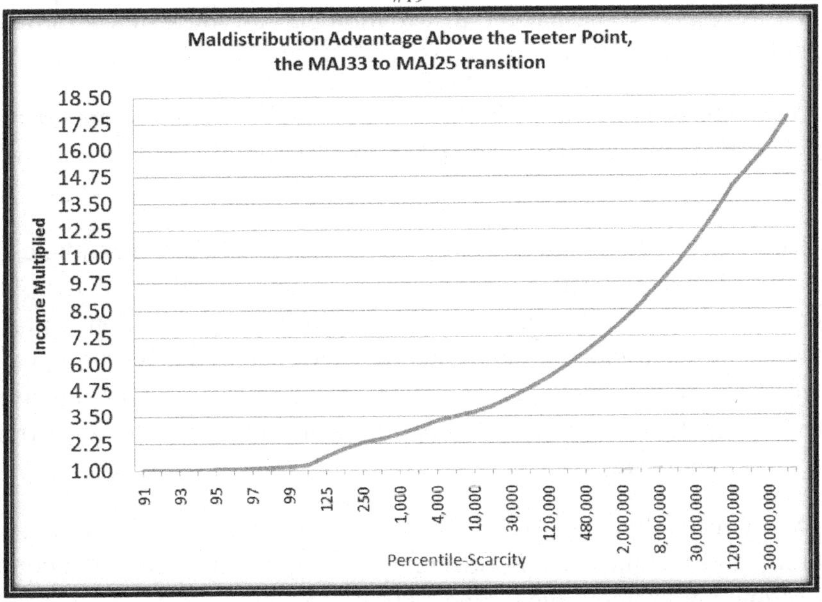

By contrast to circumstances at the MAJ, the income at the one-in-a-million-scarcity level is 7.2 times greater at MAJ25 than at the old and quaint MAJ33. Maldistribution enthusiasts have developed an economy where advantages accrue, as shown in the above graph-19.[8]

(4.5%) as that small remaining group of jobseekers who (for whatever reason – frictional, structural, or otherwise), are customarily unemployed during a thriving "full-employment" economy.

Now that you have seen key maldistribution features, but before you invest more of your time, it seems appropriate that a few remarks about the method should be provided. *But if you detest math and details, please skip the following Technical Remarks section.*

A few technical remarks.

To determine the general characteristic of the distribution in each nation, a 100-point mathematical backbone is constructed. This backbone defines the exact total percentage of income received by the MAJ segment and each of the remaining two groups (quintiles) above it. Only two specially derived technical numbers are required to define the backbone curve for each nation. The backbone always delivers the precise income shares for the above three segments of the curve – in short, the full basic distribution curve. When deviations from the backbone exist, the backbone can be bent. For example, it can be bent at the lowest quintiles (1/5ths) or at the upper reaches of the curve if data from the particular nation or other data in similar distributions warrant it. This is the logic behind the shape of the first 100 points on the income-distribution curves you will see throughout the book.

Methods originating with Pareto are usually used for analyzing the Top1% of income earners.[9] The programs I wrote do not use Pareto numbers.

The income distribution within the Top1% is of such vast range that a separate dedicated method is necessary to uncover the full distribution there. From good and recent works on income distribution within the Top1%, we have data showing income shares received by the upper and lower half of the Top1%. From this we can create a moving average Top/Bottom Ratio [Upper½%/Lower½%] trend line, and where warranted, extend or modify it.

Mathematically, the Top1% method is grounded in the precept that scarcity and income scale at different rates, and that scaling is modulated. The computer program then satisfies three objectives:

1) It anchors the low end of the Top1% curve at the one-in-a-hundred value established by the backbone and its bending.
2) It delivers a distribution curve where the Top/Bottom Ratio is substantially the same as the intended ratio. This ensures that the income allocated for the two halves of the Top1% are appropriately allocated.

3) The method accounts for income by summing the incomes of each hypothetical person in the Top1% of the population to ensure that the total of their incomes indeed exactly sums to the income share allocated to the Top1%.

Any method that cannot deliver on these three minimum requirements is footed in fiction. All the curves shown here have passed the test.

When the Top1% method is used in combination with the backbone, a complete distribution curve from top to bottom can be produced from five numbers alone: two for the backbone and three for the Top1%. If the backbone is to be bent, then the percentage received by any of the lower three quintile, the Top5%, or the Top1% can be also be used. Population size is required. Interpolation is not used within any portion of the method. That is all there is to it.

The 400 case lookup table illustrates median central tendencies – enough to approximately indicate what a distribution usually means for the complete population. The cases are also identified by the Gini index (a technical number widely used in the field to measure inequality), which is calculated for each of the distribution curves.[10] This makes it possible to cross-reference the lookup curves with distributions reported elsewhere. In historical data, there are, of course, deviations from the lookup table.

In instances where the Top1% value deviates from the represented case, a technician can readily employ the values shown at scarcity points of 100 and higher and marry them with previously known distributions to get a first approximation for distribution at high scarcity levels. This technique was never used with any data in this book, but without dedicated income-distribution computer programs, it may provide adequate first approximations. Such cutting and pasting can create distorted representations because the shape of each curve is determined by values within the Top2%. Please keep in mind the focus in this book is on the representative cases that would interest most readers, not the deviations from them.

Now we return to the business at hand.

Standard of living.

To have an intuitive grasp on how the downward transition in income distribution interacts with an average per capita growth rate of 1.5%, the following graph-22 illustrates the years required to double income, and thus presumably, standard of living.

#22

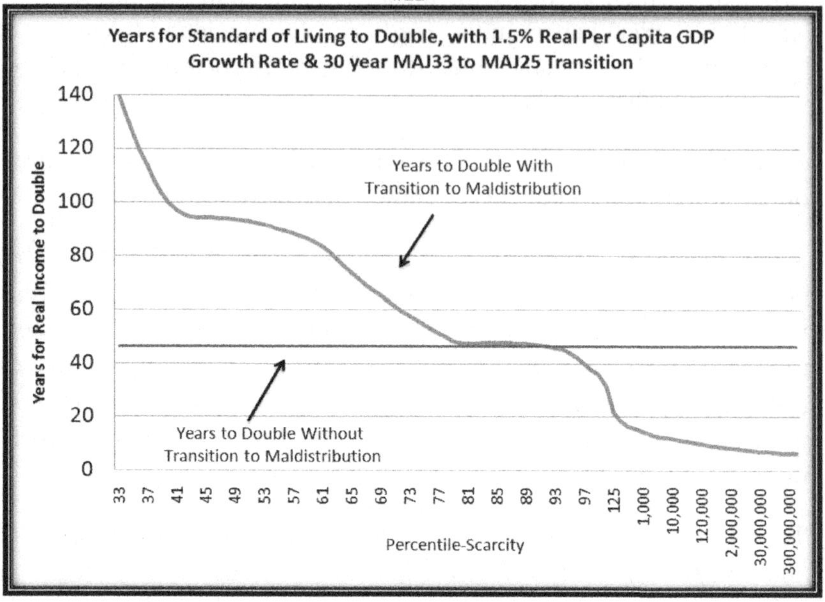

When income distribution is held constant and per capita income grows at a 1.5% rate, all segments on the distribution curve double their income in 44.6 years. However, with the maldistribution transition, the rich are able to double their standard of living much faster. At the one-in-a-thousand-scarcity level, the standard of living doubles every 21.3 years. For those at the one-in-60,000-scarcity level, income doubles every ten years. The maldistribution blessing is bestowed on them.

But for those in the MAJ, it would require a minimum of 70 years to double standard of living. For those at the 40th percentile, doubling standard of living would take a century. For those lower on the scale, the figures are so sad that I cannot bring myself to write them. If the rate of downward movement continued for a century more at the same rate as in the case of a MAJ33 going to a MAJ25 over 30 years, it would ultimately reduce the MAJ to a brutal 9.6% – a figure that a few barbaric nations have attained. Presumably the leadership is raised from its slumber before that point, and the disaster is put to an end [annual reduction in the MAJ equals 0.990459731= (25/33.33)^(1/30); 9.6= 25*(0.990459731 ^100)].

Graph-22 tells the story of how the move to maldistribution, even in the face of economic growth, influences different individuals in the economy. The way one views the future depends on rank – grim at the bottom, bright at the top.

There is a window of opportunity. If the downward transition in the majority's income share is completely halted, then there is an instant remedy, at least in part: The standard of living doubles for everyone each 46.6 years. *Maldistribution alone is evil, but a constantly increasing maldistribution is the nail in the coffin.*

Accelerating or retarding income growth rates via the maldistribution transition.

It is too easy to have inflated expectations about economic growth. Business and economic news often report glorious advances in one index or another. But over the long throw of a generation or more (including booms, busts, inflation, and population growth), the average real growth in per capita Gross Domestic Product now often falls in the neighborhood of 1.5% annually in the United States.

#23

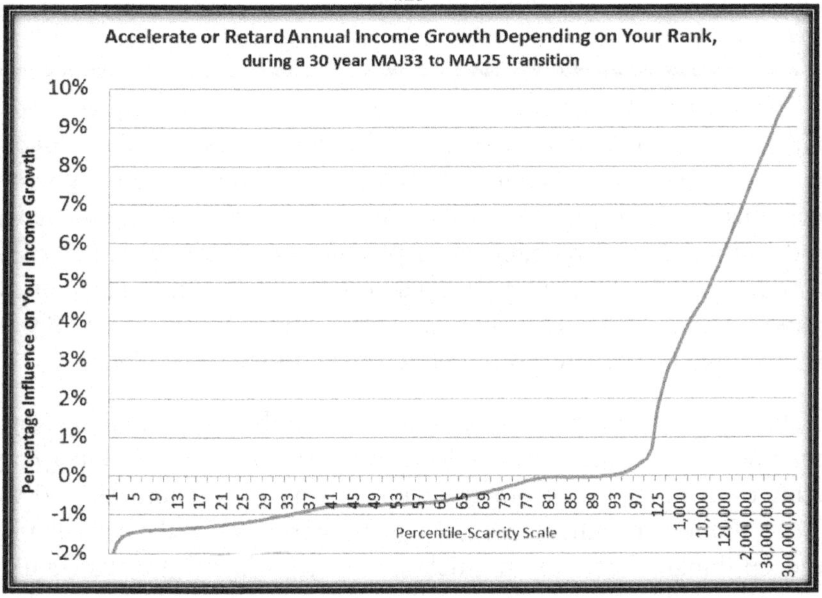

At the high perch of one-in-a-million, you would receive a windfall 6.8%+ income growth produced by the maldistribution transition alone, over and above your ordinary 1.5% GDP per capita growth (graph-23). On the other hand, for two-thirds of the population, the brakes are forcefully applied (graph-24). For them, more than a half a percent of growth is lobbed off the meager 1.5% growth. They are lucky if they can squeeze out a 1% annual growth. Most do worse.

#24

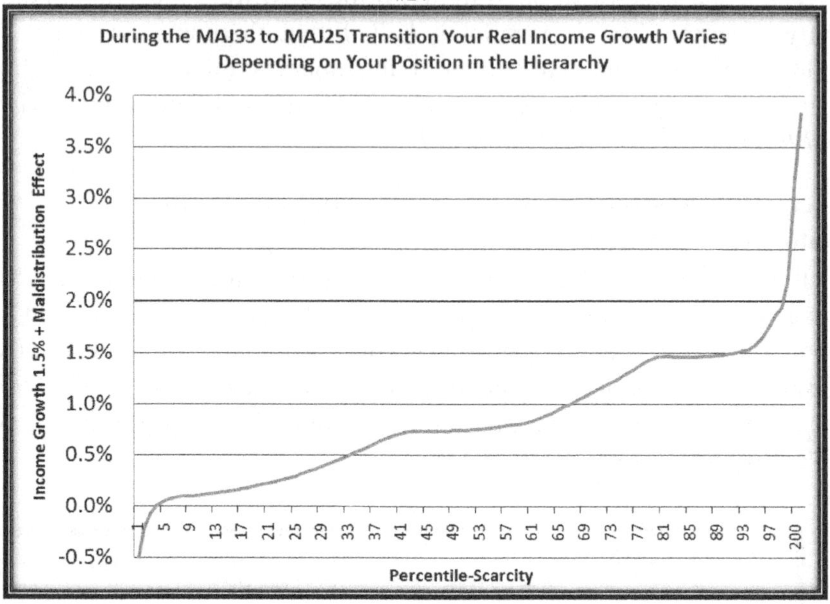

The increased rate of income growth as a consequence of the maldistribution transition is so great for the highest income groups that they receive increased immunity from periods of low economic growth and recessions. A decision-maker who is not sharing the full consequences of his decisions is well recognized as placing the entire system at risk. For example, consider an airplane mechanic who repairs an airplane on which he and his family are frequent passengers. The smart money will bet that he is likely to be particularly attentive and careful on that plane.

The high earners in a market economy are the crowd making key economic decisions. Their airplane has always flown nicely, whether they are attentive to the needs of others or not. To have decisions shaped by the maldistribution incentive – would that be perilous for the rest of us? Let the deep thinkers study it. A quick answer from the rest of us should suffice.

It is no longer exclusively a market economy for the rich. It is a maldistribution economy. Their monetary incentive is to promote it. After a 1.5% normal per capita growth rate is added to the maldistribution transition outcome, income growth across the spectrum looks like the above graph-24. The curve is truncated to focus on the majority of people.

The following graph-25 draws focus to the remarkable story that very few people experience the average growth rates reported in the news or in economic and business literature. To be precise, only one-tenth of us experience the average growth rate as evidenced by the flattening at the 1.0 multiplier.

#25

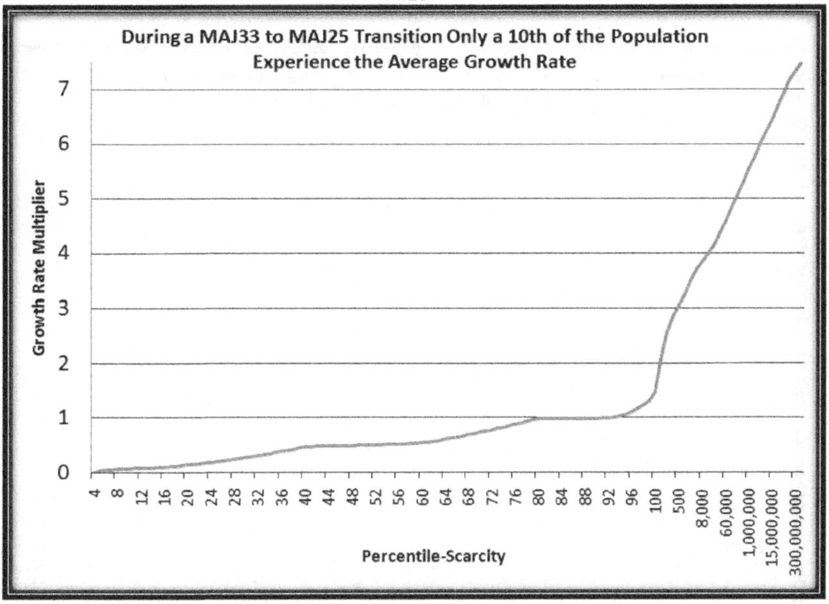

People at the one-in-125-scarcity level more than double their real income growth during the MAJ33 to MAJ25 transition. By the time you get to the one-in-a-million level, your growth rate is 5.5 times faster than the average. All key leaders in the economy above this point gain more (and in some cases much more) by promoting decisions and policies that accelerate maldistribution than they do by employing honorable means to increase their income. *Maldistribution is oligarchy capitalism. It is vastly different from equitable free market capitalism.*

The principle of equal opportunity for all is obviously sacrificed in a 30-year maldistribution transition. Those at the top advance spectacularly. Those in the bottom 75% majority are crucified. Adam Smith's free market relies on motivated self-interest to produce a desirable outcome. His guiding principle is turned on its head by ever-increasing maldistribution. A person at the high strata can achieve far more by increasing maldistribution than by pursuing customary honorable income growth.

Disruption of status among highest earners.

The fracturing of relationships between low and high earners as maldistribution progresses is well known. To the extent that social relations are enhanced when people are of roughly the same economic class and that they are reduced when people are of vastly different economic strata, maldistribution disrupts the relationship among people of certifiably high levels of scarcity and ability.

#26

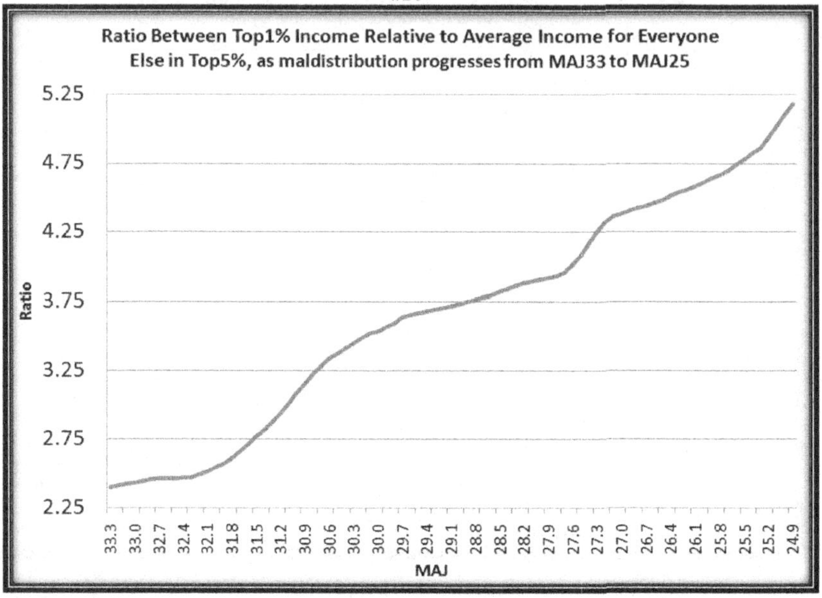

A fracturing of great importance also occurs within the Top5%. Prior to maldistribution, the ratio between the income of the Top1% and rest of those in the Top5% was about 2.5 to 1. By the time one reaches MAJ25, this ratio is almost 5 to 1. The status of everyone else relative to the Top1% plummets as illustrated in the above graph-26.

It is a common misconception that maldistribution results only because there is a great divide between people of low or intermediate status (say a person at the median) and those of elevated status and ability. True enough, there are usually vast differences in ability and justifiable differences in remuneration between these two groups which can be accentuated by lack of education and lack of abilities at the low end. However, it is wrong to think maldistribution is exclusively caused by the difference in true abilities or education, or that maldistribution can reliably be corrected by educating those of lower rank or by increasing their productivity. History teaches us that maldistribution marches to its own drummer.

A distinction should be drawn between a component like education that is needed for economic growth and the influence that education may separately have on maldistribution. Education and productivity are, of course, necessary for economies to advance, but recent U.S. history has shown increasing productivity and rising educational levels have taken place at the same time that maldistribution worsens. Maldistribution is defined by shifting incentives along the curve to disproportionately benefit the upper strata rather than any lower strata.

Ruling the roost.

Maldistribution increases the spread between those of high rank and anyone of lower rank. The increasing spread is evident within the upper reaches of the Top1% earners. This spread is especially clear when you examine the 400-case lookup table in the files accompanying this book.

#27

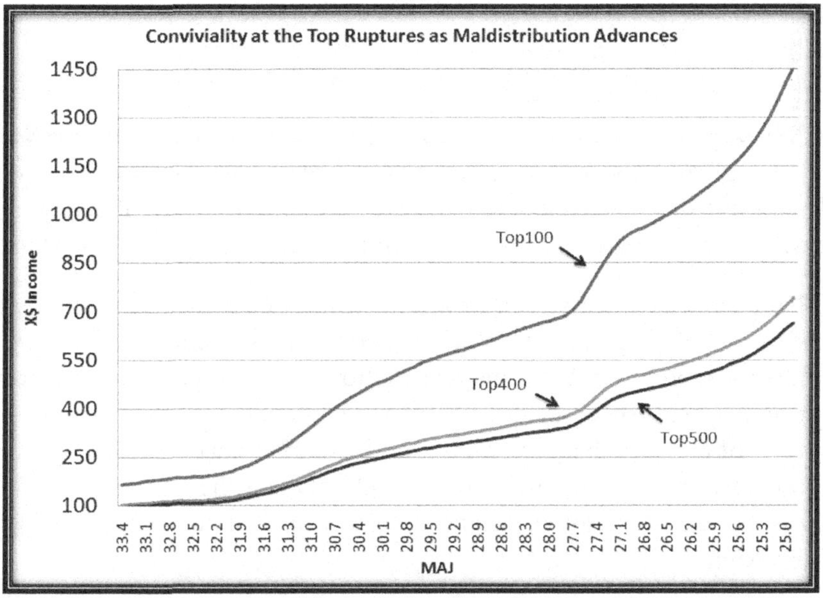

As can be seen in graph-27, at MAJ33 and thereabouts, the Top100 earners are close to others within the Top500 subgroup; but by a MAJ25 distribution, the spread increases substantially.

Similarly, the following graph-28 compares the income of a person at a one-in-500-scarcity level with a person at a one-in-240,000 level. We see that at MAJ33, the higher-income person's income is 8.3 times more than his lower-earning colleague; but at MAJ25, it is a whopping 20x greater.

#28

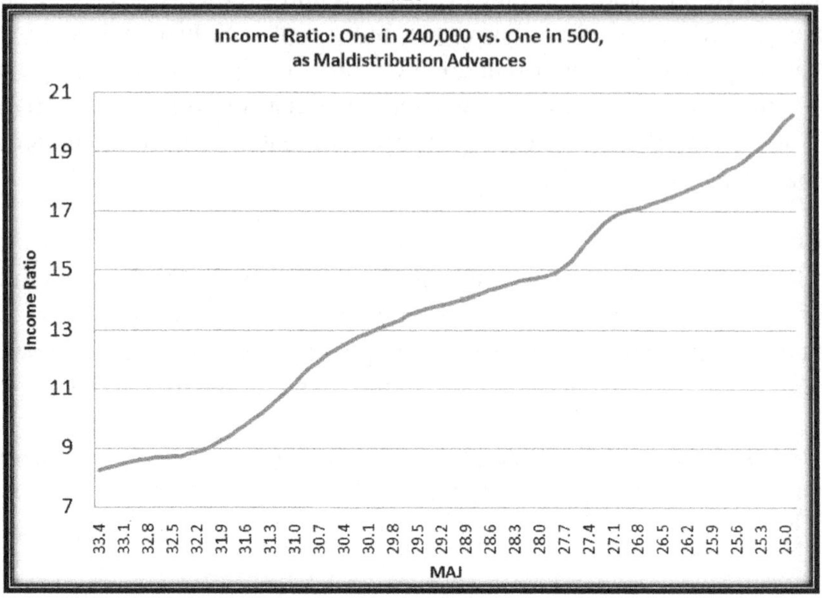

The spread between these two was always large. But ask yourself: At MAJ25 did the lower income person at the one-in-500 rank suddenly become less intelligent, less able, less productive, or less educated? Hardly.

No economic necessity or proper working of the market economy compels the increasing spread. When it occurs, it is a cultural decision – the maldistribution ethic. With maldistribution, these spreads enlarge between any higher and lower income person, independent of any change in the scarcity of abilities that are brought to the marketplace. If you want to get a visceral feeling of how great the spread between the super-rich and common folk can be in some instances, take a look at Jamie Johnson's DVD "Born Rich."

It is a dangerous spread because it increases the domination of the few (whether within the executive suites or elsewhere), and because it increases dominance of a few lucrative sectors over other sectors that may be of greater true value to the economy.

It makes it easy for a high-income bond trader to look contemptuously at a manufacturer who struggles to keep an organization together that does not bring in the big bucks, but that does employ workers and does produce a product. In view of many such businesses being abandoned, the arguments favoring maldistribution hardly benefit nations or their people. Consider career choices. A future physician may become a bond trader.

Maldistribution distorts proper relationships. Irrationality, already abundantly available, tends to become increasingly concentrated at the top. In a "wiki" thinking world where the contributions of widely diverse people, the wisdom of crowds, emergence, and complexity drive societies, a reduced incentive for the majority is antithetical.

Taking a peak at the Top1%.

We know more about the Top1% than ever before, thanks to Emmanuel Saez, Thomas Piketty, and others who have thoroughly studied top income earners.[11] They have provided a huge service to everyone by doing so. Their work has made it possible to estimate the all-important ratio between the income of the Upper½% and the Lower½% in the Top1% – a ratio which is central to the computer programs I write.

#29

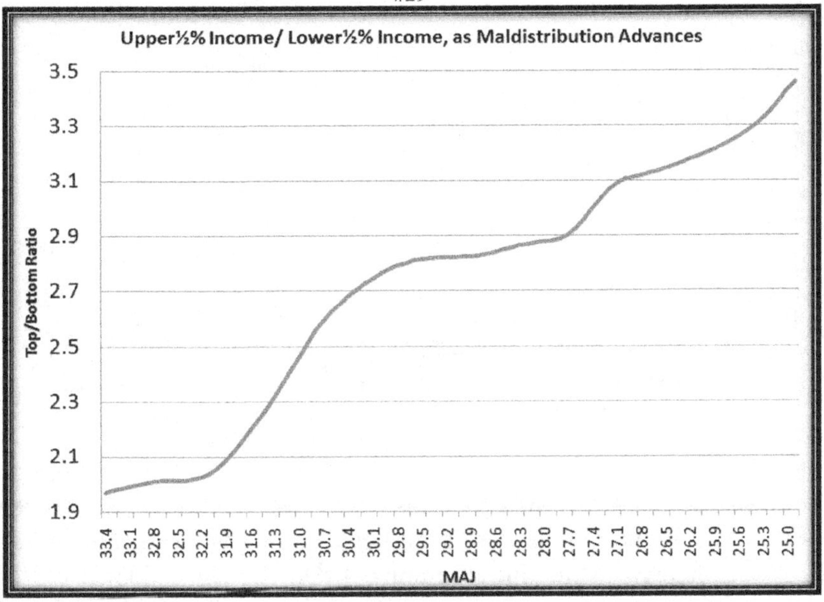

This ratio in many nations is entirely unreported and unstudied. The job of illustrating central tendencies in the Top1% will never be completely known until all governments are forthcoming. Governmental income-distribution reports need to be adequately audited and contain Top1% income data of the kind you have seen in the spreadsheets.

The above graph-29 shows an estimated smoothed trend line for the Top/Bottom Ratio. You will see those at the Upper½% not only distance themselves from mere mortals at lower percentiles, they also increasingly distance themselves from the Lower½%. The ratio becomes ever-greater as maldistribution advances.

At the distribution ranges that we have been primarily considering – MAJ33 and MAJ25 – the ratios between the Upper½% and Lower½% are approximately 1.98 and 3.40, respectively.

The ratio has a practical back-of-the-napkin importance because, without difficult computations, it can be used to quickly determine the average X$ income for the Lower½% and Upper½% sections of the Top1% [Lower½% X$= 2*(Top1%/(1+ratio)); Upper½% X$= Lower½% X$*ratio].

#30

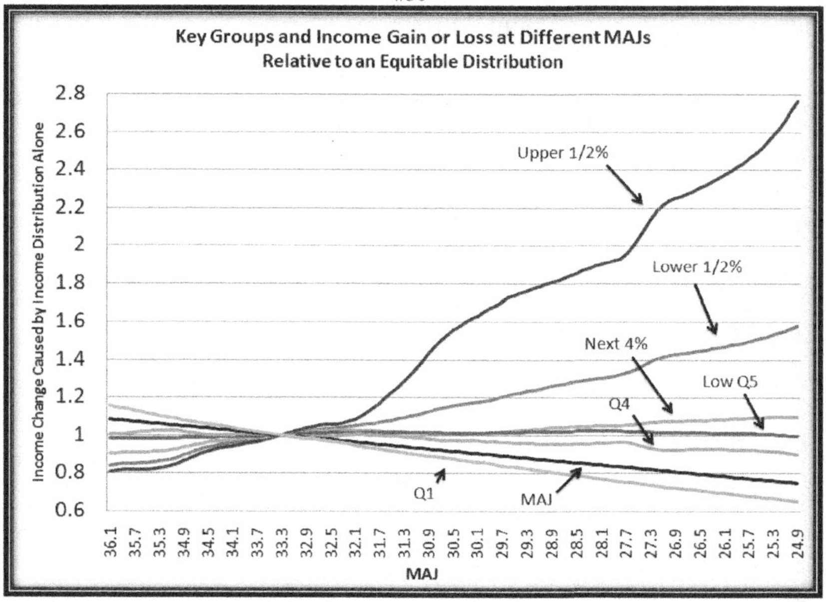

From the highest to lowest segments, all major segments of income earners are shown in the above graph-30. On the right side of the graph, they are represented in descending order from those who benefit the most to those who are hurt the most. On the left side of the graph, the graph lines are mirrored and inverted. Points in close proximity to MAJ33, whether to the right or left, are reasonably equitable.

We see at MAJ25 that the obvious maldistribution gainers, the Upper½% and Lower½% incomes, are in each year respectively 1.6 and 2.8 times higher than they would have been under MAJ33. At one step down in the hierarchy, the average income increase for the Next4% (the four percentage points beneath the Top1%) does not tend to exceed 10%. The incomes for the Low Q5 (everyone in the top 1/5 less the above top5% already graphed) are in a more ambiguous state, sometimes increasing 2% and at other times losing a half percent. All other groups are solid losers. Q4 (the next lower 1/5th of the population) loses of its 10% income. The MAJ income falls 25%. Income for Q1, the lowest 1/5th, drops 35%.

The group averages shown in the chart identify the influence on different segments; but as you have already seen, it is necessary to drill down to the X$ for each individual to comprehend the full range of incomes within any segment.

Who smiles? Happiness.

Kahneman and Deaton have done valuable work on economically induced happiness.[12] They indicate that a logarithmic principle applies to how we emotionally respond to income. This principle, Weber's Law, also applies elsewhere. For example, the relationship between stimulus and perception such as vision (brightness) and sound (intensity) is logarithmic. Kahneman and Deaton make the important observation that a person's sense of emotional well-being (happiness) in the U.S. *does not* continue to increase beyond a $75k income. But on the other hand, they observe that one's evaluation of life (sense of satisfaction) *does* continue to advance without stopping as income increases. These general tendencies have been noted to apply worldwide.

I do not pretend to be a deep thinker in the happiness field, but it struck me that the analysis here of income distribution serves nicely as a means to explore – let's call it – economically induced overall happiness. In a nub, this is the measure of happiness, shown in the upcoming graphs. It is simply the average of the "emotional well-being" and "sense of satisfaction", each being logarithmically determined [log(income)], but the former not advancing further once it reaches the designated stop point ($75k in the U.S.).

In poor, maldistributed nations, unhappiness can accrue both from a low average income for the nation and from the influence of maldistribution. In the spreadsheets, happiness is shown to reflect these influences. But in the following graphs, average income is held constant so that we can see the influence that maldistribution *alone* would be expected to have on happiness.

In the following graph-32A, 1.00 is the average national happiness at MAJ33. Even in nations with the most even of distributions, average happiness can advance no more than 2.2% above the national MAJ33 happiness. However, beneath MAJ33 maldistribution can reduce happiness in a nation by 9% in the most unequal nations.

#32A

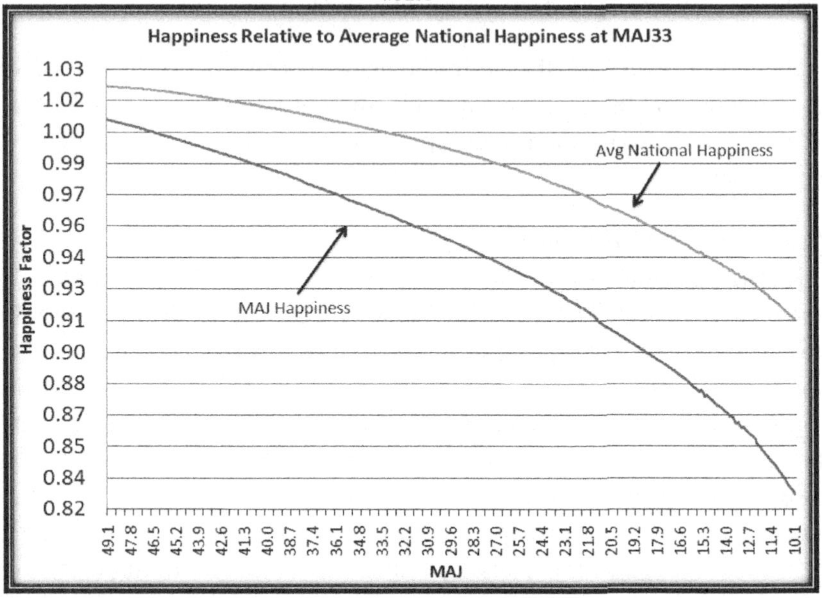

Happiness for the majority is always less than average national happiness because income at the MAJ is always less than the nation's average income. We see this principle in all lookup-table X$ curves.

In the following graph-33B, when we focus on the MAJ36 to MAJ21 range (instead of the full range shown previously) and look at the relationship in a slightly different manner, we see that national happiness falls 1.98% and MAJ happiness falls 3.18% once MAJ25 is reached. At MAJ10 (beyond the range of graph-33B), MAJ happiness drops 14% beneath the MAJ33 level.

As shown in the graph-32A and 33B, the opportunities for increasing happiness via more equal distributions exist primarily when nations are gripped by maldistribution. Once MAJ33 is reached, national happiness can only be increased slightly via changes in income distribution.

#33B

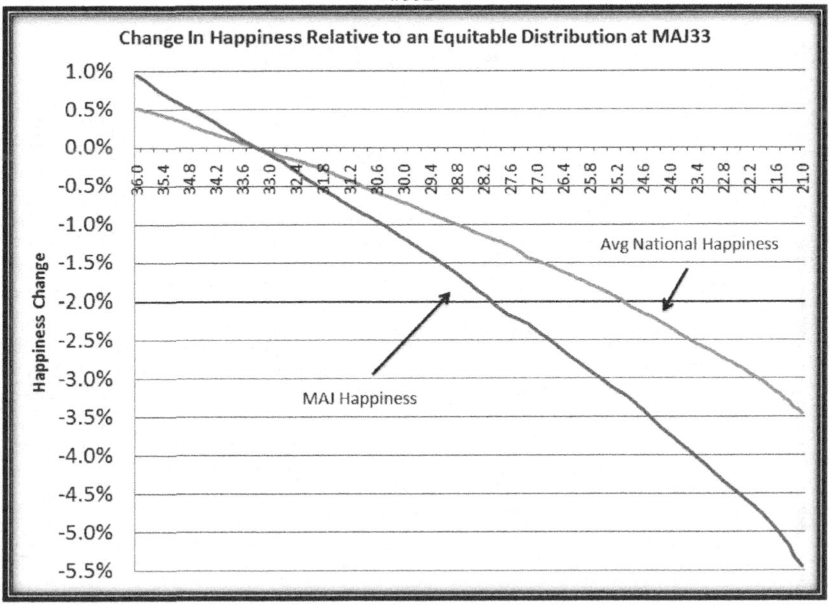

#33C

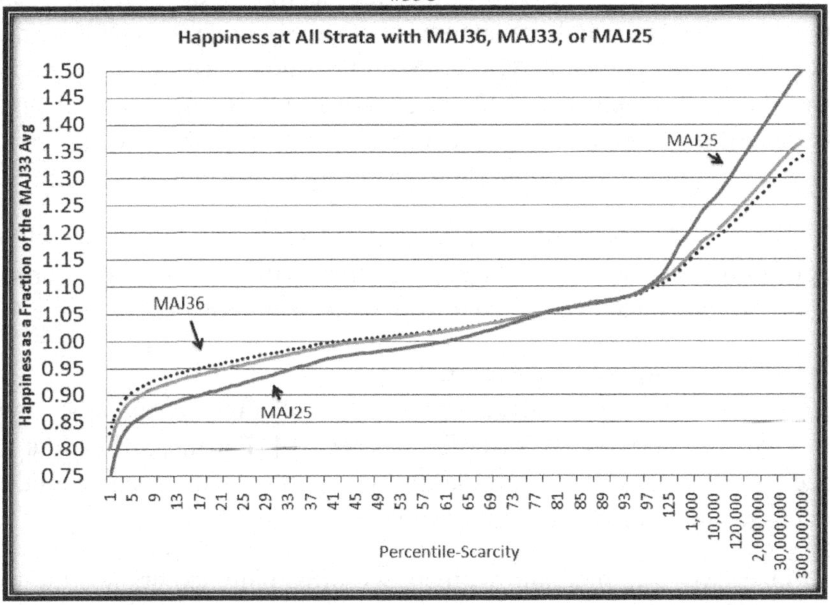

Taking a look at three curves – MAJ36 (maximum prudent equality), MAJ33 (the proposed fair case), and MAJ25 (frank maldistribution) – we see in the above graph-33C that happiness remains close throughout much of the range for MAJ36 and MAJ33.

#34D

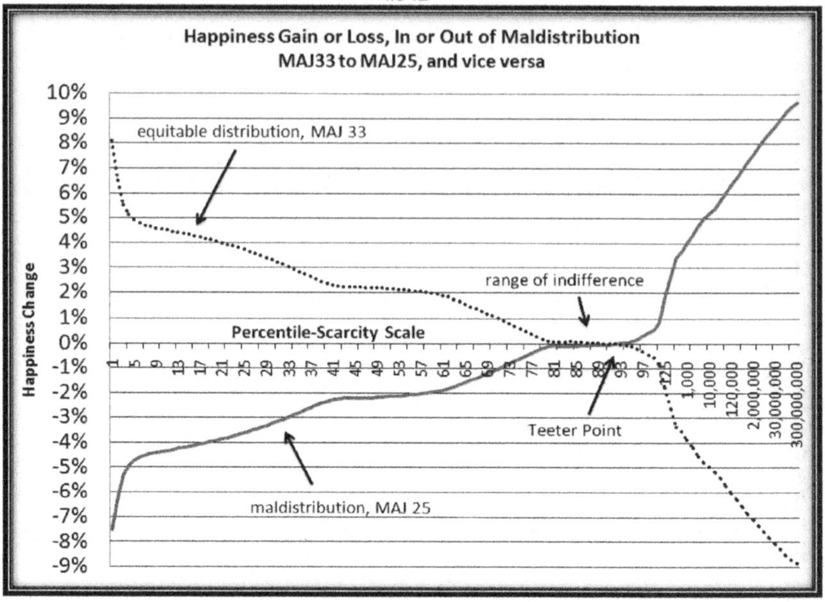

The above graph-34D shows that the happiness of all people beneath the teeter point fell, and the happiness of those above the teeter point rose with the change from a MAJ33 to MAJ25. And we can see how a change from the maldistributed MAJ25 back to MAJ33 inverts those changes to the benefit of the majority. A few unhappy pirates is the price always paid when going from maldistribution to an equitable distribution.

If maldistribution is reversed to a fair MAJ33, one can expect vigorous opposition from the Upper½% because they will be reluctant to forfeit the happiness gains that they derived from maldistribution.

The stick, stick, and the carrot.

Our instincts seldom allow us to see a full range of income distributions, such as previously illustrated in graph-14. For most of us, our reference point is apt to be more natural and closer to the income midpoint. Graph-35 attempts to duplicate this view.

For us working men and women, we principally experience the region shown here using the median as the reference point (1.0). Beneath the 50th percentile, incomes relative to the median are close; but from the midpoint upwards, they diverge appreciably.

#35

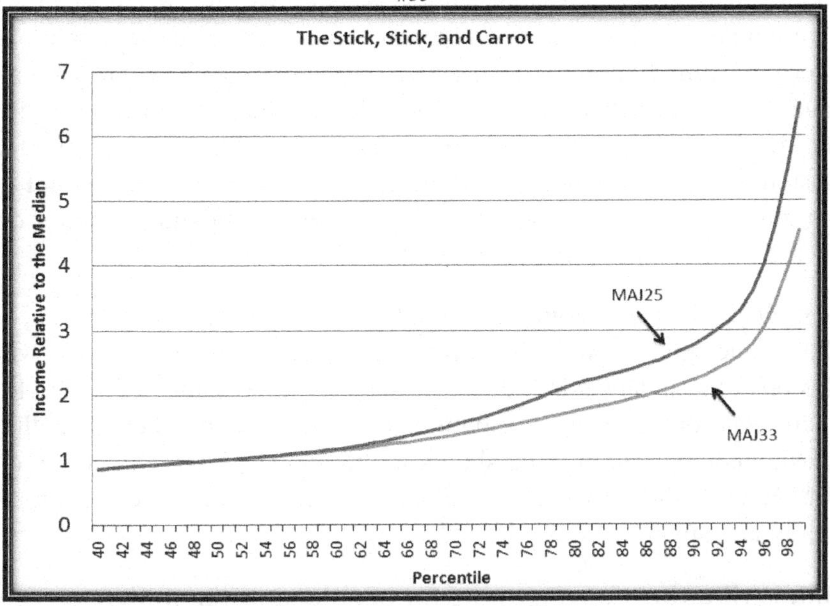

The MAJ25 and MAJ33 distributions represent two distinct compensation philosophies. Each involve the carrot and the stick: better pay for doing better, lower pay for doing worse or making a less valuable contribution. This principle conforms to the theory that high inequality is necessary to give people incentives and tends to be attractive for economists who like to see large increments associated with a particular outcome. For example, a sharply rising pay scale as scarcity increases.

In MAJ25, we see such a rise. The MAJ25 philosophy is also attractive for personalities who derive joy from dominating, and the minor potentates they collect along the way. The pirate-in-chief makes a great to-do about the rewards (carrots) and shows how far you will fall (stick) if you do not perform. The MAJ25 curve bears it out. By the 78th percentile, you make twice as much as the guy at the midpoint; and by the 92nd percentile, three times as much. It looks like MAJ25 is leaving MAJ33 in the dust.

Think again. If you believe the pirate flimflam, you have been snookered. Before anyone came into the MAJ25 game, a bigger stick had already been applied. In addition to the customary stick and carrot, the maldistributed economy adds the additional stick: a sharply rising pay scale.

As you may recall from the previous graph-14, everyone at a MAJ25 distribution beneath the teeter point (the 92nd percentile) already got a smaller income than MAJ33. The MAJ25 crowd had been fooled. They were donkeys with blinders. They were not worthy of those mentioned incomes two and three times larger than those at the median. Throughout the scale, they were actually getting a smaller income than those who elected the MAJ33 route (graph-14). Those who chose MAJ25 participated in an illusion – a more brutal one than necessary. If you have any doubt about this, turn back to graph-14 and look again at the standing of those on the MAJ25 curve beneath the teeter point

Beneath the teeter point, those on the MAJ33 curve had higher incomes. They came into the workplace ready to do a decent day's work without illusions of grandeur relative to their cohorts. They came into a workplace where everyone from top to bottom got a fair shake. Their smoothly increasing compensation scale shown in graph-35 did not contain the drama of MAJ25. It did, however, contain a sensibility and higher income completely lacking at MAJ25.

Maldistribution – paying more for people of lower ability.

#36

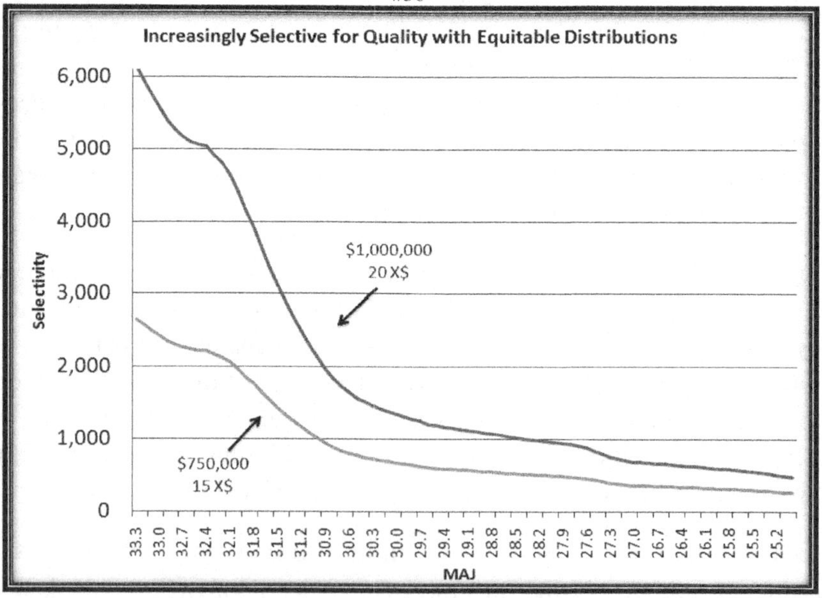

To anyone visiting or living in a country where a tinhorn potentate rules and preserves his position and those of his cronies by enforcing acute maldistribution via the power of office, it is blindingly clear that the majority of those at the top have stunningly low ability in terms of economic

usefulness. Think deeply.* Throughout the scale, there is a continuum of reduced ability as maldistribution becomes ever more intense. This continuum is the feature illustrated in the above graph-36. The concept is simple. It took the computer program less than a second to deliver all the data on this topic.

Graph-36 shows constant earning rates of 15X$ and 20X$ (corresponding to incomes of $750,000 and $1,000,000).

People earning high amounts such as 20X$ ($1,000,000) are obviously scarce, but the standards drop to low levels as an economy moves to a MAJ25. Explicitly, take the 20X$ selectivity curve. At a MAJ33, the system is highly selective allowing only one in 6,150 to attain the million dollar rank. But the profligate MAJ25 it is far less selective, paying that same relative income to a mere one-in-480. And at the 15X$ income, the selection criteria similarly drops from one-in-2,650 to one-in-265.[13]

Looking through the news, I see the Bloomberg Billionaire Index and various remarks of braggadocio. Whenever a nation proudly boasts that it has increased the number of millionaires or billionaires, the cautionary flag should wave fiercely because the mechanism for doing so is usually the drive to maldistribution. The nation typically becomes less selective for those who rise to high levels. This is especially dangerous in a free market and democracy because less able people proliferate in high decision-making positions. Those of true merit can be muscled out. High quality decision-making is one of the casualties of maldistribution.

In contrast to pure selectivity, the *selectivity ratio* illustrates selection relative to an equitable distribution base. The selectivity ratio in graph-38 indicates the degree to which high earners at the 15X$ and 20X$ income levels ($750,000 and $1,000,000) are scrutinized in the face of maldistribution.

At the fair MAJ33 distribution, only one-in-13.2 at 20X$ and one-in-10.3 at 15X$ of those who achieved their incomes in the MAJ25 case would have made the cut. As shown in graph-38, at MAJ33 the selectivity ratio is 1.0, indicating that no greater selectivity was necessary. But as

* Please do not interpret the expression "Think deeply" as a command. Many of you are, have been, and always will be in a deep thinking mode. The expression is used as punctuation for those of us who scoot along on a level of thinking just sufficient to get through the day. The "thinking deeply" is a reminder that we are approaching a curve in the road and may want to shift into another thought zone, slightly different (but no harder) than our customary cruising along.

maldistribution increases, selectivity was insufficient, corresponding to the ratios shown in graph-38.

#38

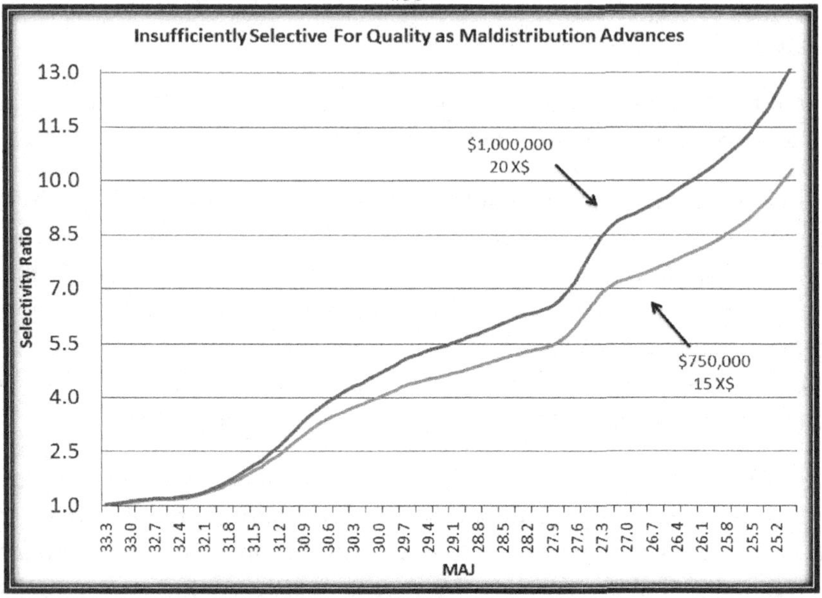

In the lookup table we see that at the one-in-a-million-scarcity level at MAJ33, the earnings are 115.1X$ ($5,755,000 in this case). Yet at MAJ25, one out of 17,627 are earning this same amount. At this point, the selectivity ratio is 56.7 – profligacy reigns. A proliferation of people of low ability in high places reduces quality of decision-making at precisely the point that a market economy requires superior decisions.

Correction without recrimination.

Revolutionaries, often through violence accompanied by a vision of an improved world, have slaughtered or removed a ruling class in a broad stroke. I believe this is wrong and counterproductive.

To look at class conditions and attempt to rectify them at the barrel of a gun is ill advised. Those who use violence seldom have the capacity to significantly advance economies. Nations in greatest distress too frequently have been driven into ever-greater misery by war. Although force and honeyed promises to a desperate people can inspire great foolishness, look at the spreadsheets. There is a trove of data that shows the impact of income and wealth at any period in history. Once the blasting and words have been given a few years to clear, the populace frequently ends up in a puddle more disagreeable than the one it left.

I do not come to this world with lily clean hands. I was raised in the segregated South in the U.S. under privileged conditions. As I saw it, the segregation we lived under was not virulently mean, as it was elsewhere. But it was unremittingly debilitating and wrong. So I know a bit about starting off with daft notions. This gives me a perspective on the capacity for change. Some will be unreservedly recalcitrant; but more often than one may be prepared to believe, opposing positions can change when reasons are compelling and persistent.

Quiet heroism is capable of rising unexpectedly. This was recently brought to my attention in the Scottsboro Boys Case. Nine rough, black, teenage hobos were wrongly accused of gang raping two white women in Alabama in 1931 during the Great Depression.[14] In that era, lynchings were frequent. The story begins at a scene where a lynching appeared to approach certainty. However, even in the intensely racist South, the Sheriff and law enforcement stood strong to prevent it – an act of courage under unfavorable odds. Then came trials that proclaimed guilt at numerous junctures but which were successfully appealed.

The point of heroism and rectitude for me came when the judge, of pure Southern tradition, set aside the jury verdict of guilty because the evidence did not support it. His decision cost him his job. Judge Horton was never elected to the bench again. He was widely opposed. Another judge handed down guilty verdicts, some of which were mitigated by parole or pardon. The larger story is that even in an imperfect world, we can move forward as long as motivations are proper. Allies like Judge Horton can be found in unlikely places. They, others, and our inner voice have the power to inspire and move us.

So be accurate. Be persistent. Be tough and strong if necessary. Be wise. It is just as impossible to reverse evolution in economics as it is in nature. Even when beneficial changes are made, you will return to a state differing from the original conditions.[15] Goals will seldom match outcomes.

Do not be violent. Too frequently the vitality of nations is laid low by the disproportionate force of a few. This wrong can be substituted for one just as great if the majority ill-advisedly resorts to violence. The majority can always triumph when guided by reason, accuracy, and fairness. I say this because I do not want the sometimes forceful words and plain picture painted here to cause evil.

In the selectivity ratio graph-38, we saw that somewhere in the neighborhood of one out of ten people at high rank possesses sufficiently great ability to justify his or her present high income. If they are removed, not only from this level of remuneration but from the decision-making process, the nation loses a valuable component required in a successful economy – broad-spread high quality decision-making. It may take more than a generation to replace it, in which case the entire society can falter, or worse.

Once an economy reaches a MAJ25, the normal selection process that would have occurred in a MAJ33 market economy has already been breached. There are no rules or easy ways to filter out or demote those who have been wrongly promoted to high income. The least worthy are apt to have the biggest mouths, have the ability to hire agents, and have sufficient contacts and power to employ governments to perpetuate their windfall.

About nine out of ten of those at the top have achieved their high income by virtue of maldistribution. As you read these pages, you may want to retain these few paragraphs in the back of your mind because if a nation is ever to get to a MAJ33 again, it needs to be done by correct and persistent means. The opposition from the unworthy will be loud, intense, ruthless, and rich.

The great danger of excessive income equality.

#40

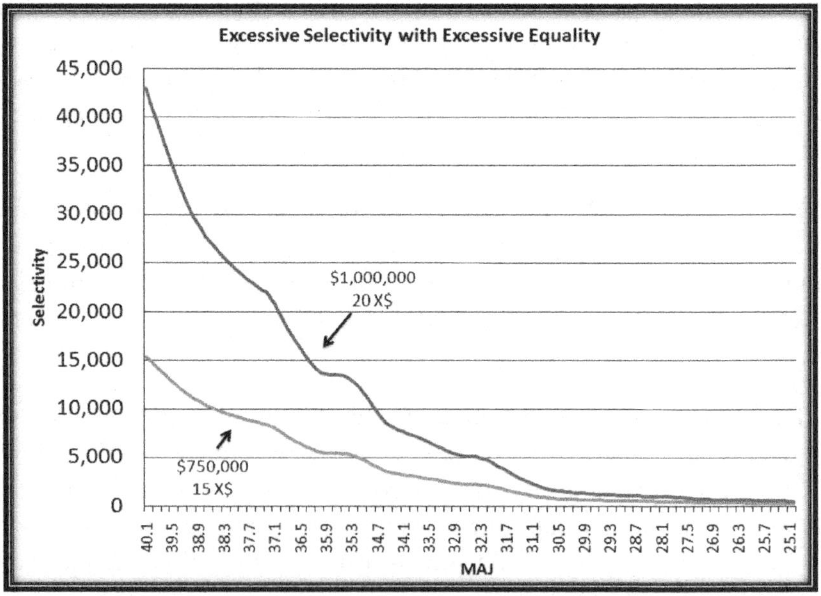

To this point, the data has decried maldistribution. Here, it will illustrate the great danger of excessive equality. Graph-40 opens the window to a *wider range* (MAJ40 to MAJ25) to show how selectivity comes into play, particularly in highly equal distributions.

In graph-40, we see that from MAJ36 through MAJ40, there is a sharp increase in selectivity at 15X$ and 20X$. this sharp rise in selectivity, especially at 15X$ ($750,000), is dangerous. If selectivity is excessively stringent, you remove precisely the kind of people necessary for quality decision-making and quality action. The economy and society suffer greatly.

I want people to be in positions of high authority who have more ability than I do. I benefit from it. I do not want to lose them. There may be fair and legitimate debate about what degree of selectivity is appropriate, but distributions significantly more equal than MAJ36 throw up a wall of dramatically increasing selectivity. It seems to me that to cross into this territory would provide little advantage to the 60% majority by way of improved income or happiness and it would create a likely prospect of reduced desirable economic activity and, perhaps, worse. The data tells us that MAJ36 is the stopping point. History tells us that MAJ33 widely works well. I like proven things that work well.

With particular reference to the above case, one of the practical advantages of defining distribution curves using MAJ numbers is that it makes it trivially easy to instantaneously determine how much better (or worse) off the 60% majority would be by a move in income distribution. It is a ready measure of how a democracy treats its people.

For example, when we consider the option between a MAJ36 (which I hold to be the maximum equality that most nations should seek) and MAJ33 (the reliable workhorse), we can easily calculate the maximum advantage the 60% majority would derive from a change in income distribution alone, before other factors are considered. The answer: 9% [9%= 36/33-1, and simple calculations of this kind can be used for any of the distributions]. However, in my mind, the 9% gained by a change of income distribution above MAJ33 would often be lost in spades by reduced economic and social vitality.

Hidden behind the Gini.

Look again at the simple calculation in the previous paragraph using MAJ numbers. You cannot perform such calculations with Ginis. [16] Most people have never heard of a Gini – with good reason. Although it is the most common measurement of income distribution, it is very cumbersome to use. We (as normal people walking down the street, in cafes, or on the job) can neither discuss it comfortably nor the income distribution to which it pertains. Even academically, it hobbles the process of modeling and understanding how economies work.

Income-distribution language has been so imprecise that the topic is practically unmanageable. By not being able to discuss income distribution or easily model it, we have been rendered powerless to understand or correct the vast adverse effects of income distribution gone awry. I disparage the Gini because I feel it has stymied valuable public and academic thinking.

Throughout the foregoing we have seen how easy it is to make calculations using MAJ numbers. We have also seen how easy it is to see how everyone from top to bottom is doing in any distribution using X$ graphs. These methods differ substantially from methods you will find elsewhere. For me, however, customary income-distribution discussions using the Gini are utterly bewildering.

Ginis are especially useless on the crucial topic of democracy. A democracy must serve and protect the majority, and it must provide a standard of fairness for all. To the extent that it does not do so, it is no democracy at all. The MAJ speaks directly to the wellbeing and status of the 60% majority, and by extension, to how fairly the remaining 40% are treated. The Gini does not.

To hide and obfuscate on a topic so vital is pedantic, perverse, and dangerous Try telling anyone what Ginis such as 34.0, 37.8, and 50.2 convey. Try telling them that the 60% majority of citizens are getting 36%, 33%, or 25% of the income earned in their nation. *Which numbers speak to you with greater clarity?*

If the majority of citizens in any nation were given complete and accurate income-distribution reporting, *would they not* be able to elect more appropriate officials? *Would they not* choose more beneficial policies? And *would not* their leaders inside and outside government be able to make better decisions ____? (Again, please fill in the blank yourself)

The Gini is no mystery. You can see its approximate relationship to the MAJ in the following graph-43. Coincidentally at 35, both are approximately equal.

#43

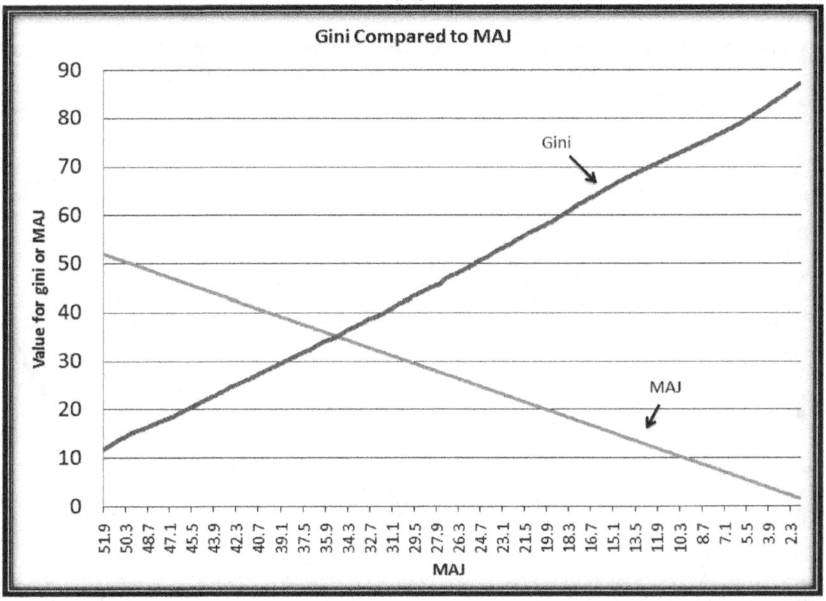

Gini numbers – such as 34.0, 37.8, and 50.2 – are dull as mud and carry little or no meaning for me, no matter how many times I see them. Granted, the Gini provides a valuable, uniform technical standard for measuring income distributions. I use it daily for technical purposes, but for conversations between normal folk – why would anyone choose to use them? [17] If you want a reliable audience for discussing Ginis, I suggest goldfish. They seem receptive.

To Gini aficionados, I might also mention that as Ginis increase linearly, people of identical ability at the high end of the scale receive incomes that expand approximately exponentially. And since people do not receive incomes in Ginis, but in real currency, it might be wiser to stay closer to the topic at hand. A small move in a Gini can spell a large change in income at the top. Focusing on Ginis is a superb way to obfuscate vast changes in top incomes and to provide little information about how the majority is doing.

The complete initial 2,500 worldwide nation-years of data available for this study is shown in the following graph-44. [18] It illustrates the real world relationship between reported MAJs and Ginis. Since it contains all the available real world quintile data, you see Ginis and MAJs at the approximate frequencies at which they occurred, with the percentage rate of occurrence also shown in the graph-44. Real world MAJ variations from the MAJ trend line tend to be small.

#44

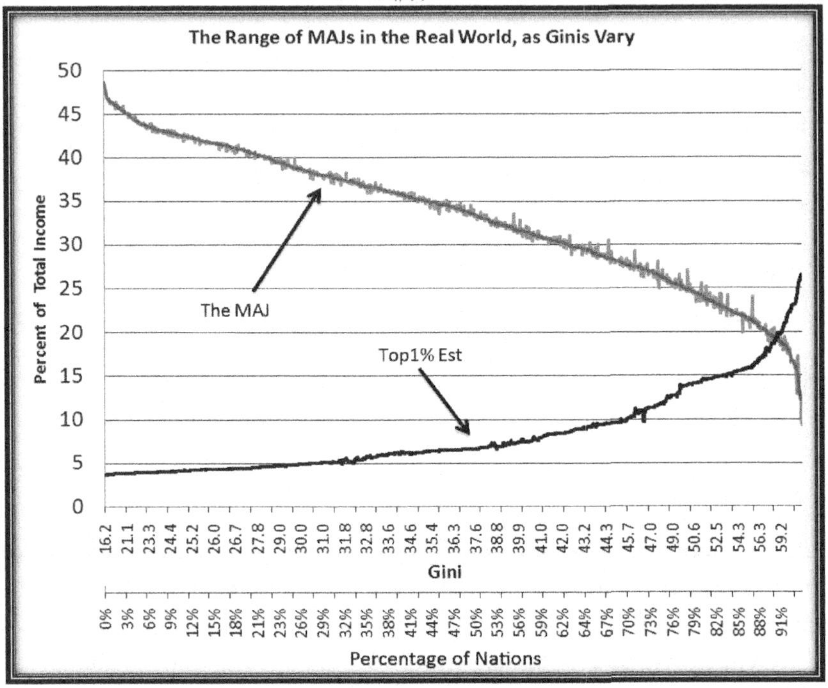

Nations that dip below a MAJ25 are outside the norm, as evidenced by the percentage designation in the graph. As can be seen at the intersection of the two curves, from a MAJ19 downward, distributions are so outlandishly inappropriate that the Top1% receives more of the total income than does the 60% majority. To have the Top1% receive a greater share of the income than the bottom 60% is an irrationality of the most grievous sort.

Frequently Gini users are remarkably inept at their craft. Ginis are so often wrongly calculated that the literature abounds with "corrected" Ginis. By contrast, income distributions are widely published in 20% increments. Given that the MAJ is the sum of the first three of them (quintiles), the MAJ gives greater assurance that the calculations are at least mathematically correct.

The fondness for imprecise income-distribution reporting is spectacular and unnecessary. If Ginis were not bad enough, try quintiles (1/5ths). That is the standard many nations use to report income distribution. Sometimes they *do* report the Top 10% or the Top5%. But reporting the Top1% ... well, for the most part, that only happens in your dreams. The U.S. Census doesn't even do that.[19]

Quintiles.

The reporting you would typically find would be the percentage income shares for each quintile. In following Table-45, the data would look like this for a MAJ33 and MAJ25 respectively:

#45

	gini	Q1	Q2	Q3	Q4	Q5
MAJ33	37.8	6.2	11.2	16.0	22.4	44.3
MAJ25	50.2	4.1	8.2	12.8	20.3	54.7
Maldistribution Influence		-34.24%	-26.82%	-19.98%	-9.67%	23.67%
Equitability Influence		52.08%	36.66%	24.97%	10.70%	-19.14%

A listing of quintiles (Q1, ... Q5) such as in Table-45 and the Gini would be as much as many governments would reveal. And the data in many instances can be decades old. Reporting percentage share is ripe for misconstrual. Governmental data certainly would not report the "maldistribution influences" and "equitability influence" shown in the table.

Take the change at the lowest quintile (Q1). The move from 6.2% to 4.1% is apt to be interpreted as a 2.1% drop in income, say over a 30-year period – hardly something to raise one's heart rate. But within the low quintile, these folk had so little income to begin with that their drop in income share would have been devastating: a full 34.2% drop in the income that they would have received if maldistribution had not occurred [34.24= 4.07 /6.19 -1]. Every year into the indefinite future while the MAJ25 prevails, the average person in this quintile gets an income 34.2% lower than it would have otherwise had at MAJ33. The real drop in status for this class was 34.2% – not the 2.1% inferred by the customary quintile reporting.

From Table-45, it is plainly apparent that with maldistribution, all quintiles were losers except Q5. But from the table, one might have inferred that the 20% of the population in Q5, principally the college educated, benefited. Wrong. You must struggle to find individuals who reap great rewards from maldistribution. They do not appear in abundance, even in Q5.

As shown in the following graph-46, no group beneath the Top1% benefited by more than 15%. All those beneath the 92nd percentile were losers. None beneath the 97th percentile benefited by more than 4.5%. How then can Q5 show a 23.7% beneficial maldistribution influence? No problem: The Lower½% got an average 56.78% benefit and the Top½% received an average 172.12% benefit. Their increases are so great that they cannot be reasonably shown in graph-46. All of this can easily be seen by dividing the MAJ25 case by the MAJ33 case in the lookup-table spreadsheet. Though the precise numbers may vary in particular cases, the maldistribution thrust remains in the same general direction.

#46

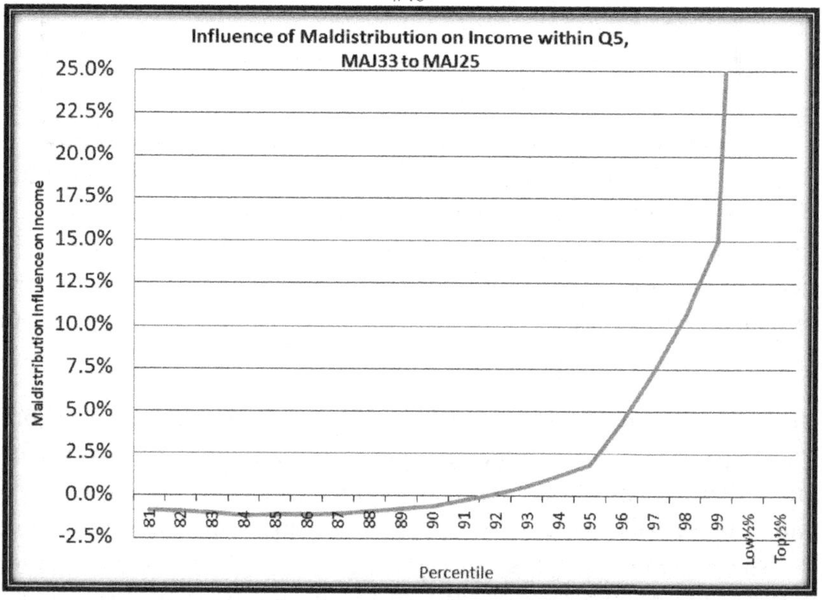

We can quickly see the consequences of falling from a MAJ33 to a MAJ25 and then returning to an equitable position at the original MAJ33 (the "maldistribution influence"). The fall results in an average 25% drop in income for the majority [25%= 25/33.333-1]. The return to an equitable distribution results in a 33% increase in income for the majority [33.3%= 33.333/25-1].

The "equitability influence" row in the previous Table-45 shows the vast benefits of returning to an equitable distribution. As previously mentioned, the reason that the return from maldistribution is more potent than the initial fall is that the base income for the majority had been reduced so greatly by maldistribution that returning to the original 33 level produces a sea change. This is one reason why the move from maldistribution is massively beneficial. It was the crucial component that pulled the USA out of the Great Depression and kept the economy vibrant. By 1939, the nation had gone from a MAJ24.6 in 1929 to a MAJ28 and real GDP was higher than pre-crash levels. The cure was well in progress, with the MAJs going ever-higher. The world of macroeconomics is now in love with interest rates, stimulus, tax policy, and financial manipulations of various kinds. The majority of these, even when appropriate and beneficial, carry a less potent influence than a break from maldistribution.

Let me show in graph-47 what quintile reporting looks like in a typical MAJ25 distribution compared to individual reporting.

#47

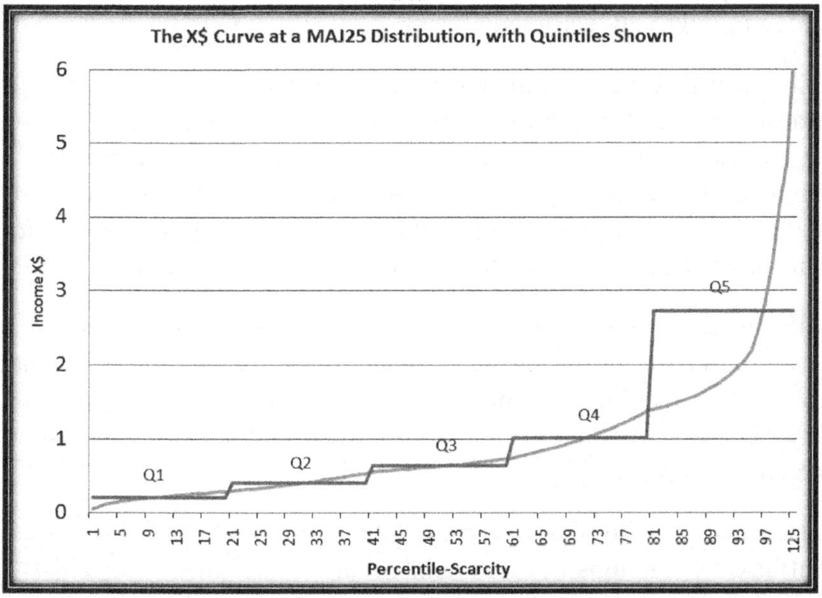

As we look at the intersection of the curve with the quintile horizontal lines, we can see that at approximately a single point, each quintile intersects with the income-distribution curve. At all other points, quintile data is erroneous. With quintile reporting alone, the spread becomes so enormous within the fifth quintile (Q5) that one cannot tell what is happening. Q5 would report a single 2.7 multiple for the entire group. A person at the low end of Q5 would be earning 1.4X$. A person at the one-in-a-hundred rank would be earning 4.7X$. By the time one reaches one-in-a-thousand, it is 28.6X$. Of course, it sharply escalates from there. All these people are within Q5. It is not the guy at the low end of Q5 that is bending the curve, but the folks at the top.

To speak of Q5 as an income-distribution group is especially useless. By not reporting the changes within the key portions of Q5, the main effects of maldistribution are almost completely disguised.

To show the data in graph-47 required an analysis that is accurate but seldom used. When you divide each of the quintile values by 20 (the number of positions in a quintile), then you get the average X$ for each quintile level shown in horizontal quintile lines in the graph.

All of this begs the obvious: Why is data reported in quintile form at all? With modern computing and file storage, the difference between 5 data points and 130 data points is trivial. Should you doubt the value of more precise reporting, take a look at the spreadsheets that my programs have created from U.S. governmental data.

It is sad that we miss many of the great stories of income distribution because income distribution is reported so convolutedly. Studies indicate that income Q3+Q4 for New England colonies in 1774 was 52.8%.[20] Such a high degree of equality at this point on the curve is unprecedented. You would know this instantly from looking either at the 400-case lookup table or histories of the 100-point distributions in particular nations.

If this figure is indeed true, we would be missing one of the great stories at the cradle of democracy – modern democracy was born under an extraordinary equitable income distribution. We would have missed the story because convoluted methods for reporting income distribution ensured our ignorance.

Gini and quintiles have a central defect. Intuitively our first instinct, and rightfully so, is to look out for "number one" – the "me." Gini and quintiles are counterintuitive because they force us to look at the general condition first and then leave us hanging without ever letting us know how the "me" is doing. The X$ curve starts with the "me" and then provides sufficient information so that you can determine how any larger group or any person elsewhere on the scale is faring.

Anyone who delves into the data will see that there is a range of highly inequitable distributions where any single description of the curve (whether it be Quintile, Top1%, Gini, or MAJ) breaks down and can no longer adequately describe the distribution. Any one of these values could stay the same or vary slightly when some other condition changes significantly. This is more than a passing theoretical point. Wealth distribution, for example, is so much more inequitable than income distribution that many of these terms often lose any significant meaning. Short of an X$ curve, you have insufficient information to understand what is going on.

#49

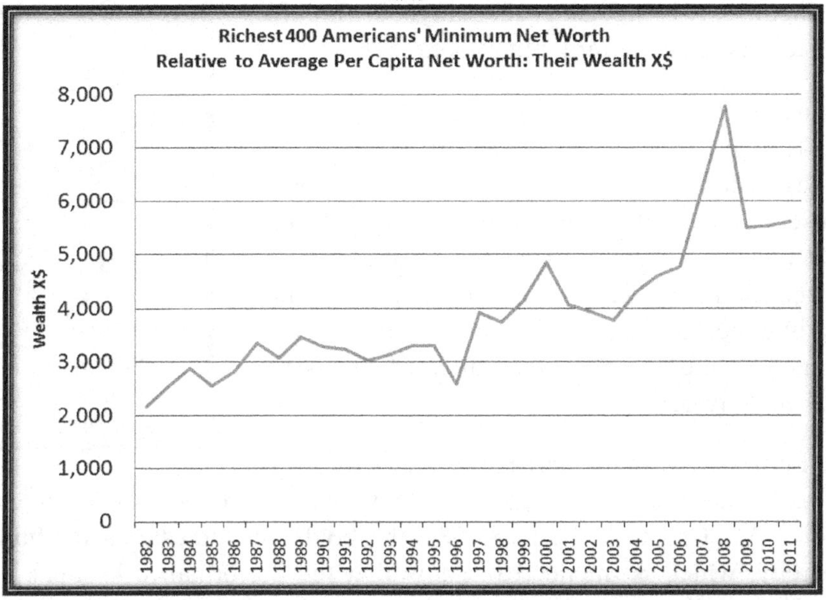

By way of example, at current population levels, only one in approximately 767,500 people are included in the Top400 wealth holders in graph-49. This is now the scarcity level for this group. In the graph, we see the ratio between the average net worth for everyone in the U.S., and the minimum net worth required to be included in the Top400. During the past decade, the U.S. MAJ has owned only about 4% to 5% of total net worth.

Without data at this level of precision, you would know very little about distribution at the extreme top, especially if you were given only the Gini. When the Forbes 400 was first reported in 1982, the minimum required net worth for the Top400 was about 2,200 times average U.S. net worth. At its peak in 2008, it was approximately 7,800. In the same period, the Gini for these distributions ranged from 71 to 84.4 – numbers which don't tell the story.

With 130 points you have sufficient detail to get a good working knowledge of the incomes and wealth of everyone from the very lowest to the very highest. Many people are doing studies of unimaginable variety and importance. They need to know the precise standing of individuals worldwide, from the lowest to the highest. Even a novelist is entitled to better information than is currently available. Quintile reporting benefits no one. It is not science. It is not reason. It certainly is not serious economics. It is hide and seek. Anyone who hides the data is not a steward, but a scoundrel.

Percentage	Scarcity
50%	**2**
75%	**4**
87.5%	**8**
90%	10
91%	11
92%	**12.5**
93%	14
94%	17
95%	20
96%	**25**
97%	33
98%	**50**
99%	**100**
99.5%	**200**
99.75%	**400**
99.88%	**800**
99.94%	**1,600**
99.97%	**3,200**
99.98%	**6,400**

Scarcity.

Though scarcity has been mentioned many times within these pages, we have not looked closely enough at it. Let's turn to it now. Income distribution is usually discussed in terms of percentages. Inadvertently, this can be seriously misleading because compensation, if fair, must be related to the scarcity and utility of the performance delivered.

Let's start with the percentage and scarcity Table-50. The points in a light-type font illustrate conventional percentiles alone. At 50%, to 75%, to 87.5%, the bold font indicates a doubling of scarcity, which is intended to show that the performance brought to the marketplace is twice as rare at each step, and compensation should reward those doublings. Similarly, doublings shown in bold occur at 92%, 96%, 98%, 99%, 99.5%, et cetera.

By way of example, looking at percentages alone in the table might suggest to you that since the percentages 99% and 99.5% are close, people at those levels should be compensated at approximately the same level. That would be wrong. The person at the one-in-200 level (99.5%) is, or at least should be, bringing a performance to market that is twice as rare as a person at the one-in-100 level (99%) [2= 200/100]. Always keep your eye on scarcity, not percentile.

Scarcity is the reason that income-distribution curves sharply rise once you get to high percentiles on the curves. A sharp rise is natural and does not imply a problem. The problem is the more delicate one that this book focuses on. When the rise is excessively sharp, the result is maldistribution. So we need also to have a fine-tuned understanding that can distinguish between an appropriately rising compensation at the high end and one that is excessive.

It is so hopelessly impractical to speak in terms of percentages within the Top1% that the only workable method for evaluating high remuneration is scarcity. When we speak in percentages at the lower end of the scale, we need to be aware that scarcity is the motor behind compensation.

The explicit purpose of the following graph-51 is to show *pure scarcity*. Previously, you have seen comparisons between MAJ33 and MAJ25, and the percentiles shown in a separate row at the bottom. But you have not seen pure scarcity. We benefit from looking at it now.

#51

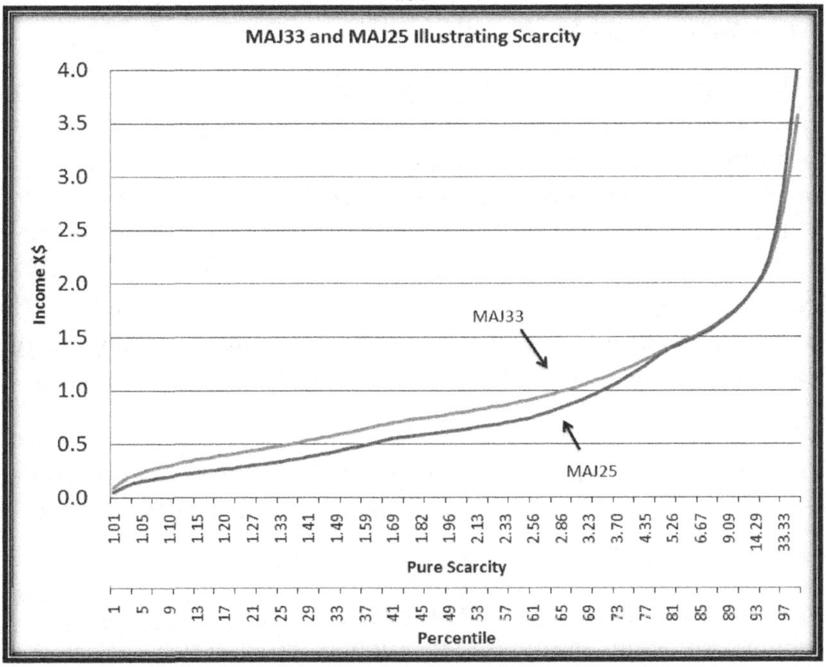

In graph-51 you see income rising slowly at the start. You also see that the pure scarcity numbers in the first row increase slowly in tandem. More to the right you see income sharply increasing as do the scarcity numbers. With graph-51 and the prior page 50 table, we get an idea of the general link between income and scarcity. And as we see in the various distribution curves, this relationship varies in form depending on which distribution prevails. By contrast, the percentile row at the bottom marches to a different drummer. It increases linearly.

For this reason, logic using percentages to describe distributions, as one might use in customary conversation to estimate appropriate norms, often tends to be wildly misleading. Although we often must talk in percentages, we need to know that at the core, scarcity directly moves distributions, not percentage. At best, percentages do so in an indirect manner [scarcity= 1/(1-percent probability)].

The dictator game.

Economist Joseph Stiglitz in his book, *The Price of Inequality*, summarizes a field of economic inquiry sometimes referred to as the dictator game.[21] At risk of further summary, here goes: There are two players. Player #1, the dictator, is given $100 and instructed to divide it between himself and player #2. The dictator usually takes the greater share and gives player #2 about $30 to $40.

The purpose of the game is to measure fairness and to see how player #2 responds. There is a limit to how much inequality player #2 will endure. When offered less than about 20% of the total ($20), player #2 revolts and refuses to accept any payment whatsoever. He would rather receive nothing than be treated unfairly. Now let's consider this in light of this chapter's heading "... one third or one fourth." The one fourth is 25% – the MAJ25 income share. If we are to assess the degree to which the 60% majority would be disgruntled, it seems they may well be nearing an arguable 20% threshold for revolt. That threshold is close to a 21.3% to which we will soon enough turn.

Oh, by the way, in the dictator game, when player #2 got about one third plus, there was no revolt. It is possible to placate the MAJ by being passably fair with us.

The time machine, now in reverse only.

Studies by King, and revised by Lindert, provide sufficient data on the 1688 income distribution in England and Wales[22] that my programs could roughly reconstruct a full range of the 300-year old distribution (with the same Gini, Q5, and Top5% as originally supplied). The program produces a MAJ21.3 distribution for 1688. Other analyses of data of the same approximate era yield similar results.

This makes it easy for us to look at and get a better understanding of income distributions of the kind that existed a century before the U.S. Declaration of Independence was written, and similarly more than a century before Adam Smith published *The Wealth of Nations* – the book which so nicely details the essence of a market economy.

The following graph-53 compares modern income distributions in a democracy and market economy at MAJ25 and MAJ33 with those of antiquity when King James II was on the throne in England, and neither modern democracy nor market economy were words on the tip of one's tongue.

#53

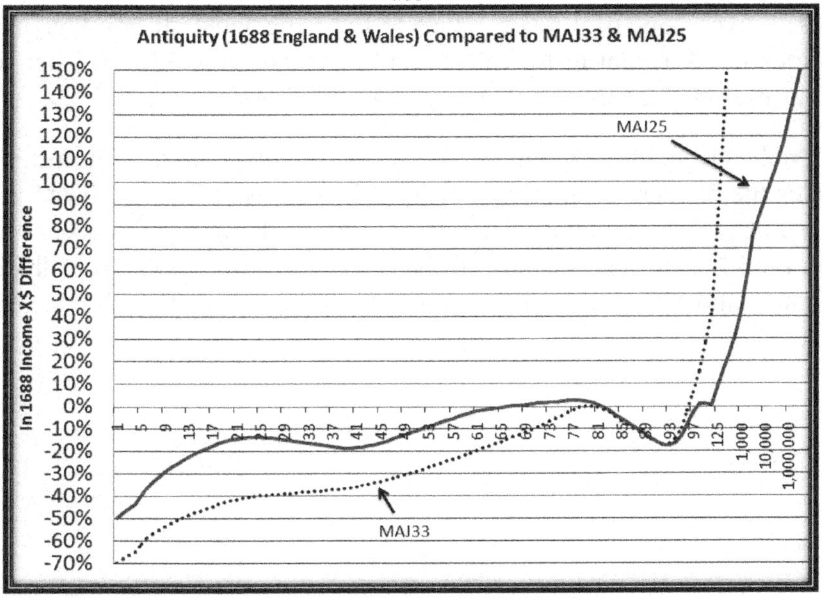

The zero line in graph-53 corresponds to conditions roughly as they existed in 1688. The graph shows that in 1688 people beneath the 80th percentile obviously faired much worse than their counterparts at MAJ33. Maldistribution proponents may argue that the recent dive into a MAJ25 maldistribution is fairer than income distribution 300+ years ago (the year 1688). Yet even there, the argument is not entirely accurate.

The recent maldistribution move to MAJ25 has put about 1/5th of the population at roughly the same relative X$ position that they would have experienced in antiquity, as evidenced by the points where the MAJ25 curve hovers near the zero point. It will take only a continuation along the current maldistribution path to bring the complete population beneath the 80th percentile to the approximate status experienced in antiquity.

Maldistribution enthusiasts are undoubtedly troubled by the observation that at the high end of the income scale, the relative status of the nobility, kings, and the like remains considerably higher than their modern counterparts under a MAJ25 regime. They need not despair. Remedy is in sight. It is still possible to move back those 300 years. The move from 33% to 25% MAJ was accomplished in 30 years. At this pace, the move from MAJ25 to MAJ21.3 can be performed within 17 years; the year 2029 or thereabouts might well be the date of interest. [16.7= ln(25/21.3) / ln((33.333/25)^(1/30)); 2029= 2012+ 16.7]. The rate at which equitable income distribution has collapsed gives hope of a quick return to the King James II era. Only 7% of nations in the recent historical record have reached MAJ21.3. Their illustrious example can inspire all King James II aficionados.

Maldistribution proponents may now proudly march with confidence under the banner "King James II in 2029 or bust." The "or bust" adds a fine folksy (if not literal) American touch to the ancient concept – don't you think? That nicely wraps up the science of going back more than 300 years in about half a century without troubling yourself with science fiction.

CH. 3

WEALTH

Wealth for the majority.

To draw attention to what Wealth is: As in a business or nation, it is net worth – the value of all your assets, less all your debt. So even though you may regard your car, house, and valuables as an indication of wealth, for true wealth, you need to subtract your debts. Net worth is an important component of economic wellbeing. Do not let income dominate your worldview to such an extent that net worth is forgotten.

As with income, wealth[23] can be estimated by using MAJ techniques. We just use the WealthMAJ rather than the IncomeMAJ (previously and customarily referred to as MAJ alone) to indicate the percentage of total wealth held by the 60% majority.

By way of introduction, the WealthMAJ is universally much lower than the IncomeMAJ. A wide difference between the two is common worldwide. In a sample of worldwide data that I had, the WealthMAJ was about 39% of the IncomeMAJ at the median (range 14% to 77%). In U.S. history, it seems to follow a path similar to the one shown in the following graph-56.[24]

As maldistribution advances, the MAJ increasingly does not have ownership. Ownership is net worth. That ownership shifts to the already wealthy. A monstrous dislocation and wrong is that *magnified reductions in net worth at the low end of the scale result from income maldistribution.* It is inevitable. And it is precisely the matter that distribution concerns itself with.

The relationships between components are not difficult to picture in your mind. If you have wealth, you are in a position to lend money and to control assets. If you do not have wealth, you are certainly in no position to lend money. Instead you are apt to become a borrower.

#56

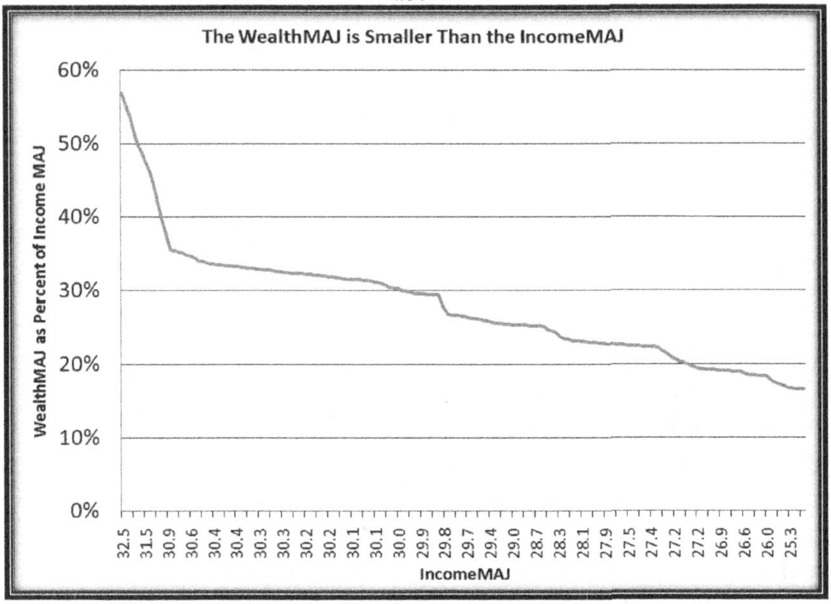

As the wealth at the low end of the scale is progressively reduced by maldistribution, those at the top are forced into unnatural machinations to lend money to people who neither have the assets nor income to support their borrowing. Their incomes can stagnate or be reduced by way of maldistribution. The MAJ's capacity to purchase may also be slight, causing them to purchase less from businesses that the wealthy own. Unholy distortions of wealth and income distribution played dominant roles in the Great Depression and the 2008 Calamity.[25]

In acute cases, the wealthy, too, are damaged by maldistribution because they no longer have means for effectively employing their assets through investments or for deriving good interest rates through sound loans. From the various combinations of these components, opportunities for crises and sharp business cycles thrive.

Guided by traditional economic thinking, I can remember many years ago being impressed by the commendable economic calming in the post WWII era through the 1970s in stark contrast to the wild swings of standard deviations in prior eras of booms, panics, and busts in U.S. economic history. I attributed this beneficial outcome largely to prudent monetary and fiscal policy. Now I tend to think another great hand was also at play: the removal of prior maldistribution.

#57

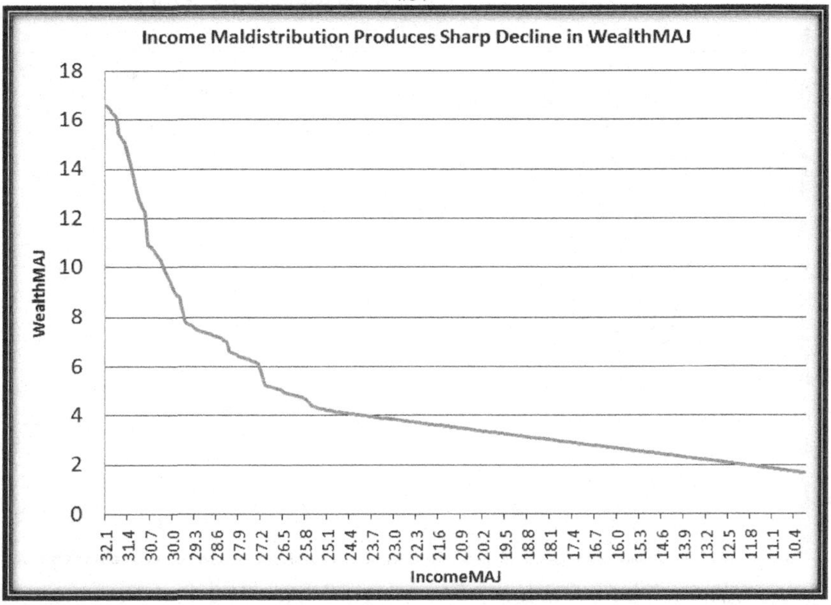

We see in the above graph-57 that wealth distribution is highly sensitive to income distribution. A small change in the IncomeMAJ is often matched by a large change in WealthMAJ. A pathetic picture appears to the right in graph-57. In the real world, the relationship is highly variable and not as ironclad as it may appear in the graph, notwithstanding that the tendencies are in the same direction. It may interest you to know that graph-57 was created by multiplying the percentages in graph-56 by the series of IncomeMAJs shown on the horizontal axis.

Lest you think that the 60% majority having a mere 4% or so of the total net worth of a nation would occur only in extraordinarily barbaric nations, you may want to observe that since 1997 the WealthMAJ has usually been less than 5% in the United States.

For half of all U.S. history, the IncomeMAJ has exceeded 29.7 and WealthMAJ has exceeded 7.8. The recent vigorous and concerted efforts of many people over many years have now moved the U.S. into rare territory. *By both distribution measures, U.S. conditions are more adverse in 2007 than in 97% of the nation's history as shown in graph-58.* And other recent years during the past decade are close to these values. In 2003, WealthMAJ was reported to be at 4%.[26]

#58

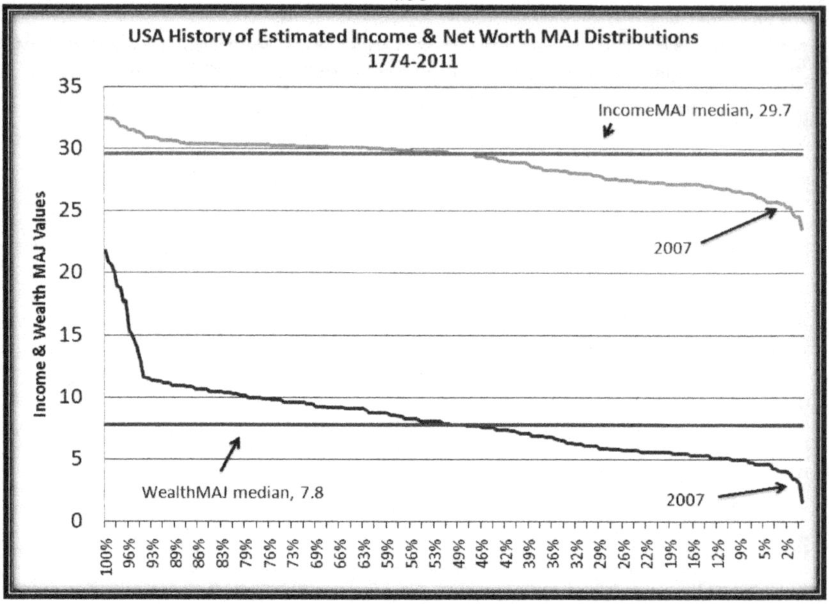

You may not be accustomed to WealthMAJs and feel that their values are so miniscule that there could be no possible remedy. Please take heart. A short mental exercise may help you to see that a solution is possible for the MAJ.

As in the methods used with IncomeMAJ, you can do quick calculations with the WealthMAJ to determine how the wealth of the 60% majority changes when the WealthMAJ changes. In the 2009-2011 period, the WealthMAJ was approximately 4. A move to the customary U.S. median WealthMAJ7.8, when other conditions remain the same, would mean that within the MAJ, wealth would be 95% larger on average [95%= 7.79/4-1].

The following graph-59 shows similar changes at other points in real world estimates for those in the 60% majority [1.948= 7.79/4]. A huge increase in wealth resulting from such changes can be looked at from the inverse perspective, too. A wealth that normally would have been available for the MAJ has been removed. The return is not so much an augmentation of the MAJ's wealth as it is a return to the approximate standard that made common economic activity possible in the past.

#59

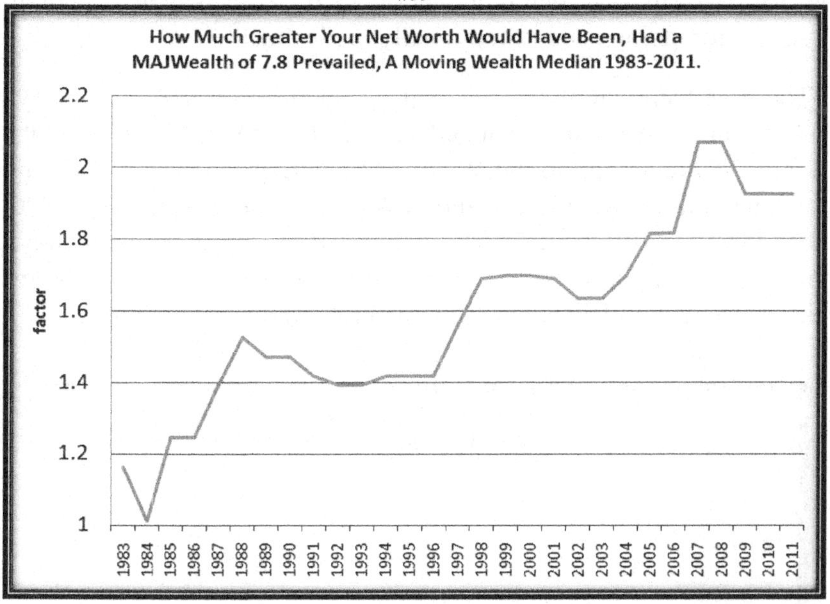

#59B

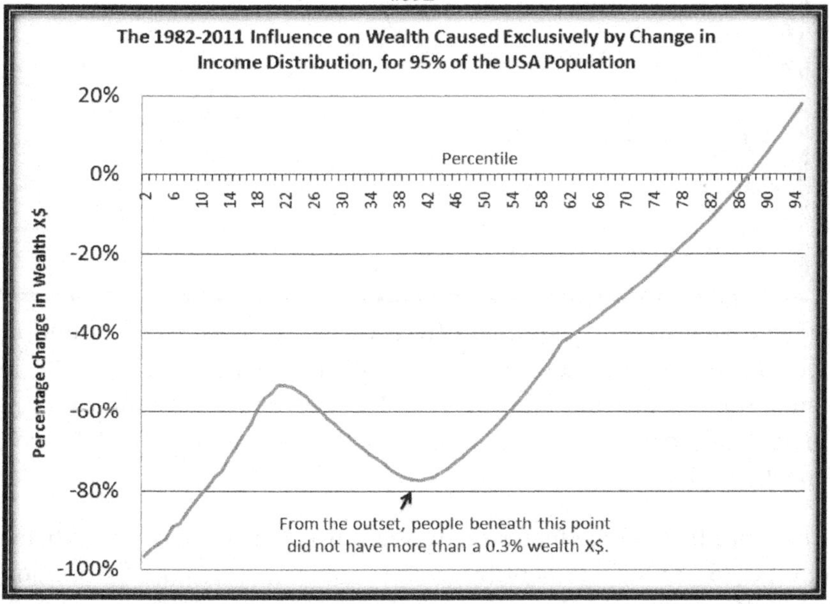

When circumstances conspire to provide the extremely wealthy with a significantly greater share of wealth than exists under median conditions, remedy is required. The MAJ needs to be provided with conditions that make it possible to accrue at least 7.8% of a nation's wealth. Otherwise, how can citizens consider their nation to be a beacon of economic fair play? The foregoing is an exceptionally modest goal.

These concepts apply to the real world in graph-59B. From 1982 to 2011, wealth distribution changed so significantly in the U.S. that there was a 65.7% reduction in the WealthMAJ during the period. The onset of this reduction of wealth for the MAJ began long ago. By 1990, the WealthMAJ had dropped 54.9%, and by 1999 the downward move had gone further south to a -61.7%. These great drops in wealth for the majority are ingredients sufficient to feed numerous future difficulties.[27]

#60

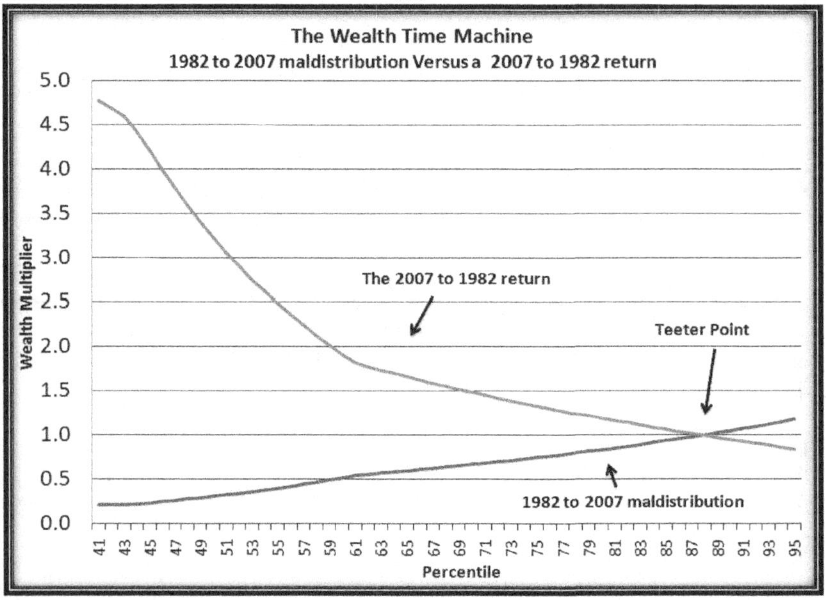

The period of most extreme difference in recent wealth distributions for which I have a consistent data series are the years 1982 to 2007 in the United States. Focusing on the 41st to 95th percentile in graph-60, we have a picture of wealth distribution changes that significantly differs from income distribution.

Beneath the *income* teeter point, there was a broad zone of indifference from the 76th to 92nd percentile, where changes in income distribution had slight influence (graph-14). With *wealth*, the picture is different.

In the graph, net worth sharply diverges at points beneath the wealth teeter point – the 88th percentile. In the income-distribution indifference range, wealth by contrast was significantly reduced by maldistribution, dropping, on average, to 84% of its former X$ level and presenting an average 1.19 wealth multiplier upon returning to the more equitable 1982 wealth distribution.

From this we see that the broad group close to the income teeter point, who initially appeared within a zone of indifference, now is significantly hit by the change in wealth distribution. The clear maldistribution losers expand to about 76% to 88% of the population, depending upon whether you take an income or wealth view.

The wealth converter.

The Wealth Converter is the ratio between wealth and GDP. It is a fundamental number for analysis, and it has practical implications in your life. Its effect can be seen in the private and public sphere.

In the late 1960s, I worked in Manhattan and lived in Brooklyn. The impact of converting money into wealth (items of long-term value) is profound. The wonderful old public library only two blocks away was a treasure, as were Prospect Park, Central Park, the museums, the art galleries, and the universities. All of these forms of wealth significantly contribute to the value of life, with unexpected results in my case.

My night courses at NYU serendipitously resulted in my becoming a director, editor, and cameraman, and later, starting a small business that manufactured motion picture editing equipment. The business, for many years, was the source of my livelihood and satisfaction. When you think back on your life, aren't there instances where wealth significantly benefited you? The prudent application of wealth touches us all.

For the past 40 years, I have lived in a section of Appalachia where most folk have, to state it politely, modest income and wealth. To state it sharply, too many of us are dirt poor. Notwithstanding poverty, one house in a nearby mountain neighborhood always stood out. The lady there had a beautifully maintained vegetable garden and flowers everywhere – a very nice place. Often even in resource-poor times, individuals and business can make extraordinary advances because they take the little bit they have and employ it to great advantage. Sweat equity becomes equity (Wealth).

And there are fluctuations in circumstances. I recall a West Virginia back road that I regularly traveled many years ago. The times were always tough there, but one year in the 1970s, folks seemed to have a little more money. That year, a striking number of homes were suddenly painted and put into reasonably decent shape.

On an international scale, you can see the capacity of some nations to more effectively convert income into wealth. A few years ago, I felt the need to quit relying on secondhand reports and made a trip around the world to see it for myself, traveling and living, much as locals do.

I recall crossing the border from Kyrgyzstan into Uzbekistan. I was struck by the number of roses, well maintained vines and homes, recently manufactured small cars and trucks, and the activity of the people in Uzbekistan. Yet upon returning and looking at statistics, both nations were shown with the same per capita income. Unless the region that I saw was doing disproportionately well, I was certain that the figures were incorrect.

A few years later the data changed to reflect the higher per capita income for Uzbekistan. Never underestimate "walk down the street" economics: people growing more roses and having the capacity to be proud of their homes and lives. That justifiable pride and order is so difficult to achieve. And once it is achieved, it is wonderful when it can be perpetuated. Such events etch on my thinking the importance of being there on site and relying on your own eyes and ears.

To make another comment on "walk down the street" economics: To significantly draw down net worth unnecessarily and often is a reliable impediment to wealth. We had a landlord in town who universally rented to the most disreputable folk. Whenever a family moved out, the yard was littered with discarded mattresses, furniture, appliances, and the like. Poverty is exacerbated by imprudent management of assets. Reducing your net worth by unnecessarily buying and replacing mattress, appliances, or covering costs of other imprudent decisions keeps the ratio between net worth and income low – in many instances a low wealth converter existing for the rest of your life.

To exclusively employ income to cover expenses of titillation and short-lived consumables can also ensure that you never have significant wealth or a nickel in the bank. Wealth requires discipline, not necessarily obsession.

So, there it goes. Just as in your own life, some people are more adept at converting income into wealth. This relationship between income and wealth as we see it in economies has powerful mathematical implications.

The U.S. Wealth Converter is equal to the ratio of net worth of households to GDP.[28] Knowing this value is fundamental to estimating wealth. Since the process is straight forward, it may interest you to know the three steps used to get both wealth and income estimates for all income strata from the lowest to the highest. The method follows:

> First, the appropriate IncomeX$ curve (shown in the foregoing curves) is multiplied by the average GDP per capita to get income estimates in dollars and cents, or whatever other currency you desire. This gives the income for each person on the curve. Second, the average GDP per capita is multiplied by the Wealth Converter (which is also GDP based), to get the average wealth per capita. Third, using the same principle as the first step with income, the above average wealth per capita is multiplied by the appropriate WealthX$ curve. And presto! The job is complete. From the lowest to the highest, you have estimates of wealth and income for everyone.

Regardless of what mechanisms are the motors behind the workings of an economy, four components ultimately determine our income and wealth: GDP per capita, the Wealth Converter, the IncomeX$ curve, and the WealthX$ curve.

From this summary, I trust you can appreciate how crucial wealth and income distribution is to our economic lives. You depend on these components. They constitute the highway to your pocketbook.

Pause. Think. When we talk of income or GDP, we think of money coming into our hands. This emotion dominates – be it personal or national.

Financial health is the consequence of income (GDP) and net worth (wealth) together. These two peas need to be in the same pod. But net worth is such an odd item. Valuations of assets may be wrong. And net worth involves an inconvenient calculation: Assets less debts equal net worth. We are so fond of forgetting that last item that we wrongly relegate it to a separate discussion, as if debt were separate from wealth. Wrong. Wealth is always another word for net worth. As inconvenient as it may be, wealth will always be assets less debts.

Wealth distribution (WealthMAJ) drives home the point: Who will be the debtors? Who will be the lenders? As long as net worth is maldistributed, lower classes will be excessively indebted to upper classes or foreign sources of funds. When a nation talks of excessive debt, it talks about a sick net worth.

And Income distribution (IncomeMAJ) tells how we value people: Which classes we elect to treat with dignity. Which classes we treat with disdain. Who we give opportunities to. Who we do not. From this we see how central both IncomeMAJ and WealthMAJ are to the financial health of people and nations.

The canary: the wealth converter.

So far we have discussed the salubrious side of the wealth converter. It also contains an unhealthy component. We see that up until about 1995, the Wealth Converter stayed within a customary range, moving about a median of 3.5. For the U.S. at the time, that was the range of wisdom. Then it exploded. Twice.

#64

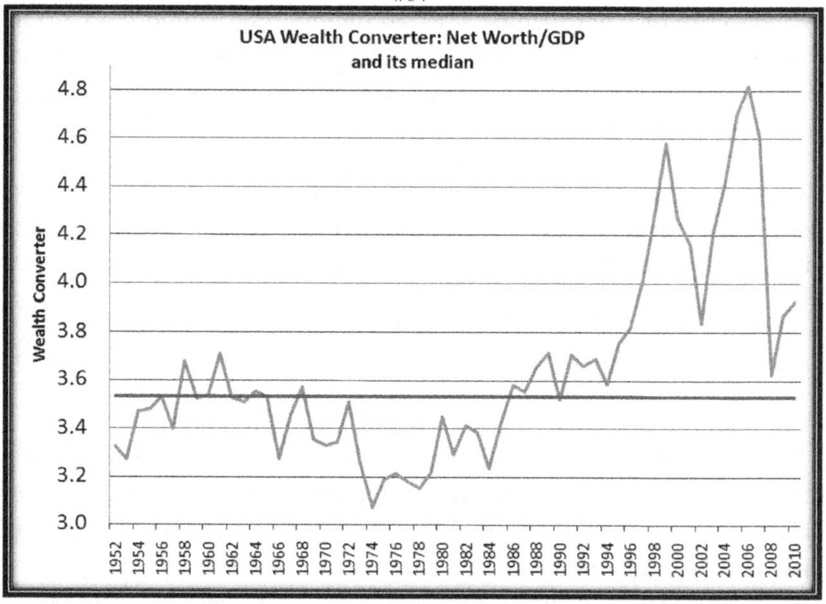

The Converter in graph-64 was trying to tell a story. Hardly anyone was listening. However, in this drama, Robert Shiller of Yale picked up on the rumbles in both instances prior to calamities. He attempted to alert the nation. In the first version (year 2000) of his book, *Irrational Exuberance*, he correctly identified (using PE ratios) a key dragon: overvaluations of stocks. In the second version (2005), his Chapter 2 spotted the second dragon, housing. In clear language, we were told why stock market and housing prices were irrationally high and doomed to fall. The books were met with widespread discussion, excitement, respect, and inaction.

In two of the most worthwhile downloadable databases on the web, Shiller provides sufficient stock market and housing data that anyone can go from the present into data that reaches as far back as the late 1800s.[29] With these databases in hand, you can see how the two bursts in the Wealth Converter occurred.

#65

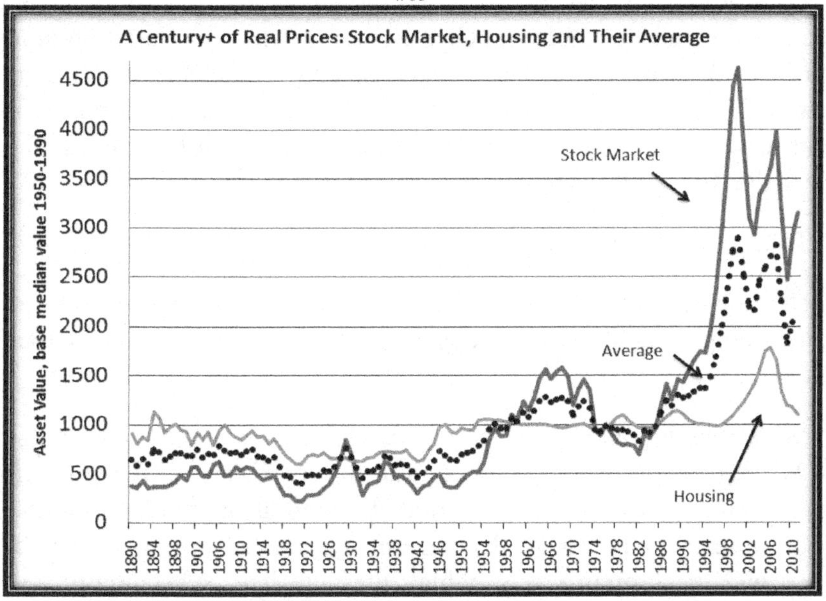

An instance in everyday life where we see the relationship between income and assets is the Home Price-to-Income Ratio. The common understanding is that to be able to afford mortgage payments, a base income sufficient to make mortgage payments is necessary. For bankers to go beyond sensible ratios and the common practice of verifying income would induce mortgage failures. In the United States, from the mid-1970s through the late 1990s, the ratio for new homes was usually between 3 and 3.5.[30] Starting in about the year 2000, the ratio rapidly rose to exceed 4.5 by the middle of the decade, systematically placing homes in the hands of owners who could not afford them. Further, a new and unconscionable form of mortgages appeared, formally called “stated income loans” (informally “liars’ loans”), in which bankers systematically did not verify the mortgage applicant’s stated income.[31] A PBS online video is persuasive, showing 2004 FBI warnings and more being ignored.[32] Mortgage failures followed.

In wealth converter history, most seriously distorted relationships between income and wealth compel correction.

The previous graph-65 is derived from the Shiller datasets. It was modified so that 1,000 would represent the median income-adjusted value in the U.S. during the 1950-1990 period. With this scaling, the graph represents the differences in prices of assets as if you started out at a median point somewhere between 1950 and 1990 with $1,000 invested.

Look at housing. The graph shows more than a century of housing price data. Never had there been such a huge burst in real (inflation-adjusted) housing values as the one that began in 1997. Suddenly it shoots up (as does the Home Price-to-Income Ratio). Not hard for competent management to spot a problem long before a crisis. Plenty of time to take corrective action by quelling the fervor.

Take a nap. Let it crash.

Now glance at the stock market (real S&P500,* scaled). I reserve comment. Being sardonic twice a day is excessively stressful. Let's touch on that later.

More relaxing and to the point, recall the twin humps that you saw in the Wealth Converter. They are similar to the average of the stock market and housing values shown by the dotted line in the graph. It is possible, but usually unnecessary, to go deeper. An analysis of key asset classes and debts, and the proportions in which they are held substantially does the same thing that the Wealth Converter does.

The Converter measures the relationship between income and wealth. When wealth unnaturally and wrongly expands, the impact is evident. The Converter is the proverbial canary in the coal mine.

The great advantage of the Converter is that, even without lengthy analysis, it is possible for management to spot trouble brewing well in advance and to take corrective action. With it, you can easily perform DIY economics and keep management on its toes.

The Wealth Converter moving standard deviation is one of the most reliable ways to spot ensuing trouble. The following graph-67 shows it.

---

* The S&P500 stands for Standard & Poor's index of 500 large companies traded in the U.S. stock market. It generally represents performance of industries in the U.S. economy.

#67

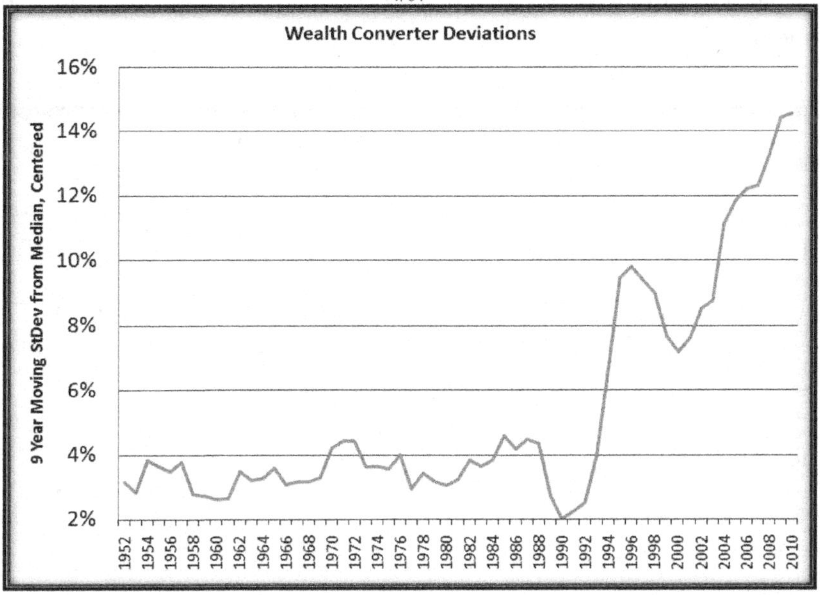

Looking at deviations is preferable to looking at absolute values because nations have vastly different Converter levels. Graph-67 focuses on unnatural deviations from the median. If the deviations cannot be explained by healthy moves in the economy, even a casual observer is forewarned. You don't need to be an expert. Keep an eye on the upswing. We will return to it much later.

Wealth worldwide.

Estimating wealth for individuals worldwide is fraught with difficulties. Net worth (wealth) data is nonexistent for many nations. About 30 of 150 nations provide some wealth distribution data, often decades old. This is in sharp contrast to the 2,500+ income-distribution cases used to develop the income-distribution curves in the lookup-table spreadsheet.

The lack of wealth reporting makes it difficult to calculate reliable Wealth Converter values. The following graph-68 shows Converters for 161 nations in the year 2000.[33] The median on the horizontal line is 3.71.

The Wealth Converters used in graph-68 cover most nations and are the only data I have access to. I use these Converters in the spreadsheets knowing that true Converter values vary from year to year. When annual Converters are not available, wealth estimates in the spreadsheets are susceptible to error. With such little reliable wealth data, I have restricted most of the wealth calculations to the spreadsheet, where perhaps you can improve on them

#68

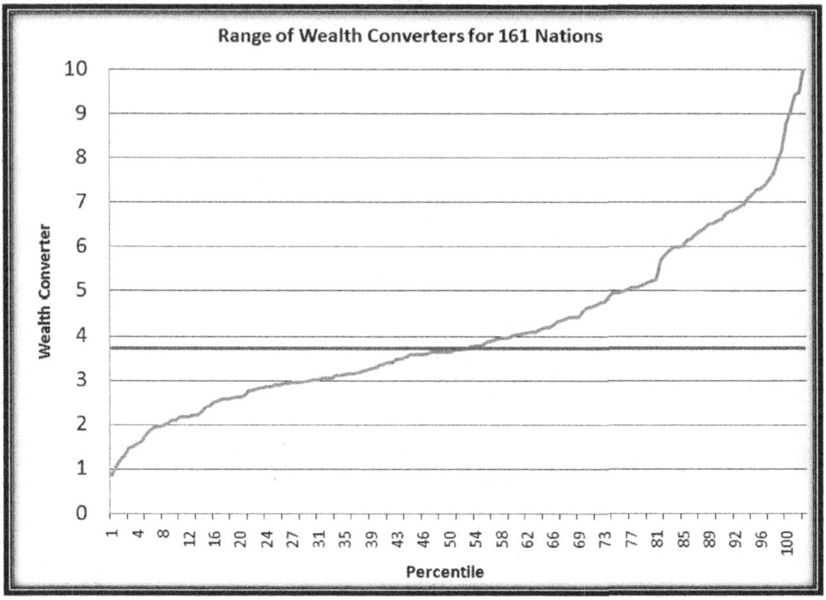

The Wealth Converter tells us how efficiently a nation converts income into wealth. This capacity varies between nations for numerous reasons. One of the less happy reasons is that in some poor nations, wealth holders invest much of their wealth outside the country where it is created.

Ancient Bolivia gives an example of conquistador wealth machinations and plunder of a kind that still continue in some regions. The *Insight Guides, South America* observed: "The amount of silver that was taken from Potosí [Bolivia] is staggering: 16 million Kg (16,000 tons) arrived in Seville between 1545 and 1660, three and a half times the entire European reserves of the day. The wealth was squandered on Spain's futile religious wars, or wasted by the extravagance of its nobles and clergymen, almost all of it ending up in the coffers of Flemish, German, or English bankers."[34] The expression "Rich as Potosí" became a synonym for wealth and opulence. The wealth came principally from a single mountain in Bolivia. Its extraction resulted in the death of thousands of indigenous Bolivians by brutal means. Effectively, none of the wealth remained in Bolivia. Exploitations of this kind do occur. The wealth converter can help ferret them out.

The wealth curve.

The Wealth Converter has a cousin. Indeed, a family of 100+ points: the Personal Wealth Converters on the Wealth Curve, as we see in the following graph-69 [achieved by dividing wealth by income at each data point].

#69

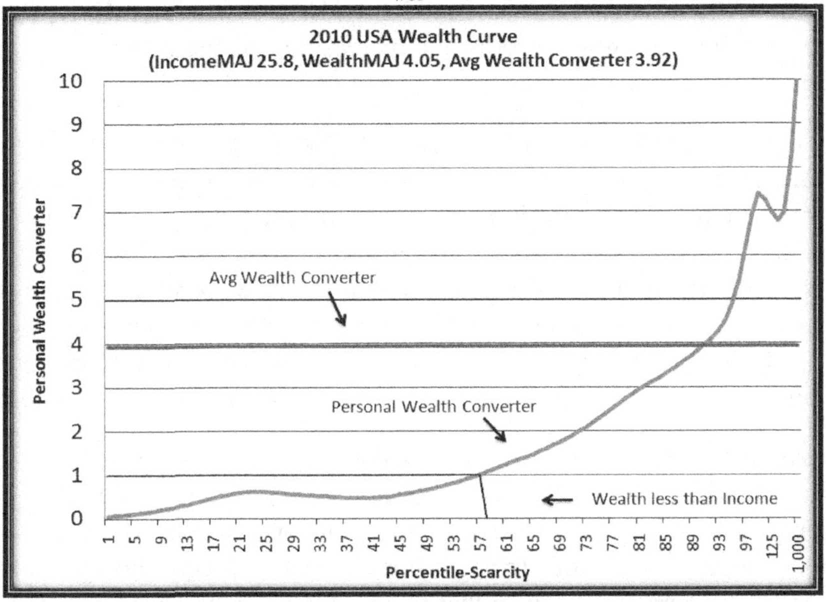

The average Wealth Converter at 3.92 is on the horizontal line. As you see, the average Converter (and by extension average wealth) tells us little about how individual people fare. The average intersects the curve at a single 92nd percentile point. For this reason, news reports of wealth approach complete uselessness. The range of wealth values are so vast that you must drill down to each point on the curve to get the drift of what is happening.

The Personal Wealth Converter curve is produced by dividing the U.S. net worth curve in 2010 by the income curve. By doing this, we can see how much wealth a person tends to have for each unit of income. The curve tells the approximate wealth relative to income for people at all points on the percentile-scarcity scale. For example, if your Personal Wealth Converter is 2, this means that your net worth is twice your income.

The wealth curve tells two stories. First, if catastrophe struck, you had no income, and you were compelled to sell all of your net worth for purposes of having enough money to live, the values on the curve indicate how many years you would be able to sustain yourself on your own resources at a level of expenditure equal to your current income. Under this scenario, 57 percent of the population has less wealth than income, as pointed out in graph-69. They would tend to exhaust their wealth within a year. Zero wealth is reached within 2 years for all beneath the 73rd percentile; within 3 years beneath the 82nd percentile; and for the person at the one-in-2,000 level (not shown on the graph-69), it would be 12.7 years. Of course, selling net worth makes one increasingly vulnerable to the point of desperation in extreme cases.

These conditions can be ameliorated by more equitable income and wealth distributions, but the magic of distribution in this area is modest. Instead of the dire scenario, people usually must adapt by having some source of income and reducing expenses. The lucky and sometimes wise few at all strata can build a more secure financial condition by having a good income, being attentive to keeping debt low, investing, and saving a sensible fraction of their income. Good luck, as well as fortunate starting circumstances, are sweet beyond a recitation of the didactically obvious.[35]

Another story told by the curve is that accumulating wealth takes time, even when one saves. The wealth curve multiples seem to be related to the average years to accumulation. It is not inconceivable that many of the very wealthy accumulated their fortunes within relatively short periods, say in about 40 years or so, given that this was the Wealth Curve value at one-in-a-million point in 2010.

A handy feature of the wealth curve is that it makes it possible to make a crude first approximation of income when net worth is known, but when income is unknown. Dividing net worth (wealth) by the corresponding point on the wealth curve gives an estimated income.

Are you better off now than you were 38 years ago?

Ah … Dear reader … Perhaps you had not hatched at such a distant date. But I trust you grasp the drift. Long, long ago in a world with many bright and blissful days, equitable wealth and income distributions were so plentifully common that we thought they came with the rising and setting of the sun. Never in a dream did we think otherwise. They were bright but ignorant times.

For practically all people, wealth comes at uncertain times and in uncertain ways, but it bears one consistent, unwavering property. To sustain wealth requires the capacity to conserve it. In an instant, wealth (large or small) can be lost through imprudence or by a turn in the wind of fortune.

Wealth can seldom withstand the constant pressure of irresponsibility. Building and sustaining wealth usually connotes responsibility and discipline.

In the USA, the necessity for a level of responsibility to have and sustain property was not lost on the Founders. They required holding property to be a precondition for voting rights. They did not want mob rule. They wanted enlightened rule. For good reasons, we no longer require the holding of property to be a precondition for the right to vote. But, correctly so – a link between wealth and responsibility will continue to exist. Long-standing wealth fosters the responsibility necessary to maintain it.

#71

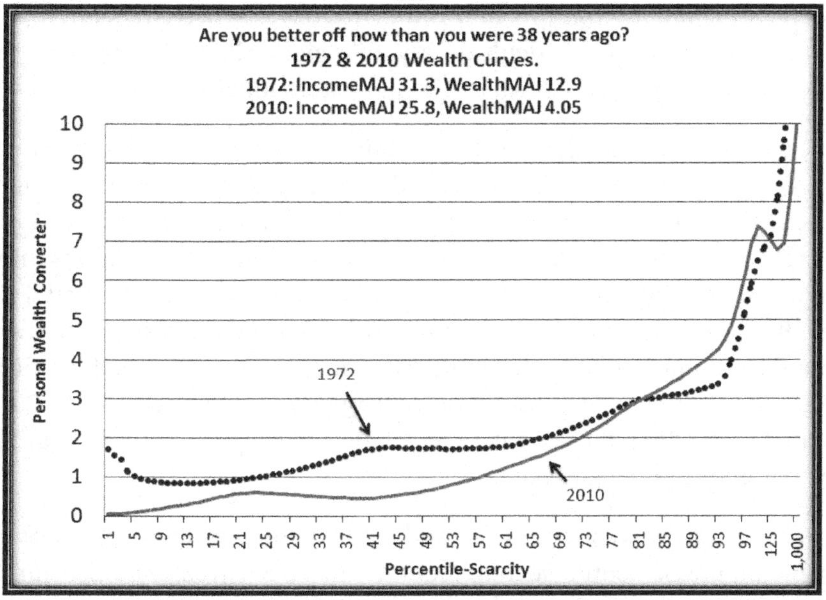

In the above graph-71, you see that beneath the 80th percentile, people had very little wealth, often not even enough to sustain themselves for one year in the event of catastrophe. By contrast, in the 1972 curve, many would have had enough wealth to sustain themselves for about two years.

The transformative impact of the 2010 curve by comparison to the 1972 curve is that modern maldistribution removes a desirable wealth-income relationship from a huge proportion of the population. The essential grounding of responsibility in wealth (even when it is a small amount of wealth) has been systematically removed by the income and wealth distribution curves.

For those not at the high strata, it was beyond the power of the individual to correct. It left a large portion of society no longer grounded by the responsibility and discipline inherent in prudently sustaining wealth. Now, the wealth for much of the nation relative to income is so slight that the ethics that were once a part of the normal social fabric necessarily change. A change I do not welcome.

Fish in the tummy. Nets.

In high school, I had the rare opportunity to have an economics teacher (Yale graduate) who was rumored to be worth in the neighborhood of thirty million (oil) – at the time, a lot of money, as it still is. He did a good job. I still recall a few of articles we studied. No customary text books. Myron Joseph's *Economic Analysis and Policy* (1963) is where we started. It was stiff reading in parts – difficult for a young high school student. The phrase I took away from the class was: "Capital is foregone consumption."

Capital can be property or invested money. Or it can be more abstract – say a Robinson Crusoe, on an island spending several days making nets instead of eating fish which he might snag by hand in tidal pools. By foregoing the immediate consumption of tidal pool fish – to take the time to build nets for catching future fish – Crusoe builds for himself capital (nets) which (until the nets need to be replaced) will make the rest of his life easier and food more readily available. By contrast, if Crusoe had continually focused on immediate consumption (snagging and eating fish), instead of expending his time building nets which became capital, his life would have been more primitive and poor.

The wealth curves provide a handy means for approximating how much people on the percentile-scarcity continuum save (invest) and consume. By these methods, we can examine the workings of the economy and see approximately how much goes to immediate consumption (fish in the tummy) and how much goes into capital (nets). Capital in the modern economy comes from savings (foregone consumption which works its way through the system to become capital). By using the wealth curve, I will show how income maldistribution has a perverse influence on a market economy.

Regardless of one's income level, a chief advantage of a certain amount of savings (and thus wealth) in your life is that it has the potential to bring tranquility. It is akin to the psychological concept of delayed gratification, which is also a measure of maturity.

But there are no easy answers. An economy requires consumption for businesses and employees to prosper. If there were a wild run to excessive savings, it would reduce necessary consumption. So it is issues along these lines to which we now turn.

CH. 4

ANALYSIS: bottom up

The aggregate versus the specific.

If, as you look up from the operating table, the last thing you see is the surgeon walking in with an ax instead of a scalpel, he has elected to treat you in the aggregate, not the specific.

To work correctly, one must use scalpel-like precision, not blunt instruments. The aggregate is blunt. Before looking at the aggregate, it is crucial to look at how each segment of the population, from bottom to top, independently influences the overall efficacy of a program at each step in money circulation. The economic usage of the term "aggregate" evolved during the 1930s when economic data was often nonexistent or primitive.[36] Keep in mind that national accounts data such as GNP and GDP did not exist then and unemployment data was unreliable.[37] The current usage of the term "aggregate" has value only to the extent that the individual components have been adequately accounted for first.

Even at the time of the Great Depression, Lauchlin Currie's then available data would have suggested that velocity of money (the average rate at which money circulates) would have been about 3 to 3.3 times per year.[38] For purposes of easily illustrating the principles involved at each step of annual circulation, the velocity is shown here as an even 3 steps per year at MAJ25.

In Table-76 shown here, we see that the average proclivities to consume for the 60% majority, everyone together, and the Top1% are respectively

98.6%, 96.5%, and 82.1%. These three groups follow the general principle that the less money you have, the less you can save. Thus your consumption rate is higher relative to a wealthier person. This principle is also seen in the wealth curves where people at the low end are compelled to spend a greater proportion of income rather than growing their net worth. Let's consider a government stimulus program, spending money that must select between five cases shown in the Table-76.

#76

Consumption Rates for the Three Target Groups:

The 60% Majority	Everybody	Top1%
98.6%	96.5%	82.1%

The Five Cases:

	Consumption Rate	Consumption at Each Step and Multiplier	Efficacy
Case 1			
MAJ only	98.6%	98.6%	
	98.6%	97.3%	
	98.6%	96.0%	
Multiplier and efficacy		**2.9**	**100%**
Case 2			
Average Only	96.5%	96.5%	
	96.5%	93.1%	
	96.5%	89.8%	
Multiplier and efficacy		**2.8**	**96%**
Case 3			
Top1% Last			
Average first	96.5%	96.5%	
	96.5%	93.1%	
	82.1%	76.4%	
Multiplier and efficacy		**2.7**	**91%**
Case 4			
Top1% first			
then Average	82.1%	82.1%	
	96.5%	79.2%	
	96.5%	76.4%	
Multiplier and efficacy		**2.4**	**81%**
Case 5			
Top1% Only	82.1%	82.1%	
	82.1%	67.4%	
	82.1%	55.3%	
Multiplier and efficacy		**2.0**	**70%**

During the three steps of the circulation cycle annually, the efficacy of the five cases can vary from 100% to 70% depending on the order of circulation and which groups are targeted. The targeting and ordering are significant. Up to roughly ⅓ can be lost by inefficient targeting [30%=100%-70%].

We can also see via the multiplier to what extent consumption can be expected to expand or contract when new money is injected into the system or when it is removed from the system (such as through debt reduction or monetary policy that reduces the supply of money). In either stimulus programs or contracting programs, multipliers act with equal force. A stimulus program that increases consumption by a multiplier of 2.9 will also reduce it by a factor of 2.9 when matching contracting policies are enacted.

In fiscal policy (government spending), programs can be targeted toward specific groups. In monetary policy, the thrust is usually broad coverage with effects accruing in rough proportion to how much money each segment controls – the Top1% being a key beneficiary.

There is no monetary or stimulus magic. Everything that has a benefit also has a cost. Long ago, Samuelson laid out the fundamentals in the 1948 first edition of his widely used textbook: "Only over the whole business cycle need the ledger be in balance." During good times, "the budget should show a surplus of tax receipts over expenditures, so that the public debt can be reduced. But when bad times come, then the budget should show a deficit of taxes over expenditures, with the public debt returning to its previous level. ... In a nutshell, that is all there is to counter-cyclical compensatory fiscal policy."[39]

Before Samuelson's first textbook, before Keynes had taken a grip, and even a month and a half before Franklin Roosevelt was sworn in as President, the University of Chicago Round Table in January 1933 stated the matter in the clearest fashion I have yet to see. Their statement had the virtue of making the analysis during time of crisis, not from the comfortable armchair of retrospect: "The balancing of budgets should be regarded as a series of long-term operations in which deficits will be incurred and debts increased during years of economic adversity, while Treasury surpluses and the rapid retirement of the public debt will be planned for years of prosperity. ... The equilibrium between revenue and expenditures is thus intentionally struck over a period of years rather than annually. ...[T]he borrowings for 1934 should not be less than the sums required to finance emergency relief, loans, investments, and public works. … The financing of recurrent outlays by borrowing can, however, be justified only as a depression measure, and it should be abandoned as soon as the country is well on the road to recovery. … [T]he failure to take advantage of a period of prosperity to build up financial reserves will tend to make … speculative booms the more pronounced."[40] Less formally, the wisdom of counter-cyclical policy was necessitated in harsh climates by storing up summer produce for winter consumption. As for long-term counter-cyclical policy, the notion predates the printing press:

> The dream: Seven cows, fat and sleek … Then seven other cows poor, very ugly, and thin. Never had I seen such ugly ones in all the land … The thin and ugly cows ate up the first seven fat cows.
>
> Reading the dream: The seven good cows are seven years … The seven lean and ugly cows are seven years of famine. There will come seven years of great plenty … After them will arise seven years of famine, and all of the plenty will be forgotten … The famine will consume the land. The plenty will no longer be known in the land because of the famine that will follow, for it will be very grievous.
>
> Joseph, the overseer: Take one fifth of all the produce of the land during the seven plenteous years … Lay up grain … That food shall be a reserve for the land against the seven years of famine that are to befall the land.[41]

In 1928, well before the Great Depression, the non-economists (but popular writers) Foster and Catchings grasped the key issues which they attempted to convey in *The Road to Plenty* – a book designed to have broad appeal to the general reader, told in the form of a novel that took place on a train journey. It had the virtue of appearing long before the 1929 Crash and Great Depression. I will liberally abridge some of it here: "Always there loomed the menacing specter of another big slump. Everywhere men talked about the next depression as though foreordained. … This country may be too prosperous, but three million workers without steady jobs don't believe it, nor do the many million more who don't know for sure whether their jobs will last another week. … We recommend when business begins to look rotten, more public spending. Projects are already before Congress for buildings, inland waterways, harbors, national highways, and parks. Construction can be pushed forward or held back, as the general business situation requires. ... When production is far below capacity, and many workers are unemployed because the demand for their products is insufficient, it is far better for the Government to spend money on public works than to use the money to pay debts. The question really is when debts should be paid – how much now, how much later?" Foster and Catchings had an understanding (albeit not rigidly accurate in places) of counter-cyclical fiscal and monetary policy.[42]

In that era the single rule of a balanced budget was the gold standard for a properly administered economy, including in FDR's mind.[43] His predispositions did not lead him toward counter-cyclical stimulatory deficit spending. In sharp contrast to popular current opinion, from 1933 to 1939 FDR ran an average deficit of 3.67%. This compares to Hoover's 1932 deficit of 4.00% and the 1981-1989 average deficit of 4.07%.[44] Keynesian deficit-spending was never fully employed in the U.S. during the Great Depression. It was employed during WWII, and then not in response to economic policy, but in response to necessity of war.

The excesses that have occurred in the name of stimulatory policy have taken place when the second and equally important phase (the paying back in good times) was left undone. When the second step is removed, it becomes a policy of profligacy, not counter-cyclical spending.

An effective stimulatory program consistently defies gravity: Trickling functions in an upward direction in economics. This is shown in the five cases in the previous Table-76. Notwithstanding that Case 3 and 4 have identical components, placing the stimulus in the hands of the Top1% first instead of last, reduced the capacity of the stimulus to increase consumption by a full 10% [10%= 91%-81%]. And the stimulus remaining in the hands of the Top1% throughout all three steps produced the least effective results. If it had been possible to confine all three steps within the 60% majority, the overall results would have been 42.5% stronger than the Top1% performance in Case 5 [42.5%= 2.9/2.0-1]. Government spending for purposes of stimulating wastes money to the degree that the Top1% is inappropriately targeted.

The table reflects what happens when new money (say through deficit spending) is put into the system. A small proportion is removed for savings at each step in the circulation (as indicated in the right hand column). By this process, each subsequent step is able to contribute less to consumption, as can be easily traced in the spreadsheet.[45]

The following often-repeated passage has given birth to one of the most pernicious notions in economics: that carelessness can be excused as long as it is stimulatory. In response to extreme conditions during the Great Depression when circumstances required a sharp increase in employment, and when the then ironclad rule of a balanced budget was contributing to economic failure, Keynes in 1935 wrote: "If the Treasury were to fill old bottles with banknotes, bury them at suitable depths …, and leave it to private enterprise … to dig the notes up again …, there need be no more unemployment and, with the help of the repercussions, the real income of the community, and its capital wealth also, would probably become a good deal greater than it actually is. It would, indeed, be more sensible to build houses and the like; but if there are political and practical difficulties in the way of this, the above would be better than nothing."[46] Too cute by half. Brilliance and clever arguments cannot be an excuse for such economic carelessness in any sector. Great care needs to be taken that government spending, as other investment spending, delivers benefits to the citizenry at least commensurate with all its costs.

When we look at the total economy, the following well-known and universally accepted relationship applies: Aggregate Demand = Consumer Spending + Investment + Government Spending + Net Export. The role of consumption is significant not only because it is the largest share of any of the components in the economy, but because the health of consumer spending drives investment, which is also a significant component.

Keep in mind the central point that personal consumption per capita reflects the economic benefits (goods and services) that citizens ultimately receive from the economy. I turn to the Adam Smith chapter in the 1961 edition of Heilbroner's *The Worldly Philosophers* that I have had since childhood: "Do not forget that the great beneficiary of the system was the consumer – not the producer. For the first time in the philosophy of everyday life, the consumer is king"[47] – a precious concept now routed, in part, by maldistribution.

What you have seen here illustrates that income distribution not only influences our lives in ways evident to us every day, it also is central to gauging how stimulus expenditures will influence economics. If you wish to diminish the effectiveness of a stimulus program, place the money in the hands of the rich.

CH. 5

PROVING ADAM SMITH: the maldistribution connection

Economic workings laid bare.

Adam Smith, in the *Wealth of Nations*, said it plainly in the quaint way of the time: "... what improves the circumstances of the greater part can never be regarded as an inconvenience to the whole. No society can surely be flourishing and happy, of which by far the greater part of the numbers are poor and miserable. It is but equity, besides, that they who feed, clothe and lodge the whole body of the people, should have such a share of the produce of their own labor ...."

And to the particular point to which we now turn, Smith states: "Consumption is the sole end and purpose of all production and the interest of the producer ought to be attended to only so far as it may be necessary for promoting that of the consumer. *The maxim is so perfectly self-evident, that it would be absurd to attempt to prove it.*" [emphasis added]

And so it has remained, unproven. Now to prove it.

With consumption and economic performance, maldistribution creates three overarching problems: 1) It takes money out of the hands of the lower classes, who have a high propensity to consume, and places it into the hands of the wealthy, who have a low propensity to consume. 2) It concentrates money in the hands of a few. Whenever an activity is concentrated in few hands, in contrast to many hands, there is greater variability – hence a greater tendency toward booms and busts in an economy. This universal phenomenon is well recognized and a key reason that in experiments, you use many samples rather than few samples before drawing conclusions – commonly known as "The Law of Large Numbers" and by its converse "The Law of Small Numbers." 3) The velocity of money, the rapidity with which money circulates, is faster in poor hands rather than in rich ones. Velocity of money slows during economically depressed times, making monetary policy a less potent corrective instrument. For all of these reasons an equitably distributed economy has inherent counter-cyclical properties to quell booming and busting and to advance more assuredly than a maldistributed one.

Let's pause and think. Savings is the "anti-matter" of consumption. When we do not spend, we save. To keep the machinery of capitalism running, a certain proportion needs to go into savings in order for capital investment (which is required for production) to advance. But if savings exceeds the proportion required to keep capitalism sufficiently well-oiled to run, then the motor runs poorly because people do not consume sufficiently – too much "anti-matter." A self-aggravating condition spiraling downward can exist when savings is excessive and consumption is thereby unduly reduced – an example of this was the Great Depression. The efficient sweet spot is when savings reaches, but does not exceed, the point where adequate consumption occurs. By way of the propensity to consume, income distribution can help to define this sweet spot.

We will approach the savings-consumption question from a perspective already implied by the wealth curves. The wealth curves suggest the proportions that each of us from bottom to top spend and, by extension, how much we save. With this information, we can prove Adam Smith's maxim and show that maldistribution stands in opposition to Adam Smith's fundamental premise.

With wealth curve data in hand, we know how income distribution inevitably defines the two prime movers in an economy – consumption and savings. All we need is a group of many varying plausible propensity-to-save curves to test how they would perform when multiplied by a variety of distribution curves – the propensity-to-save curves indicating the percentage of savings at each point, and the distribution curves indicating income in the form of X$s.

Notwithstanding that there is no necessity to have the propensity-to-save curves conform to particular rules, there is an attractive method we can use to create a sample of propensity-to-save curves. We can use as our starting point the savings rates that the U.S. has experienced over the long term. By this means, we retain the same pattern of variability experienced in the historical record. The model helps to isolate the analysis from confounding extraneous historical components. To achieve our end, we use a single Wealth Curve as the starting point.

With the above information (saving rates, propensity to consume rates, and the full range of income distributions), we substantially have the key components of the economy in hand to test the influence of maldistribution alone. The details for the model follow:

> The Wealth Curve tells us that savings are highly concentrated at the high end. We mathematically preserve this proportional relationship by using a designated factor, but manipulate the factor so that, when the resulting propensity-to-save curve is multiplied by MAJ25 and MAJ33 distribution curves, it produces the exact desired savings rate. At MAJ25, that 100-point propensity-to-save curve would always deliver the sought after savings rate. We then repeat the same process for each of the 500+ savings rates since 1959.[48] From this, we have a reasonable sample of 500 propensity-to-save curves conforming to those interest rates. Then we do the same thing again, except that we start at MAJ33 to create another 500 propensity-to-save curves. This accomplishes two purposes: It increases the number of experimental curves to 1,000, and ensures that results from MAJ33 to MAJ25 are unbiased.

The following graph-84 shows two sample average propensity-to-save curves at MAJ25 that produced 6.1% and 7.6% average saving rates.[49]

We can now let the game begin in the model by always applying the same 1,000 propensity-to-save curves to each of the distributions. To arrive at the ultimate consumption curves, we merely subtract each point on the propensity-to-save curve from one. By this means, with substantially the entire workings of the economy in your hands, you know how much each person consumes and how much is available for capital investment. You can see in isolation, the degree to which income distributions of all kinds influence the workings of the economy.

#84

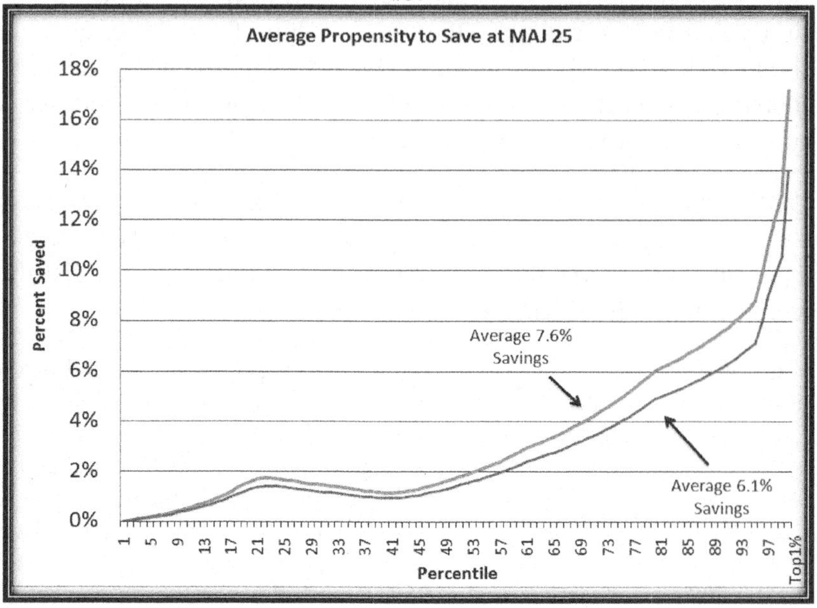

#84B

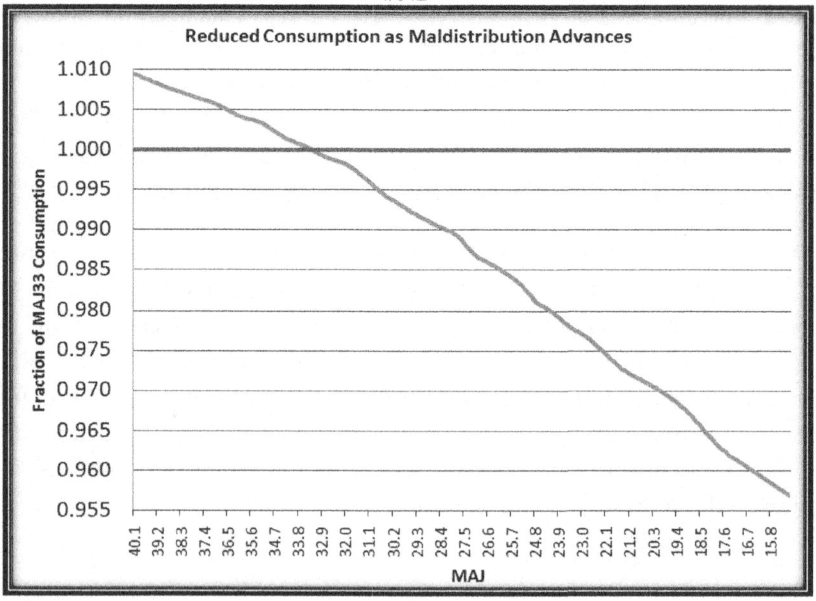

In the above graph-84B, at MAJ33, consumption for the nation is 1.00. When it falls beneath this point, the difference indicates the percentage of lost consumption. MAJ25 is at 0.98, which is equivalent to a loss of 2% consumption by virtue of the maldistribution shift [2%= 1.00-.98]. This 2%

of foregone consumption caused by maldistribution occurs year after year at MAJ25 – an unnecessary loss of wellbeing and a poorer citizenry. It is also clear that had those goods and services (2%) instead been consumed, it would have required additional employment to produce them. An estimate of the magnitude of the continuous loss of employment resulting from the lost consumption can be made (not done here). We see in graph-84B that with extreme maldistribution, consumption drops become increasingly profound.

As shown earlier in graph-51 and 84, both the distribution and propensity-to-save curves are highly inequitable and bend sharply upwards on the right hand side. Thus, when identical propensity-to-save curves are multiplied by varying distribution curves, saving variability (and thus consumption variability) is accentuated. As maldistribution increases, the economy becomes increasingly less stable as a consequence.

#85

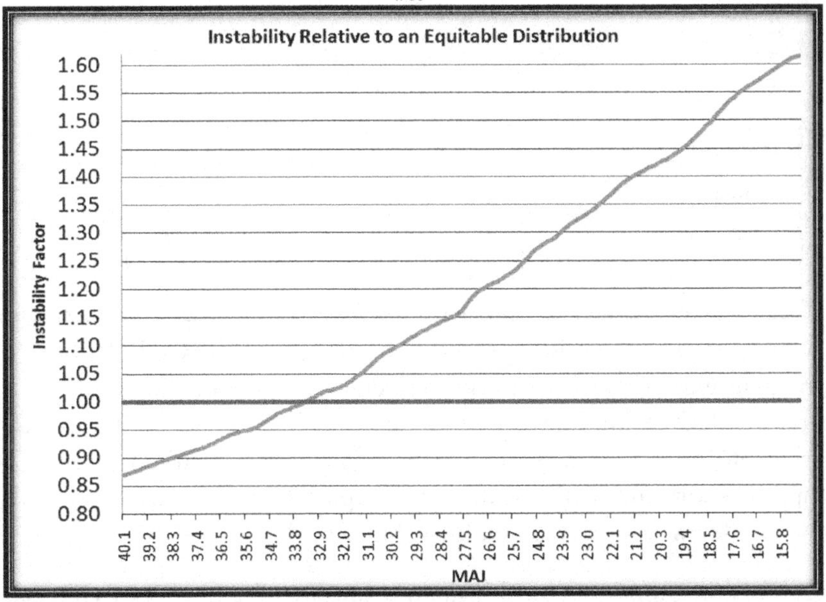

We can measure the resulting instability by using the standard deviation to compare instability at other distributions with the instability that exists at MAJ33. By this means we see in graph-85 that at a MAJ25 maldistribution, consumption is 26% less stable, which is to say more variable, than an economy at MAJ33. By the time you get to the profound MAJ15 maldistribution, consumption is fully 62% less stable. Instability can be a deal breaker for an economy.

In all distribution scenarios, there are instances of hard times. By looking at the worst of these at each MAJ level and building a chart where 1.00 represents the MAJ33 case, the following graph-86 was produced. Graph-86 shows that when crisis occurs, the extreme cases are apt to be 4% more adverse under MAJ25 than under a MAJ33 maldistribution. This might well translate into somewhere around 4% more unemployment than would have existed under an equitable distribution.

#86

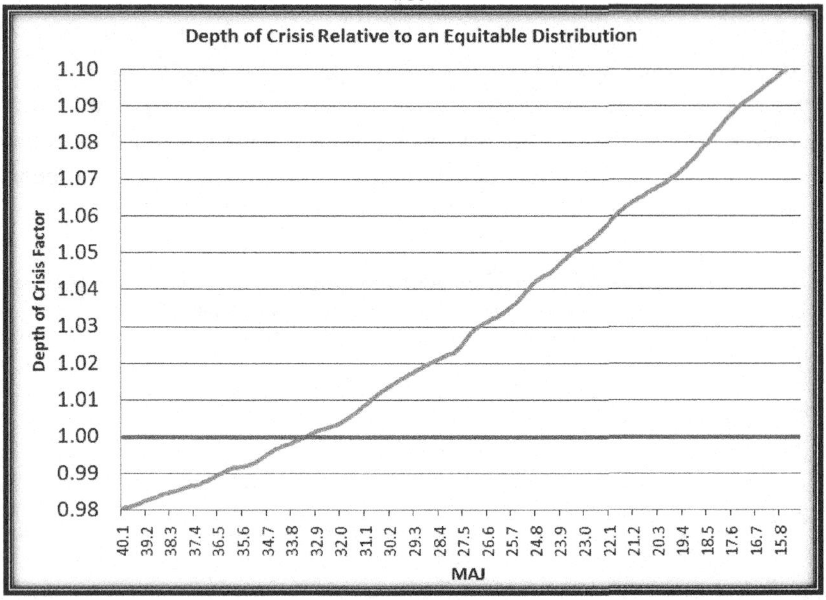

Consumer spending is the largest component of the GDP. Prior to 1980, its median was 62% of GDP. Subsequently, it has been about 67%. In the upcoming debt example, we will proceed as if it were 65%. As already discussed, at MAJ25, this degree of maldistribution resulted in a 2% consumption shortfall. In the following graph-87, we can see shortfalls become greater with increased maldistribution.

A 2% consumption shortfall in an economy where 65% of GDP goes to consumption spells a 1% loss of GDP [The 1% and 2% are rounded-off. At MAJ25 it is: -1.18%= -1.82%*65%]. If a government were to seek to offset this annual 1% reduction in GDP, the options would tend to come from one of the following components: GDP = Consumer spending + Investment + Government spending + Net export. By default, the choice would usually be increased government spending.

#87

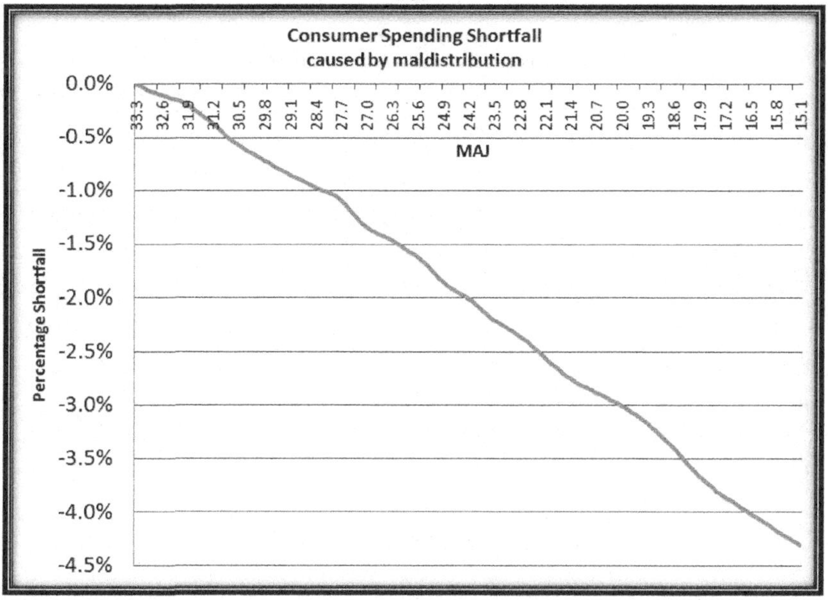

Even if by policy decision-making a nation was not aware that its GDP had dropped 1% because of maldistributribution, the nation might seek to treat social ills and loss of employment resulting from it by undertaking to annually finance an additional 1% deficit in each year. This policy, whether it be inadvertent or an intentional response to maldistribution, would have a measurable cost that would not be difficult to crudely approximate.[50]

With the given assumptions, trying to overcome the adverse effect of a MAJ25 maldistribution would create a debt equal to 10% of the GDP in 24 years. In 50 and 75 years, the debt would grow to almost 17% and 21% of the GDP, respectively. This would be huge, fully one-tenth of the GDP within 24 years, to address only a single issue – lost consumption resulting directly from maldistribution. This particular debt model could be more sophisticated and presumably more accurate. However, it helps to illustrate that counteracting the maldistribution consumption shortfall is costly to the entire nation and unremitting.

Unlike counter-cyclical fiscal policy, maldistribution is relentless, so even theoretically, there are no cyclical opportunities to pay back a portion of the debt accumulated. Nor does monetary policy offer a less painless solution. Its adverse effects under such circumstances would be more diffuse, but not less intense.

#88

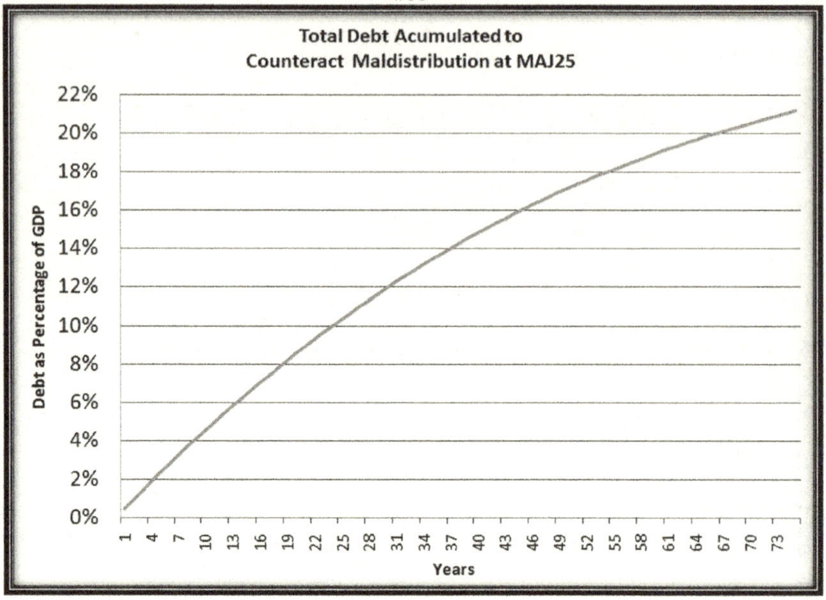

In nations with maldistribution significantly worse than MAJ25, debt consequences, given the assumptions, can be crippling – beyond the capacity of governments to meet – as you can see in the following section plucked from the spreadsheet:

MAJ	Years for Debt to equal or exceed 10% of GDP
30	not even in 150 yrs
25	24
20	14
15	9
10	8

A shortfall in consumption is an excess in savings by the same amount because that is where the money goes, say 1% of GDP at MAJ25, as has been discussed. Annually that excess savings would be approximately 0.92% of the equivalent market value of all currently reported publicly traded U.S. stock shares.

The great challenges in running a maldistributed economy are, as we have seen in the foregoing:

Maldistribution reduces consumption (and thus economic activity). It increases variability (more booms and busts). It increases the depth of crises. These combined increase unemployment. And maldistribution increases debt when management seeks to overcome its adverse impact. A management that enjoys dealing with insurmountable problems should always welcome maldistribution. It is certain to keep them busy and provide many fine opportunities for pontificating.

The big picture: maldistribution and the declining efficiency of savings.

Remember Adam Smith "… the interest of the producer ought to be attended to only so far as it may be necessary for promoting that of the consumer. *The maxim is so perfectly self-evident, that it would be absurd to attempt to prove it.* [emphasis added]" Here you can begin to cut the Gordian Knot* and move ever-closer to the proof that Smith mentioned.

Consider that the process of arriving at ultimate consumption involves all steps of finance, production, and delivery necessary to bring a product to market. When we measure the effectiveness of savings – which is a key driver in every aspect of the economy – to produce a consumed good, we are measuring the efficiency of the complete production and sales process to the point of ultimate consumption for each unit of savings [the ratio between consumption rate and savings rate].

While one might intuitively expect that savings would be a topic boring beyond words, the surprise is that it is central for comprehending how the great mysterious economy works. Savings must come in sufficient amounts to create the capital (nets) needed so that the system functions smoothly, yet it cannot come in such great proportions as to divert funds from products the consumer should properly be buying, and by extension, workers producing.

If you pick up your favorite copy of *The Concise Encyclopedia of Economics,* you are apt to see statements like, "… to economists, savings means only one thing – consuming less out of a given amount of resources in the present in order to consume more in the future. Savings, therefore, is the decision to defer consumption and to store this deferred consumption in some form of asset. … Although most people think of purchases of stocks and bonds as investments, economists use the term 'investment' to mean additions to the real stock of capital: plants, factories, equipment and so on. … By investment, economists mean the production of goods that will produce other goods. … Investment is usually the result of foregoing con-

---

* The metaphor refers to solving an intractable problem, as Alexander the Great mythically did when he encountered a famous and impossible to untie knot. Rather than attempt to untie it as previously tried, he cut it with his sword.

sumption"[51] – thus, the "capital is foregone consumption" statement drilled into me before I had facial hair.

And if you look to your friendly Wikipedia,* you may find a statement indicating that in National Income Accounting the savings investment identity requires that the amount saved in an economy equal the amount invested. That suggests the centrality of the savings-investment relationship. The objective of this conversation is not the fineness of definition, but to place the germ in your mind that savings and investments (for the production of capital) are tied together.

The money you save in the bank works its way through the system, often by loans, to make capital investments possible. And new stock issues are also instruments of capital creation, as are private business capital investments. (Sale and purchase of old stock issues are a transfer of ownership of capital, not a creation of capital.)

It is mathematically the case that one less the consumption rate equals the savings rate. By dividing consumption by savings, we can see the efficiency of savings at all distributions. To the extent that savings reflects true investment, we also see the efficiency of savings.

The plainly obvious historical and present feature of market economies is ever-increasing efficiency. From the early days of Adam Smith waxing poetic about division of labor and the wonders of the pin factory, to the modern day advantages of electronic transfer of information and computer-assisted manufacturing, efficiency has been the hallmark of capitalism. Maldistribution, shown in the following graph-91, stands in direct and dangerous opposition to the efficiency of capital.

In graph-91, the model at MAJ33 shows that, on average, every dollar saved produced $19.81 of consumption. But at the maldistributed MAJ25, each dollar of savings produced only $15.52 of consumption – savings being 21.7% less efficient at MAJ25 than at MAJ33. This relationship is the pivotal point of the analysis. [-21.7%= $15.52/$19.81-1; the dollar amounts may vary according to the model, but the percentage change and shape of the curve tends to be highly consistent.]

The efficiency gained through the capitalistic market economy can be lost in the financial sector by an excessive redirection of consumption to

* Yes, I break the rule and cite Wikipedia. Being pretentious don't work here. They do a great job.

savings. The increasing inefficiency of savings is mostly funneled into a key beneficiary: financial institutions. At the core, money that normally goes into production and consumption is diverted to savings, which is used to produce increased credit and financial instruments. With maldistribution, a disproportionate amount of money finds its way there and into stock market speculation. In the extreme case, conditions become distant from Adam Smith's world of efficient markets mainly benefiting the consumer.

#91

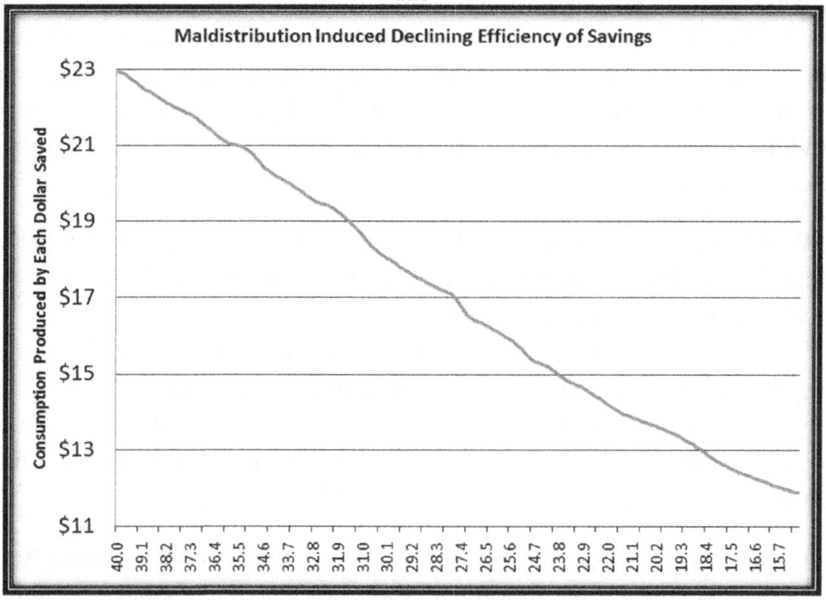

If the transition from savings to investment were to be made at no transaction cost, one would expect to see in national accounts that when consumption was divided by investment it too would yield somewhere in the neighborhood of the $20 to $15 of consumption for each dollar invested. But being realistic, the transition obviously would not be free. There would be transaction fees, some carrying costs, et cetera. A look at U.S. national GDP accounts showed each unit of investment producing only a median $4.40 of consumption during the past decade.[52] This figure suggests huge financial system inefficiencies, explicitly excessive carrying costs imposed by financial institutions, and diversions of savings into areas that are not investment. Savings is not being translated efficiently into investment, nor is investment being efficiently translated into consumption.

As one of the main beneficiaries of maldistribution, the financial sector is not only the repository of the excess savings produced by maldistribution, it can disproportionately siphon off a large portion of savings, calling it their cost of doing business. If this general thesis has merit, one might expect to see high executive compensation and periods in recent economic history when the financial sector grew considerably faster than other sectors that it was supposed to serve.

If the efficiency of capital is to move in tandem with the efficiency of savings, **the market economy requires the move toward equitable income distribution.** A downward shift in efficiency of savings, with increasing maldistribution, stands in brute contradiction to an efficient market system. If capitalism were maximally efficient, savings rates would remain static. And, if capitalism were ever more efficient, it would require less and less savings to deliver the consumed goods and services. In the previous graph-91, efficiency of savings clearly falls as maldistribution advances.

When we look at a model like this, which isolates the maldistribution effect from other real world activity, the move from MAJ33 to MAJ25 can cause the median savings rate to gradually increase from 6.1% to 7.6%. This keeps 23.3% more savings in capital markets precisely when consumption is reduced and capital investments are thus less attractive [23.3%= 7.56%/6.13%-1]. In the model, the change in savings resulted because fixed propensity to consume curves met ever more maldistributed income curves.

Long ago, the economist Arthur Okun so effectively lamented the "leaky bucket" in redistribution to the poor that it became an economic metaphor.[53] In the present case, one might reverse the metaphor to say that consumption is a leaky bucket in which a small amount in the form of savings normally drains out to nourish the capital ground. But when the savings leakage is more than the ground requires by way of maldistribution, it reduces the consumption that the economy needs to thrive, and it also distorts the workings of capital itself.

The present "leaky-bucket redistribution" goes from 92% of the population to primarily the rich few. The excess savings (about 1% of GDP) accumulating year after year is pernicious because, at least Okun's poor spent the amount they received almost instantaneously (as did most of those who received its leakage), whereas the rich place excess savings in ever-increasing amounts into capital markets, causing abnormalities there.

In the modern world, an early symptom of the widening gap between savings and investment (capital) is lowering interest rates and lower return on capital because the money invested is not worth as much. Too much extra money is out there – it is a savings glut. Later it can be expected to be called underconsumption, insufficient aggregate demand, over-production, and many of the other phrases used to describe depression. It is a recipe for serious dislocations.[54]

The stock-market capitalization to GDP ratio is a key indicator for efficiency of the market economy. It shows the willingness of the private sector to invest. Its median since 1950 has been about 0.67 to 0.72, depending on which source you use.[55] For the first time in all of U.S. history, it exceeded 1.0 in 1996 and usually stayed above this level, even reaching 1.6 in year 2000, which is to say that huge investments by the private sector were insufficient to nurse out large increases in GDP. At a 0.67 ratio we saw $1.50 of GDP for each dollar of capitalization. At a 1.6 ratio we saw only $0.62 cents of GDP for each dollar of capitalization. While the public sector (the government) has long been the whipping boy with every failure attributed to it, it need be recognized that despite the willingness of private sector to infuse money, GDP has been less responsive than anytime in U.S. history. The problem as indicated here is deeper – unrelated to the quantity of money infused either by the private or public sector.

The harsh irony is that excess savings are placed in the hands of the most wealthy – not the moderate or poor citizen who might most need it and who might well be in a position to let the growth trickle up (as in the multiplier example).

With modern financial systems, it is not necessary for savings to come from top income earners. Savings are equally useful regardless of where they originate. Savings and investments from numerous sources can easily be combined for business ventures. Anyone who has saved money can readily invest it – nobility or high status is not required. A broad range of people – from the little guy on up – can be important players in capital markets, if fairly treated.

When we think back on ancient economists, such as Adam Smith, it may be useful to recall that they were writing in brutishly difficult times when the MAJ was probably in the neighborhood of 22 or lower and capital was far less efficient than now. Even Smith's excitement about the efficiency of the pin factory would be ho-hum today. As cruel as those times were, maldistribution may have been explainable in part by a genuinely low efficiency of capital and labor. That lack of efficiency has long since disappeared in most advanced economies.

Only one lasting remedy comes to mind: a move toward equitable distribution. Short-term fixes for maldistribution-induced inefficiency of savings in a capital-efficient nation (most particularly of a credit and financial nature or international investment and credit) strike me as mainly being symptomatic nostrums, incapable of restoring the congruent relationship between income, savings, investment (capital), and consumption.

There is no mechanism whatsoever within a market economy to move to the most efficacious income distribution. Wages are a cultural decision.

> As Adam Smith wisely observed: The common wages of labor depend everywhere upon the pact between the master and the working man,
>
> "whose interests are by no means the same. The workmen desire to get as much, the masters to give as little, as possible. The former are disposed to combine in order to raise, the latter in order to lower, the wages of labor.
>
> "It is not, however, difficult to foresee which of the two parties must, upon all ordinary occasions, have the advantage in the dispute, and force the other into a compliance with their terms. The masters, being fewer in number, can combine much more easily. ... In all such disputes, the masters can hold out much longer. A landlord, a farmer, a master manufacturer, or merchant, though they did not employ a single workman, could generally live a year or two upon the stocks, which they have already acquired. Many workmen could not subsist a week, few could subsist a month, and scarce any a year, without employment. In the long run, the workman may be as necessary to his master as his master is to him; but the necessity is not so immediate.
>
> "We rarely hear, it has been said, of the combinations of masters, though frequently of those of workmen. But whoever imagines that masters rarely combine, is as ignorant of the world as of the subject. Masters are always and everywhere in a sort of tacit, but constant and uniform, combination, not to raise the wages of labor above their actual rate. To violate this combination is everywhere a most unpopular action, and a sort of reproach to a master among his neighbors and equals."[56]

Two hundred and thirty plus years ago, Smith was as on target as if he had been speaking today. Within a business, distribution of income can readily be altered to conform to a MAJ33 or another similarly appropriate income distribution without the cost of the product increasing a penny. It is only culture that bars it.

I believe most of us feel that it borders on the miraculous that modern economies function at all in view of their great complexity. But they do. And they often do so very well. There is great danger, however, in assuming that past evidence of a working economy is sufficient to indicate that the economy will and can continue to do the job well.

At all income distributions from MAJ48 to MAJ8, the position that prices, wages, and interest rates flexibly adjust in the unfettered market economy to abolish all excess supplies and demands clearly cannot hold in advanced economies. The differences in efficiencies in savings are too great across such a wide range of income distributions for this to be true. There are MAJ points where the economy can work well. There are other points where it functions poorly. In the most severe distortions, income's relationship with wealth (graph-57) becomes so distorted that economic success is unsupportable. This applies whether it is a pure market economy or a mixed economy. For all the reasons stated above: ***Maldistribution hobbles capitalism.***

Thinking about it.

The advantage of working with specific income distribution data, in contrast to working with historical cases, is that you have defined starting and ending points for people with precisely specified ability levels. And you need not concern yourself with the vagaries of inflation-adjustments and other confounding variables. With income distribution, historical data alone cannot provide the needed degree of specificity nor does it provide the ability to control consumption curves so that they can be tested under all significant income-distribution scenarios. As we already know, much high income data has always been secret and inaccessible. Only strong models can penetrate it.

It strikes me that from this analysis we can say with near certainty that the market system functions progressively worse as maldistribution advances. And we can say with certainty that the efficient market system functions at its best when income distributions are equitable.

Reduced to practice.

In patent law there is a term "reduction to practice." Actual reduction to practice refers to the item working as described. We now have evidence of the maldistribution model reduced to practice. As Stewart Lansley shows, in the 1980s the financial assets in world banks were about the same level as total productive output. By contrast in 2008, banks were so flooded with surplus capital, that financial assets ballooned to 3.5 times the value of global output. As he observed, "gradually the finance process became increasingly divorced from the national productive base ..." [57] Reportedly the U.S. banking sector went from being about one-fifth of GDP in 1960 to about 100% of GDP in 2010.[58] "Companies sought to grow not through innovation but through acquisition."[59] GDP growth relying primarily on the financial sector is far from Adam Smith and likely to be disappointing.

USA history – the 50-year advance, the 30-year collapse.

Never had the working man gained so much as he did from 1929 until about 1977 – the timeframe subsequent to World War II that became the Golden Age of Capitalism. The chief feature of income-distribution history in the U.S. is the unprecedented fifty-year increase in the MAJ and its subsequent thirty-year collapse.

#96

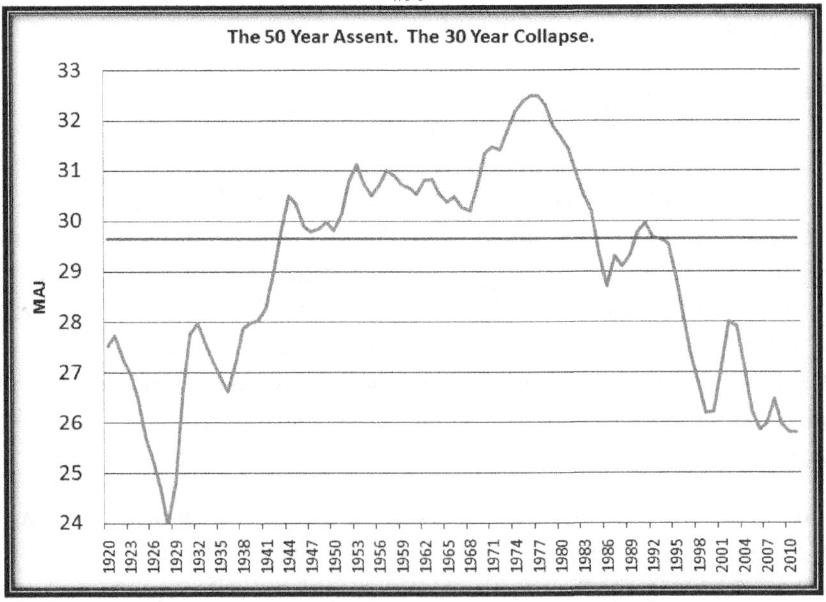

From 1921-1928, the MAJ sharply declined from 27.9 to 23.6 to welcome in the Great Depression. In the decade from 1936-1944, the MAJ increased from 26.4 to 30.6, reaching the most favorable levels of the century, as of that date.

For the forty-year period from 1943-1983, the MAJ remained above the 29.7 median, shown by the horizontal line in graph-96. From its peak of 32.5 in 1976-7, the MAJ sharply declined to 25.8 in 2007, in the range it was prior to the Great Depression.

In 1938, the MAJ was 28. Throughout the Great Depression it was lower. Historically, both in the amount and in the direction, the adverse effects of maldistribution are consistent with the earlier analysis that states: The efficient market system functions at its best when income distributions are equitable.

During the Golden Age of Capitalism, the MAJ was well above the median. At the MAJ pit, we had the Great Depression. It is counterintuitive and wrong to expect that removing income from 80% of the population will foster a healthy economy.

By the hand of maldistribution, at least 80% of U.S. citizens have been removed from the honor of fully contributing. They no longer can feel to the fiber of their being: This is the nation I helped build. I am proud of it. I am a player. If income growth reflects contribution, those words can now only be voiced with authority by the few at the top. Why did they care so little about the rest of us? Aren't they doing the math? Don't they see the numbers? Don't they know what they are doing? It is our economy. It is their economy. We all must make it work and live in it.

I make no apology for emotion. The subject is serious enough to require reason and emotion. There are occasions when individuals and groups do dastardly things. Maldistribution is one of the most monstrous of those cruelties.

If any of what is contained within these pages should strike you as passably logical, please do not expect that it might have penetrated macroeconomic thinking. As Nobel Prize winning economist Joseph Stiglitz writes, "standard macroeconomic models don't even recognize that the distribution of income matters."[60]

It may amuse you to compare your income and its advances with some of the recent bright lights. For its first two centuries, the U.S. never saw incomes at the top of the kind that are now the norm. The following graph-98 shows the inflation-adjusted annual income for those at the one-in-a-million level of income ability throughout all of U.S. history. The recent increase has put legs to the word: maldistribution. There are roughly 300 people at this general level of income in the U.S., many of whom presumably can be found among the now 400+ U.S. billionaires.

We have seen the consequences of the MAJ going from one third to one fourth of the income. In raw dollars, you can plainly spot it in the upward inflation-adjusted spike subsequent to 1980 in graph-98.

#98

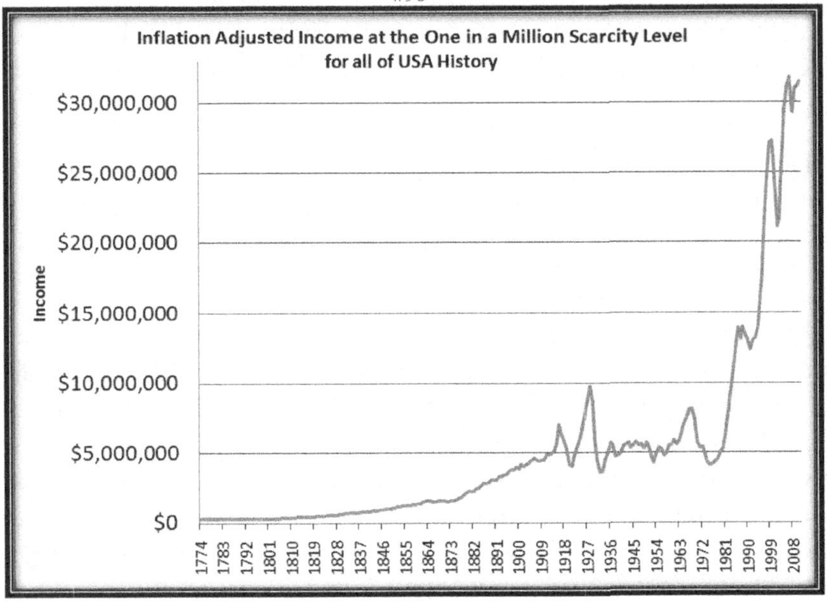

To consider the issue of economic reward, let your eyes rest on the upcoming pages.

CH. 6

THE ART OF COMPENSATION

Here we show:
CEO compensation at various income distributions.
Wealth income relative to customary income.
The roles of the KeyRatio, Productivity, and Scarcity.
The role of "Not-IQ" and its opposite.
The low and underclass & influence of income in those quarters.
The capacity of the market to limit high-income psychopaths.

The CEO.

Cut to the chase. Income distribution is how we value people.

Nowhere is high compensation more plainly obvious than executive compensation. The heads of corporations lead not only their own business, they lead the income scale culture. The standard they set moves through their business, society and the wider economy. It is wrong to think that executive compensation decisions can be made in isolation without broader influence.

The MAJ designations at the head of the columns in following Table-100 and 101 show CEO compensation at the indicated dollar amounts. As seen by moving to columns to the right, the amounts that CEOs receive ultimately define the income shares at the MAJ.

The corporate names in the tables are used as placeholders for corporations having the designated number of employees. *Do* ***not*** *attach significance to any corporate name at any particular point.* The corporation moves up or down in the table depending upon its current number of employees.

#100

	Employees	MAJ36	MAJ33	MAJ29	MAJ25	MAJ21	MAJ17
Wal-MartStores	2,055,000	$4,663,911	$7,074,322	$23,800,925	$55,649,074	$113,474,297	$175,580,965
StateGridChinaNational	1,486,000	$4,211,369	$6,328,818	$20,724,309	$47,546,388	$95,423,578	$146,220,234
ChinaNationalPetroleum	1,117,345	$3,849,786	$5,738,345	$18,348,826	$41,400,935	$81,936,686	$124,483,383
UnitedStatesPostalService	826,955	$3,501,754	$5,174,751	$16,136,212	$35,773,893	$69,763,389	$105,035,309
Sinopec	634,011	$3,220,758	$4,723,401	$14,405,758	$31,445,511	$60,529,090	$90,407,982
HonHaiPrecisionIndustry	550,000	$3,079,796	$4,498,308	$13,557,444	$29,348,988	$56,101,254	$83,437,494
Carrefour	490,042	$2,969,882	$4,323,444	$12,905,484	$27,749,842	$52,745,168	$78,174,656
SiemensAG	480,000	$2,950,586	$4,292,804	$12,791,899	$27,472,351	$52,164,762	$77,266,359
DeutschePost	475,100	$2,941,069	$4,277,700	$12,735,980	$27,335,862	$51,879,498	$76,820,150
McDonald's	465,000	$2,921,239	$4,246,243	$12,619,667	$27,052,228	$51,287,150	$75,894,047
PetroChina	464,000	$2,919,260	$4,243,104	$12,608,071	$27,023,974	$51,228,176	$75,801,879
AgriculturalBankofChina	447,519	$2,886,209	$4,190,719	$12,414,880	$26,553,715	$50,247,574	$74,270,186
Gazprom	436,096	$2,862,809	$4,153,663	$12,278,575	$26,222,531	$49,558,025	$73,194,111
UnitedParcelService	428,000	$2,845,969	$4,127,012	$12,180,727	$25,985,095	$49,064,200	$72,424,002
ChinaTelecommunications	391,864	$2,768,020	$4,003,841	$11,730,508	$24,895,998	$46,804,992	$68,906,391
Hitachi	389,752	$2,763,314	$3,996,415	$11,703,472	$24,830,777	$46,670,010	$68,696,525
InternationalBusinessMachin	386,558	$2,756,164	$3,985,135	$11,662,426	$24,731,795	$46,465,228	$68,378,191
Industrial&CommercialBanko	381,713	$2,745,242	$3,967,907	$11,599,789	$24,580,843	$46,153,081	$67,893,117
Citigroup	380,500	$2,742,492	$3,963,571	$11,584,036	$24,542,896	$46,074,645	$67,771,254
Target	366,000	$2,709,149	$3,911,025	$11,393,456	$24,084,378	$45,127,837	$66,301,184
CompassGroup	365,630	$2,708,287	$3,909,667	$11,388,537	$24,072,557	$45,103,450	$66,263,344
DaimlerAG	362,063	$2,699,940	$3,896,523	$11,340,966	$23,958,277	$44,867,760	$65,897,684
HomeDepotInc	355,000	$2,683,246	$3,870,244	$11,245,972	$23,730,267	$44,397,861	$65,168,971
SearsHoldingsCorporation	355,000	$2,683,246	$3,870,244	$11,245,972	$23,730,267	$44,397,861	$65,168,971
TATAGroup	350,000	$2,671,290	$3,851,432	$11,178,069	$23,567,440	$44,062,579	$64,649,279
VeoliaEnvironnementSA	349,000	$2,668,884	$3,847,649	$11,164,422	$23,534,732	$43,995,255	$64,544,959
Tesco	345,754	$2,661,044	$3,835,318	$11,119,967	$23,428,226	$43,776,100	$64,205,420
Sodexo	342,380	$2,652,841	$3,822,421	$11,073,506	$23,316,974	$43,547,285	$63,851,016
Volkswagen	329,305	$2,620,519	$3,771,637	$10,890,934	$22,880,426	$42,650,499	$62,463,023
FordMotorCo	327,531	$2,616,066	$3,764,646	$10,865,845	$22,820,514	$42,527,555	$62,272,869
GeneralElectric	327,000	$2,614,730	$3,762,548	$10,858,320	$22,802,547	$42,490,696	$62,215,863
Kroger	323,000	$2,604,618	$3,746,675	$10,801,409	$22,666,727	$42,212,130	$61,785,141
HSBCHoldings	322,282	$2,602,794	$3,743,812	$10,791,151	$22,642,255	$42,161,959	$61,707,580
HewlettPackardCo	321,000	$2,599,529	$3,738,690	$10,772,802	$22,598,492	$42,072,246	$61,568,906
ArcelorMittal	319,578	$2,595,898	$3,732,992	$10,752,400	$22,549,844	$41,972,540	$61,414,811
ToyotaMotor	316,121	$2,587,024	$3,719,072	$10,702,583	$22,431,110	$41,729,285	$61,038,932
AT&T	309,050	$2,568,664	$3,690,284	$10,599,708	$22,186,150	$41,227,837	$60,264,492
MatsushitaElectricIndustrial	305,828	$2,560,203	$3,677,023	$10,552,383	$22,073,574	$40,997,572	$59,909,045
LaPoste	299,010	$2,542,094	$3,648,657	$10,451,290	$21,833,325	$40,506,565	$59,151,480
ChinaConstructionBank	298,868	$2,541,714	$3,648,062	$10,449,170	$21,828,292	$40,496,282	$59,135,625
GeneralMotorsCorp	284,000	$2,501,207	$3,584,676	$10,223,975	$21,294,274	$39,406,872	$57,456,674
SamsungGroup	277,000	$2,481,631	$3,554,077	$10,115,610	$21,037,874	$38,884,784	$56,652,973
Nestlé	276,000	$2,478,807	$3,549,664	$10,100,002	$21,000,973	$38,809,699	$56,537,438
RobertBosch	271,265	$2,465,339	$3,528,627	$10,025,654	$20,825,312	$38,452,447	$55,987,893
ChinaRailwayGroup	266,474	$2,451,546	$3,507,094	$9,949,664	$20,645,959	$38,088,003	$55,427,584
MetroAG	263,794	$2,443,757	$3,494,938	$9,906,816	$20,544,908	$37,882,808	$55,112,238
EdekaZentrale	253,531	$2,413,416	$3,447,623	$9,740,378	$20,152,966	$37,087,893	$53,891,531
Sberbank	251,208	$2,406,432	$3,436,739	$9,702,172	$20,063,124	$36,905,897	$53,612,256
DeutscheTelekomAG	248,519	$2,398,292	$3,424,058	$9,657,694	$19,958,590	$36,694,248	$53,287,570
Telefónica	248,487	$2,398,194	$3,423,906	$9,657,163	$19,957,343	$36,691,723	$53,283,697
VerizonCommunications	242,000	$2,378,304	$3,392,936	$9,548,704	$19,702,727	$36,176,672	$52,494,023
FedEx	238,935	$2,368,779	$3,378,113	$9,496,879	$19,581,204	$35,931,082	$52,117,711
BankofChina	237,379	$2,363,912	$3,370,540	$9,470,424	$19,519,203	$35,805,844	$51,925,863
DeutscheBahn	237,078	$2,362,968	$3,369,071	$9,465,294	$19,507,185	$35,781,574	$51,888,686
Onex	237,000	$2,362,723	$3,368,691	$9,463,965	$19,504,069	$35,775,281	$51,879,053
BerkshireHathaway	217,550	$2,299,875	$3,271,046	$9,124,195	$18,709,997	$34,175,004	$49,431,152
UnitedTechnologiesCorp	215,000	$2,291,353	$3,257,825	$9,078,378	$18,603,221	$33,960,343	$49,103,268
CasinoGuichardPerrachon	213,000	$2,284,621	$3,247,383	$9,042,224	$18,519,021	$33,791,147	$48,844,919
LowesHomeImprovementWa	210,000	$2,274,441	$3,231,599	$8,987,626	$18,391,951	$33,535,963	$48,455,408
SaintGobainSA	208,000	$2,267,599	$3,220,994	$8,950,980	$18,306,719	$33,364,896	$48,194,385
PSAPeugeotCitroenSA	207,200	$2,264,849	$3,216,733	$8,936,265	$18,272,509	$33,296,256	$48,089,669
Safeway	207,000	$2,264,161	$3,215,666	$8,932,581	$18,263,946	$33,279,076	$48,063,463
NipponTelegraphandTelepho	205,288	$2,258,249	$3,206,506	$8,900,963	$18,190,468	$33,131,701	$47,838,686
BankofAmericaCorp.	203,425	$2,251,776	$3,196,480	$8,866,384	$18,110,152	$32,970,677	$47,593,151

#101

	Employees	MAJ36	MAJ33	MAJ29	MAJ25	MAJ21	MAJ17
Aramark	200,000	$2,239,770	$3,177,891	$8,802,335	$17,961,500	$32,672,842	$47,139,182
Oracle	200,000	$2,239,770	$3,177,891	$8,802,335	$17,961,500	$32,672,842	$47,139,182
SuperValuInc	200,000	$2,239,770	$3,177,891	$8,802,335	$17,961,500	$32,672,842	$47,139,182
AltriaGroupInc	199,000	$2,236,239	$3,172,424	$8,783,517	$17,917,852	$32,585,438	$47,006,001
FranceTélécom	191,000	$2,207,536	$3,128,024	$8,630,979	$17,564,521	$31,878,688	$45,929,854
AXAGroup	189,927	$2,203,624	$3,121,977	$8,610,243	$17,516,556	$31,782,855	$45,784,031
FederatedDept.Stores	188,000	$2,196,560	$3,111,060	$8,572,835	$17,430,063	$31,610,115	$45,521,253
ThyssenKruppAG	188,000	$2,196,560	$3,111,060	$8,572,835	$17,430,063	$31,610,115	$45,521,253
Unilever	179,000	$2,162,896	$3,059,076	$8,395,142	$17,019,926	$30,792,182	$44,278,081
LGGroup	177,000	$2,155,258	$3,047,292	$8,354,963	$16,927,354	$30,607,837	$43,998,152
JPMorganChase	176,000	$2,151,417	$3,041,367	$8,334,776	$16,880,865	$30,515,303	$43,857,671
Delphi	171,400	$2,133,553	$3,013,824	$8,241,059	$16,665,246	$30,086,449	$43,206,929
UniCreditSpA	170,000	$2,128,051	$3,005,346	$8,212,252	$16,599,034	$29,954,868	$43,007,370
Walgreen	168,600	$2,122,517	$2,996,821	$8,183,307	$16,532,540	$29,822,780	$42,807,097
PepsiCo	168,000	$2,120,136	$2,993,154	$8,170,860	$16,503,955	$29,766,015	$42,721,043
AllianzAG	167,193	$2,116,925	$2,988,207	$8,154,079	$16,465,427	$29,689,518	$42,605,092
ToshibaCorp	166,651	$2,114,762	$2,984,876	$8,142,783	$16,439,496	$29,638,043	$42,527,077
YumBrands	166,600	$2,114,558	$2,984,562	$8,141,719	$16,437,053	$29,633,194	$42,519,729
KoninklijkeAholdNV	163,866	$2,103,571	$2,967,647	$8,084,401	$16,305,564	$29,372,312	$42,124,456
FiatSpA	162,237	$2,096,964	$2,957,480	$8,049,989	$16,226,682	$29,215,901	$41,887,576
SonyCorp	162,000	$2,096,000	$2,955,995	$8,044,966	$16,215,171	$29,193,088	$41,853,026
HCA	161,500	$2,093,961	$2,952,858	$8,034,354	$16,190,859	$29,144,900	$41,780,062
SuezPublic	160,700	$2,090,689	$2,947,825	$8,017,338	$16,151,880	$29,067,656	$41,663,121
CVSCaremarkCorporation	160,000	$2,087,818	$2,943,408	$8,002,408	$16,117,690	$28,999,922	$41,560,585
WellsFargo&Co	160,000	$2,087,818	$2,943,408	$8,002,408	$16,117,690	$28,999,922	$41,560,585
CargillInc	158,000	$2,079,566	$2,930,718	$7,959,545	$16,019,581	$28,805,631	$41,266,550
DardenRestaurants	157,300	$2,076,661	$2,926,251	$7,944,469	$15,985,091	$28,737,357	$41,163,255
FujitsuLtd	157,044	$2,075,596	$2,924,614	$7,938,946	$15,972,458	$28,712,355	$41,125,427
TheBoeingCompany	157,000	$2,075,413	$2,924,333	$7,937,996	$15,970,286	$28,708,055	$41,118,923
ElectricitédeFranceSA	156,152	$2,071,877	$2,918,898	$7,919,662	$15,928,358	$28,625,083	$40,993,415
J.C.Penney	155,000	$2,067,053	$2,911,483	$7,894,663	$15,871,210	$28,512,032	$40,822,436
Gap	154,000	$2,062,845	$2,905,017	$7,872,875	$15,821,426	$28,413,580	$40,673,569
MarriottInternational	150,600	$2,048,396	$2,882,824	$7,798,187	$15,650,900	$28,076,593	$40,164,240
OAOLUKOIL	150,000	$2,045,823	$2,878,874	$7,784,906	$15,620,603	$28,016,760	$40,073,842
Starbucks	145,800	$2,027,613	$2,850,927	$7,691,080	$15,406,750	$27,594,756	$39,436,582
StarwoodHotels&Rsrts.	145,000	$2,024,104	$2,845,543	$7,673,033	$15,365,659	$27,513,735	$39,314,297
VINCI	142,000	$2,010,824	$2,825,182	$7,604,845	$15,210,516	$27,208,040	$38,853,088
LockheedMartin	140,000	$2,001,864	$2,811,450	$7,558,927	$15,106,148	$27,002,572	$38,543,256
Pemex	138,215	$1,993,793	$2,799,085	$7,517,626	$15,012,350	$26,818,031	$38,265,097
BNPParibas	138,000	$1,992,816	$2,797,588	$7,512,631	$15,001,011	$26,795,730	$38,231,487
Procter&Gamble	138,000	$1,992,816	$2,797,588	$7,512,631	$15,001,011	$26,795,730	$38,231,487
JohnsonControls	136,000	$1,983,677	$2,783,594	$7,465,949	$14,895,086	$26,587,488	$37,917,747
CréditAgricoleSA	134,000	$1,974,446	$2,769,465	$7,418,872	$14,788,356	$26,377,816	$37,601,988
WaltDisney	133,000	$1,969,796	$2,762,348	$7,395,182	$14,734,685	$26,272,433	$37,443,340
CostcoWholesaleCorporation	132,000	$1,965,121	$2,755,196	$7,371,390	$14,680,805	$26,166,680	$37,284,170
HondaMotorCoLtd	131,600	$1,963,244	$2,752,325	$7,361,845	$14,659,194	$26,124,275	$37,220,355
ElectronicDataSystems	131,000	$1,960,421	$2,748,008	$7,347,495	$14,626,714	$26,060,555	$37,124,476
RenaultSA	130,573	$1,958,407	$2,744,928	$7,337,260	$14,603,553	$26,015,124	$37,056,126
GrupoSantander	129,749	$1,954,508	$2,738,966	$7,317,454	$14,558,747	$25,927,260	$36,923,947
BestBuy	128,000	$1,946,174	$2,726,227	$7,275,176	$14,463,155	$25,739,895	$36,642,176
EmersonElectric	127,800	$1,945,216	$2,724,763	$7,270,320	$14,452,182	$25,718,394	$36,609,850
NissanMotorCoLtd	127,625	$1,944,377	$2,723,481	$7,266,067	$14,442,573	$25,699,567	$36,581,546
CanonInc	127,338	$1,943,000	$2,721,375	$7,259,087	$14,426,798	$25,668,665	$36,535,090
RWEAGPublic	127,028	$1,941,509	$2,719,098	$7,251,536	$14,409,740	$25,635,249	$36,484,857
Alcoa	123,000	$1,921,912	$2,689,167	$7,152,451	$14,186,111	$25,197,577	$35,827,263
Johnson&Johnson	122,200	$1,917,968	$2,683,146	$7,132,551	$14,141,249	$25,109,862	$35,695,547
NorthropGrumman	122,200	$1,917,968	$2,683,146	$7,132,551	$14,141,249	$25,109,862	$35,695,547
WachoviaCorporation	122,000	$1,916,979	$2,681,637	$7,127,565	$14,130,010	$25,087,890	$35,662,559
SociétéGénérale	120,000	$1,907,029	$2,666,455	$7,077,439	$14,017,094	$24,867,252	$35,331,378
TheRoyalBankofScotlandGro	120,000	$1,907,029	$2,666,455	$7,077,439	$14,017,094	$24,867,252	$35,331,378
ChinaMobileCommunications	119,000	$1,902,011	$2,658,801	$7,052,197	$13,960,273	$24,756,290	$35,164,887
INGGroupNV	115,000	$1,881,646	$2,627,757	$6,949,994	$13,730,496	$24,308,043	$34,492,743
Bouygues	113,300	$1,872,844	$2,614,348	$6,905,940	$13,631,596	$24,115,343	$34,204,002
sum (thousands)	34,545	$300,503	$429,196	$1,213,984	$2,517,723	$4,647,506	$6,769,050
MAJ33 Multiple		0.70	1.00	2.83	5.87	10.83	15.77

The number of employees is the key component.[61] It gives us a starting estimate of scarcity, given the presumption, for example, that if a person is head of a corporation with 1,117,000 employees, then he or she is at the one-in-1,117,000-scarcity level. On this assumption, as the number of employees change, so does demonstrated scarcity. In lockstep, CEO compensation changes. Within the broad scope of a functioning economy, the fewer the number of employees, the less the CEO should be paid.

No current CEO compensation for any particular company is shown. The estimated pay scales in the columns are based on the assumption that the average compensation for all of the employees, including all levels of management, is $48,000 – approximately the same as U.S. per capita GDP. Clearly this does not apply for each individual case, but there is a remedy. Use the correction factor.*

When CEO total compensation exceeds an amount shown in a column, CEO pay drives the MAJ distribution downward (as suggested by the progressive increase in pay as your eye moves towards MAJ columns at the right-hand side of the table). Over a long period of time, many companies paying salaries higher than the MAJ schedule are the motor that creates nation-wide maldistribution. The CEO pay scales here are consistent with the MAJ distributions in the lookup-table spreadsheet.

You may be tempted to say, "I do not begrudge the CEO a high salary. Look at the job that is being done. It is fantastic. It is central to the wellbeing of the company." But this well-meaning logic cannot translate all the way down the system. People at all levels do a fantastic job in a well-run company. That is why they are on the job in the first place.

If the leader takes a disproportionate amount, then people under him/her are under-compensated for the great work that they do. Those at the top are in a delicate position, since their compensation translates all the way down the scale. If their share is disproportionately large, then someone else's share is disproportionately small (whether they be in labor or management). The math is inevitable. The circumstances are far more delicate than commonly appreciated.

---

* Correction factor = "Average CompanyX Compensation" /48,000. Just multiply this number by the indicated compensations in the columns MAJ36 through MAJ17, and you will have the proposed compensations for the CEO, at the scarcity level conforming to the indicated number of employees and your chosen average compensation.

If the CEO is compensated at an amount equal to the grossly inequitable MAJ17, go study the spreadsheet lookup table at MAJ17. Look at how such compensation works its way down to the MAJ. It becomes brutally ugly once you enter the MAJ.

A business can readily select to compensate its employees according to any distribution curve in the lookup table. To do so within equitable ranges presumably promotes fair pay for all, without a necessity for labor-management bickering about the form of the curve. You can look through the curves to find the fairest ones for your business. Labor and management can have a shared destiny linked to equitable compensation curve, top to bottom. Customers can know it. Employees can know it. Stockholders can know it. The nation can know it.

Just as there are upper rational limits for CEO compensation, there are floors beneath which it should not fall. The MAJ33 is such a floor. And MAJ36 provides entirely insufficient compensation given the responsibility and difficulty of the CEO job.

The last line of Table-101 shows the position of other distributions relative to MAJ33. For example, a MAJ29 compensation is 2.83 times greater than the MAJ33 case. The next to the last line shows the sums for the previous columns. One hundred twenty-nine companies of the sizes indicated would employ more than 34 million people. At MAJ33, total CEO compensation would have been about $429 million ($1.2 billion at MAJ29), assuming a $48,000 per capita average.

There will be the few who contribute so extraordinarily that they deserve commensurately high compensation. That is the rub. The Top1% is a treasure when properly compensated; a malignancy when it is not.

Extending back as far as recent memory reaches for most people, we, in the USA, are now anchored at disproportionately high top-end incomes. But if we look in the spreadsheets at a variety of scarcity levels during the post WWII era, we get a better picture of our nation and condition that caused it to thrive.

A CEO compensation consistent with MAJ33, or thereabouts, is apt to change compensation and allocation of responsibilities throughout executive suites. Equitable distributions and a greater leveling at the higher reaches (the reduced spread between people at the top seen in earlier graphs #26 through #29 and the upcoming IQ analysis cause me to speculate that equitable distributions are conducive to improved decision-making at the top.

Income distribution does not decrease or increase the total payroll of a business. Products can sell at the same price. Competitive strength is not reduced by equitable distribution. Any constant total amount for combined labor and management, reallocated along a different curve, leaves cost of production unchanged within a business. As far as accounting is concerned, the same amount is going to company employees, just in different proportions.

If excessive compensation goes to the Top1%, beyond their true value, someone else pays for it: the customer by a higher price, the lowly worker by reduced income, the stockholder by reduced value retained in the firm and by reduced dividends, and everybody by a less vibrant business.

We have previously seen that a MAJ36 provides little likelihood of significant increases in wellbeing and happiness for the majority: It does so by insufficiently compensating the most able people at the top. To do so is wrong. The MAJ36 column in Table-100 and 101 provides the evidence that supports the argument. MAJ36 compensations are insufficient to get high quality and interesting leadership.

The MAJ29 in the tables is the midpoint between MAJ33 and MAJ25 (in the event that you are not inclined to cast your lot with either of them). The rest of the argument is that a MAJ25 maldistribution is destructive, and distributions south of it are extremely dangerous.

In a high earner's life, compensation is not made in isolation. It eventually comes back to influence the high earner's extended family. For parents in the upper 10% of income earners with three children, there is roughly a one in three chance for each of their children to end up as an adult in one of the following income groups: 1) the Top 10%, 2) the MAJ, or 3) the group in between (the respective probabilities more precisely being 29.6%, 31%, and 39.4%).[62]

You can anticipate that a maldistribution culture will ultimately disadvantage the clear majority of a high earner's descendents and extended family who in adulthood will find themselves in the MAJ or near to it. To impoverish the MAJ is to impoverish a portion of the high earner's family and its offspring in the future.

There also is roughly a one in three chance that those who come into the top 10% will come from parents from the following income groups: the Top 10%, the MAJ, or the group in between (the respective probabilities being 29.6%, 28.2%, and 42.4%).[63] The MAJ needs to be appropriately compensated in the present generation for future generations to prosper.

The ongoing health of corporations and businesses requires that leadership provide sufficient economic advantages to classes other than the top 10% because, as shown, about 70% of those in high position normally come from lower classes. The people who spend their youth in the MAJ, or nearby, need conditions where they can flourish [70.4= 100-29.6]. Explicitly, this 70% resides beneath the teeter point. They are the group damaged by maldistribution.

It is myopic and selfish in the extreme for a high earner to assert that disproportionately high compensation is his exclusive right. To whom much is given, much is expected. The maldistribution culture damages his family, his company, the economy, and the nation.

Table-100 and 101 have covered enough ground already, but it is well to keep in mind the distinction between CEO pay and CEO income. The CEO also benefits from wealth income that will result from investing his high income. What starts as narrowly considered compensation is, in practice, an entry into an income stream with a large flow coming from wealth, as well as customary compensation. Any compensation schedule carries with it the added wealth income bonus. To have money is to make money.

Wealth income.

Whenever a person earns a salary or gets income by other means, job status carries with it the income stream derived from wealth. For those of us at the low end, this wealth bonus is usually so small that we neglect to consider it. At the upper strata, the wealth bonus is often grand. In the statistics, this bonus is mixed in with the income shown in the income distribution curves. Let's try to carve it out from the whole and take a look at it.

The carving is not completely accurate, as we will soon see, but it does serve to estimate a floor for the income that would normally be generated by wealth. We multiply the ten-year bond rate in the Shiller database (listed back to 1871)[64] by the wealth indicated in the spreadsheets for all scarcity levels. This gives an estimate of the average lower limit wealth income for everybody. Wealth income, as shown here, is not necessarily received in cash each year, and may take the form of asset appreciation or indirect advantages derived from the wealth.

The following graph-106 shows a smoothed version of wealth income at scarcity levels of one-in-240,000 and one-in-a-million. An artifact of the smoothing is that the steep increase wrongly looks like it occurred about four years earlier than it actually did. The late 1970s and early 1980s experienced high interest rates that also increased wealth income. That period was followed by increased wealth inequality that kept wealth income high.

#106

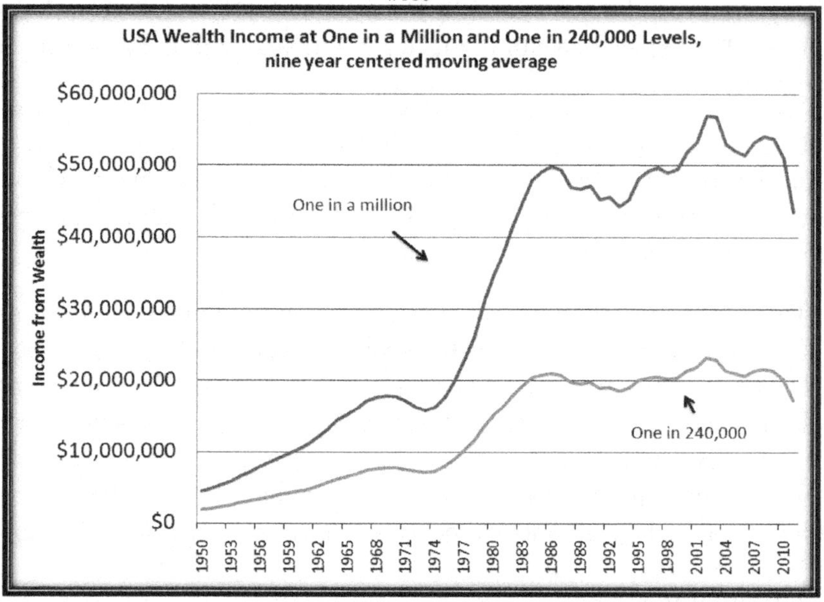

The common target for excessive compensation is the CEO. As you can begin to appreciate, the full blame should not fall on the CEO alone. As much as we may feel CEO compensation is excessive, we need to acknowledge that in most instances, the CEO has great responsibility and often great ability. The CEO presumably will seek a compensation that is keyed to those who automatically receive a high wealth income flow from their accumulated riches, which can exist irrespective of the wealth holder's ability.

In the following graph-107 for the U.S. from 1950-2011, we consider what the stream of income coming from wealth looked like compared to the customary incomes shown in the spreadsheets. As shown by the wide spread between Max and Min values in graph-107, there is great variability in the relationship between wealth income and customary income (assuming that the scarcity levels for income and wealth are identical).

#107

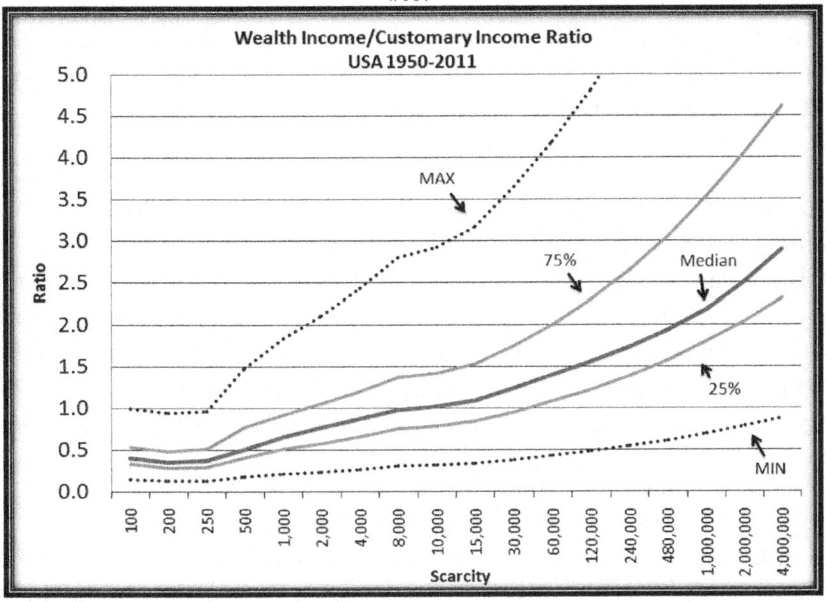

#107B

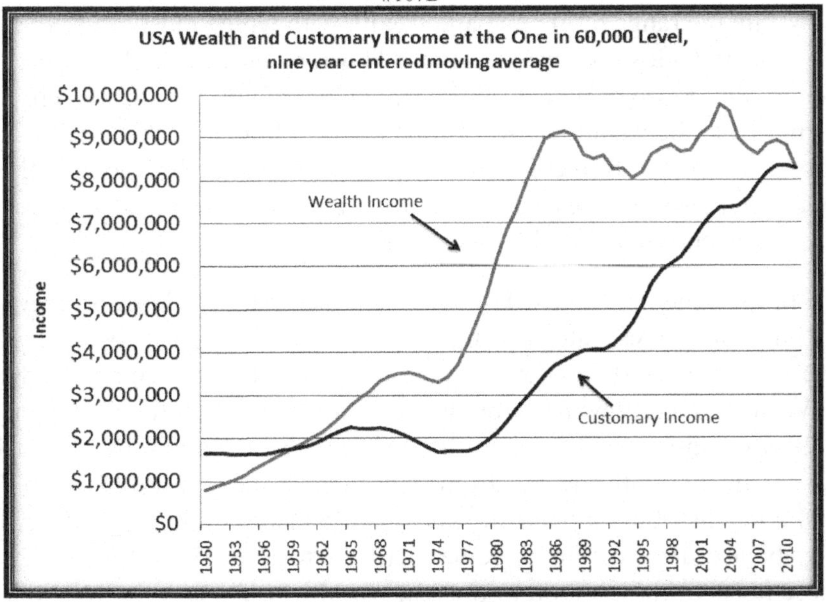

Notwithstanding, patterns emerge. At low scarcity levels, wealth income seldom approaches customary income. By the time we reach the one-in-8,000 point, the median is customarily above 1.0, indicating that from this point upwards the tendency is for wealth income alone to exceed customary income at identical scarcity levels.

By the time we reach the one-in-60,000 point, wealth income exceeds customary income in 75% of cases. We can see this particular relationship over time in graph-107B.

People with vast fortunes and exceptionally high incomes are not apt to be providing access to their private financial affairs, making mathematical probing of this kind all the more useful. The people in the above graph-107B are vastly rich. Until the mid-1960s, they often hovered in the neighborhood of $2 million annual income, coming either from wealth or conventional income. By the mid-1980s, high wealth holders had achieved most of their advantage. The high customary income earners achieved their advantage through maldistribution at a more consistent, but slower pace.

We now make a necessary distinction that we have not previously discussed. In the above graph, we are looking at two groups, separately, at the one-in-60,000 level: 1) those with vast fortunes (high wealth income), and 2) those with exceptionally high income. At times, the people in these groups overlapped, but in the main they did not.

Within the range of income and wealth with which most of us are familiar, there is a closer correspondence: Those of us with high income have high wealth; those of us with little income have little wealth – as previously implied in the wealth curves. But at the very high end, the relationship is more problematic. Sometimes those at identical scarcity levels, with very high customary incomes, make far less than those with vast fortunes that produce an enormous wealth income stream.

For example, in Table-109 let's take 1986 and 2007 USA as examples. In 1986, the interest rate was high at 7.68% producing a very high wealth income stream. And the MAJ also still had a substantial share of the wealth at WealthMAJ6.29, which provided a wealth share 1.68 times greater than its 2007 condition [1.677= 6.29/3.75]. In 1986, the wealthy were still making most of their wealth income from high interest rates rather than the acute wealth maldistribution that followed. On the income side, the MAJ in 1986 had about a 10% greater income share than in 2007 [9.69= 28.3/25.8-1]. These items draw attention to the real world where numerous relationships act in different directions to produce the ultimate outcome.

The table shows that up until about the one-in-4,000 wealth holder scarcity, customary income scarcity in 1986 and 2007 was usually less than wealth holder income scarcity. This means that up until about this level of scarcity, it was more likely that it would be easier to earn customary income rather than exclusively earning wealth income.

When we look at the very high end of the table, we see that customary income scarcities in 1986 and 2007 ballooned once wealth scarcity reached high levels. For example, at 480,000 and above, it would be nearly impossible to earn as much by conventional income as was earned by wealth income alone.

IncomeMAJ:	25.8	28.3
WealthMAJ:	3.75	6.29
Interest Rate:	4.63%	7.68%

Scarcity Level Matching Points, Where Income From Wealth Equals Conventional Income Earned

Wealth Holder Scarcity	2007 Income Earner Scarcity	1986 Income Earner Scarcity
500	136	264
1,000	203	686
2,000	975	1,780
4,000	3,424	4,620
8,000	8,891	11,988
10,000	12,095	16,300
15,000	21,141	28,492
30,000	54,918	73,952
60,000	142,697	192,007
120,000	370,779	498,386
240,000	963,376	1,293,667
480,000	2,502,569	3,359,098
1,000,000	6,878,782	9,222,942

At the one-in-8,000 wealth holder scarcity level and above, it is easier to make money by wealth income rather than by customary income. It is easy to spot this effect in the earlier graph-107 of the "Wealth Income/Customary Income Ratio." Whenever the ratio in the graph exceeded 1.0, it became more likely that it would be easier to earn income by wealth income alone than to earn it by customary income. At 1.0 and above, wealth income can no longer be carved out of conventional income by these methods as initially proposed because it exceeds it. Above 1.0, the table scarcities tell the story.

Here we see the important interplay between wealth distributions and income distributions. The high-income CEO, of great ability, is apt to be guided in his compensation demands, at least in part, by the large income-earning advantage that high wealth holders (often of lower ability) have. When wealth becomes seriously maldistributed, it holds out a tantalizing carrot-like incentive to push CEO pay higher. Income distribution, too, then edges toward being increasingly maldistributed. Where would the stopping point be? What will produce the stopping? Mull it over. Time to move on.

KeyRatio.

The lion's share of important work done by a nation is done by those between the 50th percentile level and the one-in-200 level of scarcity. This group is a bedrock of society. Many of those at the 200 level of scarcity are often capable of scoring about 670 on either the math or verbal SAT and may well have an IQ of about 140. They frequently are professional people: medical doctors, engineers, or similarly skilled professionals. Those at the 50th percentile have already made the cut to the upper half of society by being the higher one out of two.

The KeyRatio is the ratio between the incomes of these two groups: those at the one-in-200 level divided by the income of those at the 50th percentile. In order for the market economy to function, all people within this range need to be compensated at a high rate consistent with their contribution to the economy. Otherwise, the flow of income within the economy is insufficient to support consumption and the salaries of those key people who bring the product to market.

The obvious way for those at the one-in-200 level of scarcity to advance their income is to do quality work. Less obviously, it is just as important with respect to the total economy that the level of abilities of those at the 50th percentile are fully developed and appropriately remunerated, because they are the base from which the KeyRatio determines the income of those at the one-in-200 level.

The honorable way to ensure a good income for those at the one-in-200 level is to increase the contribution, productive capacity, and income for those at the 50th percentile. (The G.I. Bill after WWII is an example of this concept in practice.) By this means, when the KeyRatio is multiplied by the income at the 50th percentile, the one-in-200 level income is also proportionally increased. The dishonorable way to increase income for those at the one-in-200 level is to increase maldistribution and thereby increase the KeyRatio.

Looking at the following graph-111, you will see that the KeyRatio at MAJ33 is 7.3. At MAJ25, it balloons to 20.7. The shortsighted temptation is to ignore the people at the 50th percentile and to settle on benefitting those who prosper because they are above the teeter point. *That would not be taking care of the tribe.* A KeyRatio in the neighborhood of 7.3 serves the tribe well.

The KeyRatio is centrally important for assessing what distribution is most appropriate for a society. Superstition, primitive thought processes, poor work habits and numerous other adverse conditions may exist in a highly uneducated nation. In such a case, an equitable MAJ33, and a 7.3 KeyRatio nationwide, may be inappropriate because of an excessively large spread between abilities and performance of the 50th percentile and the one-in-200 earner.

#111

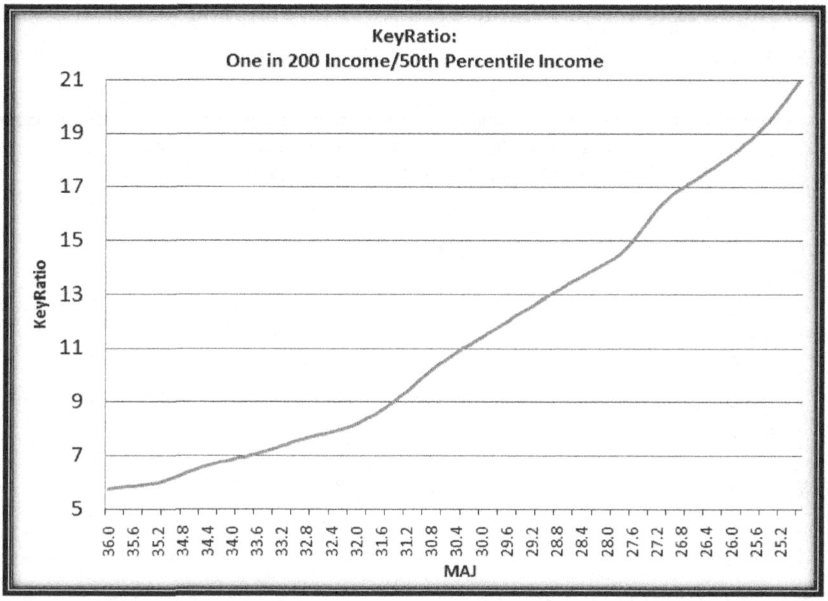

Just as there is a KeyRatio for income, corresponding KeyRatios can be constructed to measure abilities and performance brought to the marketplace. By this means, income and performance reference points together can serve to illustrate when an income KeyRatio is excessive and when it is not.

But if the starting point is a high KeyRatio, the emphasis must emphatically shift to bringing the 50th percentile up to a high standard so that the 50th percentile can receive a justifiably higher income. Lagging in this effort would suggest that the ruling class is making an insufficient effort to advance the 50th percentile, and it would suggest that the true objective is to perpetuate maldistribution and an excessively high KeyRatio, without providing any benefit to the 50th percentile.

Productivity.

In all instances, the Simon Legree School of Management holds out for "increased productivity" as a precondition for reversing maldistribution. Bunk. Productivity is important for an individual firm. I certainly kept a sensible eye on it in my business. By contrast, we can view measurements of national productivity as a means for correcting maldistribution skeptically. The dogma that if nationwide productivity in developed nations goes up, equitable income distributions will follow, is refuted by history and math. If you doubt this, look at USA MAJ history, and look at the lookup-table curves.

#112

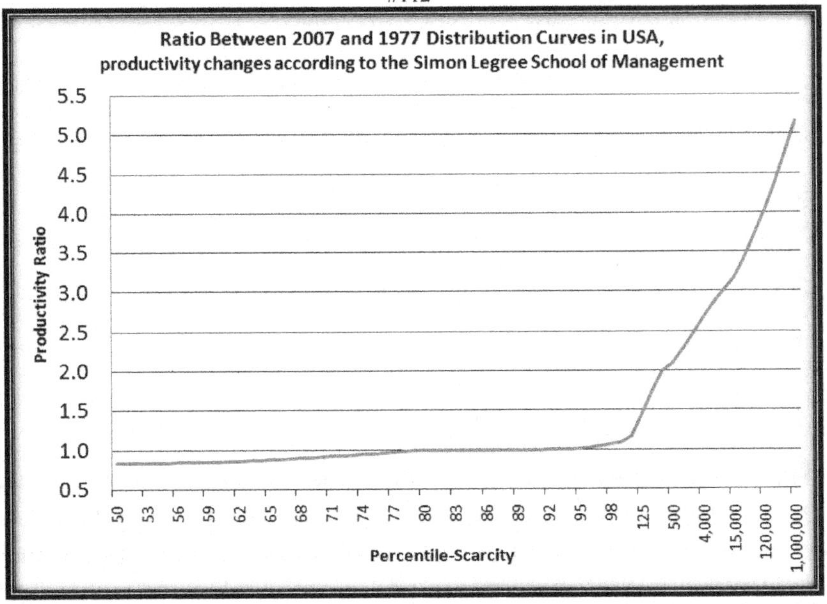

Fluidly and odoriferously, Simon Legree the fifth in his distilled, spirited manner explained the change of distribution in the U.S. during the thirty-year period from 1977 to 2007:[65]

> "Our Betterment of Legree-Like Man Society has studied the data provided in this book. We find that the above graph-112 explains the reason for the thirty-year demise of the person at the 50th percentile. That person's productivity is only 83% of what it was in 1977. The productivity of the person at the one-in-a-million increased five times during the same period. Do you expect us to pay a worm the same proportion it earned in 1977 at the very time the illustrious king of the heap has increased his productivity five-fold? I would not want the worm to touch my swizzle stick, much less give him a nickel more. I will stir my own, thank you."

The not-so-esteemed Mr. Legree *did* fish out numbers that would explain his logic. The fatal flaw is that the productivity of the average worker plainly increased since 1977, as it has done throughout U.S. economic history.[66]

#113

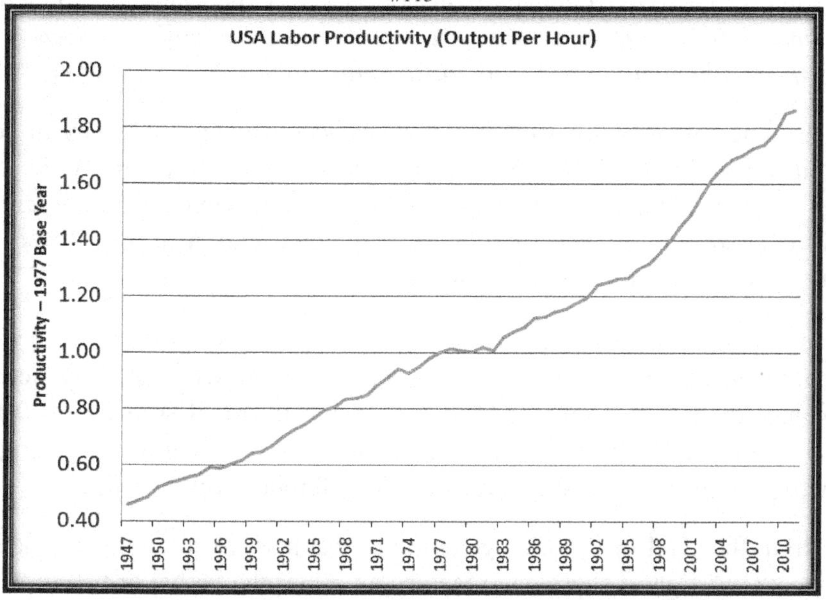

We do have firm evidence in the above graph-113 that the productivity of labor has increased about 1.86 times since 1977 – the same period in which maldistribution got legs. Productivity did not decline as Legree asserts. Productivity and maldistribution march to different drummers. In the U.S., productivity tends to consistently march upwards. Maldistribution marches to the predilections of the rich. It did so prior to the Great Depression. It is does so now.

Legree failed to show that those at the high reaches of the income ladder had increased their productivity to the extent that he asserts. This is the standard failing of those who assert that labor productivity would need to advance to quell maldistribution. The distribution curves reflect how incentives are distributed through the *complete* range – from bottom to top. Legree and his crowd ignore it.

You cannot claim that productivity on the labor portion of the curve will change the shape of the curve, without accounting for productivity at the high end of the curve. If it, too, moves in an equal upward direction, there would be no economic logic for distribution to change. The only valid economic productivity-based rationale for a more equitable distribution requires that the productivity change at the top is less than the labor productivity change.

Legree and his cohorts in all instances will always be reluctant to admit that the productivity change at the top is lower than labor's productivity change. And, *that is the precise precondition economically required to justify the productivity-cure-for-maldistribution logic.*

It is not plausible that the huge differences we have seen, say in going from a MAJ33 to a MAJ25, were caused by labor productivity deficiencies, or that labor productivity changes of a sufficient magnitude can, or will ever, reverse it. The root cause of maldistribution in the USA is culture – a Legree culture, not productivity.

Scarcity, the intuitive view.

It is often difficult to get a visceral grip on what scarcity actually means. As an aid, I developed the following informal spreadsheet Table-115. Do not take the table to be accurate. It is just a little something put together to provide a handy, albeit crude, reference while writing.

In it, the "Half SAT" college entrance exam score column is intended to indicate the highest score one receives on either the verbal or the math section.* The percentile and scarcity rankings columns refer to the total population, not just those who take the college boards or who play chess. I made estimates for chess ratings.[67] They are subject to great error. Do not take them as gospel. For percentile, SAT and IQ data, Ulf Norlinger's "Estimated IQs of some of the Greatest Geniuses" web page was used.[68]

It is ironic that economists and others employ the word meritocracy as if it conferred an advantage on a nation. Meritocracy and oligarchy have become indistinguishable.[69]

---

* A pesky point: The difference between the column, "Half SAT" rankings and conflicting SAT comments may appear confusing. The difference seems to reflect a sample size difference. The former are an expected SAT scores for a person of the indicated degree of intelligence (whether they took the test or not) and the scores in the comments indicate percentage outcomes from those who actually took the test. The differences are noticeable, most likely because many people do not take the SAT.

#115

Percent	Scarcity	IQ Stanford Binet	Half SAT	Scholastic Aptitude or Other Description
100.00%	**6,000,000,000**	201	800	Unmeasurable genius
100.00%	**240,000,000**	192	800	Highest genius
100.00%	**4,000,000**	180	800	Highest genius
100.00%	**1,000,000**	176	800	High genius; chess R. 2849. The highest ever FIDE rating was 2851, which Garry Kasparov received.
100.00%	**60,000**	166	790	High genius; chess R. 2749
100.00%	**30,000**	164	780	Genius, Nobel Prize Winners; chess R. 2649
99.99%	**15,000**	161	765	Genius, Nobel Prize Winners
99.99%	**8,000**	159	756	Genius, Nobel Prize Winners; chess R. 2549, Often having an International Grandmaster title
99.98%	**4,000**	156	741	Genius, Nobel Prize Winners; chess R. 2449, Senior Master
99.95%	**2,000**	153	727	Genius, Professors, about 99.93% (one in 1,430) of SATs lower than 800
99.9%	**1,000**	149	707	Genius, Professors , about 97% of SATs lower than 710; chess R. 2249 Life Master, National Master
99.8%	**500**	146	693	Genius, Professors, about 88% of SATs lower than 690; chess R. 2049 Expert
99.6%	**250**	142	673	Highly gifted, Intellectuals; chess R. 1949
99.5%	**200**	141	669	Highly gifted, Intellectuals; chess R. 1849 Class A
99.2%	**125**	139	659	Highly gifted, Intellectuals; chess R. 1749
99.0%	**100**	137	649	Highly gifted, Intellectuals; chess R. 1649, Class B and higher considered extremely competitive
98.7%	**75**	135	640	Gifted, University graduates, about 83% of SATs lower than 640
98.0%	**50**	133	630	Gifted, University graduates; chess R. 1449 Class C
96.7%	**31**	130	615	Chess R. 1049 Class E, bright beginner
95%	**20**	126	596	Gifted, University graduates, about 78% of SATs lower than 600; chess R. 649 Class G, slightly beneath the median chess level of 657
90%	**10**	121	572	about 72% of SATs lower than 575
72%	**3.57**	109	514	72% have not completed four years of college
60%	**2.50**	104	490	The MAJ refers to the 60% majority average income or percentage share
50%	**2.00**	100	470	about 36% of SATs lower than 475
40%	**1.67**	96	451	about 36% of SATs lower than 475
15%	**1.18**	84	393	15% have not completed High School in 2003 in USA (12 years of education); about 15% of SATs lower than 405
13%	**1.15**	82	383	Very low academic ability

In 1958, Michael Young wrote the book, *The Rise of the Meritocracy*. Young invented the word meritocracy "for purpose of damnation, not praise."[70] Indeed, in his book the protagonist is killed as a consequence of meritocracy. As the demise develops, the comment appears: "… there is nothing to be gained from social mixing, in school, in residence, or at work, because the upper class now have little or nothing to learn from the lower."[71] Young's meritocracy formula that brought about the doomed state was: Merit = Intelligence + Effort.[72]

The purpose of the prior table is not to attempt to equate income or wealth with IQ. Any attempt to find a firm, highly correlated linkage with income would be perilous from the outset.

Many years ago Judith Selvidge wrote an article that impressed me. It was about procedures for assigning probabilities to rare events. In it, she pointed out the value of "external calibration," which is to say referencing a rare event to some totally different system "whose only or main connection to the basic event is that they, too, have very small probabilities of occurrence."[73]

This is the reason for the table. Most of us know people who scored considerably better than we did on our college boards. We may also have an intuitive sense of how much smarter some people are than we are.

For example, broadly applying "external calibration," we see that a person with a one-in-four-thousand intelligence scarcity level has the mental horsepower to become a Nobel Prize winner or to make an equally outstanding contribution to society. This scarcity level implies that in many small towns (population 4,000+) and cities, there are children and adults with the mental capacity to make extraordinary contributions of Nobel Prize Winning caliber. This draws focus to the point that amazing abilities reside in unlikely places. It is a waste and a tragedy whenever maldistribution, social, or economic conditions thwart such abilities. Such people are some of our greatest resources.

The one-in-4,000-scarcity level also holds out a standard for high income earners. If you are earning an income greater than the one-in-4,000 level, you need to be making a positive contribution to society roughly proportional to a Nobel Prize winner. Otherwise you are not pulling your weight.

Table-115 is useful for viscerally "externally calibrating" what scarcity of ability means. For example, if you have a friend who scored 756 on a Half SAT, that person is rare – precisely rare at a one-in-8,000-scarcity level.

In an eminently readable fashion, Malcolm Gladwell in *Outliers: The Story of Success* points to components that delivered success to some of the greats of recent times. Ten thousand hours of hard work, deliberate practice, and effective training were a good starting point, including for John Lennon and Paul McCartney, who clearly put in their ten thousand+ hours. At 2,000 hours a year, that could occur within 5 years [365/7*40hr per week-80 hr vacation= 2005 hrs per year]. Young's meritocracy formula was: Merit = Intelligence + Effort. With a 10,000-hour threshold, it might look more like: Merit = Intelligence *multiplied times* Effort.

We see that income and intelligence are not closely aligned. Preventing maldistribution is imperative because it is impossible to know where truly great performance, talent, ability, integrity, and intelligence will arise. People at all levels must be treated fairly from birth onward because the talents we rely on as a nation will spring up in unexpected places. We never know until after the fact who will possess the vital characteristic, and who will develop it.

> "The cult of the individuals is always, in my view, unjustified. To be sure, nature distributes her gifts unevenly among her children. But there are plenty of the well-endowed, thank God, and I am firmly convinced that most of them live quiet unobtrusive lives. It strikes me as unfair, and even in bad taste, to select a few of them for boundless admiration attributing super-human powers of mind and character to them. This has been my fate, and the contrast between popular estimate of my powers and achievements and the reality is simply grotesque."
>
> – Albert Einstein[74]

With "Heritability of IQ" estimates shown in Wikipedia, we see a wide variety of possible associations, perhaps settling down to about a 0.75 heritability (where 0 indicates that none of variations in the trait is genetic in origin and 1 indicates all of the variation in the trait is genetic in origin). Although a 0.75 factor is high, it provides room for exceptions (0.25), one out of four cases. And those exceptions are often significant.

The tribe.

Pull out the napkin. Well, you may not need it. The calculations are straight forward. The reliable rule of thumb to find how much you differ from the average IQ is to divide your IQ by 100. The average IQ is 100. The peak IQ is about 200. The first percentile IQ is almost exactly half of average IQ. If you were to argue that there should be a direct proportional correspondence between IQ and income, then peak income would be twice average income and the minimum at the first percentile would be about half the average income.

In that proposed proportional IQ to income scheme, in a nation where average income was $48,000, the range of incomes would vary from $28,213 for the first percentile to $96,960 at an absolute peak IQ of 202. The Top1% would average $68,527 and a MAJ53.8 distribution would prevail. Such equality in income distribution plainly does not and never has existed in the history of nations.

Contrary to our views that have been anchored to focus on small differences at the top end, the major story is that IQ distribution within the tribe is far flatter than our emphasis on "smarts" is usually inclined to infer. And if IQ did have a direct proportional relationship with income, it would be the poor, not the rich who would primarily benefit.

#118

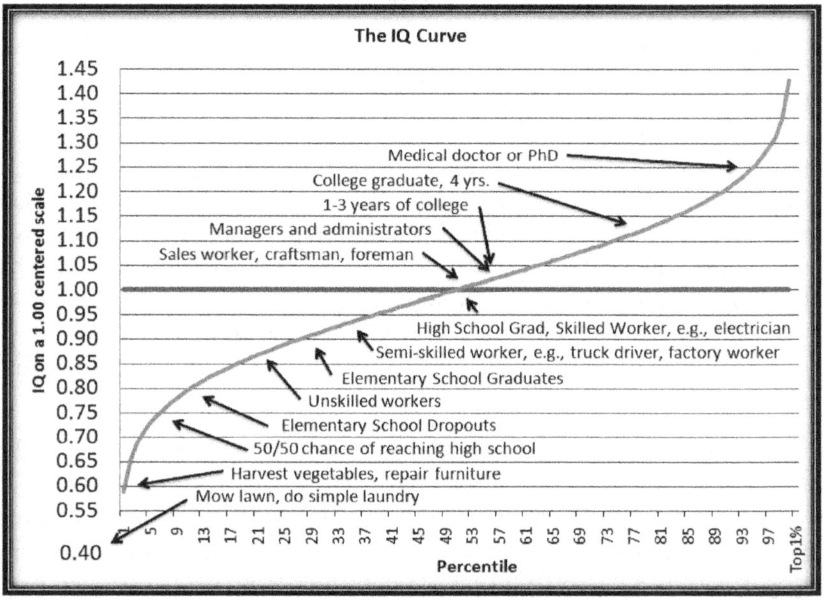

A nation, when it works well, must accommodate and provide a decent living for people of all IQ ranges, including those at the low end. To get a visual sense of IQ, some of Wikipedia's "Intelligence quotient" remarks were added to the above IQ Curve. About 4% of the population is classified as mentally retarded; 5% to 18%, as borderline intellectual functioning (below average cognitive ability).

Multiply the vertical axis in graph-118 by 100 to get IQ. Leave it as it is, to experiment with it as an X$ for determining income, as if IQ proportionately corresponds to income. However, you are apt to find such an experiment for estimating income disappointing. As shown in the following graph-119, the IQ curve is notably flat by comparison to an equitable MAJ33 income distribution.

#119

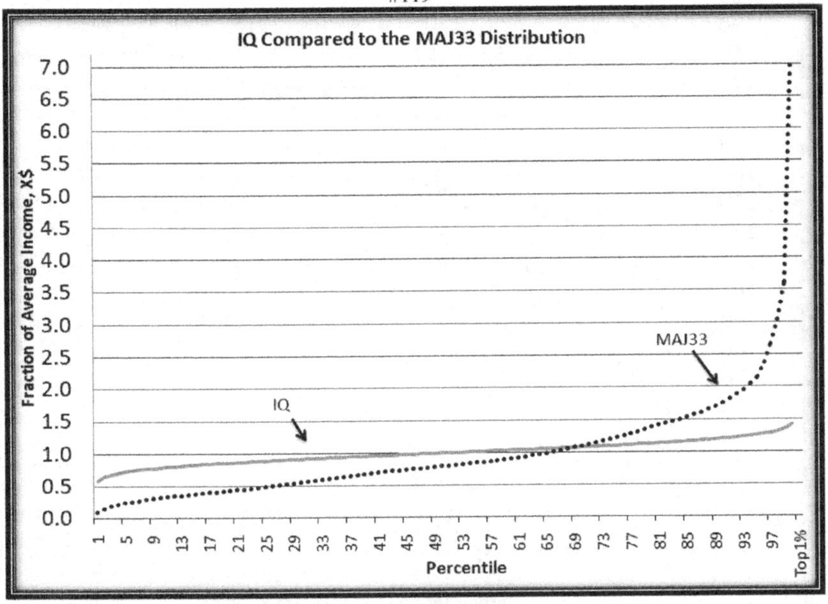

Still slugging along to find a relationship between income and IQ, the following graph-120 shows IQs that would correspond to MAJ33 and MAJ25 incomes. This graph can be made because we know the scarcity levels associated with IQ, and we know the scarcity levels associated with income. Keep in mind that Nobel Prize winners often have IQs in the neighborhood of 156+. Do you really expect the super-rich to have the extraordinarily high IQs that this graph suggests?

If you answer no, then the proposed link with income and IQ at the high end does not exist. Instead, as Gladwell has observed, once one reaches an IQ threshold of about 120, it seems that additional IQ points do not translate into an income advantages, and traits of personality and character assume increased importance.[75] About 9.1% of the population have IQs above 120.

If your answer is "yes" and you subscribe to the school of thought that the super-rich have higher IQs than Nobel Prize winners, then at MAJ33 that logic would lead to the conclusion that an approximate 156 IQ threshold for super high income would occur at an income of about one million dollars; and at MAJ25, at about three million dollars.

#120

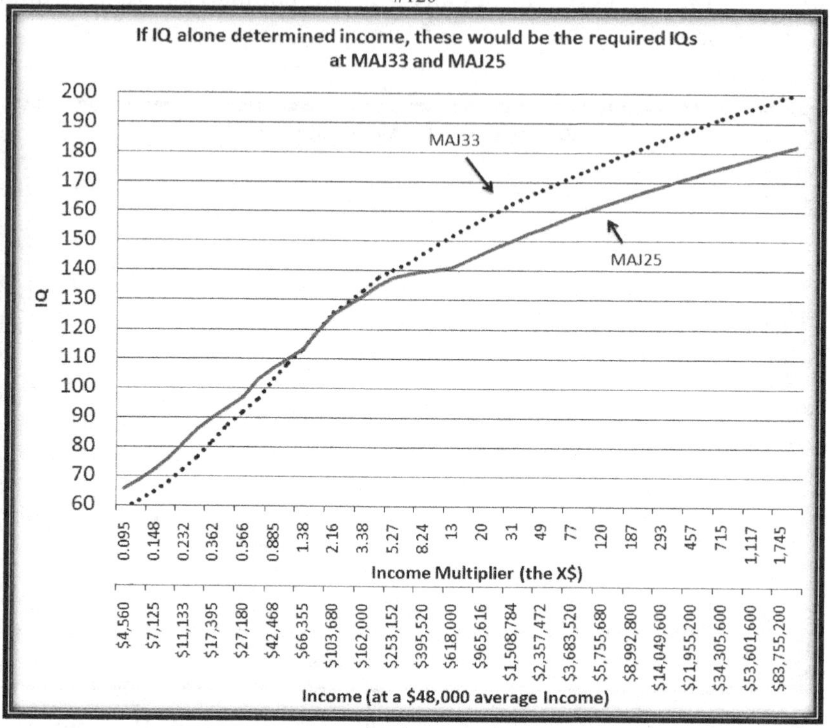

Backing away from attempting to link conventional IQ and income, perhaps there yet remains some way to hammer out a relationship. In the spirit of Selvidge's "external calibration," let's say that instead of representing conventional intelligence, IQ in the above graph-120 represents business acumen.

By this method, we see in the same graph that, at the high end of the scale, the maldistributed MAJ25 requires less ability than MAJ33, but presses for higher abilities from those at the low end – a rather twisted mentality for the MAJ25 folks.

To pay those at the top at MAJ25 more for lower business acumen – how does that strike you?

Inner Genie.

Go deep into your mind. Clear it of all heard before. Picture a world where IQ is unchanging. Picture the same world having compensations moving between MAJ33 and MAJ25. Continue thinking deeply. Ask your inner genie: "What is intelligence?" Your inner genie answers: "Intelligence, Master, is that constant quality that you have already assigned to people of the world." Ask your inner genie: "What is compensation?" Your inner genie answers: "Compensation, Master, is that changeable quality you have assigned to people of the world." As you slip out of Zen, you hear your inner genie repeating: "Constant intelligence, variable compensation. ... Constant intelligence, variable compensation. ..." As you move on, you barely hear, "Zagorsky ... Zagorsky ... Zagorsky."

Consider inner genie's brevity. A world where intelligence was largely a constant (given or developed), yet compensations went anywhere between MAJ33 to MAJ25. Clearly characteristics other than IQ are determining income variations. We do not need reams of studies to be certain of this. However, if it were possible to know baseline characteristics for compensation directly attributable to IQ, then we could estimate what fraction of income was derived from intelligence and what fraction came from characteristics other than intelligence. The inner genie's "Zagorsky" may just provide a missing link. Let's try it.

In his study, Zagorsky provides a table showing corresponding income and net worth for an IQ range of 75 to 125.[76] The computer programs I have written are able to transform Zagorsky's table into curves that explain compensation given for IQs from the 6th to 94th percentile – 89% of the population. If the data had also been available for the remaining 11%, then a full distribution curve for intelligence compensation could have been easily constructed. But the problem, as you will see, is not insurmountable. The 89% of the income curve that is available closely approximates a MAJ49 lookup-table curve. The small section of income (0.9%) beneath the 6th percentile that significantly deviates from the MAJ49 curve can be proportionally distributed to the 95th and higher percentiles without substantially changing curve shape at the backbone. By recalculating the top end with this new backbone data, the computer program gives a baseline IQ-Compensation curve (an IQ appropriate income curve) that we can compare to other distribution curves. By doing so, we can estimate how much components other than intelligence contribute to income. Don't attribute this curve to Zagorsky. Any errors are mine alone. His valuable work just made it easier for me to commit them.

To help visualize the process of creating the IQ-Comp Curve, look at the following graph-122. The data points available to me from the 6th to 94th percentile are shown in dots. The complete IQ-Comp Curve has its end points derived from the closely corresponding MAJ49 curve.[77] The final

IQ-Comp Curve was modestly less equitable than the starting MAJ49, caused partly by the difference in shape at the bottom.

#122

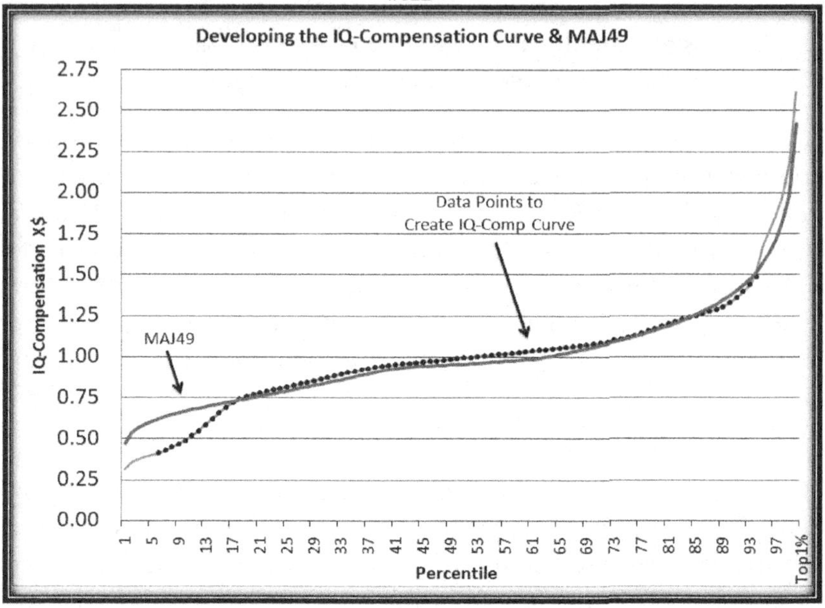

It is tempting to believe that the upper reaches of a true IQ-Comp Curve would vastly favor high IQ. I, too, would have found myself in that camp not so very long ago. But with the 6th to 94th percentile of the IQ-Comp Curve clearly defined, there is little latitude for creating other plausible shapes at the upper reaches that might greatly deviate from the shown curve. If you doubt this, try constructing a plausible curve having the same 6th to 94th percentile values, yet having other points that widely differ. Keep in mind that in the 100-point system, all points must sum to 100%. I believe you will find, as I did, that the constraints of IQ distribution and income distribution do not permit the Top1% to receive an outsized IQ advantage.

From the X$ values in the IQ-Comp Curve, we can estimate the income generated by IQ alone throughout the range. The outcome is shown in the following graph-123. This indicates about how much you would tend to be paid for IQ. The rest of your income, if higher, would come from other characteristics that the market rewards – components falling into a "not-IQ" category. *Keep the notion of "not-IQ" in mind. We can use the "not-IQ" factor to illustrate a key consequence of maldistribution.*

#123

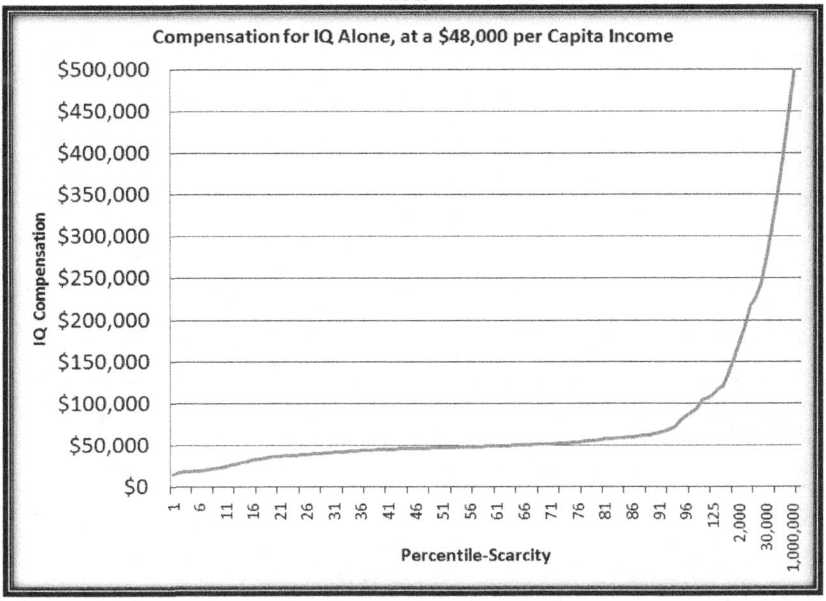

Seldom do we think it out, but IQ distribution is very flat by comparison to the huge range of incomes from top to bottom. An unavoidable consequence of the wide difference in the shape of the two curves is that people are highly compensated at the high end of the income scale for reasons that are not IQ related. They may be positive reasons, indifferent reasons, or harmful reasons – but they are not IQ. You may find the degree to which this occurs surprising

Not-IQ.

The extent to which people at the high end of the income scale are highly compensated for reasons other than IQ varies according to distribution curves. In thc following graph-124, we see that the "not-IQ" component is far, far less at MAJ33 than at MAJ25. This should not be surprising. IQ Compensation distribution is relatively flat at a MAJ48 (or if you prefer a Gini of 18.9). IQ remained the same under MAJ33 and MAJ25; the component that changed was income.

The central point remains that the greater the separation between an IQ curve and an income curve, the greater will be the "not-IQ" income component.

We can divide any given curve in the lookup table by the IQ-Comp Curve to get an approximate magnitude of the "not-IQ" influences that would tend to exist throughout the curve, from bottom to top.

#124

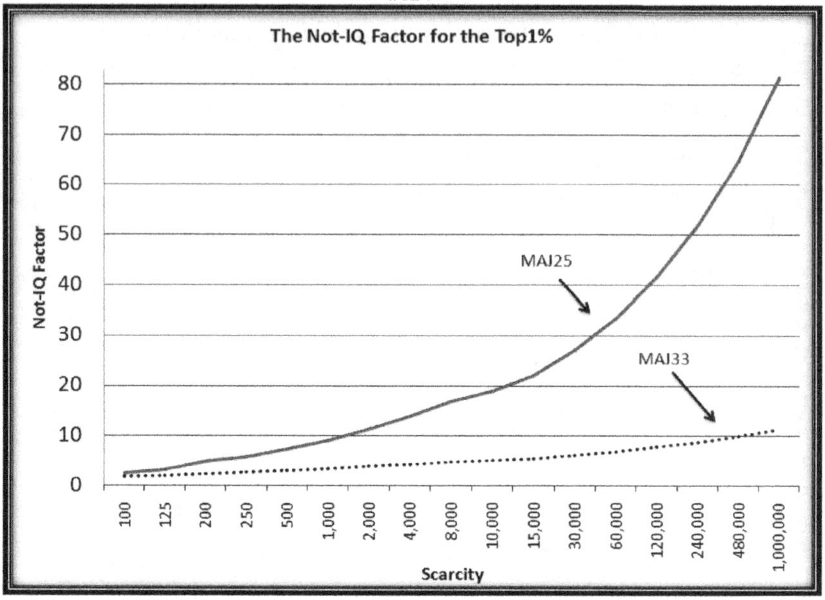

In graph-124, we see MAJ33 remains close to IQ throughout the Top1%. In sharp contrast, at MAJ25, IQ becomes a tiny portion of compensation at the high end of the curve. At the one-in-a-million-scarcity level, total compensation is more than 80 times larger than the IQ component. Obviously, this MAJ25 chasm between IQ and Income is vastly larger than the modest spread at MAJ33.

In a nation of 300 million people at MAJ33, the threshold for being in the Top500 income earners is a "not-IQ" of 10.3 – modest and sensible. At the maldistributed MAJ25 the Top500 are at a 68.3 "not-IQ." And at the highest income: a 488 "not-IQ." These guys are running on phenomenal "not-IQs."

It shows.

There is a continuum as maldistribution advances, where nations increasingly depart from intelligence-based decisions and preferences. You see this in spades when you look at a tinhorn potentate in a maldistributed economy. In such cases, in government and business, you will usually find an abundance of wing-nuts in leadership positions, and it is abundantly clear the key "not-IQ" components are coercion and a distasteful menu of items that never should have left the kitchen.

#125

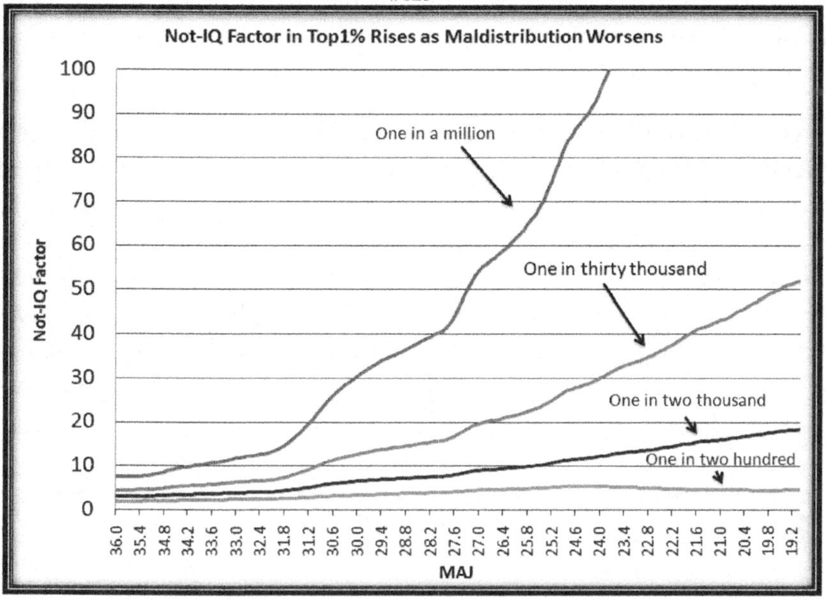

More specifically, we can see the relationship in the above graph-125. As maldistribution worsens, the high income earners at the one-in-a-million level become sharply disassociated with intelligence. The rise is quickened at MAJs beneath 31.8. It goes wildly off the scale beneath a MAJ23.7. In sharp contrast, the income earner at the one-in-200 level remains more closely grounded to intelligence with a "not-IQ" factor that ranges from about 2 to 5.5 at all points shown in the graph.

When you listen to an exceptionally wealthy person speaking in a maldistributed economy, it is well to remember that at least some of what you hear, for better or worse, is apt to be based on the "not-IQ" component. Be cautious about attributing IQ-based omnipotence to top management.

How far can economically successful nations go when enlightenment and intelligence become diminishingly small components of success? Is it not serious that as one advances to ever-higher levels of leadership, intelligence becomes an ever-decreasing component of success? Are not children the most adaptive and perceptive of us all? Will they not sense that in 73% of families, their parents are undercompensated for the intelligence they possess? Will their role models not shift increasingly away from intelligence to the more fruitful territory of "not-IQ" success? Why would a child follow the difficult route of developing education and intelligence when the plain evidence is that the greatest rewards come from the "not-IQ" (which is to say a path only slightly influenced by the classroom)? When I was in school, the window was one of the most attractive aspects of the schoolroom. But to make it the only attraction for the savvy student, would that be going too far?

As maldistribution increases, the infection of a reduced grounding in intelligence is intensely suffered almost exclusively within the Upper½%. The remaining 99½% of us are not apt to catch a debilitating case of it. It strikes with greatest force in a portion of society with whom most of us have little day-to-day social contact – the ten thousand people in the U.S. above the one-in-30,000 income level. Those at the top are the economic chiefs who indirectly determine the course of our lives. To have them making decisions without a firm and primary grounding in intelligence, would that be perilous?

#126

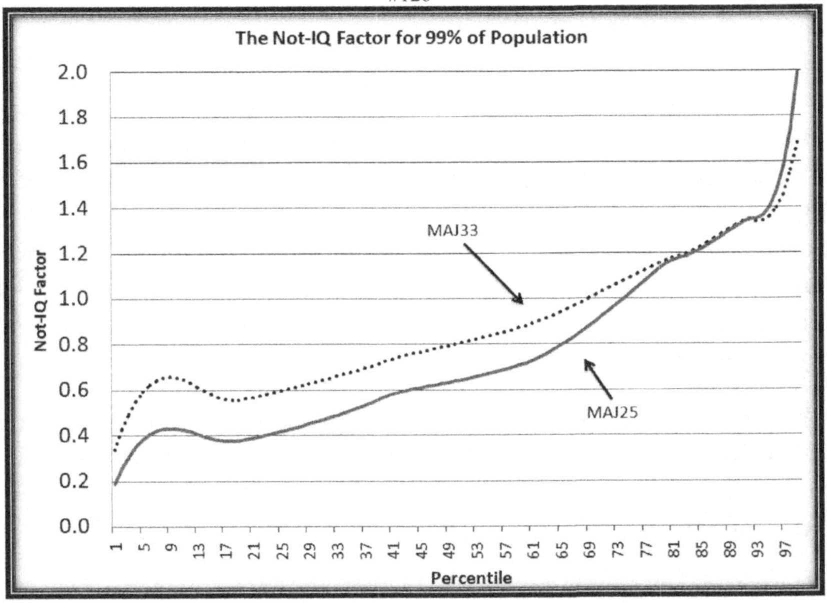

The "not-IQ" compensation that those of us in the 99% group experience does not have the drama seen in the Top1%. From about the 76th to 96th percentiles, as seen in graph-126, there is a zone of indifference between MAJ33 and MAJ25 where the differences between the two curves are about 5% or less.

When the "not-IQ" factor is equal to one, a person is compensated at an amount exactly consistent with intelligence. For MAJ33, this occurs at the 69th percentile; for MAJ25, at the 74th percentile.

When the "not-IQ" factor is less than one, a person is compensated at a rate lower than the IQ-Comp Curve. The MAJ33 keeps compensation closer to the IQ amount than does MAJ25. But no sensible distribution will keep the "not-IQ" at 1.0 throughout the range, because to do so would necessitate the nation having the same MAJ48 income distribution that intelligence does. Such a high MAJ would wrongly and dangerously undercompensate leadership, as has already been shown in another excessively equal distribution (MAJ36).

Some "not-IQ" compensation is necessary. Although a high "not-IQ" factor is deleterious, so too is an excessively low one. There are many "not-IQ" components that are valuable: integrity, hard work, discipline, desirable psychological characteristics, responsibility, conscientiousness, organizational capacity, health, creativity, experience, and the list goes on beyond the realm of didacticism to encompass numerous valuable traits, many of which we do not have the good sense to recognize.

Having said this, for a leadership to have a "not-IQ" factor of 80 (or another similarly high number) is a malady. Do you really want leadership in government and business where only $1/80^{th}$ of its characteristics for success are intelligence-based? A factor of 10 seems more likely to approach prudence. The progressive income disassociation with IQ as maldistribution advances is plainly unwise and destructive.[78]

At its core, economics is about allocation of resources. Is it an economic objective to have an intelligent society? Rewards for intelligence most certainly come under the allocation umbrella. Maldistribution devalues the single trait that distinguishes us from lower life forms. The most obvious breach of economic responsibility is to fail to reward, in proper measure, our most valuable resource – human intelligence.

Maldistribution distorts the essential relationships necessary for people and nations to thrive for the narrow purpose of benefitting a tiny few (at most, 3% of the population). We distinguish ourselves from tomatoes and such goods that can be valued and distributed exclusively according to supply and demand curves, because we are the purchasing, working, and creating engine that makes the whole enterprise workable, interesting, and useful. To keep the allocation focus on key ingredients – humans and life forms upon which they depend – would seem to be far more important than pandering to the "not-IQ" parochial interests at the top.

The instinct of the economist is to put all decision-making and value at the instant of the transaction – a paycheck. Nothing could be less appropriate. When you compensate a human, you are paying for the past (education, experiences, training, et cetera) and buying the future (the capacity to raise the next generation and care for the elders). In contrast to most animals, from infancy to adulthood, humans are exceptionally vulnerable and require a huge investment in time and resources for them to thrive. Examination of brain development during this period confirms the obvious. If compensation is reduced to a mean action to keep worker pay at the lowest achievable point, the past cannot be paid for, nor the future bought.

In its young state, the "not-IQ" factor seems to provide a standard that gives us a more accurate assessment than most of us currently have. This standard alone appears sufficient for the benchmark, especially since from the 18th to 94th percentile, it so closely matches the shape of MAJ49 and the demonstrated compensations for intelligence. So it will be included in the spreadsheets. Should it need revision, it can be revised there. Given its capacities to set a consistent standard through the wide range of MAJs and income levels that we have seen in the above graphs (#122-#126), it is hard to imagine a standard that would offer large improvements.

Return to the tribe.

The 72% of the population without a 4-year college education and the 60% majority, to which much of our discussion has been directed, are at the lower end of the scale.

As elsewhere, characteristics other than intelligence measurements play a dominant role. Responsibility, dedication, conscientiousness, study, practice, ability to put in a good day's work, and the list goes on … . These are not only of great value, they are often of preeminent value. They make more difference in many work situations than does raw initial intelligence.

I work with my hands frequently – carpentry and the like – and have a complete metal-working machine shop in my basement for prototype design (industrial lathe and computer controlled milling machine, together weighing more than most cars). Constantly good ideas come from a wide variety of people. A completely illiterate friend is a reliable source for many of them. I have been fortunate to know people of breathtaking intelligence and equally fortunate to work with ordinary folk, who on a good day, keep observations and ideas flowing.

When looking at a table or graph with 60% of the people having an IQ of 104 or lower, experience tells me that many fine decent folk can be found there. We have no reason to criticize them. They may be at 104 or lower. That is what humanity is about. Don't minimize it. It is central. When we talk about the MAJ, this fact implicitly resides in the background.

Keep in mind, though, that there is not an exact correspondence between percentile rankings and workers' IQ, especially at the lower percentiles. Highest IQ people in a household are often key income earners. Those with less marketable skills or a lower IQ may draw a lower paycheck than the key income earner, or attend to necessary duties at the home, garden, or on the farm, which may or may not generate income. A household working together, each to his or her abilities. A nice picture it is. We all have our place and our importance.

The MAJ needs sufficient opportunities. They have built, and will continue to build, great nations if they are given half a chance. They do, and can do, an honest day's work. Often they stretch beyond their God-given abilities to do exceptionally well. They may be star performers in a particular area. But they require jobs generally in line with their abilities. The MAJ should never be chastised for failing to work in heavily abstract thought of the kind you can hear listening in on graduate courses at a university. Nor should the MAJ be held hostage to vision which falls in line with some ill-conceived dreamed-up policy objectives that have little likelihood of materializing.

As shown in *Henry J. Kaiser Western Colossus*, at the shipyards, "they were a strange host, not only the healthy but the half-sick, the half-alive, the halt, the maimed, the partially blind. Thousands were 4-Fs, rejects from the draft. Thousands were women not used to heavy work they were called upon to do. Many were old, really too old to work at all, but this was war time and everyone's services were needed in one way or another. Dr. Cecil Cutting described them as a 'walking pathological museum.'" [79]

No one ever before had built a ship in fewer than twenty-four days. September 1942, Kaiser's people built one in ten days. Two months later, they did it in four days.

Back in November 1940, Kaiser had never built even one ship. His "shipyard" in 1940 was a mudflat, nothing more. From 1941 to 1945, his people built 1,490 ocean going ships – merchant ships and warships. That would be more than one ship a day, on average. Peak employment was 197,000. If you ever have any doubt about the capacity of the ordinary person, think again.

Not only could the workers be described as average, Henry J. Kaiser was a short, fat guy, who himself said "I am certain that I was less than an average boy to everyone but my mother." He left school after the 8th grade. He started off in business as a photographer. He was honest. He prohibited corruption and bribes of any kind. He hired people he had faith in, who were unproven, and who often had no prior experience in managing the jobs for which they were responsible (and these were huge jobs).

It was Kaiser's conviction, stated in the *Western Colossus*, "that every person has something to offer if given a fair chance, and if treated with proper respect. It was a microcosm of America itself – where the blending of different races and different levels of skills produces a strong and balanced economy."

Kaiser 1928: "… you can't get fine talent into your organization by simply offering high salaries. You and the men who work with you have to build yourselves up to the capacity to tackle bigger and bigger jobs,"

Kaiser 1944: "I know I speak for countless thousands when I say that both labor and management want to build. When we generalize our hopes in the thought that we want to build a better America, we really mean that we want to build a more abundant life for every American. And this, again is a Christian precept, preserved in the immortal words: 'I am come that ye might have life, and that ye might have it more abundantly.' … The only approach is the humanitarian one: the 'give and take' between men of good will; the wholehearted desire to agree; the will to work together."

As the *Western Colossus* put it, "Liking people came naturally to him. He automatically accepted people for what they were. He believed in their intrinsic goodness. He had instinctive confidence in their potential. … He accepted the role of unions wholeheartedly. … Some of his best and most lasting friendships were with union leaders …"

Dr Sidney Garfield graduated from medical school in 1933 at the depths of the Great Depression and within a few years had a small hospital. He found insurance companies haggling and challenging his fees. For non-industrial illnesses and diseases, he charged a flat $1.50 per month per company employee [about $27/month in current dollars]. Garfield found that employees were coming in early enough so that their illnesses could be controlled, instead of waiting until they were desperately ill as they had formerly done.

Kaiser questioned Garfield extensively about his preventative care program and came straight to the point, "Young man, if your idea is half as good as you say it is, it's not only good for this project, it's good for the entire country." Dr. Garfield was opposed by organized interests and Kaiser was again on point: "Nothing new or good has ever been achieved without strong opposition. If you were not opposed, it would be because you are not contributing anything worthwhile."[80]

The result: Kaiser Permanente Medical Care Program was built. His other jobs: Bonneville Dam, one year ahead of schedule and profitable, Boulder Dam, 2 years 2 months ahead of schedule and under budget; Grand Coulee Dam, a year and a half ahead of schedule and under budget.

The Schadenfruede School of Economics will always lose to the Kaiser School. It is the true and accurate belief and faith in people. It is the capacity to get your hands dirty to get the job done. It is the capacity to sacrifice to achieve an ever more noble position. These will succeed. Honor begets honor; trust begets trust; faith begets faith; and hope is the mainspring of life. The only deadly sin is cynicism.[81]

Agriculture, manufacturing, and construction made the nation great and gave us jobs populated, in large part, by the MAJ. I have done all of these manually for extended periods and loved it. Look there, and in similar areas for your MAJ to thrive.

Though many economists are fascinated with making conjectures about those at the high end of the income scale, there is need to pause and reconsider. Look around at the components that make your own life happy and at the components necessary for the perpetuation of the species.

The best portions of your home, city and town were made and put together by those of us of at the moderate scarcity range – we who did a good job.

The dose of ability and technology originating from the Top1% is indispensible, but bringing on the show usually requires the work of the ordinary guy or girl. Think about the things that bring pleasure to your life. It is often the ordinary person who was the motor behind it. Call it sophomoric, unworthy of academic consideration, and far beneath your status if you like, but calling it human and what makes the whole enterprise work is my preference.

When reduced to practicality, it takes a huge amount of time, effort, and conscientiousness to get things done. Consider how many hands-on hours it takes you to do a job well, whether it be tending a vegetable garden to feed your family, or improving or building a section of your home.

To get things right at home is a lot of work. So too, is it a lot of work in the public sphere. Walk room to room in your home; drive down each street in your town or city; you can see the job that needs to be done. The vast majority of unattended tasks in our lives and in our nation require work of the ordinary person.

The things that make a nation interesting usually involve the convergence of work and dedication coming squarely from the mainstream person of normal ability. When a nation works and is vital, it is because the game is being played well and sensibly at the middle. If this is not done, the nation is not taking care of the tribe.

When I was a child there was a beautiful phrase, the then de facto motto of the United States: "Out of many, One" (E Pluribus Unum). What a lovely way to express greatness.

The presumption in a large business or society that when 99% of the people work and deliver the end product, a preponderance of the bonus for a job well done should go to the Top1% … perhaps it's worth pondering.

In the Mayan culture, kings claimed supernatural power to deliver rain and prosperity. In return, the peasants provided lavish lifestyles replete with palaces, corn, and venison. That promise was broken when drought and climatic changes occurred. In Copán, Honduras, the royal palace was burned around 850 AD (presumably a revolt). Deforestation, periodic droughts, overpopulation, and limited food supply were key players. There were no archeological signs of anyone in the valley 400 years later.[82] Now it's a nice river valley with a small town. I have been there.

Our current economic kings claim supernatural powers to deliver a working economy. Like their Mayan predecessors, they enjoy lavish life styles. Have they got the story right? Have they got the theory right? *Are they taking care of the tribe?*

Your high school class.

In your high school class there were perhaps a few people, say one-in-a-hundred, who in your mind stood out as possessing qualities that you particularly admired. You may have felt they would be especially useful to their community, business, nation, or the world. And, deservedly they should end up in the Top1%. There was also the vast number of lower status. Perhaps the players, their abilities, and their circumstances change so greatly later that the high school assessment was perilous from the outset.

But we think back on high school because, except for the approximate one out of 7 who will not graduate from high school, it may have been the last time in our lives that we daily had visceral contact with such a wide cross section of our economy. In the economy, we are all in this enterprise together – seen and unseen. The economy must deal not only with us and people of our status, but all of us. It cannot be Gown versus Town.

The word fair. It is such a short word. And such a difficult one.

But that is what an economy must seek to be. The economy must take your high school class and those that did not graduate, and do the best job reasonably possible. Our survival and happiness depend on it. About 72% of the U.S. population do not have a four-year college degree or higher. The clear majority reside there.

The Kaiser people are of the same fiber as your high school class.

Perhaps one of the greatest advantages of equitable distributions is that people tend to be rewarded for characteristics that are valuable for society, even when they do not directly correspond to some a workplace-assessed value, or some particular intelligence or performance measurement.

Every instant of the day I am reminded that the things of great beauty and importance come from work that is not well compensated. Here at home there are numerous handmade items that required great ability to make. None of these are valuable as far as the marketplace is concerned. The majority were from eBay and cheap: Shirazi and Qashqia Persian carpets, marble murals from Lebanon, hand-painted Talavera tile from Mexico, hand-crafted leather from Oaxaca, suzanis from Uzbekistan, textiles from Guatemala, handmade wooden pens from Texas, and, when in China, a silk business suit in a style I chose, hand tailored to fit me.

With Wikipedia, Google, and the Internet, it also seems likely that many contributors are not necessarily at the high reaches on the economic ladder. At least so far, the plain message is that the contributions from a wide swath of the income scale are intellectually valuable – priceless would more accurately state it.

The message is clear. We get things of great personal value from the handwork and original contributions of others. Too frequently, there is an inverse relationship between how well such people are paid and the quality of their work. In the U.S. and throughout the world, people make huge contributions that enhance the lives of others via numerous circuitous routes. The hope of leveling unfairness to which they are subject is found in equitable distribution.

Albeit that business may be blind to it, it benefits circuitously by fair compensation because fair pay provides income used to purchase products. An equitable distribution fosters the very social vitality that makes it possible to do business.

It seems unlikely that there ever can be an exact standard for measuring the value of an individual or the capacity to contribute. At the peak, Leonardo da Vinci's remark, "men of lofty genius sometimes accomplish the most when they work the least," comes to mind.

Far more ordinarily, one of the most beneficial friendships I had in my childhood was with a tenant farmer who usually would not receive passing notice. The friendship made me a better person.

Do the powerful and beneficial relationships in your life correspond to wealth? Doesn't something about what it means to be human, something having to do with love and affection, play a larger role? The answer may suggest that it is wiser to spread the bounty widely enough to make the capacity to thrive possible.

These are not soft points. They are points that make life worth living. To unnecessarily remove the dignity to contribute from anyone removes a bit of vitality from all who come in contact with that person. To remove it from an entire class is crassly destructive – approaching insanity.

Riches to rags and …

I feel compelled to pause here and mention a perspective that drives me in these writings. For the past 40 years, I have not mentioned the following and hope it will not appear to be name dropping or posturing.

My great grandfather was a highly successful Quaker businessman in the mid-1800s. Consistent with Quaker tradition, he was noted for absolute honesty and integrity. For my family, his good fortune and financial ability benefited subsequent generations to this date. That status in my youth, albeit not extreme wealth, gave me access to circumstances that many others would not have had.

My Uncle Walter – a Member of Parliament, knighted by the queen – had a large manor home the public would visit. The family "dressed for dinner," which is to say that when a boy, I would wear everyday either a white dinner jacket or tuxedo to dinner when visiting them.

The British side of the family moved in high circles. When Chip Bohlen was ambassador to France, we were invited to the embassy to see his wife Avis, a dear friend of my aunt from the time they were children, and I might add a very interesting person, as were most of my Aunt Lenette's friends.

Notwithstanding the comfortable circumstances of the British side of the family, I liked all of them immensely, especially my cousin Minnie, who died entirely too young. So this book is not written as a diatribe against wealth. There are many fine wealthy people. There are instances where wealth is used maliciously and selfishly. There are instances where it is not.

As these words go to paper, the Internet shows that 18-year old Samantha Garvey, now living in a homeless shelter, is a semifinalist in a prestigious Intel national science competition. Her words are not those of defeatism or crying in a bucket: "There are other people out there. People my age going through the same exact thing. If I can do it, so can they. They can do just as much, if not more, than I can do."[83] I certainly wish her well. She is very interesting. If you listen to all of what she has to say in context, you also hear her words of intelligence, kindness, and acknowledgement of the deep difficulties her family is going through.

She has a fine, kind family and an enthusiastic science teacher. Of the reported 1.6 million U.S. homeless children, many are not so fortunate. If you have ever been in great poverty, you know what this means without seeing the words now in front of you. You attempt to retain pride alongside poverty – a difficult undertaking. We are so tuned to the culture of money that prudence compels myth. Myth, which at my peril, I dispel in the following.

During a particularly rough financial period slightly more than a decade ago, I worked at minimum wage for two years for two competing fast food restaurants, at times working both jobs simultaneously. It was no willful experiment with the objective of writing about it. The object was to put food on the table, to survive, and to keep and stay in my home.

A few scruffy characters work fast food. Usually they don't last. The work is demanding and difficult. Most who stick around do it well. Work often starts long before the break of day when most people are in REM sleep and it may continue to an hour that is equally inconvenient. You hardly have enough money to survive. If you work fast food, you are schooled in the art of living under extreme unremitting adversity. I do not wish that on anyone.

One of the most able people I have known worked at one of the restaurants. Chinese, at age 50, she learned English. Her daughter, of similar ability, is now a physician. Another coworker is now a math professor. To my embarrassment, a Game Theory book, borrowed from him, has yet to be returned.

Those who speak dismissively of the low-class worker are ignorant. I would pay money for the privilege of seeing them stick to the job and live off the wage it provides.

It would make a great documentary to take a 100 such cases of the decriers of the poor working person and make a film of them attempting to do the job, unremittingly day after day. Let one of them alone make 2,000+ biscuits from scratch on a busy morning, as some of us have done. I would try to edit out most of their whining. It would detract from the comedy of watching them trying to keep up with the common worker. I would, however, want to film their families now living under the bounty of a minimum wage alone. That might be instructive. Heck, look at the budgets for many of the mega-bust films. At least this one would draw a large and amused audience. And no celebrity actors or special effects would eat up the budget. Reality alone would be quite enough.

Low and underclass, closer than you expect.

We are all part of the curve. Right to the bottom.

Since 1938, the minimum wage in the U.S. has set a floor on the income for the working man that translated up the wage scale. In the following graph-137, we see that the 1938-2010 minimum wage income produced an average annual inflation-adjusted income equivalent to about $14,500 annually. The income in graph-137 results from multiplying the minimum wage rate times the customary number of annual labor hours. This annual minimum wage income reached its peak in approximately 1968. It fell to its lowest point since 1950 in 2006 – $10,200 annually.

#137

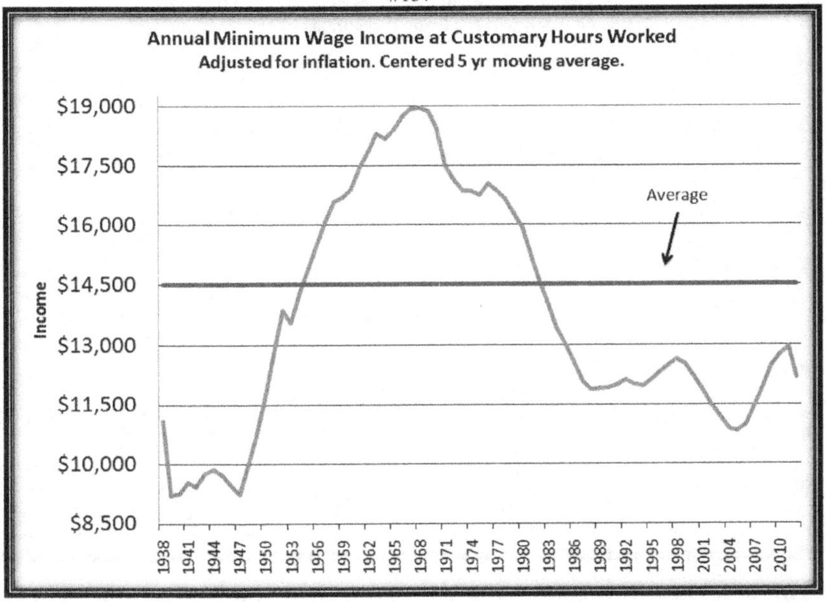

In the real world, the minimum wage worker's income is often reduced beneath the shown levels by seasonal work, unemployment, et cetera. In the year 2010, 6% of hourly workers were paid at or beneath the minimum wage – 2.5% at the minimum wage, 3.5% beneath the minimum wage.[84] The restaurant and hospitality industry have many workers beneath the minimum wage.

The minimum wage is a valuable aid to fair compensation for all workers, particularly those not represented by labor unions.[85] Its floor rate defines the wage culture. The floor dropping subsequent to the 1970s severely damaged the MAJ and non-union workers above them. They no longer had the power of government working on their behalf to keep their inflation-adjusted wage at traditional levels.

As can be seen in the lookup-table file, X$ curves often have similar shapes. If the region which most directly pertains to the minimum wage worker drops (while higher incomes do not drop), the curve is bent downward to accommodate this change. Classically and unavoidably, when a downward bend occurs in the region favorably influenced by minimum wage, an upward bend at some higher point must occur, for the plain reason that all the percentages must sum to 100%. By this logic, a drop in minimum wage income abets maldistribution.

#138

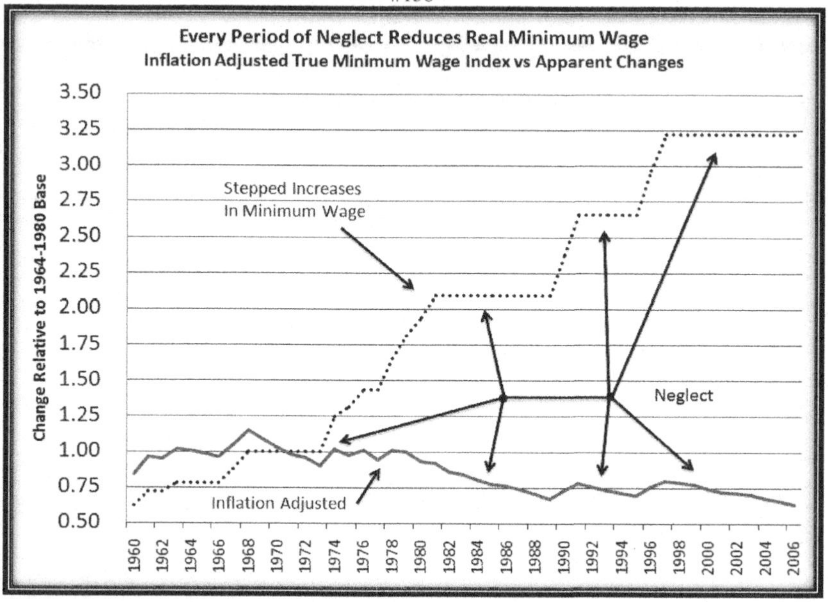

The mechanism for reducing the real inflation-adjusted minimum wage can be summarized in one word: ***Neglect!***

Look at those periods in graph-138 where the neglect arrows point. You will see a consistent repeated process that reduces the inflation-adjusted minimum wage: long lags without changes in the minimum wage. During these lags, inflation is left to eat into the worker's income. In the period 1964-1980, there had been deliberate and regular attention to adjusting the minimum wage so that the working person was protected. This process was breached in the 1969-1973 interval, but not so much so that it could not be restored.

The 1982-1989 breach was more serious and became the unrevoked trend setter. It pulled the inflation-adjusted minimum wage down 32%. From this point onward, the real minimum wage hovered in the neighborhood of being 25% lower than the 1964-1980 median. Three subsequent periods of neglect (1992-1995; 1998-2006; and 2010-2012) kept the worker down. The most devastating in 2006 pulled the worker down 37% from the base median.

All of these occurred because of lack of attention to prevent the adverse impact that inflation would otherwise wreak on the working person. Regular inflation adjustments had been the known standard of attentiveness required to prevent the gutting of the working man's wage. The failures to adjust were deliberate.

The process of periodic adjustments in the minimum wage is fraught with difficulties – neglect being just one of them. There are also instances where periodic adjustments create an excessively high minimum wage. From 1961 to 1971 the minimum wage occasionally exceeded the base line median, as can be seen in the humps in the above two graphs (#137 and #138). This was unwise.

#139

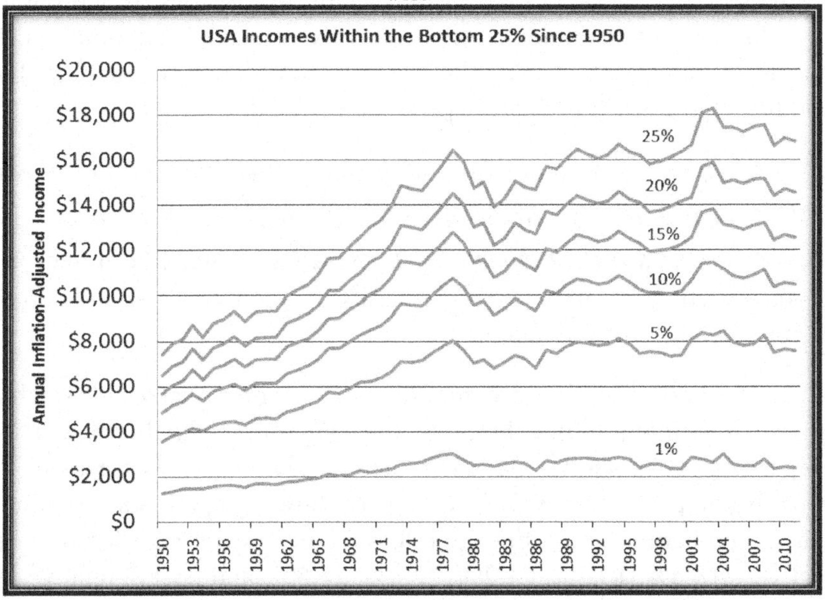

The only protection for consistent fairness for the working person and the nation at large is to have the minimum wage automatically indexed annually to inflation. To prudently return to the average $14,500 minimum wage annual income would require an inflation indexed increase plus 1.36% for ten years [1.36%= ($14,503/ $12,673)^(1/10)-1].

In the previous graph-139 we see people directly influenced by the minimum wage. Each line represents the inflation-adjusted income of the person at the designated percentile. The quick summary might well be: From 1950 to 1978, the incomes of those in the bottom quarter rose rapidly. But by 2010, their incomes were often less than their 1978 income. This summary, however, does not tell the story. To get that, you need to dig.

From 1950 through the 1970s, there was an implicit contract between the people and the government. "You, the government, lay down the rules for the economy and oversee its fairness, and we, the people, will be your productive and willing partner." Both sides took the deal seriously. It was subject to some variations and interpretations, but both parties held up to the agreement. From about 1952 to 1969, income distribution remained equitable; in some instances it was nearly constant. From 1970-1978 the lower classes received an historically increased share, after which the bumpy but sustained downward slide smashed the contract.

This slide did not occur because of latter-day theories trotted out about new information economies or other recently contrived think-tank phrases. It occurred for the same reason that downward moving income-distribution trend lines have always taken shape at the low end.

The message to the low and underclass is this: "*There is plenty of GDP, income, and wealth, and it is growing, but from this point on, you get a smaller share of it.* You had better like it and behave well or we will trash on you to a greater extent than you have ever dreamed possible. So suck up and take it."

The low and underclass are not nitwits. They don't need a crystal ball to see who is getting a larger share and who is getting a smaller one. The following graph-141 shows that their income share was worse than in the 1950s. If you prefer the explicit: In the six shown graph lines, from the 25th to the 1st percentile graph lines, the loss of income for each group was respectively 18.5%, 19.2%, 21.2%, 22.8%, 25.5%, and 35.1% relative to the moderate 1952 to 1969 median. And relative to the equitable 1978 year, the drops looked like this: 25.2%, 26.6%, 28.1%, 28.8%, 30.9%, and 41.9%. Take your pick. In either case, the game had new rules completely different from those of the 1950s, 1960s, and 1970s. Those rules moved from civilized behavior to the uncivilized.

#141

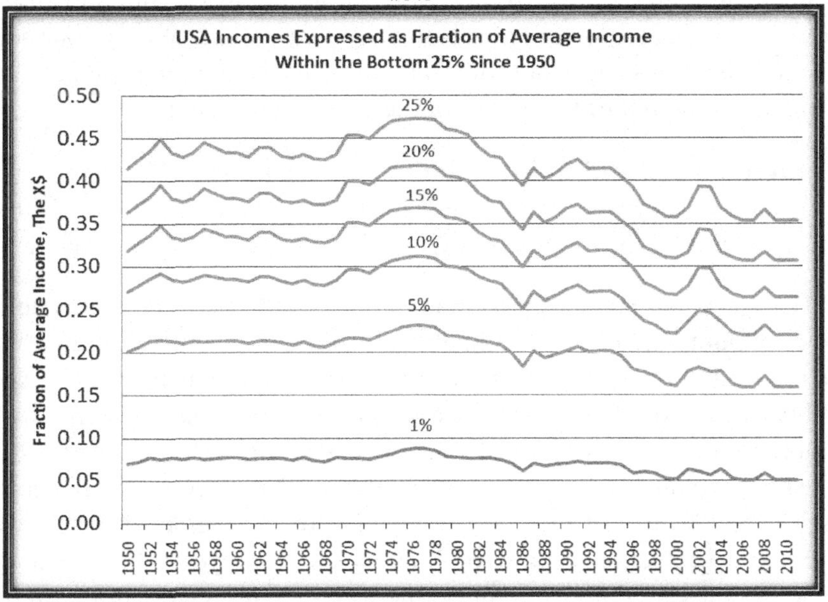

One out of four people walking down the street are in the bottom 25%. These two graphs (#139 and #141) show the consequences for this group. The group is 25 times larger than the Top1%. I repeat it: *The bottom 25% of the population has 25 times more people in it than does the Top1%.*

You trash us regardless of our actions. If we draw welfare benefits we are singled out. At least that contains a rational logic associated with free-loading. But when we do get jobs, you go out of your way to ensure that the minimum wage is far beneath levels of compensation deemed appropriate since the 1950s. By doing so, aren't you removing the very incentives necessary for us to pull ourselves up by the bootstraps? Aren't you removing the role models within our own class who we can respect for good and honorable reasons?

Are we, our families, our children, and our friends so despicable in your eyes (and you so superior) that meanness and condescension needs to be applied to us? How, by deliberately making conditions worse for us, even when we work and do our part, do you expect us, our children and our class to rise to higher levels? Has it not always been hard times for those of us in the pits? What advantage is gained by making it yet more difficult? Won't we instead adapt to the meaner prospects guaranteed by maldistribution and become more brutish and yet more recalcitrant? Aren't there enough brutes already down here? How can the evolution to a meaner and more desperate lower order benefit a great nation? Won't your actions reverse the great historical swing that all of us, as a nation, rich and poor, made marching out of the depths of the Great Depression?

Minimum wage and social spending on the poor.

The previous graphs (#139 and #141) of the bottom 25% segue into an understanding of the minimum wage and social spending on the poor.

Let's take a fixed case assumption that a $14,500 annual income from the minimum wage (as was a historical average) is appropriate in a nation having a $48,000 average income. This assumption translates into a specific threshold: a 0.3 fraction of the average income being the point at which minimum-wage protection is deemed necessary [0.3= $14,500/48,000]. This threshold would lay down an understanding that if your wage income is slightly less than ⅓ of the average income for the nation, then the nation offers you protection in law, prohibiting an employer from driving your wage further south. It also implies that we as a nation recognize that financial difficulties and distress beneath this point are likely. In the U.S. in 2010, the threshold for poverty was approximately the 0.264 X$ point.[86]

#142

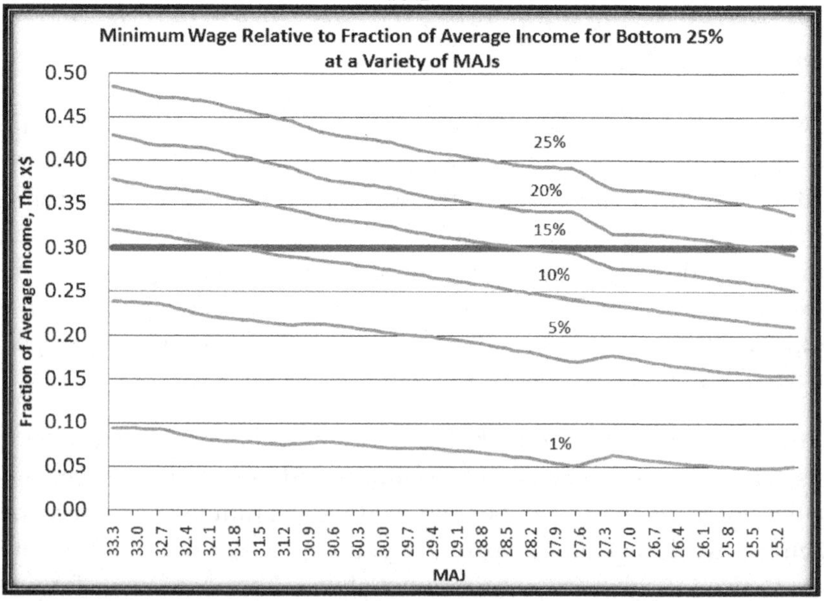

Look at the bottom 25% in above graph-142 as it would exist from MAJ33 to the maldistributed MAJ25 in the lookup table. Direct your attention to the point where the curves intersect the 0.3 horizontal line. These intersections show the point in the 0.3 scenario at which the minimum wage would start taking effect.

From this we see in constant increasing fashion that protection would be required for 10% of the population at MAJ31.8, 15% of the population at MAJ28.4, and 20% of the population at MAJ25.4. The graph is awkwardly trying to tell us a story. As maldistribution increases, social programs encompass ever-larger proportions of the nation that are unable to rise above the 0.3 threshold. This is the threshold for living a life with an income above the minimum wage – explicitly a life providing sufficient income for an honorable and fair living via normal market forces alone, without government intervention.

#143

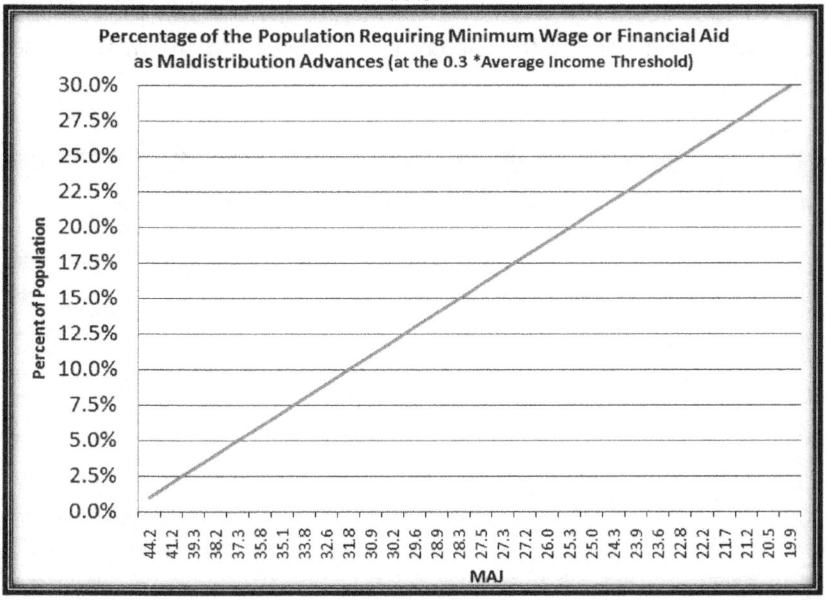

The above graph-143* more precisely shows that the number of people who come under protection of the minimum wage balloons as maldistribution advances. At MAJ33, 8.5% of the population fall beneath the 0.3 average income threshold. At MAJ25, it expands to 21% – an increase of 12.5%. In a population of 313 million, the move to MAJ25 places 39.1 million people in unnecessarily difficult financial conditions. [39.1= 313*12.5%.]

* Despite the appearances, the relationship in the graph is not purely linear, because the shown MAJ values do not increase exactly linearly.

The lookup table makes it easy to see the percent of GDP that would be required to support compensatory benefits to the lower class that fell beneath the 0.3 threshold [it is the sum of the negative values of 0.3 less the X$ for each MAJ; the X$ is a fraction of the GDP].

Maldistribution increasingly removes lower classes from the normal market economy. As such, it stands in *direct opposition to an effective market economy at the low end.* The impact is huge. While perhaps the Top3% of the nation enjoys the main market benefits from maldistribution, the market-based economy is, in large part, denied to a much larger group, the bottom 25%. By not having access to a minimum wage income sufficiently large to significantly elevate them above poverty, the twin evils of maldistribution and an inadequate minimum wage kill the vibrancy that a strong market economy would otherwise produce within the lower social orders. We see a cost of this outcome for the rest of us in the following graph-144.

#144

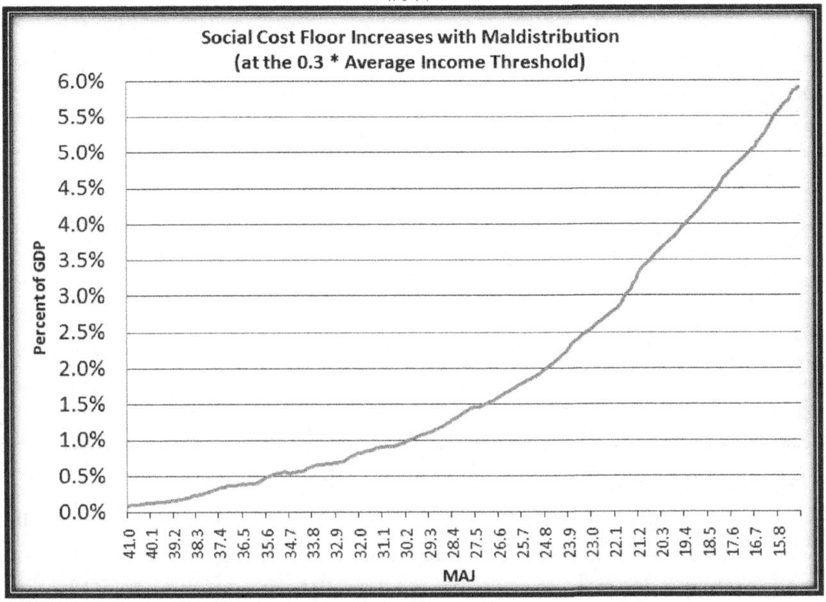

Maldistribution incrementally removes the lower classes from the income stream. Their life support then becomes increasing governmental. Income misery as a consequence of maldistribution comes at a price, not only for those that experience it, but for the citizenry who must cover the cost of the financial aid transfer, usually by higher taxes plus accumulated interest costs on any debt run up in years when the national debt is not paid down. Though the upper reaches on the income ladder are the primary beneficiary and cause of this maldistribution cost, everyone must pay for the social ills it creates. At MAJ33, the cost would have been 0.67%; at MAJ25, it shoots up to 1.93% – the difference: 1.26%, about an additional $184+ billion taxes annually on a GDP of 14.58 trillion.[87]

Each man, woman, and child in the USA appears to be paying about $587 annually to support this portion of the maldistribution program – an amount they would not be paying at MAJ33 [$586.96= $183,853,800,000/ 313,232,044]. Though these calculations are of a back-of-the-napkin character and rank no better than a first approximation, they seem to err on the low side, especially because of the zero transaction cost. The more brutal social order that accompanies maldistribution also presents additional costs in the social services infrastructure, prison costs, police force, et cetera, which in a real world analysis would need to be added in. The adverse effects come in stunning variety of areas, as Wilkinson and Pickett show in their book *The Spirit Level: Why Equality is Better for Everyone.*[88]

As you can surmise from the above graph-144, when maldistribution reaches ever more acute levels, social service expenses zoom upward. In a poor, underdeveloped, maldistributed country, the social costs can be so high that government would be unable to provide adequate assistance at the low end.

The terrible contradiction: employment or fair wage.

In the following graph-146, we see that in the U.S., minimum wage income (expressed as an X$) from its inception through the 1970s was in the range of incomes earned at the 50th and 30th percentile. Once it dropped from these levels, it transitioned to incomes approaching the 15th percentile, often dropping beneath the poverty threshold.

By 2011, incomes at the 50th, 30th, and 15th percentile were at low percentage shares not experienced since the Great Depression. It is abundantly clear that by 1987, the minimum wage played no significant role to counter maldistribution. By the year 2000, it played no role in keeping the minimum wage worker significantly above the poverty threshold.

Economists often argue that the minimum wage reduces employment. From a view of economic theory, I am sympathetic to this argument. The argument takes this form: If you set a minimum wage that exceeds the value of the work contributed by the worker, then the incentive to hire that person is reduced or extinguished. The clear underlying assumption is that the market correctly prices the worth of the worker – often called "price discovery" in efficient-market economic theory.[89] To set a minimum wage value above this point would require the employer to act contrary to economic reasoning and to pay more for the worker than he or she is worth.

#146

But the prices paid for labor, for management, and for the CEO are not reliably and exclusively determined by market forces. They are determined largely by culture. You can pick and choose between a huge variety of compensation curves that different nations have used – such as in the X$ curves in the lookup table – and find a wide variety of curves that can deliver a market economy which runs very well. The preference in this book has been for a MAJ33, but there are other curves in this same neighborhood that do quite nicely for the market economy and its citizens.

When an employer is acting in a maldistributed economy, his worldview is that the market-determined distribution curve is sacrosanct. The curve has determined his compensation correctly, and it determines the laborers compensation correctly too. Wrong on both points.

The plain case is that the market economy does not have the capacity within its workings to reverse maldistribution. And, except for the dramatic reversal from the Great Depression through the 1970s, there have been few instances where government has played a leading role to turn it around. Instead, Adam Smith's observation in the *Wealth of Nations* has dominated: "Civil government … is in reality instituted for the defense of the rich against the poor, or those who have some property against those who have none at all." Only when culture diverges from the maldistribution ethic does it vanish.

The curves that the employer sees and acts on vary greatly. Consider employers acting in two different worlds: the MAJ33 world and the MAJ25 world.

If he acts in the MAJ25 world, and labor is protected by the 0.3 minimum wage standard, the employer will start feeling put upon whenever hiring beneath the 21st percentile. By contrast, the employer in the MAJ33 world will not feel he is disadvantaged until he is dipping into workers beneath the 8.5th percentile, as indicated by the intersection with the horizontal 1.0 line in the following graph-147.

#147

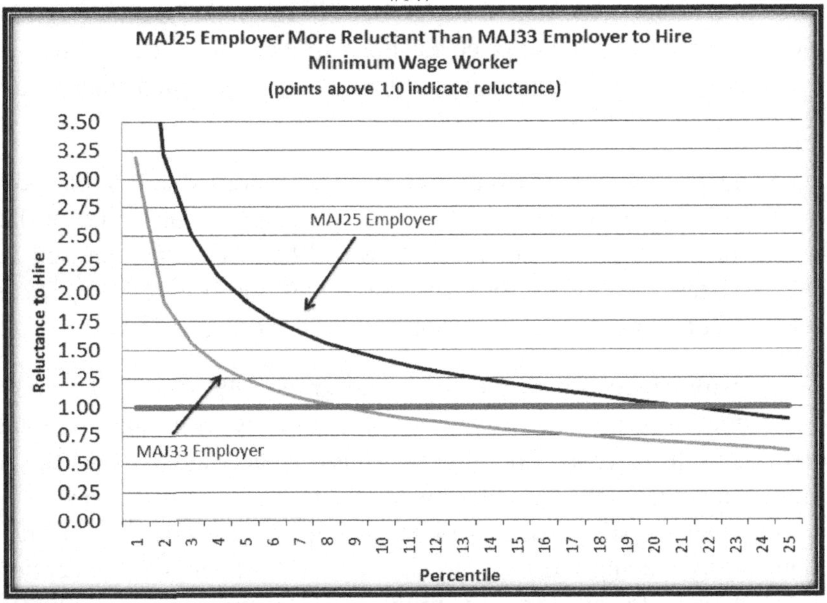

The values you see in graph-147 represent dividing 0.3 by the X$. For example, at a 1.5 value, the employer will feel he is paying 1.5 times more than he should for the worker. The emotion of the MAJ25 and MAJ33 employers are apt to be identical at the 8th and 3rd percentiles respectively. They will both feel they are paying about 1.5 times too much. Whether that 5 point percentile difference will cause the MAJ25 employer to hire, say 5%, fewer workers is a rational concern, but it is difficult to know how it will play out in practice.

The central conflict is that the minimum wage is attempting to bend the distribution curve upward at the low end, and thereby bend the upper portion of the curve down. If the employer says no to this process, then additional unemployment results. But if the minimum wage is within culturally acceptable ranges, such as it can be with inflation indexing, the impact on the employment rate may be insignificant.

Too frequently abandoning or excessively lowering minimum wage produces a Tragedy of the Markets, wherein individual firms rationally lowering wages to reduce costs and seeking to thereby increase profits destructively impact the market as a whole by spoiling revenues and thus profits that all firms together would otherwise have received.

We will touch on this later, but I suggest that the employer calculate the percentage of wage cuts saving *actually passed on in consumer price* (not your selling price). Calculate the inverse of it. Keep that number in mind. It is closely related to product price elasticity of demand, and more often than not suggests that minimum wage reductions tend to be detrimental, as you will see soon enough.

U.S. history appears to contradict the finely argued economic position that the minimum wage will increase unemployment. The inflation-adjusted minimum wage at inception was $4.04. The median since year 2000 has been $6.59. The median since 1950 has been $7.32. These respectively correspond to X$ thresholds of 0.744, 0.25, and 0.48.

The historical record in the following graph-149 shows that GDP per capita tended to grow year-to-year at faster rates when minimum wage income was high. In years when the minimum wage was less than 0.3 times average income, GDP growth slowed greatly, hovering around 1%. The minimum wage is often successful because it increases demand. It increases demand by placing money in the hands of consumers with exceptionally high propensity to consume, by properties associated with product price elasticity of demand, by increased velocity of money, by raising floor incomes throughout the wage scale, and by having lower classes that socially and economically have greater opportunities. Since GDP is another way of saying aggregate demand, the empirical evidence seems to suggest that a chief failing of the anti-minimum wage stance is that it neglects to adequately account for wage-earner consumer-generated demand created by the minimum wage.

#149

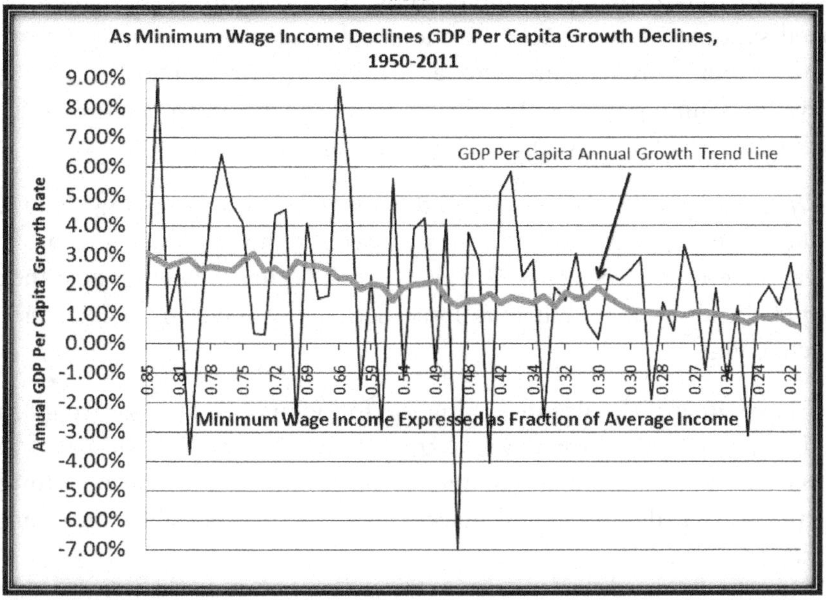

Other components – such as economic growth, long standing economic vitality, and corporate predilections – have dominant influence on employment rates. It is usually a stretch when we hear anti-minimum wage arguments trotted out at the time of accelerating maldistribution. The prime objective then usually is to bring the low class worker closer a desired point on a maldistribution curve.

Rich for unwholesome reasons.

Superficial charm
Cunning, Manipulative
Callous, Lack of empathy
Lack of remorse or guilt
Without Conscience
Abusive treatment of others
Grandiosity, Egocentricity
Emotionally shallow
Pathological lying
Anti-Social behavior
Parasitic lifestyle
Criminal versatility

"Moral Imbecile" was the ancient term used to describe a person having many such characteristics. It remains my preference. Some use the term sociopath. Wikipedia under the heading "Psychopathy" gives you a finely-honed synopsis. Do not confuse the word psychopath with the word psychotic. Both words begin with a "Psych." Their similarity ends there. Please look up the words on the Internet or other reliable source to be sure you understand the difference. They are *vastly different.*[*]

What the psychopath can do in the criminal sense is chilling. The worst of them are so far from the norm that even within prisons, they are a minority. The literature seems to indicate that no treatments reverse the psychopathic personality, but that some nations do have low occurrences of psychopaths.

I have great difficulty in writing the following because the Adam Smith business model of a firm acting to improve the lives of others strikes me as being the appropriate and usually the dominant business force. However, the freedom of the unfettered market also makes it possible for a parasitic person to thrive.

When amorality triumphs, moral disengagement and ultimately immorality prosper. Too frequently, we see moral imbecility coming out of business and economic decisions. Compensation committees seem to look upon many of the characteristics in the psychopathy checklist as being suitable, if not prerequisites, for executives. Academic attention given to the topic can be found with a Google search: "Hare corporate psychopathy." Had not a culture of corporate moral imbecility existed, it seems to me that corporations would have weeded out the CEOs that have brought too frequent disasters to their firms and to the nation.

Frank psychopaths are estimated to occur at the rate of 1% of the population in the United States.[90] Psychopaths are not delusional. They do not, as a class, suffer from lack of intelligence. They know what they are doing.

Assuming that psychopaths are evenly represented throughout the current U.S. population (including the Top1%) would imply the following: Starting U.S. 2012 population= 316,265,537; 3,162,655 psychopaths (one-in-a-hundred); 31,627 psychopaths in the Top1% (one-in-a-hundred); 15,813 psychopaths in the Upper½%. (half of the Top1%)

---

[*] I trust you get the drift. I am not an expert in the area. You can get information about it elsewhere that is far more reliable than what would come from me. Also by using those sources, we don't stray from the topic at hand.

If you wanted to crudely estimate the income of the highest income USA psychopath, consider that there are probably 3,162,655 psychopaths in the United States. Thus the highest income psychopath may well be at the one-in-3,162,655 income scarcity level. In the spreadsheets we see one-in-2-million and one-in-four-million columns. Taking the average of the two should yield a first approximation in the neighborhood of the one-in-3-million-scarcity level. By such logic, the highest income USA psychopath would tend to have an annual income of about $52,000,000 in 2011 (1,092.3X$); the wealthiest would have a net worth of about $2,463,776,000.

For many excellent reasons, pro and con, these figures can be disputed. It is open to conjecture whether the psychopathic personality could conserve such wealth for an extended period. On the other hand, the logic may under-represent the number of psychopaths in the Top1%. Because they completely lack altruistic motives, psychopaths tend to employ their energies elsewhere. Logically, the Top1% would seem to be the honey pot to disproportionately draw them. They would employ all their skills to get there and profit from it.

I know the following graph-152 is a stretch. The starting data is thin. But look, it was a kick putting it together. And perhaps it will entertain you.

But in the process of having a little fun, something more serious occurred. Assume that the dominant group within the Top1% and society as a whole normally has honorable and decent intentions and is powerful enough to exercise them.[91] Under such circumstances, it becomes likely that the equitably distributed market economy has a surprisingly powerful capacity to weed out malefactors of any kind (psychopaths or not) that otherwise would proliferate with a profligate maldistribution. That cheaters don't prosper is a boon to capitalism and the free market.

We have seen earlier at 20X$ and 15X$ earnings, via the Selectivity Ratio, that about nine out of ten were weeded out by returning to an equitable distribution. In the case of the high-income psychopath, we are presented with a person with an income equal to a 1,092X$. This is huge. Far different than the previous case of incomes of a million dollars or less.

#152

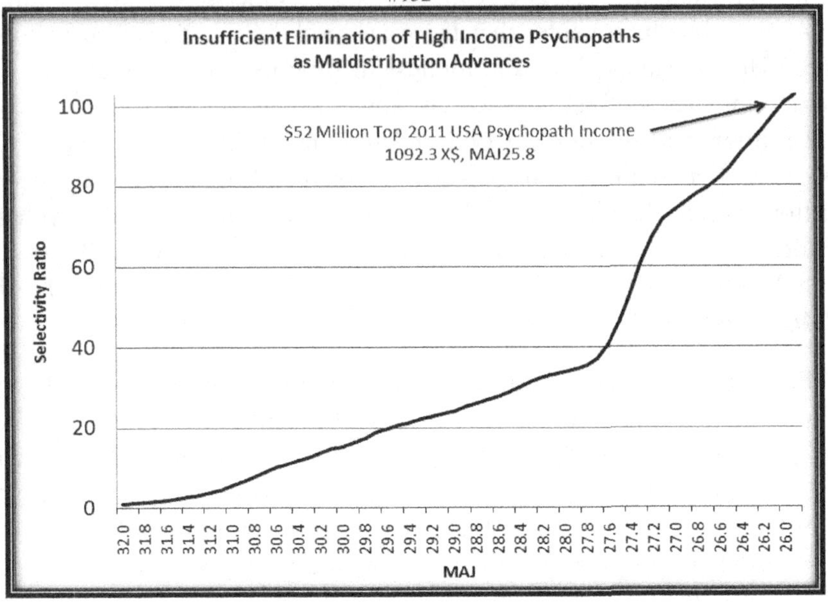

When we look at the graph-152, we see the selectivity curve for a 1092X$ income. The floodgates at MAJ25.8 (the current U.S. maldistribution) were wide open. They were letting in more than 100 times as many people to earn this extraordinarily high income than would have earned it with an equitable distribution. They were letting in so many that it became highly likely that one of them would be a psychopath.

By letting 100 times more people into this group, the policing of it by law enforcement would have become increasingly difficult and ineffective.[92] This is a direct consequence of compensation decisions in a maldistributed society. An equitable distribution would have weeded out 99 of the 100 that would have existed at the one-in-3-million level with a MAJ25.8 maldistribution.

This suggests to me that, given equitable distributions, criminality and anti-social behavior at high levels can experience a powerful self-policing performed by normal market forces, long before law enforcement needs to come into the picture. Graph-152 strongly suggests that criminality in high places is apt to be promoted by maldistribution and abated by equitable distributions. With maldistribution, the Selectivity Ratio is too high and its rise too sharp, other than to suggest serious consequences.

When I was a youngster reading economics in high school, one of the articles was entitled "The Methodology of Positive Economics" – too many syllables and too abstract. But at the core, the 1950s article sought to raise a body of systemized knowledge (alluding to science) over criteria of what ought to be (morals). This was the era of the space race, the cure for polio, and vast scientific advances that improved everyone's lives. To place economics in the category of great seriousness where equilibrium graphs and functions might reign was to align economics with science as opposed to something so quaint and old-fashioned as morals and norms.

As can be found on the Internet, the same eminent economist cloaks corporate life in the amoral:

> ...[S]hould it [the corporation] spend the stockholders' money
> for purposes which it regards as socially responsible
> but which it cannot connect to its bottom line?
> The answer I would say is no. …
>
> The corporation is amoral
> but the people who run the
> corporation are not amoral. …
>
> Can a building have moral opinions?
> Can a building have social responsibility?
> If a building can't have social responsibility, what does it
> mean to say that a corporation can't? A corporation is simply
> an artificial legal structure. It doesn't have any;
> it's neither moral nor immoral. It's simply what it is.
> But the people who are engaged in it, whether the stockholders, whether the
> executives in it, whether the employees
> they all have moral responsibilities.[93]

The notion of the corporation being a legal structure analogous to a building is wrong. Corporations have responsibilities, as witnessed by the capacity to sue them. You can't sue a building. But picking an argument there is misleading. There are bigger fish.

The psychological wellbeing of those who work in the corporate culture is injured by the carving of morality, as indicated above. And more broadly, far greater damage is done by disassociating fiduciary responsibility and corporate culture from moral frameworks required for the economy, the society, and the nation to survive and prosper.

Ethical conduct:

Right speech
Right action
Right livelihood

Ghandi:

A person cannot do right in one department
whilst attempting to do wrong in another department.
Life is one indivisible whole.

Adam Smith saw economics as a branch of moral philosophy. Quaint, but right.[94]

CH. 7

SHARED DESTINY?

"When I was a child ..." And we all roll our eyes, ready for a stretcher.

The following graph-156 may help us to gauge to what extent the eyes need to be rolled. It shows GDP, per capita GDP, and S&P500 earnings growth as if we were looking back to a time 26 years earlier.

The memory of a person looking backwards differs greatly from a present-looking perspective. The person is heavily (and correctly) influenced by the starting point just as much as the ending point. For example, looking back from 1960 would have put us squarely within the Great Depression Era, 1934. Only after 1976 were the influences of the Great Depression and WWII greatly reduced. When we make comparisons between the following three curves, we usually need not have great concern about dates because each curve is subjected to the same time period from beginning to end.

The real per capita GDP would generally reflect the story teller's perspective of people's history – how much people, on average, benefited from economic growth. On the other hand, as long as the population is growing, real GDP (which is not adjusted for population growth) always grows faster. The ambiguous item is the growth of reported inflation-adjusted corporate (S&P500) earnings.

The nation and its corporations usually had a shared destiny. We rose and fell together. Now the shared destiny is upended. Reported S&P500 earnings growth over very long periods has been rising, often sharply, at the same time that both GDP and per capita GDP have been falling. The 1990s were the turning point. We turn to them now.

#156

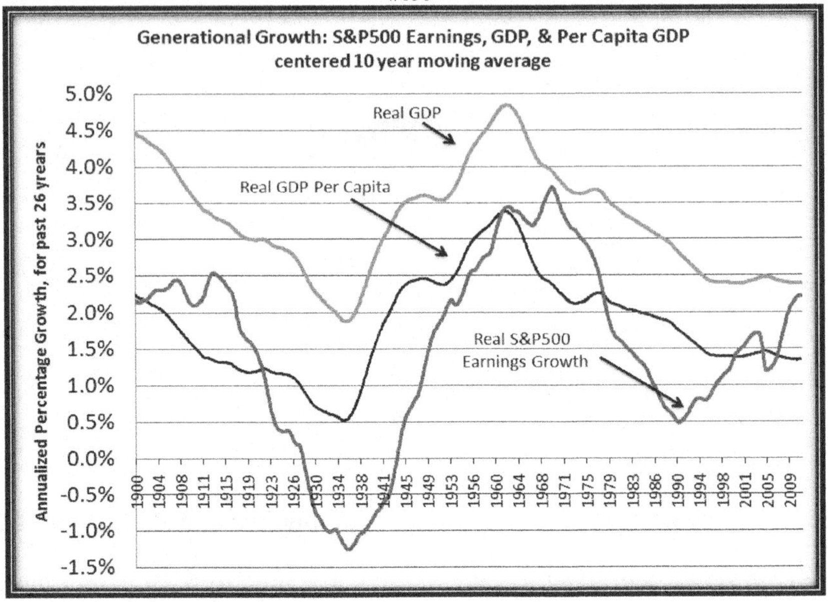

July 1991. The world changed without a whimper or a bang.

The total solar eclipse of July 11, 1991 missed the continental USA. About mid month, NYC was hotter than average, exceeding 100° F (38° C) at times. Real stock market values had grown 7.7% in a year, the best performance since May 1988. In that interval the PE ratio increased from 12.4 to 20.2. Yes, hold on. Grab your chair. I can sense already that you are stunned. Time to slow down so you can compose yourself. This is a lot to take at a single sitting. The author must be kind. He does not want to lose a reader from heart attack. Ok, the fun is up. The story was told. The reader is bored and perplexed. Time for remedy, explanation, and a graph.

The tones of great solemnity that usually accompany stock market discussions surpass absurdity, complexity, and silliness. Let's look at why it is so easy to understand the stock market, including crucially important aspects. The S&P 500 is a representative group of 500 large companies. The following formula can tell a story:

The "composite price of S&P 500 stocks" = "the as reported earnings of the companies" * "the PE ratio."

The PE ratio is the Price Earnings ratio. Take a look. Perhaps you see that the following PE ratio is redundant, no more than a restatement of the foregoing.

"The PE ratio"= "composite price of S&P 500 stocks" /"the as reported earnings of the companies."

In this instance, redundancy is crucially important. It isolates the two components that show how the megabuck world of stocks operate.

The foundation is the "earnings of the companies" (profits).[95] The ultimate price of stocks depends on earnings, via the above formulas.

The second component, the PE ratio, is a more subjective number which indicates how much the buyer is willing to pay for one unit of earnings under current conditions. (There are numerous ways this basic ratio can be distorted to create a bias toward a particular interpretation. Be careful of PE ratios that you have not calculated yourself from reliable data. Use "as reported earnings" instead of less inclusive "operating earnings.")

PE Ratio	Earnings Yield	Post 1991 Dividend Yield
50.0	2.00%	0.77%
47.5	2.11%	0.81%
45.0	2.22%	0.85%
42.5	2.35%	0.90%
40.0	2.50%	0.96%
37.5	2.67%	1.02%
35.0	2.86%	1.09%
32.5	3.08%	1.18%
30.0	3.33%	1.28%
27.5	3.64%	1.39%
25.0	4.00%	1.53%
22.5	4.44%	1.70%
20.0	5.00%	1.92%
17.5	5.71%	2.19%
15.0	6.67%	2.55%
12.5	8.00%	3.06%
10.0	10.00%	3.83%
7.5	13.33%	5.11%

It can also be expressed, in the inverse, as the earnings yield shown in Table-157, in which case it indicates the percent earnings generated by the company for a given share price.

None of this book provides investment advice!
Do not construe it as such!
We are talking about broader and more important issues here!!

Dividend yield is a function of the fraction of the earnings yield that the S&P500 corporations choose to pay, as in the table where it is based on a 38.31% payout. The PE ratio, more broadly discussed in Wikipedia as "P/E ratio," is the common term used in conversation.

To speak of stock market price without considering earnings and the PE ratio is as fruitless as to speak of timing of the tides without considering the moon. Keep an eye on PE ratios so you and the nation can prosper.

If you started where the story commenced with a PE ratio of 12.4 and within a short while it shot up to 20.2, this would mean that had earnings stayed the same, the price of your stock would have gone up 63% [63%=

20.2/12.4 -1].[96] However, earnings change, so there is seldom a lockstep relationship between price and PE ratio.

The July 1991 PE ratio increase to 20.2 portended more than anyone then (and few since) expected. In the USA, PE ratios above 20 seldom occurred as far back as 1871. When they did occur, they were usually a flash in the pan – with good reason. Once you buy into stocks at a high PE ratio, normally your complete gamble is that earnings will rise greatly because the only other mechanism to increase stock price, a significantly higher PE ratio, is unlikely, often to the vanishing point (PE ratios cannot increase to ever-higher points without stopping). At a high PE ratio, the stockholder is in a very precarious position. If other buyers lose enthusiasm (show a preference for a lower PE ratio), or if earnings grow slowly or fall, the price of stocks can languish, or fall – even dramatically. The high PE ratio is a tightrope act, daring, but difficult to sustain. The longer you are on it, the greater the chance of an error – a fall.

#158

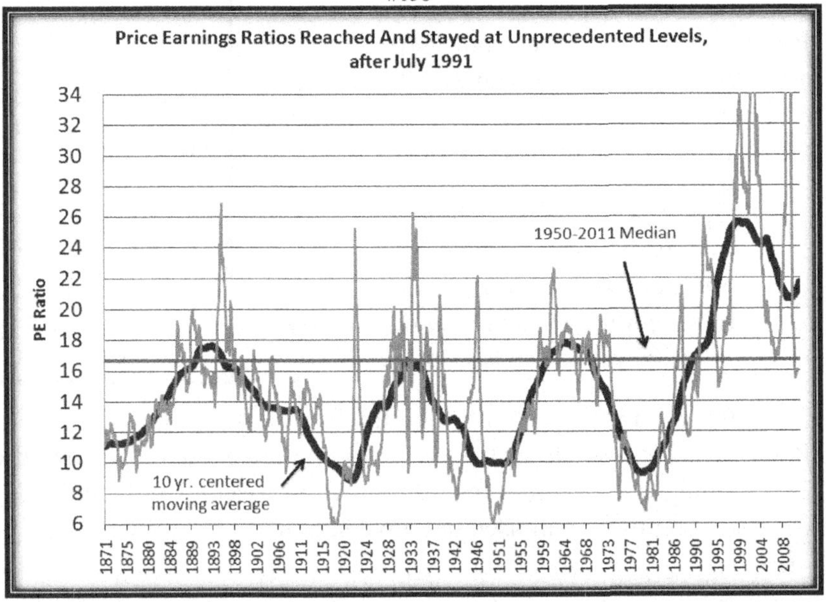

July 1991 distinguished itself because then the PE trend line went to stay in territory where no men had tread before. The tightrope act was sustained. The S&P500 PE ratios at the time of the Great Depression were not as wild as the new era, now 20 years old. By comparison, 1929 looks tame in graph-158. Where in the past the PE ratios returned to prudent regions, the market now committed itself (unwisely in my view) to high PE values.

There is an admirable logic in old-time corporate thinking referred to as "retain and reinvest." The assumption is that corporations retain a fraction of earnings so that they can reinvest them in the corporation to help it grow and innovate. Well-paid, stable blue-collar jobs thrived in this setting. But by 1992, about two million such jobs were lost, never to return, when this philosophy was largely abandoned in favor of the "shareholder value" mode of corporate thinking. The job cutting continued.[97]

#159

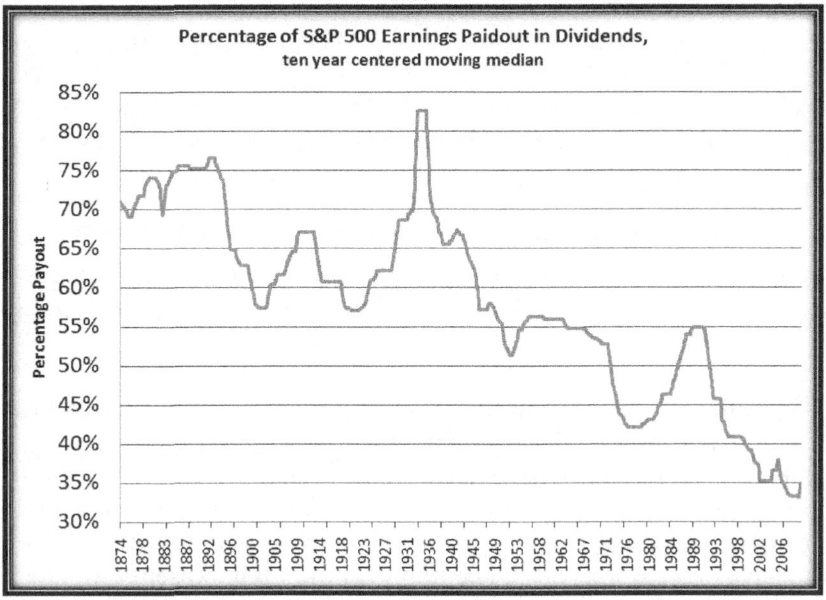

There is also an older tradition, as evidenced in the above graph-159, of the corporation paying out a large fraction of earnings so that the stockholder has firm evidence that the corporation is indeed making a bona fide profit and can lay its hands on sufficient cash to make dividend payments. These rewards to the stockholder were a nice way of guaranteeing a standard integrity and a sense of mutual benefit in corporate affairs and the progress of the nation.

Both the "retain and reinvest" and "firm evidence dividend" concepts varied and adapted over time. The ruling logic of shareholder value later, coupled with a high PE ratio regime, convolutedly transformed the relationship. At the entry into high PE ratio regime in July 1991, the decade median payout ratio was 54.5%, after which it worked its way down to a low of 33%, as shown in the graph-159. This drop in the payout, coupled with the drop in PE Ratios (see prior Table-157), pushed dividend yields down. The old-school stockholder reliance on dividends was lost. Their participation in the earnings of the corporation by way of dividends became small. Simultaneously, the standard for earnings of "being able to lay your hands on cash to make dividend payments" was greatly lowered. Removing the "firm evidence dividend" lowered the integrity bar, making it easier to cook the books and overstate earnings – a subject to which we will soon return.

By comparison to the median post-WWII PE ratio of 16.7, shown in graph-158, ratios above 20.2 gifted to those who held stock during the interval of change about 1/5 of the GDP. This is huge [21.1%= 20.182/ 16.672-1; U.S. publicly traded stock market value and GDP coincidentally can be of roughly similar size]. This boon conveyed all the advantages that wealth does, with ability to invest and use it to one's advantage.

But once these stocks were propped up (artificially in my view) by high PE ratios, a fall of value in an amount equal to one fifth of GDP (and market capitalization) would have been the logical outcome. Too much was at stake to let such an event occur. No machination was too great to prevent it.

Beneath the surface brewed a cauldron, which as of this writing has had far, far greater impact. To stay on the high wire requires a stupendous array of supports. Nothing is spared to sustain the circus.

A key player in the act is the CEO. The corporation now has a huge (excessive) vested interest in keeping PE ratio high. Absent this, stock value plummets. The compensation committee knows this, and buys a CEO with sufficient salesmanship to prop up share prices. By tying his compensation to stock price, they further secure his commitment. They are willing to pay lavishly for the actor who delivers the stock price – so lavishly that with few exceptions, the corporation becomes a chief maldistribution promoter.

The old world (the pre-July 1991 world) where PE ratios normally fluctuated between 10 and 18 had been deemed unacceptable. That is unfortunate. The shift was to short-term profits. Although "Profit" now has become one of the nastiest 6 letter words, there was no necessity for it to be so. When earnings, in proper measure, come with a long-term commitment to delivering a good product and treating the workers who produce it civilly, it is a boon to all.

Are you mystified by continuous discussions of the stock market? So am I. There is a trivially simple formula that can show, to the penny, how much the stock market will appreciate. It exclusively uses the two components stressed here: PE ratio and earnings. Try it out on the Shiller database of stock prices. Playing with it exactly explains all S&P500 composite price moves from the 1870s to the present. For me, that is good enough. The great advantage of "***The Formula***" is that it frees up time that might otherwise be spent in the morose or comic (depending on your perspective) world of economic and business pontification for more useful activities. Ping pong, for example.

"*The Formula:*"

S&P 500 Annual Rate of Appreciation =
((PE2/PE1)^(1/years) * (1+annual earnings growth rate))-1

and if you like you can play with it in this corresponding form:

S&P 500 Annual Rate of Appreciation =
((PE2/PE1)^(1/years) * (Earn2/ Earn1)^(1/years))-1

In plain words, the formula boils down to multiplying the PE ratio growth factor times the earnings growth factor and subtracting one, to state the rate of S&P500 composite appreciation in percentage form. End of story. Less precisely, it is generally assumed that PE ratios vary up and down within a customary range, and the base (earnings) grows in a growing economy. Use it a few times with the Shiller data. Once you are comfortable with it you will be stunned at its to-the-penny accuracy and forever question why so much stock market chatter goes far afield from plain logic.

PS. The starting PE ratio is PE1. The PE ratio at the end of the period is PE2. Both PE ratios are determined by dividing S&P500 price by the corresponding S&P500 earnings. The years are determined by subtracting the exact difference between years down to the fraction of a year for the corresponding period. Earn1 and Earn2 similarly correspond to matching earnings.

The following graph-162 takes a ten-year view. It uses "***The Formula***" to illustrate why it is easy to lose money when PE ratios reach 20 or higher.

Here we optimistically assume that earnings growth will be 73.2% of GDP growth (a median, but high, value since 1960). Basing earnings on a history of GDP performance is intended to overcome endemic inaccuracies in reported earnings. Graph-162 shows a range of earnings growth rates – from the 5th, 25th, 50th, 75th percentile up to the Top estimated earnings rate. Under all of these conditions, it indicates the consequences of starting with a PE ratio of 20, and ending ten years later with one of the PE ratios on the horizontal axis. On the vertical axis the resulting annual inflation-adjusted rate of S&P500 appreciation is shown.

#162

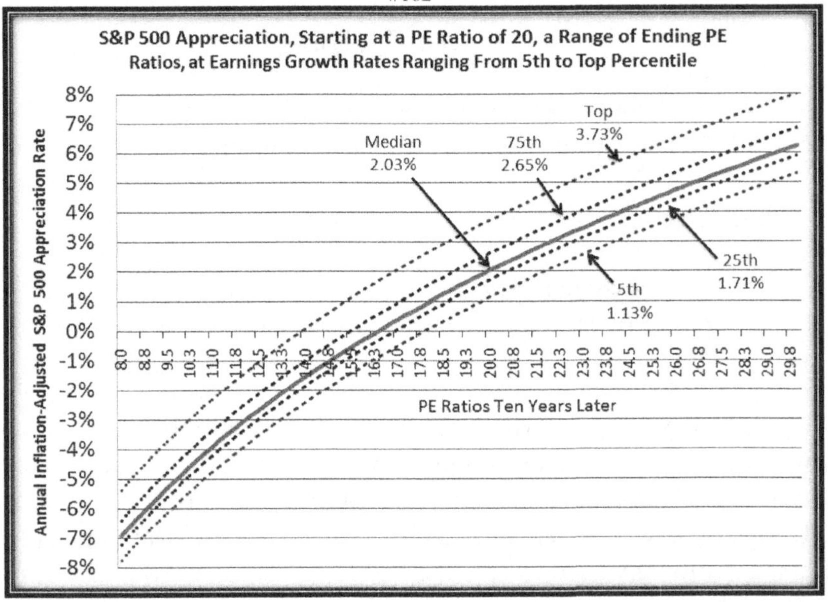

Your first thought may be that as long as earnings are growing for ten years, a S&P500 investment at the end of the period should also appreciate in real value. This assumption would be reliably accurate only if the starting PE ratio did not fall. The S&P500 investment would lose value in 75% of cases, if the PE ratio at the end of ten years fell beneath 15.25; in 50% of cases, if it fell beneath 16.25; in 25% of cases, if it fell beneath 16.75; and in 5% of cases, if it fell beneath 17.75. Even at the Top earnings rate, the investment would be apt to lose if the PE ratio fell beneath 13.75. When investors start at a PE ratio of 20, the capacity of the S&P500 to fall in so many instances should raise red flags.

The investment would also have very small appreciation or drop in value in 50% of cases, if PE ratio moved within ten years to the *long-term well-respected and prudent range of 15.25 to 16.75.* This is perhaps a chief indictment of how wrong and inappropriate the high PE ratio mentality and practice is. It enforces a nationwide regime of investment imprudence.

These statements contrast with rosy proclamations coming from nearly all quarters during times of boom. Highly favorable reports in such periods are usually short-term and not inflation-adjusted. Routinely, they are based on exaggerated earnings reports that widely differ from long-term earnings performance and from GDP growth rates. And, they wrongly assume that the PE ratio will not significantly fall. In short, they fail to account for each of the components that are at the heart of the analysis. "***The Formula***" nicely cuts away emotions that frequently lead a nation astray.

At a PE ratio of 20, you enter a gambling casino. The house always wins. You and the nation may not. At PE ratios closer to 16, you have left the casino and your prospects improve considerably. So do those of the nation.

The philosophy and culture of managing companies to produce short-term profits to satisfy shareholder value objectives carries with it the less salubrious aspects of a desperation to hit short-term earning targets. The unsavory aspects are now so virulent that they can be spied in national economic statistics.

Earnings subject to arbitrary determination.

When you look at the following graph-164, keep in mind that in 1929, a peak of 3.5% existed. Peaks back then were few.

It is impossible for true S&P500 earnings growth to consistently exceed GDP growth on a sustained basis in a normally operating economy, except when given cataclysmic events such as the Great Depression and WWII.

The reader speaks. Well, is graph-164 an instance of "open mouth, in-sert foot?" To these eyes it looks like earnings growth for sustained 10-year periods surpassed GDP growth. Ok, maybe in the pre-1990s era, earn-ings did not have the mojo, but look at the 1990s onward. The brew was different. What do you say to that – you author of many words?

#164

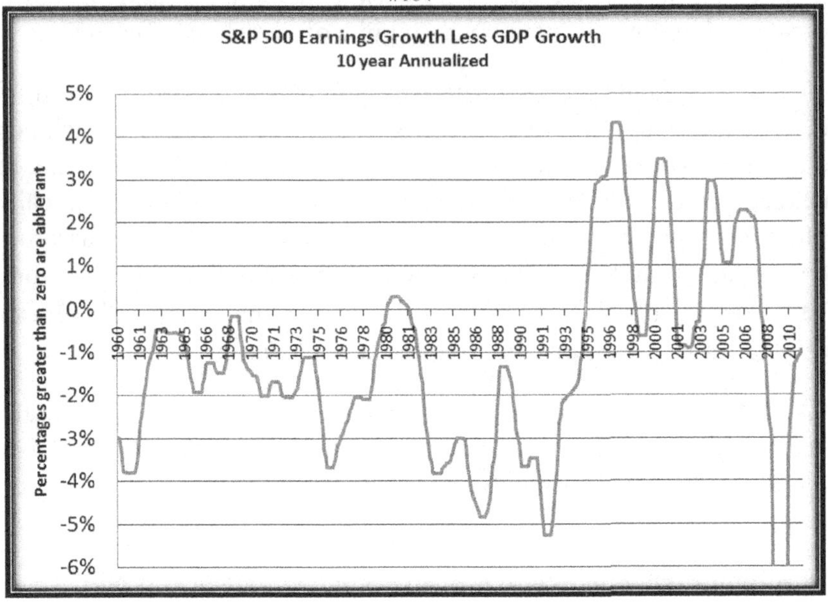

Author of many words speaks. It pains me to say it because, in my view, the corporation is a great, necessary, and indispensable tool to pool money and abilities to get the job done. But the corporation also must carry with it honor and fair play for workers, stockholders, and customers. Graph-164 bears testimony to a failure in that sphere. You choose the words: fraud, creative accounting, hitting the numbers, deception, deceit, swindle, cooking the books, corporate maneuverings, stealing from the firm by raiding pension funds, ____ (You who have the Savings and Loan crisis, the 2008-2009 bust, Enron, WorldCom, or corporate downsizing dancing in your eyes, of course, may fill in the blank. My scope is insufficient.). It seems that components of that ilk would have been necessary to manufacture (cook up) profits so great that they would have exceeded the growth of the general economy. The sporadic nature of the mojo peaking further suggest inappropriate components in contrast to fundamental structural changes such as global trade.

GDP is made up of a number of components, including wages, the cost of the input, government spending, and profits. If profits grow faster than GDP, something else loses out.[98] If general economy growth were to truly lag corporate earnings, it would be a sad and dangerous commentary on the nation and on the corporation because the corporation derives its earnings from the GDP. When it exceeds GDP growth, it is predatory or cooking the books.

If the stock market had the capacity to grow faster than GDP on a sustained basis, then many people would profitably buy stock and abandon their own businesses because the stock market would provide a better rate of return than the work their modest GDP life provided. Happily, we can be confident that GDP grows faster than corporate earnings and that fraud and other temporary untoward components are apt to be the reason for disproportionately high earnings reports.

The 2003 surge in graph-164 is supported by David Bianco's observation in a New York Times article at the time, *Earnings Are Worse Without The Icing*: "The quality of earnings for the S&P 500, from an accounting standpoint, is the worst it has been in more than a decade." He cites aggressive accounting practices in three areas: special charges or one-time events, not subtracting the costs of stock options, and inflating pension earnings or masking pension costs. He goes on to estimate that earnings adjusted for so-called "funny stuff" were *41% less than the profits reported to investors*.[99]

Similarly Bernstein and Arnott, in 2000, estimated that when three sources of earnings overstatement ("aggressive pension accounting, failure to expense stock options, and outright fraud") are removed, peak S&P500 earnings were effectively ⅓ less than the stated amount.[100]

Consider that a S&P500 PE ratio of 30 is an extraordinarily high number. That at best would normally provide a slim rate of return for the stock purchaser. Time to pull out the napkin and write at the top "The Crashes That Should Have Occurred & The Unwholesome Means That Prevented Them." Imagine if earnings had been reported at a true value that was ⅓ less than published earnings. Dream that the S&P500 was priced at 1000 with a PE ratio of 20. This would mean that reported earnings were 50. If those earnings of 50 were wrongly stated, and true earnings were ⅓ less at 33.33, then all investors would instantly know that the market was operating at a PE ratio of 30 and be primed for a fall [50= 1000/20; 33.33= 50*(1-⅓); 30=1000/33.33]. Stockholders would bail out en masse. Deception, coated with doses of fraud, was the modest requirement to sustain market value.

Cutting to the chase: The hypothetical case prevented a severe drop, as have the other subsequent real instances of deception coated with fraud, where earnings growth exceeded GDP growth for sustained periods as shown in the previous graph-164. Albeit many years later, riding the waves of fraud and deception culminates in a downward surf to reality – a low stock price commensurate with true unadulterated earnings (for example, with a price closer to a value that might have been suggested by the formerly unreported PE ratio of 30).

The unhappy picture is that what should have been an economically sound mechanism for participating in the growth of the economy, has been transformed into a game no better than a variation on "musical chairs" where at some unsuspecting point, players are left with no place to sit when phony earnings are jerked out from under them.

The great advantage for a citizen is that neither PE ratio nor "earnings growth less GDP growth" require complex analysis. The data is publicly available. Via such data, it is easy to keep tabs on corporations and raise flags when danger points exist. There is no need to repeatedly play 1929. Have you ever seen a Border Collie dog herd sheep? When I was a child, "Pat" was my pet Border Collie. We also had sheep. Pat provided great lessons in corporate herding. Her example is an inspiration. She kept sheep where she wanted them. YouTube has some examples nearly as good as she was. The megabuck corporate herd, too, can be kept in line. Honor your inner dog. Let her run. These guys have run far afield. They need to be brought home.

Think back on the PE ratio formulas. The two components that move stock price are PE ratio and reported earnings. If they do not move, the stock price does not move. The PE ratio is susceptible to growing under the pressure of a great sales pitch. Reported earnings can hit the target when the accounting department is given sufficient incentive to perform machinations or shift expenses and revenues to produce a desired profit target. If the corporation, by whatever means it uses, can sufficiently advance the two components that determine stock price (PE ratio and reported earnings), then share price follows suit. This may not be good for the wellbeing of the company, the workers, the customer, the long-term stockholder, or the nation, but it is apt to bring joy to executive suites, directors, and short-term stock traders. The 1990s onward mojo, which made it possible for reported earnings to so spectacularly exceed GDP growth, appears to have been voodoo of the vile sort, just as it was in 1929.

Benjamin Graham is an ancient god of investment analysis. Long before the recent mojo era, he wrote two pieces of advice to the investor: "The first is: Don't take a single year's earnings seriously. The second is:

If you do pay attention to short-term earnings, look out for booby traps …"[101]

In his 1934 bible, *Security Analysis*, he observed: "Earnings Not Only Fluctuate but Are Subject to Arbitrary Determination … It will be illuminating if we summarize, at this point, the various devices legitimate and otherwise, by which per-share earnings may *at the choice of those in control* be made to appear larger or smaller [emphasis in the original]." And, speaking directly to the PE ratio, he decreed: "We would suggest that *about sixteen times average earnings* is as high a price as can be paid in an *investment* purchase of a common stock… *[P]eople who habitually purchase common stocks at more than about sixteen times their average earnings are likely to lose considerable money in the long run.*" [emphasis in the original][102] As Graham's writings indicate, there has always been an incentive to overstate profits. For the modern era to stimulate it in the name of increasing shareholder value is wrong and counterproductive.

Our experience with pre-1990s corporate history would have lead us to expect earnings' deviations to be modest, with a prompt return to rates consistent with GDP trend lines. In the new era, those sensibilities are completely absent. There is no shared destiny.

Since 1995 earnings growth often exceeded GDP growth for decades. The relationship now strongly suggests the "arbitrary determination" of earnings Graham warned of. That it has been accompanied by PE ratios far above Graham's maximum redoubles the injury.

Business confidence depends on rational S&P500 appreciation. Rationality exists only if it is GDP-based. Together, outsized PE ratios and outsized earnings reports, as have been prevalent since 1991, are unprecedented in U.S. stock market history. Business and consumer confidence depend on a return to the old S&P500 GDP-based rationality, prior to the shareholder value mindset, the High PE Ratio regime, and phony earnings reports. Without the guiding hand of GDP for earnings, we live quite literally as subjects to a myth factory.

The following graph-168 indexes both real absolute GDP and S&P500 earnings (not growth rates) to their approximate 1991 values, so that the starting point is 1.0. Never does GDP significantly exceed 1.5. Yet earnings grow to approximately 3.75 prior to the 2008-2009 financial calamity and recession resulting from it, caused by these folk and their kin – obviously at great expense and hardship for us citizens. The deep concern is that no lesson has been learned. A subsequent peak in 2012 that was the highest ever reported and the outgoing 3.5 peak in graph-168 indicates a return to prior flimflam.

#168

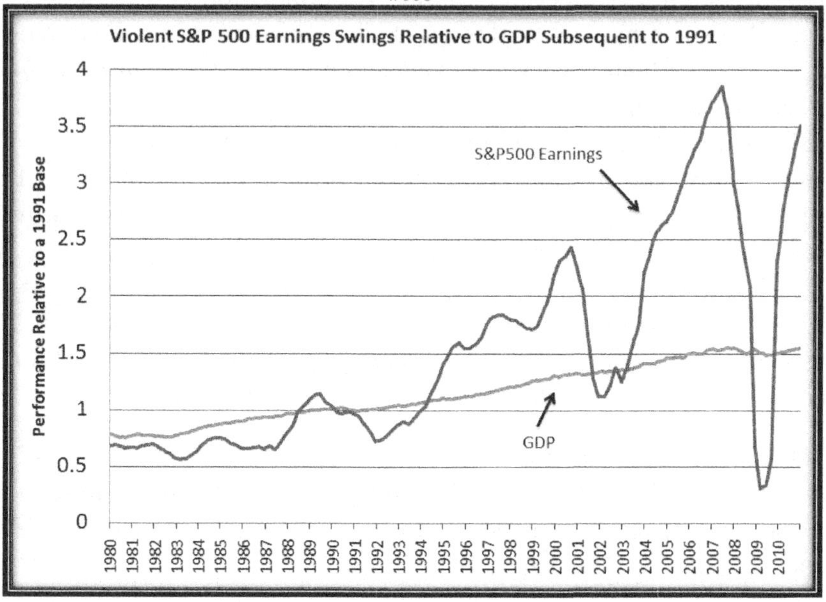

Look at this graph. Pause. Think. A market economy, when working, relies on rationality. Rationality is derived in the main from GDP. In sharp contrast, starting in about 1995, outsized earnings reports occurred which grew ever-larger, completely disassociated with GDP. This corruption of the market economy is profound. "*The Formula,*" the PE ratio, and earnings are the central determiners of stock market value. For rationality to exist in stock market values, earnings must be stated accurately and have a rational relationship with GDP. Otherwise profound misallocations of wealth result. Reports in the news that the "market has rebounded" more often than not are unwelcome reports that mean stock market gains are again outsized and not are carrying a rational relationship with GDP.

Wealth transformations have vast reaches. When earnings become mythical, the presumed rationality is no longer rational at all, but is instead an instrument of myth. The plain GDP progression that should drive the markets is subordinated – no, made irrelevant – by outsized earnings reports. When this occurs, market allocations throughout the economy are transformed. The increased apparent wealth causes us to make decisions we otherwise would not have made. We would have known those same decisions to be imprudent had market values moved in response to GDP.

The nursery rhyme "The Three Little Pigs" comes to mind. Remember the line, "I'll huff, and I'll puff, and I'll blow your house in." The first house was of straw, the second of sticks, the third of bricks.

The GDP house is of brick. The Myth House is of straw or sticks. Take your pick.

The PE ratio hits us all.

The real world was not polite enough to give us a crystal clear picture, but it did give us enough in the following graph-169 to get started.

#169

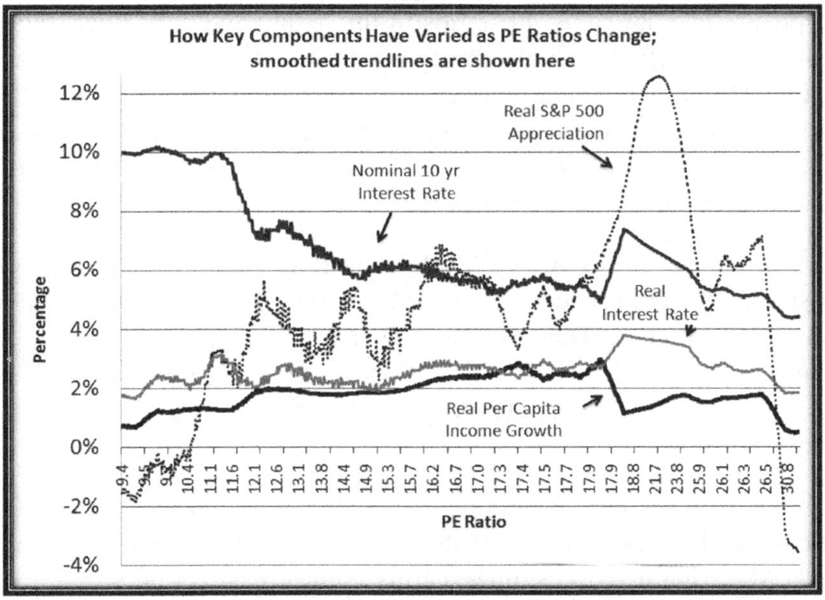

The data varies widely but when heavily smoothed, it seems to give an approximate estimate of conditions that have existed since the 1960s to the present. Graph-169 deliberately does not use earlier data in order to stay clear of possible influences from Great Depression and WWII rebounds.

Nominal interest rates (the rates we see in the news before they are inflation-adjusted) and real S&P appreciation (increase in value after inflation adjustments) are both important components. They determine how much everyone (not just the rich) makes from their savings and investments. They also influence financial institutions, including insurance companies, to whom we pay premiums. Real interest rates, those adjusted for inflation, tend to be more constant. It has been a tribute to the Federal Reserve that in the 1960s and subsequently, the wide swings in real interest that used to occur during the wild boom and bust eras in earlier U.S. history no longer exist.

The previous graph-169 suggests to me that when PE ratios range from about 12.1 to 17.9, the values of most of the components seem to stay within an appropriate range.

If this were condensed to a rule, it would read: "A PE ratio of 15 plus or minus 2.9 is acceptable." Albeit an unremarkable rule that many people have generally spoken, their thoughts are correct. Outside this range, the picture is confusing. Beneath 12.1, the values seem to indicate a slowing, particularly in the real GDP per capita, which affects us all. Above 17.9, the picture is ambiguous. PE ratios in this range allow for huge appreciations in real S&P500 but also bring huge falls. Above 17.9, the lower per capita GDP growth would seem to hurt us all. Both nominal and real interest rates also seem to go excessively low, making conditions difficult for people who rely on good sources of fixed income and for financial institutions that depend on good interest rates.

A key advantage of a 15 ±2.9 PE ratio rule is that it vastly reduces the possibility of booms and busts in the S&P500. You can see this by pulling out your calculator. The maximum swings about the median caused by changes in PE ratios would be confined to 19% [19.3%= 2.9/15]. Nations can withstand such fluctuations without serious injury, as the previous graph-169 shows.

No need to be dull. Marching in the streets whenever the S&P500 PE ratio exceeds 17.9 would probably serve nations well. A day off from work. Make it a party, costumes, carnival, theatre, street fairs, and the like. Might as well have some fun. A national holiday. Better yet, a national holiday once a week until the PE ratio falls beneath 17.9. *The partying would accomplish what no government or psychiatrist has done: prevent stock market madness.* Picture it. The PEparty anticipation. The release of absolute joy when the day arrives. May Day, Christmas, Thanksgiving, Valentine's Day, all national holidays worldwide rolled into one. The possibility of it occurring several times a year. Put that on your Happiness Index. A jet set traveling nation to nation, staying in continuous party mode. CEOs of the greatest companies leading the parades. Dream. Dream. Dream. Joy. Joy. Joy.

Badness index.

The Badness Index used here does not encompass all corporate sins. It confines itself to the two components we have been dealing with: high PE ratios and high reported earnings growth relative to GDP growth. It is an important concept because *either earnings growth or PE ratio growth, if exaggerated, can wrongly increase stock price. Sins in either area can be equally potent. By identifying the most egregious departures, we more easily see their combined effect.*

By using a technique that employs multiple data sorts, we can determine instances where the greatest improprieties occur.[103] Based on this method, ranked according to badness, the following graph-171 shows the most egregious excesses in either PE or earnings on the right, and the mildest expressions on the left.

#171

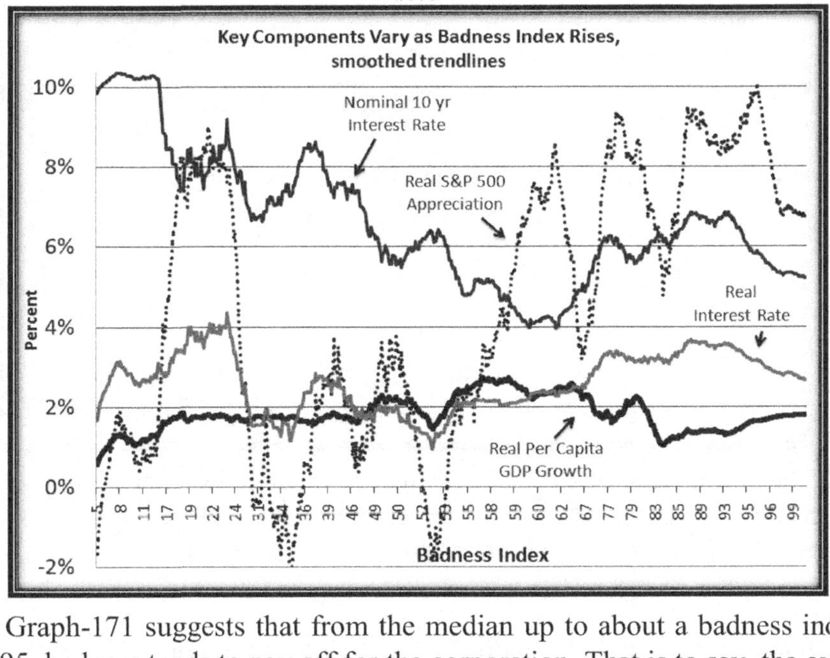

Graph-171 suggests that from the median up to about a badness index of 95, badness tends to pay off for the corporation. That is to say, the overstatement of earnings and jacking up PE ratios does seem to accelerate S&P500 appreciation. Notwithstanding that it is dishonorable, it would be consistent with a model of a rational amoral corporate culture seeking to advance shareholder-value.

But the results are inconsistent. Very high appreciation occurs also at the benign region of about an 18-22 badness. As to whether high interest rates can abate badness, it seems that nominal interest rates in the neighborhood of 6.2-6.8% and real interest rates in the neighborhood of 3.3-3.5% on the right side of graph-171 do not control it, but very high nominal interest rates (7+%) on the left-hand side may.

A badness index above 66 appears to be associated with lower per capita GDP growth rates and increases in real interest rates. So it is referred to as a threshold for harm. Beneath this point, GDP growth seems strong until a badness of 18. The data used here is not sufficiently abundant to draw firm conclusions.

#172

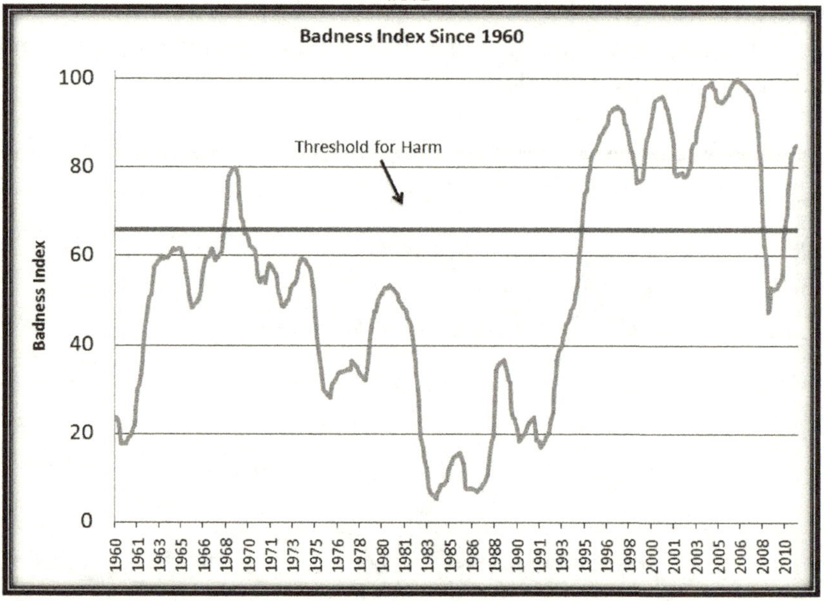

The chronology of PE and earnings badness show interesting changes in badness in graph-172. From about 1982-1993, PE ratio and earnings badness were very low – less than 40. From 1963-1974, badness remained close to 60, except for 1968-69, when it exceeded the threshold for harm.

Interestingly, at the inception of the high PE ratio regime in 1991, badness was quite low at 17.4, until three years later when it jumped above the threshold for harm. The badness regime then continued significantly above the threshold until the market collapse in 2008. Exceeding the threshold again in 2010 is a cause for concern.

This measure of badness was preceded by a great evil that later operated concurrently with it. Often under the name of promoting shareholder value, companies wildly cut employees and restructured, using all manner of devices at their disposal to provide short-term high returns to stockholders. General Electric alone, during the tenure of CEO Jack Welch (1981-2001), eliminated 120,000 of its employees, reportedly increasing earnings by $7.8 billion, the bulk of which were estimated to have occurred on the backs of laid-off workers.[104]

Was this vilified? No. Jack Welch clones continue to proliferate among MBAs and CEOs. Welch worshipers and the like are more frequently the rule, rather than the exception. It is not hard to spot the palpable joy – no, outright bliss – in the financial press when downsizing, layoffs, shedding labor costs, corporate restructuring, and the like are announced. Restructuring became a sanitized word for fewer workers, fewer jobs.

The Schadenfruede School of Economics reigns. The MAJ's meager share of net worth dropped about 29% between 1983 and 1991. By 2011 it had dropped another 25%.

For decades, any excess, any stomping on labor for short-term, stockholder gain, was held out as the dominant, if not the only acceptable, corporate culture/ideology. Hostile takeovers, mergers, leveraged buy-outs, proxy fights – these added to the amusement. When the S&P stagnated for decades on end, or the S&P500 crashed, only then did it seem to abate. Thanks to this culture, too frequently near zero or negative decade-long inflation-adjusted stock value growth has also become a rule, rather than an exception. The presumed beneficiaries, the stockholders, too, were harmed.

The suffering at the MAJ during this period can be seen in the following graph-174. Already well in progress prior to July 1991, the additional PE ratio and earning reporting machinations continued to apply downward pressure on the working person. By 1991, the MAJ income share had fallen 2.63 points from its peak. After 1991, it fell another 3.6 points.

The economist James Galbraith makes the point that "inequality in the structure of incomes largely follows the stock market."[105] When advantages are achieved in the stock market by unwholesome means, the MAJ and all those beneath the teeter point are harmed. To be indifferent to stock-market machinations is to abet maldistribution.

#174

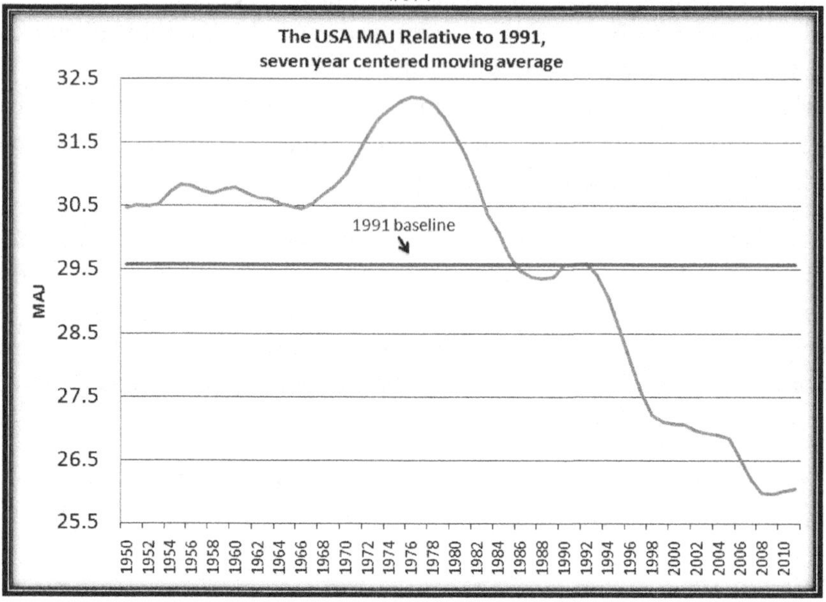

Myth or GDP. Please choose.

Time for a thought experiment. This one needs to be computer-assisted. A spreadsheet can do the job. No need for sophisticated programming. We have looked at high PE ratios and dubious earnings reports from several angles, but we have yet to tie them together well enough to know what the world might have looked like if such excesses had been erased from history.

Let's see if we can show the picture. We will do a simulation with two rules. 1) PE ratios will be the same as those that occurred in history, except that they will be capped at the 17.9 danger point. 2) We will start with the same inflation-adjusted earnings that existed in 1900 and have them grow at a fixed proportion of annual GDP growth so that by 1991, estimated earnings will equal true 1991 earnings. The Rule-Based stock value will equal these GDP-based earnings multiplied by the 17.9 capped PE ratios (using the same process that is used in real world formulas).

The following graph-175 shows the inflation-adjusted S&P500 along with the Rule-Based S&P500. The Rule-Based earnings were again substantially equal by March 2009.

The two curves diverged in the Depression and WWII era. From 1950-1995, they reflected the same characteristics. Beginning in about January 1995, the obvious and expected departure occurred. And it was huge. Once the high historical inflation-adjusted peaks occurred, falls from them or subsequent stagnation became inevitable.

#175

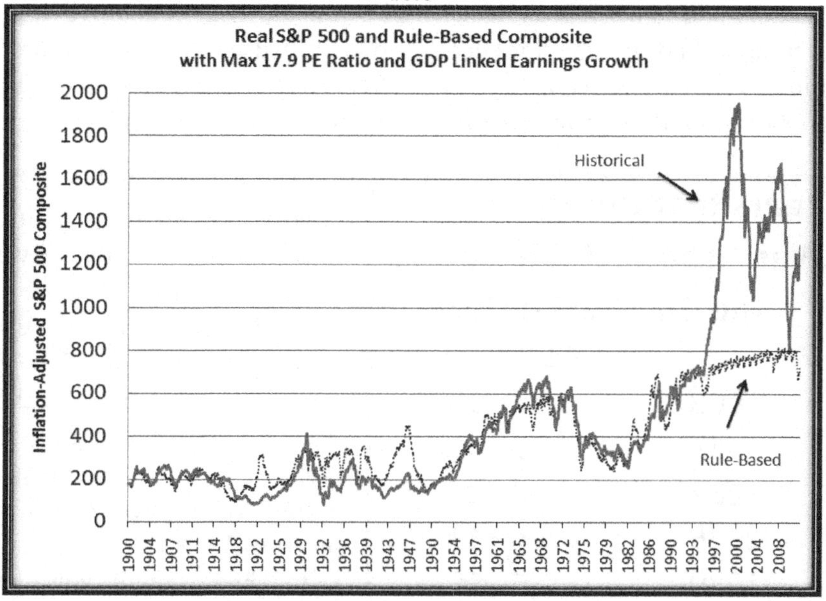

The point made in this chapter is that PE ratios and exaggerated earnings reports were responsible for the huge boom in stock prices. Graph-175 tells the same story, but with greater clarity. If the huge boom was responsive to GDP alone, the historical curve would have behaved approximately as the Rule-Based curve did. On average, subsequent to 1991, real world PE ratios were 1.52 times higher and reported earnings were 1.26 times higher than in the Rule-Based model. During the period since 1991, the lack of the two moderating components raised average stock price by a factor of 1.665 higher than they would have been under Rule-Based conditions. The simple two-rule model would have had no boom and no crash. It would have preserved a shared destiny with GDP. The two rules, whether incorporated by culture or other mechanisms, are potent.

Investors cannot and should not expect to be rescued by outsized GDP growth. Real GDP growth rates subsequent to 1995 have not been the mechanism behind spectacular stock values. The magical mechanisms that have rescued investors have been, and continue to be, outsized earnings reports and outsized PE ratios.

It would be all well and fine if force-feeding the rich was free of adverse consequences. To believe it is of such benign character is to be wrong. The CIA World Factbook shows the USA in 2011 had a $15.04 trillion GDP and a $17.14 trillion market value of publicly traded shares (14% larger than GDP).* The S&P500 is in the index of leading economic indicators and is considered a bellwether for the U.S. economy. If, as the last time around, the market becomes overvalued by a factor of 1.665 and again drops to a level consistent with GDP growth, it could readily result in a $6.84 trillion drop in wealth (46% of GDP). Would caution be in order?

Years that the Fall In GDP Was Greater Than During the 2008 Calamity

	GDP Growth
2008	-3.11%
1958	-3.74%
1982	-4.03%
1946	-4.41%
1980	-6.99%
1947	-8.73%

The unwarranted boom, now almost 20 years old, and its kin, placed a huge amount of wealth into the hands of a few. It skewed economic decision-making and culture. People relied on precarious wealth – a wealth disassociated from GDP realities. The mechanisms required to support it, too, have profoundly adverse consequences to which we will return later.

By 2008, the U.S. had built an edifice designed to fall. That is precisely what it did. There were insufficient controls and oversight throughout. There have been other larger falls in GDP since the Great Depression, but this was the most devastating because the housing crash, the stock market crash, the banking crash, and the crash of many large institutions coincided. In the prior major drops in GDP since the Great Depression income was more equitably distributed, making recovery easier. As measured by increased deficit spending, the 2008 Calamity has been disproportionately costly to contain. And inexpensive and effective recovery measures, such as key regulatory mechanisms that would prevent a repeat and would lay a framework for a strong economy, are not in place.

Market economics has the potential for great nobility. But when it goes far afield from prudent income and wealth distributions and from appropri-

---

* In contrast to all of prior U.S. history, since about 1997, market value (i.e., capitalization) has customarily exceeded GDP and at its peak was about half again as large as GDP. According to the website VectorGrader and others, the investor, Warren Buffett, reportedly regards the "Market Capitalization to GDP" ratio as "probably the best single measure of where valuations stand at any given moment." Keep in mind that Market Capitalization is another way of saying PE ratio * earnings.

ate securities (stock market and bond) practices, it can be a cruel and unforgiving master.

When you take a look, you will see that in the previous graph-175, for a brief instant, the stock market returned to levels consistent with GDP growth. Here was the opportunity to begin anew and join in a shared destiny with GDP. That opportunity appears to have been lost in preference to wrongly promoting another unwarranted stock market surge, which can be expected to be as damaging as the prior ones.

The culture of myth and outsized gains has accrued benefits for a tiny minority. This disproportionality invades all economic decisions. Manifestations of disproportionality come in many forms. Maldistribution of income and wealth are abetted, as are all points where tentacles of economic impropriety reach.

Pause. Think of the damage. How easy it would have been to have avoided it. Embarrassingly easy.

CH. 8

THE USA: drama, engine, & triumph

The wonderful blank.

> It is only half a century since ______ emerged from colonial dependence ...The number of large fortunes in the country is quite small, and capital is still scarce. Yet no people on earth has made more rapid progress ... The greatest industrial ventures are completed without difficulty because the entire population is involved in industry, and the poorest citizen willingly joins forces with the most opulent to ensure its success. It is a source of constant surprise to see what vast projects are carried out easily by a nation that in a sense has no rich people. ... They have stood the whole natural order on its head ...[106]

"Scarce capital," "in a sense ... no rich people." Yet as he states, "The longest railroad lines that have been built to this day are in America." ... "They are today the second leading maritime nation in the world." His praises literally fill volumes.

Alexis De Tocqueville in 1831-1832 writing *Democracy in America* was impressed with the young nation's equality so much so that he used "equal" or "equality" 622 times – an average of once every page and a half.

His observations, though, were not Panglossian:

> The territorial aristocracy of centuries past was obligated by law, or believed itself to be obliged by mores, to aid its servants and to assuage their miseries. But today's manufacturing aristocracy, having impoverished and brutalized the men it uses, abandons them in times of crisis and turns them over to public assistance to be fed. ...

> All things considered, I believe that the manufacturing aristocracy that we see rising before our eyes is one of the harshest that has ever existed on earth. …
>
> …[F]riends of democracy must keep an anxious eye peeled in this direction at all times. For if permanent inequality of conditions and aristocracy are ever to appear in the world anew, it is safe to predict that this is the gate by which they will enter.[107]

If we are to honor the wise warning to keep our eyes peeled, we need reliable data. The long history of absent economic data at critical junctures in U.S. history is legendary.

Bluster.

To a striking extent, books prior to and during the Great Depression often sought to carry the argument primarily by bluster and force of personality, without a grounding in fact. In a measure, it is pardonable because in the primitive conditions existing at the time, facts (especially accurate statistical facts) were frequently absent.

During the Great Depression and the years leading up to it, readily available and coherent governmental data was missing precisely in areas that needed to be well-managed in order to evade or mitigate the huge economic difficulties of the time. Key actors did not have the data.

An instance concerning a hero of mine, Frances Perkins,[108] comes to mind. Franklin D. Roosevelt (FDR), not yet President, was still Governor of the State of New York; and Perkins was the State's Industrial Commissioner. Page One of the *New York Times*, January 22, 1930 read:

> President Hoover stated today that the trend of employment had changed in the right direction. …
>
> Secretary Davis [Department of Labor] said, 'we can expect a great deal of business in 1930,' and that the present year 'should see us well on the way to complete recovery' from the depression during the last few months of 1929.
>
> Jan. 1 actually marked the turn upward in employment, the Secretary said, but it was not entirely evident until Jan. 6, when reports show a steady gain. Since then, he continued, the strides toward industrial recovery have been maintained.

Perhaps the statement would have sufficed for the camp-following eunuchs, but it was plainly implausible. And Perkins knew it. The assertion that a short January 1 to 6 interval was a sufficient basis for a grand recovery was silly. Her office was showing vastly different data. She responded in the *NYT* January 23 and February 11, with detailed data, that in New York State in January 1930, were 2% fewer jobs than in December 1929, and 6% fewer than in November 1929. Since October 1929, 100,000 factory jobs had been lost in New York.

In the *NYT* January 25, 1930, Secretary Davis stuck to his story, "There is no disputing ... the fact that there was a very appreciable trend upwards on Jan. 6 as compared with Dec. 30. [This would have been worthy of an Onion News satire, had it been around then. A mere week portending a turnaround – what absurdity.] ... The fact remains, as stated by the President and myself, that Jan. 6 showed the first tangible evidence of returning employment."[109]

According to a March 1, 1930 *NYT* article "the Federal Bureau of Labor Statistics *refused to make public* the detailed figures on which the optimistic statements were made. [emphasis added]"[110]

This foray into silliness underlines a greater problem. At the time there were no national reliable, readily available, and coherent governmental data for unemployment, GNP, GDP, income distribution, and key monetary data.

National account numbers such as GDP did not exist. Four years later, in 1934, Simon Kuznets first presented estimates for the 1929-1932 period to the Senate. Under the exigency of wartime planning, with his good work, Gross National Product data was developed by the Department of Commerce in 1942. But it was not until July 1947 that the data achieved maturity.

Velocity of money and money supply data were scarce or absent, depending upon your view. Lauchlin Currie, in 1934, was a first in that sphere.[111] Even as late as 1975, stunningly large corrections had to be made on Great Depression employment data.[112]

Keep in mind that major economic theories developed during this period were often blind to accurate antecedent and current statistics at pivotal points. Bluster by default was a commanding component – too frequently only randomly correct, in policy and in theory.

Numbers in the Great Depression.

One of the greatest economic dramas of all times was the Great Depression. In the United States, it was the era of saving Democracy and Capitalism from the far right and the far left – a job well done, even with its faults.

For reasons beyond my comprehension, most economists prefer mainly to look elsewhere for economic answers. I find the story of economic success squarely within it, and often widely applicable for all times. Here is the story of a form of government (Democracy) which (through its economy) delivered to the people a path out of misery of no less dramatic proportion than Moses' parting of the waters. Ah, you say: Exaggeration. Look at the data. Then see what you think. After repeatedly seeing it, I remain amazed.

The Depression years and their antecedents speak to the present with surprising clarity. Let's first look at it through the eyes of money supply. That will clarify key economic features as we probe the era for insight into our current maldistribution spawned difficulties.

The 1915-1933 period serves as a rare money supply laboratory in a free market setting with little government spending. First, money supply shot up. Then it crashed down. Here we are able to see the power of money supply, its weakness, its calamity. This was a drama of first order. There never again will be such a laboratory. It would be considered unethical human experimentation.

In 1934 Lauchlin Currie wrote a major book on money supply.[113] He ranged from being a monetarist working on banking laws, under which we still operate today, to being a New Deal economist at the center of economic decision making. Trained at Harvard, he served initially in the Treasury Department, then at the Federal Reserve, and ultimately as FDR's White House economic adviser (a forerunner of today's Council of Economic Advisors). Few, if any, economists had such scope during the crucial period.[114]

He attributed initial difficulties in the Great Depression to monetary policy. Now that we have greater body of data developed from his work, it is not hard to see why.

In the following graph-183 we see a massive downturn in money supply beginning in 1927. It precipitated the Great Depression. Monetary contractions of this magnitude were unprecedented.

If the money supply is not growing but the economy is growing (producing more goods and services), then there is insufficient money available. With a smaller amount of money spread over a larger number of items sold, prices must go down (deflation). Perceiving that prices will continue to go down, buyers tend to delay purchases in hopes that they can strike a deal at a future date at yet a lower price. Reluctance to purchase can readily become a self-feeding process that reduces the amount of products coming to market, which contributes to recession or depression.[115]

#183

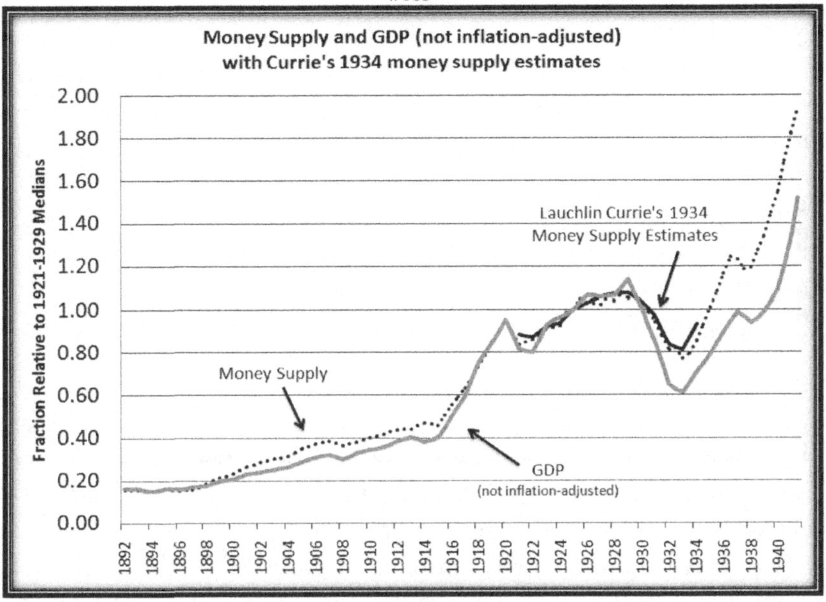

Money supply growth stalled in 1926. By early 1929 it commenced its deep fall. It did not surpass its 1926 level until 1936 – a full decade.[116] Look at the length and depth of this fall in the above graph-183. It guaranteed depression and deflation. Both of which came. The money supply data you see here was not available until 1943. The GDP data came much later. Data and theory were inadequate to meet the challenge. To a large extent, people acted on hunches. Little more. Too frequently, incorrect.

On the other hand, with excessive monetary growth, a larger amount of money chasing the same number of goods at market, tends to produce inflation. Inflation, the direct opposite of deflation, creates a stimulus to buy goods now before they increase to a yet higher future price.

Money supply management was so misguided from 1915 to 1933 that, on one hand, the vast growth in money supply from 1915 to 1920 produced the doubling of prices shown in the following graph-184. And then from 1930 to 1933, money supply acted in the opposite direction to quickly deflate prices by 25%. Both shocks were enormous, the latter being sufficient to vastly deepen the Great Depression.

#184

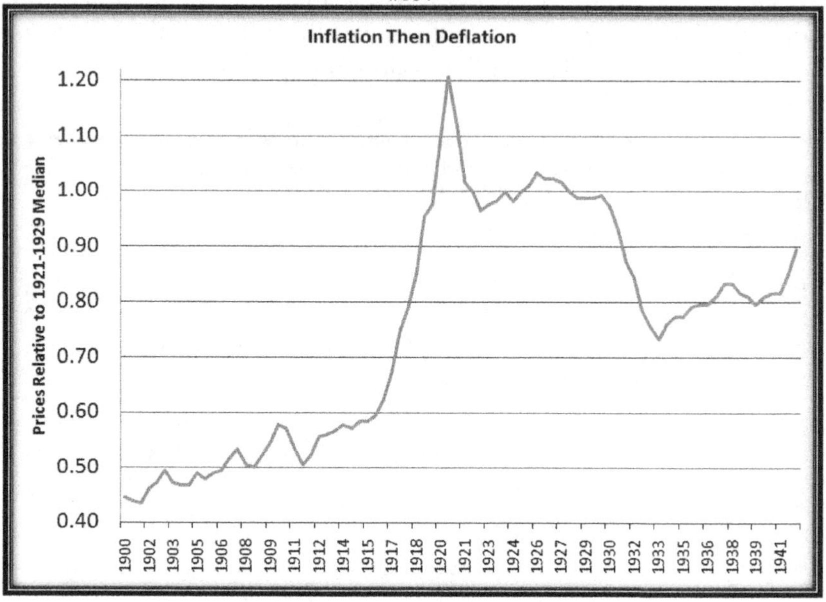

Very mild inflation is generally desirable because it produces a slight incentive toward economic growth. With this in mind, the prudent objective is to have money supply growing slightly faster than expected real economic growth. But the caveat is that there is an addictive hazard when governments create excessively high monetary supply growth. In such a case, the inflation engine is apt to run out of control, sometimes reaching hyperinflation.

Finely-tuned reasoning relies on good data – data unavailable during most of the period shown in the following graph-185. The consequences were inflation and deflation rates that varied from a negative 3.9% to plus 10.2% (for eight-year periods from 1892-1941).

For those who are great friends of the unfettered marketplace, look closely at graph-185. It shows annualized growth over 8-year periods, as if you were comparing your present position to a time 8 years earlier. Government intervention then was often slight to nonexistent.

An economically aware uncle of mine, who lived in the early 1900s, pointed out to me that throughout his childhood, including when he was at Harvard, classmates often were forced to drop out of school because their parents had lost everything they had in one panic or another. Those same panics take on an undeservedly cool representation in the GDP troughs shown in graph-185.

#185

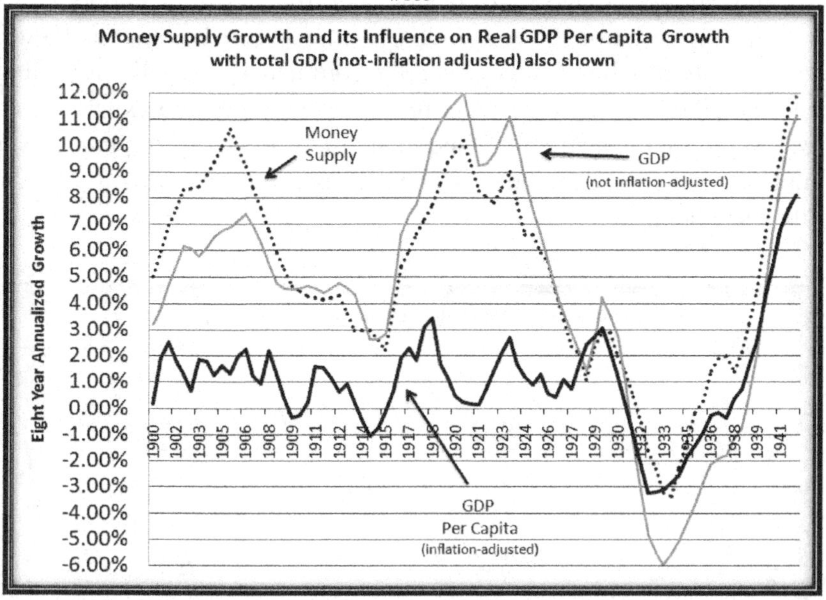

The real GDP per capita growth in graph-185 is a good reference point because it flushes out the inflation and deflation influences that accompany large money supply moves, thereby letting you see how the economy is actually doing. The inflation-adjusted GDP per capita shows numerous steep drops, several approaching, or falling beneath, a zero growth rate. These frequent catastrophes are not nearly as attractive as rhetorical arguments for completely unfettered markets may suggest.[117] Going back in history to sometime in the distant past of supposed perfection often requires evading inconvenient details – such as stating the MAJ value that free market buccaneers regard as appropriate for their idealized state.

You can see in the previous graph-185, money supply during this period grew and declined at very fast rates. Sustained money supply growth rates significantly exceeding 5% produced no advantage during the period, as can be seen in real GDP per capita which moved, as if oblivious, to many of the high monetary growths. But, a sharply declining rate of money supply growth, such as at the 1914 trough and the Great Depression, appear to have been adverse – profoundly so in the case of the Great Depression. If money supply had grown at the constant rate of 5.2% (the average for the 1892-1941 period), the cycle of booms and panics would likely have been less extreme.

To cast money supply as a guiding and necessary thread for economic wellbeing is appropriate. But to push on the string … Try that one at home.

Money supply is causative, but not curative.* Money supply can drag you into vast inflation. It can drag you into great depressions. But once money supply reaches levels generally commensurate with sustaining rational real GDP per capita growth, to increase it more and expect it to grow an economy, that is a stretch. Once in an appropriate region, money supply cannot go further to cure slow or negative real income growth. The causes reside elsewhere.

#186

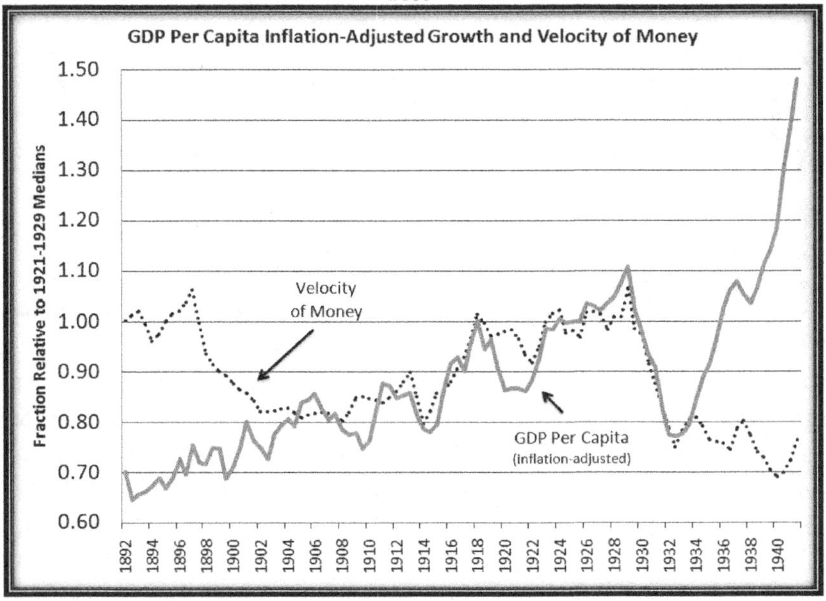

You can see in the above graph-186 that velocity of money declined at the same instant that real per capita growth did. Slow turnover of money was especially evident from the onset of the Great Depression onward [turnover of money can easily be measured by dividing GDP by money supply]. At these times, even if an increase in monetary supply were desired, the infusion would have occurred at reduced effectiveness. In the graph it would have been 70% to 80% less effective after 1932. A slowing of the rate of turnover (velocity of money) tends to be symptomatic of unrelated underlying economic problems that cause downturns.

---

* See graphs 183 onward where money supply prior to 1920 increased greatly but inflation-adjusted GDP per capita did not. Also see the Great Depression increase in money supply during the recovery which did little more than to bring money supply to suitable levels after the previous disastrously wrong money supply contraction.

One of the reasons money supply, in times of desperation, is such a weak curative actor is that the velocity of money tends to decline greatly in adverse times. Precisely when a cure is most needed, monetary policy is least able to provide the cure because money has commenced circulating more slowly.

A few remarks by Currie in his memoirs suggest why monetary policy (even when appropriately managed) requires other helping components:

> "Although banking reform was the first order of business, my main interest and concern had been for some years centered on the problem of securing full employment – of making the economic machine produce the ever-increasing volume of goods and services it was potentially able to produce. From 1930-1933 I had felt increasing frustration and impotence as I listened to the foolish things which were said and watched the equally foolish things that were done. This feeling was not relieved by the policy of wholesale bank closings and the ill-starred National Recovery Act in 1933. The first ray of hope for me came from the relief and public works appropriations. …"[118]
>
> "… [I]ncreased expenditures wait on increased demand and increased demand waits on increased expenditures …. The most feasible way in which this deadlock may be broken is for the Government through its expenditures to increase incomes, and hence demand for goods … This very simply, is the theory of pump priming operations …
>
> "… [W]ell in advance of the publication of Keynes' monumental General Theory of Employment, I was aware that savings had to be spent if the monetary circulation was to be maintained …"[119]
>
> "The year 1936 had witnessed a very substantial measure of recovery. … From 1933 to 1936 inclusive, the main factor responsible for the recovery movement was the excess of federal expenditures over tax revenues. This led to an expansion of money, an expansion of incomes, an increase in the demand for goods, and a secondary expansion of incomes."[120]

Monetary circulation (velocity of money) and money supply both depend on economic vibrancy elsewhere. There is an interesting banking concept called "fractional reserve banking," which multiplies money deposited in banks. Wikipedia has a good description of it, as does khanacademy.org on YouTube. The mechanism by which it works is straightforward.

If you are not an economist, you may be surprised to know that the actual currency in circulation is only a small portion of money supply because of fractional reserve banking. In other words, the central bank for the nation requires a specific percentage of total deposits to be held in reserve. For example, if 20% is held in reserve, then the initial existing currency is capable of producing total deposits that are 5 times greater; if 10%, it is 10 times greater [multiplier= 1/"reserve percentage"; 5= 1/20%; 10= 1/10%]. The money supply used here and by Currie is the sum of all bank deposits plus currency (similar to the M1 designation that economist are familiar with). Deposits multiply because banks loan out money. Then through intermediate transactions in the marketplace (when borrowers spend the money) the money is again redeposited in banks. By this mechanism, money supply grows. In most instances, this benefits everyone.

There is no great need to make the discussion complicated by deeply studying the process. It is enough to know that banks loaning money causes money supply to grow. From personal experience, I can tell you that when a businessperson goes to the bank for a loan to purchase additional machinery or to cover receivables (money owed to him by customers), and he has his house and everything he owns as collateral to back up loans with the bank, his chief concern is that he will indeed be able to repay the bank loan he takes out. He would be a fool to borrow if he did not have a high degree of certainty that he would be able to pay off the loan.

This brings us to economically distressed times when income for the businessman is uncertain. The predilection is not to borrow, or else to borrow in only small amounts. Multiply that by many parties not taking out loans. Money supply as a consequence contracts. In an instance, such as during the Great Depression, it is beyond the reach of monetary policy alone to overcome the businessman's and other borrowers' justifiable caution sufficiently for them to risk borrowing or investing in quantities large enough to restore a moribund economy.

Returning to Currie's remark, the increased federal expenditures *led to an expansion of money*, an expansion of incomes, and an increase in the demand for goods. It led to an expansion of money because it helped to keep bank deposits up. The increased demand for goods helped to restore customary economic activity.

Put yourself in the position of an economic potentate stuck in the middle of a deep depression. You are looking at the sum of Consumer Spending plus Investment, which has precipitously fallen. You know that Aggregate Demand = Consumer Spending + Investment + Government Spending

+ Net Export. If you were to cut Government Spending, then Aggregate Demand (GDP) goes further south. Ask, what will fill up the pocketbook sufficiently for Consumer Spending to increase? If businesses are in a depressed state where they are unable to profitably sell goods that their present capital can already produce, what reason would they have to hire more workers or to increase Investment further? In such conditions, by default, Government Spending is the most likely curative agent.

From 1933 through the 1970s, decisions were not flawless but increasingly, they did sensibly combine monetary policy and fiscal policy (government spending) to produce an outstanding economic outcome for the workingman which no prior or subsequent period has equaled. Monetary and fiscal policy were not opposing hands, but two hands working together. Clap. With two hands? Why not?

Fascism, Socialism, Communism, saving the Democracy.

With characteristic precision, twenty years before the darkest years of the Great Depression, the economist Allyn Young pointed out two especially potent sources for the appeal of socialism: 1) "… [I]n many American cities … a vote for the socialist ticket has often been the only way of lodging an effective protest against things as they are." And, 2) "Certain elements of the socialist movement … seem to be based on little more than … the envious spleen of those who have not against those who have."[121] The latter being particularly evident in radical elements whose preference for going on strike and disrupting social order seemed to outweigh their interest in performing bona fide work under improved conditions.

On a more positive note, beginning in the 1880s and peaking in the 1920s, settlement houses and the like appeared in many U.S. cities – 423 settlement houses in 1913.[122] Here, the poor, often the immigrant poor, could come for language lessons, classes, culture, and social life, intended to alleviate their condition and help them to integrate into and prosper in the U.S. The houses also became the training grounds for many social workers and socially concerned citizens. Many of them later became professionals in the field and directly involved in government administration and policy. Many illustrious names in U.S. history came both from the ranks of the poor who benefited from these houses and from the ranks of the social workers and citizens who worked there.

A 40-hour workweek, no child factory laborers, worker safety, old age security, and unemployment insurance are now mainstream. All these originated from long-fought-for demands from labor unions, socialists, and socially concerned citizens. It is too often forgotten that good ideas can and have originated from sources with whom we may disagree. All of these were resisted by the then rich classes and often by Federal Law, usually for silly reasons. For example, a reasoning behind child labor was that factories needed the small hands of children in cotton mills to service looms and other machinery.[123]

The pronouncements from officialdom were no better. In 1918, the Supreme Court of the United States ruled that Congress could not enact child labor laws because they were a state matter, unrelated to interstate commerce. In 1923, the Court ruled it was illegal to set a minimum wage for women. In 1905, it ruled that worker hours could not be restricted to ten hours a day because it violated workers' right to contract their own hours.[124] As for the 40-hour workweek, contrary to the wishes of the National Association of Manufacturers, it gained credence when Henry Ford doubled worker pay and cut shifts to eight hours a day in 1914. The logic: "Every hour you work over 40 hours a week is making you less effective."[125] The Supreme Court and the ethic of the wealthy thwarted progress on these crucial points, which today are taken for granted. At the time, there was no certainty that FDR could move beyond troglodyte rulings of the time.

To mention socialism, communism, or fascism as an alternative to the American Way is to excite the greatest of emotions – the most profound testing of which came during the Great Depression. Even to the patriotic it looked as if capitalism was broken. Farming, a preeminent economic sector, had been in distress for a decade and was heading further south. Real housing values had been in a longstanding decline (graph-65). Many people who had money in the bank found themselves broken when thousands of banks failed. This contrasted to Canada whose banking laws resulted in no bank failures.[126] Those who were already broken could not find work or, often, food. Too frequently, industrial workers were laid off or cut back. The intellectual foothold of capitalism appeared so weak that justifiable desperation lead one's mind elsewhere – either to the right or to the left. Even fascism was considered.

Columbia Pictures in 1933 released the Fascistly friendly film "Mussolini Speaks" narrated by the popular CBS broadcaster Lowell Thomas. It was a box-office success that grossed $1 million at a time when a movie ticket sold for fifteen cents; a ticket price which suggests that 6.7 million

Americans paid to see the film [6,666,667= 1,000,000/0.15]. Columbia Pictures' screen dedication stated: "To a man of the people whose deeds for his people will ever be an inspiration to mankind – Benito Mussolini."[127]

FDR's first presidential term began March 4, 1933. Ten days later, on March 13, a *New York Times* review read: "… 'Mussolini Speaks' presents the career, achievements and ambitions of the Italian dictator in an interesting and instructive way. Lowell Thomas … translates the fiery words of Mussolini … so that even those in the audience who are not Italians cannot resist a surge of patriotic feeling. … [T]he camera moves out over the country to illustrate what has been done … and how Mussolini has kept his promises to his people."

The newspapers of William Randolph Hearst employed Mussolini and Hitler as foreign correspondents. Hitler proved unsatisfactory because he failed to meet submission deadlines. And Hearst's wife, Millicent, visited with Mussolini in Rome and wrote favorably of him.[128]

A few weeks after the release of "Mussolini Speaks," on March 31, a film was released to which we still have access and about which FDR made suggestions during its making.[129] "Gabriel Over the White House" provides a picture of a near dictatorial president. The *Nation* titled its review of it as "Fascism over Hollywood." My take is that this is one of the few films that was greatly improved by censorship (because the original script was so ghastly).[130] In its reconstructed form, the film powerfully stated the democratic challenge that then faced the nation, notwithstanding that it included the distasteful aspect of martial law. The Gabriel President was clear to Congress: "A plant cannot be made to grow by watering the top alone and letting the roots go dry. The people of this country are the roots of the nation …" Those plain words and the image of a decisive President working to better conditions for the people were apt to have been the hope and sentiment that the audience had when they walked out of theatres in 1933. A feeling, transcending ideology, that they were one step further from utter despair.

Through the power of indirectness, knowledgeable people on occasion transmit lasting meaning. For me, one such statement about Communism stands out. Karl Radek, a radical from at least 1904 onward and a prominent Bolshevik in the early days of the Russian Revolution, commented to Chip Bohlen in Russian, "You Westerners will never understand Bolshevism. You consider Bolshevism as a hot bath whose temperature can be raised and lowered to suit the taste of the bather. This is not true. You are either a hundred percent in the bath and a hundred percent for it, or you are a hundred percent outside and a hundred percent against it."[131] The rigidity can be of spectacular proportions. Radek, himself, was purged and murdered a few years later – removed, shall we say, from the bath.

In 1931, the U.S. Communist Party had 8,000 members. Its impact outweighed its numbers.[132] The party's objective and method converge in the plain statement that "ends can only be attained by the forcible overthrow of existing social conditions."[133] Yet, it aligned itself with many worthwhile progressive causes: anti-lynching laws, improved racial conditions, labor movement, and the like. Its objective was not so much to ameliorate or improve social conditions as so widely hoped for during the Depression, but to advance the triumph of the "bath" and all that came with it. The testing of Communism and Democracy in the USA came at the Great Depression.

Bolshevik theory presumes uniting the workers of the world. At no time in all of U.S. history were workers in such great distress and had such dim prospects as in the early years of the Great Depression. FDR provided palpable change that from the outset addressed the worker. Bringing real success to the worker undercut and triumphed over Bolshevik rhetoric.

The trajectory: bottom up, not top down.

In his "Forgotten Man" speech in the spring of 1932 before he was elected President, FDR's trajectory – bottom up, not top down – was set, as he clearly stated:

> These unhappy times call for the building of plans that rest upon the forgotten, the unorganized but the indispensable units of economic power [and] for plans like those of 1917 [World War I] that *build from the bottom up and not from the top down, that put their faith once more in the forgotten man at the bottom of the economic pyramid.*
>
> … It is the habit of the unthinking to turn in times like this to the illusions of economic magic. People suggest that a huge expenditure of public funds by the Federal Government and by State and Local governments will completely solve the unemployment problem. But it is clear that even if we could raise many billions of dollars and find definitely useful public works to spend these billions on, even all that money would not give employment to the seven million or ten million people who are out of work. Let us admit frankly that it would be only a stopgap. A real economic cure must go to the killing of the bacteria in the system rather than to the treatment of external symptoms.

> … The result of loss of purchasing power is that millions of people engaged in industry in the cities cannot sell industrial products to the farming half of the Nation. This brings home to every city worker that his own employment is directly tied up with the farmer's dollar. No Nation can long endure half bankrupt. Main Street, Broadway, the mills, the mines will close if half the buyers are broke.
>
> …Every man and woman who gives any thought to the subject knows that if our factories run even 80 percent of capacity, they will turn out more products than we as a Nation can possibly use ourselves. The answer is that if they run on 80 percent of capacity, we must sell some goods abroad. …
>
> [The current administration] has sought temporary relief *from the top down* rather than *permanent relief from the bottom up.* It has totally failed to plan ahead in a comprehensive way. It has waited until something has cracked and then at the last moment has sought to prevent total collapse.
>
> It is high time to get back to fundamentals. It is high time to admit with courage that we are in the midst of an emergency at least equal to that of war. Let us mobilize to meet it. [emphasis added] [134]

The test was not to be an easy one. The spectators along the parade path all interjected their say. Explicitly to counter Roosevelt, the Liberty League was formed in August 1934 by a group of wealthy and influential leaders, promising an "unremitting" fight against "government encroachments upon the rights of citizens."[135] William Graham Sumner, a professor of sociology, was a Social Darwinist of great influence. Although he died 20 years before the Depression's trough, he provided the grist for much of the rhetorical opposition. Such lively comments of his as the following illustrate his stance: "Before the tribunal of nature, a man has no more right to life than a rattlesnake; he has no more right to liberty than any wild beast; his right to pursuit of happiness is nothing but a license to maintain the struggle for existence …"[136]

For those inspired by such sentiments, may I suggest *The Forgotten Man's Almanac*? For each day of the year you can wake to inspiring words from Sumner (the book is arranged according to days of the year). For example, when you arise from your bed on May 21 of any year, you can be greeted by: "The world of human society is what has resulted from thousands of years of life. ... To talk of making another system is like talking of making a man of [age] sixty* into something else than what his life has made him."[137] FDR and those close to him offered a different tone, and an alternative – a successful one. It rankled his opponents.

Although my library is filled with academically-couched books on the topic, turning the pages of Robert McElvaine's two volumes of the *Encyclopedia of the Great Depression* provides a constant reminder of the breadth and richness of the era – an expression of which resides in McElvaine's well-aimed statement:

> One result of the use of eighteenth-century theories to deal with twentieth-century reality was a growing maldistribution of income in twenties America. *No cause of the Great Depression was of larger importance* [emphasis added].[138]

A shout out from maldistribution.

As De Tocqueville cautioned, friends of democracy must keep an anxious eye peeled. As Gabriel warned, a plant cannot be made to grow by watering the top alone. Yet even as this pen goes to paper, we in the USA still do not have vital income-distribution data in front of us.

We understand neither maldistribution's role in the Great Depression, nor its role in the current U.S. economy. Surprisingly, as will be dealt with later, Census Household data for the Top1% and Top5% for approximately the past 30 years has been too flawed to be useable. Fortunately, the Congressional Budget Office in 2011 published data which is credible. Other data sources, such as Emmanuel Saez and Edward Wolff, are invaluable and are giving us an ever-better picture of USA income and wealth distributions.

The decision-makers during the Great Depression were as ignorant of the catastrophically mismanaged money supply from 1915 to 1933 as they were of income distribution. And we now find that for the past 30 years, we too have not had good data and have catastrophically mismanaged U.S. income distribution. It has been a long saga of ignorance and its consequences.

---

* Sumner died in 1910. At the time male life expectancy was 50.2 years. By 2004 it was 50% longer, 75.7 years. Sumner never got the drift. Things change.

For starters, try this for size. The year was 1916:

> "We are a long way, of course, from knowing at all accurately just how property and incomes are distributed among the 21,000,000 or more families in this country. We do not even know whether the average family income is as low as $1200 or as high as $1600. We are not sure whether the share of the aggregate national income going to the richest 2 per cent of our families is more nearly a fourth, or a fifth, or a sixth of the total. The poorest half of our families may possibly get a fourth or perhaps, three tenths of the national dividend — just what the proportion may be is uncertain."[139]

This is where we begin: *uncertainty* – a 1916 paper presented at the joint meeting of the American Economic Association and the American Statistical Association. Allyn Young,* an economist of extraordinary insight and ability, delivered the above words. Thirteen years later the Great Depression commenced. Yet, as with money supply, maldistribution data was still unavailable.

The USA now has had two economic crises of recent memory: the 1929-1939 Great Depression and the 2008-_?_ Calamity, in which a root cause for both was maldistribution. The first time around, income-distribution data and theory were no better than when Young spoke in 1916.† The second time around, the data was marginally better but still uncertain and profoundly inadequate. More dangerously, there was no theoretical consensus linking maldistribution with economic calamity. Although there have been intelligent musings and noble words here and there, nothing has been done to ameliorate or reverse maldistribution since the 1970s.

The magical MAJ. The engine that drives the nation.

The relationship is unmistakable. When MAJ income grows, so too does the per capita GDP for the nation. This is not a touchy-feely pronouncement. It is the historical case. It is obvious nationally and internationally.[140] A nation does not thrive if the MAJ does not thrive.

---

* President of the American Statistical Association (1917) and President of the American Economic Association (1925)

† The first plausible income distribution estimate came from the Brookings Institution in 1935 well after the onset of the depression – an estimated MAJ26.3 for the year 1929.

Look at the following graph-196.* You will see that when MAJ income growth is high, per capita GDP growth is also high. You will also see that the variation about the trend line is slight for values above 1.3%. *When MAJ income growth exceeds 1.3%, nationwide growth exceeds its median growth rate. This is the ironclad threshold for success.* If the nation does not meet it, it courts danger.

#196

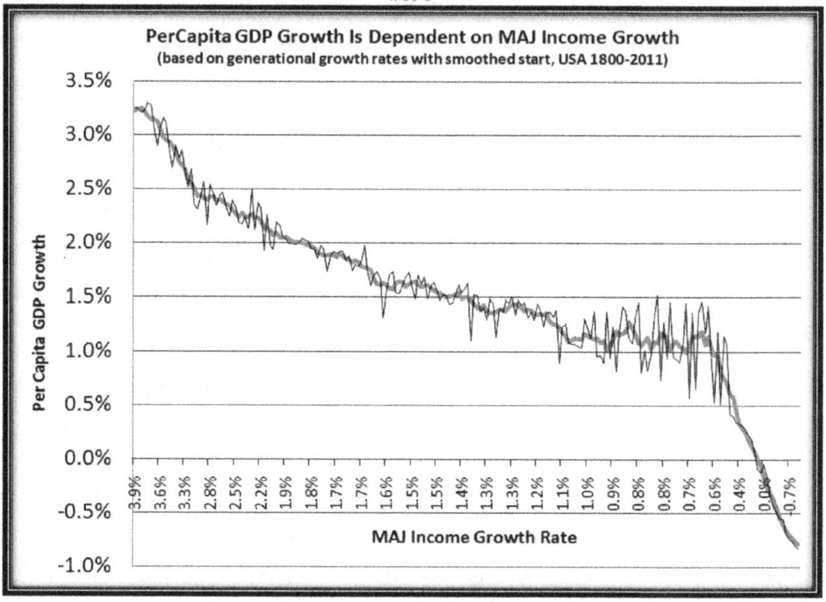

The MAJ has only 25% to 33% of the income at its disposal, yet long-term successful per capita GDP growth for everyone completely depends on its success. Such a strong influence from the MAJ is disproportionate to its income share. You can see it when you look at long-term generational data. There is a lot more going on here than equilibrium graphs and the kind of equations that economists are so fond of would suggest. Textbook economic theories fail to account for it. Yet, it is central to economic success by way of the "Dem Bones Theory of Economic Interconnectedness."

---

* All graphs from here up to graph-236 use the following techniques for all of U.S. history: They take a generational view (annualized growth over the past 26 years) to minimize the impact of annual fluctuations. The method is designed to produce representative data less influenced by transitory components. Since a deviant first data point can distort outcome, an eleven year centered moving average is used instead for the first data point. All the data (MAJ, Upper½%, and Per Capita GDP) are subjected to same process with the intent of delivering a fair representation of U.S. history. Like graphs throughout the book, data is inflation-adjusted unless otherwise indicated.

… The toe bone connected to the foot bone,
The foot bone connected to the ankle bone,
The ankle bone connected to the leg bone,
Shake dem fine bones.

The leg bone connected to the knee bone,
The knee bone connected to the thigh bone,
The thigh bone connected to the hip bone,
Shake dem fine bones. …[141]

The MAJ is fully 60% of the economic body. It may not receive much by way of income, but its interconnectedness is vital to the body, just as in the old spiritual "Dem Bones." It must flourish for the body to flourish. The trajectory for economic success is only and always bottom up – the trajectory that FDR enunciated in his Forgotten Man Speech.

Upper½% silliness versus the MAJ Threshold for Success.

#197

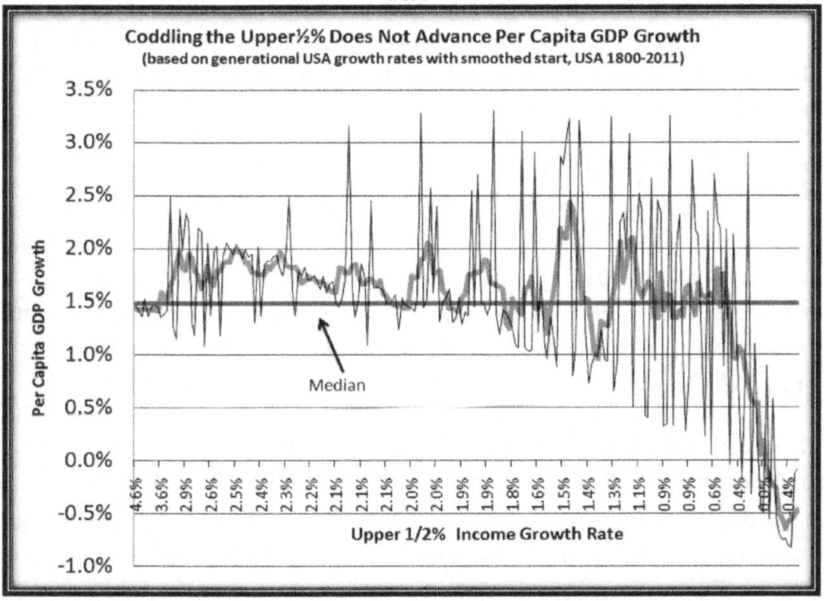

Much silliness is uttered about the Upper½%, the need to cater to it, its capacity to trickle down and leave tidbits for the rest of us, the prerogative of its members not to pay their fair share, the freedom for its members to do whatever may cross their minds, et cetera. Those at the upper reaches are obviously important to the nation, but economic growth in those quarters is decidedly of slight beneficial influence on the nation as a whole. In sharp contrast to the MAJ influence in the prior graph-196, *whether the Upper½% income grew at 4.5% or 1.0% annually had no discernible influence on per capita income growth rate,* as shown in graph-197. As you can see, the variability about the trend line is huge, and the relationship between the Upper½% and per capita GDP growth is weak to non-existent. *There is no trickling down. The trickling is from bottom up.* You can see this in the strong relationship between MAJ and per capita GDP – a relationship totally absent between the Upper½% and per capita GDP.

Nick Hanauer, an early venture capitalist investor in Amazon.com, got it right:

> We've had it backward for the last 30 years. Rich businesspeople like me don't create jobs. ... If the typical American family still got today the same share of income they earned in 1980, they would earn about 25% more and have an astounding $13,000 more a year. ... Only consumers can set in motion this virtuous cycle of increasing demand and hiring. In this sense, an ordinary middle-class consumer is far more of a job creator than a capitalist like me. Anyone who's ever run a business knows that hiring more people is a capitalist's course of last resort, something we do only when increasing customer demand requires it. In this sense, calling ourselves job creators isn't just inaccurate, it's disingenuous.[142]

The MAJ Threshold for Success.

In the following graph-199, we see how the data points were spread through U.S. history. First, both classes (the MAJ and Upper½%) suffered greatly in the economic turmoil after the American Revolutionary War. By about 1832, they both experienced growth patterns that were sustained until about 1897, with the Upper½% growing on average about 0.61% faster than the MAJ.

It is well to keep in mind that 1890 was a turning point in U.S. history. Census declared 1890 to be the end of the American frontier. Westward expansion was complete; the frontier closed. The homesteading and growth from expansion was still on the minds of many people 40 years later when the Great Depression struck. A lingering doubt remained whether vast agricultural changes and the absence of the economic vitality from the westward expansion were reducing economic growth.

#199

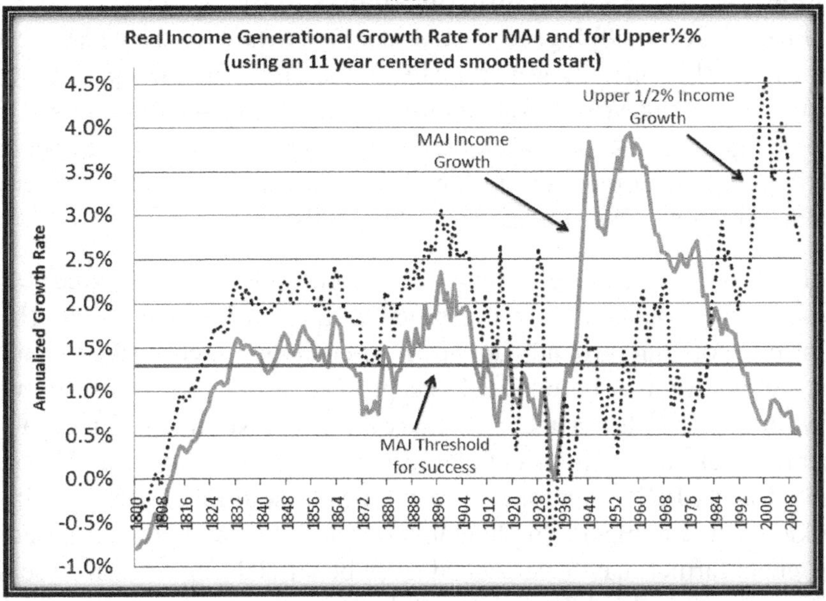

From 1889 to the Great Depression, income growth trended ever-lower for the MAJ (and more variably for the Upper½% also). By 1912, MAJ income dropped beneath the "MAJ Threshold for Success" and with the exception of WWI boom years, remained there until 1938. MAJ income growth had been trending downward for 30 years by the time the Great Depression struck, and the MAJ had been continuously beneath the Threshold for Success since 1920. Similarly in our time, the MAJ had been sharply trending downward for 30 years prior to 2008 and had been continuously beneath the MAJ Threshold for Success since 1993.

The MAJ Threshold for Success is a potent leading indicator. For 17 years, from 1912 to 1929, the nation was ignorant – not knowing that this silent disease was eating away at its potential for success. The dosage of neglect at the MAJ was sufficient that by 1929 the nation unraveled.

There is a lesson here. The economists were not looking at income distribution or how it affected the MAJ. There was no data or theory along those lines. Yet once the bottom up trajectory was applied to the MAJ in 1933, MAJ income growth rate shot up, as did in tandem per capita income. Until 1979, MAJ income growth rate remained above its highest previous growth rate experienced in 1897. We all benefited. But by not giving sufficient attention to the MAJ in recent years, we again find ourselves in a disagreeable puddle.

Highest GDP per capita growths, thanks to the MAJ.

From 1936 to 1982, generational income growth for the MAJ exceeded the Upper½%'s income growth. This is the only extended period of U.S. history where the MAJ prospered to such an extent. As you will see in the upcoming graph-201, it is also the period where the highest U.S. per capita GDP growth occurred on a sustained basis. It was the era of the reversal of maldistribution – The Golden Age of Capitalism.

FDR and those close to him were responsible for the engine that unleashed and sustained the success that carried on into the 1970s. He was right on economic grounds unknown to economic theory (then or now) – not the dole (which he opposed except when relief was absolutely necessary) but because he gave the little guy a chance. Nothing like this had ever occurred before, and its beneficial influence was long-lived. For his economist Currie, FDR's approach was at times frustrating. As for myself, now looking at the numbers, his humanitarian instincts and conversations with his tenant farmer may have packed more beneficial impact than a room full of theories of the kind that existed at the time:

> "The basic conflicts of the period had their counterpart in Roosevelt's own mind. He was torn between his earlier concepts of 'sound economics' [balanced budget] and his strong humanitarian impulses and his itch 'to get things done.' … He was glad to use economic arguments for the proposed Public Works Administration legislation but I always believed that his decision really turned on his humanitarian impulses … He was distrustful of abstract reasoning … He would interrupt an overall economic argument to relate a conversation he had had with his tenant Smith [a farmer]. Sometimes I felt the views of his tenant were a more important influence on policy than all our memoranda. … he was the first President to accept the responsibility of the Government for achieving and maintaining the economic health of the community. He also was the first American president to accept the duty and responsibility of the State to shield the worker from the economic hazards of unemployment, sickness and old age and the farmer from certain hazards beyond his individual control."[143]

From 1979 to 2011, an un-American pattern, not seen in all of U.S. history, emerged. The two classes moved in diametrically opposite directions in a manner never seen before. As shown in the prior graph-199, starting in the early 1980s, Upper½% income growth shot up to unprecedentedly high levels at the same time that MAJ income growth rates collapsed. For 18 years (1993-2011) the MAJ income growth rate has been beneath the "MAJ Threshold for Success" – a potent and an evil portent for us all.

The only time in all of U.S. history that generational MAJ income growth was lower than in 2011 were the years 1932, 1933, 1934 and years before 1819 when we were still recovering from the economic depression after the American Revolutionary War.

GDP per capita down. Upper½% up.

In recent times, all of us, not just the MAJ, have suffered as shown by the generational GDP per capita growth rates in the following graph-201. In 2011, the per capita growth rate over a 26-year period was the lowest it has been since 1939.

#201

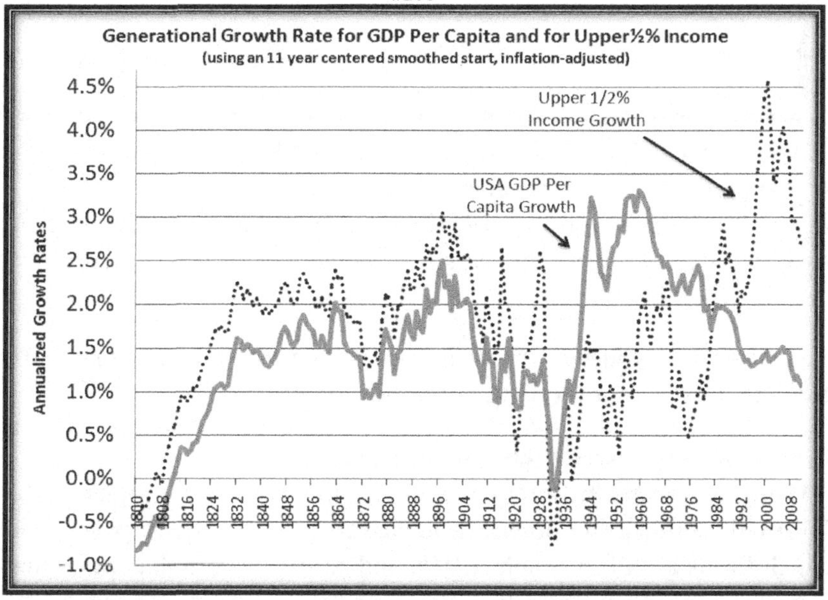

Don't despair. The Upper½% has done quite nicely. We can live vicariously through them. It saves so much trouble from having to live a real life.

As a result of the previously shown income growth rates, those of us in the MAJ have had a great deal of experience watching the Upper½% double their standard of living (reflected by doubling of income) much quicker than we did. As shown in the following graph-202, up until the early 1930s, the MAJ lagged a median 14 to 15 years behind the Upper½% in the years it took to double income.[144] Since 1984 we have lagged a median 67 years.

#202

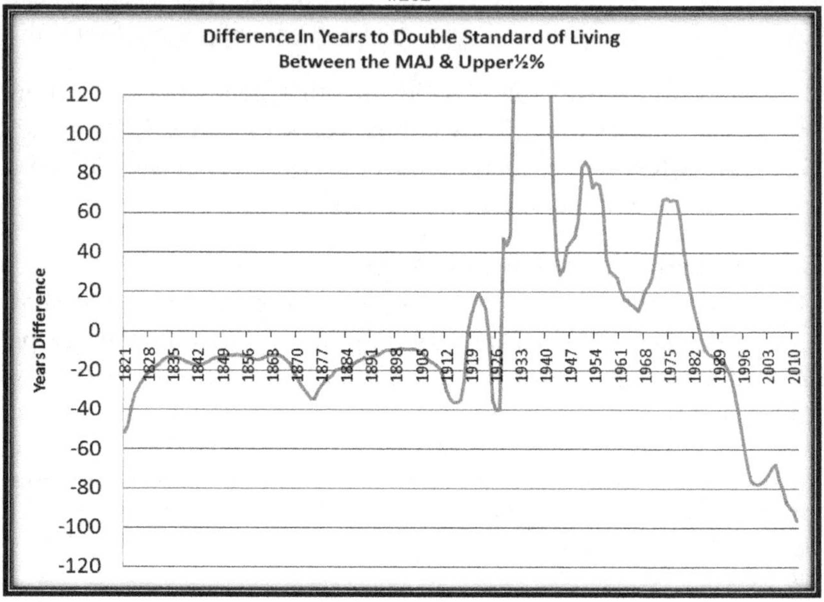

It sure feels a lot different than the 1930-1984 period when we doubled our standard of living a median 49 years quicker than the Upper½% did. We are still working on that vicarious living thing. So far it just ain't cutting it. In 2011, we were 96 years behind them. This sets a record for all of U.S. history. It hurts.

For those of you who revel in the chance to manage a maldistributed economy, this is your moment in the sun.

Growth in MAJ share fuels the engine.

Using a slightly different technique, the next two graphs (#203 and #204) will confirm the potent influence that the MAJ exerts on economic growth for us all. Prior graphs (#196 and #199) showed that when the actual growth of MAJ income (not necessarily MAJ share) exceeded a given threshold, economic growth accelerated.

Here, we explicitly see that when MAJ income share increases, GDP grows much faster than it customarily does. I emphasize that growth in MAJ share is the key component, say going from MAJ25 to MAJ29.25. A move of this magnitude in the graphs would be referred to as a 17% growth (horizontal axis) or a 1.17 change (vertical axis) in the MAJ share over 26 years [29.25= 25*1.17; or 29.25= 25+17%*25].

The upcoming graph-203 uses data for MAJ share and for GDP per capita over 26-year periods. It employs centered 11-year smoothed averages for both the start and end points. Instead of looking at the years to double GDP per capita as in the previous graph-202, we will simply look at the total growth of GDP per capita and MAJ income share over a generation for all years since 1840.

The following graph-203 covers 172 years of U.S. economic history. Only in 28.5% of those instances (49 years) did the MAJ share grow. The graph shows that the MAJ share was not static – it was either growing or decreasing. The dominant tendency in U.S. history has been to reduce MAJ share. The increasing maldistribution seen in the past 30 years is an acceleration of this tendency. It is not unique. Just old school on steroids.

#203

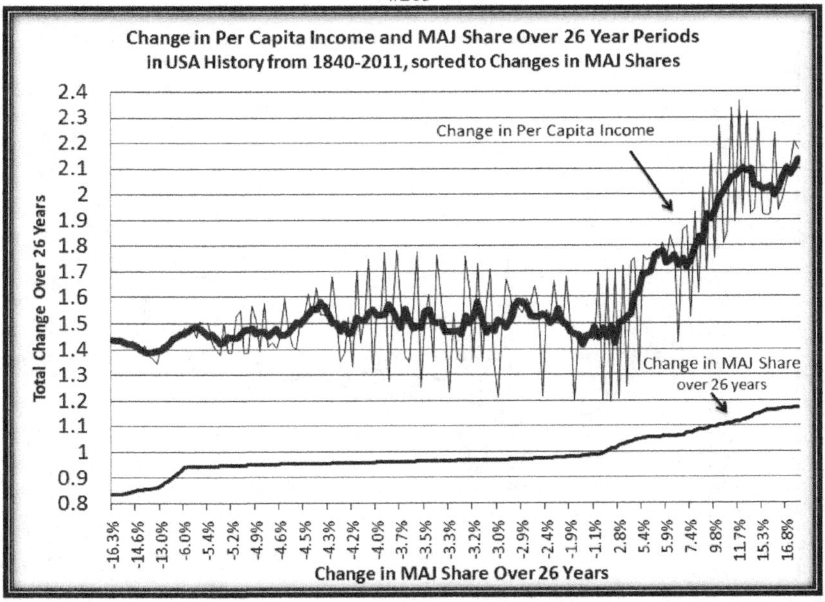

The only generations in U.S. history where GDP per capita grew exceptionally fast were those in which MAJ shares increased. You can clearly see in the graph that when MAJ share increased, economic growth accelerated. Many generations benefited. At the trend lines, even the Great Depression was insufficient in some instances to quell high generational GDP growth so long as MAJ share increased – a few examples: 1917-1943, 1918-1944, 1922-1948, 1923-1949, 1926-1952, 1928-1954, 1943-1969, and 1945-1971. In those few years when MAJ share increased, GDP per capita (standard of living) grew an average 1.85 times larger – growing 25% faster than in the years when MAJ share was decreasing. With sufficiently fast MAJ share increases, it was even possible to double standard of living within a generation. But during the years of decreasing MAJ shares, standard of living on average grew only 1.49 times larger in each generation. Empirically and theoretically, *a contracting MAJ share is typically one of the most pernicious economic activities that a nation can engage in.*

Macroeconomists (economists looking at the big picture of how a whole economy functions) are wedded to interest rates, monetary policy, fiscal policy, and a variety of arcane matters. *In front of their face stands a MAJ, which, when provided increasing shares of income, drives a formerly maldistributed economy forward – often far faster and more effectively than the tools they choose to employ.* Why the great predilection to look elsewhere?

#204

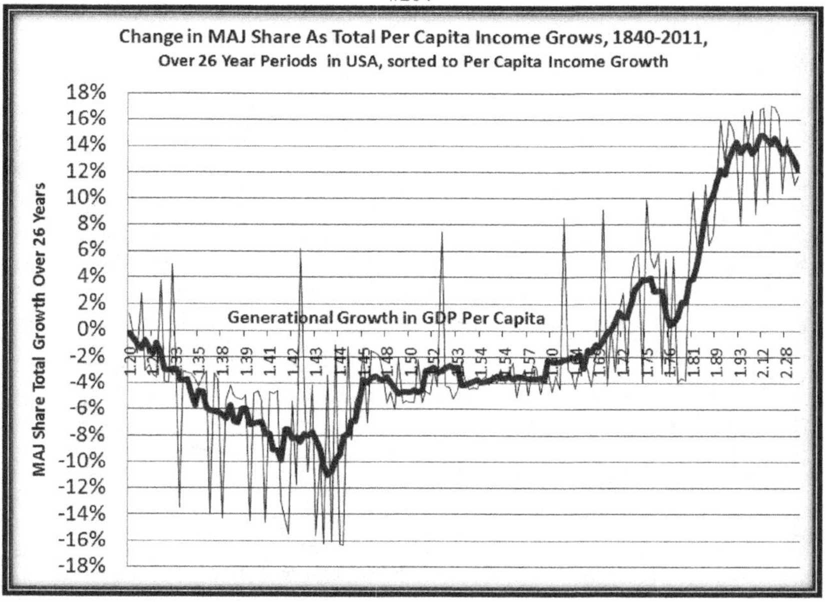

In the above graph-204, we look at the identical data but instead, sort it to growth in GDP per capita to see if any special MAJ-share-growth requirements exist. There is no period in U.S. history where the standard of living grew faster than 1.82 times in a generation in which MAJ share did not grow 5.9% or more during the same period. At the other extreme, when MAJ share contracted at a rate of 8.4% or more in a generation, there was no period in U.S. history when per capita income grew faster than 1.45 times in a generation.

Let's look at the two defining philosophies: 1) Stomp-on-the-MAJ and 2) Advance-the-MAJ. The Stomp-on-the-MAJ approach yielded a 1.42% annual GDP per capita growth rate or slower. The Advance-the-MAJ approach yielded a 2.31% annual GDP per capita growth or faster – at least 0.89% greater than when the MAJ was hobbled [1.42%= 1.443^(1/26)-1; 2.31%= 1.813^(1/26)-1; 0.89%= 2.31%-1.42%].

The 92% solution.

Our focus has been on the MAJ. It comprises 2/3 of the people beneath the teeter point. Let's look at all of U.S. history and expand the view to include all those beneath the teeter point – explicitly 92% of the population. The year 1928 was the most maldistributed year in all U.S. history and the welcoming point for the Great Depression. In the following graph-205 we look at income share relative to that year to indicate when we are dangerously close to catastrophe.

#205

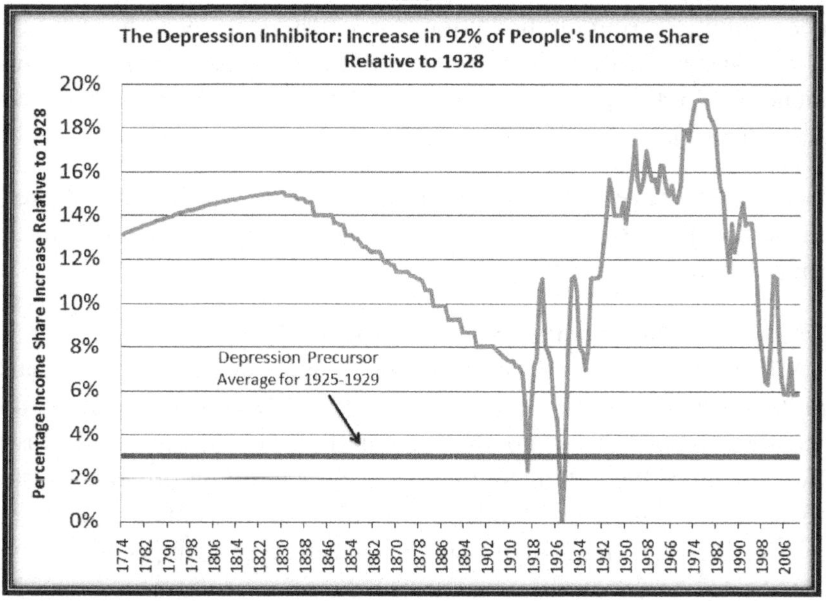

As I look at graph-205, I am reminded of a remark that Currie made about economists during the Great Depression:

"[N]o criticism was meted out to those professional economists who through this tragic decade betrayed their trust and continued to talk nonsense about balancing the budget and restoring confidence. They were promoted … The penalties for non-conformity were harsh. It is not surprising, therefore, that the New Deal secured so little support or

> help from economists as a class and that Roosevelt had a quite justifiable distrust of economists in general. ... For these various reasons, economists as a class made little contribution to the solution of the most critical economic situation that ever confronted the American people. On the whole, they were silent in those tragic years ... [I]t is not a record to which economists can point to with pride."[145]

In graph-205 it is plain that 92% of people in recent years have had an ever-reducing share of national income than they customarily receive. The life-blood of the economy is consumer income. You can employ infusions of government spending and increases in money supply to your heart's content to replace it, but my take is that *sucking the life blood out by way of maldistribution and then seeking to replace it with infusions of other kinds is silly and futile.*

For off-the-cuff thresholds: A Depression Inhibitor score in the above graph-205 needs to be 14% or higher to have a healthy economy; 12% for an economy teetering on disruptions; and 10% or lower to hear the clarion call of disaster. At that point, too much blood has been extracted from the patient. At 3.04% you are at the 1925-1929 average and can expect the same future that awaited those folks.

Those who revel in managing an increasingly maldistributed economy will be required to become magicians. Excuse me. I believe the proper term would be illusionists.

Not looking. Not caring. Not knowing.

A few pages back we saw how poorly monetary policy was managed and how it contributed to deepening the Great Depression. Data sufficient to create those charts was not available until the 1940s or later. To the great disadvantage of the nation, simple decision-making on obvious points was impeded, and some cases made impossible, because data and theory were not available. The Great Depression came full force unimpeded.

It would be nice if we could regard such poor economic data scenarios as the province of bygone eras only. That is not the case. One of the key contributors to economic catastrophe is, and has been, maldistribution – in the Great Depression and now. In both periods, crucial and timely data from responsible sources have been absent or wildly contradictory. The uncertainty that Allyn Young expressed in 1916 has been insufficiently removed. The consequences still hit full force unimpeded. Take a look at the history of MAJ data. When it declines, we as a nation decline just as readily as we did in the 1920s.

Prior to 1929, MAJ data is, and has been, unavailable from major sources. There remains a vast spread between recent minimum and maximum MAJs reported by major sources. With such a rat's nest of ambiguous data, the citizen and the economist are rendered powerless to take corrective action. In the face of dire lack of adequate data, all but a vanishingly few economists have cared enough to take action.

In October 2011, the Congressional Budget Office published the **first credible series** of income-distribution data for years subsequent to 1979. Bureau of Census household income-distribution data has been so seriously flawed that it is unusable. The following graph-207 illustrates the extent to which Census understates the Top5% income share relative to the better-supported Congressional Budget Office data [Percent error= Congressional Top5%/ Census Top5%-1].

#207

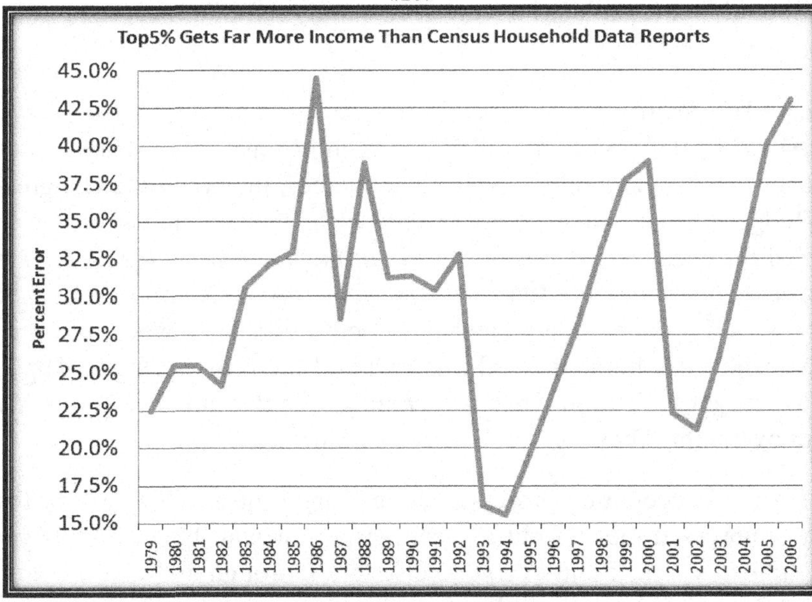

The discussion of distribution estimates and the severe failing of the Bureau of Census are serious and detailed, so it is placed in the Appendix, page 353. Should the matter concern you, you may want to look there.

A few pages back we started by illustrating that having inadequate monetary supply data and inadequate theory led to financial crises (particularly the Great Depression). You may have well thought, "How yesterday is that? Why not forget and move on?" A good reason not to forget is that recent Census data has been similarly defective. It would have been impossible to form competent theory or solutions based on it.

No criticism was meted out to those professional economists who through this past tragic decade betrayed their trust and continued to talk nonsense about monetary theory's capacity to cure the nation's ills. They were promoted. The penalties for non-conformity were harsh. It is not surprising, therefore, that income-distribution considerations secured so little support or help from economists as a class, and that the public had a quite justifiable distrust of economists in general. For these various reasons, economists as a class made little contribution to the solution of one of the most critical economic calamities that ever confronted the American people. On the whole, they were silent, providing neither prevention nor cure during those tragic years. It is not a record to which economists can point to with pride.

Should that remark strike you as uncannily familiar, may I suggest page 205.

Ought We Audit?

Always. The vast conflict between Census household income-distribution data and other responsible sources, including the Congressional Budget Office, makes it abundantly clear that we have been seriously misled for decades. *The problem did not involve fine points of deep thinking. It involved getting 100 numbers right (the backbone).* Census failed because it did not get the highest 5 of them right. They were not even held to a sufficiently high standard that required them to report the Top1%. If so, we might have seen what was coming. We did not. There was insufficient oversight. They were not held to a high standard.

I had an accounting professor, John King, who made a remark that always impressed me. "Audit to keep an honest man honest."[146] If you do not subject yourself and everyone else to a thorough audit, you court danger. A little fudge here, a little fudge there can lead to vast impropriety in a business. Your ship must be tight, whether in a storm or not.

In 1965, at the National University of Mexico I had another professor (economics), Edmundo Flores. He was a visceral, hands-on man. He embodied the difference between a primary source and a secondary one. He was distinctly primary – a player. He worked on many land reform programs throughout Latin America. A story of his sticks with me. He recited a textbook-perfect case of land reform where all the paperwork was in order and the offices were spotless and well managed.

He recited another. The offices were decrepit. Throughout the country they were filled with campesinos (peasants). Chaos reigned. The offices stank from body odor. There were so many fleas that you had to bathe often and frequently take more aggressive measures to keep them off you.

Which program worked? The latter. The reason. Success smells. Whenever real reform is involved, the stakes are high. In the former case, the paperwork and public affairs were unctuously handled. The peasants were not players. In the latter case, the peasants were players. They were unceasing to see that real land reform took place.

Though my accounting professor and Edmundo Flores were polar opposites, they reflected the same view. The process must be audited to keep it honest. If the data is fudged, a vested interest will lose – whether it be the upper 8% or the bottom 92%. With income and wealth distribution, the stakes are high. Parties high and low, labor and management, stockholder and consumer, national and international, all must have their independent option of audit. Without this basic activity, someone will be snookered. There will be no honest data. The data will be phony – the Census Top1% for example.

CH. 9

THE USA: to leave depression then & now

USA Great Depression recovery relative to leading nations.

For the five-year period prior to the Great Depression, 1923-1928, the dozen nations with highest GDP per capita in the world were, in ranked order: the United States, Switzerland, Australia, Netherlands, New Zealand, United Kingdom, Belgium, Denmark, Canada, France, Argentina, and Germany. Here we look at those nations during the antecedent years as well as during the U.S. recovery.[147]

#211

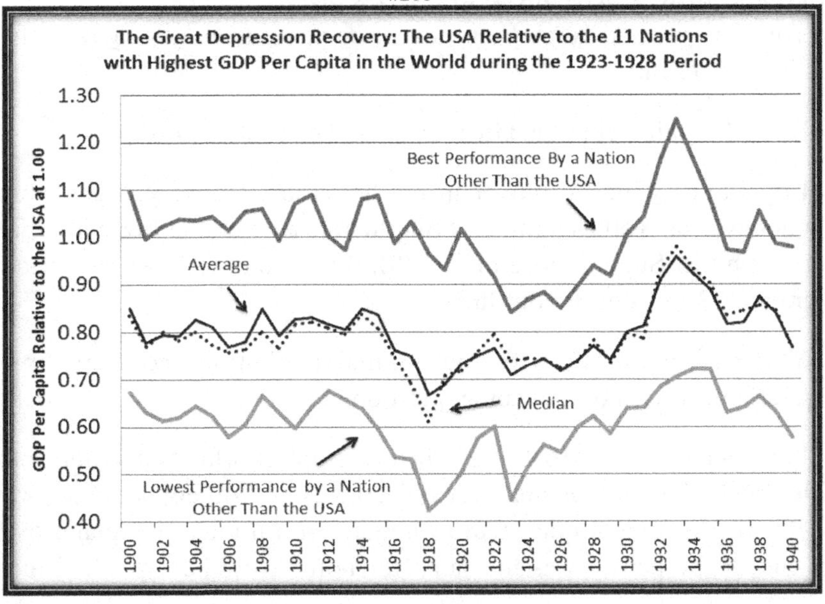

The U.S. GDP per capita is represented by 1.00 in graph-211. To have had a higher GDP, a nation would have needed to exceed the 1.00 threshold. From 1900 to 1915, Australia, New Zealand, and the United Kingdom at times did. In the post-WWI era, the U.S. was unsurpassed from 1921-1929. However, from about 1924 to 1933, all four graph lines show a decidedly upward trajectory indicating that most of the other nations were growing faster than the U.S. up until FDR's presidency.

After FDR took office, all four lines declined indicating that the U.S. recovery was exceeding the growth rates of the other nations in all four categories. In the 1930-1935 period, those nations which had a higher GDP than the U.S. were from time to time Switzerland, Australia, Netherlands, or the United Kingdom. In 1936, 1937, 1939, and 1940, the U.S. was unsurpassed.

A cult of economists is fascinated with Austria. For their benefit, the following is provided. In years discussed here, Austria did not provide a worthwhile example. In the 1920s, Austria ranked 15th in GDP per capita after Uruguay and better than Chile. From 1930-1938, its GDP per capita was 58% of the United States, and its trajectory was undistinguished. Austria is an admirable nation now, but for the Great Depression era, the effective performance of the U.S. provides the lesson plan, not Austria.

Then and now. Forty-one years. Jived up.

Tom Sawyer and Huck Finn juiced, on steroids, way-way over the top, and in the present:

Hey. You talk about the Great Depression. That is so yesterday.

Boy I ain't going to quiver in my boots just 'cause you got words. If you got eyes as well as a mouth train them here. Let that big mind of yours work with me. Superimpose the 1970-2011 era on the 1900-1941 era. Like in graph-213 in front of your face.

You start to jive me with your ok-maldistribution, monetarist, modern wonder boy stuff and I got some questions for you.

Put your eyes on 1929-1939. In the graph world, that is the same as 1999-2009. You let that sink in real deep. Unless you got some wizardry of the 9th dimension that I don't know about, don't it look like total growth by the end of the period was the same for both? New boy, you tell me that.

Don't your eyes tell you that ***the economy grew no more in the 1999-2009 period than it grew in the 1929-1939 period?***

#213

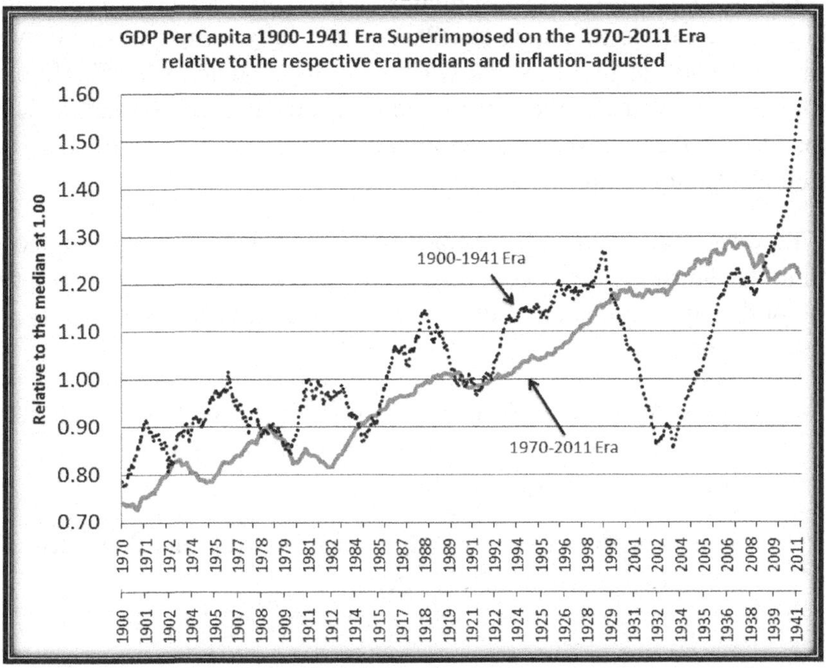

It was in the Mama of Depressions and they jumped out. It was pure crash. The real thing, when your pants ain't got no round nickel in 'em.

Hey, you so fond of dumping on the Man. 'Dose guys was in the pits. Where in all of U.S. history has there been such a quick, large, and sustained jump out? Don't your eyes show you that the jump out was well in hand before any war? And you tell me that when the Man gave the little guy a fair chance, it don't matter. You is illegal. New boy, you so wise, why you ain't done no better?

You run on about free this and free that. Well put your eyes on 1900-1941. You look at the bounce downs. Those old times was panics. You know, the boom bust. Just look at that line doing the total free market jump. It don't show that on those jump downs that it was the people that was getting stomped on. But that was what it was. It happened regular. 'Dem know it.

You put your eyes on the 1970-2011 line. You see that got smoother. In 1959, when the jump out way was still in progress Mikie called it "modified capitalism"[148] it gave fast growth, the little guy got a fair shake, and there was fewer bumps.

You think electric now. Oscillate like that old line. Try a few syllables. I know you can do it: Capacitor. When electricity jumps up and down and you don't want to jump in that way, you put a capacitor on the line. Sure enough you can make the juice calm so it don't jump as much. They got capacitors and resistors of more kinds than you can think of to change how much electricity jumps up and down. [149]

You see that graph line getting smoother. They put capacitance on it and took 'dat ripple out. Economists like other words. Boy I tell you this, if it smoothes it out, they are mostly in the capacitance business whether they know it or not.

Now some of those guys have got such big heads that they think they are mostly in the generator business. They don't know that they just in the capacitor business. They just big farads.[150]

Now you hear this. Don't you tell 'em this. It ruins their strut. They ain't no fun to look at when that happens.

Jobs.

In 1936, relief employment created 3.7 million jobs. Excess money supply growth may not grow jobs by itself, but the difficult and messy business of actually hiring people certainly does. Prior to 1933 and after 1941, relief jobs constituted less than 1.7% of total employment. The Great Depression distinguishes itself from all other periods in U.S. history because it had the nation's only large and effective public works jobs program. The amount of work accomplished and the benefit of these programs is stunning. The distance of roads that were paved in this period stands out in the records. The West Wing of the White House and numerous public buildings, parks, hydroelectric and flood control projects, and the like remain monuments of its success.[151]

The objective was jobs. All of my data include the military. From 1934-1939, the number of relief jobs created exceeded 6.6% of total employment, except for the year 1937 where job numbers were reduced to 5.7%.[152] In that year, a mini-recession occurred, presumably in response to reduced Federal spending and a tightening of money supply. FDR's Administration had prematurely reduced stimulus in that year, feeling that the 1936 rate of recovery was substantial and sustainable (1936 had produced an exceptionally high 12.5% GDP per capita growth). As you see in graph-215, at its peak, the extent of public works employment exceeded World War I military employment and was almost double Cold War military employment. The relief jobs were paid so little that up until 1976 they were not even counted among the employed.[153] It was a huge and remarkable undertaking to have been carried out on short notice and as a temporary measure. All of which was efficiently done vis-à-vis more recent deficits, especially those from 1980 onward.

#215

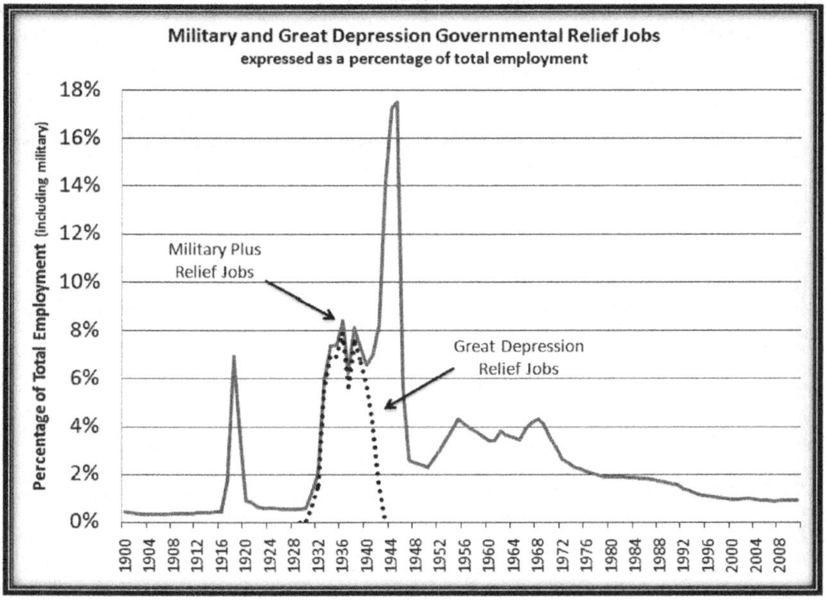

Following it came the World War II military employment which was far larger. Military employment peaked at 17.5% in 1945. Two years later, in 1947, it was 15% less – only 2.6%. The great miracle was that the economy did not nosedive in the post-WWII era.

Competent monetary, fiscal, income-distribution, and 40-hour work-week policies were great contributors. Then and now, workweek length is crucial because it creates jobs in a way that may surprise you. We will soon enough consider why, but let's return to the pre-Depression era to see if it has a story of its own to tell.

Put yourself in the minds of the people at the time of the Great Depression. As already observed, the Census declared 1890 to be the end of the American frontier. The common man was looking at the jobs picture getting progressively dimmer. This view can be understood when we look at the rate of job growth in the following graph-216. In the early 1900s, job creation was slowing and was largely unresponsive to money supply moves, already seen in graph-185 – the exception being the deep slump created by the mindless money supply contraction that accelerated and deepened the Great Depression. Well before then, growth in jobs was precipitously slowing. By 1927, job growth was lower than population growth, as shown in the following graph-216.

We need to focus on the point that the vast increases in money supply in the early 1900s did not stem the job growth decline. Both now and prior to the Great Depression, monetary policy has not rectified severe structural job growth problems.

#216

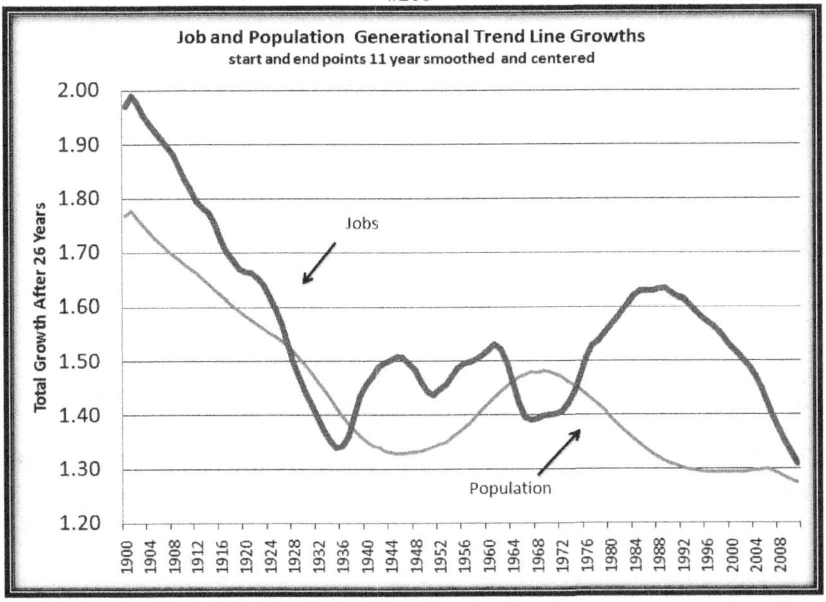

Prior to the 1980s, it was well within the ability of government to smoothly manage the equitably distributed economy, and to keep the economic growth ripples within acceptable ranges. In a maldistributed economy, a full employment mandate, either for the FED or for governmental spending, is problematical and may well be asking these entities to deliver corrective acts which are beyond their capabilities. In recent years, there have been only about 30% more jobs (1.3) than there were a generation ago. Not since the Great Depression has there been such a prolonged and deep long-term slowing in job growth.

Like the pre-Great Depression era, by 1989 the nation again turned the corner into the next great slump in job growth. It too was unresponsive to monetary policy. Keep in mind that these are generational long-term trends and not circumstances that are apt to appear much different in tomorrow's news.

#217

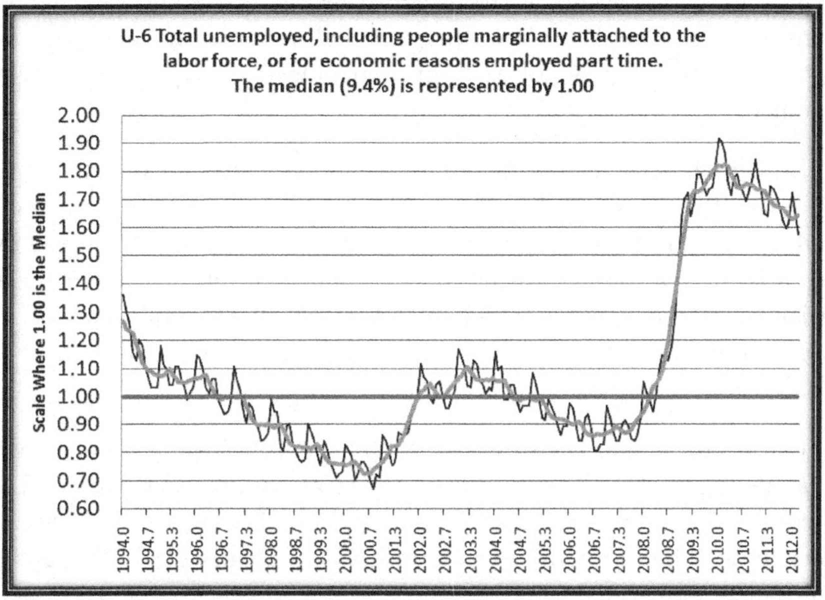

When I look at the above curve, I can't help but think that it looks like a dragon. The head, tail – the whole thing. But let's leave Rorschach notions behind and get down to business. The opposite of job creation is unemployment. The unemployment rate that we see in the news is the official unemployment rate: U-3 Total unemployed, a percent of the civilian labor force unemployed (e.g. 8.2%, in early 2012). The U.S. Bureau of Labor Statistics also publishes a less well-known, but more comprehensive rate: U-6 total unemployed (graph-217), which includes all persons marginally attached to the labor force and total employed part time for economic reasons (e.g., 14.5%, in early 2012).

The minimum U-6 unemployment since 1994 was 6.3% in the fall of year 2000. Its peak was 18.0% in the winter of 2009. Prior to the 2008 Calamity it seldom exceeded 11.3% (1.20 on the scale). At the height of the calamity U-6 was 80% larger (1.80) than customary conditions. A downward trajectory is in place. But the damage caused was so massive that we need to be rock-solid sure that such events are prevented.

GDP Growth = Jobs. Wrong or irregular? You bet.

To add each new job to the economy by way of GDP growth requires a large increase in GDP. It is not nearly so natural, easy, consistent, or automatic as some economists seem to suggest.

The creed is that GDP growth produces job growth. It is implicit that Okun's Law closely ties GDP growth rates with reduction in unemployment rates.[154] That 1962 law being revised periodically is perhaps a hint that the relationship is not as tight as people like myself had previously assumed.

Both monetary and fiscal policy presuppose that by expanding GDP, job growth follows in turn. Economic theory preponderantly relies on the GDP-Jobs relationship. After many years of taking the relationship between GDP and jobs as gospel, I was stunned to find that there is a huge variability in the extent to which normal GDP growth produces jobs. Often disproportionately large amounts of GDP growth are allocated to areas other than job creation.

Friends of the market economy, such as myself, have been too generous in assuming that a roughly consistent relationship exists between GDP growth and job creation. That is not the case. There is a disconnect. The capacity for GDP growth to create jobs varies greatly depending upon circumstances at the time.

I took all years of U.S. history where there was employment data and subjected it to two simple rules. The method looked at all years which shared two features: 1) positive GDP growth and 2) positive job growth. I then divided that incremental GDP growth by the incremental increase in jobs to get the average GDP increase needed to produce each added job during the year. The GDP increase per job was then divided by per capita GDP to have a consistent standard across years.

To keep the discussion realistic, consider the following example. In the year 2007, GDP increased $357 billion dollars, and jobs increased by 1.6 million, thus each GDP increase of $218,032 produced one added job. When we divide $218,032 by the GDP per capita of $49,514 we get the 4.4 multiplier referred to in the following graphs [$218,032= $354,501,944,130/ 1,625,917; $218,032/ $49,514= 4.40]. If you, like me, had expected this multiplier to be passably regular, you too would have been in for a surprise. As you can see in the following graph-219, even filtering using medians leaves huge variability. The disconnect between GDP growth theory and actual job production is great.

#219

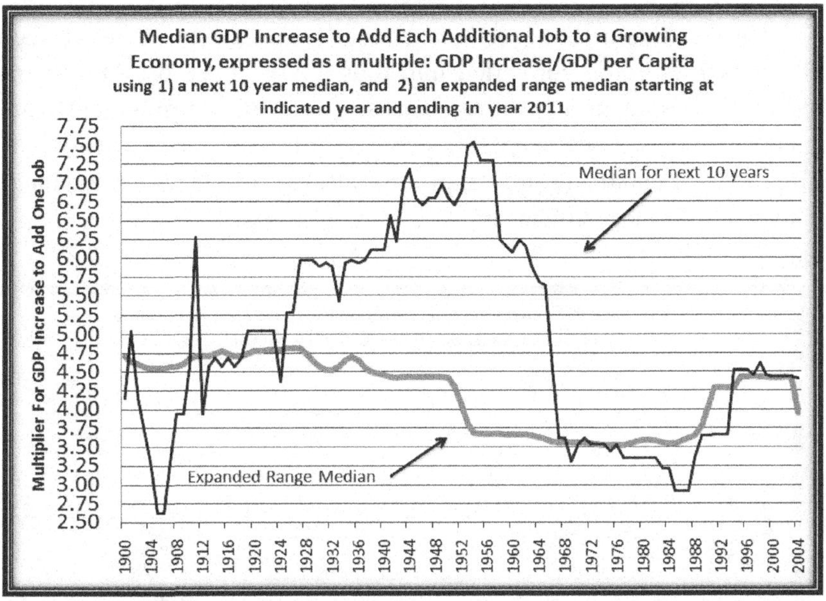

When it was most important for GDP to grow jobs, it was often difficult to do so. In the 1933-1939 period, FDR faced a multiplier of 5.45. The 1923-1929 median multiplier at 5.28 was not much different. In more prosperous times, it was often lower. The 1960-1979 median was 4.65, which was close to the 2007 4.4 multiple. The expanded range median graph line suggests that multipliers in a low range of 3.5 to 3.75 have been widely observed since 1952, but after 1995 they moved higher to a median of 4.5 – job creation getting a lower share of GDP growth. The rise in the multiplier may be contributing to the slowing of generational job growth previously shown in graph-216.

GDP Job Growth Allocation

Multiplier	Efficiency	Performance Relative to the 3.6 Base
5.7	0.63	-36.8%
5.6	0.64	-35.7%
5.45	0.66	-33.9%
5.28	0.68	-31.8%
4.8	0.75	-25.0%
4.5	0.80	-20.0%
4.4	0.82	-18.2%
3.6	1.00	0.0%
3.5	1.03	2.9%
3	1.20	20.0%
2.8	1.29	28.6%

A high multiplier indicates that new advances in GDP are going disproportionately into areas other than job growth. At 7.3 million added jobs in two years, President Jimmy Carter delivered the highest peacetime two-year job growth in all of U.S. history [1977, 3.26 million new jobs; 1978, 4.02 million]. He kept the multiplier within a 2.8 to 3.07 range during those years. In numerous recent years, GDP allocations have been heavily in areas other than jobs, as evidenced by their multipliers, for example: 2004, 5.7; 2003, 5.6; 1999, 5.6; 1998, 4.8; 2005, 4.5; and 2007, 4.4.

At least by this method we have a standard so we know how effectively GDP growth is being converted into jobs. GDP diversion into other areas may be justifiable in a healthy economy near full employment. But in a floundering one, or one desperately in need of increased job growth, a high multiplier is a canary requiring prompt attention [efficiency= 3.6/multiplier; Relative Performance= efficiency-1].

#220

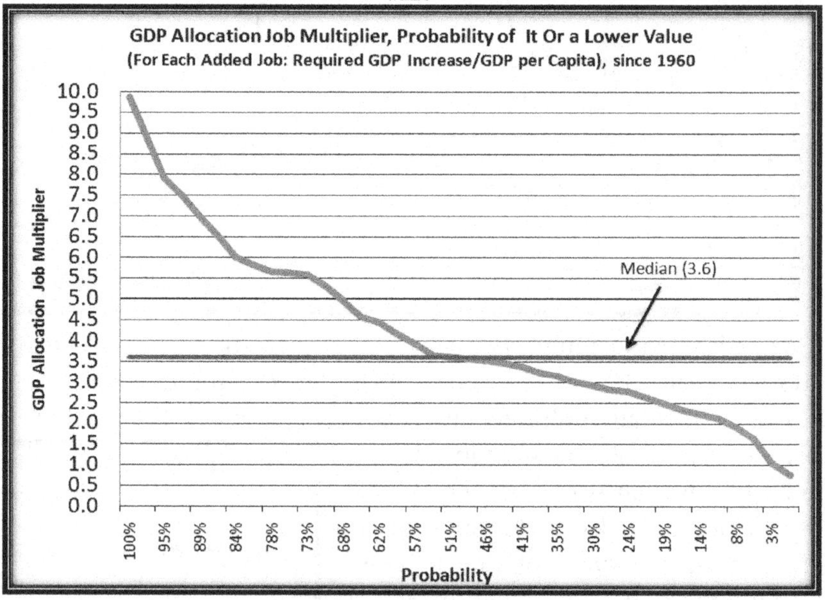

As seen above, the median multiplier has been 3.6 since the 1960s. Graph-220 also shows that to date, there has been a 73% chance that the multiplier would be less than 5.6. But in the same period, there was less than a 24% chance that the multiplier would be lower than 2.8. [Probability was determined by sorting the data and ranking it according to percentile.]

We now can take this analysis to the next level to see the GDP growth that would be required under the shown conditions to add 12.7 million people (the number of unemployed in early 2012) to the ranks of the employed. The advantage of using methods of this kind is that it becomes easy to evaluate whether management has done a superior job of adding new jobs.

The general muddy assumption that job growth systematically follows GDP growth too gracefully allows sloppy opinions to proliferate. A greater appreciation for identifying circumstances contributing to long-term job growth makes each of us a better and more informed player. With the data necessary for calculations being so easily available, DIY economics becomes possible.

#221

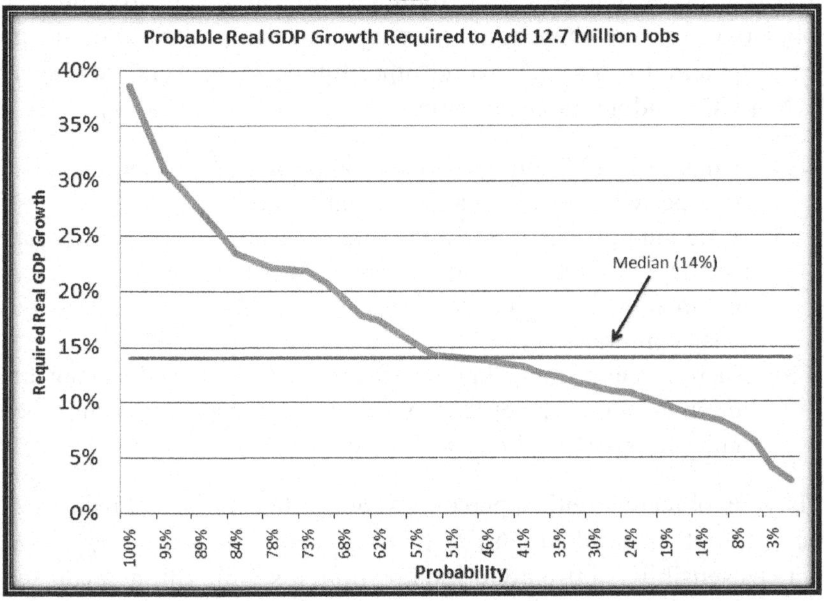

We see in the above graph-221 the *total* GDP growth rates necessary to add 12.7 million jobs, given the multipliers previously shown. These total growth rates would require several years of economic growth. The following table illustrates how we can anticipate the number of years of GDP growth that will be required to add the 12.7 million jobs.

To Add 12.7 Million Jobs Starting in 2012

Probability	Multiplier	Total GDP Growth	Years at 2.6% Annual GDP Growth Rate	Million Added Jobs Per Year
73%	5.6	22%	7.7	1.651
50%	3.6	14%	5.1	2.477
24%	2.8	11%	4.0	3.169

We have no way of knowing future GDP growth rates, but to the extent they vary from the 2.6% in the table, you can readily compute the corrected number of years it would take to employ 12.7 million [for example, 7.7 years= log(1+22%)/ log(1+2.6%), as in the first row]. Each of the rows correspond to the previous probability cases in the graphs, and refer to the probability of the outcome being at least as favorable as indicated.

In records not shown here, during the period 1993-2007, a median 1.872 million jobs were created in each year of growth; the multiplier was 4.4. Maximum job creation was 3.398 million. At the rate of 1.872 million new jobs a year, it would take 6.8 years to employ an additional 12.7 million people. This analysis can be tightened up mathematically and economic objectives may be changed (not hiring all of the 12.7 million, just getting unemployment down to 4.5% after other future job seekers are also included). Notwithstanding, three core messages can be carried away:

1) Bringing in 12.7 million workers into the ranks of the employed can be expected to be a long and difficult process.
2) If the multiplier is significantly higher than 3.6, then a disproportionate share of GDP is going into areas other than job creation. Depending upon the times, it is necessary to evaluate whether a high multiplier is appropriate.
3) There is a huge range in how effectively GDP growth is converted into job creation. The efficiency and proportional relationships between multipliers and the 3.6 baseline show it.

If your objective, either personally or while running a business during times of high unemployment, is to have your own spending and hiring practices sensibly contribute to job creation, a simple formula can serve as a general guide: The increase in your income or profit divided by "GDP per capita*3.6" minimally indicates how many new workers you would need to add to your payroll [$171,383= GDP per capita*3.6= 47,606*3.6]. If the result is a fractional number, then multiply it by 365 to find the number of additional days per year to employ an additional person. It then remains to be clever enough to find appropriate work to be done, and to have the person/people do it.

Relying on GDP alone to create jobs, and to take it as an article of faith that an appropriate number of jobs will be created, is hazardous. It is useful to consider ways that the employee and employer together can make job creation more efficient, less burdensome, and arguably more profitable. Let's look for ways of doing it, including in the following.

Workweek matters.

Economists are customarily dismissive about the capacity for workweek length to favorably influence employment. Their thoughts are driven mainly by ancient literature. I suggest doing the math and looking at the data, especially the role that the workweek played subsequent to the Great Depression.

Shorter workweek hours mean more jobs. I take the position that workweek length is central to managing an effective economy, whether it be during a Depression or any other time. If you should be eager to be old school on this, please continually ask your inner genie as you thumb through the following pages what unemployment might have looked like if the average workweek remained stuck at an average 52+ hours as it was in the early 1900s (the 1.3+ level on the following graph-223).

#223

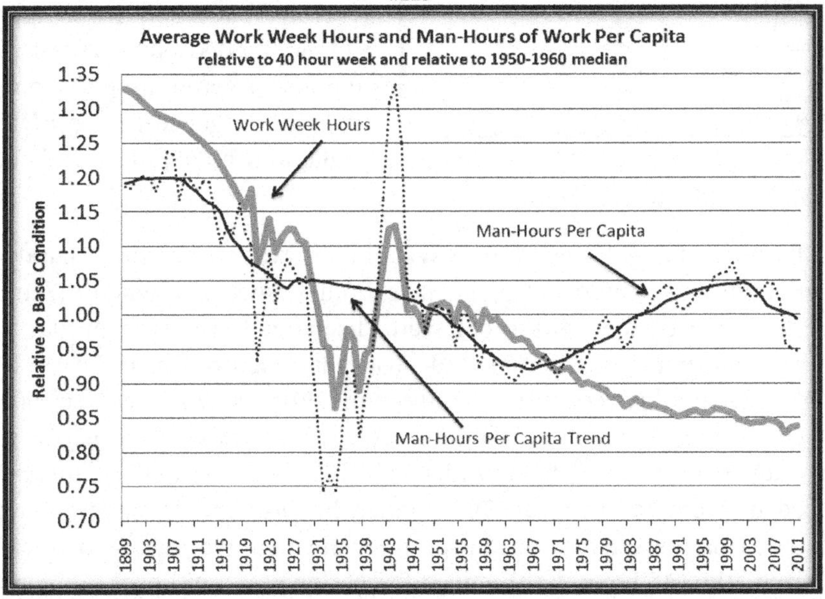

It does not take a great deal of math to see that the average workweek was 10% longer (1.10) in 1928 than it was in the 1950s. Workweek length was not falling fast enough in view of increased employee efficiency (man-hours per capita) [man-hours per capita = employed labor force * average hours worked annually / population]. The Fair Labor Standards Act of 1938 established time and a half overtime pay after 40 hours.

From that point onward, the 40-hour workweek became an integral part of American culture. The Fair Labor Standards Act of 1938 was 10 years too late. Had it been enacted in 1928, it would have required 10% more workers to perform the same work (man-hours of work) at the onset of the Great Depression. By not acting at that time, the adjustment took a cruel form later: a 10% boost in unemployment during the Great Depression. Vast unemployment was a defining feature of the Great Depression.

Summary of FDR Evaluation in Life Magazine June 27, 1938	FDR in General	His Personality	Wages & Hours
Southwest		98%	91%
The Poor	75%	93%	79%
Lower Middle Class	62%	89%	72%
Upper Middle Class	53%	85%	60%
Northeast		80%	57%
The Prosperous	39%	74%	45%
Average Labor	77%		
Unemployed	70%		
Houskeepers	64%		
Farmers	61%		
White Collar	59%		
Professionals	46%		
Students	39%		
Executives	35%		

In the week that FDR signed the Fair Labor Standards Act into law, *Life Magazine* provided a thorough and interesting FDR opinion poll. I summarize a portion that relates to his wage and hour policy in the table here.[155] Where wage and hour data were not available, the table shows a positive opinion of FDR in general. Wage and Hour approval ratings tended to exceed these amounts. Even among the prosperous, who in general rated FDR low (39%), 45% seemed to approve of his wage and hour policy and feel he was a likeable guy (74%).

To stress it again, after World War II there was no certainty that depression conditions would not again take hold – especially when 9.8 million people (15% of the workforce) were discharged from the military after WWII. The numerous booms and busts that occurred in the early 1900s might have readily reoccurred. Without the 40-hour workweek culture produced by the Fair Labor Standards Act, the workweek probably would have again lengthened to its old level (10% higher) and in tandem produced an unemployment rate 10% higher. In 1947, the President of General Motors, Charles Wilson, was pushing for the legal workweek to be extended from 40 to 45 hours.[156] We need to get down on our knees and thank all of those who brought about the Fair Labor Standards Act and kept it in force. Absent that change in work-hour culture, there would never have been a Golden Age of Capitalism.

A great miracle of capitalism is that it is so efficient. As measured by man-hours per capita, workers were required to deliver in the neighborhood of a median 840 hours of work to support each person in the population (child, parent, elder, or anyone else) during the 1950-1960 period – represented by the 1.00 in the prior graph-223. At the beginning of the century, it had taken 20% more hours to support each person (1.20). It achieved its post WWII peak in year 2000 at 900 hours and its minimum in 1964 at 760 hours.

Man-hours are not a question of ideology, for the right or for the left. They are central to understanding jobs. The man-hours of work per capita are a measure of how much work is required in a nation to support all people, working and non working. Less salubriously, it is also vacillates when economic activity changes, as you can see in its moves relative to the trend line. When it plummets in economically lean times, it tends to reflect a lower quality of life. If we pause and think in the grand scheme of things, the smoothed out man-hours of work per capita provides a reasonable picture of how much work was required to support lives at an acceptable standard of living for the era. It also may reflect changes in new segments coming into the workforce or the composition of nonworking members, such as children and the aged. We only need to multiply these figures times population to know approximately how many total man-hours of work a nation will need to deliver. By this means, the total work of a nation can be defined in man-hours.

A laudable objective is to put few hours into work, but to work efficiently and well in those hours so that you have more free time to do as you please. Between 1950 and 1990, the fewest man-hours of work per capita were 760 man-hours in 1964, and in that era there were several years close to it. The year 1964 was indeed good. The Index of Consumer Confidence employs it as its base year for its index. Since 1978, only 12% of months ranked higher. On the other hand, the month of August 2011 was the third lowest on record since 1978.[157]

By the man-hours per capita measure, 1960s capitalism was operating at a high degree of efficiency, with fewer hours than customary required to support each life. Most middle-class families at that time had *Life Magazine* on the coffee table, for its pictures of course. My coffee table remains stuck in the era with the February 14, 1964 edition on it. As I thumb through its many pictures, I see a 10-page long article: "The Emptiness of Too Much Leisure." In it I find, "Akron rubber workers had a 36-hour week for years ..." and various discussions of the prospect of suffering excessive man-hours of leisure, summed up by: "Problems, problems."[158] That was the era of the Affluent Society, where coping with efficiency was challenging. Little did they know how radically different the current economy would be.

The last word in efficiency is to support high quality life with few hours worked. The elusive "quality" divided by "hours-worked" ratio is subject to whimsical interpretations. What I regard as "quality" and "work" may differ greatly from a sane person. For example, writing this book. Much of it was just "playing." Portions of it were crushingly difficult. For that I am working on developing a less capacious memory that will remember it all as play. You see the quality/work ratio is nicely malleable. I will raise it by all means available to me. It is vastly preferable to the expression "utility" used in economics, which is even more malleable but certainly less fun. Ok, so much for that. Let's get practical.

#226

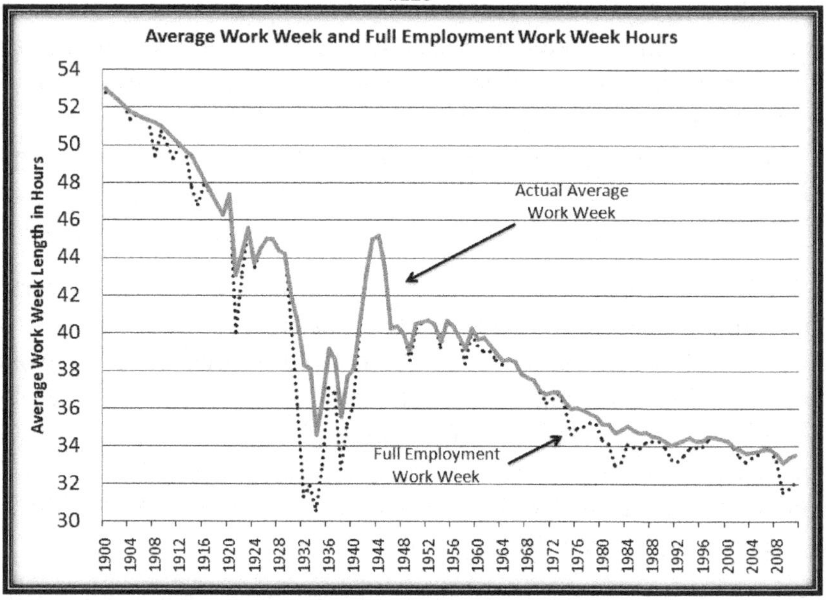

The above graph-226 may look plain, but there is a lot going on here. All of it is important, especially the full-employment dotted line that you see. While we may have a 40-hour workweek in our mind as a standard, we see that the average number of hours per week for all workers is a great deal less, considering holidays, vacations, and many people working reduced hours. As we saw in the earlier graph-223 , from about 1911-1924 there was a sharp decline in the number of hours worked per capita after which the improvements became more modest and variable. While some sectors could adapt to a 40-hour workweek, it still required a large number of hours of work to deliver a satisfactory living standard, which is to say conditions remained too primitive to adopt a shorter workweek nationwide without imperiling the standard of living. By the late 1920s, efficiency had advanced sufficiently that the 40-hour work week was appropriate.

We see in the above graph-226 that in 1929, the average workweek was 44.2 hours. By then, man-hours per capita had dropped greatly and the workweek needed to fall further. But even in retrospect, it is difficult to pinpoint when and by how much it should fall. When the market forces ultimately did exert their voice, it was done with a roar – then too late and with insufficient clarity.

On December 1, 1930, Kellogg's, the largest manufacturer of ready-to-eat cereals in the world, instituted a six-hour work day, which in part remained in effect until 1985. As the company owner stated, "if we put in four six-hour shifts … instead of three eight hour shifts, this will give work and paychecks to the heads of three hundred more families in Battle Creek." [Both are a 24 hour day: 24= 4*6; 24= 8*3.] The company president went on to state that the Depression had but one "remedy … shorter work periods."[159] Six hours a day, five days a week is a 30-hour workweek. By 1931, profits were double those of 1928.[160] In 1935, Kellogg stated, "39% more people were working at Kellogg's than in 1929." … "This isn't just theory with us."[161] In 1935 and 1939 they were boasting that the program was "an unqualified success"[162] A 1932 U.S. Department of Labor study looking at women workers, found that 85% preferred Kellogg's six-hour shift. Less pay was a key reason that 11% preferred the eight-hour shift.[163] Kellogg was not alone. In April 1933, Senator Hugo Black's Bill for a 30-hour workweek passed the Senate by a vote of 53-30, but was blocked in the House. To my taste, its language was too rigid. It prohibited in interstate commerce all goods produced by establishments where the workweek was more than five days and the work day more than six hours.[164]

This brings us to the crux of the problem in all ages: how to provide substantially full employment in a way that does not unduly strait-jacket other desirable aspects of the normal free market. Too frequently, economic changes cannot be anticipated, or programs to deal with them cannot be brought on-line fast enough. This is a great and constant problem for counter-cyclical policy. But keep your eyes open: Workweek hours may offer a rare opportunity for prompt, efficient market adjustments at extraordinarily low cost.

The full-employment workweek.

If the workweek were adjusted to the number of hours shown by the dotted line in the prior graph-226, there would have been substantially full employment in all years. For example, in 2011, the unemployment rate was 8.88% and the average workweek was 33.56 hours. If the objective were to pull the unemployment rate down to 4.5% (a normal full-employment structural unemployment rate), it would require reducing unemployment by 4.38% [4.38%= 8.88%-4.5%]. This correction occurs at a 32.09 hour workweek, as shown on the dotted line in graph-226 [4.38%= 32.09/33.56-1]. So we are best off following a simple rule: Let workweek hours vary in an upward way as they normally do, but whenever unemployment exceeds 4.5%, then shorten workweek hours. The dotted line in graph-226 shows the degree of workweek correction that would have been required at all points since 1900 to have achieved substantially full employment in the United States.

Unemployment stands in opposition to an effectively functioning market economy. Consumption comes from having jobs and paychecks. Without them, there is no market. When facing a downturn, or when seeking to increase profits or create special advantages for the owners, a business – even in good times – may lay off workers. Acting independently and rationally according to perceived self-interest, companies often dismiss employees even when it is clear that it is not in the best interest for the market as a whole for this to happen. Oblivious to the reduced revenues spawned by the parsimony, the market is damaged for all of us through excessive job cutting and the concomitant reduction in purchasing power.

An ancillary problem is that in a maldistributed economy, the worker's purchasing power is already so low that the corporation feels it can reduce their buying power further without seriously impacting corporate revenue. The 75-year old Fair Labor Standards Act needs to be amended to create flexible workweek lengths consistent with ever-evolving conditions. This is required to counter the tendency to drive the worker further south and to ensure that it is in the self-interest of the firm to employ an optimum number of employees – for both the firm and the market economy at large.

One day less for full employment.

You may already see where this is going. To summarize: We have a certain number of man-hours of work that must be performed. We have a workforce of a designated number of citizens who want to work who are divided into two sections: 1) those who work (the employed); and 2) those who don't (the unemployed). The average workweek defines the two classes: the employed and the unemployed. As the workweek lengthens, fewer people are needed to complete the work because each worker works more hours. As the workweek shortens, more people are required to complete the work because each worker works fewer hours.

As we saw in the previous graph-226, there were numerous points where the market had indeed produced full employment and there was no need for intervention. Here we will look at a method that would help to define workweek hours in a manner similar to the dotted full employment line in the graph. The following Table-229 describes with numbers the basis for the full employment program.

#229

One Day Less for Full Employment Program

Unemployment threshold	4-week Overtime Threshold	Fraction of 40-hour work week	Maximum Increase in Employment	Calc Days 2 weeks Normal	Calc Days 2 weeks Reduced
4.5%	40.0	100.0%	0.0%	10	10
5.0%	36.0	90.0%	10.0%	10	9
5.6%	35.6	88.9%	11.1%	9	8
6.3%	35.0	87.5%	12.5%	8	7
7.1%	34.3	85.7%	14.3%	7	6
8.3%	33.3	83.3%	16.7%	6	5
10.0%	32.0	80.0%	20.0%	5	4
12.5%	30.0	75.0%	25.0%	4	3
16.7%	26.7	66.7%	33.3%	3	2
25.0%	20.0	50.0%	50.0%	2	1

The first two columns in the table are key. The last two need not concern you. They are used to generate the appropriate fraction of a 40-hour week, which in turn illustrates the maximum increase in employment [e.g., 88.9%= 8/9; 11.1%= 1-88.9%; 35.6 hours= 40*88.9%. The one day less moniker results from this relationship in the last two columns.]. The program reduces the overtime threshold as unemployment increases. The employer has an option to hire more workers or to pay more to those he already has by way of overtime.

As long as unemployment is less than 5.0%, there is no need for additional intervention. Once the unemployment thresholds exceed 5.0%, the objective is for businesses to quickly promote job creation and to take incrementally more vigorous job creation at each of the steps shown in the above table.[165] This would be done not by requiring the firm to incur an increased man-hour load, but by creating an incentive for the employer to have more workers perform the man-hours of work already available.

The method is self-extinguishing, which is to say that since each step upward would reduce the unemployment rate, it would become increasingly difficult for unemployment to further increase. The tendency would be for unemployment to fall to the lowest achievable rate under existing conditions. And once normal structural unemployment of less than 5.0% resumed again, there would be no difference between this program and the current 40-hour week, 8-hour a day overtime standard.

However, if the market over an extended period was unable to support the 40-hour workweek standard at full employment, the workweek overtime standard would automatically become the then applicable 4-week Overtime Threshold listed in the second column. If businesses prefer the 40-hour week scheduling, together they will need to hire enough employees to keep unemployment less than 5.0%.

Passed in 1938, six years after unemployment had reached 15.5%, the Fair Labor Standards Act had its major effect subsequent to WWII, not at the onset of the Depression when prompt action was required. The difficulty, as we saw with the Great Depression, is that few activities other than direct relief or military employment took quick and effective action to reduce unemployment, and these were costly. The 40-hour ceiling on the normal workweek was slow in coming. An economy must be able to adjust its work culture so that workers and employees migrate to the number of workweek hours appropriate for both of them.

Any program, to be effective nationwide, needs to allow for an hourly daily unit divisible into the 24-hour day. Six or eight hours are fine, but eight hours are often preferable because of 25% less time spent commuting. Importantly, the employer needs to have sufficient scheduling flexibility within an extended accounting period so that even-length 8-hour work units will be compatible with what – under extreme circumstances – could be 10 steps for overtime pay determination (as indicated in the Overtime Threshold in the second column). To do this, the accounting period for overtime pay must to be no less than 4 weeks.

Except for the still-standing 40-hour overtime provisions resolved weekly, overtime excesses caused by exceeding the reduced-schedule hours listed in the table (less than 40 hours) would be paid after the end of each of the 4-week accounting periods. The employee would still collect a his/her customary check, with customary 40-hour-week and 8-hour day overtime included. But the portion of overtime resulting from the reduced schedule's overtime threshold would be determined at 4-week intervals.

One of the great impediments to flexible work scheduling of less than 40-hour weeks, is that the employer needs to have a designated number of work hours delivered, sometimes scheduling an employee for a different number of days in each week. For example in the 5.0% unemployment threshold case, working 9 days in two weeks (4 days in one week and 5 days in another) an average 36 hours of work per week. Easy enough. But at a the 5.6% unemployment threshold and 35.6 hours, the employer seeking to avoid overtime pay would need to schedule 13 days over three weeks in which: 1) in two weeks the employee worked 4 days; and in one week, 5 days; or, 2) in two weeks 5 days and in one week 3 days. The fine gradation within workweek threshold options and unemployment thresholds is necessary to have a method that is consistently and proportionately responsive to changes in unemployment.

Since in many instances, such as the above, the additional overtime could not be resolved in a period less than 3 weeks, it becomes clear that a one-week overtime accounting period for the short hours would be hopeless for many desirable average workweek lengths. This may well be a reason that the workweek standard has remained stuck at 40 hours for 75 years. It strikes me as mathematically impossible to migrate to an appropriately shorter week overtime standard within existing law which is based on a short 7-day accounting period.

#231

Unemployment threshold	Average work week hours in 4 weeks	Eight hour days in 4 weeks worked without overtime	Six hour days in 4 weeks worked without overtime	Hours worked in 4 weeks without overtime	Number of employees to deliver 16,000 man-hours, no overtime
4.5%	40.0	20.0	26.7	160	100
5.0%	36.0	18.0	24.0	144	111
5.6%	35.6	17.8	23.7	142	113
6.3%	35.0	17.5	23.3	140	114
7.1%	34.3	17.1	22.9	137	117
8.3%	33.3	16.7	22.2	133	120
10.0%	32.0	16.0	21.3	128	125
12.5%	30.0	15.0	20.0	120	133
16.7%	26.7	13.3	17.8	107	150
25.0%	20.0	10.0	13.3	80	200

In the above Table-231, we see the program from both the view of the employer and the employee. For illustration, as in the above table, take an employer who needs 16,000 man-hours over four weeks. At 40 hours a week, he is able to do this with 100 employees [16,000= 40*4*100]. The next step at the 5.0% unemployment threshold is deliberately the largest for the purpose of keeping the economy at full employment and promptly quelling tendencies for employment to rise much above the range of structural unemployment. Here, the average workweek drops to 36 hours, and the employer needs to hire 11% more employees than he otherwise would in order to meet his required man-hours to avoid paying overtime [11%= 110/100-1].

The table shows that as unemployment thresholds advance, the need to hire additional workers is modest, only a few at each step within the range of unemployment customarily experienced. The program does not impose an onerous burden on business, yet it gets unemployment down.

The continuous lowering of the average workweek overtime threshold creates a modest but constant pressure to increase overtime expenses, thus keeping pressure on the employer to reduce unemployment, even in cases where the actual number of employees shown in the table does not appear to change much. The small gradations help to keep the employer's eye open to spreading the man-hours of labor over more workers whenever unemployment rises.

There are numerous strategies the employer can use to reduce unemployment and to also reduce his potential overtime burdens. 1) Ahead of any increase in unemployment, hire a few workers in amounts suggested in the table, at say 6 hours a day, who can become familiar with company operation and be ready to fill in 8-hour slots as needed and to keep nationwide unemployment down. This gives on-the-job training, flexibility for promotion, and the ability to meet surges, and keeps unemployment low nationally. 2) Encourage employment in other firms and government. Hiring workers elsewhere by anyone, government or private, benefits you. It reduces the chance of unemployment rates rising. Treat companies and people who needlessly cut jobs as pariahs.

A culture of identifying work that needs to be done and hiring people to do it needs to prevail. By doing so, the chance of high unemployment and a moribund economy is reduced. As an employer, you benefit from a culture of job creation, not job destruction. How else will the market for your products grow? Many people now have never had a job and their parents, too, may be equally inexperienced. To give them a chance is potent medicine. The presumption is that intelligent management is just that. Intelligent. It can find opportunities for profit of all kinds and employees of all kinds who can deliver profits to improve the company and the country.

As for most of us who are the employees, the first step to a 36-hour week at 5.0% unemployment is the greatest. As with the employer, the objective is to quickly reduce likelihood of unemployment getting a toehold. In a 4-week period, you would customarily work twenty 8-hour days. Instead, on the reduced schedule, you would work 18 days and take 2 days off every 4 weeks. This first step needs to be a large one. The average workweek has already migrated far south of 40 hours and about half of all jobs are not hourly. Thus, even with a large step, its proportional influence on job growth is apt to be considerably less than the maximum 10% reduction in employment that you see in Table-229. If unemployment continues to require additional downward pressure on it, you make additional reductions (many of which are small after the first step).

Now you, as an employee, have a conversation with yourself: "How much more will I be asked to sacrifice?" We have already seen the answer in a disguised form. The smoothed man-hours per capita has largely varied ±5% since the 1950s, as we saw in the graph-223. So within the larger economy, those man-hours of work are out there. The ±5% fluctuations in employment exist mainly within a range that can be cancelled out in the early steps of the program. The first step you take may be sufficient to reduce unemployment by the customary 5%. Since 1950, the maximum spread between the full employment level and actual unemployment was 5.05% in 2010.

But if, in that conversation with yourself, you still are not persuaded, put in your mind a scenario of going from working 40 hours a week to working 30 hours a week (working 15 days instead of 20 in a 4-week period). The Kellogg workers made a single step move into the 30-hour week. Many of them found that going directly from the 8-hour day to the 6-hour day to be positive (a 40-hour week to a 30-hour week), notwithstanding the lower paycheck. In the program here, the steps are gradual, seeking in each step, to find the minimum dose of workweek correction necessary to effect the unemployment cure.

In that conversation with yourself, you may have consulted the graph-226. There you would have seen the floor for the full-employment workweek was 32.09 hours in 2011 – a rare case, which except in recent times, has not been seen since 1938. Perhaps this is a hint. Running a maldistributed economy has been trickier than some seem to think. So you were wise to keep probing. The times now are unusual. They require solutions that are not usual. Figuring on a low of 32 hours in a maldistributed economy would seem to be a current possible worst case. By removing the constraints that maldistribution now places on the market economy, I believe you will find the MAJ again having strong incomes, and capitalism producing the jobs that create them.

Further, by quenching maldistribution, those in the MAJ often would find their average income undiminished. To take an example, working 10% fewer hours and going from a MAJ25.8 maldistribution to a more equitable MAJ28.7 would have reduced unemployment, yet MAJ income would have remained constant [28.7= 25.8/.9]. On your own, you can readily do various combinations of workweek length up to MAJ33. I believe you will find numerous combinations that produce a thriving market economy with strong consumer demand, low unemployment, and a shorter workweek.

A shorter workweek gives birth to opportunities outside your main job. In the mountains where I live, many people, work a full-time job to supplement income from their small farm. Similarly, if you have other interests (playing in a band, running a small business, inventing things, growing a garden to have fresh vegetables, et cetera), having that steady paycheck coming in gives you sufficient economic security to allow your personal interests to thrive. With a shorter workweek, you have the advantage of a steady paycheck and more time to devote to your other life – a life from which you and others can benefit.

A workweek of improperly long length is responsible for the two classes: the employed and the unemployed. The greater the impropriety, the greater the unemployment. In times of economic downturns, GDP and man-hours of work drop. The means of reduction is normally to throw people out of jobs. These will always be harder times, but for the unemployed, it can become utter deprivation rather than just hard times. Harry Hopkins, FDR's man and no academic wallflower, put the case clearly "Hunger is not debatable. ... People don't eat in the long run, they eat every day."[166]

They also, every day, have families, children, confidence (called consumer confidence in the leading economic indicators), work relationships, networks of friends, trajectories of success (schooling, work, et cetera) that reach far out into the future, and more. The interruption and destruction of these is unpardonable. By a workweek that automatically shortens, the pain is at least shared, not heaped in undue proportion on the unemployed alone.

On a less equitable note, I am reminded of two observations Currie made during the Great Depression:

> "One of the findings, which I had to publish in rather guarded fashion, was on the nature of the deposit withdrawals that precipitated bank closings. The popular impression fostered by newspaper photos, was that banks were forced to close because of the host of small depositors who ran on banks in a fit of unreasoning (and unreasonable) panic. We found, on analysis, that in bank after bank the damage had been done by large withdrawals by people with inside information considerably before the final runs started. This abuse of trust by directors and their friends is not a pretty chapter in American financial history."[167]

> "… [A]t the end of 1935 the demand deposit of consumers were probably no more than one-sixth of the total. The remainder was distributed among business, finance and public groups. … [B]etween the end of 1933 and 1935 business and finance increased their money holdings substantially, which indicated a failure to pass on all their receipts from the public."[168]

Even as I write now, the hoarding of cash and the simultaneous refusal to hire more workers is widely reported in the financial news and by friends – temp workers, consultants, outsourcing. Anything but putting people on the payroll is the rule. Corporations need an incentive to get people on the payroll, and the prospect of additional overtime charges if they do not do so must be in place long before unemployment rates increase. The corporate culture needs to look at any massive layoffs and plant closings by one of its cohorts as an evil that will increase their own in-house overtime pay as a consequence of national unemployment rising.

The grotesque nature of the current hiring process, regimented first by resumes of such an arcane nature that their word soup formulation is demeaning, is then exceeded by the humiliation of computer robots refusing to consider the overwhelming majority of applications. The *Wall Street Journal* (January 2012) caught the spirit of the undertaking in an article's title "Your Résumé vs. Oblivion."[169] Too often and for too many, it is hopelessly difficult to get a job.

It is good capitalism to adapt to an appropriately short workweek. Henry Ford got it right: "Where people work less they buy more."[170] It worked in the past. It works now. It reduces the dole and puts people on payrolls. Those newly added from the ranks of the unemployed have exceptionally high propensities to consume. All of this may help to provide a leg-up during recovery. But the chief gain is not pecuniary, it is the vitality of having a job that makes it much more likely that you and your family will possess ethical values that provide the essential weave in the social fabric that distinguish a successful nation from one that is not.

Recall those the 10,000+ hours that John Lennon and all other greats in their own fields put in. When you do not grant employment, and when you take people out of employment, you are removing them from the future capacity to contribute. This is too great a price for any nation to pay. As Michael Yates put it, "As we work, we not only make useful things, we also make ourselves. Through our work, we become what we are."[171] It cannot be unemployed versus employed. For us all, it's a shared destiny. We work. We do it to the best of our capacity. We do it in a way of mutual respect and dignity. The way of honest work.

Those who discourage it need to be met with opprobrium, not reward or respect.

Fair wages and employment are not a bane to an economy but its sustenance. As Adam Smith quaintly put it in 1776:

> The demand for those who live by wages … necessarily increases with the increase of the revenue … of every country, and cannot possibly increase without it. … The demand for those who live by wages, therefore, naturally increases with the increase of national wealth … It is not, accordingly, in the richest countries, but in the most thriving … that the wages of labour are highest. … The wages of labour … are *much higher in North America than in any part of England.* … [T]he real command of the necessaries and conveniencies of life which it [wages of labor] conveys to the labourer, must be higher in a still greater proportion. … North America is not yet so rich as England, [but] it is much more thriving, and advancing with much greater rapidity … [emphasis added] [172]

If the above does not move you, try the math.

Let's look at two cases: 1) the descent that has occurred since arguably the most efficient year during the Golden Age of Capitalism, 1964; and 2) the descent from 1920 into conditions that contributed to (or brought on, depending upon your view) the Great Depression. In the first case we see that by 2011 the MAJ share fell to 84.6% of its prior level, and work hours fell to 87.1% of their former level. If maldistribution had not occurred, the MAJ income would have been 1.821 times greater, and each work hour would have been worth 1.357 times more.

As shown in the table, the Great Depression transition components were *less* severe than those that we have experienced since 1964. Explicitly, in case #2, if maldistribution had been reversed, the gain for the MAJ would be less at 1.168. Similarly, the work hour value multiplier was less at 1.254. The strategy of reducing the workers' share of income was an abject failure in both cases. Period.

Golden Age vs. 2011

	2011	1964	2011/1964
gini	48.9	42.0	
MAJ	25.8	30.5	84.6%
Avg. Hours	33.6	38.5	87.1%
Reversing the Maldistribution Advantage			1.1821
Hourly Pay Advantage			1.3571

Pre Great Depression Transition

	1928	1920	1928/1920
gini	52.5	45.9	
MAJ	23.6	27.6	85.5%
Avg. Hours	44.2	47.4	93.2%
Reversing the Maldistribution Advantage			1.1697
Hourly Pay Advantage			1.2544

The other way. Cut your pay.

Graph-238 covers 108 years. In 48 of them, the hourly income for the MAJ was substantially stuck and not advancing. Specifically, the years of MAJ wage stagnation can be found in six periods (length indicated in parentheses): 1903-1909 (6), 1924-1934 (10), 1946-1951 (5), 1978-1987 (9), 1990-2000 (10), and 2003-2011 (8), the last of which is still in progress.

We see that hourly inflation-adjusted MAJ income averaged $1.85 per hour during the ten years from 1924-1934 – $14.80 per eight-hour day. That is in today's dollars.

Let's be clear on this. It means that in today's marketplace of goods and services you would need to feed yourself, your family, pay the rent, pay the cost of getting to and from work, and all else on $14.80 a day. That was the 1924-1934 standard. It was the average hourly income that existed in the "roaring twenties" and the early years of the Great Depression.

The roaring twenties that you hear about … it roared for the rich, but not for the MAJ. The 60% majority was stuck at a substantially stagnant inflation-adjusted hourly pay, and it was a paltry low one at that – too feeble to support the demand necessary to fuel the economy, as became plainly evident with the onset of the Great Depression.

Many economists routinely dismiss the advantage of a rationally short work week. You might then ask, what is their solution for reducing unemployment. It may startle you. So if you are, say, standing on a subway while reading, or in some other precarious position, I urge you to put this book down instantly and wait until you are comfortably seated in a suitably soft chair. This one might knock you to the floor.

#238

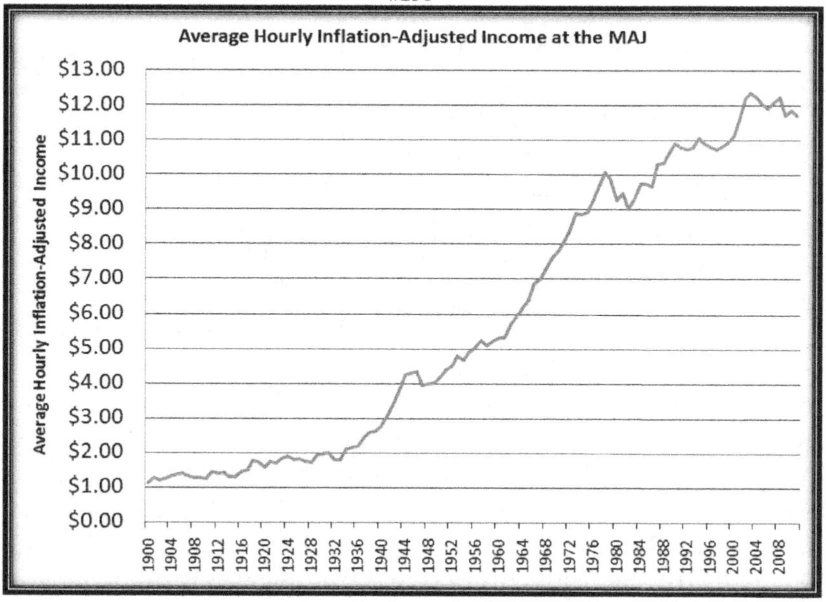

Ok, I trust you are now comfortable and prepared. I will dish it out. To solve the unemployment problem during the Depression, the learned economist takes the person earning $14.80 a day and cuts his wages, say to $12.58 a day [$12.58= $14.80*(1-.15); a 15% pay cut]. Do not throw this book. This was not my idea. Huge numbers of economists look at demand and supply curves day and night. They are well paid. They know all about things like this. They study and teach it to vast numbers of people. Their position is that if you cut pay, then you reduce unemployment. Cut pay any way you can. Throw out minimum wages. At any increase in unemployment, cut wages quickly. A wage of $14.80 a day can easily be cut lower. But as an employer, don't go beneath the point where frank and obvious death by starvation occurs or where rotten eggs and tomatoes might be tossed at you.

The old term for the borderline starvation practice is "The Iron Law of Wages."[173] The mention of suitably-aged eggs and tomatoes brings to mind their uncommonly persuasive properties. In the sailing boat era, Chinese pirates would carry a sufficient quantity of stench-producing material that, when buckets of it were flung on their victim ships, they could take over the complete ship while the crew fled from the smell.[174] So as you see, even "Iron" is malleable when a sufficient stink is raised. A modern stink is to primarily purchase from firms that provide fair bottom-to-top compensation distributions, and to shun firms that don't.[175]

Cost cutting to abolish unemployment goes something like this, although the numbers certainly will vary: You have 17 people earning $14.80 a day, costing the employer $251.60 a day. Unemployment reaches 19.5%, as in the Great Depression, and you want to reduce unemployment to 4.5%, which means you need to hire about 15% more workers.*

Let's take this sick thinking step by step. The Great Depression was caused primarily because the income going to the 60% majority was reduced to less than 25% of total earned income (the MAJ25 condition that we have so frequently discussed on past pages). When unemployment needs to be reduced 15%, you then reduce the workers' pay yet further from $14.80 a day to $12.58 a day. By doing this, the employer will hire 20 instead of 17 workers, thereby keeping his total payroll at $251.60 and getting about 15% more man-hours of work. In a depression, there are so many people desperate for a job that even an offer of a low wage is presumed to be sufficient to attract an employee. This reduction in pay takes worker income which is already pitifully low (MAJ25) and reduces it yet further. It also requires the worker to work as hard as before, but to get paid less for it. (No time off here. Keep the nose to the grindstone.)

When the worker refuses to accept the deal, your academic economist refers to his wage as being "sticky." I suggest another "s" word: "sensible" – as in "sensible worker." The issue is hardly moot. In Ben Bernanke's year-2000 book, *Essays on the Great Depression*, we find:

---

* $251.60=17*$14.80; $251.60=20*$12.58; 15%=19.5%-4.5%; 20=17/0.85; 15*1.15=19.55, rounded off to 20 workers. Actually 17.6%=20/17, thus the following illustrations will understate the adverse consequences of attempting to reduce unemployment by cutting wages by referring to 15% changes in quantity when 17.6% changes in quantity would be more likely.

> [W]hy didn't the 'normal' stabilizing mechanisms of the economy, such as the adjustment of wages and prices to changes in demand, limit the real impact of the fall in aggregate demand …?[176]
>
> In particular, if the nominal wage is 'too high' relative to labor market equilibrium both the employer and the worker (who otherwise would be unemployed) should be willing to accept a lower wage, or to take other measures to achieve an efficient level of employment … reconciling wage-price stickiness…[177]
>
> [I]t is hard to understand how nominal wages could have been so unresponsive. Wages had fallen quickly in many countries in the contraction of 1921-22. In the United States nominal wages were maintained until the fall of 1931…[178]
>
> The tendency of real wages to rise despite high unemployment was especially striking in the major depression cycle (1929-37) … Why real wages should rise when the demand for labor is presumably very low is difficult for any existing approach, equilibrium or disequilibrium, to explain …[179]
>
> The New Deal era, 1933-41, was a period of general economic growth, set back only by the 1937-38 recession. This economic growth occurred simultaneously with a real wage 'push' engineered in part by the government and the unions. As we normally think of higher real wages as depressing aggregate supply, how can these two developments be consistent? … Maybe Herbert Hoover and Henry Ford were right: Higher real wages may have paid for themselves in the broader sense that their positive effect on aggregate demand compensated for their tendency to raise costs.[180]

If you did not catch it, in economic theory, the general thread starts with the belief that the worker should accept lower pay so that supply and demand curves meet at a point that reduces unemployment. FDR and his associates grew the economy by increasing wages. It continues to spawn economic befuddlement, despite the success.

You will find in the spreadsheets that the concern about wage stickiness was preceded by a far greater stickiness in the Top1% throughout the 1920s, when they grabbed a disproportionately large share of total income. That is where true stickiness was. It was sufficiently great to reduce the 60% majority's income share to a paltry MAJ23.6 by 1928 (the lowest on record). The learned economists do not have the income-distribution spreadsheets of the kind we consider so frequently here, nor have they taken the trouble to develop the estimates on their own. Their immutable theories are too often wrong and of stunningly ancient origin. The worker, and often his employer, were far wiser than the trained economist for refusing to cut wages.

Let's pause to think of the 1920s. Not only were MAJ wages substantially stagnant in the 1920s, but general economic growth for the entire nation seems to have been slowing relative to other nation's performances during the 1920s, as shown earlier in graph-211. The evidence of slowing growth relative to other nations coupled with the stagnant MAJ hourly income was warning that demand was becoming increasingly insufficient. To have continued with stagnant wages or to have accepted frankly falling ones would have been a maldistribution prolonging disaster and would have deadened the 1933 onward recovery.

It was well known in the Great Depression that there was already a tremendous glut of goods on the market that people could not afford to buy. To reduce worker pay so that yet more goods would be produced by formerly unemployed workers would neither profit the employer nor the employee – goods must be sold to be profitable. If you argue that the price of the goods would fall to a sufficiently low price to induce the needed demand, we will soon enough see why that would not be the case.

The wage cut fallacy.

Wage cuts are not fully passed on as price cuts for the consumer. And it is the consumer price that must be changed in order for the quantity demanded (sold) to increase. Middlemen, owners taking off a fraction of the wage cuts to increase their profits, and labor being but one of many costs of running a business, all tend to make the labor wage reduction component of the store shelf price far more modest than the initial 15% labor wage cut. At a labor cost of 30% of market price, it would be highly optimistic to assume that a 4.5% price reduction enabled by the wage cut will induce a 15% increase in demand. To the contrary, the glut with vanishingly few exceptions will increase [4.5% price reduction= 15% reduced labor cost*30% (if optimistically, all of the labor savings is passed through); with 20 instead of 17 workers, 15% more goods would be coming to market assuming labor efficiency does not change. PED= 3.3= 15%/4.5%].

The ineffectiveness of wage cutting to reduce unemployment becomes transparent when we get precise. Here, **Price Elasticity of Demand (PED)** is equal to the absolute value of the percentage change in the quantity sold divided by change in price [PED= %QuantityChange / %PriceChange]. Estimated price elasticity of demand for various items are shown in the following table.[181] These roughly indicate customary market conditions, but can decrease greatly in a depression and can vary according to market conditions.[182] For example, in the table, housing decreased from a 1.5 PED to a 0.3 PED when the market turned sour.

	Price Elasticity of Demand ABS (PED)	Price Reduction to Get 15% Quantity Increase	Price Reduction to Get 10% Quantity Increase
Housing (poor market)	0.3	50.0%	33.3%
Gasoline (long run)	0.31	48.4%	32.3%
Egg (Canada)	0.35	42.9%	28.6%
Beef	0.4	37.5%	25.0%
Physician Services	0.75	20.0%	13.3%
Clothing	1	15.0%	10.0%
Furniture	1	15.0%	10.0%
Books	1.4	10.7%	7.1%
Housing	1.5	10.0%	6.7%
Marijuana	1.5	10.0%	6.7%
Restaurant meals	2.3	6.5%	4.3%
Compact car	2.8	5.4%	3.6%
Soft drink like Coca-Cola™	3.8	3.9%	2.6%
Foreign travel	4.1	3.7%	2.4%
Tomatoes	4.6	3.3%	2.2%

Necessities tend to have low PEDs and luxury items or items that require a large proportion of the consumer's income tend to have high PEDs. The simple rule is that as a PED increases, ever-smaller price reductions have a mathematically increasing capacity to increase quantities sold. This becomes especially evident when a PED exceeds 1.0. When a PED is less than 1.0, even large price changes can be insufficient to greatly increase the quantity sold.

For example, eggs at a PED of about 0.35 have an inelastic demand. Lowering the price 42% would bring only about 15% more of them to market. Even substantially greater price reductions typically won't result in consumers buying vast quantities of eggs. After eggs for breakfast, lunch, dinner, an egg snack while watching TV, munching on eggs while on the phone, slurping on eggs while driving, et cetera. At some point you and the market reach the egg limit.

You get the drift. Many items, particularly the staples we daily rely on, do not much increase quantity sold once the basic need is met.

So from the outset we know a great deal. Any policy based on reducing the item's price by lowering the cost of its labor component will have a highly uneven influence across industries. Industries with low PEDs will experience triflingly small increases in quantity sold. Even with high PED luxury goods, the wage cutting program is unlikely to restore full employment. Let's see how the worm works.

We focus on the 15% column in the table because when 15% more workers are employed, it is likely that they will produce 15% more items to be sold. This is the key column because it corresponds to the contention that 15% more workers (the formerly unemployed) can be brought into the workforce so long as you cut wages sufficiently. The 10% column is added only for your general interest and is not referenced here. A price cut of 4.5% would be an optimistic assumption.

Stop. Think. In the table, there are only three items that would be sufficiently responsive to a 4.5% price cut to produce a 15%+ increase in the quantity. These are tomatoes, foreign travel, and soft drinks when PEDs exceeded 3.3 [PED= 3.3= 15%/4.5%]. And this is based on PEDs in a normal market. So the grand strategy of cutting labor pay to counter unemployment, works adequately for these 3 items in a normal market. But it fails for all other listed products. And in depression times, it may fall for all items if their PEDs fall to less than 3.3.[183]

Let's consider a labor-intensive business where labor's percentage of revenues is 66%, and thus the cut in product price might be as much as 10%. [PED= 1.5= 15%/10%; 10% price reduction= 15% reduced labor cost*66%]. Now let's search for labor intensive industries with a PED higher than 1.5. I see only three on the list that might qualify: marijuana, restaurants, and tomatoes. Marijuana is somewhat edgy. With a PED of 1.5, it might fall off the list, caused by a depression tendency to drop PEDs. So even there the program is apt to be a bust.

There are very few instances, even theoretically, where there was some chance that wage cuts might overcome 15% unemployment, and that the goods produced with the larger work force would actually be sold. The program fails miserably in most instances. The worker is right to be sticky – for his interests and for the interests of the nation.

It is brightly clear why cutting wages to reduce unemployment is a doomed strategy because it goes through steps roughly similar to the following:

1) Countering unemployment requires reducing wages by a percentage amount roughly equal to the unemployment to be corrected. The resulting increased employment increases quantity produced (q%).
2) Price reduction is only a small fraction (f%), say 30%, of the cut in wages (w%) because there are many other input costs other than labor in a product.

3) If q% is about the same as w% and the percentage of labor-saving cuts passed on in consumer price is about 30%, then only a very narrow band of goods, those with a high PEDs, can respond successfully to the strategy. This can be seen in w%= q%; PED= w%/(w%*f%)= 1/f%. Where f%= 0.3, PED= 1/0.3= 3.33. So as we see, even in an optimistic case, the only products that can benefit from a wage cutting to reduce unemployment program will be those with a PED higher than *the inverse of the fraction in the cut in wages that is passed on to the consumer (f%)*. Since staple goods have low PEDs, and since products have many input costs other than labor, attempting to restore national unemployment by wage cutting is a dubious proposition from the outset. The math can be more finely stated. The conclusion will remain the same.

To grow, wages must grow, whether it be in a nation or a firm.

The wage cutting illness is strange. It persists when the national reduction in GDP growth shows its damage. It persists when it is in the interest of the firm to pay a fair wage. When a firm looks at PEDs, the resounding cry is that in many instances there is only slight chance of achieving great growth developed from ever-larger price reductions coming from cutting worker pay. And that growth spurt *comes only in the same year as the price reduction.*

Once the approximate price range consistent with present technology is established for a product or a service, few future growth opportunities exist via price cuts that come from cutting wages. You then must sell on the basis of quality and meeting consumer needs and desires. You get what you pay for. If you are doing it on the cheap, nastiness and inefficiency will be endemic within management and labor. The customer will be one of the first to sense it. You need good people. And the emphasis is on the word "good," as in decent, able, honest, good performers. And you need a culture that knows that a wage or salary is paying for the past and buying the future. Such a world does not exist at MAJ25, either within a firm or within a nation.

Oh, you may have noticed that when we were discussing PEDs, the wage cutting strategy was limitedly successful with goods with high PEDs, in short *luxury goods*. Could there be a fit – high PEDs, luxury goods, and maldistribution together? Long before you picked up this book, you may have observed that in a maldistributed economy, the rich purchase *boatloads of luxury goods* vis-à-vis your minimum wage worker and other common folk. I would not be one to suggest that the rich are myopic and that they are merely *applying luxury-goods PEDs purchasing strategies to their assumption that cutting wages is a desirable across the board strategy*. No. No. No. Someone else will need to make that suggestion. I would never suggest that the intuitions of the rich might be flawed in any manner whatsoever. Not me. I don't go there.

During the acceleration of maldistribution nationally over the past few decades, wage cutting did not pull the economy out of a puddle. It just created a yet more disagreeable puddle containing less employment, more deeply impoverished workers, and a slowing growth of aggregate demand.

In economic language, the Wage Cut Fallacy looks something like this, except as we have already seen, even the salubrious aspects of purported increased employment are much in doubt, making the fallacy evermore certain:

> "If workers in the widget industry take a pay cut, this will lead to lower prices of widgets relative to other things, so people will buy more widgets, hence more employment.
> "But if everyone takes a pay cut, that logic no longer applies. The only way a general cut in wages can increase employment is if it leads people to buy more across the board. … [But] wage cuts do nothing to increase demand." – Paul Krugman[184]

During the Great Depression, the slim hope was to increase demand. Hourly MAJ income increased and consumer demand grew in tandem. FDR did this through public works projects, by gradually improving distribution of income and by other means.

Those with unstoppable misanthropic tendencies will cherry-pick cases where wages need to be reduced for the betterment of the firm. There certainly are instances in which wages do need to be reduced for the betterment of the firm. However they are confined to cases where the firm's compensation schedule is far more equal than a MAJ33 distribution. That is not the case with a MAJ25 maldistribution during a depression. For this reason, wages in the 1930s needed to rise for the nation to thrive. They had been too low for too long.

Look at the earlier graph-238, particularly the two periods 1934-1946 (12) and 1951-1978 (27). These were uninterrupted periods of hourly MAJ income increases: the first for 12 years and the second for 27 years. Those years provide the object lesson in how to grow an economy. You increase MAJ hourly wage. That increases your demand. Gluts disappear. You restore the proper relationship between production and consumption.

You cannot grow a nation by lowering MAJ wage levels, the minimum wage, or other worker pay. To do so impoverishes the majority and creates a moribund economy – whether it be during a Great Depression or now. The reason lowering wages so reliably destroys an economy is that healthy consumer demand comes from an adequately compensated MAJ. They are workers. They are consumers.

Maldistribution is just another word for reduced sustainable consumer demand.

At least a million more jobs. Sustainable consumer demand.

From its founding up until the early 1830s, and then again from 1944-1983, the nation hovered in an equitable income-distribution range near the MAJ 30.5 that existed in 1964. By the early 1850s, the moves toward increasing maldistribution were established and became increasingly acute.

#246

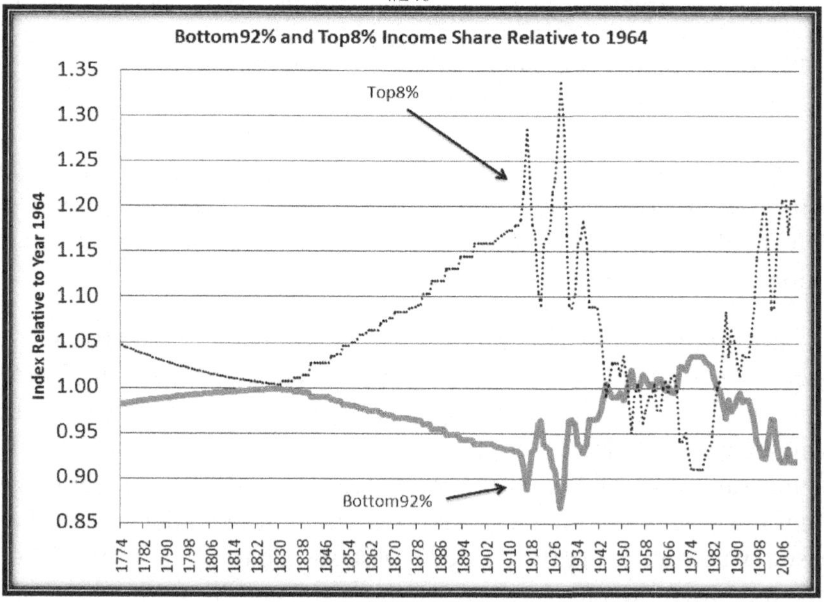

It was not until Saez 1913 income tax data became available that my data could show annual variations. Prior to 1913, the above graph-246 required interpolation. The year 1964 is taken as the base year because it reflects, as previously indicated, a year of high degree of efficiency during an era when the market economy functioned well.

Graph-246 focuses on those beneath the teeter point (the Bottom92%) but it also shows the Top8%. The average income relative to 1964 for the 1925-1930 period was 0.91 and for the 2005-2011 period it was 0.92, which is to say that income in those years was respectively 9% and 8% lower for the Bottom92% than it would have been under a 1964 income distribution.

At the start, the nation was mainly agricultural. Even in 1870, an estimated 70% to 80% of the population was employed in agriculture.[185] In an agrarian economy, some of the influence from the larger economy could be buffered by food from garden, livestock, and a high degree of self sufficiency, but farmers too increasingly depended on the overall economy. As urban America became an ever-greater share of the population, economic success relied completely on consumer demand.

In graph-246, we can easily see why the Golden Age of Capitalism was confined to a short period of U.S. history. While the nation has had a mature economy, it has been only during a brief period that income distribution stayed within an equitable range. The nation has paid a steep price for the divergences.

The point is a practical one. The modern market economy relies on consumer demand. The Bottom92% have a higher average propensity to consume than the Top8%. My computer programs have an ability that the real world does not. They can hold the consumption habits constant and vary only income distributions as have existed in the past.

For example, people at the 52nd and 98th percentiles in the computer program always respectively spend 98.0% and 87.5% of their incomes in all of the distributions, and all other people along the continuum also retain their spending characteristics. It is just their income shares that change. By this method, we are purely testing the influence of distribution apart from all other components, and this is done for all the years for which we have income-distribution data. In sum, the computer program subjected all years to a single propensity-to-consume schedule based on percentile rank, consistent with a 6.7% savings rate at a MAJ 30.5.

It was then able to show that even when each consumer retained the original propensity to consume, it caused the amounts that would have been consumed nationwide to vary relative to year 1964 as shown in the following graph-248. With this information, we can do the accounting for some key areas to see the influence that maldistribution has had on the Bottom92% and the nation as a whole.

During the 2005-2011 period, the Bottom92%, as previously shown in graph-246, was at 0.92 of the customary 1964 performance. The average income for the Bottom92% was $34,708 in those years. The first and most obvious loss for the Bottom92% is that their average income would have been $2,967 higher under the 1964 distribution [$37,676= $34,708/ 0.9212; $2,967= $37,676-$34,708].

But the loss for the nation as whole is greater. Let's start with the year 2011. As shown in graph-248, in 2011, consumption was reduced 0.94% by maldistribution. The last time it was that low was during the 1929-1930 transition when it was respectively 1.29% to 0.75% beneath the 1964 level. In only 13 years of all U.S. history has the consumption disadvantage been so acute. Those were years of poor performance. It remains to be seen whether a mature maldistributed economy can succeed over the long term. It has not been done in the past.

#248

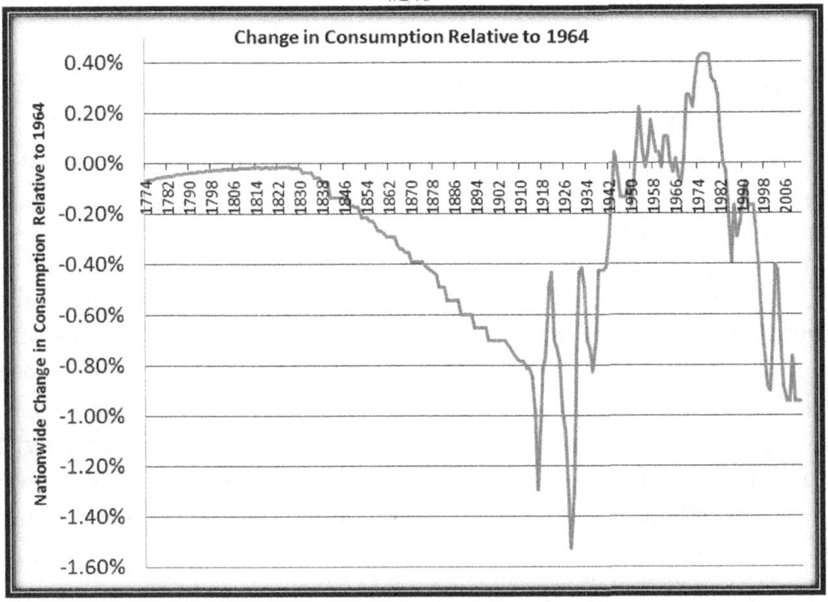

Let's consider the job implications for the United States. The 0.94% reduction in consumption translates into a GDP reduction of approximately the same amount, since the economy is consumer-driven. This would mean that by doing away with maldistribution and going back to 1964, income distributions would transform the 2012 GDP of $15,461.8 billion into a $15,608.7 billion GDP, an increase in size of $146.93 billion [$15,608.73= $15,461.80/ 0.990586908]. As we have seen in the job analysis, when a 3.6 multiplier is used, each $171,383 increase in GDP adds one permanent job for the nation. This would mean at the median that 857,298 jobs are added (701,426 jobs at a minimum, if a 4.4 multiplier is used and a $209,468 GDP increase for each job prevails). [857,298 jobs= $146,926,381,131/ $171,383; $171,383= 47606*3.6].

Confined just to these components and not considering other benefits, making this transition from maldistribution can be expected to produce 701,400 to 857,300 permanent jobs and provide a standard of living 0.95% higher for the USA [0.95%= 1/0.990586908-1].

If we think deeply about this, we find nice analytical points. A chief problem in fiscal and monetary policies for growing an economy is that many points are ambiguous. Actions are assumed to increase GDP. The GDP is assumed to increase jobs. Whether the undertaking is sustainable is problematic. One uncomfortable assumption is piled upon another. And together it is doubtful whether they will actually produce pump priming.

The "pump priming" metaphor may require some explanation that my farm-boy heritage can speak to. On many a cold day I have had to prime an ancient water pump that no longer took water from the well to the house. To do so, you insert a small amount of water into a pump chamber after which the pump runs fine, as if it had never failed in the first place. In truth, economic "pump priming" is false, but advertisingly potent. In contrast to true pump priming, which requires only a tiny amount of water, the metaphorical economic equivalent requires huge infusions. Too frequently those large infusions are continuous, just to keep a moribund economy functioning – all vastly different from the tiny cup of water carried to the pump house.

The nice maldistribution analytical point is that removing maldistribution lets the economy return to a natural state where it automatically generates the consumer demand necessary to sustain it; and on the supply side, it minimally and permanently employs 700,000 more people. This is closer to pump priming that has vast and sustainable effect.

By contrast, maldistribution sucks too much out of customary free market consumer demand for the motor to function optimally. All that is needed is to make a maldistribution-extinguishing valve adjustment so that the economic motor runs smoothly – a consumer demand motor matched with the number of jobs to produce the product. A nice analytical composition.

If we go one step further and use the base year 1977 instead of 1964, we see the optimum possibility available within the realm of past U.S. income distributions. It is well to note that 1977 was not an aberrant year. The 1975-1978 years had approximately the same distribution.

#250

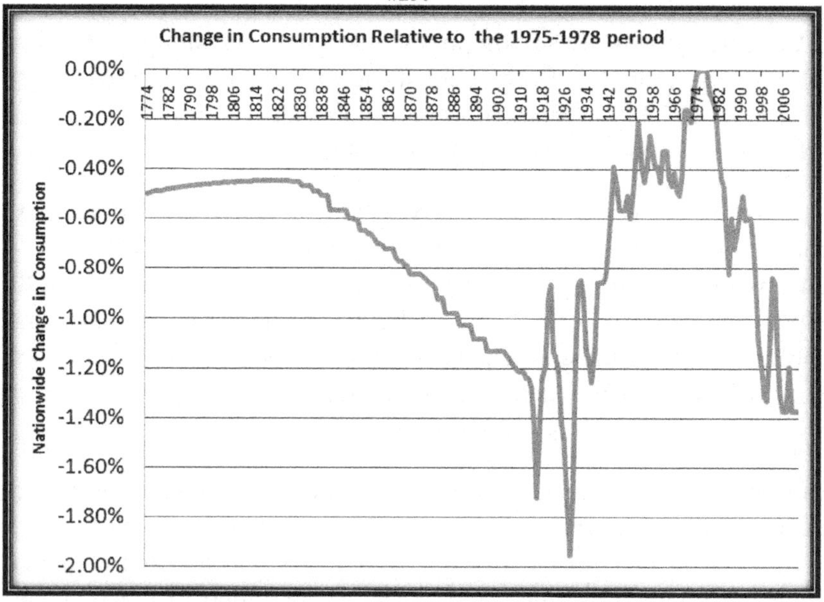

By moving from a MAJ25.8 in 2012, to the 1977 MAJ32.5 (instead of the 1964 MAJ30.5) we see the true job capabilities that the nation can generate when it returns to its best performing MAJ. Using the same sequence of calculations as previously, we see that under normal conditions, the change would produce 1,253,150 more jobs; and 1,025,300 more jobs if the 4.4 multiplier prevailed [$15,676.57= $15,461.80/ 98.63%; $214.77=$15,676.57-$15,461.80; 1,253,149 jobs= $214,768,513,734.43/ $171,383; $171,383= 47606*3.6].

You may recall that several pages ago, job multipliers in graph-220 occurred at various probabilities. The following graph-251 shows that when those multipliers are applied here, the above number of jobs tend to be created. When the probability is high, you can be confident that the historical multiplier record would tend to produce *at least* the shown number of jobs. And when the probability is lower (which is to say that the event is less likely), say 24% (as in President Jimmy Carter's high job creation era), many more jobs would tend to be created. The one to 1.25 million job estimates respectively reflect the multiplier in recent years, and in the median year.

To summarize, the U.S. would tend to have one to 1.25 million additional jobs created and filled by returning to its old MAJ32.5. Pipe dream you say? Not hardly. It has been done before. Going from the 1929 MAJ24.6 to the 1976 MAJ32.5 required an additional 7.9% to be added to the MAJ. That is certainly less than the 6.7% addition required for going from the 2011 MAJ25.8 to a MAJ32.5 [7.9%= MAJ32.5-MAJ24.6; 6.7%= MAJ32.5-MAJ25.8]. Play with the numbers. I believe you will find increasing job numbers subsequent to 1933 that were substantially aided by breaking with maldistribution. Worse yet, consider what they might have looked like if maldistribution had persisted unabated from 1928 onward.

#251

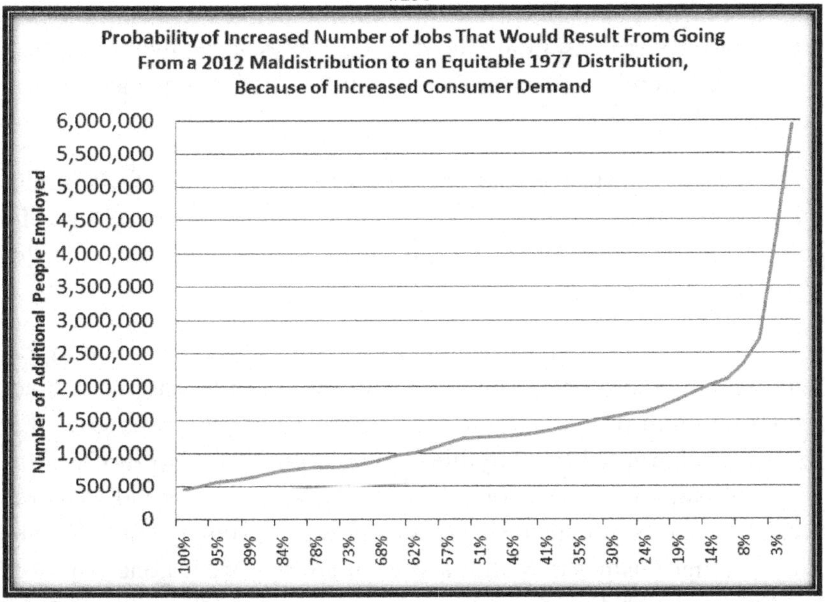

How did the MAJ lose?

I came from the farm. My business was manufacturing. I got my start at Dickinson College, Carlisle, Pa., where I was fortunate, at a crucial point in life, to know men and women students of great ability. They opened my eyes to what thinking was all about and what made a worthwhile life. In the finest sense of the word, it was a Liberal Arts education well-delivered.

Those were times when studying economics was primarily an exercise in understanding how agriculture and manufacturing built economies. The process back then was so successful that a friend once asked me why would I ever want to study economics, the implication being that there were more interesting and refined topics of far greater value than studying something that was already working in a clockwork-perfect manner. We could all easily get summer jobs. Our parents were doing ok. And it looked like our economic future, and that of our nation, would be inevitably and unavoidably bright. I too shared that view. I undertook the study because my experience in Mexico persuaded me that developmental economics – what makes nations grow and succeed – is vastly important.

Even at this late date I cannot but think that agriculture and manufacturing are fundamental. My business, which started in the 1970s, began on a shoestring. But over time it came to rely on key suppliers. Prisms, electronic components, electric motors, extruded aluminum, and the like came from various suppliers. We made most of the parts in-house, but those that we purchased were essential. By the late 1970s, an unwholesome, previously-unseen trend crept in and then came with a vengeance: mergers or takeovers.[186]

The way we worked is that I would order a few tons of aluminum. We would spend about six months on a production run making parts for our film editing machines. We needed to make the parts in sufficient quantity to be competitive and efficient.

About twice a year I would load up the truck and personally drive it down to an anodizing plant in North Carolina (a firm that puts a black finish on aluminum parts). For me that truckload of parts was gold. I would have been bankrupted had anything gone wrong. The North Carolina anodizing company did a fantastic job for many years, and it did so at a decent price. They had boatloads of business and were thriving. They were bought out by another business. Within a year or so they were gone – out of business. I never again found their equal. Mergers and takeovers destroyed so many of my suppliers that the instant a merger occurred I would make provisions for finding an alternate supplier.

There was a machine shop within a few miles of my business that did extraordinarily good work. An engineer there of unusual brilliance, George Wendell, was especially helpful to me. Everyone in the shop did a fine job. In these manufacturing businesses you have highly educated people working side by side with people with high school educations. All doing good work. All respected. And should you think that being a machinist would not be mentally challenging and interesting, my experience taking Machine Shop, taught by Bob Gibson at New River Community College in the 1970s, was just as challenging and interesting as any graduate course I have taken.

Yet George's shop started to fade. Within a decade, it was gone. Foreign trade was not the killer. I got about 20% of my business from sales abroad and could beat foreign competitors. George's shop and the anodizing business were not eliminated by foreign trade. It was something closer to home.

I am trying to say that what I saw was not an Adam Smith process of the best surviving and prospering. The uneconomic nature of the process was plainly apparent. A new mindset was targeting and killing businesses and the people that worked for them – a mindset that attacked not only the worker, but that also attacked the educated people who were the builders.[187]

Barry Bluestone and Bennett Harrison in 1982 were among the first to tell the story. They wrote the book, *Deindustrialization of America: Plant Closings, Community Abandonment, and the Dismantling of Basic Industry*. The title tells the story. It wasn't so much the sweeping economic rationales that were the cause. It was something brutal. The way they saw it:

> … capital – in the forms of financial resources and of real plant and equipment – has been diverted from productive investment in our basic national industries into unproductive speculation, mergers and acquisitions, and foreign investment.[188]

From age 13 to 25 I worked on many jobs, frequently as a laborer, where the MAJ can be found: farming, building Interstate 95, working as a roughneck on an oil rig, building a water treatment plant, building a Federal Reserve Building, building a nuclear power plant, running a print shop for NYU Medical Center, and working as a feature writer for the *Orange Review*. Often these were summer jobs. Seldom did I see college-bound kids working on them. The lack of visceral day-to-day contact that educated people (liberal and conservative) had with the MAJ has always struck me as notable. Always ready to supply theories about the MAJ, they too frequently had not been there.

I also noticed this when I went into manufacturing. Educated college friends were mainly unfamiliar with it and were focused elsewhere. In that light it is not surprising that as Bluestone and Harrison say, "much disinvestment is invisible to all but those who work on the shop floor or to the managers who actually plan it …"[189] The process of deindustrialization and disinvestment was so insidious, so gradual, so distant from the visceral concerns of the leading classes, and so far out of the educated eye that it proceeded unabated. Too frequently, close contact between the MAJ and upper classes did not exist. As the MAJ descended, they had too few friends in high places who were committed to their success.

As always, about 35% of purchases are and have been manufactured goods. Yet in the U.S. manufacturing now accounts for only 12% of GDP.[190] If you were to conclude this is the fault of the MAJ, you would be wrong. Let me give you an example. As Charles Ferguson indicated, in 1982, General Motors closed an assembly plant in California, dubbing it unprofitable, presumably because of its unionized labor force. Yet in a joint venture with Toyota in 1984, the plant reopened with the same workers, doubled productivity, and produced higher quality cars.[191] With high quality management, we can do a great job. Just let us. The failure in manufacturing has been at the top, not at the MAJ. We lost our manufacturing GDP by sloppy management, a sloppy national agenda, and frank destruction. The sanitized word for the process was often "restructuring."

Ironically Joseph Schumpeter's phrase "creative destruction" has been adopted by MBAs and free-market economists to justify gutting the lifeblood of the MAJ. It is ironic for two reasons: First, the phrase originated with the alleged arch villain of free markets, Karl Marx.[192] Second, Schumpeter saw capitalism not as a model that would succeed, but as one which would be supplanted. Schumpeter had his chance to participate in solving the greatest threat capitalism ever faced (the Great Depression). Instead, he was pathetic during the period – hardly a person MBAs should emulate. For a taste of his thinking published soon after the Depression in 1943, feast your eyes on the following (which was proven way wrong by the 1950s through 1970s):

> Can capitalism survive? No, I do not think it can. … its very success undermines the social institutions which protect it, and 'inevitably' creates conditions in which it will not be able to live and which strongly point to socialism as the heir apparent.[193]

The MAJ has always been at the heart of core production, agriculture and manufacturing. Once they and their educated cohorts were "creatively destroyed," the vast shift toward maldistribution became inevitable. The nation lost the jobs that the MAJ relied on for its livelihood.

Outgunned: business vs. core production.

Should you be skeptical of anecdotal stories such as mine, may I suggest the following graph-255 for your consideration.[194] As many of my readers have business degrees, please accept my apologies in advance. But the data so plainly illustrates changes since the 1970s that I am compelled to include it.

The fields of study that I refer to as Core Production in the following graph-255 are: engineering, biological and biomedical sciences, health professions and related clinical sciences, mathematics and statistics, agriculture and natural resources, architecture and related services, engineering technologies, and transportation & materials.

#255

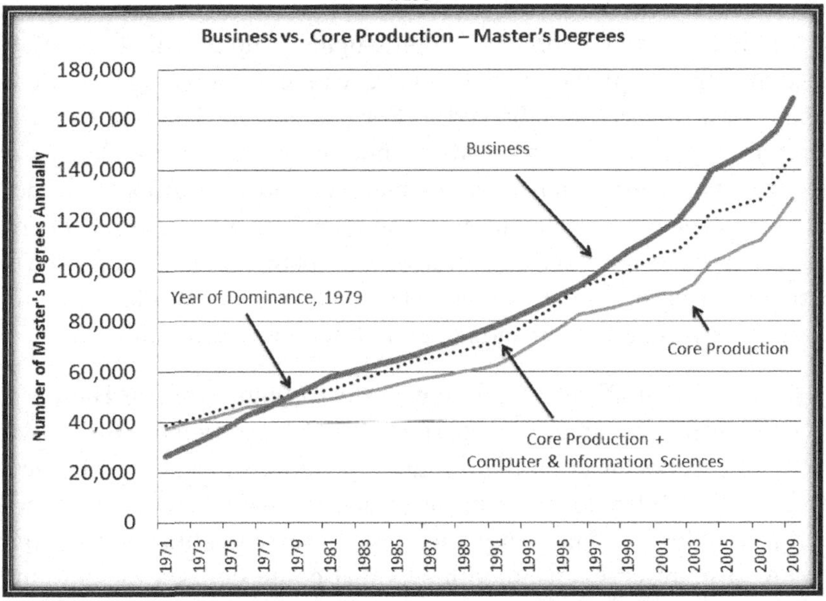

In 1971, at the start of graph-255, the number of Master's Degrees awarded in Core Production in 1971 outnumbered Master's Degrees awarded in business by a factor of 1.4 times. This was right and proper. Then, in a sudden burst, by 1979 Business degrees dominated Core Production. By 2009, there were fully 31% more Master's Degrees in Business than all of Core Production. I believe students have correctly spotted the winning team – much to the disadvantage of Core Production and the nation. Each person with a high level of capacity in Core Production had 1.3 Business graduates riding herd on him. Too many cowboys, too few cows.

You could see them coming. And they weren't on ponies. One morning in the early 1980s, I had a meeting at a local corporation. As I walked to the parking lot of mainly modest cars and pickup trucks, I recall an ungodly expensive car charging into the lot with "Ride of the Valkyries" blasting. The owner, in an equally phony power suit, stormed into the building. Another MBA on the loose, another parade to be rained on. They were not players. They were not folks that made businesses run and thrive. They were inflated egos on legs. True to form, they destroyed much in their path and were never wise enough to know it. They were too impressed with themselves to be inquisitive, patient, or truly creative. There is a huge difference between builders and trashers. They trimmed us out. We lost jobs, success, businesses. Now it is PhDs in the sciences – neuroscience and the like – that cannot find jobs in their fields.[195] The trimming continues.

Mel Brooks, who supplies us with laughter, supplied them in 1968 with the term for one of the chief tools: "Creative Accounting."[196] Meant for humor, they in earnest embraced it. For example in the book *Creative Accounting Exposed*, you can find the not surprising observation, "Companies that make very intense use of mergers and acquisitions are the most likely to use creative accounting techniques," or a full chapter devoted to "Subjectivity in the Consolidation of Companies," or passages on incorrectly deferring sales in a merger process, et cetera.[197] Working in a few tax advantages was also swell and made it all the more profitable.[198]

Abraham Briloff, an accounting professor and writer in Barron's, was an early critic of loose accounting. In *Unaccountable Accounting*, he wrote: " … Because of their high P/E ratios, the new conglomerates achieved the ability to make instant 'merger profits' by taking over firms with low ratios. … The conglomerates … become attracted to firms possessing large reserves of liquid assets that could be used to shore up their … financial structures."[199] So here we have it. Those low PE ratios, which as I have shown to be advantageous for stockholders and for providing increased financial stability, are the precise item that cause a firm to be targeted and taken over – in short, to be made less stable.

Perhaps you get the drift. When you build a product, when you run a tight company and when you have real employees doing real work, the process of making a profit, growing a company, and building a nation is a lot different from the paper magic to which firms increasingly dedicate themselves, abetted by newly minted MBAs. The 1971-1979 MBA assent from an ordinary position to a dominant one was palpable. The MAJ's descent began in 1979. The data show it.

You also may have already seen some of the recent videos concerning the 2008 Calamity and how the financial sector unraveled the market economy. If not, you may want to put them on your play list: Inside Job (DVD); Bill Moyers' Journal: William K. Black: CSI Bailout (Liars' Loans online video); Frontline: The Warning (DVD and online); Frontline: Secret History of the Credit Card (DVD and online); and Frontline: Inside the Meltdown (DVD and online).

Investments, interest rates, stimulus, deficits.

The transformation since the equitable distributions in the pre-1980s era has had two thrusts: the destruction of the MAJ and the twisting of customary financial conditions.

#257

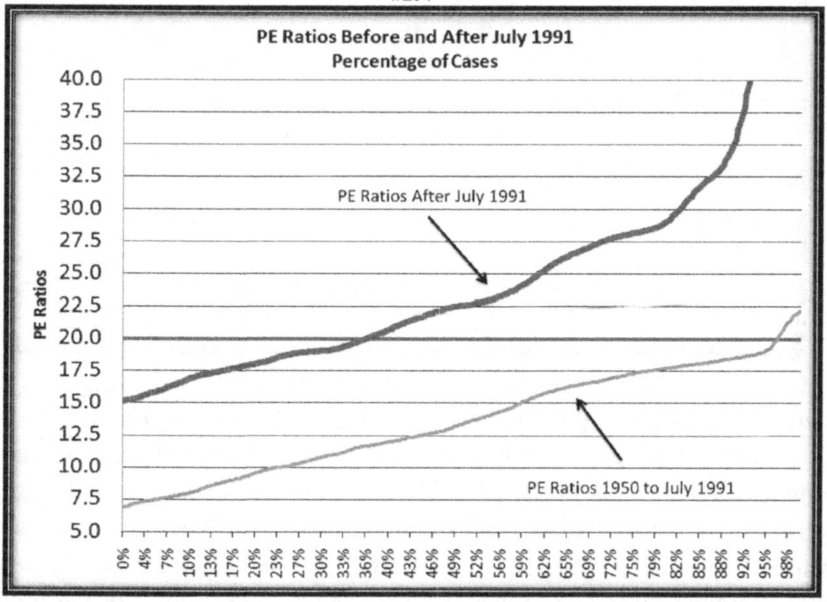

The S&P500 PE ratio shows the ratio between capitalization and each unit of profit. When you ask yourself, "Why is vast capitalization now necessary to support lower earnings?" The answer is unpleasant: Systematically, business is no longer converting capitalization into profit as efficiently as it once did in the low PE ratio era. This requires that more funds go into capitalization, thus less money for use elsewhere.

As earlier illustrated, after July 1991, the transformation of the stock market (the S&P500) was profound. In the above graph-257 we see that fully 7.30% of the PE ratios were so bizarrely high that they exceeded 40. From 1950-July 1991, only in 3.2% of cases did the PE ratio even exceed 20. By contrast, from July 1991 to 2011, 63.5% cases exceeded 20. [3.21%= 1-96.79%; 63.52%= 1-36.48%; 7.30%= 1-92.70%]. *At the median, the difference between the pre- and post-July 1991 world would have put 1.7 times more wealth into the hands of stockholders for each unit of profit.* [1.686= 13.37/22.547].

#258

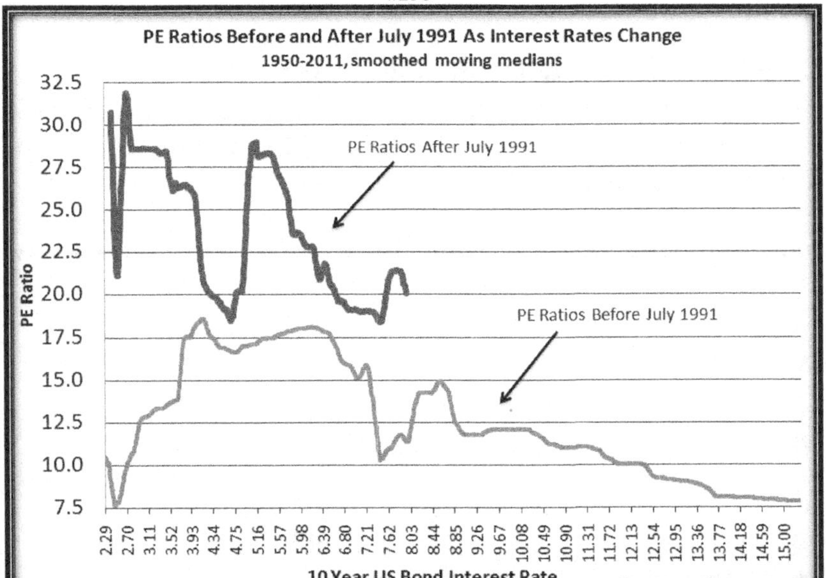

Perhaps you, like me, might have felt that this quick overview could have misrepresented the case because it did not account for interest rates, which were different in the two periods. So let's look at PE ratios matched to interest rates in the graph-258. The post-1991 era curve had PE ratios on average 1.54 times greater than the pre-1991 era curve when the cases are matched for interest rates [1.54= 23.60/15.28]. *When matched for interest rates, the post-1991 era placed 1.54 times as much wealth in the hands of stockholders for each unit of profit.* In the post-July 1991 era, PE ratios were plainly higher even when matched for interest rates. The post-July

1991 curve is truncated because it did not experience some of the high interest rates that the pre-1991 era did.

In both curves there is an unsteady but generally consistent relationship: As U.S. bond interest rates exceed 5.1%, PE ratios fall. In the post-1991 era, PE ratios, and consequently the stock market, have been propped up by low interest rates. On the other hand, the prospect of increasing interest rates strikes fear into the hearts of stockholders because, plainly stated, high interest rates mean their stock wealth is apt to fall.

Monetarist interest-rate decisions greatly influence our lives. They can be so powerful as to have far greater economic sway than do the political leaders who ostensibly stand at the head of government. The source of this power in the U.S. is the Federal Reserve Board (FED). It is no accident that the stock-market rides on the latest pronouncement of the FED chairman, whether it be Greenspan, Bernanke, or anyone else. It does so for good reason. It knows who butters its bread. We need not go into great detail, but I would like to give explicit examples that show how interest rates touch all of our lives, whether it be directly or indirectly.

You may recall "***The Formula***" from a few pages back. It looked like this:

S&P 500 Annual Rate of Appreciation =
((PE2/PE1)^(1/years) * (1+annual earnings growth rate))-1

If we add an estimate of dividends to that formula, we have total estimated annual income from a stock investment. We can very quickly make a first approximation of such dividends using PE ratios and a number related to the dividend payout ratio [+(2/(PE2 + PE1)*0.46] which then gives us:

S&P 500 Annual Rate of Return = ((PE2/PE1)^(1/years) * (1+annual earnings growth rate))-1+(2/(PE2 + PE1)*0.46

For the post-July 1991 era, the median interest rates and PE ratios were respectively 5.11% and 22.55; for the 1950-July 1991 era, they were 6.31% and 13.37. We can gain an appreciation of how low interest rates, used as a stimulus in monetary policy, can influence rational decision-making. I argue that customary median interest rates are preferable to propping up unnaturally high PE ratios via expansionary monetary policy and low interest rates.

The method is straightforward. We use "***The Formula***" with its dividend rate estimate to determine the customary average rate of return over time, as if a 20% drop in stock market value occurred in the last year. We can easily do this in the formula by taking the median post-July 1991 era PE ratio (PE1 22.55) and reducing it 20% to a PE2 of 18.04 [18.04= 22.55*.8]. The method uses an Earnings Growth Rate of 5.5%, and Years shown later in the table columns [annualRateOfReturnOnInvestment= (((PE2/PE1)^(1/Years)* (1+EarningsGrowthRate))-1)+(2/(PE2+PE1)* 0.46)]. Let's call all of this using "***The Formula***" Side 1.

For Side 2, we calculate allocations (bond% and the remainder in stocks) using the bond rates shown in the tables and fixed long-term stock-market rate of return (7.54%). Our breakeven point is where the bond allocation for Side2 (the normal steady state condition) [normalRateReturn= allocation* BondRateOfReturn+(1-allocation) * StockRateOfReturn] is equal to Side 1 (the market performing normally but with a 20% crash).

I remember a talk Herbert Simon gave about 35 years ago in which he remarked, as I paraphrase here: "When have you seen people you know and see every day perform in the way that economic models suggest?" The implication being that people in everyday life perform vastly differently from many rational models.

So when I think back on Herbert Simon, I am reminded that no matter how correct an analysis may be, responsible people in the field to which it centrally pertains will not necessarily be rational. They are bounded by tradition, habit, and self-interest. Notwithstanding, the underlying formulas in the following are so potent that some of their logic inevitably filters through to show the direction markets move.

For the benefit of those of you who have the good sense to concern yourselves entirely in areas other than finance, let me give you a brief and hopefully painless introduction to a healthy "normal" market: Treasury bonds offer a fixed rate of return. The stock market offers a rate of return, which is more variable but often higher. The wise investor will allocate a fraction of his total investment to bonds (for security), and allocate the balance to the stock market (hoping to get a higher rate of return). The optimum allocation would give the highest rate of return that can be achieved for a given period while retaining an appropriate level of security from the fixed rate Treasury bond and while also taking advantage of the presumably higher stock market rate of return. By looking at allocations, we can begin to appreciate what causes people to put money into the stock market, and conversely what causes them to pull it out.

Since most of us do not suffer from various preconceptions found in the financial press, we can instantly spot that the allocations in each of the rows in the following tables vastly vary depending upon interest rates.

For example, in the first table, ask yourself, "How many years will it be before the market experiences at least a 20% drop in a single year?" For the record, in the 21 years since 1991, it has happened twice: 2001-2003 and 2008-2009. Let's say that you guess another 20%+ drop* is apt to occur within 11 years. Your strategy at the 11-year mark and at a bond rate of 2.71 would be to put 39.2% in bonds and the rest in stock, but at the same 11-year mark, if the interest rate was 6.31%, you would put 100% into bonds.† I think you can see here how interest rates greatly influence rational investment decisions. Even if you were highly optimistic, I believe you would be dreaming to assume that a 20% drop would remain 21+ years into the future.

Years to a 20% Drop In Stock Value	Bond Allocation As Interest Rate Changes			
	2.71%	3.91%	5.11%	6.31%
1	100.0%	100.0%	100.0%	100.0%
3	100.0%	100.0%	100.0%	100.0%
5	90.7%	100.0%	100.0%	100.0%
7	63.9%	85.0%	100.0%	100.0%
9	48.8%	65.0%	97.0%	100.0%
11	39.2%	52.2%	77.9%	100.0%
13	32.5%	43.3%	64.6%	100.0%
15	27.6%	36.7%	54.8%	100.0%
17	23.8%	31.7%	47.3%	93.5%
19	20.9%	27.7%	41.4%	81.8%
21	18.4%	24.5%	36.6%	72.3%
23	16.4%	21.9%	32.6%	64.4%
25	14.8%	19.6%	29.3%	57.8%
27	13.3%	17.7%	26.5%	52.2%
29	12.1%	16.1%	24.0%	47.4%
31	11.0%	14.7%	21.9%	43.1%
33	10.1%	13.4%	20.0%	39.4%
35	9.2%	12.3%	18.3%	36.1%
37	8.5%	11.3%	16.8%	33.2%
39	7.8%	10.4%	15.5%	30.6%

So you see in the table that a high degree of optimism and low bond rates are key motivations for investing predominantly in the stock market. Governmental and corporate leaders use low interest rates to prop up the stock market. Money can go into or out of the stock market quickly depending on interest rate moves.

---

* For example coming from a drop in PE ratios.

† You might then wait out the market for it to drop 20%, whereupon you might sell bonds and buy stock in a allocation consistent with when you guess the market would again fall 20% further. Eventually you ratchet PE1 and PE2 to points you are comfortable with.

These examples are based on starting with a 22.6 PE ratio of the kind that existed in the post-1991 era. The propping up via low interest rates is especially precarious because if interest rates rise (say due to inflation or components beyond the control of policymakers), PE ratios are apt to fall and send the stock market south. In the pre-1991 era with PE ratios of say 13.4 to 15, the props were not necessary because the market was already in a rational relationship with earnings, and great drops were less likely; thus optimism was more justified and the market was more rational and more stable.

What I am trying to illustrate here is that when interest rates are low, there is great pressure to buy stocks rather than bonds, and this tends to push PE ratios higher. We can see it in our own decisions. We can see it in national decisions. And conversely, when interest rates rise, we can expect a disincentive to buy stock and for PE ratios to fall, just as we saw empirically in graph-258.

Age	Time Horizon In Years	Bond Allocation As Interest Rate Changes 2.71%	3.91%	5.11%	6.31%
40	39	7.8%	10.4%	15.5%	30.6%
42	37	8.5%	11.3%	16.8%	33.2%
44	35	9.2%	12.3%	18.3%	36.1%
46	33	10.1%	13.4%	20.0%	39.4%
48	31	11.0%	14.7%	21.9%	43.1%
50	29	12.1%	16.1%	24.0%	47.4%
52	27	13.3%	17.7%	26.5%	52.2%
54	25	14.8%	19.6%	29.3%	57.8%
56	23	16.4%	21.9%	32.6%	64.4%
58	21	18.4%	24.5%	36.6%	72.3%
60	19	20.9%	27.7%	41.4%	81.8%
61	18	22.3%	29.6%	44.2%	87.3%
62	17	23.8%	31.7%	47.3%	93.5%
63	16	25.6%	34.1%	50.9%	100.0%
64	15	27.6%	36.7%	54.8%	100.0%
65	14	29.9%	39.8%	59.4%	100.0%
66	13	32.5%	43.3%	64.6%	100.0%
67	12	35.6%	47.4%	70.7%	100.0%
68	11	39.2%	52.2%	77.9%	100.0%
69	10	43.6%	57.9%	86.5%	100.0%
70	9	48.8%	65.0%	97.0%	100.0%
71	8	55.4%	73.8%	100.0%	100.0%
72	7	63.9%	85.0%	100.0%	100.0%
73	6	75.1%	99.9%	100.0%	100.0%
74	5	90.7%	100.0%	100.0%	100.0%
75	4	100.0%	100.0%	100.0%	100.0%
76	3	100.0%	100.0%	100.0%	100.0%
77	2	100.0%	100.0%	100.0%	100.0%
78	1	100.0%	100.0%	100.0%	100.0%

In the table here, our allocation selections change as we age. A young investor with a long time horizon who does not mind increased risk can invest over the long term with somewhat less attention to bond allocations. But as the investor ages, the time horizon changes – in most instances arguing for a high bond allocation.* These tables illustrate how interest rates influence the way the economy functions, and more particularly how interest rates impact us as we age.

*** Again, I stress this is NOT investment advice. Do NOT use it as such. There are vast considerations including inflation rates and other factors that make it dangerous for you to consider it to be investment advice. See a professional. Not this. I am not an investment advisor.**

In 2005, with his $4.2 million total personal assets, Federal Reserve Chairman Alan Greenspan invested primarily in Treasury bonds and bond funds ($3 million).[200] From this we see that 71.4% of his assets were safely in bonds [71.4%= 3/4.2]. On one hand, it is an age-appropriate allocation. On the other, it certainly *does not display a high degree of confidence that a drop of 20% in the stock market would be much postponed.* It would not be a surprise to learn that many of the truly knowledgeable financial leaders similarly had a large proportion of their assets in bonds when the market tanked in 2008-2009. Undoubtedly, they would have done calculations similar to those you see here. While they talked about a healthy economy publically, privately, their inner voice most likely warned them to be more prudent in their personal accounts. We also see that Greenspan's wealth was a modest $4.2 million. I say modest because in the maldistributed world of the mega-rich that came to exist on his watch, he was but a comparatively poor servant for their amusement and benefit.

Indeed the vastly wealthy often prefer not to directly deal with banks or stock and bond markets, as we mere mortals do. Their wealth is now too huge for cumbersome institutions like banks and stock markets. Instead, shadow banking (now twice as large as regulated traditional banking)[201] and private equity are often their tools of choice.

Maldistribution & the monetarist.

There is a school of thought that seeks to impoverish government to such an extent that the only remaining economic instrument of public policy is monetary. They have attributed the Great Depression exclusively to a contraction of money, and have denied that there were fundamental structural causes in the economy prior to the Great Depression. On the other side, the Keynes flag has been planted. There, government spending is often proposed as an economic cure. Neither has adequately addressed income distribution. We can say this with confidence because long-term income-distribution data, of the kind you see in graph-264 have not existed previously. In it we can see the economic strength of the MAJ in 1964 and 1977 relative to pre-Great Depression conditions. Contrariwise, we can also see the MAJ's current danger.

How close can you get to 1928 before you have 1929? That is the game of economic chicken now being played. In the following graph-264, two-thirds of the population in 2011 is within 10% of the 1928 point (0%). The MAJ now is only receiving a 9% income share above 1928. The 2011 income distribution is even more unequal than the 1910 distribution – one hundred years ago. Graph-264 was constructed by dividing the X$ curves for each of the shown years by the 1928 X$ curve.

#264

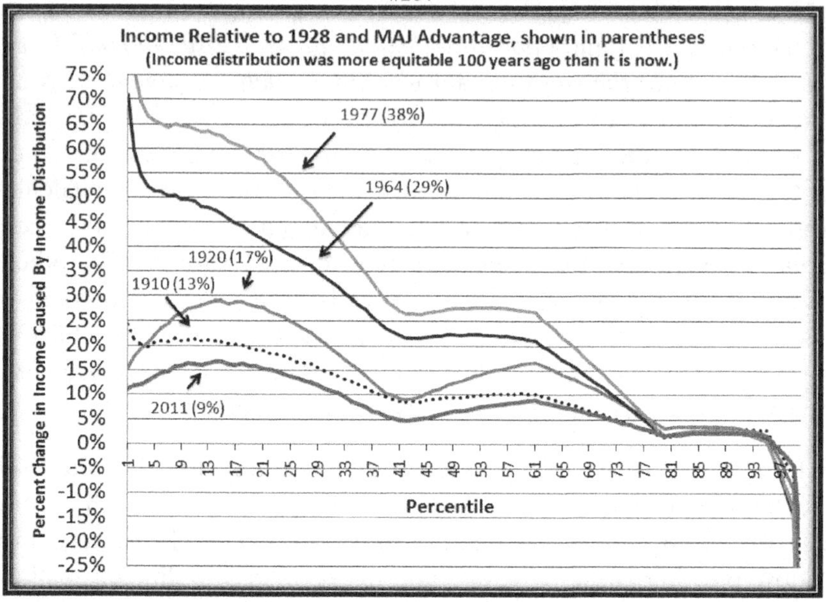

In 1964 and 1997, the MAJ respectively had a 29% and 38% greater income share than the 1928-Depression-producing distribution. Keynes never saw 1964 or 1977. We have. Nor did he see the GDP per capita growth rates associated with them. We have. We can learn. The lack of aggregate demand so widely fretted about during the Great Depression was caused in large part by maldistribution.

Consider history relived with a Depression-producing MAJ in 1964 and 1977. How would you, your parents, or your ancestors have fared if the 29% or 38% increased income coming from equitable distributions had then been removed from the MAJ? Those lives would have been vastly different, vastly inferior, and far less educated. During the Great Depression, aggregate demand was poisoned by maldistribution, and so were lives. The post-WWII era made the wise decision to move to increased equality. Had the 1950s returned to a 1928 MAJ23.6, do you honestly believe the great post WWII economic advances would have occurred? Yet none of this penetrates current economic planning.

The approach, now called Keynesian, correctly saw the problem as a demand problem. It saw Government spending as the method for increasing aggregate demand. That may be plausible and even effective; but if the objective is to get maximum therapeutic effect at a minimum dosage, it is necessary to reverse maldistribution. The maldistribution reversal will bring increased demand. Also by reconfiguring the incentive structure, it promotes improved human interaction and decision-making. Over the long run, the combination is potent. We need to again recall the mindset that produced success:

> "It is our duty now to begin to lay the plans and determine the strategy for ... the establishment of an American standard of living higher than ever before known. We cannot be content, no matter how high that general standard of living may be, if some fraction of our people – whether it be one-third or one-fifth or one-tenth—is ill-fed, ill-clothed, ill-housed, and insecure. This Republic had its beginning, and grew to its present strength, under the protection of certain inalienable political rights – among them the right of free speech, free press, free worship, trial by jury, freedom from unreasonable searches and seizures. They were our rights to life and liberty.
>
> "As our nation has grown in size and stature, however – as our industrial economy expanded – these political rights proved inadequate to assure us equality in the pursuit of happiness."
>
> "We have come to a clear realization of the fact that true individual freedom cannot exist without economic security and independence. "Necessitous men are not free men."[202] People who are hungry and out of a job are the stuff of which dictatorships are made. *In our day these economic truths have become accepted as self-evident. We have accepted, so to speak, a second Bill of Rights under which a new basis of security and prosperity can be established for all – regardless of station, race, or creed.*
>
> "Among these are:
>
> "The right to a useful and remunerative job in the industries or shops or farms or mines of the nation;
> "The right to earn enough to provide adequate food and clothing and recreation;
> "The right of every farmer to raise and sell his products at a return which will give him and his family a decent living;
> "The right of every businessman, large and small, to trade in an atmosphere of freedom from unfair competition and domination by monopolies at home or abroad;
> "The right of every family to a decent home;

"The right to adequate medical care and the opportunity to achieve and enjoy good health;

"The right to adequate protection from the economic fears of old age, sickness, accident, and unemployment;

The right to a good education.

"All of these rights spell security. … we must be prepared to move forward, in the implementation of these rights, to new goals of human happiness and well-being.

"America's own rightful place in the world depends in large part upon how fully these and similar rights have been carried into practice for all our citizens."

FDR, Jan. 11, 1944, State of the Union Address[203]

This approach cannot be subordinated to economics or ideology. Both must work within it. President Eisenhower and others had the good sense to keep these principles in mind and thus created the Golden Age of Capitalism. In more recent times, breaching the basic equitability, which made past success possible, has undermined the economy and nation.

The surprise.

#266

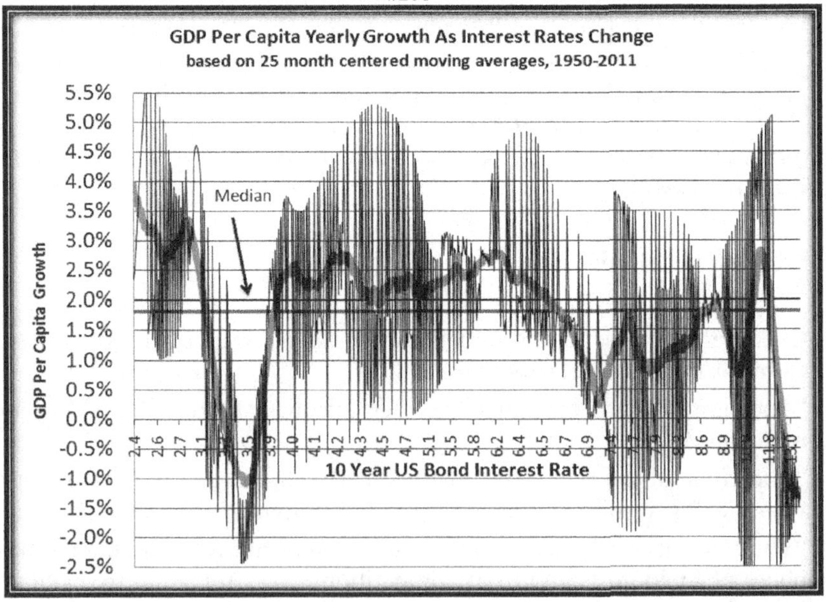

My training and instincts had always led me to believe that low interest rates promoted GDP per capita growth. In my mind, this held the status of axiomatic economic knowledge. Yet when I look at the data shown in the above graph-266, I see a more ambiguous story.

When examining trend-line data points, we see that only 10% of them are at a 3.05% interest rate or lower. This group did produce a GDP per capita growth rate greater than 2.5% – at the median 3.11%. If you focus on that tiny area, yes, you can say growth rates are higher. But such a focus would distort the case. All of the successful data in this region occurred during the 1950-1956 period – a period that benefited greatly from equitable income distribution. It would seem unwise to draw firm interest rate conclusions based on such an unusual sample and such a small one at that (10% of the data). Making the low interest case weaker, nearby low interest rates in the range of 3.2% to 3.5% delivered profoundly substandard growth rates.

By contrast, a wide swath of interest rates (fully 33% of the data) from 4% to 6.3% produced a GDP per capita growth rate that was often in the neighborhood of 2.5%. For this midrange interest rate group, the median GDP per capita growth was a respectable 2.38%. True, this is 0.73% less than the presumed highly stimulatory low interest rate [0.73%= 3.11%-2.38%]. But in my view, interest rates in that range are unambiguously more reliable and come with fewer side effects.

#267

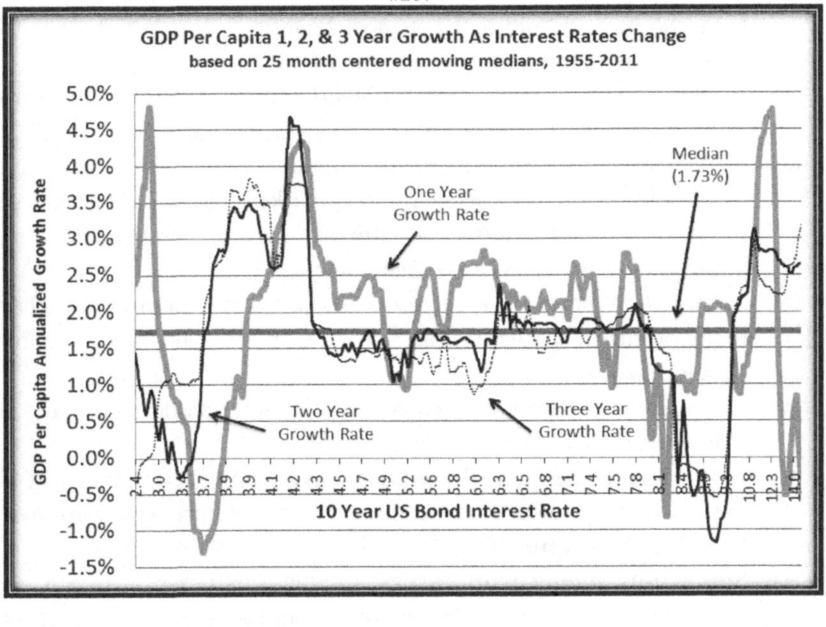

Using a slightly different technique, the above graph-267 yields substantially the same conclusions. If you want an effective low interest rate to support GDP growth, those exceeding 4% do quite nicely.

The low interest rate regime has been oversold – disingenuously so in my view. Its purpose is to prop up the stock market. To take the dubious stance that a 0.73% growth increase is a justifiable excuse for low interest rates would be to ignore their many profoundly unwelcome side effects. We have been too quick to accept economic theory and equilibrium economics. At best, low interest rates are suitable only for short-term adjustments.

It seems unlikely that long-term low interest rates would benefit the MAJ. The growth killing maldistributions that have existed in recent years will not be cured by low interest rate monetarism. For as long as the stimulatory monetarist regime exists, we can expect the nation to falter. Long-term, low-interest rate, stimulatory monetarism, as the exclusive solution for GDP growth, seems doomed to fail.

1) The chief harm of low interest rates is that they reallocate between interest-benefiting activities and investment activities. More often than not, the distortions disproportionately favor imprudent decision-making.
2) Stimulatory monetarism feeds the rich, not the poor.[204] Those who have the most money get the most benefit. It is a top-down response to problems that require bottom-up answers.
3) A chief (albeit often unstated) objective of stimulatory monetarism is to prop up high PE ratios and inflate stock market values.[205] The practical examples of how it distorts wealth can be found in the housing boom and bust and in inflated stock market values. It fosters a variety of excessively speculative investments, mergers, and financial manipulations – all of which are unwelcome.
4) Stimulatory monetarism disproportionately restructures the economy to favor financial institutions rather than truly productive economic development.
5) A low interest rate is the voice that financial markets use to tell you that your money is not worth much.
6) Low interest rates hurt the prudent saver. They especially hurt the elderly who rely on (and expect to live on) interest on wealth accumulated over a lifetime of work.[206]
7) Stimulatory monetarism creates a dangerous nexus between government and low interest rates. A government policy of low interest rates

- is a self-feeding mechanism leading government to take on excessive debt. A government has an unwelcome incentive to take on excessive debt when it is cheap to do so. At some future date, interest rates will rise. Government then can face a crippling interest rate burden when debt is refinanced. In the interim, it may be unable to finance worthy and necessary public functions. In short, a weaker nation.

8) Stimulatory monetarism does not provide a sustainable cure for anemic consumer demand. It is not restorative. It is not curative. At best it is palliative care for a chronic malady – just pushing on a string.
9) Stimulatory monetarism accelerates the growth of wealth relative to the growth of income. This expands the debtor class again distorting housing and stock market valuations.
10) At customary midrange interest rates, the least profit-worthy projects are filtered out because only sounder operations can afford the higher interest rates. But when interest rates are abnormally low, so too is the bar of prudence. This brings forth additional investment in less profit-worthy projects. A weaker economy, not a stronger one, is created when marginally profitable endeavors proliferate.
11) Compared to midrange interest rates, history shows that exceptionally low interest rates do not generally produce sufficiently higher growth in GDP per capita to warrant incurring their adverse side effects.
12) Stimulatory monetarism risks inflation. With inflation comes higher interest rates. If the transition between low and high rates is quick, dislocations and economic difficulties can be massive.
13) Low interest rates in the U.S. foster international borrowing in U.S. capital markets, extracting capital from the U.S. that is needed at home. High or moderate interest rates are apt to bring in foreign capital or be more neutral.
14) Stimulatory monetarism addresses symptoms. It is not symptoms that require patching. It is core problems that require fixing. Monetarism only delays the day of reckoning.

The second tool.

Typically the second major tool in a macroeconomist's toolbox is fiscal policy (government spending, taxation, deficit spending). Before getting into it, let's look at Federal Government expenditures over time as in the following graph-270.[207]

When Federal spending is about 20%, it follows that the economy is 80% market economy, 20% government. In this case, when tax revenue is about 20% of GDP, there is no deficit. Having about a one-fifth federal role in the economy (20%) provides continuity and absorbs shocks (capacitance to use an electrical analogy). In the seven-years-of-plenty, seven-years-of-famine analogy, it is interesting to note that a one-fifth* taking, there too provided an advantage.

#270

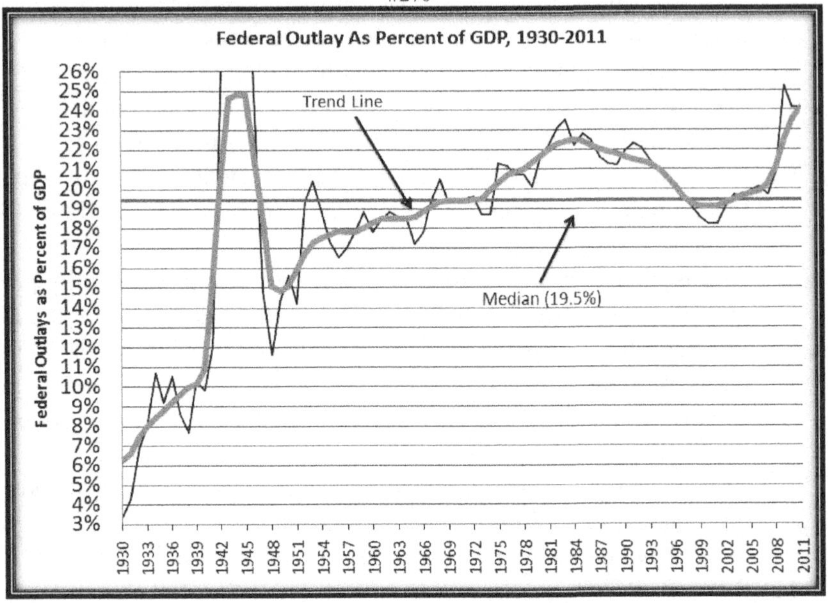

In the 1980s, Federal outlays averaged 22.2%. There is a lively and often silly debate about how much government spending is appropriate. Often nirvana would seem to be achievable if we were to swallow hook line and sinker the line of some of the louder voices in the arena. But history presents a calmer picture. Good growth rates were achieved independent of government size. The GDP growth rate trend line is strikingly near the median at Federal outlays between 17% and 21%.

On the small government side, those instances beneath a 17% outlay that had high GDP growth rates occurred during the period from 1934 to 1957. The high growth rates in those years were a consequence of vastly improving income distributions, not small government, per se. Indeed, government was growing in those years.

A more appropriate debate can be directed toward deficit spending. Primarily deficit spending results for two reasons: tax cuts or increased

---

* "Take one fifth of all the produce of the land during the seven plenteous years … Lay up grain … That food shall be a reserve for the land against the seven years of famine that are to befall the land." – Genesis 41:34

Federal spending. When tax collection is appropriately raised and sufficient tax revenue results, deficits are reduced. You will notice that the median deficit was 2.55% of GDP. Even a 1% increase in tax revenue would have greatly reduced deficits.

#271

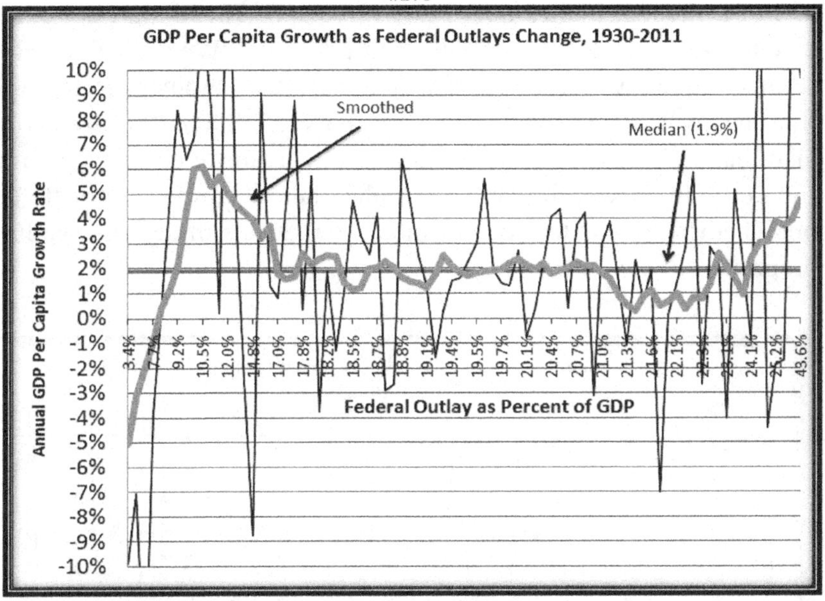

#271B

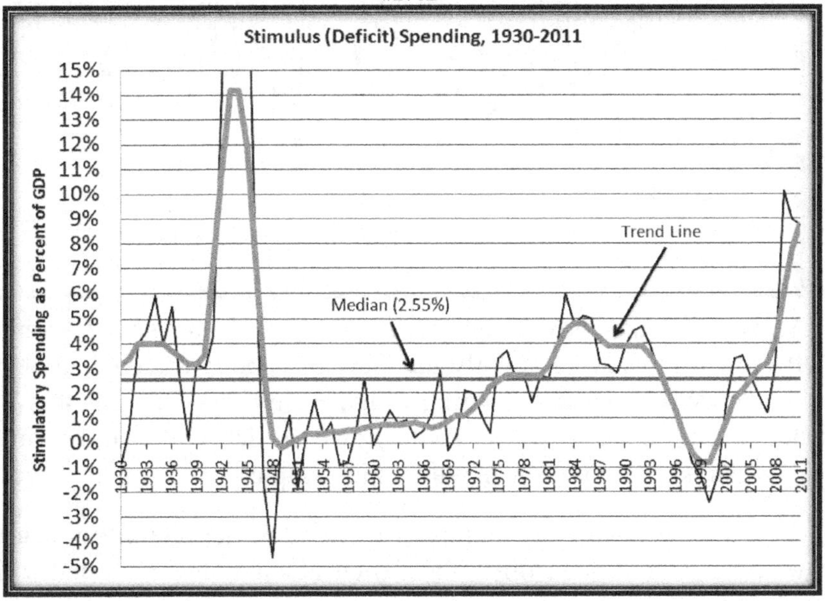

There is much confusion about when large peacetime deficits occurred in U.S. history. From 1933 to 1939, FDR ran an average deficit of 3.67% of GDP. The objective then was to pull us out of the Great Depression and to let the MAJ (which was on the brink of starvation) live and thrive. The next large peacetime deficit, 1981-1989, averaged 4.07%. It was four tenths of a percent higher than FDR's average. Those high deficits were later cited to indicate that deficits don't matter. "We won the mid-term elections, this is our due," was a widely reported comment in that regard. Unfortunately U.S. mismanagement in the years 2000-2008 was so spectacular that the world's economy came within a hair of completely unraveling in 2008. In answer to that catastrophe, there is now a legitimate debate about whether the low-tax regime and current levels of deficit spending are appropriate.

#272

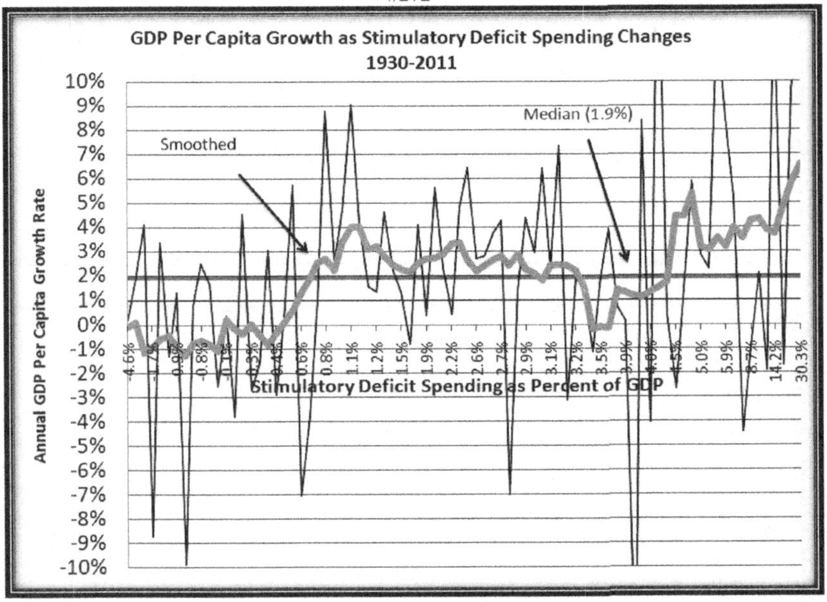

As we see in the above graph-272, from about 0.6% to a 3.2% stimulus, GDP growth rates were slightly and variably above the median. A wide variety of deficits were delivering roughly similar GDP growth. With a pronounced negative stimulus (paying down the debt), there did seem to be a significant slowing in growth within this sample.

With a Keynesian-style multiplier of say 2.5, the premise is that GDP grows by 2.5 multiplied times the deficit amount. It can be more finely stated, but we see in the upcoming graph-273 that the multiplier notion does not hold. At a wide range of deficit spending rates, GDP growth rate does not respond in a systematic multiplier fashion. And this is the case whether we look at average growth rates over 1, 2, or 3 years.

Currie, in the Great Depression and later, expressed doubts about the Keynes multiplier.[208] Skepticism is justified. In my view, the Keynes multiplier does not exist – in the sense that it is now useless for economic stimulus projections.

In only 38% of the cases in graph-273 did the multiplier exceed one [38%= 1-62%]. In only 25% of cases was the increase in GDP twice as large as the government deficit, which is to say that about 25% of deficit spending cases are supportable based on GDP outcome. In 32% of the cases it was between 0 and 1, which is to say that the increase in GDP was less than the deficit that the Federal government ran up. In these instances, deficit spending was a bust.

In the 30% of cases where the multiplier was negative, GDP and deficit moved in opposite directions. This can be advantageous in instances where the deficit is negative but growth is positive.

The Keynesian Multiplier is widely variable and usually unsuitable for justifying tax cuts or for justifying increased government spending. If either of these are worthwhile, they need to stand on their merits alone.

#273

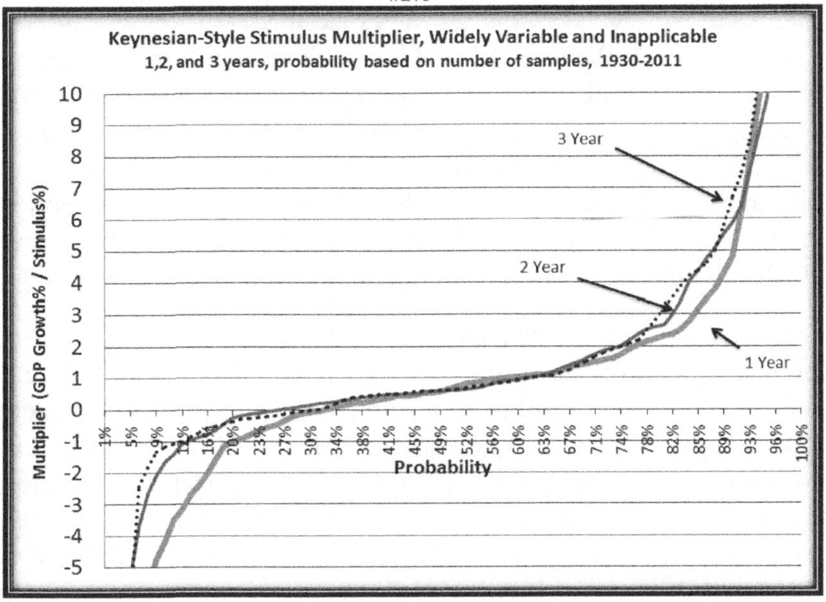

Probability, as in graph-273, is insufficient to give the answer. For that we must dig. In the following graph-274, we see numerous instances before 1972 where the multiplier exceeded 2, at least providing some justification for stimulatory deficits in those instances. However, subsequent to the late 1970s, a completely different picture emerges where the deficits were seldom supportable for purposes of stimulus.

#274

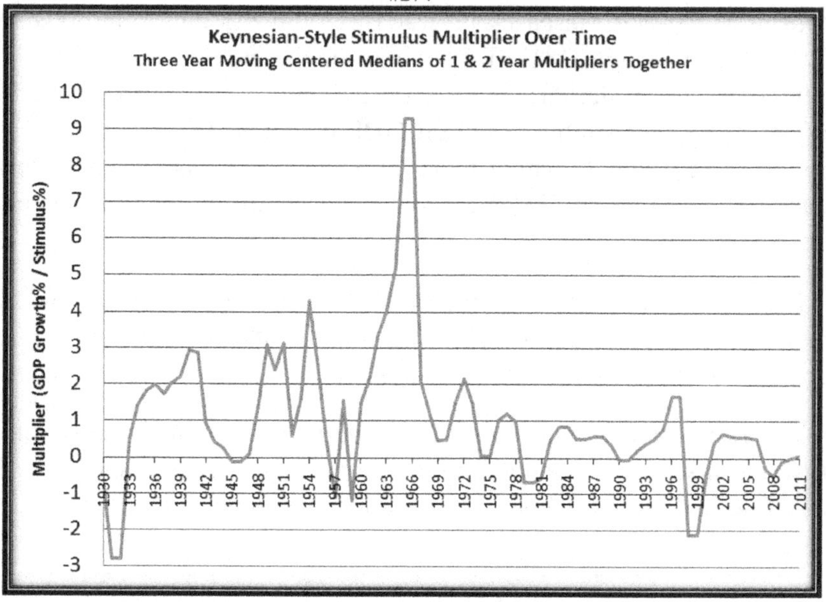

When the multiplier is between 0 and 1, it means that the government is injecting more into the economy (by way of deficit) than the economy is producing in growth. With few exceptions, this seems to have been the case since the late 1970s. Unless deficits are explicitly targeted to worthwhile endeavors, they do not work. In the current economy, the notion of a stimulus multiplier where a significantly greater output (GDP growth) results from a stimulus input (Federal deficit) is seldom valid.

Deficits, (by way of tax cuts or by increased government spending) even when they work, are a transitory stimulus solution with lasting repercussions. If deficits are not periodically paid down (in a true countercyclical fashion), then interest expenses eventually become quite large. Not only will interest expenses grow, but in times of high interest rates, they may grow to assume cripplingly large proportions of the budget. And when deficits are disproportionally large relative to GDP growth, the adverse impact is accentuated.

Government is a servant of the people. Deficits do not reliably produce economic growth. If government functions are disproportionately consumed in interest payments on debt, then government has insufficient financial strength to be a good servant elsewhere. And, when accumulated debt is large, government also loses the ability to effectively use deficit spending counter-cyclically as may be required during adverse economic times or in crisis. All of this together cautions against excessive debt.

None of this should be construed as an argument for reducing expenditures of an appropriately sized government that is making rationally beneficial decisions. Explicitly, governmental expenditures do not go into a black hole. Like the private consumer, it is an economic player who circulates money. It just does so on a larger scale. The argument made here is for being more attentive toward being sure that government is adequately funded and that, when deficits occur, they are appropriately sized.

Now what?

The common story you hear is stunningly misleading:

> President John F. Kennedy adopted the principles of Keynesian economics in 1961 … He proposed substantial tax cuts to lift the economy out of a slump; after these were enacted, the economy grew rapidly. … The 1980s provided another dramatic demonstration of how fiscal policy works. In 1981 Congress passed [tax cuts]. … The fiscal expansion helped pull the American economy out of the deep recession of 1981-1982. …[209]

It sounds like a nice unified story of success. Wish it were so. Take a look at the table.[210] You will see that the two cases are vastly different. In the 1961-69 example, stimulus spending was only 0.80% of GDP. By contrast, in 1981-1989, the deficit spending was huge – five times larger at fully 4% of GDP. It was the largest U.S. peacetime deficit since the Great Depression.

Period	Stimulus (Deficit Spending) Median % of GDP	GDP Per Capita Growth Median for 1st & 2nd Year	Multiplier
1961-1969	0.80%	3.58%	4.48
1981-1989	4.00%	2.29%	0.57
factor	5.00	0.64	0.13
FDR, Great Depression			
1933-1937	4.50%	8.37%	1.86

Now look at efficacy. In the 1961-1969 period, the multiplier was 4.48. This was sufficient to justify the tax cut. In sharp contrast, the 1981-1989 deficit spending was only 13% as effective. The multiplier was a puny 0.57. By a large margin, the 1981-1989 Government stimulus expenditures exceeded the GDP growth that resulted from it, explicitly a 4.0% cost to gain 2.29% in GDP. The 1981-1989 deficit spending tax-cut program was an abject failure. It cost the nation more than the nation reaped. We still pay for it.

It is astoundingly remarkable that economists continue to call for large deficit spending. Since the late 1970s, there have been vanishingly few cases where the gain in GDP growth has exceeded the cost of the deficit. Such recommendations are old school. They had merit long ago – not now.

To put the 1980s deficit spending in perspective, when FDR came to power in 1933, the GDP per capita for the prior three years had fallen: -9.87%, -7.05%, and -14.73%. The nation was in crisis. Even under those extreme conditions, FDR's average deficit spending averaged 3.67% from 1933-1939. By comparison, in 1980 and 1982, GDP had fallen less severely: -6.99% and -4.03%. Strong counteracting measures were needed. However, instead of deficit spending being applied for a short corrective burst, stimulatory deficits remained in place at disproportionately high levels in most years up until the present.

In the healthy economy from 1950 to 1979, real total GDP grew at an average 4.00%; in the same period deficits averaged 1.06% annually, effectively a 3.77 multiplier [3.77= 4.00%/1.06%]. This was prudent governance. In sharp contrast, during the period of decline *from 1980 to 2011, real total GDP grew at an average 2.2%, while deficits averaged 3.2% of GDP annually, effectively a 0.69 multiplier – deficits exceeding growth by a large margin.*

Focus on the 3.2% of deficit growth being greater than the 2.2% GDP growth. This indicates that since 1980, the nation has accumulated more in federal debt than it has in GDP growth. Macroeconomists should have been wildly waving the cautionary flag of prudence. High deficits consistently exceeding GDP growth are a radical departure from the good governance and the healthy economy that existed prior to 1980. Since the bulk of GDP growth came from the Federal deficit, Washington = Honey Pot became the well-known formula that attracted a stunning variety of primates.

Before going further, we need to catch our breath and do some deep thinking. The multiplier was probably a flawed concept from the outset. It is plain that numerous forces act upon an economy: money supply, interest rates, changes in income distribution, social conditions, trading patterns, et cetera. To expect deficit spending to systematically override all the many other components of the economy is, at best, misguided. The low efficacy of deficit spending over the past 30+ years may relate to 1) how government is spending the money; 2) deficits used continuously instead of just for recovery; 3) changes in how the economy is operating; or, perhaps most importantly, 4) structural relationships between deficit and customary GDP growth rates.* In any case, we can no longer proceed with the hubris that deficit spending per se is a sound policy. That reflexive rationale lost validity about 40 years ago.

From this mess we may be able to salvage something. The multiplier may no longer be useful for projections, but it remains useful for retrospective analysis and planning.

We can learn a lot from looking at the distribution of GDP per capita growth rates.[211] Regarding good governance, we would know from the outset (the next graph-278) that in only 34% of cases did GDP per capita growth exceed 3.2%. So if a nation were running an average 3.2% deficit, as the U.S. did in the 1980-2011 era, it should have known from the outset that there was only a remote possibility that the multiplier would have exceeded 1. In other words, in the post-1980 era, competent management would have known that deficits would have exceeded GDP growth by looking at the distribution in a graph similar to the one you see below. Competent management would have then increased taxes and/or reduced expenses, depending on which of those options was most desirable to get the deficit to a level having a higher multiplier.

There is a simple rule for deficits: Deficit as a percent of GDP should not exceed one half of expected GDP growth. If this plays out, you have a multiplier of 2, and you attain a status of being a competent manager. In short, the higher your multiplier, the higher your status. Also you do the nation a favor because in times of crisis you leave your successor the op-

---

* This last point is particularly important. For example, if an economy customarily grows at approximately 2.2% over the long term, deficits (especially if they are regular deficits) significantly in excess of 2.2% of GDP are apt to be a failure, which is to say they are likely to have a multiplier between 0 and 1. Deficits are best used only in moderation or for addressing infrequently acute problems.

tion of employing deficits with greatest force when they truly are needed. This is the simple plan. Now for the more carefully-tuned one.

Levels of deficit spending are often referred to ambiguously as a "stimulus." Paying the debt down in good times is even more ambiguously referred to (if at all). For the various scenarios a nation is apt to face throughout its history, there has been no consensus about appropriate amounts of stimulus or appropriate payback schedules. Especially in poor nations that are hard-pressed to serve their people, there may be excessive pressure to try a "stimulus" without knowing what size is appropriate.

Whether rich or poor, a more detailed view of appropriate deficit schedules is required. The history from 1930 to the present, shown in the following graph-278, provides sufficient information about potential GDP outcomes, both good and bad. For the appropriate deficit, graph-278 uses the 1950 to 1979 period (where deficits averaged 1.06%) as the desirable long-term deficit objective. This period is also an appropriate reference point because it was an era of equitable income distribution, the objective of this book.

#278

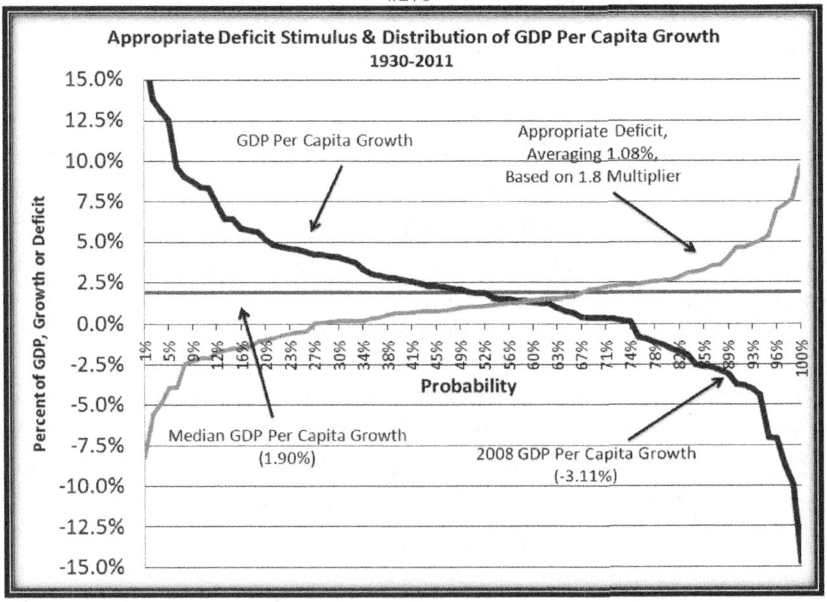

Sorting the GDP per capita growth curve in reverse order and dividing it by a 1.8 multiplier, creates the "appropriate deficit" curve shown in graph-278.* Negative numbers indicate when and by how much the debt is paid down. The curve provides stimulus, when needed, and cools down the economy when it overheats. It also meets the standard of having an average 1.08% deficit for all of history. Since the adjustments occur in sync with GDP and since many of the adjustments are small (less than 1%), they are amenable to tax adjustments (lower taxes in bad years, increased taxes in good years).

The important point is not about details but the need to abolish the present regime where deficits exceed GDP growth and to return to a standard that has produced a high growth rate and high citizen satisfaction in the past (1950-1979). By basing the deficit curve on a 1.8 multiplier across all scenarios, the pony is shifted from government providing all of GDP growth via deficits to the private sector providing an increasing share, much as it did in other successful periods of U.S. history.

#279

You probably have the drift of it. We can see how effectively government is using deficit by looking at the multiplier. When the multiplier is high, the nation is delivering a great deal of GDP growth with a small amount of deficit. When the multiplier is between zero and one, the con-

* The reverse sort is especially effective because it identifies past periods of greatest growth and matches them with periods when greatest growth is required. It then employs the desired multiplier and consequently the desired deficit to produce that growth.

verse is true. The method is not completely satisfactory because negative multipliers (particularly paying down debt or negative GDP growth) muddy it up. Notwithstanding, the above graph-279 should give you a partial picture of when governments performed well and when they did not. The high spikes often resulted when debt was paid down. For a practical example consider the year 1964, which we have previously represented as a year of great economic success. In that year the Good Governance Indicator was between 4.5 to 5.7, depending upon your perspective.

#280

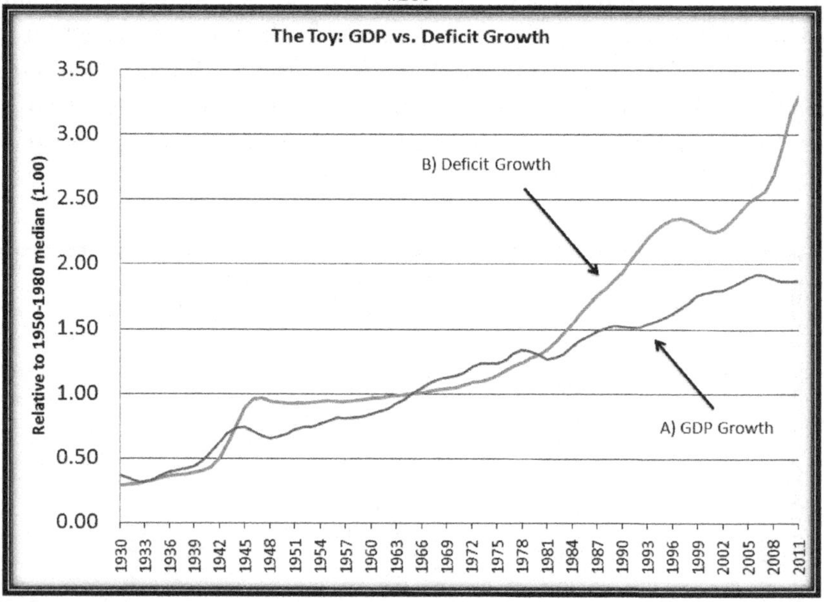

Just playing around for my amusement, I created two nations. Nation A was a nation with the same GDP per capita growth rate as the United States. Nation B was a hypothetical nation whose GDP per capita growth rate was equal to the United States deficit expressed as a percent of GDP. Then I stepped through Nation A and B's growth rates (a product series) to get their cumulative growth. Since I was particularly interested in the difference between the post- and pre-1980 eras, I normalized both curves, so that their medians for the 1950-1980 period equaled 1.00. The graph toy that resulted is graph-280. Thought it might interest you. It illustrates when and to what degree governmental attitude toward debt changed. True to form, Nation B (the deficit nation) outpaced Nation A (the GDP nation), as we all too well knew it would – the winner in this instance being the loser.

Some aspects of this are not a toy. In the foreground, we have deficit growth. But subsequent to 1980 and in the background we also have had the burgeoning class of the spectacularly rich, who grew in measures never before seen in all of U.S. history. All of this as the MAJ and the jobs they depend on were destroyed.

Sorting it out.

I have been troubled many times while writing this book to find my expectations overturned by the evidence. I had expected strong immutable relationships between low interest rates and GDP growth, stimulatory deficits and GDP growth, jobs and GDP growth, stock market values and GDP, and the list goes on. In all of these, the relationships were ambiguous, complex, or difficult to penetrate. It has been humbling to have been corrected so often by the data. My training had misled me.

However, I did have a forewarning that it might. I purchased many introductory economic textbooks to see how economics was now being taught. I slogged through one. When I got to about page 700, there were two graphs. They both had differently shaped demand and supply curves purportedly representing the same condition. One of the graphs represented the Monetarist position; the other the Keynesian position. Then my little brain said, "Whoa!" These are the two main approaches to macroeconomics. To have a page-700 debate about the shape of the curves – that is stunning. These guys don't know the shapes of the fundamental demand and supply curves. The representations were little more than a mental exercise. If the page-700 graphs had been on page 5 (when the reader was still alert), he or she might have had the good sense to put the book down and do something more worthwhile, like _____ (well, you fill in the blank on this one, perhaps using the word "armpit").

Notwithstanding much fine work, I do think the profession is both insufficiently inclusive and insufficiently accurate. It is too quick to look to the aggregate before understanding the specific. It has completely failed to develop a theoretical consensus about appropriate relationships between income and wealth distributions. And its prevailing theories are insufficiently protective where great harm is likely (e.g., years 2008±). By having preconceived notions about equilibrium curves and aggregates, I sense that much is lost. Some of which is vital.

When I see biological systems or the miracles of human physiology, I am struck by a sense of beauty – how economically well designed they are. I suspect the features of those designs have much to say about economics. In the late 1980s and early 1990s, regulation of the autonomic nervous system greatly interested me. In those years before the Internet I drove from medical library to medical library searching studies related to it. I have several thousand copies of journal articles that I made during the period and that I hope to get back to (unrelated to economics) in the not too distant future. In short, it was an obsession, which seems to be returning.

The autonomic nervous system is the portion of your nervous system beneath the level of consciousness that automatically regulates organs – the heart being one of them. There is a field of study that concerns itself with variability of heart rate.[212] Contrary to what you might expect, a highly regular beat-to-beat interval is not a marker of health. Instead an unnaturally regular heart rate is associated with numerous maladies. Conversely, states of health are often related to heart rate variability produced by a well-regulated autonomic nervous system.

By way of clarification, the heart rate variability about which I am talking is not what you see on EKGs in the doctor's office or what you might be able to discern by taking your pulse rate. Instead, heart rate variability usually requires rather sophisticated mathematical techniques to analyze it. But in the analysis one can see how the two halves of the system are acting.

One half of the autonomic nervous system is for slowing down the heart (or to state it another way, for conserving energy). When functioning properly, the slowing acts quickly within milliseconds. Its function is customarily critical for preserving health.

The other half of the autonomic nervous system is for stimulating (speeding up) the heart. The greatest danger lies there. When it is overactive, it is destructive. In illness there is a tendency for it to be overactive. Beta blocker pills may be taken to control it. These remarks are for giving a snapshot, not for conveying academic accuracy and certainly not for medical advice.

By contrast to traits which culture seems to admire, the autonomic nervous system acts in precisely the opposite fashion. It normally rewards the portion of the system that slows down (which is to say conserves energy) and punishes an overactive stimulatory system.

If we were to apply the language of the autonomic nervous system elsewhere, many of the stimulatory acts that we admire in culture, in success, and in economics would be apt to be punished (reduced longevity or frank illness). In the language of the autonomic nervous system, the capacity to conserve (and I mean this in the literal sense, not the political one) is vital for the preservation of the organism.

But it is a mix. Both halves are required for the organism to function well, neither the conserving nor the stimulatory half alone will suffice. It is the way they work together that defines health. I cannot but feel that a great deal of life and economics is much the same.

I view excessive and sustained monetary or fiscal stimulus with skepticism. I doubt that they are health-giving. In these past few pages we saw, contrary to expectations, that mid-range interest rates exceeding 4% delivered strong economic growth, and very low interest rates, at least in my view, produced more ambiguous outcomes. And when it came to deficit spending, again contrary to initial expectations, we saw that more moderate deficits often were the most efficient (highest multipliers). The economic system may be like our heart in the way it functions, requiring variability, but not rewarding extremes.

CH. 10

THE WORLD

Since antiquity the rich have lived in splendor. Today nations may have trophy buildings and the like. These biceps of achievement are fine, inspiring, and perhaps necessary. But a nation has little distinction if it serves only the rich. For distinction, one must look elsewhere.

The Modernity Timeline.

We need to know how the MAJ is doing in each nation, but GDP per capita does not account for income distribution. For this reason, GDP per capita fails to give a reliable picture of the incomes of the majority in each nation. The methods we have been using here, however, make it trivially easy to see how successfully each nation provides incomes for its majority.

We can easily find the position on the Modernity Timeline using the following method: Match the MAJ income for any nation with the last year in U.S. MAJ income history when that nation's MAJ income was at least as great as the U.S. MAJ income [MAJ income= MAJ/60*GDP per capita]. Doing so gives the Modernity Year that you see in the following table. Table-286 provides one of the most reliable methods for gauging a nation's economic success.

#286

The Modernity Timeline

MAJ Income Rank	Percentile Income Rank	Nation	Modernity Year	Years Relative to USA	MAJ Income Rank	Percentile Income Rank	Nation	Modernity Year	Years Relative to USA
1	1%	Qatar	2091	79	57	36%	Azerbaijan	1940	-72
2	1%	Luxembourg	2060	48	58	37%	Seychelles	1939	-73
3	2%	Norway	2043	31	59	38%	Mexico	1939	-73
4	3%	Sweden	2025	13	60	38%	Panama	1938	-74
5	3%	Singapore	2024	12	61	39%	Iran	1938	-74
6	4%	Austria	2023	11	62	39%	Tunisia	1938	-74
7	4%	Switzerland	2021	9	63	40%	Albania	1938	-74
8	5%	Netherlands	2021	9	64	41%	CostaRica	1937	-75
9	6%	Iceland	2021	9	65	41%	Macedonia	1937	-75
10	6%	Canada	2018	6	66	42%	Ukraine	1937	-75
11	7%	Denmark	2018	6	67	43%	Algeria	1936	-76
12	8%	Germany	2018	6	68	43%	Kosovo	1936	-76
13	8%	Finland	2018	6	69	44%	Peru	1935	-77
14	9%	Australia	2017	5	70	45%	China	1934	-78
15	10%	Belgium	2015	3	71	45%	Maldives	1934	-78
16	10%	Ireland	2013	1	72	46%	Botswana	1933	-79
17	11%	Taiwan	2013	1	73	46%	Jamaica	1933	-79
18	**11%**	**UnitedStates**	2012	**0**	74	47%	Turkmenista	1933	-79
19	12%	France	2008	-4	75	48%	Suriname	1932	-80
20	13%	UnitedKingdc	2004	-8	76	48%	Bosnia and I	1932	-80
21	13%	Japan	1999	-13	77	49%	Dominican R	1931	-81
22	14%	Korea,South	1998	-14	**78**	**50%**	**Brazil**	**1930**	**-82**
23	15%	Slovenia	1989	-23	79	50%	Egypt	1919	-93
24	15%	Greece	1988	-24	80	51%	Guyana	1918	-94
25	16%	CzechRepubli	1988	-24	81	52%	Thailand	1913	-99
26	17%	Malta	1988	-24	82	52%	Ecuador	1907	-105
27	17%	HongKong	1986	-26	83	53%	Armenia	1906	-106
28	18%	Spain	1986	-26	84	54%	Colombia	1903	-109
29	18%	Italy	1975	-37	85	54%	Belize	1901	-111
30	19%	Israel	1973	-39	86	55%	Jordan	1896	-116
31	20%	NewZealand	1973	-39	87	55%	SouthAfrica	1895	-117
32	20%	Slovakia	1971	-41	88	56%	ElSalvador	1895	-117
33	21%	Cyprus	1968	-44	89	57%	SyrianArabR	1894	-118
34	22%	Portugal	1965	-47	90	57%	Angola	1891	-121
35	22%	Hungary	1964	-48	91	58%	Bhutan	1889	-123
36	23%	TrinidadandT	1962	-50	92	59%	Georgia	1889	-123
37	24%	Estonia	1961	-51	93	59%	Morocco	1888	-124
38	24%	Poland	1961	-51	94	60%	Indonesia	1886	-126
39	**25%**	**Croatia**	**1959**	**-53**	95	61%	SriLanka	1882	-130
40	25%	Belarus	1953	-59	96	61%	Paraguay	1880	-132
41	26%	Lithuania	1952	-60	97	62%	Mongolia	1880	-132
42	27%	Latvia	1948	-64	98	62%	India	1879	-133
43	27%	Russia	1945	-67	99	63%	Guatemala	1877	-135
44	28%	Kazakhstan	1945	-67	100	64%	Swaziland	1877	-135
45	29%	Gabon	1943	-69	101	64%	Congo,Rep.	1877	-135
46	29%	Mauritius	1943	-69	102	65%	Uzbekistan	1876	-136
47	30%	Serbia	1943	-69	103	66%	Vietnam	1875	-137
48	31%	Romania	1942	-70	104	66%	Philippines	1874	-138
49	31%	Uruguay	1941	-71	105	67%	Bolivia	1867	-145
50	32%	Malaysia	1941	-71	106	68%	CapeVerde	1866	-146
51	32%	Argentina	1941	-71	107	68%	Pakistan	1866	-146
52	33%	Montenegro	1941	-71	108	69%	Djibouti	1864	-148
53	34%	Chile	1940	-72	109	69%	Yemen	1864	-148
54	34%	Bulgaria	1940	-72	110	70%	Timor-Leste	1863	-149
55	35%	Venezuela	1940	-72	111	71%	Moldova	1862	-150
56	36%	Turkey	1940	-72	112	71%	Laos	1861	-151

An IMF report shows that more than 75% of major economic powers have worsened their income distributions in the Mid-1980s to Mid-2000s interval. Only a quarter of the nations in the study remained substantially constant or became more equitable.[213] With the maldistribution contagion in progress, measuring nations using MAJ income becomes increasingly important.[214] The Modernity Timeline tells us how we are doing.

The Modernity Timeline (continued)

	MAJ Income Rank	Percentile Income Rank	Nation	Modernity Year	Years Relative to USA
113	113	72%	Honduras	1860	-152
114	114	73%	Kyrgyzstan	1858	-154
115	115	73%	Ghana	1855	-157
116	116	74%	Nicaragua	1854	-158
117	117	75%	Nigeria	1852	-160
118	**118**	**75%**	**Tajikistan**	**1852**	**-160**
119	119	76%	Mauritania	1848	-164
120	120	76%	Cameroon	1847	-165
121	121	77%	Namibia	1846	-166
122	122	78%	Bangladesh	1843	-169
123	123	78%	PapuaNewGi	1842	-170
124	124	79%	Cambodia	1842	-170
125	125	80%	Senegal	1842	-170
126	126	80%	Chad	1835	-177
127	127	81%	Coted'Ivoire	1832	-180
128	128	82%	Benin	1832	-180
129	129	82%	Gambia,The	1831	-181
130	130	83%	Tanzania	1828	-184
131	131	83%	SaoTomeand	1825	-187
132	132	84%	Kenya	1824	-188
133	133	85%	Micronesia,Fe	1820	-192
134	134	85%	Guinea-Bissa	1820	-192

MAJ Income Rank	Percentile Income Rank	Nation	Modernity Year	Years Relative to USA
135	86%	BurkinaFaso	1818	-194
136	87%	Mali	1817	-195
137	87%	Ethiopia	1817	-195
138	88%	Afghanistan	1815	-197
139	89%	Zambia	1814	-198
140	89%	Uganda	1812	-200
141	90%	Nepal	1810	-202
142	90%	Guinea	1810	-202
143	91%	Togo	1808	-204
144	92%	Lesotho	1802	-210
145	92%	Malawi	1798	-214
146	93%	Mozambique	1796	-216
147	94%	Rwanda	1794	-218
148	94%	Madagascar	1792	-220
149	95%	Haiti	1788	-224
150	96%	Niger	1773	-239
151	96%	Comoros	1771	-241
152	97%	SierraLeone	1766	-246
153	97%	Liberia	1766	-246
154	98%	CentralAfric	1756	-256
155	99%	Zimbabwe	1752	-260
156	99%	Burundi	1745	**-267**
157	100%	Congo,Dem.	1740	-272

Notwithstanding the simplicity of the method, you have crucial development information. You can see the current relative MAJ position of nations along a continuum of MAJ income growths that were historically achieved [and when necessary, by a trend line extending it into the future or distant past]. By doing so, you can see the number of years of growth required to raise the MAJ income for any nation to a designated higher level (if nations are destined to follow the growth path that the United States did). The timeline gives an appreciation of the true task of moving nations through history and into the future.

Affection throughout the timeline.

This Modernity Timeline section is a very difficult section for me to write. It can easily enflame emotions inappropriately. Hopefully, this will not occur. As I type these words I wrestle with how to say it.

I'll begin by mentioning a motorcycle trip I took to Mexico in 1965. … Graduated from high school…. A dreadful Spanish student. … Fearful of failing Spanish in college. … I liked economics, so I struck out on my own to study economics and Spanish at the summer session of the National University in Mexico City. The trip was a coming-of-age eye opener. I flew from Virginia to Tennessee. Then on the cheap, took a bus to Houston. I was a naive farm boy who believed (as I still do) in stewardship, conservation of soil, and decency. Flying over Tennessee, I saw as far as the eye could see mountains strip-mined bare. It was a shock. I've yet to get over it. … Never knew people could be so cruel to the land.

The plan was to buy a used Honda 305cc motorcycle in Houston, but none were to be found. A dealership had a new 160cc Honda. I had never ridden a motorcycle. The salesman took me for a test ride, flying through downtown Houston weaving through as many cars as he could find. Terrified, I screamed again and again: "I'll buy it. I'll buy it." It turned out to be an excellent bike for the trip. I saw Mexico at a slow pace, close up – so close that in my mind's eye, I still see individual grasshoppers as I rode along.

Edmundo Flores, my economics professor in Mexico, drove home a pivotal concept: "Underdevelopment is a Madison Avenue advertising phrase. There is no such thing as underdevelopment. It is poverty." He is right. It was poverty then. It is poverty now. Anyone who lives it knows it.

From that trip onward, I have loved Mexico. The people, the land – it is a close emotional bond. A similar feeling occasionally comes when visiting other countries of roughly the same economic status. I live in a working-class neighborhood in Appalachia, once in a while going elsewhere. The fancy bright lights of economic success are ok for an occasional visit, but plain and less troublesome ways are my preference. There are attributes to not living at the budding edge of modernity. Many people throughout the world know it.

I am reminded, when thinking back on my grandparents' home, how nice it was on the screen porch with neighbors coming in and out. That was the 1950s. Looking at the classic films from the 1920s and 1930s similarly shows fully developed lives and ways of living. Reading authors of the 1800s again provides a reminder that much of the old times were attractive and interesting. Ability, intelligence, and humor obviously are not newly born children of modernity.

Clearly as creatures of the present, we benefit greatly from modernity, but treasures of the past and other ways of living are plainly evident, often appealing. But if you are poor, your view is apt to be more conflicted because you can see modernity, but your nation and present income may compel you to live an entirely different life.

For each nation, we can see in the graph-289 how modernity (as measured by the income of the 60% majority) plays out. In half of the nations of the world, the majority of people live at an income level equal to or greater than their MAJ counterparts in the U.S. experienced in the year 1930.

In nearly all remaining nations, the MAJ is living at an income level lower than the U.S. MAJ income in year 1919. One quarter of nations are above year 1959. One quarter of nations are beneath year 1852. The range is huge and you can see it in graph-289.

#289

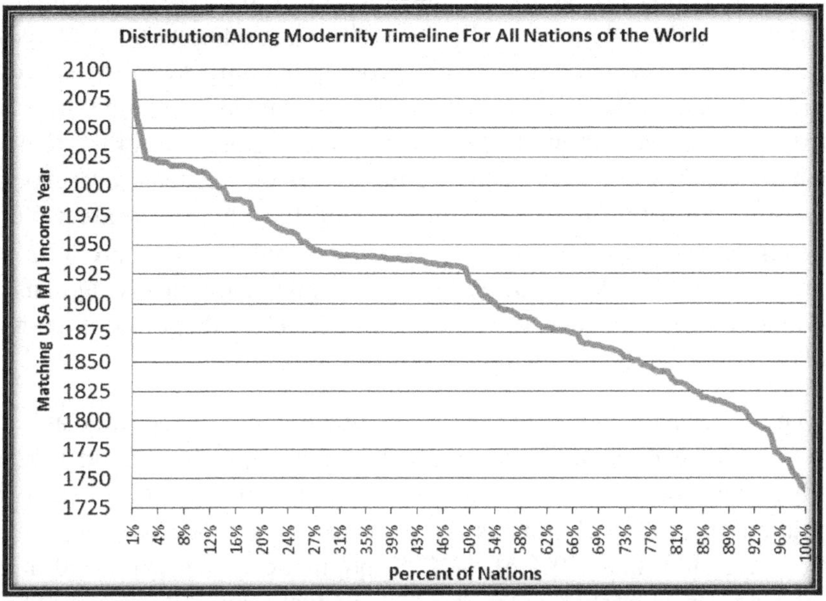

The timeline tends to define your life whether you are in the MAJ or above it. If maldistribution is acute and modernity primitive, an element of meanness, dismissiveness, and dominance too frequently is imbedded in the upper class's treatment of the MAJ.

Geography and the USA MAJ.

It is hardly the magic of economics alone that propels U.S. success. Contrary to extravagant economic claims, the U.S. advantage is, in large part, a blessing of geography and attitude.

O beautiful for spacious skies,
For amber waves of grain,
For purple mountain majesties
Above the fruited plain!

America! America!
God shed His grace on thee,
And crown thy good with brotherhood
From sea to shining sea! …

America! America!
God mend thine ev'ry flaw,
Confirm thy soul in self-control,
Thy liberty in law.[215]

The advantages of geography are implicit in the lyrics. By climate, by absence of tropical disease, by agricultural productivity, by access to oceans and by navigable waterways, geography confers enormous economic advantages on the United States. Should you doubt geography's influence on economics, think deeply. Worldwide regions within the temperate zone and within 60 miles (100 kilometers) of the seacoast or a navigable waterway constitute only 8.4% of the world's inhabitable area. Yet this tiny region contains 22.8% of the world's population and produces more than half of the world's GDP (52.9%).[216] It goes without saying that population and economic success would be more widely dispersed if geography and economic success were not so potently linked.

The U.S. has a variably shaped coastline on both the Atlantic and Pacific Ocean with good harbors. It has the Mississippi River and tributaries midway, and the Great Lakes to the north, all of these aiding water transportation and heavy shipments. With access to two oceans along much of its border, more than 50% of the U.S. population lives within 50 miles of the oceans or navigable waterways.[217] The many benefits provided by water are central to the economic workings of a nation.

The temperate zone in the U.S. reduces parasites and provides favorable climates for farms and for healthful living. Parasites are so severe in many poor, hot nations that intestinal worms and tropical diseases are major reasons that children do poorly in school. There, deworming children is often key to improving school success. The U.S. also once shared similar conditions. From 1910 onward, the Rockefeller Foundation fought hookworms in children in the American South.[218]

The U.S. also has vastly different regions, thus a setback in one area can often be offset by a favorable outcome in another. These are silent but persistent and substantial advantages. No nation in the world has the United States' great geographic advantages. It is a gift. Its long-standing economic can-do spirit is outstanding. Alexis De Tocqueville in his 1830s writing on the U.S. was also struck by it.

Even with its huge geographical advantages, the U.S. ranks 18th in the world on the MAJ Modernity Timeline. Since most nations do not possess the U.S. advantages, it is clear that their strategy must be economically smarter about economic development and ensuring that it indeed does benefit their MAJ. It is only by superior methods that they can advance quickly up the timeline. They do not have the luxury of error.

Even if U.S. MAJ income growth rates were grafted onto other nations, in more than half of the nations it would not be sufficient for them to reach current U.S. MAJ income levels within an 82-year lifetime, as can be seen in the prior table at the 50th percentile point. Twenty-five percent of the nations would not even be able to reach the current standard in 160 years at the historical U.S. MAJ growth rates.

It is mean-spirited and wrong to hold out hope that past U.S. growth rates and a market economy are alone the answer for people in desperately poor nations. Poor nations require greater wisdom to succeed – to live smart, to grow smart, and to avoid big mistakes.

Highest priority: population growth less than job growth.

If population growth greatly exceeds job growth, a moribund economy and a vast, idle population is the outcome.

#291

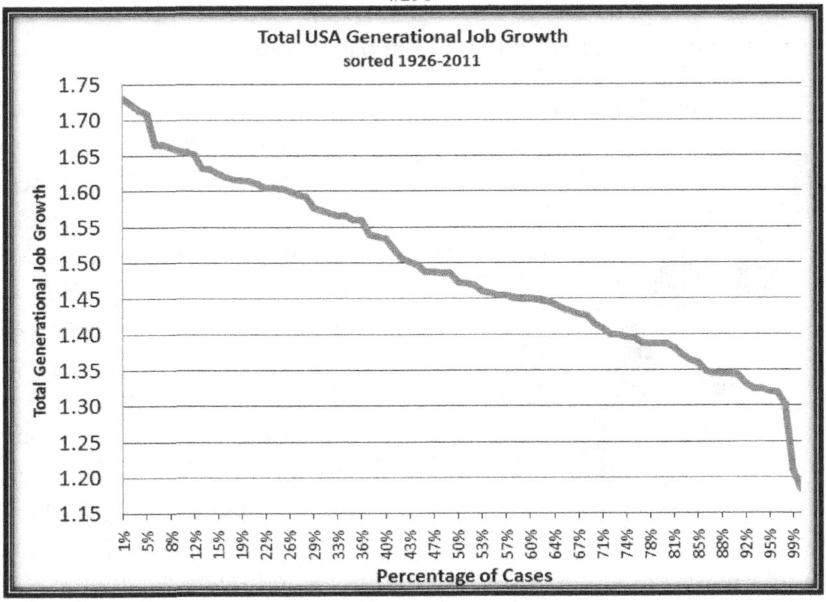

U.S. job growth history provides a ready standard for the number of jobs that can be created over a generation in a prosperous nation. At the median in all years since 1926, job growth in the U.S. has been slightly less than 1.5x over a generation as shown in the above graph-291. At this writing it is about 1.3x. *Long-term population growth should not exceed long-term job growth in any nation. Period.*

The ladies determine economic success.

Generational population growth provides a reference point from two perspectives. First, it encompasses a woman's primary child bearing years. Second, the period is long enough for analysis and yet young adults can still recall its approximate starting point (or know that it occurred no more than a few years before their birth).

If we consider three 26-year generations (total 78 yrs), each with a 2x growth rate in each generation, the outcome, at the end of the period, is a population 8x larger than it was at the time of our birth [8= 2^3]. Imagine the infrastructure: highways, traffic, and so on that might well be required under those conditions. This is untenable.

In several nations, average lifespan exceeds 78 years – three generations. In many instances, this means that our children and their children will be alive at the time of our death. At the end of the 78-year period, each woman having two children in each generation not only replenishes the population when she and her spouse are gone, but she produces a population growth considerably higher than most people would intuitively expect.

The graphic seeks to tell to tell a story. The ladies are the conduit for population growth. The graphic shows an exact 50% chance of a female birth in each generation, daughters being born at 26 year intervals,[219] and each lady in her generation giving birth to two children, who survive a full life. If this sequence persists into the indefinite future, population growth would be 3x every 78 years – the initial 2 parents dying soon after age 78 and leaving behind 6 descendants [3= 6/2] … the male children marrying ladies from other families and being accounted for by a similar process there.

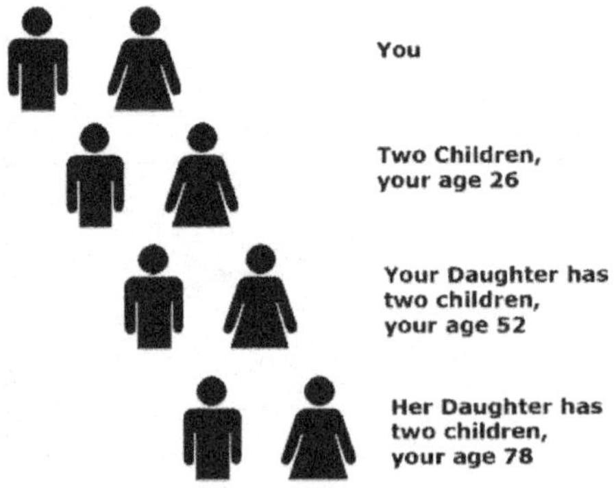

This 3x growth over 3 generations is equal to a 1.44x population growth per generation [1.44= 3^(1/3)]. A 1.44x generational population growth exceeds recent generational job growth capacity in the U.S. and in many other nations. *For each and every lady, two babies each is too many. By exceeding job growth capabilities, many children of average ability in adulthood will be idle, without jobs, and in economic distress.*

In the real world, the average interval between female births, the average number of children each lady has, average lifespan, and immigration and emigration and other components influence population growth. The way population growth transpires from generation to generation can vary greatly. But coincidentally, the population growth in the graphic did not differ greatly from the 78-year experience from 1933 onward, when world population grew 3.22 times larger, at a generational population growth averaging 1.48 [1.476= 3.22^(1/3)]. Yet you hear in the news: 4.6, 6.1, and 6.4 children per woman in Rwanda, the Congo, and Uganda. That won't work. National boundaries will burst; civilized life, fracture.

Except in a vanishingly few exceptionally rich nations such as Saudi Arabia, a generation population growth exceeding 2x clearly presents a huge obstacle to normal economic and social wellbeing. Consider all the problems of raising a family, having adequate schools for your children to flourish, and adequate jobs for decent incomes for parents.

As abundantly seen already, incomes are a function of scarcity. If population grows faster than jobs, those who are at low education and skill levels invariably suffer. And suffer greatly. It is doubly unfortunate that the poorest people and poorest regions in nearly all nations give birth to the most children. As overpopulation progresses, it cements them into poverty.

You can see in the following table (population in millions and growth rates over the previous 26 years) that seventeen nations exceeded 2x growth in 2010 and many others were not far behind. This creates a huge drag on per capita income. It requires that roughly 2.8% to 3.6% be subtracted from GDP growth to get per capita income growth [3.65%= 2.54^(1/26)-1; 2.8%= 2.0^ (1/26) -1]. That hobbling of per capita growth is, in many instances, sufficient to destroy a nation.

	Nation	Population 2010, Millions	Generation Population Growth 2010	Generation Population Growth 2030, est
1	Saudi Arabia	27.4	2.19	3.75
2	Yemen	24.1	2.57	2.48
3	Uganda	33.4	2.33	2.65
4	Niger	15.5	2.36	2.44
5	Congo Dem. Rep.	66.0	2.19	2.75
6	Malawi	14.9	2.14	2.55
7	Angola	19.1	2.17	2.48
8	Tanzania	44.8	2.12	2.43
9	Burkina Faso	16.5	2.07	2.27
10	Kenya	40.5	2.14	2.10
11	Senegal	12.4	2.05	2.23
12	Madagascar	20.7	2.17	1.93
13	Chad	11.2	2.24	1.78
14	Mali	15.4	1.95	2.34
15	Guinea	10.0	2.08	2.03
16	Iraq	32.0	2.10	1.95
17	Afghanistan	34.4	2.05	1.97
18	Ghana	24.4	1.96	1.97
19	Nigeria	158.4	1.89	2.06
20	Guatemala	14.4	1.85	2.04
21	Zambia	12.9	1.97	1.81
22	Syria	20.4	2.00	1.73
23	Sudan	43.6	1.90	1.87
24	Ethiopia	82.9	2.09	1.50
25	Cameroon	19.6	1.92	1.78
26	Cote d'Ivoire	19.7	1.96	1.27
27	Mozambique	23.4	1.77	1.52
28	Egypt	81.1	1.64	1.72
29	Algeria	35.5	1.65	1.66
30	Nepal	30.0	1.81	1.29
31	Philippines	93.3	1.77	1.35
32	Pakistan	173.6	1.88	1.13
33	Malaysia	28.4	1.85	1.17
34	Ecuador	14.5	1.63	1.57
35	Venezuela	28.8	1.70	1.42
36	Australia	22.3	1.44	1.85
37	Cambodia	14.1	1.87	0.98
38	Bolivia	9.9	1.70	1.29
39	Uzbekistan	28.2	1.59	1.45
40	Azerbaijan	9.0	1.38	1.79
41	Colombia	46.3	1.58	1.35
42	Dominican Repub.	9.9	1.57	1.37
43	Iran	74.0	1.65	1.14
44	Spain	46.1	1.20	2.02
45	Haiti	10.0	1.60	1.16
46	**India**	**1170.9**	**1.56**	**1.23**
47	Turkey	72.8	1.50	1.31
48	Sri Lanka	20.9	1.30	1.69
49	Bangladesh	148.7	1.66	0.97
50	Mexico	113.4	1.52	1.23
51	Vietnam	86.9	1.51	1.19
52	Indonesia	239.9	1.46	1.26
53	**Total World**	**6817.4**	**1.44**	**1.29**
54	Tunisia	10.5	1.50	1.17
55	Morocco	32.0	1.47	1.21
56	Peru	29.1	1.53	1.07
57	Canada	34.1	1.33	1.42
58	Chile	17.1	1.44	1.16
59	Brazil	194.9	1.46	1.06
60	Somalia	9.3	1.45	1.06
61	Argentina	40.4	1.35	1.14
62	Thailand	69.1	1.35	1.08
63	Italy	60.5	1.07	1.62
64	**United States**	309.1	1.31	1.13

High population growth is how you can be poor and stay poor, and how your children can be poor and stay poor without remedy. There is little reason to expect job growth to exceed about 1.5x per generation even under very favorable circumstances. It is apt to be far lower. A nation with population growth higher than job growth produces an increasingly large number of unemployed and concomitant problems that come with them – often called failed states.[220]

Population growth is not an ancillary consideration. It is central, often beyond the reach of prudent national economic management. Once on the slippery slope of excessive population growth, circumstances rule, not man. The lives of many kind and decent people are defined by the central failure of the society to control population. The distribution of lives hits them hard and with a grasp that does not release.

The first 25 nations listed in the table have acute population growth now and their population growth trends since 1995 are insufficiently corrective, as can be seen in the 2030 column.[221] Many other nations further down on the list have prospects that are not much better.

The table ranks nations in a systematic order that roughly suggests the degree to which they need to be attentive to population growth. Ninety-four percent of the world's population resides on this list. Most nations with a population exceeding 9 million are included.

	Nation	Population 2010, Millions	Generation Population Growth 2010	Generation Population Growth 2030, est
65	North Korea	24.3	1.32	0.99
66	Belgium	10.9	1.10	1.40
67	China	1338.3	1.29	1.01
68	France	64.9	1.15	1.27
69	Myanmar	48.0	1.35	0.87
70	United Kingdom	62.2	1.10	1.32
71	Greece	11.3	1.14	1.07
72	South Korea	48.9	1.21	0.83
73	Netherlands	16.6	1.15	0.91
74	Cuba	11.3	1.13	0.93
75	Poland	38.2	1.03	1.11
76	Portugal	10.6	1.07	0.97
77	Romania	21.4	0.95	1.18
78	Japan	127.5	1.06	0.90
79	Germany	81.7	1.05	0.86
80	Russia	141.8	0.99	0.95
81	Ukraine	45.9	0.90	1.08
82	Hungary	10.0	0.94	0.97

The first 30 listed nations together have a population of one billion; the first 49 have a population of three billion. Nearly all of these have serious population growth problems. The 60% majority in the first 49 nations comprise 1.8 billion people, who in the main live under difficult conditions. The magnitude of the population growth problem is huge.

The combined population of Europe and the U.S. is 1.14 billion – far fewer than the distressed majority in nations with dangerous population growth. These are people, not just numbers. They need a chance for full and productive lives. Excessive population growth cripples them.

White's Law.

An adult male can deliver about 75 watts of muscle energy.[222] Not much more than a light bulb – about 1/10 of a horsepower. All other energy that makes our culture possible must come from elsewhere. Energy use separates us from primitive conditions. Culture is defined by it.

For most of our time on earth, we humans lived in Stone Age conditions without harnessing much energy except a fire to warm us and to cook our food. Later we also used energy supplied by domesticated animals for farming and transportation – the donkey, ox, horse, and other beasts of burden. Reportedly sailboats harnessed the wind as early as 3000 BC. Watermills began about the 2nd century BC. Windmills started appearing in Europe in the 1300s. All of these used small amounts of energy compared to the First Industrial Revolution (1750) and the age of steam that came with it. It then became plainly clear that energy defined culture. For the first time in history, the living standards of the masses underwent sustained growth. By 1870, the work done by steam exceeded that done by animal and human power together.[223]

The above snippet is intended to draw attention to the degree to which energy use has defined the culture we now take for granted. Without energy we return to near Stone Age conditions. However competent a people may be, when energy sources or access to them are removed or lessened, culture becomes more primitive, ever-closer to the human-muscle-power and beast-of-burden eras of the past.

White's Law, as follows, focuses on the relationship between culture, energy, and population:

> [C]ulture evolves as the amount of energy harnessed ***per capita*** per year is increased, or as the efficiency ... of putting the energy to work is increased. [emphasis added][224]

Consistent with White's Law, when energy sources are finite or declining (as are fossil fuels), increasing population reverses culture. Nations with insufficient energy efficiency, insufficient energy sources, inappropriate population size, or inappropriate population growth reverse culture.

Richard Duncan indicates that world energy per capita from 1945 to 1973 grew at 3.45% per year; from 1973 to 1979 it grew at 0.64% per year; from 1979 to 1999 it declined 0.33% per year.[225] To mismanage energy production, energy efficiency, or population endangers a nation. This is territory ripe for pessimists, but it is also ripe for solutions and sensibility – little of which unfortunately is in evidence so far.

If you would like to reduce the relationship to a formula, it looks something like this:

Energy_Induced_Culture = Energy_Source x Efficiency / Population

High population damages culture. It has the potential to obliterate it.

Low on Modernity Timeline & high in population growth.

The great concern is that many nations with acute population growth have population growth patterns that are not significantly changing for the better. To the contrary, many nations are so far off track that their prospects are alarmingly bad. Especially in nations low on the modernity timeline, the higher the rank on the list, the greater the chance of serious economic and social disruptions resulting from excessive population growth.

Table-297 ranks fifty nations and attempts to show where, at greatest intensity, the twin problems of excessive population growth and low income for the MAJ can be found.* There are one billion people in the first 27 nations; 2.6 billion in the first 36, and 3.5 billion in the first 50. The table should not be used as a scorecard because it is not that precise and because many moderately smaller nations were not included. But you can be confident that those nations listed near the top do require immediate attention to the twin evils of low modernity ranking and excessive population growth – the latter being especially tenacious.

Population Growth & Modernity Rank Combined

1	Congo Dem. Rep.
2	Uganda
3	Malawi
4	Madagascar
5	Guinea
6	Burkina Faso
7	Tanzania
8	Kenya
9	Mali
10	Yemen
11	Afghanistan
12	Senegal
13	Chad
14	Zambia
15	Mozambique
16	Ethiopia
17	Nepal
18	Nigeria
19	Ghana
20	Angola
21	Cote d'Ivoire
22	Cameroon
23	Haiti
24	Guatemala
25	Cambodia
26	Pakistan
27	Philippines
28	Syria
29	Bolivia
30	Niger
31	Uzbekistan
32	Egypt
33	Bangladesh
34	Ecuador
35	Algeria
36	India
37	Colombia
38	Vietnam
39	Sri Lanka
40	Dominican Repub.
41	Venezuela
42	Indonesia
43	Malaysia
44	Morocco
45	Iran
46	Azerbaijan
47	Mexico
48	Turkey
49	Brazil
50	Peru

Catholic Church.

Colombia ranks #37 in the table of acutely troubled nations (Table-297). During the 1967-68 school year, I studied economics at the National University of Colombia and took a course in social work where I worked in an exceptionally poor barrio with Catholic nuns, for whom I had great respect, and who I felt were doing a fine job. The poor folk I was working with were not only decent and kind, many were outstandingly intelligent, but only a thin few were able to get responsible jobs – electric company lineman, et cetera. On a personal level, I liked everyone I knew there. The majority were unable to get work of any kind and remained at the door of destitution. Colombia's population then was already large and barely capable of providing a living for its people.

All forms of birth control were quashed by the Catholic Church. In that era and reportedly up through the 1980s, Catholic authorities were even unwilling to distribute a Vatican pamphlet on the rhythm method. Such intransigence contributed to the Colombia population growing 2.5 times larger than it was in 1967. By way of comparison, in the same period the U.S. population grew 1.5 times larger – far, far less.

* The table was formed by using the average of the adverse ranks of modernity year and of population growth (including expected future growth) as the sort key.

As can be seen in Wikipedia's page on condoms, in the 1930s the Anglican Church and the Federal Council of Churches in the U.S. sanctioned the use of birth control by married couples. The Roman Catholic Church responded by issuing the encyclical Casti Connubi affirming its opposition to contraceptives, a stance it never reversed. At the time of its 1930 ruling, the world population was roughly 2 billion and growing at a generational rate of 1.22x, neither of which appeared to constitute a grave problem. *Population at that time was controlled by hazards of life: high child mortality and short life spans.*

If world population growth had continued at that rate, world population now would be 55% of its present size – 3.88 billion, not its present 7 billion. The Catholic hierarchy who made the decision were unable to foresee the population explosion that resulted because of their decision. *When hazards of life are mainly removed from the population equation, then willful human decisions must be inserted to provide needed control.* Without this, world population growth radically increases. That is precisely what happened, beyond what could have been known in 1930 when the Church initiated the decision to oppose contraception.

Remembering the apology of Pope John Paul II for the role of Christians in the Holocaust (an event rooted in roughly the same era as when the Catholic Church rejected contraception), we can see that rectification on this matter may be possible in the not too distant future.[226] As clearly vile and intentional as the Holocaust was, it seems inevitable that population growth (albeit not so obviously) wields a considerably more vicious hand – ever-growing billions of people repeatedly suffering and many dying into the infinitely distant future because of unquelled and excessive population growth.

The Church could now play a positive role to improve the spiritual wellbeing of its flock by removing the damage that its stance on contraception has already caused. Today there are about one billion Catholics worldwide. Many of them are in Latin America, where excessive population growth results in vicious poverty and social disorder, as is evident from the above lists.

Population growth & Modernity Timeline linked.

We can see in the following smoothed graph-299 that high generational population growth rates – such as 1.6x and greater – are a spoiler. With them, the economic wellbeing of the 60% majority tends to be equivalent to a life spent in the 1870s or earlier. Not until 1.58x growth rates and lower does the MAJ enter an economic wellbeing consistent with the 1900s. And not until 1.4x are they into the 1950s.

#299

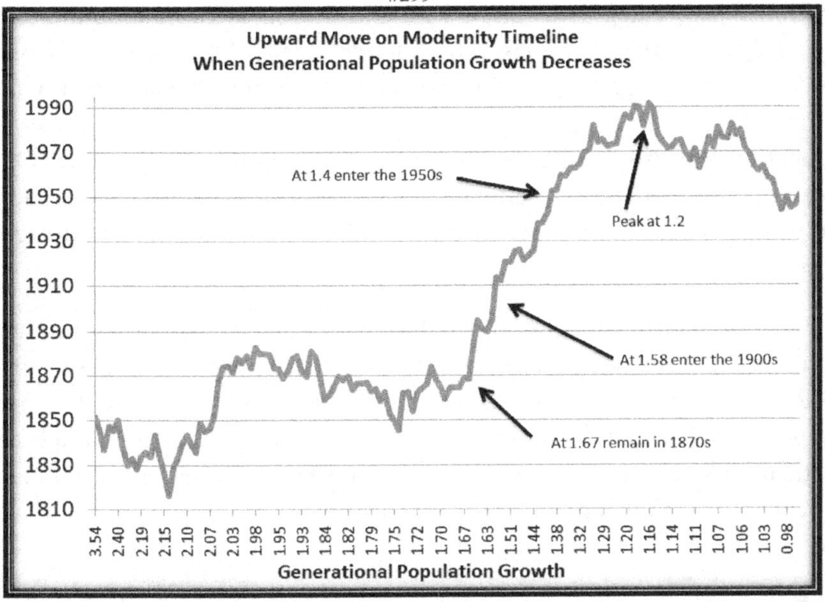

These are not ironclad points of transformation (there is huge variability in the data). The central inescapable point, though, is that the majority suffer when population growth rates are disproportionately high. It takes a sharp reduction in high population growth rates to help propel the majority wellbeing upward – often far sharper than commonly appreciated. Societal and economic structures have large enough difficulties adapting to modest changes, but huge accelerations in population simply outstrip resources, abilities, and social norms.

The Modernity Timeline and the "Successful States Index."

The Modernity Timeline is a method that ranks nations according to their MAJ income. It accounts for both economic vitality and income distribution. As shown in graph-300, the ranking performs much like the well-developed and reputable Failed States Index (2012) published by the magazine *Foreign Policy* and the Fund for Peace.[227] The Success Rank here is formed by inverting Failed States Ranks so that successful nations are ranked first.

The Failed States Index is developed by evaluating the following categories in each nation: Demographic Pressures, Refugees and Internally

Displaced People, Uneven Economic Development (including distribution of income), Group Grievance, Human Flight and Brain Drain, Poverty and Economic Decline, State Legitimacy, Public Services, Human Rights and Rule of Law, Security Apparatus, Factionalized Elites, and External Intervention. These categories can be best understood by evaluating the original report. But to give examples: The Factionalized Elites category would include Power Struggles, Defectors, Flawed Elections, and Political Competition. The Public Services category would include Policing, Criminality, Education Provision, Literacy, Water & Sanitation, Infrastructure, Quality Healthcare, Telephony, Internet Access, Energy Reliability, and Roads. As confirmed here, the conduct of elites and basic public services are crucial to success.

Generally corresponding to the Failed-States nomenclature, the Success Rank uses the following rank categories: 1-12 are Most Stable/Sustainable; 13-23 are Stable; 24-45 are Moderate/Borderline; 46-126 are Warning/In danger; and 127-151 are Critical/Alert. These categories are marked on the vertical rank axis in the graph. As you can see, many nations are under significant stress. Few nations are deemed stable.

#300

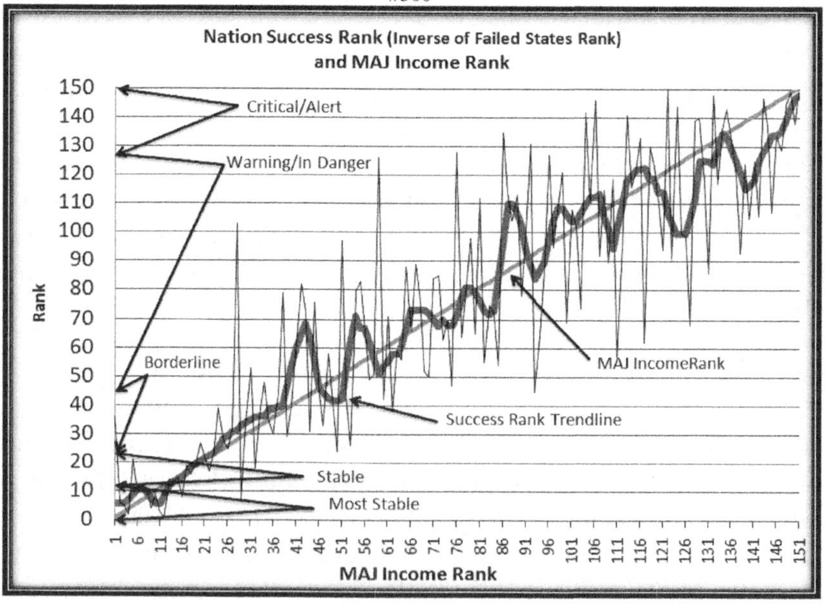

The MAJ Income Rank (and thus the Modernity Timeline Rank) are shown on the diagonal in graph-300. The Failed States Index is sophisticatedly developed. It was of interest that the simple MAJ income ranking also tended to follow its same path. The valuable features that distinguish successful nations seem to be closely intertwined with MAJ income.

#301

Nation	Modernity Timeline Year	MAJ Income Rank	Success Rank	Success Rank Diff.	Nation	Modernity Timeline Year	MAJ Income Rank	Success Rank	Success Rank Diff.	Nation	Modernity Timeline Year	MAJ Income Rank	Success Rank	Success Rank Diff.
Qatar	2091	1	36	-35	Azerbaijan	1940	51	97	-46	Philippines	1874	101	108	-7
Luxembourg	2060	2	6	-4	Bulgaria	1940	52	43	9	Bolivia	1867	102	102	0
Norway	2043	3	5	-2	Chile	1940	53	26	27	CapeVerde	1866	103	74	29
Sweden	2025	4	2	2	Turkey	1940	54	80	-26	Pakistan	1866	104	142	-38
Singapore	2024	5	21	-16	Venezuela	1940	55	83	-28	Djibouti	1864	105	111	-6
Austria	2023	6	10	-4	Mexico	1939	56	67	-11	Yemen	1864	106	146	-40
Iceland	2021	7	12	-5	Seychelles	1939	57	49	8	Moldova	1862	107	92	15
Netherlands	2021	8	11	-3	Albania	1938	58	51	7	Laos	1861	108	115	-7
Switzerland	2021	9	4	5	Iran	1938	59	126	-67	Honduras	1860	109	90	19
Canada	2018	10	9	1	Panama	1938	60	42	18	Kyrgyzstan	1858	110	119	-9
Denmark	2018	11	3	8	Tunisia	1938	61	71	-10	Ghana	1855	111	57	54
Finland	2018	12	1	11	CostaRica	1937	62	38	24	Nicaragua	1854	112	96	16
Germany	2018	13	14	-1	Macedonia	1937	63	59	4	Nigeria	1852	113	141	-28
Australia	2017	14	13	1	Ukraine	1937	64	56	8	Tajikistan	1852	114	116	-2
Belgium	2015	15	15	0	Algeria	1936	65	88	-23	Mauritania	1848	115	122	-7
Ireland	2013	16	8	8	Peru	1935	66	66	0	Cameroon	1847	116	133	-17
UnitedStates	2012	17	19	-2	China	1934	67	89	-22	Namibia	1846	117	62	55
France	2008	18	16	2	Maldives	1934	68	77	-9	Bangladesh	1843	118	130	-12
UnitedKingdc	2004	19	20	-1	Botswana	1933	69	52	17	Cambodia	1842	119	123	-4
Japan	1999	20	27	-7	Jamaica	1933	70	50	20	PapuaNewGu	1842	120	110	10
Korea,South	1998	21	22	-1	Turkmenistar	1933	71	84	-13	Senegal	1842	121	94	27
Slovenia	1989	22	17	5	Bosnia and H	1932	72	85	-13	Chad	1835	122	150	-28
CzechRepubli	1988	23	23	0	Suriname	1932	73	63	10	Benin	1832	123	91	32
Greece	1988	24	39	-15	Dominican Re	1931	74	70	4	Coted'Ivoire	1832	124	144	-20
Malta	1988	25	28	-3	Brazil	1930	75	47	28	Gambia,The	1831	125	100	25
Spain	1986	26	25	1	Egypt	1919	76	128	-52	Tanzania	1828	126	99	27
Italy	1975	27	32	-5	Guyana	1918	77	64	13	SaoTomeand	1825	127	68	59
Israel	1973	28	103	-75	Thailand	1913	78	81	-3	Kenya	1824	128	139	-11
NewZealand	1973	29	7	22	Ecuador	1907	79	98	-19	Guinea-Bissa	1820	129	140	-11
Slovakia	1971	30	34	-4	Armenia	1906	80	65	15	BurkinaFaso	1818	130	118	12
Cyprus	1968	31	53	-22	Colombia	1903	81	112	-31	Mali	1817	131	86	45
Portugal	1965	32	18	14	Belize	1901	82	55	27	Afghanistan	1815	132	148	-16
Hungary	1964	33	37	-4	Jordan	1896	83	75	8	Zambia	1814	133	117	16
TrinidadandT	1962	34	48	-14	ElSalvador	1895	84	72	12	Uganda	1812	134	136	-2
Estonia	1961	35	35	0	SouthAfrica	1895	85	54	31	Guinea	1810	135	143	-8
Poland	1961	36	30	6	SyrianArabRe	1894	86	135	-49	Nepal	1810	136	132	4
Croatia	1959	37	44	-7	Angola	1891	87	114	-27	Togo	1808	137	120	17
Belarus	1953	38	79	-41	Bhutan	1889	88	104	-16	Lesotho	1802	138	93	45
Lithuania	1952	39	29	10	Georgia	1889	89	113	-24	Malawi	1798	139	124	15
Latvia	1948	40	40	0	Morocco	1888	90	78	12	Mozambique	1796	140	105	35
Kazakhstan	1945	41	60	-19	Indonesia	1886	91	101	-10	Rwanda	1794	141	125	16
Russia	1945	42	82	-40	SriLanka	1882	92	131	-39	Madagascar	1792	142	106	36
Gabon	1943	43	73	-30	Mongolia	1880	93	45	48	Haiti	1788	143	147	-4
Mauritius	1943	44	31	13	Paraguay	1880	94	61	33	Niger	1773	144	137	7
Serbia	1943	45	76	-31	India	1879	95	87	8	Comoros	1771	145	107	38
Romania	1942	46	46	0	Congo,Rep.	1877	96	127	-31	Liberia	1766	146	134	12
Argentina	1941	47	33	14	Guatemala	1877	97	95	2	SierraLeone	1766	147	129	18
Malaysia	1941	48	58	-10	Swaziland	1877	98	109	-11	CentralAfrica	1756	148	145	3
Montenegro	1941	49	41	8	Uzbekistan	1876	99	121	-22	Zimbabwe	1752	149	149	0
Uruguay	1941	50	24	26	Vietnam	1875	100	69	31	Burundi	1745	150	138	12
										Congo,Dem.I	1740	151	151	0

Table-301 includes nation names, the Modernity Timeline, the Success Rank Difference, and data shown in the graph. Whenever the Success Rank is of higher status than the MAJ Income Rank (i.e., Success Rank Difference being positive), those nations based on Failed-State criteria are delivering a higher quality of life than other nations with similar MAJ economic strength, and they must be vigilant not to slip backwards. On the other hand, when the Success Rank Difference is negative in the table, those nations are advised that they have the economic strength to deliver a higher quality of life to their citizens than they are doing. If they were doing as well as they should, their rank among nations would be raised by the absolute value of the indicated Success Rank Difference. And since quality of life and national well-being grow in conjunction with MAJ income, all nations are well advised to focus on advancing the MAJ. Nations that inhibit MAJ income do so at their peril.

As in the table, graph-300 also indicates when nations are delivering a higher quality of life than other nations with similar MAJ incomes. Whenever a nation is beneath the diagonal, it is delivering a higher quality of life than commonly associated with its MAJ income. Conversely, whenever a nation is above the diagonal, it is delivering a lower quality of life than it should, given the strength of its MAJ income.

To those who are wedded to the unfettered free market: Your position more often than not is married to elites, not to the MAJ. Yet it is the market economy at the MAJ that advances nations. In many of these nations, elites are unconstrained. Look at the hundreds of nations listed here. Where do you find your success stories? There are numerous cases to choose from. I don't see the bright stories of success emanating from the unfettered elites. I do see them coming from the top dozen stable states and from equitable, mixed, capitalistic economies similar to those that existed in the USA during the 1950s, 1960s, and 1970s – all of which gave a fair shake to the MAJ. The ample and increasing freedoms and opportunities there are quite sufficient to produce successful nations. To free market buccaneers, your voice may charm others, but my preference remains with demonstrated performance. For the world at large, it is the MAJ and prudence that offer the greatest rewards.

Population growth too frequently high & staying there.

In its distant past, the U.S. also had high generational population growths (which included immigration) exceeding 2.0x (graph-303). It took 70 years (1870-1940) for it to go from a 2.0x to a 1.35x population growth. Nations now do not have the luxury of lethargy. Many are already on the precipice.

As a mantra, economists assert that with economic growth, population growth slows. Yes, it slows. But does it slow fast enough, and particularly does it slow fast enough in key nations? My answer is a resounding, "No." Sir David Attenborough refers to the failure to address population control as the "absurd taboo." He is right – brilliantly so – in his "People and Planet" speech available on YouTube.[228]

#303

#303B

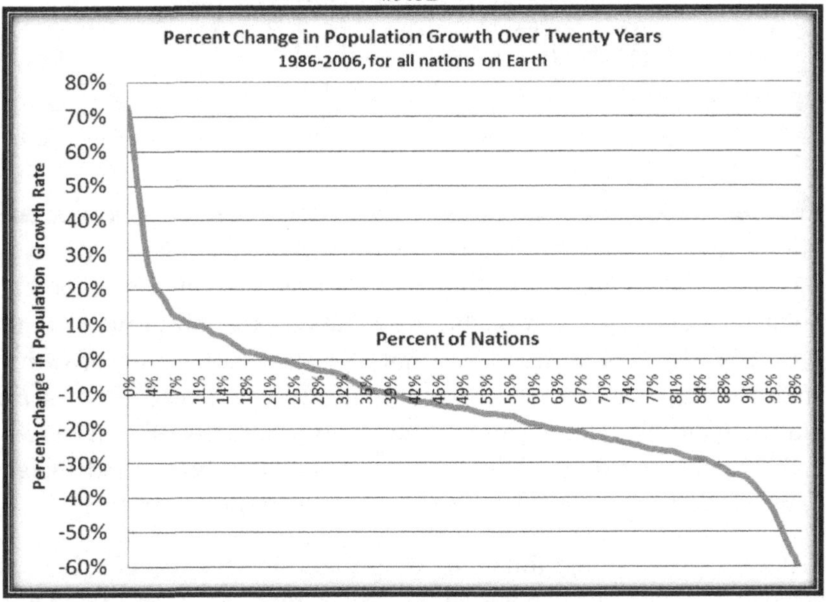

In the above graph-303B, looking at the 20-year (1986-2006) interval in generational growth rates for all nations, we see many of the worst offending nations' populations are growing at an unchanged rate or only slowing slightly [the 1986-2006 interval being more precisely median 1984-88 to median 2004-08 data points]. Graph-303B shows that generational population growth changed slowly. In 23% of nations, population growth increased. In 39% of nations, it has not even decreased 10%; in 63%, not even 20%; in 86%, not even 30%. Only in 6% has it decreased 40%. Only in 4% has it decreased more than 50%. But this summary does not tell us which nations are doing what. Since we are most concerned with problem population growth (nations at 1.35+ per generation), let's look at the following graph-304 of all of those nations worldwide.

#304

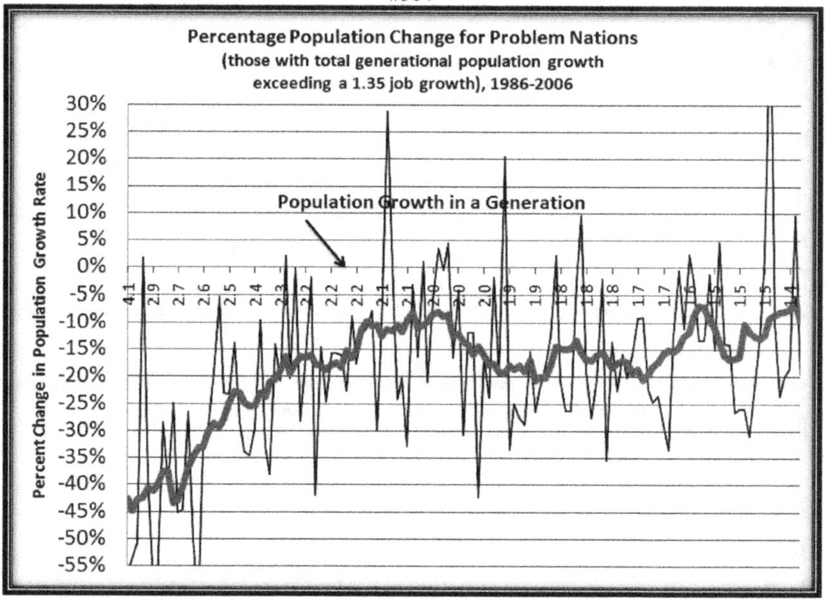

In the above graph-304, we see that the trend line only bent downward significantly at points exceeding a 2.3 growth. Even when population growth far outstripped reasonable expectations for job growth (explicitly 1.7 to 2.3), the general trend was not to reduce population growth more than 20% – leaving population growth rates that will continue to seriously harm the majority. The outcome is so vastly destructive that it makes you cry. These are decent people placed in untenable economic and social conditions by wildly inappropriate population growth rates.

As we can see in the following graph-305, in 1986 exactly 66% of nations had a generational population growth that exceeded reasonable expectations for job growth. Twenty years later in 2006, 57% of nations still remained over the 1.35 threshold. A 9% improvement, but an improvement coming too slowly and leaving numerous nations far above the job threshold. This is a core reason unemployment grows.

#305

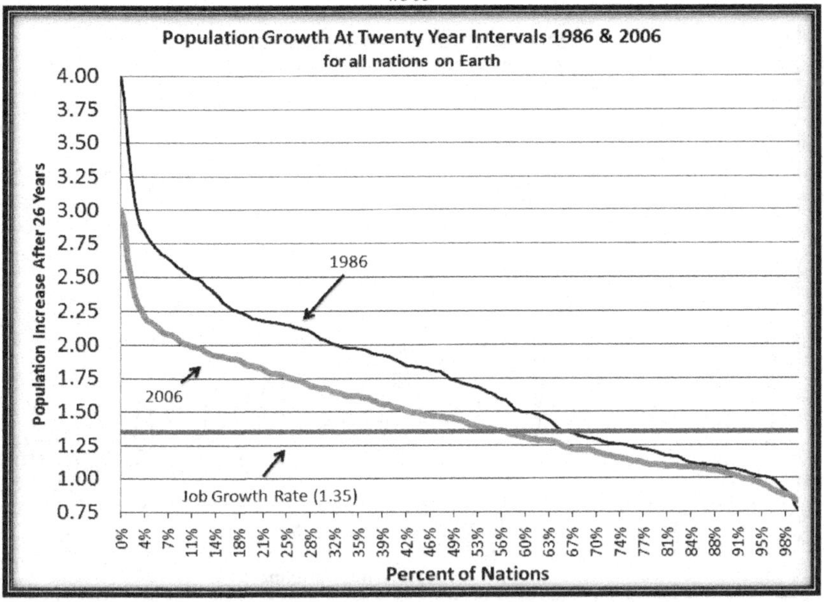

Idle population. Population growth vs. job creation.

Job creation adjusted for hours worked grew at 1.35x generationally (every 26 years) from 1900 through 2011 in the United States. Its slowing is caused by fewer hours worked. Yet further increasing efficiencies may slow it more. It is perilous and foolish for population to grow at a rate faster than potential job creation. To do so will certainly increase the number of idle people within a nation or force them to migrate to other nations.

It would be optimistic to assume that poor economies can produce the above 1.35x generational job growth that the U.S. did. U.S. growth was delivered under highly favorable conditions. The difference between the 1.35x generational job growth and the generational population growth will minimally equal the growth rate of the idle population not having jobs in adulthood. You can expect growth in the idle population to exceed this amount.

If present rates were to continue, within a generation forty-three nations could expect to produce an idle population in an amount greater than 20% of their present total population (43% at the median). That percentage is about 2.25x greater in two generations and about 3.75x greater in three generations. The number of idle people produced is simply huge in these nations. This is unfair to the people born and to the nation as a whole.

#306

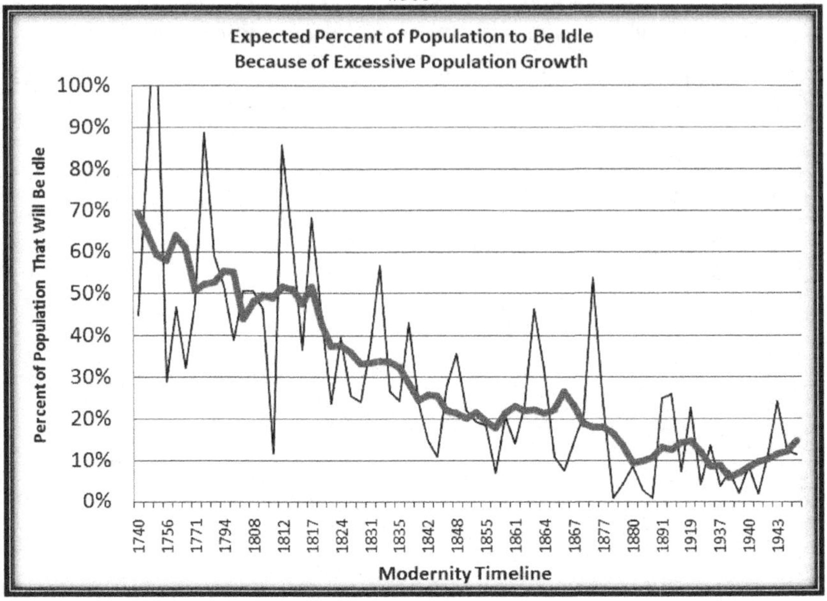

At the median, these forty-three nations are at year 1817 on the Modernity Timeline (125 years behind nations not reporting population growth exceeding 1.35x generationally). Their population growth has forced their people to live primitively and will continue to do so until they take effective population growth action.

The above graph-306 contains all nations where expected population growth exceeds 1.35x per generation. It shows the idle population produced within a generation and the nations' position on the Modernity Timeline. Nations low on the Modernity Timeline have too few resources to withstand a vastly increasing idle population. Yet they have them in greatest measure because of excessive population growth.

We began with a song.

God mend thine ev'ry flaw,
Confirm thy soul in self-control,
Thy liberty in law.[229]

Its line, "Confirm thy soul in self-control" is universal – success giving.

Flesh on the planet.

As Ian Roberts remarked: "[People] immediately focus on population. Actually, when it comes down to it, it's not how many mouths there are to feed, it is how much flesh there is on the planet."[230]

It is flesh and numbers that make up human biomass. BMI is a weight measurement that adjusts for height. Comparing two prosperous nations, the U.S. and Japan, we see that the U.S. BMI was 28.7 and Japan's was 22.9, which is to say that the average adult U.S. citizen, after adjusting for body height, is carrying 25% more weight than the average Japanese [25%= 28.7/22.9-1].[231]

Although nations that have rapidly increasing population are creating problems, those of us in the economically advanced nations, by increasing our size, are also placing disproportionate pressure on the land. Our increased size requires increased food to support it.

Biomass. 45% for humans after 3X growth.

There are numerous ways civilizations can collapse. Overpopulation is one of the most reliable.

Using a portion of the data in a table under Wikipedia's Biomass (ecology) heading, I put together this informal table to get a first approximation of some consequences of a 3x human population growth.

Species	Biomass by Weight in Million Tonnes, 2011	Percent Biomass, 2011	After 3x Human Population Growth, Biomass by Weight in Million Tonnes	After 3x Human Population Growth, Percent Biomass
Ants	1,000	20.63%	1,000	14.51%
Marine fish	1,000	20.63%	1,000	14.51%
Cyanobacteria (apicoplankton)	1,000	20.63%	1,000	14.51%
Cattle	520	**10.73%**	1,560	**22.63%**
Termites	445	9.18%	445	6.46%
Antarctic krill	379	7.82%	379	5.50%
Humans	350	**7.22%**	1,050	**15.23%**
Sheep and goats	105	**2.17%**	315	**4.57%**
Chickens	48	**0.99%**	144	**2.09%**
Blue whales	1	0.01%	1	0.01%
Total	4,848		6,894	
Percent of human related biomass		**21%**		**45%**

The table here lists key non-plant biomass. If cattle, sheep and goats, and chickens (which exist primarily to satisfy the human diet) were to grow at 3x in tandem with humans, then this group would comprise 45% of the listed biomass, in contrast to its present 21%. This optimistically assumes that the other listed species would remain at current levels.

Consider the plants on which humans and their livestock depend. The following are listed in ranked order according to their percentage of approximate total weight of food produced worldwide. The vast majority of them would seem to generally increase in response to population growth: sugarcane 24.5%, wheat 11.6%, rice 11.6%, maize (corn) 10.8%, potato 6.0%, sugarbeet 5.6%, cassava 3.4%, barley 3.0%, sweet potato 2.9%, soybean 2.6%, banana/plantain 1.8%, tomato 1.8%, cottonseed 1.2%, orange 1.2%, grape 1.2%, sorghum 1.1%, apple 1.1%, coconut 1.0%, cabbage 1.0%, watermelon 0.8%, onion 0.8%, rapeseed/canola 0.7%, yam 0.7%,

Population Per Square Football Field of Arable Land

Rank	Nation	Football Field Number
1	Djibouti	657.7
2	Seychelles	69.6
3	Maldives	61.3
4	Qatar	49.2
5	TrinidadandT	43.1
6	Malta	41.0
7	Iceland	35.2
8	Japan	24.4
9	Korea,South	24.4
10	Jordan	24.4
11	Egypt	21.8
12	PapuaNewGu	21.5
13	Israel	18.5
14	CostaRica	17.5
15	SriLanka	17.0
16	Jamaica	16.9
17	Colombia	16.7
18	Switzerland	15.2
19	SaoTomeand	14.7
20	Bangladesh	14.4
21	Philippines	14.1
22	Netherlands	13.0
23	Yemen	13.0
24	Malaysia	12.0
25	Mauritius	11.1
26	Vietnam	10.7
27	Belgium	10.4
28	Slovenia	9.6
29	Nepal	9.6
30	Dominican Re	9.4
31	China	9.2
32	Chile	9.2
33	Indonesia	8.7
34	Ecuador	8.7
35	UnitedKingdo	8.6
36	Venezuela	8.4
37	Haiti	8.2
38	Suriname	8.1
39	Cyprus	8.1
40	NewZealand	8.0
41	Georgia	7.7
42	CapeVerde	7.5
43	ElSalvador	7.4
44	Congo,Dem.F	7.1
45	Guatemala	7.0
46	Tajikistan	7.0
47	Liberia	6.9
48	Rwanda	6.7
49	Comoros	6.6
50	Botswana	6.6

oats 0.6%, peanuts 0.6%, millet 0.6%, sunflower 0.6%, rye 0.5%, mango 0.4%, and beans 0.4%.[232] And although not listed, cotton accounts for 2.5% of arable land (land used for growing crops).[233]

Arable land.

There is only a limited amount of arable land. The number of nations whose population far outstrip the capacity of the soil is stunning. Picture in your mind an American football playing field: 100 yards long (almost 100 meters). Mark off land that is approximately one square football playing field (100 yds. x 100 yds.).[234] The table you see here lists nations in rank order of population intensity per square football field of arable land based on 2000-2009 median World Bank data.

The top dozen on the list would require the square football field to feed more than 20 people. Perhaps you have grown a garden that you relied on to feed your family. We have something in common. I would hazard a guess that, you too, would find it inconceivable to expect a square football field garden, with some livestock and a few chickens to reliably feed that many people. Without food imports, it is obvious that people would starve in a heartbeat. Wealthy nations can import; poor nations less so. Jared Diamond attributed Rwanda's genocide to population competition over land.[235] Rwanda is now 48th on the list with 6.7 people per square football field. In the worst of times it was at 7.5. Points above this exceed the threshold of danger. As you see, this is not an issue of population growth leading to untenable conditions. It is a question of already untenable conditions becoming yet more untenable.

#309

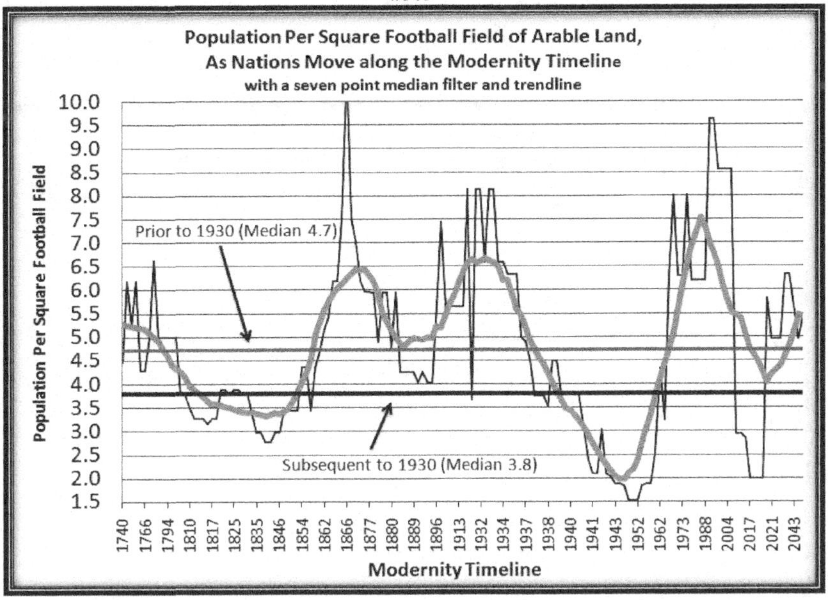

The pressure that nations place on arable land, as shown in above graph-309, assumes variable shapes about which it is risky to draw conclusions. There are obviously both rich and poor nations that put high pressure on the land. However, using the original data, we find that the football field median was 4.4 for all nations, but prior to a 1930 Modernity Timeline position, it was 4.7, and for the nations above 1930 on the Timeline, it was 3.8; thus suggesting that poor nations are putting about 25% more pressure on the land [25%= 4.7/3.8-1]. Poor nations are at the mercy of this pressure because they have less buying power to acquire food internationally when their own crops become insufficient.

Arable land, what's left of it.

David Montgomery's splendid book *Dirt: The Erosion of Civilizations* tells the story of civilizations rising and falling according to the health of their soil. It is an ancient and predictable process that applied to the Romans, the Greeks, and the Mayans, just as much as it does today.

Since 1945, erosion worldwide has degraded an amount of agricultural land equal to the combined size of China and India. Today about a third of China's cultivated land is being seriously eroded. I have seen it. Montgomery indicates that arable land is declining at a rate of about 1% a year.[236] In fairness to the topic, there are a variety of opinions out there. But for brevity, the following graph-310 summarizes only the consequence of an uninterrupted 1% continuous decline.

#310

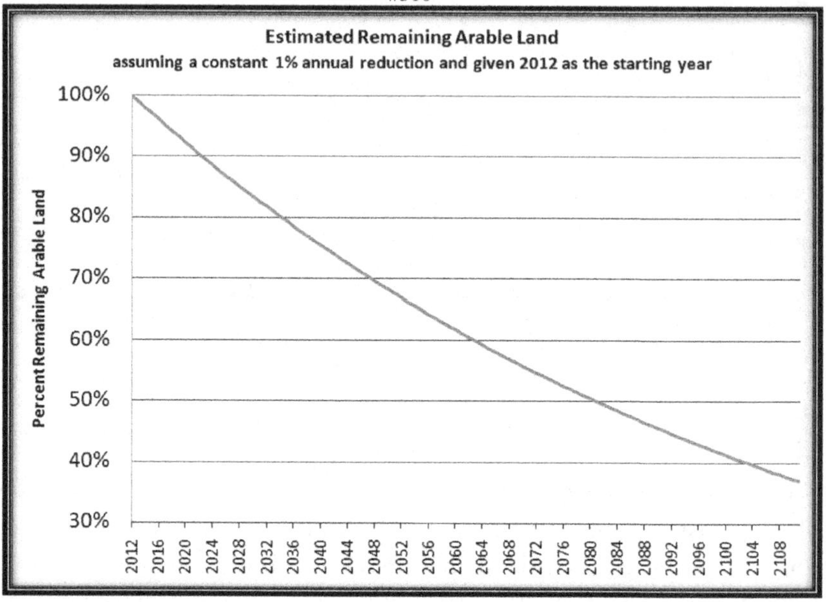

Table-311 attempts to show where, at greatest intensity, the twin problems of high pressure on arable land and low income for the MAJ can be found.* However, farmland_1 is not equal to farmland_2, which is to say there is a huge variety of soil and farm quality. To lump them all under a single phrase "arable land" is at best misleading and often frankly inaccurate. Much of the land being farmed is already marginal land of poor quality and low yields.[237]

Further, if farmland is created by deforestation, as it is in many places, the health of the land is degraded. While that land may be deemed "arable" for a short while, usually it will soon be worthless for farming. The value of trees is inescapable, whether in agriculture or in urban settings.

Trees are a marker for income inequality. Wealthy neighborhoods have them in abundance. Poor neighborhoods do not. Satellite images from Google Earth bear this out.[238] One of the smartest transitions from poverty to wealth is to plant and maintain trees.

---

* Table-311was formed by using the average of the adverse ranks of modernity year and square football field number as the sort key.

General trends through history take two forms: A civilization first populates fertile river valleys. As population expands, it moves into increasingly marginal land, ultimately into sloping land prone to erosion. With the expanding population, excessive pressure is placed on the land to produce food. Land is cleared of trees. The soil becomes depleted. Erosion intensifies especially on the sloping land. Unable to produce sufficient food, the civilization crashes or fails.[239]

Pressure on Arable Land and Modernity Year Combined

Rank	Nation	Modernity Year	Football Field Number
1	Congo,Dem.F	1740	7.1
2	Nepal	1810	9.6
3	Haiti	1788	8.2
4	PapuaNewGu	1842	21.5
5	SaoTomeand	1825	14.7
6	Djibouti	1864	657.7
7	Liberia	1766	6.9
8	Bangladesh	1843	14.4
9	Comoros	1771	6.6
10	Burundi	1745	6.2
11	Rwanda	1794	6.7
12	Yemen	1864	13.0
13	Philippines	1874	14.1
14	Madagascar	1792	5.0
15	SriLanka	1882	17.0
16	Lesotho	1802	5.4
17	Vietnam	1875	10.7
18	Jordan	1896	24.4
19	SierraLeone	1766	4.3
20	Tajikistan	1852	7.0
21	Kenya	1824	5.6
22	Maldives	1934	61.3
23	Egypt	1919	21.8
24	Colombia	1903	16.7
25	Ethiopia	1817	4.9
26	Mauritania	1848	6.3
27	Coted'Ivoire	1832	5.4
28	CapeVerde	1866	7.5
29	Mozambique	1796	3.8
30	Indonesia	1886	8.7
31	Seychelles	1939	69.6
32	Uganda	1812	3.9
33	Jamaica	1933	16.9
34	Guatemala	1877	7.0
35	Georgia	1889	7.7
36	Malawi	1798	3.5
37	CostaRica	1937	17.5
38	Guinea-Bissa	1820	3.9
39	Honduras	1860	5.4
40	Pakistan	1866	6.2
41	Ecuador	1907	8.7
42	Dominican Re	1931	9.4
43	ElSalvador	1895	7.4
44	Timor-Leste	1863	5.1
45	Gambia,The	1831	3.8
46	Congo,Rep.	1877	6.0
47	Zimbabwe	1752	2.7
48	Zambia	1814	3.3
49	China	1934	9.2
50	India	1879	5.9

Another sequence is for farmers to ruin the land, soon abandoning it to move onward onto new land. Even at the founding of the United States, George Washington and others sharply criticized this land destruction practice, which was massive especially in the South. As Montgomery relates, "After five years of tobacco cultivation the ground was too depleted in nutrients to grow much of anything. … [F]armers just kept on clearing new fields."[240] Even without modern mechanization, the destruction was massive. To this date, damage remains in many regions.[241]

Albeit serious, in these scenarios (civilizations failing or farmers moving on to deplete new land), the damage was regionally confined. The distinction now is that the population pressure is global, not regional – thus consequences are global, not just regional.

For 129 of the nations on the Modernity Timeline, sufficient World-Bank arable land data was available to draw the following conclusions.[242] For the 1960-1969 period, the median for the nations represented in the following graph-312 was 2.4 people per square football field. By 2000-2009, it had increased to 4.9 –

twice as many people per unit of land. By 2000-2009, 81% of nations exceeded the previous 2.4 median.

#312

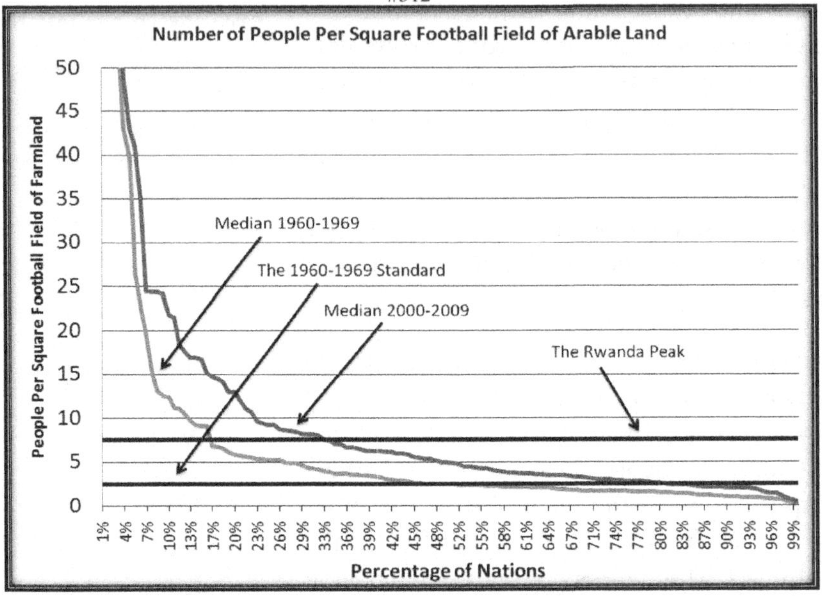

Over 40 years, the pressure on the land increased at a rate of 1.8% per year [2.024= 4.92/2.43; 1.78%= 2.024^(1/40)-1]. Eleven percent of nations were above 20. As Jared Diamond indicated, land disputes, genocide, and Rwanda were a nasty brew. At its worst, Rwanda had 7.5 people on each arable square football field. In 1960-69, only 16% of nations put this much pressure on the land. By 2000-2009, 33% of nations were at this testy point. Some were rich enough that they could import food with ease. Many were not.

Farming by extraction: soil and oil.

I come with prejudice. I grew up and worked on a farm. If it had been profitable, my preference would have been to remain there. The work is satisfying. Not great, just a nice way of living. A farming orientation fosters a sharp attention to the care of the land. I cannot describe the depth of revulsion when seeing eroded land. It is the first job of stewardship to care for the land, and, when the soil is out of repair, to do all in one's power restore it. In many nations this job is simply unattended to.

Look to the stars and planets above – then the earth below. The earth beneath your feet surpasses all treasures. It gives the life found nowhere else. Michael Wood's visit to Uruk in "The Cradle of Civilization" (on

YouTube and DVD) dramatically and clearly shows the path that was taken there.[243] From once being the verdant giver of life for our long-ago ancestors, the literal cradle of civilization has made the full run to an endpoint of being a blasted landscape. We too risk the same journey.

There is nothing in the entire known universe which brings and supports the life that the subsoil beneath our feet provides. We are tied to soil. Being remote from it does not remove our dependence on it. When it is lost, so too is life.

I am uncertain how to begin. In an attempt to convey it, I have cut a hair from my head and measured it with a micrometer. It's three thousandths of an inch thick. My waist circumference is 33 inches. I have checked to see the diameter of the earth. It is approximately 7,926 miles. Topsoil, what plants predominately live in, is usually 2 to 8 inches thick. For ease of example, I am going to call it a foot. If we were to consider the topsoil to be the skin of the earth, which we and substantially all creatures rely on for life, how should we think of it? After doing the calculations, it would be as if the skin around my waist was 12,000 times thinner than a human hair – that is the narrow skin of the earth. Our civilization, our life, is held together by this very fragile and thin integument – extractable, yet irreplaceable.

Topsoil loss is so great that the U.S. Department of Agriculture has a poster to illustrate the extent of topsoil loss in the State of Missouri. In it they give an example that for every 100 bushels of corn that are produced, the equivalent of 100 bushels of topsoil are lost. They also state, "It takes about 500 years for nature to create one inch of topsoil."[244] But at an erosion rate of 5.6 tons per acre annually, one inch of topsoil is lost within 30 years. Not a comforting picture. A bushel of topsoil gone for each bushel of corn sold; topsoil lost in 30 years that takes 500 years to create. Those underling properties stand in opposition to the bucolic notion of farming. Instead now at the core, farming too frequently is a process of extraction, slowly mining the land – removing its life and its capacity to give life.

When population increases indefinitely and the resource topsoil is finite, there is a pause for consideration. Food comes from topsoil. That applies whether we are urban or rural. No distance from it is sufficient to remove us from our dependence on it. It lets us live, or alternatively, if we ignore it, it lets us die. If you have any doubt about its importance worldwide, go to a barren desert. Look around. Or, reconsider Haiti and other examples of deforestation. Such devastation is too easily achieved. It does not feed people.

Rigoberta Menchú made a comment about her Mayan tradition, which I translate as: "We cultivate corn and a few beans. Before beginning to plant we have a ceremony for the seeds and the land. We ask for permission from our mother earth for the wound that we are going to inflict on her by planting the corn."[245] That tradition and wisdom of honoring the soil strikes me as appropriate. As Wendell Berry says, we must grow like a tree, not like a fire.[246]

Albeit indirectly, farming is now an exercise in extraction – first extracting topsoil as we have seen, and second extracting fossil fuels, as we will now see.

Calories are energy. Each calorie of food that we eat is literally the energy that makes it possible to live. Less obviously, each calorie that we consume also requires energy consumption to grow the food source, and take it through all of the steps that bring it to our table. In today's mechanized world, that energy is enormous. Since 1974, it has been estimated that approximately 9.5 calories are expended to produce one food calorie.[247] These industrial calories come principally from fossil fuels. For every calorie we ingest, we effectively consume about 8+ calories of fossil fuels.

Though we intellectually assume that the farm, with its natural process of plant and animal growth, is the source of our food, the reality now is that oil extraction is what delivers food production. One estimate suggests that in the United States, each person is effectively "eating" the equivalent of about 1.1 gallons of oil a day, 400 gallons a year.[248] It took about 20 to 650 million years to create the fossil fuels that we now use at a furious rate to drive modern agriculture.

Those fuels seems to be expended in roughly the following proportions: 31% for manufacturing fertilizer, 16% for transportation, 13% for irrigation, 10% for operating farm machinery, with the balance going to raising livestock (not including feed), crop drying, pesticide, et cetera. In part, these heavy energy expenditures arise from the Green Revolution (1950-1984). Worldwide, it is estimated to have increased grain production about 250%, but its methods necessitate high fossil fuel use.[249] Thirty percent of oil consumption goes to agriculture. [250] The revolution in food production staved off famine, but adversely, it also made huge population increases possible. Having food production dependent on topsoil and fossil fuel extraction in great quantities warns us that population at current levels is already perilous. To yet grow population further would seem to bring only vast misery.

How much population growth can the earth absorb before human growth completely overreaches earth's capabilities? The impact on plant kingdoms on which our food-source animals depend would even be more massive than our present non-plant biomass consumption. The prospect of new food sources technologically created from fungus, genetic modification, and other yet to be imagined sources to meet the food needs of humans swarming the earth … This would not seem to represent progress. It would not seem to conform to our spiritual, intellectual, or religious purpose for being on this earth in the first place. A human species transformed into an instrument of thorough and complete predation and extraction – doesn't that stand in stark opposition to the very meaning of the word Civilization?

Ozymandian Economics

In the desert, on the sands, a pedestal stands.
And on the pedestal these words appear:
'My name is Ozymandias, king of kings:
Look on my works, ye Mighty and despair!'
Nothing beside remains. Round the decay
Of that colossal wreck, boundless and bare
The lone and level sands stretch far away.
Percy Bysshe Shelley, 1817, modified and abridged

Farming can work. Decency can work.

I have visited various organic farms, Polyface Farms of *Omnivore's Dilemma* fame, and of course, with my own farm background numerous others, many of which had great merit.[251] However, the standout I stumbled on in 2007, not even knowing it was a farm when I arrived, and certainly not anticipating the sensational job it did.

Environmentally, Selva Negra in Matagalpa, Nicaragua is the soundest farming operation I have seen. Nicaragua, despite its many fine characteristics, presents formidable geographic difficulties of dry weather and soil depletion. Selva Negra distinguishes itself because it thrives in precisely such a setting. It is a 300-acre farm and nature reserve. Its forests were carefully planted with plants and a variety of trees with different root structures. Grasslands and forest work together – one must have the other.

The result over time is that Selva Negra has developed its own microclimate with numerous flowing springs in an otherwise dry region. The forest is stunningly beautiful, unlike much of the rough land leading up to it. The forest brings the climate and water on which the farm thrives. The Selva Negra cabins, lodge, and layout are an architectural dreamland, not so much for their novelty, but for how comfortably they and their plantings fit into the setting. You would be perfectly happy if you saw no more than this. At least that is how I felt when I arrived.

Walking further down the hill, I saw the school house and homes of the people who worked on the farm; and further down, the dairy cows. Every day, without exception, the cows are rotated into a small new field. This vastly increases the productivity of the land because the grazed field has time to heal, the new grown grass grows quickly and new grass is also preferred by the cattle. That single innovation made it possible to literally double herd size using the same amount of land. And the land was in better ecological shape because of it. The farm had far more lessons to teach than I could properly relate. I do not hold it out as utopia. But to my eyes it provides encouragement that the sensible marriage of forest with smart farming can work, and work well, even under adverse conditions. I was also encouraged that it had been a long-term endeavor stretching back to the early 1900s. It had achieved its outcome, not through a shot-in-the-pan academic dream, but by continuous trial and error, shepherded by the hand of intelligence, creativity, and persistence.

There are a few instances of sustained successful agriculture: some sections of China, 4,000+ years;[252] Egypt prior to the damming of the Nile, 7,000 years;[253] *terra preta* in the Amazon, 2,000 years;[254] Colca Valley, Peru, 1,500 years;[255] the island Tikopia, 1,000+ years;[256] Tsangpo valley, Tibet, 1,000+ years.[257] These isolated stories of success are matched by the success of the Dutch after catastrophic medieval famines and plague. As David Montgomery relates:

> [T]he Netherlands are covered by quartz-rich dirt ill suited for agriculture. … [T]he Dutch began mixing manure, leaves, and other organic waste into their dirt. … [O]ver time they built up dark, organic-rich soils to as much as three feet thick. Lacking land they made soil.[258]

Successful land management is labor intensive and personal. From what I have seen of it, absentee decision-making and ownership do not work. Geographical and human considerations are regional. They are best addressed with that in mind, explicitly favoring the hand of caution. The marriage of forest, farm, dedication, and intelligence that Selva Negra showed is an example of the elements which in combination are potent. Not perfect, but good enough.

(In the real world, what is ever perfect? Except you, dear reader.)

(Dear perfect reader, My praises to you are infinite. Don't let anyone tell you otherwise. Ok, this chatter ends. You can let your eyes move down the page.)

On a more levelheaded note, please observe that income-distribution spreadsheets for nearly all of the nations of the world are available at Dilives.com (as in Di$_{\text{stribution of}}$Lives).

CH. 11

PROGRESSIVE? Not Hardly.

Always a difficult word, the presumption is that taxation should be **fair.** It is especially difficult if fairness is to rest on profound income-distribution ignorance. As I believe you have seen, we have known too little about income distribution. Citizens and governments need to have a precise understanding of income distribution before there can be any hope of constructing a system of fair taxation.

Even the knowledge we now have has been insufficiently implemented. In the old USA, taxation schemes were constructed far more wisely than they are today. Let's see what has happened and why.

The notion of the "margin" has permeated income tax construction since 1913. Economists have a predilection for looking at the marginal. The origin, I believe, can be traced to primitive economics. To give a little background, the "Marginal Revolution" in economics appeared in the 1860s and 1870s, and was given a huge boost by Alfred Marshall's publication of *Principles of Economics* in 1890.[259] All of this, for economists, gave rise to the "margin" having great academic importance. Our marginal tax rate structure retains those vestiges of academia that give "the margin" pretensions of importance.

However, the margin is of little use in taxation. A list of average taxation at each point would do just as well and would be far easier to understand. Using a marginal structure too readily hides the true form of taxation. The margin is subject to manipulation, demagoguery, and chicanery.

Worst of all, we citizens cannot grasp the income tax picture with such a confusing presentation.

By contrast, average taxation lets you see exactly how much people are being taxed at every point. As you will see, these pages will soon enough distance themselves from the margin. But before doing so, we need to understand how the marginal tax has been applied to the top income bracket. We need a clear picture of how those at the high economic strata now benefit relative to past periods of taxation.

The tax code has several points of philosophical change. The initial philosophy was to have gradations of taxation all the way up to very scarce incomes. In about 70% of the years from 1913 to 1941, the threshold for applying the top bracket exceeded one in a million; and in 20% of the years, the scarcity threshold was so high that it was unlikely that any taxpayer would attain such a high income. Population was 134 million in 1942, so few, if any, taxpayers were actually taxed at the highest bracket rate. The particulars can be seen in Table-322. In this 1913-1941 period, which I call Stage I, there seems to have been a bona fide effort to distinguish between high-income taxpayers all the way up to the very top.

"Tax at the Threshold" refers to the Top-Bracket income tax threshold above which further marginal tax rate increases don't occur. For the rich, this causes a flattening of tax above this point. The measurement is handy because it cuts across time and conditions; and by stating this flat-tax threshold in X$s, it simultaneously accounts for tax rate, inflation, and changes in income distribution.*

	Period	Median Tax at the Thresh-old in X$s	Median Scarcity
Stage I	1913-1941	1,499	8,293,482
Stage II	1942-1964	132.5	150,364
Stage III	1965-1981	32.0	11,981
Stage IV	1982-2011	8.2	144

The short story of the past century of income taxes can be understood by looking at the 4 stages of income-tax top-bracket philosophy. As shown in the table here, Stage I (1913-1941) is a period in which the taxation

* "Tax at the Threshold in X$s" is equal to the "Top Bracket Income Threshold in X$s" multiplied by "Top Tax Rate." It is not a tax rate that is paid, but it is a marker for how Top Income Bracket taxing is structured, because it illustrates the level of taxation upon entering the Top Bracket. And as indicated previously, please keep in mind that scarcity is based on full population, not number of tax filers. For example, one-in-4,000 would refer to one person in a town of 4,000, not one tax filer in 4,000.

gradients reached very high levels well in excess of one million (8.2 million at the median). In all subsequent stages, the gradations significantly dropped, as did tax at the threshold. Notwithstanding, Stage II (1942-1964) was sufficient to prevent maldistribution from gaining a foothold.

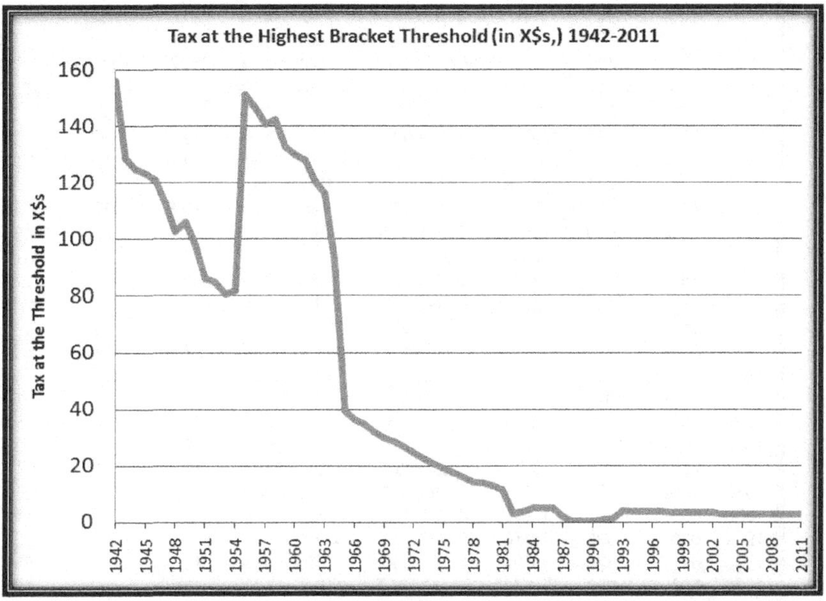

#321

I never thought I would be writing this, but what we now need is a bald guy about 5' 10.5" tall, who weighs somewhere between 175-185 pounds, and who plays golf at every opportunity he can get, specifically: Eisenhower. Look at his Presidential term 1953-1961 within graph-321 and the tables here. His median threshold tax was 145.8 and his median gradations reached up to the one-in-225,160 scarcity level (see Table-322). As shown in graph-321, that was one of the last times in the post WWII era that taxation greatly impeded the accumulation of vast income and wealth at the top. From then on, it was a downward slide.

Stage IV (1981-2012) completely opened the flood gates. The top tax rate dropped to the lowest it had been since 1931. There was no taxation impediment to maldistribution whatsoever. The tax rates for those at the pinnacle were trivially low and maldistribution came apace.

#322

Ninety-nine Years of USA Top Tax Rates

year	Top Tax Rate	Bracket Income Thresh-old in X$s	Tax at the Thresh-old in X$s	Scarcity	year	Top Tax Rate	Bracket Income Thresh-old in X$s	Tax at the Thresh-old in X$s	Scarcity
1913	7%	1,390	97	6,236,945	1962	91%	132	121	209,206
1914	7%	1,499	105	6,860,184	1963	91%	127	116	189,992
1915	7%	1,452	102	4,929,279	1964	77%	120	93	127,891
1916	15%	4,729	709	29,207,839	1965	70%	56.4	39	18,271
1917	67%	3,989	2,673	35,083,928	1966	70%	52.0	36	17,127
1918	77%	1,586	1,221	8,293,482	1967	70%	49.9	35	12,953
1919	73%	1,435	1,048	7,337,321	1968	70%	45.8	32	10,151
1920	73%	1,293	944	11,712,122	1969	70%	42.8	30	10,551
1921	73%	1,530	1,117	19,806,234	1970	70%	41.0	29	21,245
1922	58%	317	184	293,665	1971	70%	38.3	27	17,699
1923	58%	279	162	217,097	1972	70%	35.3	25	11,981
1924	46%	683	314	1,344,178	1973	70%	32.0	22	14,154
1925	25%	134	33	31,595	1974	70%	29.7	21	15,412
1926	25%	127	32	25,705	1975	70%	27.4	19	12,381
1927	25%	130	32	20,272	1976	70%	24.9	17	9,465
1928	25%	130	33	15,069	1977	70%	22.8	16	7,406
1929	25%	123	31	17,756	1978	70%	20.4	14	5,348
1930	25%	139	35	46,062	1979	70%	19.6	14	3,689
1931	25%	167	42	123,488	1980	70%	18.5	13	2,889
1932	63%	2,172	1,368	45,099,223	1981	70%	16.4	11	1,802
1933	63%	2,318	1,460	44,054,715	1982	50%	6.3	3.2	144
1934	63%	2,026	1,276	16,949,361	1983	50%	7.5	3.8	201
1935	63%	1,829	1,152	13,167,606	1984	50%	10.1	5.1	258
1936	79%	8,068	6,374	268,309,351	1985	50%	9.9	5.0	201
1937	79%	7,376	5,827	285,819,935	1986	50%	9.8	4.9	201
1938	79%	7,829	6,185	853,704,982	1987	39%	4.8	1.8	144
1939	79%	7,453	5,888	762,506,518	1988	28%	1.5	0.4	30
1940	79%	6,856	5,416	629,521,082	1989	28%	1.5	0.4	30
1941	81%	5,599	4,535	414,561,519	1990	28%	1.5	0.4	30
1942	88%	178	156	181,529	1991	31%	3.6	1.1	87
1943	88%	146	129	140,071	1992	31%	3.6	1.1	87
1944	94%	133	125	187,076	1993	40%	10.1	4.0	258
1945	94%	131	123	150,364	1994	40%	9.6	3.8	201
1946	91%	133	121	111,365	1995	40%	9.5	3.8	201
1947	91%	124	113	94,039	1996	40%	9.3	3.7	201
1948	91%	113	102	75,340	1997	40%	9.1	3.6	201
1949	91%	117	106	96,612	1998	40%	8.9	3.5	144
1950	91%	107	98	65,161	1999	40%	8.6	3.4	144
1951	91%	95	86	58,585	2000	40%	8.3	3.3	144
1952	92%	92	85	84,432	2001	39%	8.4	3.3	144
1953	92%	88	81	131,837	2002	39%	8.5	3.3	201
1954	91%	90	82	65,790	2003	35%	8.3	2.9	201
1955	91%	166	151	268,562	2004	35%	8.1	2.8	144
1956	91%	161	147	303,558	2005	35%	7.9	2.7	144
1957	91%	155	141	455,780	2006	35%	7.7	2.7	144
1958	91%	156	142	316,367	2007	35%	7.7	2.7	144
1959	91%	146	133	218,126	2008	35%	7.8	2.7	144
1960	91%	143	130	225,160	2009	35%	8.4	2.9	144
1961	91%	140	128	177,869	2010	35%	8.1	2.8	144
					2011	35%	8.0	2.8	144

I am tired of saying X$. It is too formal. Instead I will say this guy is earning a 1,000 people (or whatever other X$ applies). You have turned enough pages in this book to get the drift. And I rather like saying "He earned a 1,000 people." I can easily picture such an income kingdom and can have some fun saying it.

By Stage IV, a guy with a 1,000 people income, would be facing a substantially flat tax subsequent to the 8th or 9th person. The Upper½% begins at the one-in-200 level. Thus, the Stage IV median scarcity at 144 served to flatten the tax for the entire Upper½%. As we have seen, this is where the greatest maldistributions occurred (e.g., graph-30). Yet the stopping point for high bracket increases occurred before it even reached the Upper½%.

If you were to cherry-pick years of iniquity,[260] the prize winners are 1988-1990 at 0.4 on Tax at the Threshold as seen in Table-322. We did not even reach a full person on that one (0.4). It was also insufficient to fund government.

Stage IV is how you transform a democracy into an oligarchy. It is the lesson plan. Nowhere in USA tax history has there been anything like it. Every day now, the news and our own eyes witness its impact.

It built incomes for the profligately rich. It built governmental debt for the rest of us.

The booby prize: It lowered our standard of living. The anti-tax brigade won the battle. The super rich were safe to grow. And that is what they did.

Preventing maldistribution before it gets a foothold.

Explicitly, high taxes at pinnacle incomes are ***not about redistribution***. They are about setting tax levels that prevent maldistribution from occurring in the first place. Few people were ever taxed at the 91% margins that existed in the 1950s. These taxes were a preventative measure that guaranteed that excessive income and wealth were not widely accumulated at the top.

By taxation setting those ceilings, corporations were advised in advance that inappropriately high compensation was pointless because it would go into taxes anyway. So they moderated their pay packages. Similarly, a private business person was advised by taxation that beyond a certain point, his or her after-tax income would not increase greatly if activities were disproportionately remunerative. High tax bracket rates thus ensured that a winner-take-all ethic did not pervade. It gave everybody a fair shot at getting a good (even a high) after-tax income, but it prevented oligarchy. It prevented plutocracy. It prevented monopoly incomes.

We need not look as far back as our founders for wisdom. Just looking back to FDR, Truman, and Eisenhower is enough. They built and maintained a culture of taxation and compensation wisdom that was the foundation of a capitalism that thrived as never before.[261] When you remove that ethic, you increasingly have oligarchy, plutocracy, and monopoly. You also impoverish the MAJ and reduce the incomes of 92% of the population. FDR, Truman, and Eisenhower saw to it that we prospered together. The incremental chipping away at their ethic reversed that destiny.

Looking at the stages.

#324

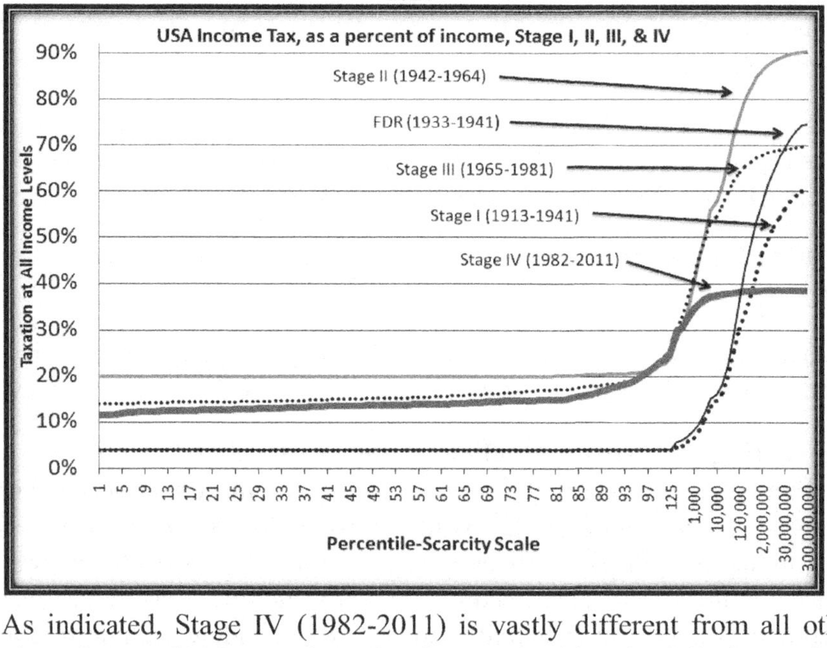

As indicated, Stage IV (1982-2011) is vastly different from all other previous forms of U.S. taxation. Graph-324 provides the full picture from bottom to top, showing median curves for each of the four Stages. As you can see, there was a profound flattening in Stage IV that became pronounced at about the one-in-4,000 scarcity level. At this level and higher, taxation provided no impediment to maldistribution. A person at the one-in-4,000 level would be earning about 50 people a year (approximately $2.3 million). A small town with a population of about 4,000 people might have one person at this level. Stage IV taxation exists to benefit these people and those of higher rank.

By contrast, within the Top1%, Stage IV taxation did not reduce taxes by more than 2.2% for people lower than the one-in-250 level. Many pages back (graph-30) we saw the sharp increase in Upper½% incomes as maldistribution advanced, but a far more moderate increase in Lower½% incomes. The dividing line between the Upper½% and the Lower½% is the one-in-200 point. Stage IV was designed for the Upper½%, not the Lower½%.

In the early years of Stage IV (1985), the Americans for Tax Reform was founded. It developed the Taxpayer Protection Pledge that binds its signers to ***never support a tax increase.*** As of this writing, it has been signed by 238 of the 242 House Republicans (98%) and 41 of the 47 GOP senators (87%).[262] So if you like Stage IV, you know where you can get more of it. Just give them a call. Send them a few million dollars. And we can run a Stone Age economy backed by Stone Age logic. There are enough of them. They are well funded. They are sufficiently enthusiastic that they can preserve oligarchy until its last quivering pulse. It now appears that this crowd has greater power than the President to determine our destiny.

The take and give.

#325

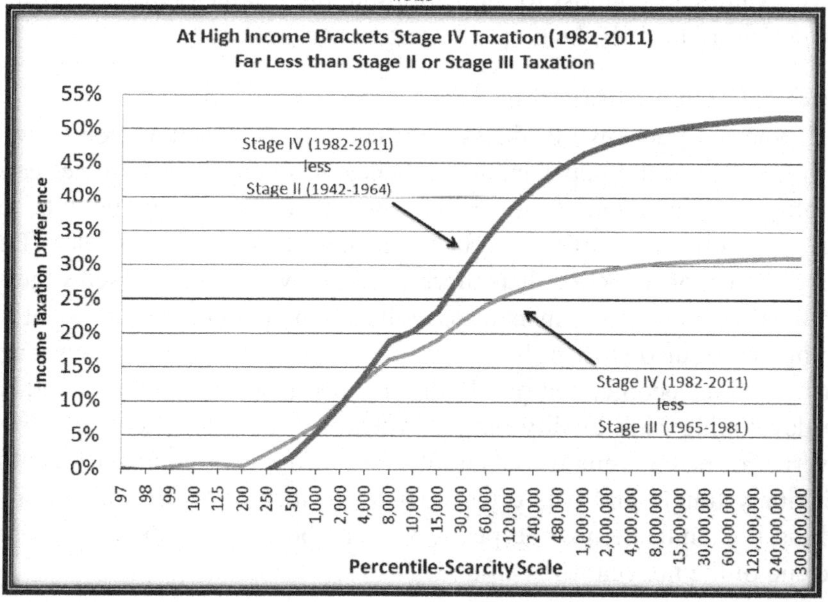

We have spent a great deal of time in this book on the maldistribution transition which took 25% of the income from the MAJ [-¼= (25/33.3333)-1]. That taking took 30 years to perfect.

But with the stroke of a pen, a giving of 25%+ took place. It did not go to the MAJ. It went precisely in the opposite direction – to the already wealthy, specifically to those at the one-in-120,000 scarcity level and above. And this giving has occurred once a year for 30 years now. Since the tax gift occurs to those who are already feverishly wealthy (earning 250+ people per year, $11.6+ million), there is no need for them to spend it on necessities. They can sock it away in investments, becoming ever-richer as those investments grow.

For this small elite, the gift is a wealth and power-creating machine. An additional 25%+ each year for 30 years provides a spectacular boost. This is the consequence of replacing Stage III tax policy (Johnson, Nixon, Ford, Carter) with Stage IV tax policy (Reagan, Bush1, Clinton, Bush2, Obama). It can be seen in graph-325.

If we were to look further back to compare Stage II (FDR, Truman, Eisenhower, Kennedy) with Stage IV, the scenario is transformed into a 38%+ yearly advantage at the one-in-120,000 level and above, as can be seen in graph-325. Not only did Stage IV fail to collect enough taxes to fund government (thus enormous deficits and debt), it developed elite-driven values in contrast to the nation-building values that existed during Stage II and Stage III. Its greatest damage was done there.

Practical. Then ruminating.

If you ran your own business prior to Stage IV taxation, you knew that high taxation at the upper income reaches was beneficial to lower earning employees. When you, as the owner, knew that you were going to be taxed like crazy on high profits, you had a strong incentive to pay subordinates more (better an expense than more profit now). Money which otherwise would flow into governmental tax collector hands now could benefit and strengthen your own firm by paying workers well, starting a new project, hiring quality people, and purchasing needed machinery. You could focus on developing high quality output instead of being tempted to hoard and divert profits for your own benefit alone. Though running a business is genuinely tough, and it is often difficult to turn a profit, once things get rolling it is amusing how desperate you can become to moderate profits as the end of the tax year rolls around.

High bracket taxation also keeps the demon within in check. If you are earning at the one-in-120,000 level, you are earning about 250 people a year. Do you really think you are that good? If so, do you think the question might be open for debate, say if 10 unbiased people who knew you best were to silently vote their opinion without adverse repercussions?

The fierce battle to preserve the Stage IV tax perks for the elite is amusing. If their logic had been plainly incorporated into the first sentence of the Declaration of Independence, how many soldiers would have appeared at Valley Forge? How many people would have widely supported such perks of wealth? As I understood it, there was some objection to a monarchy at the time. I don't see that substituting distant monarchy for a de facto local monarchy of wealth would have been all that appealing. But then I have been surprised at the enthusiasm for Stage IV goings on for some time and may have underestimated the capacity for economic self-flagellation.

I don't get it. Show me what's progressive.

Framing the debate: Almost exclusively, opposition to higher tax at the income pinnacle is stated relative to a person's income, not his or her capacity to pay. If you are vastly wealthy, you know that income is only a small reflection of your capacity to pay income tax. Your wealth is so much greater than your income that dipping into it to pay income taxes is often only a modest inconvenience.

We can chuckle in harmony as the super-rich cast the story of taxation as if their interests and those of the common man were aligned. Those of us at the low end are more hard-pressed to pay income tax than the wealthy.

Graph-328 shows the sharp decline in the income tax burden as one becomes ever more wealthy. For us common folk, it may be difficult to grasp, but when one is vastly wealthy, income fluctuations in a day or a week are often immense. For each million dollars invested, the stock market going up or down 5 percentage points means a ±$50,000 change, more than the average person makes in a year. And when a person is vastly rich, they have many millions of dollars invested in various assets. Most of their conversation about these big numbers they don't make public. They are used to vast changes and are fine-tuned to minimizing the ones that are adverse to them.

If you are at the 80th wealth percentile, your income taxes may be about 5% of your wealth (graph-328). But at the one-in-120,000 scarcity level, it may be closer to 1.3% of that person's wealth. You are more hard put upon to pay income tax than the highly wealthy person. It is a burden about 3.75 times as great for you to pay income tax than it is for the high earner [3.8= 5%/1.3%].

#328

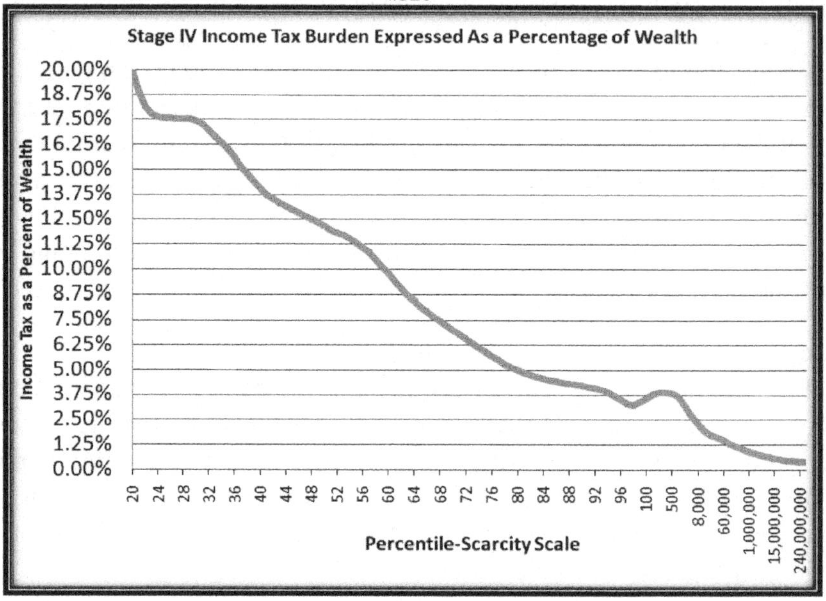

The high earner is an expert at winning arguments. He will hammer home that he paid $4.2 million in taxes. He will repeat this until he sees tears coming to your eyes. Then he will stop. He knows when to stop. For example, he will stop before getting around to mentioning that his net worth is about $312 million. So long as he sees those tears in your eyes, he knows you will argue on his behalf to lower income taxes yet further. The one thing he prefers above all else is an agent acting freely on his behalf. He hates to pay his servants.

Education.

> The fact is that income inequality is real; it's been rising for more than 25 years. The reason is clear: We have an economy that increasingly rewards education, and skills because of that education.[263]
>
> – George W. Bush, 2007

One of the favorite ploys of the elite is to focus on the deplorable state of education in all classes lower than their own. This old saw has played its tune for centuries. Since childhood I can recall complaints about education, the majority of which were valid. The truth be told, many of us, when children, went to schools that were flawed in one aspect or another, and too often we did not do as well as we should have because of our own failings, as much as those of the schools.

The rich, though, have another motive for focusing on the sorry state of education, unrelated to the welfare of the lower classes. They can claim educational differences are the cause of low incomes at the bottom and conversely, in view of their superior education, the cause of super high incomes at the top.

On that point it is they, not us, that need the education. So for those of you who purchased the gold-plated, diamond-studded edition of this book, I urge you to look closely at the following graphs and experience the bliss of education. We will start by looking at differences between the Top4% in 1979 and 2007, using Congressional Budget Office (CBO) data subjected to my computer programs (as discussed in the Appendix). You will observe in graph-329 that when matched for people of equal status, very high incomes in 2006 were far greater than in 1979 but at the lower end of the scale, they were much closer together.

#329

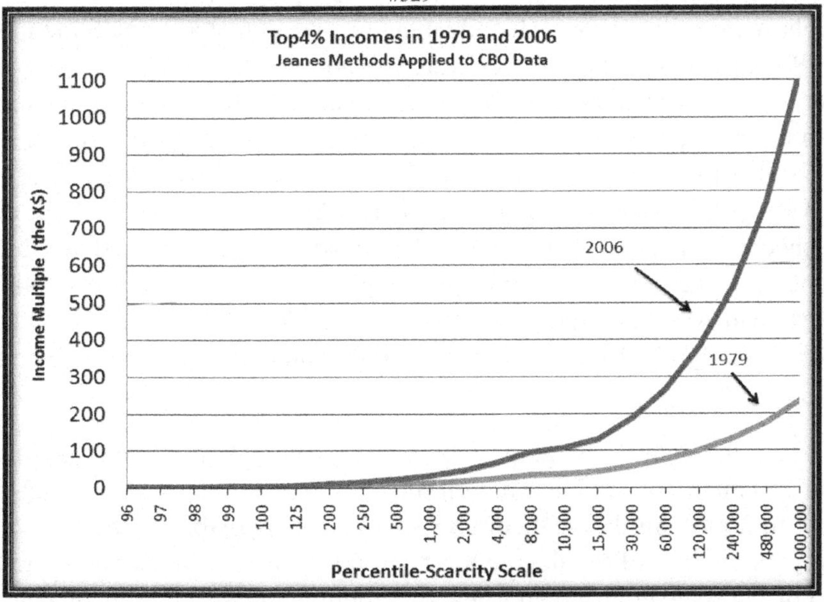

To be specific, the point that escapes me in the elite's maldistribution-because-of-education argument is that at the one-in-240,000 scarcity level, what was so deficient about folks at that level in 1979 in contrast to the new 2006 elite at the identical scarcity level? What was the education-on-steroids program that produced the sensational difference? The old education saw does not seem to explain the difference at this point on the scale or the differences elsewhere within the Upper½% which we see in graph-329.

I offer the thesis that favorable tax treatment, not educational difference, was the reason that the super-rich advanced so spectacularly. And that it is disingenuous to assert that education was responsible for their spectacular rise vis-à-vis their 1979 peers.

With that out of the way, we now can crack the nut.

Cracking the nut.

The shape of the tax advantage curve in graph-331 appears much like the one in the Stage III-to-Stage IV transition that we saw earlier in graph-325. But unlike prior comparison of philosophies, here we focus on the specific changes from 1979 to 2006.

Using the modified Congressional Budget Office (CBO) data, the Top4% of the population, above the teeter point is the group that benefited from maldistribution. Graph-331 shows the 1979-2008 tax advantage at all levels within this group. The advantage was calculated by subtracting the 2008 tax rate from the 1979 tax rate (based on average income tax paid at each level). The tax advantage was less than 6.7% for those at points lower than the one-in-200 scarcity point (the threshold point for entering the Upper½%). At higher points on the scale, the advantage was spectacular. And it was an advantage received annually. At the one-in-10,000 point, it reached a 25% tax advantage. And the tax advantage continued to grow the higher you went, as can be seen in graph-331. To have your tax bill 25% lower than was customary is indeed a sweet deal. But it was too sweet to spread widely; so those at the one-in-10,000 and above were the few to get it.

From the data in the graph-329, we can calculate the fractional income change caused by maldistribution alone that occurred at each point from 1979 to 2006. Similarly, WealthX$ data is also available. With the two, we can get a picture of the degree to which favorable tax treatment at the high end of the scale contributed to maldistribution. We can do this by calculating the average annual increases in the two X$ measurements [average annual change=fraction^(1/(2006-1979))-1] and charting them in graph-331.

At the one-in-240,000 scarcity level, because of maldistribution transition alone, income grew an additional 5.3% annually; and wealth, an additional 3.5%. Graph-331B exists for those of you who might be making a first approximation of what fraction of the Tax Advantage translated into income and wealth growth. So far at the median it's about 18%.

#331

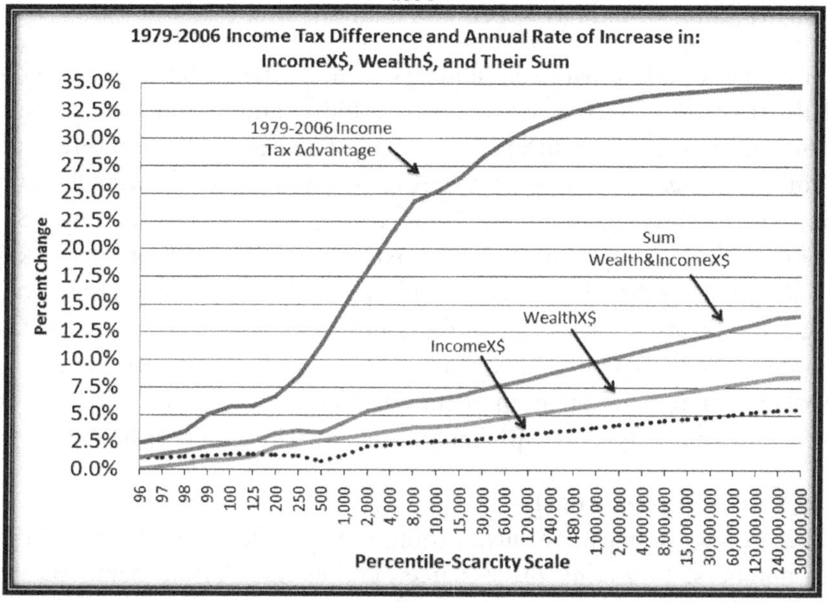

#331B

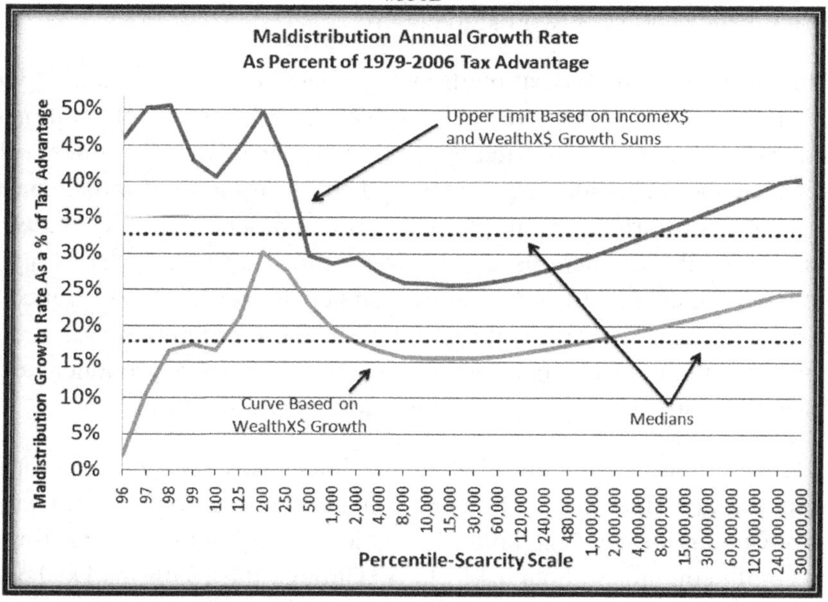

A word of caution: I believe the relationship in graph-331B is more complex than a simple multiplier. The numbers there just describe potential tax-induced wealth increases during the 1979-2006 period. Summing wealth and income in the graphs was done only to define an upper limit estimate. Some portion of income is included in wealth; thus, we can be reasonably confident that the total income and wealth tax-induced maldistribution would have been less than this figure.

The huge tax advantage and its concomitant pressure to increase maldistribution stands in opposition to the central point that neither the IncomeX$ nor the WealthX$ should have been growing in the first place. A competent manager seeking to preserve an appropriate income distribution will closely monitor the rate of change in the IncomeX$ and WealthX$, especially at all levels above the one-in-4,000 point. He knows that it is undesirable that an equitable income distribution perish. Over the long-term, the average change at these high levels should not exceed 0%. If it does, he knows that taxation at the high levels is insufficient to quell maldistribution. That taxation at the high levels is then ratcheted upwards until the equitability of wealth and income distribution is assured.

The Madison mish mash.

I am going to pause because I think it is wise to. We can get too deeply into numbers, forgetting the essence. The essence is the democracy. The democracy which from the outset was never certain to survive, or to use Lincoln's nice choice of words: to endure.

In its first decade, the nation did not yet have the Constitution on which the whole enterprise now rests. In 1787, the proposed Constitution had been drafted, but not yet ratified by the states. There were arguments about whether it should be adopted. To strengthen the argument for the Constitution, a series of articles were published now known as the *Federalist Papers*. The tenth of which, used here, was penned by James Madison anonymously. It concerned itself with the danger of mob rule and argued that the representative government embodied in the Constitution was the best available option in an imperfect world. Madison, as a proponent of the Constitution, was keenly aware of the imperfectability of man.

He was writing at a time when the horse was the quickest form of transportation. The nation was predominantly agricultural. Manufacturing was advancing in New England. And income distribution in New England was highly equitable (about a MAJ35). Through the 1830s, as De Tocqueville observed, equality among freemen was the nation's defining characteristic. Madison's writings do not seem oriented toward changing circumstances so much as seeking to set a stage where wisdom in government would have the greatest chance of success.

In the following, I will be unfair to Madison because his original argument without my tampering is the best representation of his thoughts. Here, however, I reorder his language to shorten and draw attention to issues that he considered, many of which today, we also address, using a slightly different vernacular.

> "... By a faction, I understand a number of citizens, whether amounting to a majority or a minority of the whole, who are united and actuated by some common impulse of passion, or of interest, adverse to the rights of other citizens, or to the permanent and aggregate interests of the community.
>
> "... the most common and durable source of factions has been the various and unequal distribution of property. Those who hold and those who are without property have ever formed distinct interests in society. Those who are creditors, and those who are debtors, fall under a like discrimination.
>
> "...The regulation of these various and interfering interests forms the principal task of modern legislation, and involves the spirit of party and faction in the necessary and ordinary operations of the government.
>
> "... The apportionment of taxes on the various descriptions of property is an act which seems to require the most exact impartiality; yet there is, perhaps, no legislative act in which greater opportunity and temptation are given to a predominant party to trample on the rules of justice. Every shilling with which they overburden the inferior number, is a shilling saved to their own pockets.
>
> "... the public good is disregarded in the conflicts of rival parties, and that measures are too often decided ... by the superior force of an interested and overbearing majority.
>
> "... A republic, by ... representation takes place, opens a different prospect, and promises the cure ... in controlling the effects of faction.
>
> "... the delegation of the government ... to a small number of citizens elected by the rest... to refine and enlarge the public views, by passing

> them through the medium of a chosen body of citizens, whose wisdom may best discern the true interest of their country, and whose patriotism and love of justice will be least likely to sacrifice it to temporary or partial considerations. … On the other hand, the effect may be inverted. Men of factious tempers, of local prejudices, or of sinister designs, may, by intrigue, by corruption, or by other means … betray the interests, of the people. … Besides other impediments, it may be remarked that, where there is a consciousness of unjust or dishonorable purposes, communication is always checked by distrust in proportion to the number whose concurrence is necessary.
>
> "… Does it, in fine, consist in the greater obstacles opposed to the concert and accomplishment of the secret wishes of an unjust and interested majority?
>
> "The influence of factious leaders may kindle a flame … but will be unable to spread a general conflagration… A rage for … any … improper or wicked project, will be less apt to pervade the whole body of the Union than a particular member of it…" [264]

It would be possible to call attention to numerous passages that relate to the present. The one I would like to draw attention to is "taxes … which seems to require the most exact impartiality."

Please keep "the most exact impartiality" in mind. That is where we will try to go.

The rich were too heavily taxed. Yes, I mean it.

The singular message is that the long throw of USA tax history has provided no consistent standard for taxes at the high end. This can be seen in graph-335. In summary, Stage I, II, and FDR in the main provided taxes that were commendably within ±5% of the equitable standard up until the one-in-15,000 point. But at the higher levels, they tended to overtax the rich a median 10%.

Stage III and IV are bipolar. Starting at the one-in-200 point, Stage III overtaxed a wide swath of the Upper½%, a median 12.8%. The most egregious of all USA tax history remains Stage IV taxation, which did not kick in its main benefits for the elite until the one-in-1,000 point at 7.5%, after which the advantages came with a vengeance, peaking at about 42%. From the 91st percentile to one-in-125 point, Stage IV provided no tax advantage in order to achieve the boon for those at the top.

#335

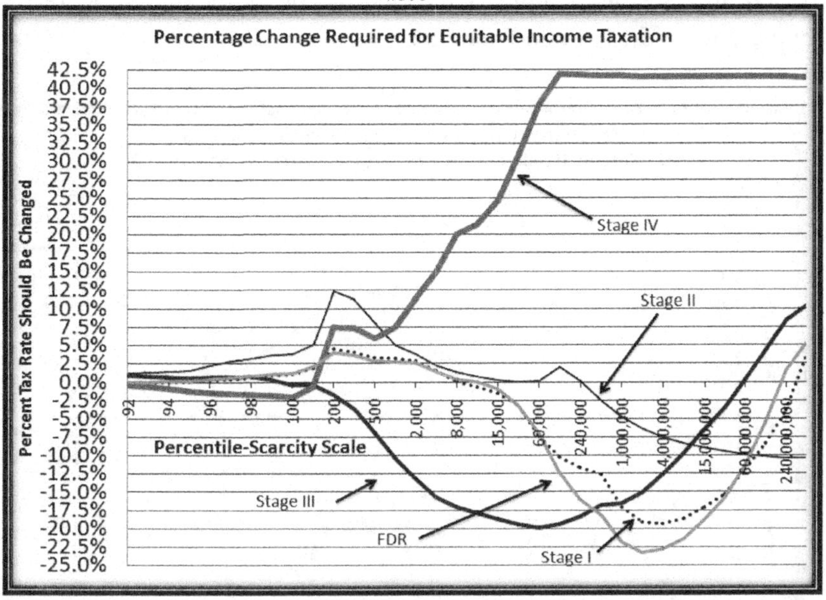

#335B

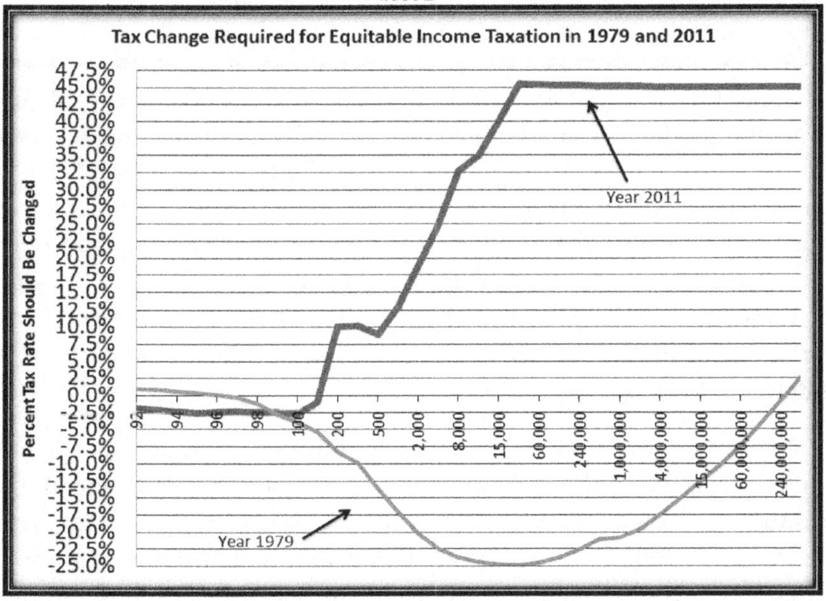

More specifically, we look at two years in the Stage III-to-Stage IV transition: 1979 and 2011 in graph-335B. Income taxation in 1979 over-taxed the Top2% a median 17%. A broad swath of the Top2% were over-taxed, often approaching 25%. This was too much for the rich to stomach. In revenge, they saw to it that the elites prospered. Income taxation in 2011 provided an 8.9% advantage at the one-in-500 point that shot up rapidly from there to a 45.5% tax advantage.

#336

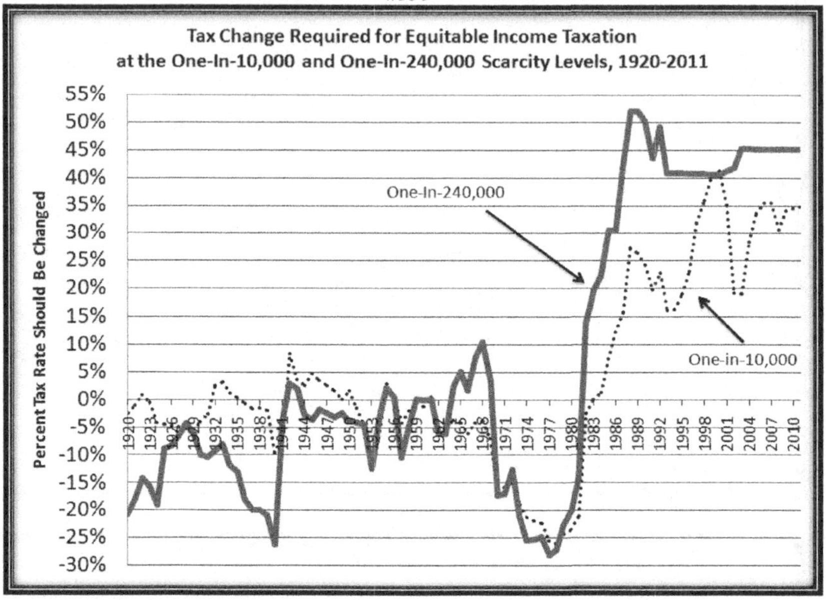

Graph-336 tells a story similar to the former graphs, except it focuses on people at the one-in-10,000 and one-in-240,000 income levels from 1920 to 2011. Within these groups from 1920 to 1970, most of the variation occurred within the range of a 5% under-taxation to a 10% overtaxation. And occasionally the two groups found themselves on opposite sides of the line in the same year, for example 3.1% and -7.9% in 1933. For these two groups, the two great taxing errors were a median 21.5% overtaxing from 1970 to 1981 and the median 40.4% under-taxing from 1986 to 2011.

The lesson is plain. Once an appropriate income distribution is achieved, such as in the 1970s, those who promote a fair or liberal agenda need to be careful above all else that they do not wrongly overtax the rich. The message from 1979 and Stage III taxation is that the rich were being overtaxed. It was suicidal to overtax them because they had the money, power, and ultimately vengeance to respond. The Stage III-to-Stage IV transition and the 1979-2011 case are evidence of it.

Given the favorable income distributions for the MAJ, the rich in 1979 were overtaxed. The rich responded by reducing their taxes to a point about 45% beneath where they should have been. Not only did they get disproportionately favorable tax treatment by this move, they dragged into place an oligarchy of the kind the USA has not seen previously. Along with it came the concomitant ills for all those beneath the teeter point. For that taxation error in the 1970s, the nation paid deeply. In good times and bad, a democracy requires attentive tax management at the high end of the scale. Without it, the MAJ is imperiled. The nation is imperiled. The democracy is imperiled.

The most exact impartiality.

Too frequently, tax discussions devolve into a zeal for different opinions, mutual animosities, frivolous or fanciful distinctions, factious tempers, prejudices, sinister designs, and various mischiefs more disposed to vex and oppress rather than to cooperate. Yet taxation is the instrument that makes government possible. It is beneficial – no, necessary – to be enlightened statesmen and citizens to ensure this great enterprise that we call democracy works, and works for all of us. Taxation is at the heart of it.

My family's farm is within 5 miles of President Madison's home and within 30 miles of President Jefferson's home. From childhood onward it was impressed upon me that government was a serious and beneficial exercise; and public service, noble. I believe those lessons were correct and worthy of aspiring to. Please turn the page to consider a technique for implementing Madison's "most exact impartiality" in our modern democracy.

CH. 12

BIG ROCKS: adaptive taxation.

Long ago I had a conversation with Dietrich Fischer. Through the filter of memory, the story he told goes much like the following. I will call it the Big Rocks Story:

> You are given two piles of rocks: big rocks and small pebbles. You are given a jar in which to put them. There are enough big rocks that they alone would fill the jar to the brim.
>
> How can you most effectively fill the jar?
>
> Try starting with the pebbles. Try starting with the big rocks.
>
> If you start with pebbles, the big rocks will not fit into the jar.
>
> Starting with big rocks is the most effective way to fill the jar. The pebbles can be fitted around them.[265]

Similarly, this applies to big issues. If we consistently address the great non-issues of our time and trivial details (the pebbles), the outcome is likely to be disappointing, because the important issues (the big rocks) never find their way into the jar.

Our democracy was built on getting the big rocks into place. We were fortunate that it happened at the outset and that, when later required, at great decision points, the big rocks were properly attended to. Our less glorious moments were spent with the pebbles.

This author is drawing to a close. The work is now in the citizen's hand. We have trekked through many pages. You may well have anticipated we would land here and may also have anticipated the remaining pages. As you moved through the book up to this point, you have seen that we really knew very little about income distribution and that its principal measures, such as Ginis, quintiles, and the like, were useless for arriving at solutions or for letting us understand our place in this great enterprise that we call an economy.

Most particularly, a subset of that economy, taxation, has been hobbled by our lack of knowledge about income distribution and its effect. Even with the best intensions at exceptionally high incomes, taxation drifted away from appropriate standards. At best it was hit and miss. Sometimes getting it right; more often, not.

Fair taxation and income distribution are inexorably linked. We intuitively grasp this when we visit polar-opposite nations, say one nation that is unusually equitable (at MAJ36 for example) and another nation, which is oppressively cruel (at MAJ8).* In a heartbeat, we would join hands to say that the rich in the cruelly oppressive nation should be placed under a heavier tax burden than the rich in a patently fair nation, whose income already comprises a far smaller share of national wealth.

Even if we were unmoved by ethics, the exigencies of pragmatism would motivate us to give the wealthy in any nation ample incentive to ensure that the nation would naturally move to a position that was as equitable as was reasonably practicable within a well functioning capitalistic system.

Adaptive taxation.

Graph-341 (overall 16% average tax) and graph-341B (overall 20% average tax) illustrate adaptive taxation. The only difference in the graphs is that the latter is designed to produce about 4% more tax revenue. In both graphs, as income distribution becomes ever more equitable, the average tax rate for the elite is reduced, ultimately reaching a substantially flat tax at the far left-hand side of the graph where the difference between the high and low curve is slight.

---

* At MAJ8, there is only a pauper's share of income for the majority, a mere 8% of the income for 60% of the people.

You have already seen adaptive taxation in action. It was referred to as "equitable taxation" in graph-335 and subsequent graphs. Those graphs showed how adaptive taxation compared with our history of past taxation. It would have eliminated the egregious over-taxation of the rich in the 1970s and would have prevented the vast Stage IV under taxation.

#341

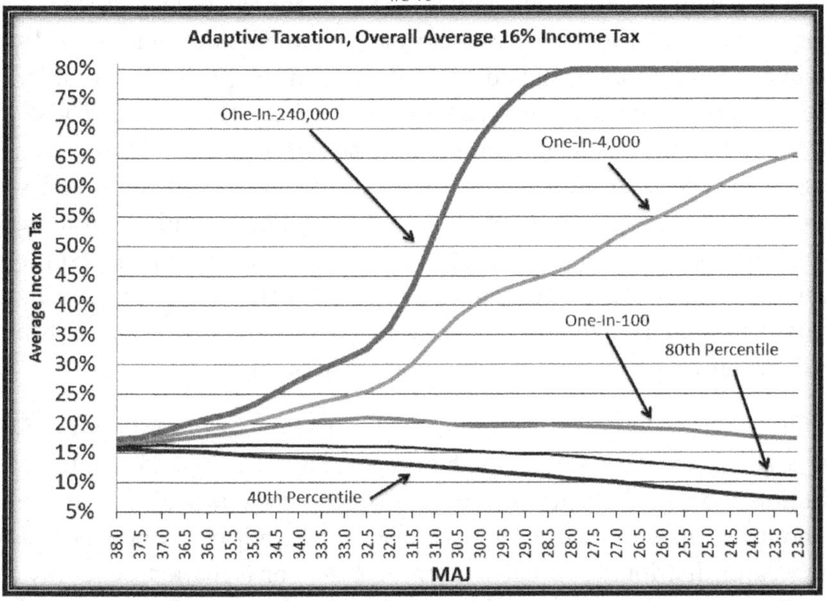

#341B

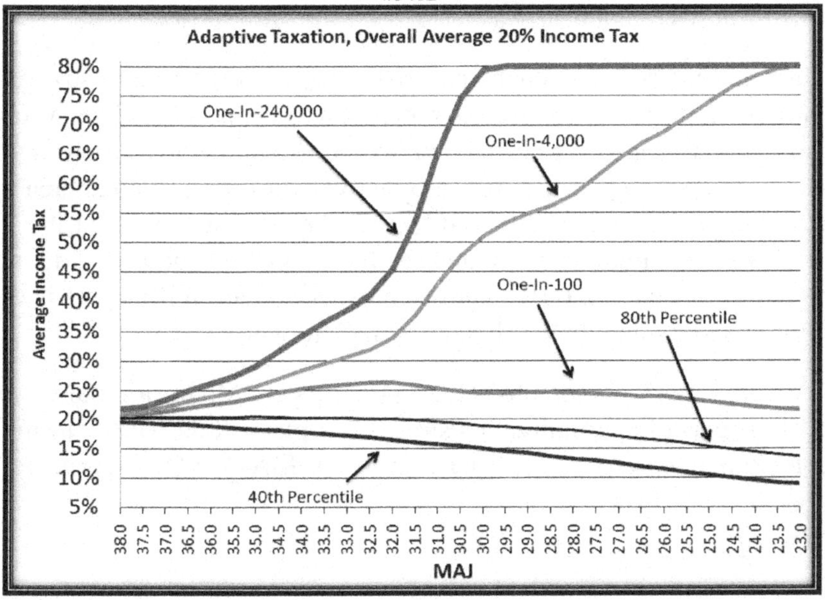

Adaptive taxation is the bridge that directly connects the elites to the wellbeing of the MAJ. Producing a prosperous MAJ cuts taxes for the Top1%.[266]

The remedy.

The plain point is that when a nation elects to have a maldistributed economy, it chooses to concentrate wealth and income in a few hands. Those beneath the teeter point who have neither much income or wealth become severely subordinated, directly or indirectly, to the wealthy. The wealthy benefit because they are holders of money that is lent. Those at the low end, having reduced income by way of maldistribution, are hard-pressed to pay those debts. Together, the interplay of income and wealth under such circumstances is precarious and subject to failure. Within these machinations, the financial sector disproportionately grows, sometimes dwarfing productive sectors. The financial sector not only concentrates wealth, its chief actors and minions profit from it.[267] It becomes a maldistribution between sectors and between people.

These observations are pragmatic. Long ago, in graph-57 and 58, we saw a sharp and ever-reducing share of wealth at the MAJ as income distribution worsened. When the 60% majority is a full player in the U.S. economy as it was in the 1950s-1970s, the relationship between income and wealth distribution creates a strong base for a market economy, for a capitalistic system, and for a democracy. That base has been chiseled apart by men who were not nearly as wise as they professed to be.

Just as Madison was concerned with elected officials and structure of government, we now must turn our attention to the modern elites who govern the private sphere of our nation. We need a structure that ensures that our private governing elites, too, are motivated to act in the national interest, not just for their exclusive self benefit. They must serve the tribe. They derive their strength from it and in turn must be motivated to return strength to it. That the 60% majority prosper and are full players is essential for this system that we call a democracy to work.

Adaptive taxation (graph-341 & 341B) meets Madison's objective for the "most exact impartiality." Its structure is plain. It derives its form from the lookup table curves. The base curve is MAJ39. Each curve for the

MAJs in graph-341 or 341B is divided by the base curve.* The outcome provides a predictable in-place adaptive schedule based on income share. The taxpayer, in advance, knows that the income tax that he or she pays will vary according to changes in income distribution and can look to the curves to see how much the changes will be.

The objective is for the economy over time to find its best functioning natural income distribution on its own. Adaptive taxation is intended to instill responsibility in all classes. As maldistribution becomes less intense, those at the low end have their taxes increase. They also receive larger incomes (higher MAJs) and are thus able to pay the taxes and still be net gainers. In short, they are full and responsible players as much as anyone else and not just organisms for receiving government largess.

Those at the high end are also held to a high standard, as they should be, because they make the decisions that determine how the rest of us fare. If their greed devolves primarily to their benefit alone without filtering advantages down to lower classes, then they must pay a burdensome tax. If they treat the MAJ fairly, their taxes are reduced. If a particular individual makes a hobby of amassing huge fortunes, whether it be for good or indifferent reasons, that person may do so. He or she just must pay a very high average tax not exceeding 80%. There is no need to vilify this person, for he or she is contributing mightily to the government treasury and thus is making a bona fide contribution to the nation's wellbeing.

Adaptive taxation delivers the message to the high reaches of the Upper½%: You may have your low taxes, but you may not impoverish 60% of the population and simultaneously have your low taxes. If you want low taxes, you must provide a fair income share for the 60% majority.

We have too long argued taxation and income distribution. It is time to give the noise a rest. A known adaptive taxation schedule provides the incentive in advance to avoid maldistribution. More positively, it provides

---

* The resulting array of ratios are the key. To illustrate how unbiased and uncomplicated the method is, the subroutine is called with this simple statement:
CALL GetAdaptiveTax(MAJ, OverallTaxRate, population, AdaptiveTax())
The key subroutine line for determining the resulting OverallTaxRate is:
sum=sum+(BASEadjust*Ratio(x)*CurrentDistributionCurve(x))
The BASEadjust is a constant designed to yield the particular OverallTaxRate (called the sum when it is being applied throughout the backbone).
When this condition is met: AdaptiveTaxAtEachPoint(x)=BASEadjust*Ratio(x)
Required adjustments are subsequently made at the top end, and the highest average tax is capped at 80%. If MAJ>39 then it is a flat tax = OverallTaxRate. The final array is then sorted..

the rich with an incentive to migrate toward income distributions that are wholesome for the MAJ, the nation, and the rich alike.

Outside the direct reach of taxes, the workings of adaptive taxation indirectly motivate the rich in their customary business practices to encourage more regular and more remunerative employment for the MAJ because a prosperous MAJ lowers their personal tax bill. As the historical record illustrates, a prospering MAJ carries with it a thriving economy. By such a combination of means, we all prosper, whether we are beneath or above the teeter point.

Thank you Madison. Thank you Smith.

Our nation and our economy are now vastly different from when Madison wrote the *Federalist Papers*. His focus was on government and creating a Constitutional design for it. Now government and the economy are so intertwined that even sufficient Constitutional measures are insufficient to ensure national success.

Taking the cue from Madison, adaptive taxation can offer the "most exact impartiality." It is so plainly simple that, if they elect to do so, the citizenry can amply monitor it, widely audit it, and appropriately implement it. By bringing many people into the process, the fractious impulses which Madison so greatly lamented and so greatly feared can be reduced.

Adaptive taxation takes a second cue from the same era. That cue comes from Adam Smith's observation that we benefit by addressing enlightened self-interest.

They said it all. It is now time for this author to stop.

ACKNOWLEDGEMENTS

To claim this work as mine alone would be an exaggeration. It has been transformed by others. Mary Geisenhoff, with each draft, gave it a thorough going over, cleaning up originalities in spelling, grammar, punctuation, and more. It was a stroke of fortune to have her reliable and helpful observations. Patricia Grenseman continued in that vein, adding in her linguistic abilities, organization, and (again) more. It was a great pleasure to have her hand in the pie. And the ever self-deprecating Aoife Herlihy who insists that she cannot be called a physicist (because she studied that too long ago), who's job title is quality engineer (not civil engineer), and who is completely Irish but now in London, who notwithstanding all of the foregoing made her well-aimed and indispensable contributions – exactly where they were needed. And Lorie DeWorken worked her magic on the ebook, notwithstanding formidable impediments. And to others who bask in privacy: Thanks all. Every person on this project went beyond the common call of duty. The contributions, all coming from vastly different perspectives, was a much needed bonus. Even with such energetic and able help, my wild pen managed to slip in a few items to drag it down to the low level that I am comfortable with. For all of it, I take full responsibility.

I am also indebted to a person who never knew this book was being written. Bob Zale wrote and has been the mainstay behind PowerBasic – the computer language I used for writing the computer programs that are the foundation on which this work rests.

There are billions of people in the world. My programs looked through substantially each of them, at times for hundreds of years, examining thousands of potential outcomes before arriving at the best fit for each year. To do this required programs at least as fast as C++ computer programs. The PowerBasic Console Compiler delivered this and more.[268] It has a deceptively plain screen, but what is under the hood is reliable and pure muscle. It can easily handle vast amounts of data. It is especially well suited for economic analysis and modeling.

This book is about fairness and virtues being rewarded. To the extent that I am familiar with the company, PowerBasic conforms to those precepts. For the customer, its business practices are those that I associate with integrity: fair pricing, fair updating, and providing the user with a fair shake – in my case for almost 20 years. The way I see it, in this instance, the little guy triumphed. Bob and those at PowerBasic did a better job than many software conglomerates.

Along these lines, it strikes me as fitting that they were at the heart of this work.*

* A necessary disclosure: Bob Zale does not know me from Adam. I do not have, nor will I have a financial intermingling or any compromising relationship with his company. However, I do expect to continue to be a customer, as I have been in the past.

APPENDIX 1. Lookup table

In Chapter 2, spreadsheet lookup-table data illustrated the consequences for the MAJ that occurred as a result of going from a one third income share to a one quarter income share. Lookup-table data lets you understand the approximate form that all income and wealth distributions take. This is not to say that the table is a rigid standard. It is to say it is a reasonable guide that seeks to illustrate central tendencies based on information now available, processed by my computer programs. About 2,500 income-distribution cases worldwide and a small number of wealth distribution cases were used.

When you download the lookup-table spreadsheet, its header row contains the following listed information in sequence. Excluding the columns with the headings, "MAJ, KeyRatio, Gini, Population, and Top/Bottom Ratio," all the data beneath the headings are in X$s. Regardless of what nation you live in or the currency you use, you can multiply the X$s by your GDP per capita to understand how incomes at all points from bottom to top influence your nation, depending on income distribution. Separately, if you know your nation's average net worth per capita, you can multiply it by the X$s in the lookup table. That will show how wealth tends to change from bottom to top as wealth distributions change.

Descriptors: MAJ, KeyRatio, Gini, Lower½%, Upper½%.
Backbone: Top1%, 1, 2, 3, 4, 5, 6, 7, 8, 9, 10, 11, 12, 13, 14, 15, 16, 17, 18, 19, 20, 21, 22, 23, 24, 25, 26, 27, 28, 29, 30, 31, 32, 33, 34, 35, 36, 37, 38, 39, 40, 41, 42, 43, 44, 45, 46, 47, 48, 49, 50, 51, 52, 53, 54, 55, 56, 57, 58, 59, 60, 61, 62, 63, 64, 65, 66, 67, 68, 69, 70, 71, 72, 73, 74, 75, 76, 77, 78, 79, 80, 81, 82, 83, 84, 85, 86, 87, 88, 89, 90, 91, 92, 93, 94, 95, 96, 97, 98, 99.
Scarcity levels within the Top1%: 100, 125, 200, 250, 500, 1,000, 2,000, 4,000, 8,000, 10,000, 15,000, 30,000, 60,000, 120,000, 240,000, 480,000, 1,000,000, 2,000,000, 4,000,000, 8,000,000, 15,000,000, 30,000,000, 60,000,000, 120,000,000, 240,000,000, 300,000,000, 480,000,000, 1,000,000,000, 7,000,000,000.
Top-end threshold categories: Top500, Top400, Top100, 10th, 3rd , 2nd, 1st
Details: Population, Top/Bottom Ratio.

A word of caution: The lookup table is calculated based on a population of 307 million. This closely approximates the United States. But for significantly different population sizes, you cannot use the Top-end threshold data (Top500 to 1st). All of these references are highly populations sensitive. For Top-end threshold data, you are best advised to consult spreadsheets pertaining to your nation or other nations of approximately the same population size.

The abridged lookup table is spread over the next 4 pages. In contrast to the complete downloadable lookup table, it is abridged to fit the space available and contains the following headings.

Descriptors: MAJ, Gini, Lower½%, Upper½%.
Backbone: Top1%, 1, 5, 10, 15, 20, 25, 30, 35, 40, 45, 50, 55, 60, 65, 70, 75, 80, 85, 90, 95.
Scarcity levels within the Top1%: 100, 200, 500, 1,000, 30,000, 120,000, 1,000,000.
Top-end threshold categories: Top400, Top100, 10th, 1st

The table starts with an excessively equitable MAJ49 income distribution and ends with an excessively inequitable wealth distribution (MAJ1.6). In the downloadable version at Dilives.com, the MAJ values are shown at 0.1 increments. Here they are shown at 0.25 increments (except for MAJ33.3 which was added to exactly match the base case so often referred to in the text).

To those of you who turned to the Appendix before reading the book, the MAJ refers to the percent of income (or wealth) received by the bottom 60% of the population. On page 350, the income MAJ range we have principally discussed (MAJ36 through MAJ25) is shown and the key rows are highlighted (MAJ36, MAJ33.3, MAJ25). On page 352, MAJs lower than 13.25 are shown. They pertain mainly to U.S. wealth distribution, which in recent years has ranged from about MAJ6 to MAJ4.

Once you have familiarized yourself with the lookup table by dividing a row into other rows to see how much changes in distribution influence conditions, and once you have summed various sections of the backbone to see the percent of income received in various segments, you will be the autodidact on the way to becoming a useful DIY economist. Print up your own degree. Hang it wherever you like. An appropriately sized mural of it is always nice.

Never forget. Only sum numbers within the backbone. (All of them together sum to 100.) If you sum other numbers (Lower½%, Upper½%, scarcity levels within the Top1%, or Top-end threshold categories), you are honor bound to tear up your degree and start over.

MAJ	Gini	Lower ½%	Upper ½%	Top1	1	5	10	15	20	25	30	35	40	45	50	55	60	65
49.00	16.1	2.1	2.7	2.4	0.47	0.61	0.67	0.71	0.75	0.79	0.83	0.88	0.92	0.94	0.95	0.97	0.98	1.02
48.75	16.4	2.2	3.0	2.6	0.46	0.60	0.66	0.71	0.75	0.79	0.83	0.87	0.91	0.93	0.95	0.96	0.98	1.02
48.50	16.7	2.2	3.2	2.7	0.45	0.59	0.66	0.71	0.75	0.79	0.83	0.87	0.91	0.93	0.94	0.96	0.98	1.02
48.25	17.0	2.2	3.3	2.7	0.44	0.59	0.65	0.70	0.75	0.78	0.82	0.86	0.90	0.92	0.94	0.96	0.99	1.02
48.00	17.3	2.2	3.3	2.7	0.44	0.58	0.65	0.70	0.74	0.78	0.82	0.85	0.89	0.92	0.94	0.96	0.99	1.02
47.75	17.5	2.2	3.3	2.8	0.43	0.57	0.65	0.70	0.74	0.78	0.81	0.85	0.88	0.91	0.93	0.96	0.99	1.03
47.50	17.8	2.2	3.3	2.8	0.42	0.57	0.64	0.70	0.75	0.78	0.81	0.84	0.87	0.90	0.93	0.96	0.99	1.04
47.25	18.1	2.2	3.4	2.8	0.41	0.56	0.63	0.69	0.74	0.78	0.81	0.83	0.86	0.89	0.92	0.96	1.00	1.04
47.00	18.3	2.2	3.4	2.8	0.40	0.55	0.63	0.69	0.74	0.78	0.80	0.83	0.85	0.88	0.92	0.96	1.01	1.05
46.75	18.7	2.2	3.4	2.8	0.39	0.54	0.62	0.68	0.73	0.77	0.80	0.83	0.85	0.89	0.93	0.97	1.01	1.06
46.50	19.1	2.2	3.5	2.8	0.38	0.53	0.61	0.67	0.72	0.76	0.79	0.82	0.85	0.89	0.93	0.97	1.01	1.06
46.25	19.5	2.2	3.5	2.9	0.37	0.52	0.60	0.66	0.72	0.76	0.79	0.82	0.85	0.89	0.93	0.97	1.01	1.06
46.00	19.8	2.2	3.6	2.9	0.36	0.51	0.59	0.65	0.71	0.75	0.79	0.82	0.85	0.89	0.93	0.97	1.02	1.07
45.75	20.2	2.3	3.6	2.9	0.35	0.50	0.58	0.65	0.70	0.75	0.78	0.82	0.85	0.89	0.93	0.97	1.01	1.06
45.50	20.5	2.3	3.7	3.0	0.34	0.50	0.58	0.64	0.70	0.74	0.78	0.81	0.85	0.88	0.92	0.97	1.01	1.06
45.25	20.9	2.3	3.7	3.0	0.33	0.49	0.57	0.63	0.69	0.73	0.77	0.81	0.85	0.88	0.92	0.97	1.01	1.06
45.00	21.2	2.3	3.9	3.1	0.32	0.48	0.57	0.63	0.68	0.73	0.77	0.80	0.84	0.88	0.92	0.96	1.01	1.06
44.75	21.6	2.4	4.0	3.2	0.31	0.47	0.56	0.62	0.68	0.72	0.76	0.80	0.84	0.88	0.92	0.96	1.01	1.06
44.50	22.0	2.4	4.2	3.3	0.31	0.47	0.55	0.61	0.67	0.72	0.76	0.80	0.84	0.88	0.92	0.96	1.01	1.06
44.25	22.4	2.4	4.4	3.4	0.30	0.46	0.55	0.61	0.66	0.71	0.75	0.79	0.84	0.88	0.92	0.96	1.01	1.06
44.00	22.7	2.4	4.4	3.4	0.29	0.46	0.54	0.60	0.66	0.71	0.75	0.79	0.83	0.87	0.91	0.96	1.01	1.06
43.75	23.0	2.5	4.5	3.5	0.29	0.45	0.53	0.60	0.66	0.70	0.74	0.78	0.82	0.87	0.91	0.96	1.01	1.06
43.50	23.4	2.6	4.6	3.6	0.28	0.44	0.53	0.60	0.65	0.70	0.74	0.78	0.82	0.86	0.91	0.96	1.01	1.06
43.25	23.8	2.6	4.8	3.7	0.27	0.44	0.52	0.59	0.64	0.69	0.74	0.78	0.82	0.86	0.91	0.95	1.00	1.06
43.00	24.2	2.7	4.9	3.8	0.27	0.43	0.52	0.58	0.64	0.69	0.73	0.78	0.82	0.86	0.90	0.95	1.00	1.05
42.75	24.6	2.7	5.0	3.9	0.26	0.43	0.51	0.57	0.63	0.68	0.72	0.77	0.82	0.86	0.90	0.95	0.99	1.05
42.50	24.9	2.8	5.1	3.9	0.26	0.42	0.51	0.57	0.62	0.67	0.72	0.77	0.82	0.86	0.90	0.94	0.99	1.05
42.25	25.2	2.8	5.1	4.0	0.25	0.42	0.50	0.57	0.62	0.67	0.72	0.76	0.81	0.85	0.90	0.94	0.99	1.05
42.00	25.5	2.9	5.3	4.1	0.24	0.41	0.50	0.56	0.62	0.67	0.71	0.76	0.81	0.85	0.89	0.94	0.98	1.04
41.75	25.9	2.9	5.3	4.1	0.24	0.41	0.50	0.56	0.61	0.66	0.71	0.76	0.80	0.85	0.89	0.93	0.98	1.04
41.50	26.2	2.9	5.4	4.2	0.23	0.40	0.49	0.55	0.61	0.66	0.70	0.75	0.80	0.84	0.88	0.93	0.98	1.04
41.25	26.5	3.0	5.5	4.2	0.22	0.40	0.48	0.55	0.60	0.65	0.70	0.75	0.79	0.84	0.88	0.93	0.98	1.04
41.00	26.9	3.0	5.5	4.3	0.22	0.39	0.47	0.54	0.59	0.65	0.69	0.74	0.79	0.84	0.88	0.93	0.98	1.05
40.75	27.3	3.0	5.6	4.3	0.21	0.38	0.47	0.53	0.59	0.64	0.69	0.74	0.79	0.84	0.88	0.93	0.98	1.05
40.50	22.6	3.1	5.7	4.4	0.21	0.38	0.46	0.53	0.58	0.63	0.68	0.74	0.79	0.84	0.88	0.93	0.98	1.04
40.25	28.0	3.1	5.8	4.5	0.20	0.37	0.46	0.52	0.58	0.63	0.68	0.73	0.79	0.83	0.88	0.92	0.98	1.04
40.00	28.4	3.2	5.9	4.6	0.20	0.37	0.45	0.52	0.57	0.62	0.68	0.73	0.78	0.83	0.87	0.92	0.97	1.04
39.75	28.7	3.3	6.0	4.6	0.19	0.36	0.45	0.51	0.57	0.62	0.67	0.72	0.78	0.82	0.87	0.92	0.97	1.04
39.50	29.0	3.3	6.1	4.7	0.19	0.36	0.45	0.51	0.56	0.62	0.67	0.72	0.77	0.82	0.86	0.91	0.97	1.04
39.25	29.4	3.4	6.2	4.8	0.18	0.35	0.44	0.50	0.56	0.61	0.66	0.71	0.77	0.81	0.86	0.91	0.97	1.03
39.00	29.7	3.4	6.4	4.9	0.18	0.35	0.44	0.50	0.56	0.61	0.66	0.71	0.76	0.81	0.86	0.91	0.96	1.03
38.75	30.1	3.5	6.4	4.9	0.17	0.34	0.43	0.49	0.55	0.60	0.65	0.71	0.76	0.81	0.85	0.91	0.96	1.03
38.50	30.4	3.5	6.5	5.0	0.17	0.33	0.42	0.49	0.55	0.60	0.65	0.70	0.76	0.80	0.85	0.91	0.96	1.03
38.25	30.8	3.6	6.6	5.1	0.16	0.32	0.42	0.48	0.54	0.60	0.65	0.70	0.75	0.80	0.85	0.90	0.96	1.03
38.00	31.2	3.6	6.7	5.1	0.15	0.32	0.41	0.47	0.53	0.59	0.64	0.70	0.75	0.80	0.85	0.90	0.96	1.04
37.75	31.5	3.6	6.7	5.2	0.15	0.31	0.40	0.46	0.52	0.58	0.63	0.69	0.75	0.80	0.85	0.91	0.96	1.04
37.50	31.8	3.6	6.8	5.2	0.14	0.30	0.39	0.46	0.52	0.57	0.63	0.69	0.75	0.80	0.85	0.90	0.97	1.04
37.25	32.1	3.7	6.8	5.3	0.14	0.30	0.39	0.46	0.52	0.57	0.63	0.68	0.74	0.79	0.84	0.90	0.97	1.04

MAJ	70	75	80	85	90	95	100	200	500	1,000	30,000	120,000	1,000,000	Top400	Top100	10th	1st
49.00	1.06	1.11	1.17	1.26	1.37	1.56	2.0	2.3	2.6	2.9	4.9	6.1	8.5	8.1	10.1	14.0	21.0
48.75	1.06	1.11	1.18	1.26	1.38	1.58	2.0	2.3	2.9	3.5	6.3	8.1	11.9	11.4	14.5	22.0	33.0
48.50	1.06	1.12	1.18	1.27	1.39	1.59	2.0	2.4	3.1	3.9	7.6	10.0	15.2	14.4	19.0	30.0	47.0
48.25	1.07	1.12	1.19	1.28	1.40	1.60	2.0	2.4	3.1	3.9	7.7	10.1	15.3	14.5	19.1	30.0	47.0
48.00	1.07	1.13	1.19	1.28	1.40	1.61	2.0	2.4	3.1	3.9	7.7	10.1	15.4	14.6	19.2	30.0	48.0
47.75	1.08	1.13	1.20	1.29	1.41	1.62	2.0	2.4	3.2	4.0	7.8	10.3	15.7	14.9	19.7	31.0	49.0
47.50	1.08	1.14	1.21	1.30	1.42	1.62	2.0	2.4	3.2	4.0	7.8	10.3	15.8	14.9	19.7	31.0	49.0
47.25	1.09	1.15	1.22	1.30	1.42	1.62	2.0	2.4	3.2	4.0	8.0	10.6	16.3	15.5	20.5	32.5	52.0
47.00	1.10	1.16	1.23	1.31	1.43	1.62	2.0	2.4	3.2	4.1	8.1	10.8	16.6	15.7	20.8	33.0	53.0
46.75	1.11	1.16	1.23	1.32	1.43	1.62	2.0	2.4	3.3	4.1	8.3	11.0	17.0	16.1	21.3	34.0	54.5
46.50	1.11	1.17	1.24	1.33	1.45	1.65	2.0	2.4	3.3	4.2	8.5	11.3	17.6	16.7	22.2	36.0	58.0
46.25	1.11	1.17	1.24	1.33	1.45	1.66	2.1	2.5	3.4	4.3	8.7	11.6	18.0	17.1	22.8	37.0	59.5
46.00	1.12	1.18	1.25	1.34	1.46	1.65	2.1	2.5	3.4	4.3	8.7	11.7	18.2	17.2	23.1	37.0	61.0
45.75	1.11	1.18	1.25	1.34	1.47	1.68	2.1	2.5	3.5	4.4	9.0	12.1	18.9	17.8	24.0	39.0	63.5
45.50	1.12	1.18	1.26	1.35	1.48	1.69	2.1	2.5	3.5	4.4	9.1	12.3	19.3	18.3	24.6	40.0	66.0
45.25	1.12	1.18	1.26	1.35	1.49	1.71	2.1	2.6	3.6	4.5	9.5	12.8	20.3	19.2	25.9	43.0	70.5
45.00	1.12	1.18	1.26	1.36	1.50	1.72	2.1	2.6	3.7	4.7	10.0	13.7	21.9	20.7	28.2	47.0	79.0
44.75	1.12	1.19	1.27	1.37	1.50	1.73	2.1	2.7	3.9	5.0	10.9	15.0	24.4	23.0	31.6	53.5	91.5
44.50	1.12	1.19	1.27	1.37	1.51	1.74	2.2	2.7	4.1	5.2	11.6	16.1	26.6	25.0	34.8	60.0	104.0
44.25	1.12	1.19	1.27	1.37	1.51	1.74	2.2	2.8	4.3	5.4	12.4	17.4	29.1	27.3	38.3	67.0	117.5
44.00	1.12	1.19	1.28	1.38	1.52	1.75	2.2	2.8	4.3	5.5	12.7	17.8	30.1	28.2	39.6	70.0	123.0
43.75	1.12	1.20	1.28	1.38	1.52	1.76	2.3	2.9	4.4	5.6	13.0	18.4	31.1	29.1	41.1	73.0	129.5
43.50	1.13	1.20	1.29	1.39	1.53	1.76	2.3	2.9	4.5	5.7	13.3	18.9	32.2	30.1	42.7	76.0	136.0
43.25	1.12	1.20	1.29	1.39	1.53	1.77	2.4	3.1	4.7	5.8	13.9	19.7	33.9	31.7	45.1	81.5	146.0
43.00	1.12	1.19	1.29	1.39	1.53	1.78	2.4	3.1	4.8	6.0	14.4	20.6	35.6	33.2	47.6	86.0	157.0
42.75	1.12	1.19	1.29	1.39	1.54	1.80	2.5	3.2	4.9	6.1	14.8	21.1	36.8	34.3	49.3	89.5	163.5
42.50	1.12	1.20	1.29	1.40	1.55	1.82	2.5	3.2	5.0	6.1	15.0	21.5	37.6	35.1	50.4	92.0	169.0
42.25	1.12	1.20	1.29	1.41	1.56	1.83	2.5	3.2	5.1	6.2	15.3	22.0	38.5	35.9	51.8	95.5	175.0
42.00	1.11	1.20	1.30	1.41	1.57	1.84	2.6	3.3	5.2	6.3	15.6	22.6	39.8	37.1	53.6	99.0	183.0
41.75	1.11	1.20	1.30	1.41	1.58	1.86	2.6	3.4	5.3	6.4	16.0	23.2	41.0	38.1	55.4	102.5	190.5
41.50	1.11	1.20	1.30	1.42	1.59	1.87	2.6	3.4	5.4	6.5	16.2	23.6	41.9	39.0	56.7	106.0	197.0
41.25	1.12	1.20	1.31	1.42	1.59	1.88	2.6	3.4	5.4	6.6	16.5	24.1	42.9	39.9	58.1	108.5	203.5
41.00	1.12	1.21	1.31	1.43	1.60	1.88	2.7	3.5	5.5	6.6	16.8	24.5	43.8	40.7	59.5	112.0	210.0
40.75	1.12	1.21	1.31	1.43	1.60	1.89	2.7	3.5	5.6	6.7	17.1	25.1	44.9	41.8	61.3	115.0	217.0
40.50	1.12	1.21	1.32	1.44	1.61	1.90	2.8	3.6	5.6	6.8	17.5	25.7	46.2	42.9	63.1	119.0	226.0
40.25	1.12	1.21	1.32	1.44	1.62	1.92	2.8	3.7	5.7	6.9	17.9	26.3	47.6	44.2	65.1	124.0	236.0
40.00	1.12	1.21	1.32	1.45	1.62	1.93	2.8	3.7	5.8	7.0	18.2	27.0	49.0	45.5	67.2	128.0	246.0
39.75	1.12	1.21	1.32	1.45	1.63	1.93	2.9	3.8	5.8	7.1	18.7	27.7	50.6	47.0	69.6	134.0	257.5
39.50	1.12	1.21	1.33	1.45	1.63	1.94	2.9	3.9	5.9	7.2	19.1	28.4	52.1	48.3	71.7	139.0	268.0
39.25	1.12	1.21	1.33	1.45	1.63	1.95	3.0	3.9	6.0	7.4	19.6	29.2	53.8	49.8	74.4	144.5	280.5
39.00	1.12	1.21	1.33	1.46	1.64	1.95	3.1	4.0	6.1	7.5	20.0	30.0	55.5	51.4	77.0	150.0	294.0
38.75	1.12	1.21	1.34	1.46	1.65	1.97	3.1	4.1	6.2	7.6	20.4	30.6	56.9	52.6	78.9	154.5	304
38.50	1.12	1.22	1.34	1.46	1.65	1.96	3.1	4.1	6.2	7.6	20.8	31.2	58.3	53.9	81.0	160.0	314
38.25	1.12	1.22	1.34	1.47	1.65	1.97	3.2	4.2	6.3	7.7	21.0	31.7	59.2	54.8	82.5	162.5	322
38.00	1.12	1.22	1.35	1.48	1.66	1.98	3.2	4.2	6.3	7.8	21.3	32.2	60.4	55.9	84.3	167.0	331
37.75	1.12	1.23	1.35	1.48	1.67	1.99	3.2	4.3	6.4	7.8	21.5	32.5	61.1	56.5	85.4	169.0	336
37.50	1.13	1.23	1.36	1.49	1.67	2.00	3.2	4.3	6.4	7.9	21.8	33.0	62.2	57.5	87.0	173.0	345
37.25	1.13	1.24	1.37	1.49	1.68	2.00	3.3	4.3	6.5	7.9	22.0	33.3	62.9	58.2	88.1	176.0	350

MAJ	Gini	Lower ½%	Upper ½%	Top1	1	5	10	15	20	25	30	35	40	45	50	55	60	65	70	75	80	85	90	95	100	200	500	1,000	30,000	120,000	1,000,000	Top400	Top100	10th	1st
37.00	32.5	3.7	7.0	5.3	0.13	0.29	0.38	0.45	0.51	0.57	0.62	0.68	0.73	0.79	0.84	0.90	0.96	1.04	1.13	1.24	1.37	1.50	1.69	2.01	3.3	4.4	6.5	8.1	22.6	34.3	65.2	60.7	91.5	183.0	368
36.75	32.9	3.8	7.1	5.5	0.13	0.29	0.38	0.45	0.50	0.56	0.62	0.67	0.73	0.79	0.84	0.89	0.95	1.03	1.12	1.23	1.36	1.50	1.70	2.04	3.3	4.5	6.7	8.3	23.5	35.8	68.5	63.2	96.6	195.5	395
36.50	33.3	3.8	7.3	5.6	0.13	0.29	0.38	0.44	0.50	0.56	0.61	0.67	0.73	0.78	0.83	0.89	0.95	1.03	1.12	1.23	1.36	1.50	1.71	2.06	3.4	4.6	6.8	8.5	24.2	37.2	71.6	66.0	101.3	206.0	421
36.25	33.7	3.9	7.5	5.7	0.13	0.29	0.37	0.43	0.49	0.55	0.61	0.67	0.73	0.79	0.83	0.88	0.94	1.01	1.11	1.22	1.36	1.50	1.72	2.10	3.4	4.7	7.0	8.7	25.0	38.6	74.8	68.9	106.2	218.0	448
36.00	**34.1**	**4.0**	**7.6**	**5.8**	**0.13**	**0.28**	**0.37**	**0.43**	**0.48**	**0.54**	**0.60**	**0.67**	**0.73**	**0.78**	**0.83**	**0.88**	**0.93**	**1.01**	**1.10**	**1.21**	**1.36**	**1.51**	**1.73**	**2.12**	**3.5**	**4.8**	**7.1**	**8.8**	**25.7**	**39.7**	**77.4**	**71.3**	**110.3**	**228.0**	**470**
35.75	34.3	4.0	7.6	5.8	0.12	0.28	0.36	0.43	0.49	0.54	0.60	0.66	0.72	0.77	0.82	0.88	0.94	1.02	1.11	1.23	1.37	1.51	1.73	2.10	3.5	4.8	7.1	8.8	25.7	39.8	77.5	71.3	110.3	227.5	470
35.50	34.6	4.0	7.6	5.8	0.11	0.27	0.36	0.42	0.48	0.54	0.59	0.65	0.71	0.77	0.82	0.88	0.95	1.03	1.12	1.24	1.38	1.52	1.72	2.08	3.5	4.8	7.1	8.8	25.7	39.7	77.4	71.2	110.2	227.0	469
35.25	34.9	4.1	7.7	5.9	0.11	0.26	0.35	0.42	0.48	0.53	0.59	0.65	0.70	0.76	0.82	0.88	0.95	1.03	1.13	1.24	1.39	1.52	1.72	2.08	3.6	4.9	7.2	8.9	26.1	40.5	79.1	72.7	112.8	233.5	484
35.00	35.2	4.2	7.9	6.0	0.11	0.26	0.35	0.41	0.47	0.53	0.58	0.64	0.70	0.76	0.81	0.88	0.94	1.03	1.13	1.24	1.39	1.52	1.73	2.08	3.6	5.0	7.3	9.1	27.0	42.1	83.0	76.3	118.9	248.0	519
34.75	35.7	4.3	8.3	6.3	0.11	0.26	0.34	0.41	0.46	0.52	0.58	0.64	0.71	0.76	0.81	0.87	0.93	1.01	1.11	1.23	1.38	1.52	1.73	2.10	3.8	5.2	7.6	9.5	28.9	45.3	90.5	83.0	130.4	276.0	585
34.50	36.2	4.4	8.6	6.5	0.11	0.26	0.34	0.40	0.45	0.51	0.57	0.64	0.71	0.76	0.81	0.86	0.92	1.00	1.10	1.22	1.37	1.52	1.73	2.12	3.9	5.3	7.8	9.8	30.4	48.1	97.0	88.8	140.6	301	646
34.25	36.5	4.5	8.7	6.6	0.11	0.26	0.34	0.39	0.45	0.50	0.57	0.63	0.71	0.76	0.80	0.86	0.91	1.00	1.10	1.22	1.37	1.52	1.74	2.13	3.9	5.4	8.0	10.1	31.3	49.6	100.7	92.2	146.5	316	682
34.00	36.8	4.6	8.9	6.7	0.10	0.25	0.33	0.39	0.44	0.50	0.56	0.63	0.70	0.75	0.80	0.85	0.92	1.00	1.10	1.23	1.38	1.52	1.74	2.12	4.0	5.5	8.1	10.2	31.9	50.8	103.6	94.8	151.0	327	709
33.75	37.2	4.6	9.0	6.8	0.10	0.24	0.33	0.39	0.44	0.50	0.56	0.62	0.69	0.75	0.80	0.85	0.92	1.00	1.10	1.23	1.39	1.53	1.74	2.13	4.0	5.6	8.2	10.4	32.6	52.1	106.6	97.5	155.7	330	738
33.50	37.5	4.7	9.2	6.9	0.10	0.24	0.32	0.38	0.43	0.49	0.55	0.62	0.69	0.74	0.79	0.85	0.91	1.00	1.10	1.23	1.39	1.53	1.75	2.14	4.0	5.7	8.3	10.5	33.6	53.8	110.9	101.3	162.5	356	780
33.30	**37.8**	**4.7**	**9.3**	**7.0**	**0.09**	**0.24**	**0.32**	**0.38**	**0.43**	**0.49**	**0.55**	**0.62**	**0.69**	**0.74**	**0.79**	**0.84**	**0.91**	**0.99**	**1.09**	**1.22**	**1.38**	**1.53**	**1.76**	**2.16**	**4.1**	**5.8**	**8.5**	**10.7**	**34.5**	**55.6**	**115.1**	**105.1**	**169.2**	**373**	**823**
33.25	37.9	4.7	9.4	7.1	0.09	0.24	0.32	0.38	0.43	0.49	0.55	0.61	0.69	0.74	0.79	0.84	0.90	0.99	1.09	1.22	1.38	1.53	1.76	2.16	4.1	5.8	8.5	10.8	34.7	56.0	116.1	106.0	170.8	377	833
33.00	38.3	4.8	9.6	7.2	0.09	0.24	0.32	0.37	0.42	0.48	0.54	0.61	0.68	0.74	0.78	0.84	0.89	0.98	1.09	1.22	1.38	1.54	1.77	2.19	4.1	5.9	8.7	11.0	36.0	58.2	121.7	111.0	179.7	400	890
32.75	38.7	4.9	9.8	7.3	0.09	0.24	0.31	0.37	0.42	0.47	0.54	0.61	0.68	0.73	0.78	0.83	0.89	0.97	1.08	1.21	1.38	1.54	1.78	2.21	4.1	6.0	8.9	11.3	37.1	60.3	126.7	115.5	182.7	421	943
32.50	38.9	4.9	9.9	7.4	0.09	0.23	0.31	0.37	0.42	0.47	0.53	0.60	0.67	0.72	0.77	0.83	0.89	0.98	1.09	1.22	1.39	1.55	1.78	2.20	4.2	6.1	8.9	11.3	37.4	60.8	128.0	116.6	189.8	426	956
32.25	39.2	4.9	9.9	7.4	0.08	0.23	0.31	0.37	0.42	0.47	0.53	0.59	0.66	0.72	0.77	0.83	0.90	0.99	1.10	1.23	1.40	1.55	1.78	2.19	4.2	6.1	8.9	11.3	37.5	61.0	128.6	117.2	190.7	429	963
32.00	39.5	5.0	10.2	7.6	0.08	0.22	0.30	0.36	0.41	0.47	0.52	0.59	0.65	0.71	0.77	0.83	0.90	0.99	1.10	1.23	1.40	1.55	1.78	2.19	4.2	6.2	9.1	11.7	39.0	63.9	135.8	123.6	202.3	459	1,040
31.75	39.9	5.0	10.8	7.9	0.08	0.22	0.30	0.36	0.41	0.46	0.52	0.58	0.65	0.71	0.76	0.82	0.89	0.98	1.09	1.23	1.40	1.55	1.78	2.20	4.2	6.5	9.6	12.4	42.7	70.7	153.0	138.9	230.1	532	1,231
31.50	40.3	5.1	11.4	8.3	0.08	0.22	0.30	0.35	0.40	0.45	0.51	0.58	0.65	0.70	0.76	0.82	0.89	0.98	1.09	1.23	1.40	1.55	1.78	2.20	4.2	6.7	10.1	13.1	46.6	78.1	172.1	156.0	261.5	617	1,454
31.25	40.7	5.2	12.1	8.7	0.08	0.21	0.29	0.35	0.40	0.45	0.51	0.57	0.64	0.70	0.75	0.81	0.88	0.97	1.08	1.22	1.40	1.55	1.78	2.20	4.1	7.0	10.7	13.9	50.9	86.3	193.5	174.9	296.7	714	1,717
31.00	41.1	5.3	13.1	9.2	0.08	0.21	0.29	0.34	0.39	0.44	0.50	0.57	0.64	0.70	0.75	0.81	0.87	0.96	1.08	1.22	1.40	1.55	1.78	2.20	4.1	7.3	11.4	15.0	56.8	97.8	224.3	202.2	348	858	2,116
30.75	41.6	5.4	13.9	9.6	0.08	0.21	0.29	0.34	0.38	0.43	0.50	0.57	0.65	0.70	0.75	0.80	0.86	0.95	1.06	1.21	1.39	1.54	1.78	2.21	4.1	7.7	12.1	15.9	62.3	108.5	253.8	228.3	398	1,001	2,520
30.50	42.0	5.5	14.6	10.0	0.08	0.21	0.28	0.33	0.38	0.43	0.49	0.56	0.64	0.70	0.74	0.79	0.85	0.94	1.06	1.20	1.39	1.54	1.78	2.22	4.1	8.0	12.6	16.7	66.6	117.1	277.6	249.3	438	1,120	2,860
30.25	42.3	5.5	15.0	10.3	0.07	0.21	0.28	0.33	0.37	0.43	0.49	0.56	0.64	0.69	0.74	0.79	0.85	0.94	1.06	1.20	1.39	1.54	1.78	2.21	4.1	8.2	13.0	17.2	69.8	123.6	295.9	265.3	470	1,212	3,129
30.00	42.6	5.6	15.5	10.6	0.07	0.21	0.28	0.33	0.37	0.42	0.48	0.55	0.63	0.68	0.73	0.78	0.85	0.94	1.06	1.20	1.39	1.54	1.77	2.20	4.1	8.4	13.3	17.7	73.2	130.3	315	282.20	503	1,311	3,420
29.75	43.0	5.7	15.9	10.8	0.07	0.20	0.27	0.32	0.37	0.42	0.48	0.55	0.63	0.68	0.73	0.78	0.84	0.93	1.05	1.20	1.39	1.54	1.78	2.21	4.1	8.6	13.7	18.2	76.1	136.1	332	296.70	531	1,398	3,677
29.50	43.4	5.8	16.3	11.0	0.07	0.20	0.27	0.32	0.36	0.41	0.48	0.55	0.62	0.68	0.72	0.77	0.83	0.93	1.04	1.19	1.39	1.54	1.78	2.23	4.2	8.8	13.8	18.6	78.2	140.6	345	308	554	1,466	3,882
29.25	43.8	5.9	16.5	11.2	0.07	0.20	0.27	0.31	0.36	0.41	0.47	0.54	0.62	0.67	0.72	0.77	0.83	0.92	1.04	1.19	1.39	1.55	1.79	2.24	4.2	9.0	14.1	18.9	80.0	144.3	355	318	572	1,523	4,054
29.00	44.1	5.9	16.7	11.3	0.07	0.20	0.26	0.31	0.35	0.41	0.47	0.54	0.61	0.67	0.71	0.76	0.82	0.92	1.04	1.19	1.39	1.55	1.79	2.25	4.2	9.1	14.2	19.1	81.6	147.4	365	326	589	1,573	4,204
28.75	44.5	6.0	17.1	11.5	0.07	0.19	0.26	0.31	0.35	0.40	0.46	0.53	0.61	0.66	0.71	0.76	0.82	0.92	1.04	1.19	1.39	1.55	1.79	2.25	4.3	9.4	14.4	19.4	83.8	151.9	378	337	611	1,644	4,419
28.50	44.8	6.1	17.3	11.7	0.06	0.19	0.25	0.30	0.35	0.40	0.46	0.53	0.60	0.66	0.70	0.76	0.82	0.91	1.04	1.19	1.39	1.55	1.80	2.26	4.3	9.5	14.6	19.7	85.7	155.8	389	347	632	1,707	4,613
28.25	45.2	6.2	17.7	11.9	0.06	0.18	0.25	0.30	0.34	0.39	0.45	0.52	0.60	0.65	0.70	0.75	0.82	0.91	1.04	1.19	1.40	1.55	1.80	2.25	4.3	9.7	14.9	20.1	88.2	161.0	404	360	658	1,790	4,867
28.00	45.4	6.2	17.9	12.0	0.06	0.18	0.25	0.30	0.34	0.39	0.45	0.52	0.59	0.64	0.69	0.75	0.82	0.92	1.04	1.20	1.40	1.56	1.80	2.24	4.3	9.8	15.0	20.3	89.5	163.8	413	368	673	1,837	5,013
27.75	45.7	6.3	18.1	12.2	0.05	0.17	0.24	0.30	0.34	0.39	0.45	0.51	0.57	0.63	0.69	0.75	0.82	0.92	1.05	1.21	1.41	1.56	1.79	2.23	4.4	10.0	15.2	20.6	91.0	166.8	422	376	689	1,887	5,167
27.50	46.2	6.4	19.0	12.7	0.06	0.17	0.24	0.29	0.33	0.38	0.44	0.51	0.58	0.63	0.68	0.74	0.81	0.90	1.03	1.19	1.40	1.55	1.79	2.24	4.4	10.4	15.8	21.5	97.7	180.9	464	413	764	2,126	5,917
27.25	46.9	6.6	20.3	13.5	0.06	0.18	0.24	0.28	0.32	0.37	0.43	0.51	0.59	0.64	0.68	0.72	0.78	0.87	1.00	1.16	1.38	1.54	1.79	2.26	4.5	11.0	16.8	23.1	108.2	203.2	532	472	886	2,524	7,185
27.00	47.3	6.7	20.9	13.8	0.06	0.18	0.23	0.28	0.32	0.37	0.43	0.50	0.59	0.64	0.67	0.72	0.77	0.87	1.00	1.16	1.38	1.53	1.78	2.26	4.5	11.2	17.2	23.7	112.6	212.5	561	497	939	2,695	7,741
26.75	47.6	6.8	21.2	14.0	0.06	0.17	0.23	0.27	0.32	0.37	0.43	0.50	0.58	0.63	0.67	0.71	0.77	0.87	1.00	1.16	1.38	1.54	1.78	2.25	4.5	11.4	17.5	24.1	115.0	217.7	578	511	968	2,793	8,060
26.50	47.9	6.9	21.6	14.2	0.06	0.17	0.23	0.27	0.31	0.36	0.42	0.49	0.57	0.62	0.66	0.71	0.77	0.87	1.00	1.17	1.38	1.54	1.78	2.24	4.5	11.5	17.7	24.4	117.7	223.5	596	527	1,001	2,905	8,428
26.25	48.2	6.9	22.0	14.4	0.05	0.16	0.23	0.27	0.31	0.36	0.42	0.49	0.56	0.61	0.66	0.71	0.77	0.87	1.00	1.17	1.39	1.54	1.78	2.24	4.6	11.7	18.0	24.8	120.8	230.2	617	546	1,039	3,033	8,848
26.00	48.6	7.0	22.4	14.7	0.05	0.16	0.22	0.27	0.31	0.36	0.41	0.48	0.55	0.61	0.65	0.70	0.77	0.87	1.00	1.17	1.39	1.54	1.77	2.23	4.6	11.8	18.3	25.3	124.1	237.3	640	565	1,081	3,173	9,314
25.75	48.9	7.1	22.9	15.0	0.05	0.16	0.22	0.26	0.31	0.35	0.41	0.47	0.55	0.60	0.65	0.70	0.76	0.86	0.99	1.16	1.39	1.54	1.77	2.23	4.6	12.1	18.7	25.8	128.0	245.7	667	589	1,130	3,340	9,871
25.50	49.4	7.2	23.7	15.5	0.05	0.16	0.22	0.26	0.30	0.35	0.41	0.47	0.54	0.60	0.64	0.69	0.76	0.86	0.99	1.16	1.39	1.53	1.75	2.20	4.7	12.4	19.2	26.7	134.8	260.6	714	630	1,218	3,642	10,889
25.25	49.7	7.3	24.2	15.7	0.05	0.16	0.21	0.26	0.30	0.35	0.40	0.47	0.54	0.59	0.63	0.69	0.75	0.85	0.98	1.16	1.38	1.53	1.76	2.21	4.7	12.6	19.6	27.3	138.9	269.7	744	656	1,273	3,832	11,534
25.00	**50.2**	**7.4**	**25.4**	**16.4**	**0.05**	**0.16**	**0.21**	**0.25**	**0.29**	**0.34**	**0.40**	**0.46**	**0.54**	**0.59**	**0.63**	**0.68**	**0.74**	**0.84**	**0.97**	**1.14**	**1.38**	**1.52**	**1.75**	**2.20**	**4.7**	**13.0**	**20.4**	**28.6**	**149.0**	**292.0**	**817**	**719**	**1,409**	**4,308**	**13,172**

MAJ	Gini	Lower ½%	Upper ½%	Top1	1	5	10	15	20	25	30	35	40	45	50	55	60	65	70	75	80	85	90	95	100	200	500	1,000	30,000	120,000	1,000,000	Top400	Top100	10th	1st
24.75	50.7	7.5	26.5	17.0	0.05	0.15	0.21	0.25	0.29	0.33	0.39	0.46	0.54	0.59	0.63	0.67	0.73	0.83	0.96	1.14	1.37	1.51	1.73	2.18	4.7	13.4	21.2	29.7	157.9	312	883	776	1,532	4,746	14,702
24.50	51.0	7.6	26.9	17.2	0.05	0.15	0.20	0.25	0.28	0.33	0.39	0.45	0.53	0.58	0.62	0.67	0.73	0.83	0.97	1.14	1.38	1.51	1.73	2.16	4.8	13.5	21.4	30.1	161.2	319	909	797	1,579	4,915	15,297
24.25	51.3	7.6	27.2	17.4	0.04	0.14	0.20	0.24	0.28	0.33	0.38	0.45	0.52	0.57	0.61	0.67	0.73	0.83	0.97	1.15	1.38	1.51	1.72	2.15	4.8	13.6	21.7	30.5	163.9	325	929	815	1,618	5,053	15,782
24.00	51.7	7.6	27.9	17.7	0.04	0.14	0.20	0.24	0.28	0.32	0.38	0.44	0.52	0.57	0.61	0.66	0.72	0.83	0.96	1.14	1.38	1.51	1.73	2.16	4.8	13.3	22.1	31.2	169.7	339	973	853	1,701	5,356	16,859
23.75	52.2	7.5	28.8	18.2	0.04	0.14	0.19	0.23	0.27	0.31	0.37	0.44	0.52	0.57	0.61	0.65	0.71	0.81	0.95	1.13	1.37	1.50	1.73	2.18	4.8	13.1	22.8	32.2	178.1	357	1,038	908	1,824	5,803	18,463
23.50	52.7	7.5	29.5	18.5	0.04	0.14	0.19	0.23	0.26	0.31	0.37	0.44	0.52	0.57	0.60	0.65	0.70	0.80	0.94	1.12	1.36	1.50	1.73	2.19	4.8	12.9	23.2	33.0	184.8	373	1,091	954	1,924	6,173	19,806
23.25	53.0	7.5	30.1	18.8	0.04	0.14	0.18	0.22	0.26	0.31	0.36	0.43	0.51	0.56	0.60	0.64	0.70	0.80	0.94	1.12	1.36	1.50	1.73	2.18	4.9	12.7	23.7	33.7	190.3	385	1,134	991	2,007	6,481	20,928
23.00	53.3	7.5	30.4	18.9	0.04	0.13	0.18	0.22	0.26	0.30	0.36	0.43	0.51	0.55	0.59	0.64	0.69	0.80	0.94	1.12	1.37	1.50	1.73	2.18	5.0	12.5	23.9	34.0	193.2	392	1,158	1,011	2,053	6,651	21,551
22.75	53.7	7.5	30.8	19.2	0.04	0.13	0.18	0.22	0.25	0.30	0.35	0.42	0.50	0.55	0.59	0.63	0.69	0.79	0.93	1.12	1.36	1.50	1.72	2.17	5.0	12.3	24.3	34.7	198.2	404	1,198	1,046	2,129	6,939	22,614
22.50	54.2	7.5	31.4	19.5	0.04	0.13	0.18	0.21	0.25	0.30	0.35	0.42	0.50	0.55	0.58	0.63	0.68	0.78	0.92	1.11	1.36	1.49	1.72	2.17	5.2	12.1	24.7	35.3	204.3	418	1,248	1,089	2,226	7,304	23,966
22.25	54.6	7.6	32.2	19.8	0.04	0.13	0.17	0.21	0.25	0.29	0.35	0.41	0.49	0.54	0.58	0.62	0.67	0.78	0.92	1.10	1.35	1.48	1.69	2.12	5.4	11.8	25.4	36.4	213.7	440	1,325	1,155	2,376	7,874	26,098
22.00	55.0	7.7	32.7	20.2	0.04	0.12	0.17	0.21	0.24	0.29	0.34	0.41	0.49	0.54	0.57	0.61	0.67	0.77	0.91	1.10	1.35	1.48	1.69	2.12	5.5	11.7	25.8	37.1	219.5	453	1,373	1,196	2,469	8,231	27,442
21.75	55.5	7.8	33.4	20.6	0.04	0.12	0.17	0.20	0.24	0.28	0.34	0.41	0.49	0.53	0.57	0.61	0.66	0.76	0.90	1.09	1.35	1.46	1.66	2.07	5.7	11.5	26.5	38.1	228.6	475	1,451	1,262	2,620	8,814	29,656
21.50	55.9	8.0	34.0	21.0	0.04	0.12	0.16	0.20	0.23	0.28	0.33	0.40	0.48	0.53	0.56	0.60	0.66	0.26	0.90	1.09	1.35	1.45	1.63	2.02	6.0	11.5	27.0	39.0	236.8	494	1,521	1,322	2,757	9,349	31,702
21.25	56.3	8.1	34.4	21.2	0.03	0.11	0.16	0.19	0.22	0.27	0.32	0.40	0.48	0.53	0.56	0.60	0.66	0.76	0.90	1.09	1.35	1.44	1.62	1.99	6.1	11.5	27.4	39.6	242.1	507	1,566	1,361	2,846	9,700	33,057
21.00	56.7	8.2	34.7	21.4	0.03	0.11	0.15	0.18	0.22	0.26	0.32	0.39	0.48	0.53	0.56	0.60	0.66	0.76	0.91	1.10	1.36	1.44	1.61	1.97	6.2	11.5	27.7	40.1	247.0	518	1,609	1,397	2,930	10,028	34,326
20.75	57.0	8.2	34.9	21.5	0.03	0.10	0.15	0.18	0.22	0.26	0.32	0.39	0.47	0.52	0.55	0.60	0.66	0.26	0.91	1.10	1.36	1.45	1.61	1.97	6.3	11.4	28.0	40.6	251.3	528	1,646	1,429	3,004	10,322	35,468
20.50	57.3	8.1	35.2	21.7	0.03	0.10	0.14	0.18	0.21	0.26	0.31	0.38	0.46	0.51	0.55	0.60	0.65	0.76	0.90	1.10	1.36	1.45	1.62	1.99	6.3	11.2	28.4	41.3	257.9	544	1,705	1,478	3,119	10,779	37,253
20.25	57.7	8.1	35.5	21.8	0.03	0.10	0.14	0.17	0.21	0.25	0.31	0.38	0.46	0.51	0.54	0.59	0.65	0.75	0.90	1.09	1.36	1.45	1.63	2.00	6.3	11.1	28.9	42.1	265.0	561	1,768	1,532	3,244	11,281	39,227
20.00	58.1	8.2	36.1	22.2	0.03	0.10	0.14	0.17	0.21	0.25	0.30	0.37	0.45	0.50	0.54	0.59	0.64	0.75	0.90	1.09	1.36	1.44	1.61	1.97	6.5	11.1	29.1	43.3	276.5	589	1,872	1,620	3,450	12,112	42,519
19.75	58.4	8.2	36.2	22.2	0.03	0.10	0.14	0.17	0.20	0.24	0.30	0.36	0.45	0.50	0.53	0.58	0.64	0.74	0.89	1.09	1.36	1.45	1.63	2.01	6.4	11.0	29.1	43.5	278.7	594	1,891	1,637	3,489	12,270	43,147
19.50	58.8	8.3	36.6	22.5	0.03	0.10	0.13	0.16	0.20	0.24	0.29	0.36	0.44	0.49	0.53	0.57	0.63	0.74	0.89	1.08	1.35	1.45	1.62	2.01	6.6	11.1	28.5	44.2	285.3	610	1,952	1,688	3,610	12,763	45,118
19.25	59.2	8.4	37.1	22.8	0.02	0.09	0.13	0.16	0.19	0.23	0.29	0.36	0.44	0.49	0.52	0.57	0.62	0.73	0.88	1.08	1.35	1.44	1.62	2.00	6.7	11.2	28.0	44.9	292.3	627	2,016	1,743	3,740	13,293	47,250
19.00	59.6	8.5	37.6	23.1	0.02	0.09	0.13	0.16	0.19	0.23	0.28	0.35	0.43	0.48	0.52	0.56	0.62	0.72	0.87	1.07	1.35	1.44	1.61	1.99	6.8	11.3	27.5	45.6	299.4	645	2,082	1,799	3,872	13,836	49,443
18.75	60.1	8.8	38.2	23.5	0.02	0.09	0.13	0.16	0.18	0.22	0.28	0.35	0.43	0.48	0.51	0.56	0.61	0.72	0.86	1.06	1.34	1.43	1.59	1.96	7.0	11.6	27.6	46.3	306	660	2,142	1,849	3,992	14,334	51,463
18.50	60.6	9.1	38.8	24.0	0.02	0.09	0.13	0.15	0.18	0.22	0.27	0.34	0.43	0.48	0.51	0.55	0.60	0.71	0.86	1.06	1.33	1.41	1.56	1.91	7.3	12.0	27.8	46.8	311	674	2,194	1,893	4,097	14,770	53,241
18.25	61.1	9.5	39.5	24.5	0.03	0.09	0.12	0.15	0.17	0.21	0.27	0.34	0.42	0.47	0.50	0.54	0.59	0.70	0.85	1.05	1.33	1.39	1.53	1.86	7.6	12.4	28.1	47.4	317	687	2,245	1,937	4,201	15,203	55,016
18.00	61.6	9.9	40.1	25.0	0.03	0.09	0.12	0.14	0.17	0.20	0.26	0.33	0.42	0.47	0.50	0.53	0.58	0.69	0.84	1.04	1.32	1.37	1.50	1.81	7.9	12.8	28.4	47.9	322	700	2,295	1,979	4,302	15,626	56,753
17.75	61.9	9.8	40.4	25.1	0.03	0.09	0.12	0.14	0.16	0.20	0.25	0.33	0.42	0.47	0.49	0.53	0.57	0.68	0.83	1.03	1.31	1.38	1.52	1.85	7.9	12.9	28.6	48.3	325	708	2,327	2,006	4,366	15,893	57,854
17.50	62.4	10.3	41.1	25.7	0.03	0.09	0.12	0.14	0.16	0.19	0.25	0.32	0.42	0.46	0.49	0.52	0.57	0.67	0.82	1.02	1.31	1.36	1.48	1.79	8.3	13.3	29.1	48.7	330	720	2,374	2,045	4,461	16,293	59,506
17.25	62.8	10.3	41.4	25.9	0.03	0.09	0.12	0.14	0.15	0.19	0.24	0.32	0.41	0.46	0.48	0.51	0.56	0.66	0.81	1.01	1.30	1.36	1.49	1.81	8.3	13.4	29.4	49.1	333	728	2,404	2,071	4,523	16,553	60,583
17.00	63.2	10.4	41.8	26.1	0.03	0.09	0.12	0.13	0.15	0.19	0.24	0.31	0.41	0.45	0.47	0.51	0.55	0.65	0.80	1.00	1.29	1.36	1.50	1.84	8.4	13.5	29.7	49.4	337	736	2,436	2,098	4,588	16,831	61,738
16.75	63.6	10.4	42.1	26.3	0.03	0.09	0.11	0.13	0.15	0.18	0.24	0.31	0.40	0.45	0.47	0.50	0.54	0.64	0.79	0.99	1.29	1.36	1.51	1.86	8.4	13.6	30.0	49.7	340	744	2,465	2,123	4,647	17,081	62,778
16.50	64.0	10.5	42.5	26.5	0.03	0.09	0.11	0.13	0.14	0.18	0.23	0.30	0.40	0.44	0.46	0.49	0.53	0.63	0.78	0.99	1.28	1.36	1.52	1.88	8.4	13.7	30.3	50.0	343	752	2,499	2,151	4,716	17,371	63,987
16.25	64.4	10.6	42.8	26.7	0.03	0.09	0.11	0.12	0.14	0.17	0.23	0.30	0.40	0.44	0.46	0.48	0.52	0.62	0.77	0.98	1.27	1.36	1.53	1.91	8.5	13.8	30.7	50.3	346	760	2,528	2,176	4,776	17,629	65,069
16.00	64.8	10.6	43.2	26.9	0.03	0.09	0.11	0.12	0.13	0.17	0.22	0.29	0.39	0.44	0.45	0.48	0.51	0.61	0.76	0.97	1.26	1.36	1.54	1.93	8.5	13.9	30.9	50.6	349	768	2,559	2,202	4,840	17,900	66,201
15.75	65.3	10.7	43.5	27.1	0.03	0.08	0.10	0.11	0.13	0.16	0.21	0.29	0.39	0.43	0.45	0.47	0.51	0.60	0.75	0.96	1.26	1.36	1.55	1.96	8.6	14.0	31.3	50.9	353	776	2,592	2,230	4,907	18,185	67,400
15.50	65.7	10.8	43.9	27.3	0.03	0.08	0.10	0.11	0.12	0.16	0.21	0.29	0.39	0.43	0.44	0.46	0.50	0.59	0.74	0.95	1.25	1.36	1.56	1.99	8.6	14.1	31.7	51.2	356	784	2,623	2,256	4,970	18,459	68,549
15.25	66.1	10.9	44.2	27.5	0.05	0.08	0.09	0.10	0.12	0.15	0.21	0.28	0.38	0.42	0.44	0.46	0.49	0.58	0.74	0.93	1.24	1.35	1.57	2.04	8.7	14.3	32.2	51.4	357	788	2,639	2,270	5,003	18,600	69,142
15.00	66.4	10.2	45.3	27.8	0.07	0.08	0.09	0.10	0.12	0.15	0.20	0.28	0.37	0.42	0.43	0.45	0.48	0.58	0.73	0.91	1.24	1.36	1.56	2.07	8.1	13.5	33.1	53.1	375	833	2,820	2,422	5,375	20,201	75,930
14.75	66.8	10.2	45.7	28.0	0.07	0.07	0.08	0.10	0.11	0.15	0.20	0.27	0.37	0.41	0.43	0.45	0.48	0.57	0.73	0.90	1.24	1.36	1.57	2.09	8.1	13.7	33.7	53.4	378	839	2,844	2,442	5,425	20,420	76,864
14.50	67.1	10.3	45.9	28.1	0.07	0.07	0.08	0.10	0.11	0.15	0.20	0.27	0.36	0.40	0.42	0.44	0.47	0.57	0.72	0.90	1.23	1.36	1.57	2.10	8.1	13.7	34.0	53.4	379	842	2,855	2,451	5,447	20,515	77,268
14.25	67.6	11.0	45.7	28.4	0.06	0.07	0.08	0.09	0.11	0.14	0.19	0.26	0.35	0.39	0.41	0.44	0.47	0.55	0.72	0.90	1.20	1.34	1.62	2.17	8.8	14.6	34.0	52.8	371	823	2,778	2,386	5,288	19,825	74,330
14.00	68.0	11.1	46.0	28.5	0.06	0.07	0.08	0.09	0.11	0.14	0.19	0.26	0.34	0.38	0.40	0.43	0.46	0.55	0.72	0.89	1.20	1.34	1.63	2.18	8.8	14.6	34.1	53.0	374	830	2,808	2,412	5,349	20,092	75,465
13.75	68.3	11.1	46.3	28.7	0.04	0.07	0.08	0.09	0.11	0.14	0.19	0.25	0.34	0.38	0.40	0.42	0.45	0.54	0.69	0.89	1.19	1.35	1.61	2.20	8.9	14.7	34.3	53.3	378	839	2,842	2,440	5,419	20,396	76,760
13.50	68.6	11.3	46.5	28.9	0.02	0.07	0.08	0.09	0.11	0.14	0.18	0.25	0.34	0.38	0.39	0.41	0.44	0.54	0.68	0.89	1.20	1.36	1.62	2.15	9.0	14.9	34.3	53.4	379	841	2,851	2,448	5,440	20,484	77,135

MAJ	Gini	Lower ½%	Upper ½%	Top1	1	5	10	15	20	25	30	35	40	45	50	55	60
13.25	69.0	11.0	42.1	29.0	0.04	0.07	0.08	0.09	0.11	0.13	0.18	0.24	0.33	0.37	0.38	0.41	0.44
13.00	69.3	10.6	47.8	29.2	0.06	0.06	0.07	0.09	0.10	0.13	0.18	0.24	0.31	0.35	0.38	0.40	0.44
12.75	69.6	10.7	48.0	29.4	0.05	0.06	0.07	0.08	0.10	0.13	0.17	0.23	0.31	0.35	0.37	0.40	0.43
12.50	70.0	11.3	47.7	29.5	0.05	0.06	0.07	0.08	0.10	0.13	0.17	0.23	0.30	0.34	0.36	0.39	0.43
12.25	70.3	11.7	47.7	29.7	0.03	0.06	0.07	0.08	0.10	0.13	0.17	0.22	0.29	0.33	0.35	0.39	0.42
12.00	70.6	11.7	47.9	29.8	0.01	0.05	0.07	0.08	0.10	0.13	0.16	0.22	0.29	0.33	0.35	0.38	0.42
11.75	71.0	11.8	48.1	30.0	0.01	0.05	0.07	0.08	0.10	0.12	0.16	0.21	0.28	0.32	0.34	0.37	0.41
11.50	71.3	11.9	48.4	30.1	0.01	0.05	0.07	0.08	0.10	0.12	0.16	0.21	0.27	0.31	0.33	0.37	0.41
11.25	71.6	11.9	48.6	30.2	0.01	0.05	0.06	0.08	0.10	0.12	0.15	0.20	0.26	0.30	0.32	0.36	0.41
11.00	71.9	12.0	48.8	30.4	0.01	0.04	0.06	0.08	0.10	0.12	0.15	0.20	0.26	0.29	0.32	0.35	0.40
10.75	72.3	12.0	49.1	30.6	0.01	0.04	0.06	0.07	0.09	0.12	0.15	0.19	0.25	0.28	0.31	0.35	0.40
10.50	72.6	12.1	49.4	30.7	0.01	0.04	0.06	0.07	0.09	0.11	0.14	0.19	0.24	0.28	0.31	0.34	0.40
10.25	73.0	12.1	49.6	30.9	0.01	0.04	0.05	0.07	0.09	0.11	0.14	0.18	0.23	0.27	0.30	0.34	0.39
10.00	73.3	12.2	49.9	31.0	0.01	0.03	0.05	0.07	0.09	0.11	0.14	0.18	0.23	0.26	0.29	0.33	0.39
9.75	73.6	12.3	50.2	31.2	0.01	0.03	0.05	0.07	0.08	0.11	0.13	0.17	0.22	0.25	0.29	0.33	0.38
9.50	74.0	12.3	50.4	31.4	0.01	0.03	0.05	0.06	0.08	0.10	0.13	0.16	0.21	0.25	0.28	0.32	0.38
9.25	74.3	12.4	50.7	31.5	0.01	0.03	0.05	0.06	0.08	0.10	0.12	0.16	0.21	0.24	0.27	0.32	0.37
9.00	74.7	12.5	51.0	31.8	0.00	0.03	0.04	0.06	0.08	0.10	0.12	0.15	0.20	0.23	0.27	0.31	0.37
8.75	75.0	12.5	51.3	31.9	0.00	0.03	0.04	0.06	0.08	0.10	0.12	0.15	0.19	0.22	0.26	0.30	0.36
8.50	75.3	12.6	51.6	32.1	0.00	0.02	0.04	0.06	0.08	0.09	0.12	0.14	0.18	0.21	0.25	0.30	0.36
8.25	75.7	12.7	52.0	32.3	0.00	0.02	0.04	0.06	0.07	0.09	0.11	0.14	0.17	0.21	0.24	0.29	0.35
8.00	76.0	12.8	52.3	32.5	0.00	0.02	0.04	0.05	0.07	0.09	0.11	0.13	0.16	0.20	0.23	0.28	0.35
7.75	76.4	12.8	52.6	32.7	0.00	0.02	0.04	0.05	0.07	0.09	0.11	0.13	0.16	0.19	0.22	0.28	0.34
7.50	76.7	12.8	52.9	32.9	0.00	0.02	0.04	0.05	0.07	0.09	0.10	0.12	0.15	0.18	0.22	0.27	0.34
7.25	77.0	12.9	53.2	33.0	0.00	0.02	0.03	0.05	0.07	0.09	0.10	0.12	0.14	0.17	0.21	0.26	0.33
7.00	72.4	12.9	53.5	33.2	0.00	0.02	0.03	0.05	0.07	0.08	0.10	0.11	0.14	0.16	0.20	0.25	0.33
6.75	72.8	13.0	54.1	33.5	0.00	0.01	0.03	0.05	0.07	0.08	0.09	0.11	0.13	0.16	0.19	0.25	0.32
6.50	78.1	12.9	54.8	33.9	0.00	0.01	0.03	0.04	0.07	0.08	0.09	0.10	0.12	0.15	0.19	0.24	0.31
6.25	78.5	12.9	55.7	34.3	0.00	0.01	0.03	0.04	0.06	0.08	0.09	0.10	0.11	0.14	0.18	0.23	0.31
6.00	78.9	12.9	56.7	34.8	0.00	0.01	0.02	0.04	0.06	0.08	0.08	0.09	0.11	0.13	0.17	0.23	0.30
5.75	79.3	12.9	57.9	35.4	0.00	0.01	0.02	0.04	0.06	0.07	0.08	0.09	0.10	0.13	0.16	0.22	0.29
5.50	79.8	12.8	58.8	35.8	0.00	0.01	0.02	0.04	0.06	0.07	0.08	0.09	0.10	0.12	0.16	0.21	0.28
5.25	80.2	12.8	59.6	36.2	0.00	0.01	0.02	0.03	0.06	0.07	0.07	0.08	0.09	0.11	0.15	0.20	0.27
5.00	80.6	12.8	60.4	36.6	0.00	0.01	0.02	0.03	0.05	0.06	0.07	0.08	0.09	0.11	0.14	0.19	0.26
4.75	81.1	12.8	61.2	37.0	0.00	0.01	0.02	0.03	0.05	0.06	0.07	0.07	0.08	0.10	0.13	0.18	0.26
4.50	81.5	12.7	62.2	37.5	0.00	0.01	0.02	0.03	0.05	0.06	0.06	0.07	0.07	0.09	0.13	0.18	0.25
4.25	82.0	12.6	63.9	38.2	0.00	0.01	0.01	0.03	0.05	0.06	0.06	0.06	0.07	0.09	0.12	0.17	0.24
4.00	82.5	12.4	65.6	39.0	0.00	0.00	0.01	0.03	0.04	0.05	0.06	0.06	0.06	0.08	0.11	0.16	0.23
3.75	83.0	12.3	67.3	39.8	0.00	0.00	0.01	0.02	0.04	0.05	0.05	0.06	0.06	0.08	0.11	0.15	0.22
3.50	83.4	12.1	67.6	39.8	0.00	0.00	0.01	0.02	0.04	0.05	0.05	0.05	0.05	0.07	0.10	0.14	0.21
3.25	84.0	12.2	69.6	40.9	0.00	0.00	0.01	0.02	0.04	0.05	0.05	0.05	0.05	0.06	0.09	0.13	0.19
3.00	84.4	12.2	70.2	41.2	0.00	0.00	0.01	0.02	0.04	0.04	0.04	0.04	0.05	0.06	0.08	0.12	0.18
2.75	84.9	12.2	70.8	41.5	0.00	0.00	0.01	0.02	0.03	0.04	0.04	0.04	0.04	0.05	0.08	0.11	0.17
2.50	85.4	12.1	71.4	41.8	0.00	0.00	0.01	0.02	0.03	0.04	0.04	0.04	0.04	0.05	0.07	0.10	0.16
2.25	85.9	12.1	72.1	42.1	0.00	0.00	0.01	0.01	0.03	0.03	0.03	0.03	0.03	0.04	0.06	0.09	0.15
2.00	86.4	12.1	72.8	42.4	0.00	0.00	0.00	0.01	0.02	0.03	0.03	0.03	0.03	0.04	0.05	0.08	0.13
1.75	87.0	12.0	73.5	42.8	0.00	0.00	0.00	0.01	0.02	0.02	0.02	0.02	0.03	0.03	0.05	0.07	0.12
1.60	87.3	12.0	74.0	43.0	0.00	0.00	0.00	0.01	0.02	0.02	0.02	0.02	0.02	0.03	0.04	0.07	0.11

MAJ	65	70	75	80	85	90	95	100	200	500	1,000	30,000	120,000	1,000,000	Top400	Top100	10th	1st
13.25	0.54	0.69	0.88	1.21	1.36	1.61	2.18	8.7	14.6	34.8	54.4	389	866	2,953	2,534	5,649	21,397	81,050
13.00	0.53	0.69	0.86	1.21	1.36	1.61	2.22	8.4	14.2	35.4	55.3	399	892	3,055	2,620	5,861	22,324	85,036
12.75	0.53	0.68	0.86	1.20	1.36	1.61	2.23	8.4	14.4	35.8	55.5	401	897	3,075	2,637	5,903	22,511	85,842
12.50	0.52	0.68	0.86	1.21	1.35	1.62	2.22	9.0	15.0	35.6	54.6	392	874	2,986	2,561	5,717	21,694	82,322
12.25	0.51	0.67	0.87	1.20	1.35	1.64	2.23	9.3	15.4	35.7	54.3	388	865	2,948	2,530	5,639	21,355	80,864
12.00	0.51	0.66	0.88	1.19	1.36	1.64	2.21	9.3	15.5	36.0	54.5	390	871	2,970	2,548	5,685	21,552	81,709
11.75	0.51	0.66	0.87	1.19	1.36	1.65	2.22	9.4	15.6	36.3	54.7	392	875	2,987	2,563	5,720	21,708	82,381
11.50	0.51	0.66	0.87	1.19	1.36	1.65	2.23	9.4	15.7	36.6	54.8	394	879	3,006	2,578	5,759	21,878	83,111
11.25	0.51	0.65	0.87	1.19	1.36	1.66	2.24	9.5	15.8	36.8	55.0	396	884	3,025	2,595	5,799	22,056	83,872
11.00	0.50	0.65	0.87	1.19	1.37	1.66	2.26	9.5	15.8	36.9	55.2	398	890	3,049	2,615	5,848	22,268	84,796
10.75	0.50	0.65	0.86	1.19	1.37	1.67	2.27	9.5	15.9	37.1	55.5	400	896	3,072	2,634	5,897	22,483	85,722
10.50	0.50	0.65	0.86	1.19	1.37	1.67	2.28	9.6	16.0	37.2	55.6	402	902	3,095	2,653	5,944	22,690	86,619
10.25	0.49	0.64	0.86	1.18	1.37	1.68	2.29	9.6	16.1	37.3	55.9	405	907	3,118	2,673	5,991	22,900	87,528
10.00	0.49	0.64	0.86	1.18	1.37	1.68	2.31	9.7	16.2	37.4	56.1	407	913	3,142	2,693	6,042	23,125	88,504
9.75	0.48	0.63	0.85	1.18	1.37	1.69	2.32	9.7	16.3	37.6	56.4	410	920	3,172	2,718	6,103	23,394	89,669
9.50	0.48	0.63	0.85	1.18	1.37	1.69	2.33	9.8	16.4	37.7	56.6	413	928	3,201	2,743	6,165	23,666	90,853
9.25	0.48	0.63	0.85	1.18	1.37	1.70	2.34	9.8	16.4	37.9	56.9	415	935	3,230	2,767	6,225	23,933	92,016
9.00	0.47	0.62	0.84	1.17	1.37	1.70	2.34	9.9	16.6	38.1	57.2	419	944	3,267	2,798	6,303	24,279	93,525
8.75	0.47	0.62	0.84	1.17	1.37	1.70	2.36	9.9	16.6	38.3	57.5	422	952	3,300	2,826	6,371	24,583	94,853
8.50	0.46	0.61	0.83	1.17	1.37	1.71	2.37	10.0	16.7	38.5	57.8	426	962	3,340	2,859	6,454	24,952	96,471
8.25	0.46	0.61	0.83	1.16	1.37	1.71	2.38	10.1	16.8	38.7	58.2	430	971	3,380	2,893	6,537	25,325	98,106
8.00	0.45	0.60	0.83	1.16	1.37	1.71	2.39	10.1	16.9	38.9	58.5	434	981	3,421	2,927	6,624	25,711	99,805
7.75	0.45	0.60	0.82	1.16	1.37	1.72	2.40	10.2	16.9	39.1	58.9	438	992	3,466	2,965	6,712	26,130	101,647
7.50	0.44	0.59	0.82	1.15	1.37	1.72	2.42	10.2	16.9	38.7	59.3	443	1,005	3,518	3,009	6,827	26,624	103,830
7.25	0.44	0.59	0.81	1.15	1.37	1.73	2.44	10.3	16.9	38.4	59.7	448	1,017	3,569	3,052	6,935	27,111	105,984
7.00	0.43	0.58	0.81	1.14	1.37	1.74	2.46	10.3	17.0	38.0	60.2	453	1,030	3,622	3,096	7,046	27,610	108,201
6.75	0.43	0.58	0.80	1.14	1.37	1.74	2.46	10.3	17.1	38.4	60.8	460	1,048	3,699	3,161	7,208	28,346	111,475
6.50	0.42	0.57	0.79	1.13	1.37	1.75	2.49	10.2	17.1	39.6	61.4	466	1,065	3,769	3,219	7,354	29,012	114,448
6.25	0.41	0.56	0.79	1.13	1.37	1.75	2.50	10.2	17.2	41.0	62.1	473	1,084	3,848	3,285	7,522	29,775	117,866
6.00	0.40	0.55	0.78	1.12	1.36	1.75	2.51	10.1	17.4	41.4	62.7	482	1,105	3,936	3,359	7,708	30,630	121,708
5.75	0.39	0.54	0.77	1.11	1.36	1.75	2.53	10.0	17.6	41.9	63.6	491	1,130	4,044	3,449	7,937	31,679	126,444
5.50	0.38	0.53	0.75	1.10	1.35	1.75	2.55	10.0	17.4	42.8	65.0	508	1,173	4,226	3,601	8,323	33,465	134,558
5.25	0.37	0.52	0.74	1.09	1.34	1.75	2.56	10.1	17.2	42.0	66.7	527	1,225	4,446	3,785	8,793	35,656	144,588
5.00	0.36	0.51	0.73	1.07	1.33	1.75	2.58	10.1	17.0	39.6	68.5	549	1,281	4,689	3,988	9,314	38,103	155,885
4.75	0.35	0.50	0.72	1.06	1.33	1.75	2.59	10.2	16.9	38.0	70.1	569	1,334	4,918	4,179	9,806	40,436	166,749
4.50	0.35	0.49	0.71	1.05	1.32	1.75	2.60	10.2	16.7	36.1	72.7	600	1,417	5,281	4,481	10,591	44,196	184,428
4.25	0.33	0.47	0.69	1.03	1.30	1.74	2.61	10.1	16.4	34.2	68.5	653	1,562	5,924	5,016	11,994	51,021	217,048
4.00	0.32	0.46	0.67	1.02	1.29	1.74	2.62	10.0	16.2	32.7	62.1	714	1,728	6,674	5,638	13,643	59,197	256,860
3.75	0.31	0.44	0.66	1.00	1.28	1.73	2.63	9.9	16.0	31.6	57.8	783	1,919	7,558	6,370	15,607	69,145	306,340
3.50	0.29	0.43	0.64	0.98	1.28	1.77	2.76	9.7	15.7	31.2	57.2	799	1,963	7,762	6,539	16,063	71,474	318,041
3.25	0.28	0.41	0.62	0.96	1.25	1.74	2.70	9.8	15.8	30.7	53.8	891	2,221	8,980	7,543	18,804	85,731	390,862
3.00	0.27	0.39	0.60	0.93	1.24	1.75	2.78	9.8	15.7	30.5	53.0	922	2,308	9,397	7,887	19,751	90,729	416,787
2.75	0.25	0.38	0.58	0.91	1.23	1.77	2.86	9.8	15.7	30.4	52.4	954	2,401	9,847	8,257	20,773	96,173	445,252
2.50	0.24	0.36	0.55	0.88	1.22	1.79	2.94	9.7	15.7	30.3	51.8	990	2,503	10,340	8,662	21,901	102,224	477,134
2.25	0.22	0.34	0.53	0.85	1.20	1.80	3.04	9.7	15.7	30.3	51.7	1,014	2,571	10,673	8,936	22,664	106,346	499,003
2.00	0.20	0.32	0.50	0.82	1.19	1.82	3.14	9.7	15.7	30.3	51.7	1,029	2,616	10,895	9,118	23,174	109,113	513,745
1.75	0.19	0.29	0.47	0.78	1.16	1.84	3.27	9.6	15.6	30.2	51.8	1,047	2,666	11,142	9,321	23,243	112,212	530,316
1.60	0.18	0.28	0.45	0.76	1.15	1.85	3.35	9.6	15.6	30.2	51.8	1,058	2,700	11,311	9,459	24,132	114,334	541,701

APPENDIX 2.

THE USA: the fib, its danger, its correction

The great difficulty is that if one were cherry-picking data, or just randomly taking government data that came up in web searches, there is a high probability of being misled. You can see that there is a huge difference between minimum and maximum values in the following graph-353 and in each of the rows in the upcoming Table-355.

#353

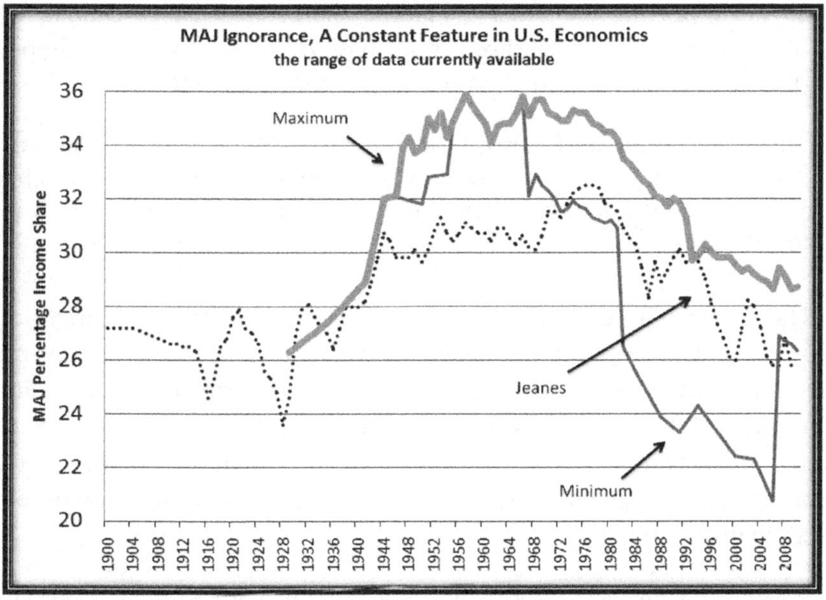

In many nations, there is a great incentive for governments (and politicians who want to preserve their electability) to understate the extent of maldistribution. Without diligent third party audits and careful data collection, we may never know precise distributions. Even in the USA with many studies making bona fide responsible analyses, we do not yet have adequate income-distribution data around which a consensus can be formed.

The Census Bureau's Current Population Survey (CPS) underreports high incomes.[269] Its highest listed survey category is vaguely stated as an income greater than $999,999. Roughly one in 659 people in 2011 were at a scarcity level sufficient to live in households with an income higher than this amount. This is precisely the group that the Census survey does not even look at. At this scarcity level, approximately 475,000 people were living in the USA at these high income levels. They slipped beneath the Census Bureau radar [475,314= 313,232,044/659]. This is the section of the population where the most dramatic maldistribution occurs. Census data misses it under the rubric of "top-coding." A top-coded dataset is one in which the upper bound is not reported, often to preserve the anonymity of people participating in the survey. The result: a huge amount of top income is missed. In truth, it cannot be claimed to be top-coding for the sake of preserving anonymity. With approximately 475,000 citizens at this level, anonymity is assured. Since anonymity is not the excuse, what is?

By not reporting the Top1% income share, the Census Bureau leaves the citizen completely without information about the most important maldistribution component. As Piketty and Saez explicitly state:

> ...the Census Bureau figures, based on data which cannot measure top 1% incomes, miss the extraordinary gains going to the top 1%, which is perhaps the most striking change in the U.S. income distribution in recent decades.[270]

The Census Bureau is not properly doing its income-distribution job. You can pick it up in the language they use and in the data they report. Take the term "income dispersion," a palatable term to express variance which has started to creep into their language, when what they are really talking about is increased concentration of income at the top and increased inequality. Call it what it is: inequality or concentration of income – not "income dispersion."

As for the Census data, look at the following Table-355.[271] You will see that the Congressional Budget Office (CBO) not only reports the Top1% (which the Census is silent on), but their data shows that in the period 1982-2006 Census failed to report a 6% average share that went to the Top5% [6.1%= 26.1-20.0%].[272] This is a large and serious omission that would significantly influence the shape of the entire distribution curve.

In 2003, the media took notice. Piketty and Saez's article "Income Inequality in the United States, 1913–1998" in the *Quarterly Journal of Economics* got traction. Census data received its shot over the bow. The public became increasingly aware that there was a huge high income problem that Census was not reporting. To take the metaphor to the next level, the aims with subsequent salvos have been lowered. Soon they should properly be low enough to blow the hull out of the water. We need good, responsibly-supported data. Not fiction.

#355 *

1982-2006 Income Shares According to Various Sources

	Min Other	Census Family	Census Household	Jeanes	Budget Office Congress	Saez, excluding capital gains	Wolff, Federal Reserve Study	Saez, including capital gains	Max Other
					Averages				
MAJ	23.5	30.8	28.3	28.5	28.6		23.5		30.8
Top5%	18.9	18.9	20.0	24.3	26.1	27.8	30.9	30.7	30.9
Top1%	13.3			12.0	13.6	13.3	16.5	16.2	16.5
					Medians				
MAJ	23.6	30.0	27.7	28.9	28.9		23.6		30.0
Top5%	20.1	20.1	21.0	23.6	25.4	27.9	30.3	29.5	30.3
Top1%	13.3			11.4	13.3	13.5	16.0	15.5	16.0

To their credit, as can be seen in Table-355, Census Household data and the Congressional Budget Office did have MAJs that were close. If you were to be a casual observer of data and saw Family or Household reports of income shares, you might initially expect them to be close. However the family unit (two or more people related by birth, marriage, or adoption), according to Census data, appears more stable at the low end, garnering a 30.8% share for the MAJ in contrast to the 28.3% for households (all people who occupy a housing unit regardless of relationship). In the previous graph-353, the maximum reported MAJ was customarily the Family (as opposed to Household) MAJ.

Family data is useful when studying family life alone. The spreadsheets (but not the charts here) show that prior to 1983, the family data had a MAJ that was an average 3.2 points higher than household data, consistent with the view that the family economic unit (by its binding of kinship) is stronger than a household unit of not necessarily related people. But that family advantage diminished to an average 2.4 points for the period after 1983.

---

* In the Table "Min Other" and "Max Other" refer to minimum and maximum for row data other than Jeanes. I emphasize in the tables and in the graphs the estimates and interpretations are mine alone and not necessarily those of the authors of the original studies. The Bureau of the Census, The Congressional Budget Office, The Federal Reserve Board, Thomas Piketty, Emmanuel Saez, and Edward N. Wolff provided source material and analysis of their own. They are not responsible for anything that appears here. Any errors here are my own. In some instances my position will conflict with the author's analysis, notwithstanding the merit of the original work.

The lowest MAJ came from Wolff's Federal Reserve work, which studied FED data since 1982. The Federal Reserve Board's (FED) Survey of Consumer Finances (SCF) tends to oversample the rich and is made available once every three years.[273] We see that Wolff's study of SCF (after my programs interpolated the data for absent years) tended to show a very low average MAJ23.5. But on the other hand, in the high range (Top5% and Top1%) his data was very close to Saez's income with capital gains. Saez's studies so far are of high income earners and do not provide MAJ data. But since Wolff and Saez are close at the top end, Wolff's study would seem to reflect a Saez-like MAJ, had Saez reported one.

I hope that this discussion reflects that data sampling favoring either the low end or the high end produces vastly different results. This is a key cause of the great differences between sources that we see in the graphs. The family-household difference is best put aside in favor of focusing on individual or household data when looking at national economics. The Jeanes data is individual (whole population) data and thus its scarcity levels will not correspond to the sampling used in Saez tax-based data.

#356

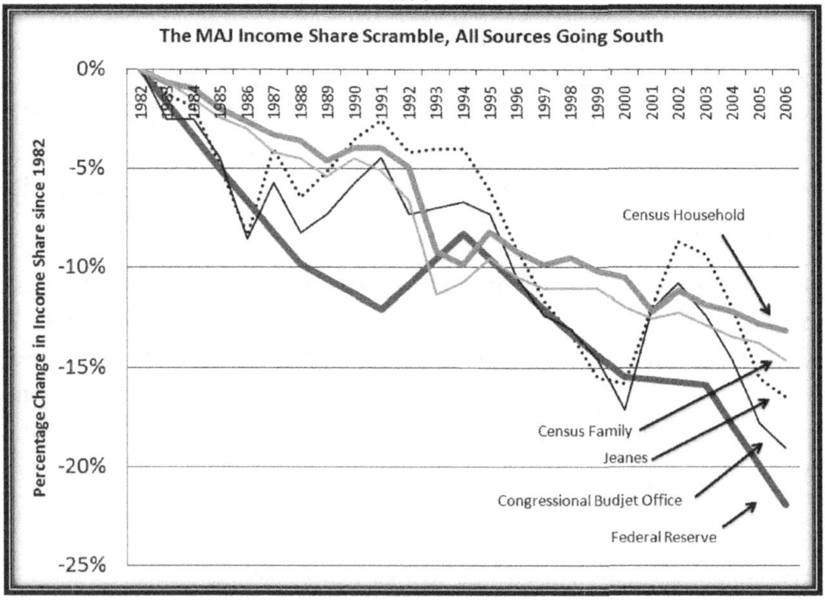

Notwithstanding the vast ranges of reported MAJs in the 1982-2006 period, there is no series that stands in opposition to the blindingly obvious reduction in MAJ share since 1982.* In the above graph-356, all sources saw MAJ income share declining, the degree of decline depending upon the source: Census Household, 13.1%; Census Family, 14.6%; Jeanes, 16.5%; Congressional Budget Office, 19.0%, and Wolff's Federal Reserve Study, 21.9%. The consensus is that there is a MAJ decline. The only debate is how great.

Congressional Budget Office. A nice balance.

My hunch is that the Congressional Budget Office (CBO) has struck a balanced position between Census Household data at the low end and Saez and Wolff's high-end data. I argue that Jeanes has set the floor. The MAJ decline is at least as great as Jeanes graph lines indicate.

#357

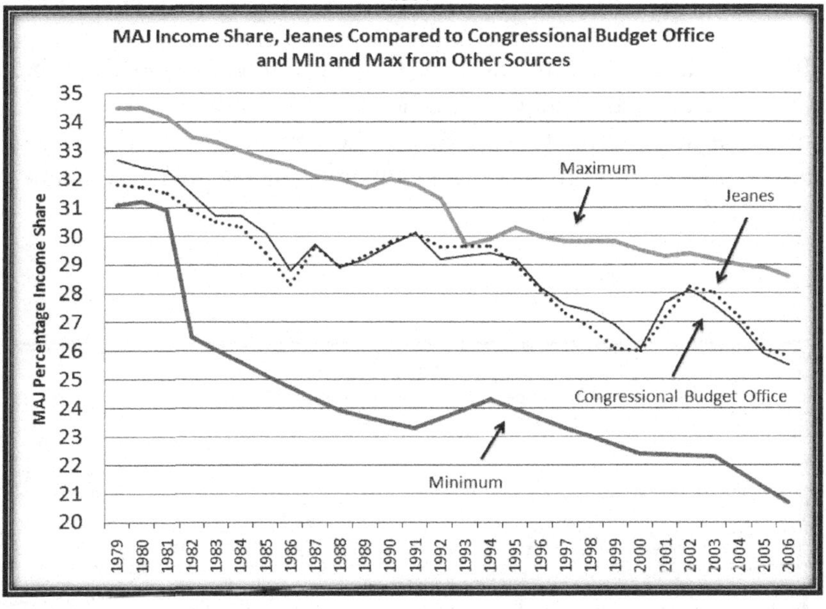

In the above graph-357, you see that my estimates of MAJ (Jeanes) are quite close to the CBO. The method I use provides a fortuitous way for estimating MAJ distributions without over sampling either high or low end data. Saez is the only source providing U.S. income-distribution data back to 1913, and there is no continuous data series from 1929 to the present other than his data. The continuous lines you see in the graphs using other data often required interpolation. At the start of my work years ago, I tried

*The starting year is 1982 because this is the first year that the Federal Reserve SCF and Wolff's data covered.

to stitch the wide variety of sources available with vastly different data to create a continuous series. The various outcomes were primitive and unreliable.

Then one day the light bulb flashed. My programs could dig into Saez data at a variety of scarcity levels to develop curves of the kind that you see in the lookup table. By this means, a continuous series of income-distribution data could be formed from 1913 to the present. [274] These curves tend to reflect the characteristics of the Congressional Budget Office MAJ data. Fortunately, the CBO provided data from 1979 to 2006. *Their MAJs ranged from 25.5-32.7, closely approximating the MAJ33 to MAJ25 transition on which the second chapter was based.* More importantly, this range was also sufficient to describe nearly all U.S. distributions since 1776, which in my estimates have ranged from 23.6-32.5.

If you find a MAJ estimate that, in your opinion, is more reliable than mine, you can readily adjust income data by methods we have already seen. Say a MAJ estimate is 32.5, but the believed true value is 33. This would require increasing estimated incomes in the MAJ by about 1.5% [1.5%= 33/32.5-1].

#358

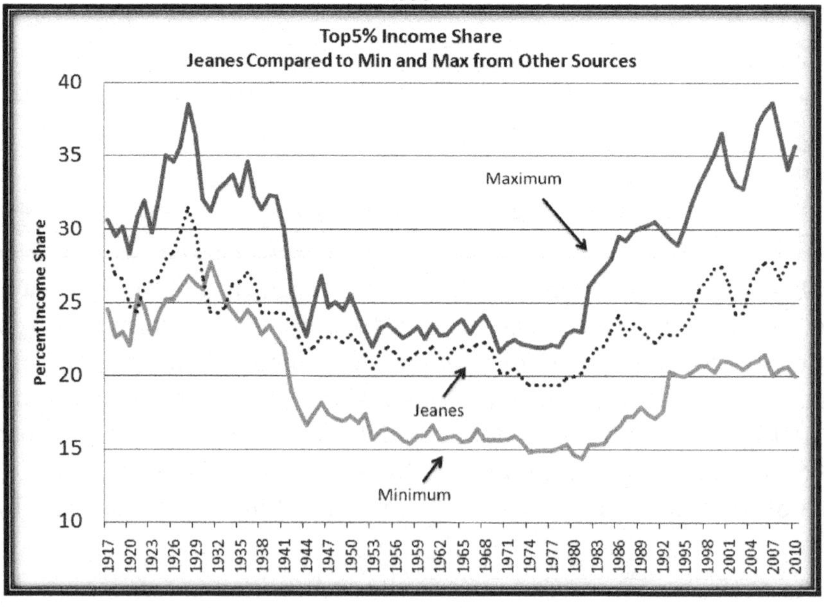

In the prior graph-358, we see that Jeanes' estimates for the Top5% income share were mainly between the minimum and maximum values from other sources back to 1917. However, unlike the close agreement between Jeanes and the Congressional Budget Office at the MAJ, Table-355 shows that at the Top5%, Jeanes' average Top5% was 24.3 while Congress showed 26.1. This 1.8% difference would result in Jeanes understating Top5% income by about 7% [1.8= 26.1-24.3; 7%= 26.1/24.3-1].

You will note that the Jeanes' MAJ estimates in the graph-353 are lower than Census data estimates, particularly from the mid 1940s to mid-1970s. But on the other hand, during the same period, Jeanes' estimates were close to maximum Top5% estimates during the same period shown in the above graph-358.

The following graph-359 of the Top1% drills deeper. Here we also see a long period where Jeanes' data is close to the maximum, but especially after the late 1980s, it is lower than all other reported data. During the 1982-2006 period, the Jeanes' Top1% was about 1.6% beneath the Congressional Budget office (Table-355). With that in mind, if you wanted to get Top1% data in the 1982-2012 period that tended to more closely conform to the Congressional Budget Office figures, you would be well advised to multiply Jeanes' Top1% incomes by 1.13 [1.6=13.6-12.0; 1.13= 13.6/12.0].

#359

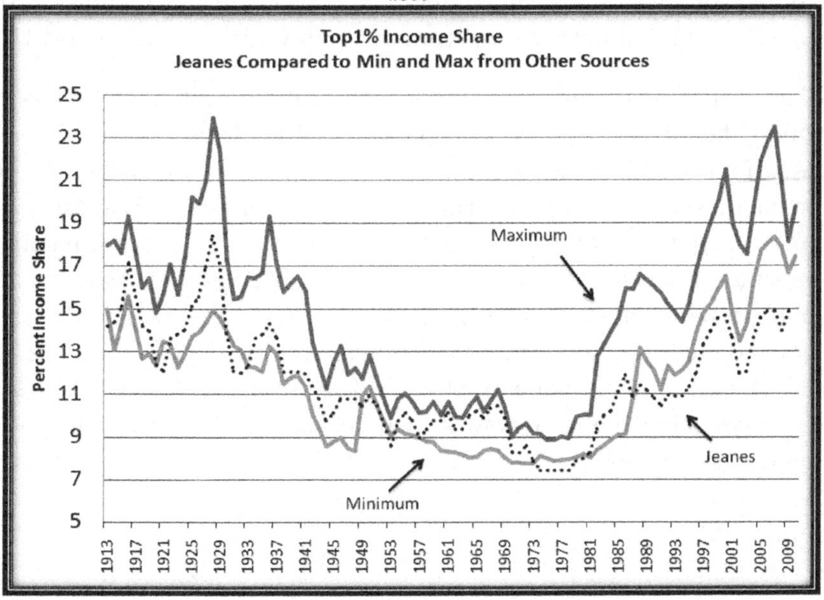

I submitted all the original data from the mentioned sources to my computer programs. They showed the following estimates for high-end incomes. The huge differences that you see in the table reflect the vast dispute that would exist if the published data were subjected to the test of rational analysis. We see that the estimates, based on Census data, would have produced a woefully low highest income (1st). It is not hard to cite a handful of CEOs who customarily earn far more than $80 million annually. And, that is before we consider the silent income that flows from vast wealth and capital appreciation. Census should have computer programs at least as good as mine. This should have been obvious to them.

#360

	Year 2006, USA	
	Top400	1st
Census Family	$6,952,228	$62,704,450
Census Household	$8,195,564	$79,516,867
Jeanes	$27,950,643	$467,228,794
Congressional Budget Office	$46,830,401	$984,357,233
Federal Reserve Based	$63,481,536	$1,527,046,409

Again, my preference is for the Congressional Budget Office data, which seems to do a credible job at the high and low end. The standard which should be met at the high end is that the threshold for the Top400 in the prior table must be accurately defined. The estimate for the highest position (1st) would of course vary from the highly variable real-world 1st.

The Jeanes' data, while it previously met the objective of satisfactorily defining the MAJ, had a low Top5% and Top1% in instances of acute maldistribution. When this portion of the backbone is understated, it greatly impacts top-end computer calculations. My programs require that the Top2% be stated with high accuracy, the Top1%, of course, having the dominant influence. Notwithstanding these observations, Jeanes and the Congressional Budget Office were nearly always within ±10% of each other prior to entering the Upper½%. You can see the degree of variation between them in the following graph-361: data from Wolff's Federal Reserve Study suggesting higher incomes than Jeanes and Congress, and Census being excessively low.

#361

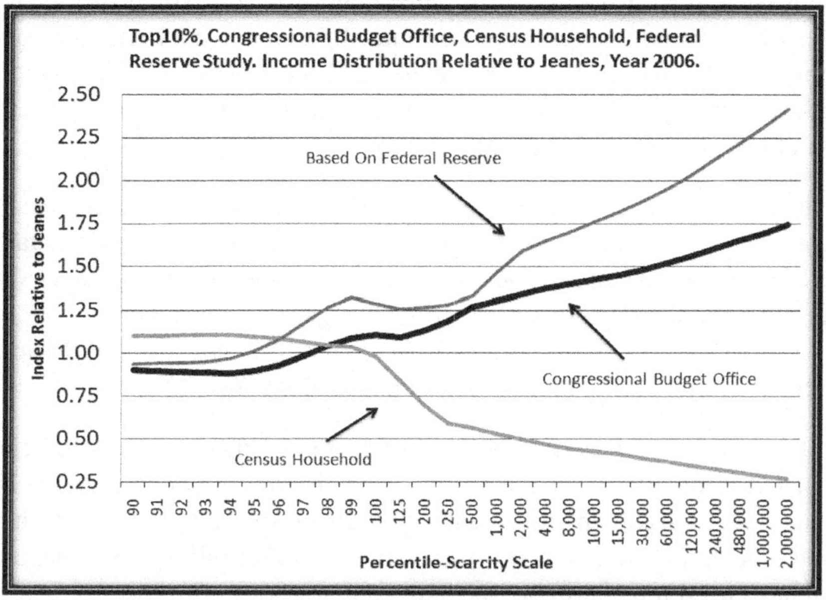

The comparison of different reports for the purpose of finding the most accurate is a risky business. Fortunately, we have an aid. The threshold wealth for the Forbes400 and Jeanes' estimated wealth for the Top400 are close. Also we know that GDP per capita adjusted for inflation grew an average 1.8% annually. And we know real inflation-adjusted bond yields because of TIPS bonds. If we look at the silent income expected from the vast fortunes in the Top400 wealth holders, we see that the estimated Top400 income/Top400 wealth would have produced the rates of return shown in the following table. The less reliable 1st position is also shown.

Average Required Inflation-Adjusted Return on Wealth Years 1982- 2006 in USA

	Top400	1st
Census Family	0.73%	0.15%
Census Household	0.88%	0.19%
Jeanes	2.57%	0.92%
Congressional Budget Office	3.28%	1.32%
Federal Reserve Based	4.81%	2.27%

As expected, Census is implausibly low. Jeanes, Congress, and Federal Reserve studies suggest rates of return higher than per capita GDP growth. Such silent income calculations combined with the list of known CEOs within the Top400 income rank may suggest to you which of the studies ultimately best define very high incomes. I do not have a definitive answer. Prior to entering the Upper½%, Jeanes and the Congressional Budget Office were nearly always within ±10% of each other. It is only after that point that substantial differences occurred.

In conclusion: If you are one of the Top1% wealthy, everything you have read so far disparaging maldistribution based on Jeanes data may have been candy-coated. The well-balanced Congressional Budget Office report seems to suggest that the Top1% is getting far higher incomes than has been shown in the previous pages. If this is so, the maldistribution problem is graver than represented within these pages.

The advantage of taking the lines of reasoning that this book has chosen is that it is operating on the safe side of the line of debate. You cannot sugar-coat an argument sufficiently to say that the rich have been unfairly treated here. To the contrary – the evidence is that within these pages, the rich have been too charitably treated.

Candy coating removed.

To be clear, the data you see here in the Appendix was not prepared by the CBO. Both Jeanes and Congressional Budget Office data were produced by my programs when given the available published public information. The difference between the two is a consequence of the initial data – not a difference in computer processing.

To the casual eye it would appear that for the bottom 99% in 2006 Jeanes and CBO were close in graph-363A. However, within the Top1% it becomes clear in graph-363B that Jeanes is significantly lower at the high end. For example, at the one-in-a-million level Jeanes shows an income 661 times larger than the average, but the CBO curve shows a much higher 1,121X$. The summary graph-364C shows the degree to which CBO and Jeanes differ throughout the range from the first percentile up through the one-in-60-million scarcity point. From the 5th to 32nd percentile and from the 51st to 97th percentile, Jeanes' estimate of income was higher than the CBO, but for all other points, especially within the Top1%, the CBO curve was usually considerably higher for the year 2006.

#363A

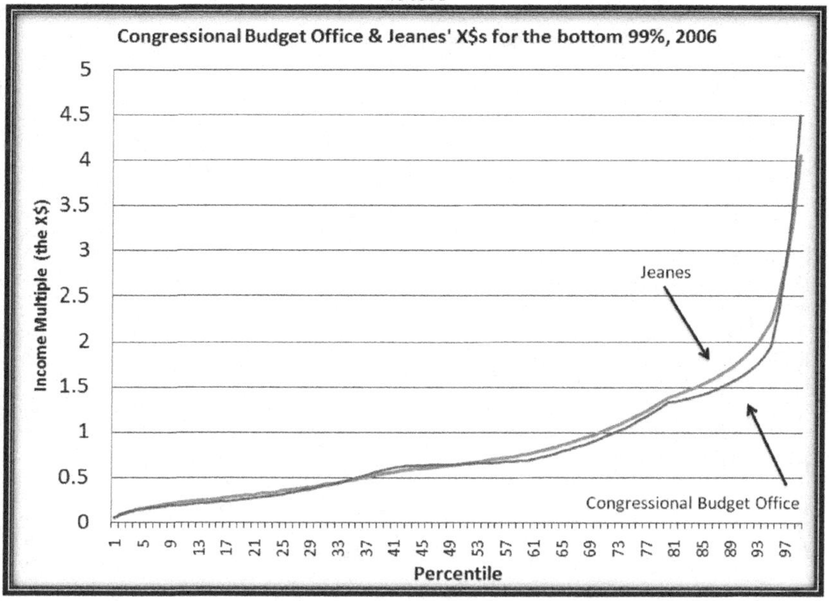
Congressional Budget Office & Jeanes' X$s for the bottom 99%, 2006
Income Multiple (the X$)
5
4.5
4
3.5
3
2.5
2
1.5
1
0.5
0
Jeanes
Congressional Budget Office
1
5
9
13
17
21
25
29
33
37
41
45
49
53
57
61
65
69
73
77
81
85
89
93
97
Percentile

#363B

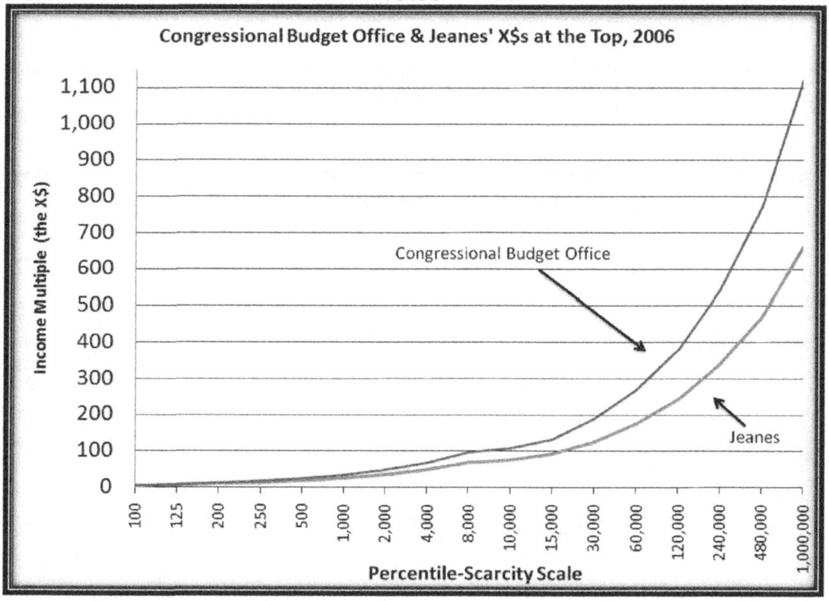
Congressional Budget Office & Jeanes' X$s at the Top, 2006
Income Multiple (the X$)
1,100
1,000
900
800
700
600
500
400
300
200
100
0
Congressional Budget Office
Jeanes
100
125
200
250
500
1,000
2,000
4,000
8,000
10,000
15,000
30,000
60,000
120,000
240,000
480,000
1,000,000
Percentile-Scarcity Scale

#364C

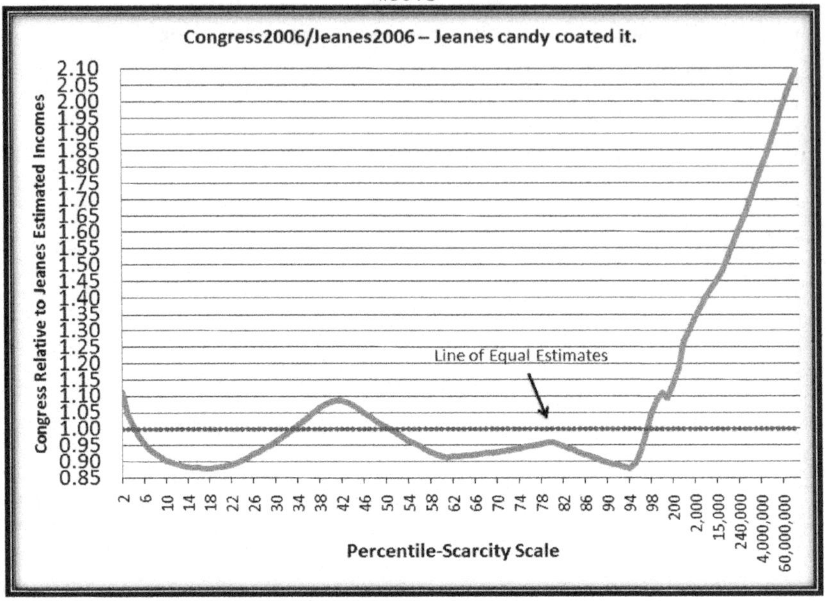

This book has been deeply concerned about the transitional impact of maldistribution. The 1979-2006 CBO data presents a more grim view than Jeanes has. While Jeanes showed a zone of indifference beneath the 92nd percentile teeter point, in graph-364A, the CBO graph line shows the teeter point at a higher point – the 96th percentile.

#364A

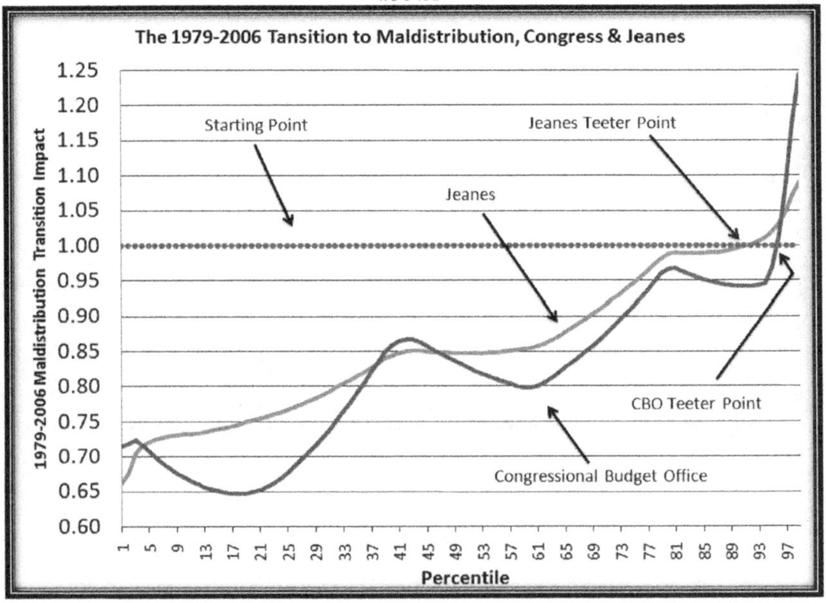

#365B

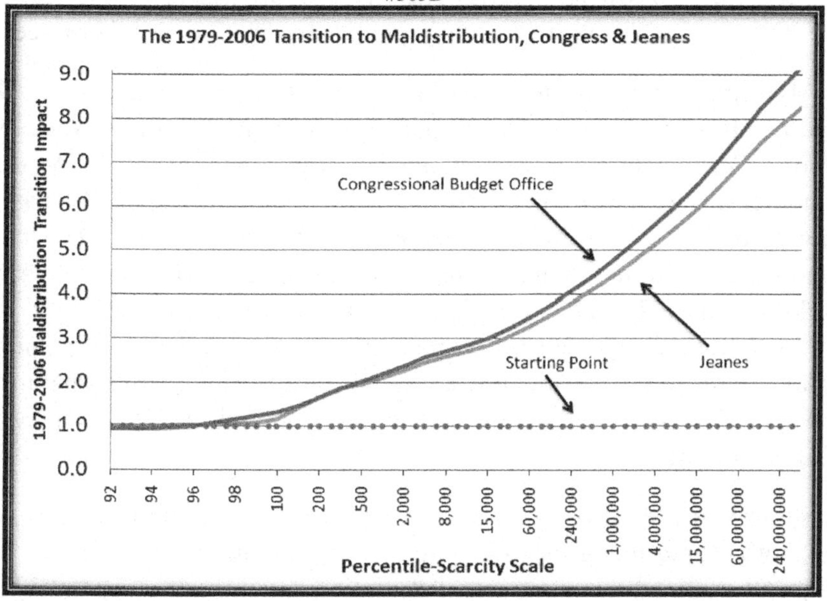

The point of flattening in the CBO graph line (comparable to the zone of indifference in Jeanes) occurs at a 5% reduction of income. To stress the point, in the CBO curve, the bottom 95% are definitive losers as a consequence of the maldistribution transition. Especially at the low end, which in better times benefited from a fair minimum wage, the maldistribution looses there were far sharper than Jeanes suggested.

At the other end of the scale: Within the Top1% in graph-365B the CBO gains at the one-in-a-million point were modestly higher than Jeanes (4.77 vs. 4.43). CBO indicates a more acute case than Jeanes, throughout the range from bottom to top. Together this suggests that reversing maldistribution is likely to be more beneficial than Jeanes suggested.

The worldwide numbers problem.

As for the Jeanes' discrepancies, they would have disappeared had the backbone been bent upward at the high end. However, the lookup table was designed to reflect income distributions worldwide, not just for the United States. The reported Top5% worldwide data available to me did not warrant further bending. The objective in the lookup table was to conform to median trend line conditions found in the worldwide historical record. The lookup table met that objective. If the curves had been further bent at the top to conform the U.S. Congressional Budget Office (CBO) data that I now have, they would have produced Ginis higher than those customarily suggested by worldwide reports. The CBO report was not available to me until October 29, 2011, after having spent years with other data sources.

My saga began with the UNU-WIDER World Income Inequality Database (WIID) which covers 159 countries, in some instances from 1960-2006.[275] When I started, I was a neophyte. I believed what I saw. A cursory computer-program examination of worldwide data revealed a few cases so implausible as to be obviously incompetently created, or to be outright fraudulent, but in the main, the data seemed ok, even after a few years of working with it. The chief objection that I have had (and continue to have) is that WIID data has not been updated since May 2008. The lethargy to update seems to reflect how low a priority nations and international institutions place on reporting income distribution and their disinterest in considering its import.

What you see before you now is a revelation that until a short while ago, I was lured like a fish, the angler being the master. I fell hard. Now I frequently suspect much income-distribution data is a lure: unpalatable and often best ignored rather than taken in a full bite. That Census so greatly misrepresented the case astounded me (and still does). Of the thousands of worldwide cases I have been studying, why should I expect other nations to be more reliable than Census has been?

Let me take yet another case in point. The most recent CIA World Factbook understated U.S. inequity. It reports a Gini of 45 for the year 2007. The Jeanes' USA Gini for 2007 is 48.9. As we have seen, the CBO provides sufficient data that my programs could construct complete curves based on its data and determine corresponding Ginis for them. In 2006, the Gini based on CBO data was 50.1. The CBO calculations I have suggest that the last time a USA Gini of 45 occurred was between 1995 and 1996 – sixteen years ago. This is for a major world power that should have ample and prompt income-distribution data available. How much more vulnerable are we to inaccurate reporting in less affluent or less able nations worldwide?

I hope you can appreciate the frustration a serious student of income distribution has. Major sources report implausible data. You start your work believing the data. Then you find it to be wrong. In such shifting sands, building a stable edifice is indeed challenging. My approach was to have my programs ride Saez stable tax-based data, but to do so in a way designed to generally reflect Congressional Budget Office MAJ reports. I believe that technique provides the best method for assessing distribution from bottom to top for a major swath of U.S. history.

There is a danger of my getting into excessive minutia. I am making the curves I developed from Census Family, Census Household, Jeanes, Congressional Budget Office, and Wolff's Federal Reserve data available in the spreadsheets so that you can consider them there.

I hope that people from a variety of disciplines will put income distribution under the microscope. There is no justification now for advancing a dogma – mine or anyone else's. Richard Feynman's principle comes to mind, "You must not fool yourself – and you are the easiest person to fool." Along the same lines, Jason Zweig nicely commented, "Remember that the smarter you are, the more easily you can fool yourself," and similarly, he points out that the more vehemently you ridicule a competing idea, the more likely you yourself are wrong.[276] If the subject comes under enough eyes, soon enough we should be able to be broadly confident that the prevailing data will be reliable.

Too little is now known. Too few methods have been tried. Being mindful of the great work done in high-end digital cameras, weather forecasting, medical technology, and in understanding and manipulating images, it seems that, in a wiki way, we can get to a better place than where we now are. With a new consensus, income-distribution analysis can become as easy and reliable as point-and-shoot photography. We all will be better off for it. Our economies will not function optimally otherwise.

Although it is quick and to the point, I can't tell you how weird it felt to use the third person ("Jeanes") in the above graphs and discussion. Try it yourself "Smith," "Jones," "Bernanke," or whatever name your parents or spouse saddled you with.

INDEX

1

2

3

4

5

9

A

B

C

D

E

F

G

H

I

N

O

P

Q

R

S

T

U

V

W

X

Y

Z

ENDNOTES

---

[1] For Colonial Economic History and distributions see: P. H. Lindert and J. G. Williamson, "America's Revolution: Economic Disaster, Development, and Equality," *VOX.* VoxEU, http://www.VoxEU.org/index.php?q=node/6751 .

[2] Spreadsheets are downloadable at Dilives: http://www.Dilives.com .

[3] This applies to the graphs. Tables may not be published without the publisher's consent. They are often in context with the text and subject to misinterpretation when that context is removed. Please note that the book is copyrighted. Making graphs available shall not be interpreted as reducing copyright protection.

[4] See USA spreadsheets at Dilives.com.

[5] Nations widely report GDP, thus it is a readily available standard that can be used as a base for X$ calculations. The calculations use GDP per capita, multiply it by the X$, and call the outcome income. More precisely, it is approximately the GDP contribution made at the point. And, in my view, that is the most important component. How much a person is able to contribute to the enterprise that we call the economy. To the extent that it is different from income received, the user can usually find a point on the curve that does match their current income and then view in the lookup table how that income changes as distributions changes. (An ancillary concern: How much those at the bottom receive on the dole is often a consequence of a dysfunctional economy that fails to integrate those at the bottom into the working economy.)

[6] A generation is the average time between a mother's first offspring and her daughter's first offspring – 30 years in Germany, 25 years in the U.S., and fewer years in most poor countries. This book will use 26 years as a standard when referring to a generation, with the understanding that different generational lengths exist. Indeed, lengths vary between the states in the U.S. and over time. The more backward states in the U.S. often show low generational years and only slight increases over time. See Wikipedia title "Generation" and its references.

[7] William Lazonick and Mary O'Sullivan, "Maximizing Shareholder Value: A New Ideology For Corporate Governance." *Economy and Society,* 29, no. 1 (2000), 29.

[8] For a lively view of maldistribution enthusiasts see Jacob S. Hacker, Paul Pierson, *Winner-Take-All Politics: How Washington Made the Rich Richer – And Turned Its Back on the Middle Class*, (New York: Simon & Schuster, 2010).

[9] "Vilfredo Pareto," Wikipedia, http://en.wikipedia.org/wiki/Vilfredo_Pareto ; "Pareto distribution," Wikipedia, http://en.wikipedia.org/wiki/Pareto_distribution .

[10] The Gini Index, as commonly used, is a theoretical number, which when divided by 100, ranges from zero to 1. It reflects the gradation between two outcomes: Zero is equivalent to everyone having equal incomes. A value of one indicates all the national income is going to a single person.

[11] Thomas Piketty and Emmanuel Saez, "Income Inequality in the United States, 1913–1998," *Quarterly Journal of Economics*, 118, no 1 (2003), 1-39; A. B. Atkinson and Francois Bourguignon, *Handbook of Income Distribution* Volume 1 (Amsterdam: Elsevier North Holland, 2007); Thomas Piketty and Emmanuel Saez, "Income and Wage Inequality in the United States 1913-2002" in A. B. Atkinson and T. Piketty, *Top Incomes over the Twentieth Century. A Contrast Between Continental European and English-Speaking Countries*, Chapter 5, (Oxford University Press, 2007); "The World Top Incomes Database," http://g-

mond.parisschoolofeconomics.eu/topincomes/ ; see additional material at Emmanuel Saez homepage: http://elsa.berkeley.edu/~saez/ .

[12] Daniel Kahneman and Angus Deaton, "High Income Improves Evaluation of Life but Not Emotional Well-being." *PNAS,* 107, no. 38 (2010).

[13] Christopher Hayes illustrated the transformation from meritocracy to oligarchy in *Twilight of the Elites.* He remarks on page 155, "[Extreme inequality] makes elites less accountable, more prone to corruption and self-dealing, more status-obsessed and less empathetic, more blinkered and removed from informational feedback crucial to effective decision-making. For this reason, extreme inequality produces elites who are less competent and more corrupt than those in a more egalitarian social order ..."

[14] *Scottsboro: An American Tragedy*, DVD, directed by Barak Goodman and Daniel Anker (PBS, 2005).

[15] *Naturalist E. O. Wilson - Lord of the Ants*, DVD, directed by David Dugan (PBS, 2008).

[16] "Gini coefficient," Wikipedia, http://en.wikipedia.org/wiki/Gini_coefficient .

[17] For a quick approximation within the MAJ33 to MAJ25 range, the following formula is often within a tenth of a MAJ value in the 400 case lookup table: Gini*-0.6687+58.506=MAJ.

[18] UNU-WIDER, WIID2C.xls Download, http://www.wider.unu.edu/research/Database/en_GB/wiid/ ; http://www.wider.unu.edu/research/Database/en_GB/wiid/_files/79789834673192984/default/WIID2C.xls .

[19] A pleasant exception is that the US Congressional Budget Office is now reporting the Top1%. It is reporting with greater accuracy than prior U.S. government reports. http://www.cbo.gov/publications/collections/tax .

[20] P. H. Lindert t and J. G. Williamson, "America's Revolution: Economic Disaster, Development, and Equality," *VOX.* VoxEU, http://www.VoxEU.org/index.php?q=node/6751 .

[21] Joseph E. Stiglitz, *The Price of Inequality,* (New York: W.W. Norton & Co., 2012), 126-127.

[22] P. H. Lindert , "Three Centuries of Inequality in Britain and America" , in *Handbook of Income Distribution*, ed. A. B. Atkinson and Francois Bourguignon, *Handbook of Income Distribution* Volume 1 (Amsterdam: Elsevier North Holland, 2007), 175.

[23] For wealth data, I rely mainly on four sources:
1) Table 1 and 2 in Working Paper No. 589 in Edward N. Wolff, "Recent Trends in Household Wealth in the United States: Rising Debt and the Middle-Class Squeeze— an Update to 2007" (March 2010). *Levy Economics Institute Working Papers Series No. 159.* SSRN.
2) Tables 1 and 3 in James B. Davies and others, "The World Distribution of Household Wealth," (November 2007). http://escholarship.org/uc/item/3jv048hx .
3) particularly Table 3 in *Handbook of Income Distribution*, ed. A. B. Atkinson and Francois Bourguignon, *Handbook of Income Distribution* Volume 1 (Amsterdam: Elsevier North Holland, 2007), 188.
4) "World Distribution of Wealth," Wikipedia, http://en.wikipedia.org/wiki/World_distribution_of_wealth .

[24] Technicians should note that great variability exists in the IncomeMAJ and WealthMAJ relationship. A somewhat tighter relationship exists at the Top1% income and wealth shares.

[25] Michael Kumhof and Romain Rancière, "Inequality, Leverage and Crises" , IMF Working Paper, WP/10/268, November 2010, www.imf.org/external/pubs/ft/wp/2010/wp10268.pdf .

[26] See Table 2 -- 3rd and "bottom" columns – in Working Paper No. 589 in Edward N. Wolff, "Recent Trends in Household Wealth in the United States: Rising Debt and the Middle-Class Squeeze — an Update to 2007" (March 2010). *Levy Economics Institute Working Papers Series No. 159.* SSRN.

[27] The seemingly irregular moves beneath the 40th percentile are, in part, a consequence of this group having so little wealth that any change has the capacity to produce unexpected results.

[28] The ratio can be derived by dividing "Net worth of households and nonprofit organizations" by GDP as given in the Federal Reserve Flow of Funds Accounts of the United States. The ratio should not be confused with the ratio of household net worth to disposable personal income reported by the US Bureau of Economic Analysis at: http://www.bea.gov/national/nipaweb/Nipa-Frb.asp .

[29] Robert J. Shiller, *Irrational Exuberance* (New York: Broadway Books, 2000 and 2005, updated). Home page: http://www.irrationalexuberance.com/
http://www.econ.yale.edu/~shiller/data/ie_data.xls (S&P500 data)
http://www.econ.yale.edu/~shiller/data/Fig2-1.xls (Housing market data)

[30] "Home Price and Income Ratio Chart," Seeking Alpha, http://seekingalpha.com/article/117085-home-price-and-income-ratio-chart .

[31] If liar's loans strike you as excessive, there were worse. Consider Christopher Hayes' report in *Twilight of the Elites*, p. 95: "As the housing bubble expanded, Countrywide maintained its competitive edge by pushing suicidally dangerous products like a mortgage that would – get this – allow borrowers to choose how much they would pay every month, adding the unpaid balance to their principal." As Hayes reports, the CEO got a $22.1 million compensation plus $121.5 million by exercising stock options; and (p.97) between 2001 and 2006 he received $470 million total compensation.

[32] Bill Moyers' Journal. *Watch & Listen*, PBS Apr 3, 2009 – William K. Black interview. Video (Liar's Loans): http://www.pbs.org/moyers/journal/04032009/watch.html ; YouTube also has numerous liar loan videos; see "Stated income loan," Wikipedia, http://en.wikipedia.org/wiki/Stated_income_loan . A leading rating agency even went so far as to have a state law prohibiting reckless and predatory mortgage failures overturned. See Stiglitz, *The Price of Inequality*, 192. Charles Ferguson, *Predator Nation: Corporate Criminals, Political Corruption, and the Hijacking of America*, (New York: Crown Business, 2012), 58-59.

[33] The graph is based on data from "World Distribution of Wealth" at http://en.wikipedia.org/wiki/World_distribution_of_wealth .

[34] Natalie Minnis, *Insight Guides: South America,* (London: Langenscheidt Publishing Group, 2003), 174.

[35] Michael Lewis, "Princeton Baccalaureate 2012 Michael Lewis," YouTube, http://www.youtube.com/watch?v=CiQ_T5C3hIM&list=UUcBYSgQTxc126-lj_gdrO8Q&index=1&feature=plcp

[36] It is difficult to appreciate how primitive the field was. There were no governmental statistics for GNP or GDP. In 1920, there were only 22 doctoral degrees in economics conferred in the US; by 1937, it was roughly 100. U.S. Census Bureau, *Historical Statistics of the United States Colonial Times to 1970*, (1975), 388.

[37] Also see page 181 in this book.

[38] Lauchlin Currie, *The Supply and Control of Money in the United States*, (Cambridge: Harvard University Press,1935), 6 (velocity of currency plus demand deposits). I will also reference Lauchlin Currie later. He was a Great Depression era economist at a time when accurate data was scarce (the government did not even have GDP figures), when economic theory was in some key areas in its infancy, and when the greatest economic catastrophe of the modern world was within a hair's breadth of tearing apart our democracy. Real decisions and action were required. Then and later in WWII, he worked in that real world (leaving us with some of the banking policy that we still have) and stayed abreast of changes in economic theory (e.g., Keynes, sometimes supporting, and at other times, taking a critical stance). Currie had a strong background in monetary policy and wrote the first major book on the supply and control of money. At Harvard he was a student of Allyn Young, an open-minded economics professor of unusual ability who published little but who was instrumental in teaching a generation of economists and who was an advisor to Benjamin Strong, governor of the Federal Reserve Bank NY, later widely commented on. In government, Currie first worked closely with, and admired, the Republican head of the Federal Reserve, Marriner Eccles. In 1939, Roosevelt asked Currie to come to the White House to be his personal economic advisor. Currie's body of work (from his early years through his work in developmental economics in Colombia) falls within the mainstream of high quality American economic thinking – hardly radical, despite FBI files and McCarthy Hearings, where he was accused by a person who had never met him. Where I might take issue (his decision on Stillwell in China and his 1937 changes on reserve requirements), I have the unfair advantage of hindsight, and even there I believe the issues would be inconsequential from a historical perspective. In Colombia South America his developmental economics were cautious mainstream and quite sensible. I believe he was out of the country when I was there. In 1967-68, I was studying at the National University of Colombia and am personally familiar the widespread interest students in the Economics department there had in Marxist economics. These students in the main were eager, well-meaning people sincerely anxious to improve conditions within their own country and dubious of capitalism's capacity to advance their lot. Concurrently, they had a conflicting respect for both Robert and Jack Kennedy. Ciudad Kennedy, a major section of Bogotá, was named after Jack Kennedy. Robert Kennedy was killed while I was there. Many students expressed their deep distress and emotions to me when he was killed. I also recall one leftist leaning student and friend whose father had been killed in La Violencia (pushed out of an airplane while still alive). He expressed a great admiration for the can-do attitude of Americans of all status, which he drew attention to in a story about an American engineer: A necessary part on a drilling operation had fallen into a crude oil drum. Colombian workers were standing around the drum, and the job had come to a halt. The American engineer in charge of the project in a white shirt inquired what had happened. When he learned, he silently took off his shirt, reached into the filthy barrel, pulled out the part, silently handed it to the workers, and left to clean up. Currie's work and writings were so far from leftist sentiments (widely in evidence in Colombia) as to be laughable to accuse him of leftist leanings. Currie, has had a wide swath of critics who have never read his works or been in conditions where he worked. Even academics well aware of his work have not had the courage to cite him, when they obviously relied on his work. I cite him. The complete body of his work stands in opposition to the de facto blacklisting to which he has been subjected – a blacklisting in stark contrast with his work for President Roosevelt, for the USA, and for

---

serious students of monetary policy and of the Great Depression. I might add that the proclivity now for people such as Congressman Allen West to state on April 11, 2012, "There are about 78 to 81 members of the Democratic Party that are members of the Communist Party" is a rebirth of nonsense and should be quickly scrutinized.

As for those who are proponents of the McCarthy hearings, blacklisting, and the like, I feel compelled to point out a section of John Lewis Gaddis, *George F. Kennan: An American Life*, (New York: Penguin Press, 2011), p. 499: George Kennan: "People who have 'what you might call genius of some sort, intellectual or artistic,' find it hard to arrange their relationships 'in a manner which is wholly conventional.' ... Such a person could be 'profoundly honest and yet ... have associates and friends who may be misguided and misled.' ... 'I would say that when gifted individuals come to a maturity of judgment which makes them valuable public servants, you are apt to find that the road by which they have [traveled] may have had zigzags in it of various sorts.'" My view: When you presume some idealized state with zigzags filtered out, you do not have the Abraham Lincolns or the majority of the greats. Instead you have boring intellectual eugenics. Life without zigzags too frequently is life by imitation alone. The real world fortunately has zigzags and is richer for it.

[39] Paul A. Samuelson, *Economics: An Introductory Analysis*, 1st ed. (New York: McGraw Hill, 1948), 411.

[40] *Balancing The Budget Federal Fiscal Policy During Depression Statement by University of Chicago Round Table*, (Chicago: University of Chicago Press, January 16, 1933), 11, 29, 8, 11.

[41] The abridgment was based on: Bruce M. Metzger and Roland E. Murphy, *The New Oxford Annotated Bible with the Apocryphal/Deuterocanonical Books,* Genesis 41, (New York: Oxford University Press, 1991), 53-4.

[42] William Trufant Foster and Waddill Catchings, *The Road To Plenty*, (Cambridge: Houghton Mifflin Press, 1928) 10, 9, 194, 201.

[43] Especially during his first campaign and first term he was a strong proponent of balanced budgets. Both his budget Director Lewis Douglas and, later his secretary of Treasury Henry Morgenthau, were forceful balanced budget advocates. The Economy Act, passed within days of FDR's being sworn in, gave him broad authority to cut the federal government employee salaries, which he did. Balanced budgets preoccupied him. He was not by disposition a deficit spending advocate. Also see following endnote 143.

[44] Fiscal Year 2013 Historical Tables, Budget of the U.S. Government, Office of Management and Budget, 24-25, http://www.whitehouse.gov/sites/default/files/omb/budget/fy2013/assets/hist.pdf .

[45] The mechanics are: At the starting step, the consumption rate is multiplied by 1 and placed in the right column. Subsequently, each right column is multiplied by the left column lower position and that number is placed in the right column. At the end, the right column is summed to get the multiplier for these steps, as shown in the spreadsheet.

[46] John Maynard Keynes, *The General Theory of Employment, Interest, and Money*, (London: Macmillian, 1936), Chapter 10. The marginal propensity to consume and the multiplier, part VI. Please note that in this book I exclusively and purposely use only *average* propensity to save and consume, not *marginal*.

[47] Robert Heilbroner, *The Worldly Philosophers*, (New York: Time Incorporated, 1961), 67.

[48] U.S. Department of Commerce: Bureau of Economic Analysis, *Personal Saving Rate*, Series ID: PSAVERT. By using this series of savings rates, we are basing the analysis on characteristics of the U.S. economy.

[49] Unlike distribution curves which are always ascending, consumption and savings curves can vary in shape according to increased debt repayment or debt assumption at portions of the curve. In this instance, the alteration in shape takes place at relatively low incomes where the amount of savings is low; thus the influence is small.

[50] These are the assumptions: Consumption as fraction of GDP: 65%; Real interest rate to finance debt: 2.2%; real GDP growth rate 3.2%; Keynes Multiplier: 2.5. This optimistically assumes that the multiplier works. If not, outcome can be markedly more costly. Assumptions can be easily modified in a spreadsheet.

[51] David R. Henderson, *The Concise Encyclopedia of Economics*, (Liberty Fund, Inc, 2008), Saving, p. 456, Investment, p. 304.

[52] Table 1.1.5 in U.S. Bureau of Economic Analysis, *Gross Domestic Product*, (May 2011).

[53] Arthur M. Okun, *Equality and Efficiency The Big Tradeoff*, (Washington: The Brookings Institution, 1975), 91: "... the money must be carried from the rich to the poor in a leaky bucket. Some will simply disappear in transit, so the poor will not receive all the money that is taken from the rich."

[54] Maldistribution apologists may seek to employ a technical argument that when the lower 80% receive a greater share of income, then they too, will save more and the consumption curve will change. There is a twofold response: 1) Is it undesirable that the 80% who were struggling to make ends meet might have a little extra savings – an economic cushion, some economic tranquility in their lives? 2) If the model is altered to employ the proposed different consumption curve over all the different MAJ distributions, you will still see the declining efficiency of savings with increasing maldistribution. The numbers may be slightly different; the direction is not.

[55] http://lh4.ggpht.com/_cwHfePkadc4/TJth3RjDSSI/AAAAAAAAA5A/9DiYUdF-0nl/s1600-h/image%5B14%5D.png ;
http://www.vectorgrader.com/indicators/market-cap-gdp ;
http://www.ritholtz.com/blog/wp-content/uploads/2011 .

[56] Book I, Ch. 8 in Adam Smith, *Wealth of Nations,* (New York: P.F. Collier & Son, 1776).

[57] Stewart Lansley, *The Cost of Inequality: Why Economic Equality is Essential for Recovery*, (Gibson Square, January 19, 2012). Chapter 4, Figure 4.1, p. 92, Kindle locations 1470-95.

[58] Lansley, Chapter 5, Fig. 5.1, p. 106, Kindle location 1742-48.

[59] Lansley, Chapter 5, p. 107, Kindle location 1751-60.

[60] Stiglitz, *The Price of Inequality,* 243. Similarly, James Galbraith points out in *Inequality and Instability*, (Oxford University Press, 2012), 4: "In the classification system of the *Journal of Economic Literature* there was (and is) no category for work relating inequality to the financial system. In other words, both inequality and financial instability were largely blank spots in dominant theory; neither concept was important to mainstream economics, and the relationship between them was not even thought of." And on page 5: "[The] study of inequality was divorced, entirely from the study of economic dynamics, and it therefore posed no challenge to the dominant doctrines."

[61] Internet searches: "FORTUNE 500 2007 Top Companies - Biggest Companies By Employees"; "Global 500 2008 Top Performers – Biggest Companies Employees"; "World's

---

Largest Companies – World's Largest Companies by Employees"; "Blue Chip Largest Company List."

[62] Derived from: Tom Hertz, "Rags, Riches, and Race, The Intergenerational Economic Mobility of Black and White Families in the United States," in *Unequal Chances, Family Background and Economic Success* , ed. Samuel Bowles, Herbert Gintis, and Melissa Osborne Groves, (New Jersey: Princeton University Press, 2005), 186. Table 5.10 Decile Transition Matrix for the Pooled Income Distribution.

[63] Hertz, 186.

[64] See endnote #29.

[65] "Uncle Tom's Cabin," Wikipedia, http://en.wikipedia.org/wiki/Uncle_Tom%27s_Cabin . Simon Legree is the cruel slave owner character in *Uncle Tom's Cabin*.

[66] U.S. Department of Labor data normalized to 1977.

[67] "Elo rating system," Wikipedia, http://en.wikipedia.org/wiki/Elo_rating_system ; USCF Ratings Distribution Charts, http://archive.uschess.org/ratings/ratedist.php .

[68] Wikipedia's "Intelligence quotient" page is also a good reference.

[69] Christopher Hayes, "Why Elites Fail," *The Nation*, June 25, 2012, http://www.thenation.com/article/168265/why-elites ; Christopher Hayes, *Twilight of the Elites: America After Meritocracy*, (Crown, 2012).

[70] Nicholas Lemann, *The Big Test: The Secret History of the American Meritocracy*, (New York: Farrar, Straus and Giroux, 2000), 118.

[71] Michael Young, *The Rise of the Meritocracy*, (Transaction Publishers, 1999). 95.

[72] Young, 84.

[73] Judith Selvidge, "A Three-step Procedure for Assigning Probabilities to Rare Events," in *Utility, Probability, and Human Decision Making Vol. 11*, ed. Dirk Wendt and Charles Vlek, (Dordrecht: D. Reidel Publishing Company, 1975), 205.

[74] Albert Einstein, *Ideas and Opinions*, (New York: Crown Publishers, 1963), 4.

[75] Malcolm Gladwell, *Outliers*, (New York: Little, Brown and Co., 2008), 79.

[76] Jay L. Zagorsky, "Do You Have to Be Smart to Be Rich? The Impact of IQ on Wealth, Income and Financial Distress." *Intelligence* 35, no. 5 (2007), 489-501. Table 2, p. 495, with IQ 105 values removed, because of inconsistencies. Curves developed using interpolated IQ-income and IQ- wealth values mapped to known IQ percentile relationships. See Zagorsky's Fig. 1 and 2 scatter plots for income and net worth.

[77] A distribution close to the known points was located in the lookup table, MAJ49. For those points not available to me beneath the 6th percentile I employed points that were in the same fractional relationship with MAJ49 as was the last available data point. Then the adjustment at the top discussed in the previous paragraph was used.

[78] In a different context, Richard Lynn and Tatu Vanhanen, *IQ and Global Inequality*, (Augusta, Ga.: Washington Summit Publishers, 2006), 195-198, observe: "National IQ seems to explain quite well the relatively low level of income inequality in nearly all economically developed market economies and democracies."

[79] At the indicated page numbers in approximate sequence, all Kaiser references can be found in: Albert Heiner, *Henry J. Kaiser Western Colossus*, (San Francisco: Halo Books, 1991), 86, 128, 118, 152, 1, 135, 43, 203, 204, 77, 78, 82, 96.

[80] Please see above note for page numbers that apply to the foregoing quotations.

[81] Starting with "honor begets honor" are the words of Henry L. Stimson, *On Active Service in Peace and War*, (New York: Harper, 1948), 671-672. (paraphrased in some instances).

[82] Jared Diamond, *Collapse: How Societies Choose to Fail or Succeed*, (New York: Viking Penguin, 2005), 167-70.

[83] Long Island News, Homeless Science Whiz Gets a Home, ABC 7. Intel semifinalist; and Newsday, "Intel Semifinalist: Samantha Garvey of Brentwood High School," YouTube, http://www.youtube.com/watch?v=-UjX6OKWF2c .

[84] U.S. Bureau of Labor Statistics, Characteristics of Minimum Wage Workers: 2010; also Wage and Hour Division, History of Federal Minimum Wage Rates Under the Fair Labor Standards Act, 1938-2009.

[85] We have long known that de-unionization contributed to inequality, e.g., Sheldon Danziger and Peter Gottschalk, *Uneven Tides Rising Inequality in America*, (New York: Russell Sage Foundation, 1993),134

[86] "Poverty threshold," Wikipedia, http://en.wikipedia.org/wiki/Poverty_threshold . 15.1% of the population in 2010. 0.264 is the corresponding X$ in the accompanying USA spreadsheet.

[87] An aside: A pure transfer of 1.26% of the GDP to the damaged citizens at the low end at zero transaction costs would have erred on the side of excessive optimism. And an overestimate of the initial transfer (based on 0.3 of the average income, rather than the 0.264 poverty threshold) is offset by an underestimate of ancillary costs at the 0.3 threshold.

[88] Richard Wilkinson and Kate Pickett, *The Spirit Level: Why Equality is Better for Everyone*, (Penguin Books, 2010).

[89] Stiglitz, *The Price of Inequality*, 164.

[90] Robert D. Hare, *Without Conscience: The Disturbing World of the Psychopaths Among Us*, (New York: The Guilford Press, 1999). Jon Ronson, *The Psychopath Test: A Journey Through the Madness Industry,* (New York: Riverhead Books, 2011). Martha Stout, *The Sociopath Next Door,* (New York: Broadway Books, 2006). On page 6 and related endnote, she indicates that 4% of the USA population are sociopaths. More positively on page 136 and endnote, she shows a 0.03% to 0.14% rate for Taiwan; and relatively rare occurrences for certain East Asian nations, such as Japan and China. Paul J. Zak, *Moral Markets: The Critical Role of Values in the Economy*, (Princeton: Princeton University Press, 2008), 268. Oxytocin released in the brain influences moral behavior. Zak suggests that about 2% of subjects did not have a normal response and that this was roughly the proportion of sociopaths in the population.

[91] A deeper analysis of honesty can be found in Dan Ariely, "Why We Lie," *Wall Street Journal*, (May 26-27, 2012), C1.

[92] David Schwab and Elinor Ostrom, "The Vital Role of Norms and Rules in Maintaining Open Public and Private Economies"; Oliver Goodenough, "Values, Mechanism Design, and Fairness" in Paul Zak, *Moral Markets*, 204,247, 270. Schwab: Observe that in the former Soviet Union many policy analysts expected that rapid development would occur with privatization and free market institutions. This did not happen. The influence norms were underestimated. Goodenough : High policing costs depress overall productivity.

[93] At 41 minutes 30 seconds into "The Corporation," DVD, directed by Mark Achbar and Jennifer Abbot (2003); Milton Friedman. http://hellocoolworld.com/files/TheCorporation/Friedman.pdf . Also see Stewart Lansley,

---

The Cost of Inequality: Why Economic Equality is Essential for Recovery, p.32, Kindle location 522-31: Friedman, "Few trends could so thoroughly undermine the very foundations of our free society as the acceptance by corporate officials of a social responsibility other than to make as much money for their stockholders as possible."

[94] Paul Zak, *Moral Markets.* See Lynn A. Stout, "Taking Conscience Seriously" p157-172.

[95] The Shiller database of inflation-adjusted values, used here, lets you see S&P500's full unvarnished history. It uses "as reported earnings," which factor in write-offs and restructuring charges not included in less inclusive "operating earnings," often reported elsewhere. On average from 1988-2011, operating earnings have been 17% larger than "as reported earnings."

[96] In the real world case, this did not happen because earnings dropped from May, 1988 to July, 1991. So even though the crucially important earnings had indeed dropped in the interval, the stock sold at a higher price.

[97] Lazonick and O'Sullivan, "Maximizing Shareholder Value: A New Ideology For Corporate Governance." *Economy and Society* 29, no. 1 (2000), 13-35.

[98] This remark was made on a web page many years ago, which no longer seems to be available. David Teitelbaum, http://www.moneybalance.com/search/display.asp?ID=35 . It is very tough to grow earnings more rapidly than the economy.

[99] Gretchen Morgenson, "Market Watch; Earnings Are Worse Without The Icing" *New York Times* July 13, 2003, http://www.nytimes.com/2003/07/13/business/market-watch-earnings-are-worse-without-the-icing.html .

[100] William J. Bernstein and Robert D. Arnott, "Earnings Growth: The Two Percent Dilution," *Financial Analysts Journal* 59, no. 5, 47-55.

[101] Benjamin Graham, *The Intelligent Investor*, (New York: Harper and Row, 1973), 165, 167.

[102] Benjamin Graham and David L. Dodd, *Security Analysis*, (New York: McGraw-Hill, 1934), 352, 453. Other pages of note: 372, 395, 433, 451, 378.

[103] The method sorts all the data shown according to each of the two key components (PE ratio and earnings departure from GDP). After each sort, two separate columns, from one to the ending number, rank each of these components. Then in a third column, it sums the prior two malefactor rankings to create total badness number. It then sorts all columns based on this number. After having done this, each badness number is divided by the highest badness number to give the badness index number.

[104] Alan A. Kennedy, *The End of Shareholder Value: Corporations at the Crossroads*, (Cambridge: Perseus Publishing, 2000), 54.

[105] Galbraith, *Inequality and Instability: A Study of the World Economy Just Before the Great Crisis*, 127.

[106] Alexis De Tocqueville, *Democracy in America*, translated by Arthur Goldhammer, Volume 2, Chapter 19, (The Library of America, 2004), 646-647.

[107] De Tocqueville, 652.

[108] Kirstin Downey, *The Woman Behind the New Deal: The Life of Francis Perkins, FDR's Secretary of Labor and His Moral Conscience,* (New York: Doubleday, 2009); Adam Cohen, *Nothing To Fear: FDR's Inner Circle and the Hundred Days That Created Modern America*, (New York:Penguin Press, 2009), 157-194.

[109] "Employment Gain Reaffirmed By Davis," *New York Times*, (Jan. 25, 1930), 3.

[110] "Assails Hoover Forecast. Mary Van Kleeck Criticizes Federal Statements on Unemployment," *New York Times*, (Mar 1, 1930), 11.

---

[111] Ben S. Bernanke, *Monetary Aggregates and Monetary Policy at the Federal Reserve: A Historical Perspective,* at the Fourth ECB Central Banking Conference, Frankfurt, Germany, November 10, 2006.

[112] See endnote 152.

[113] Lauchlin Currie, *The Supply and Control of Money in the United States,* (Cambridge: Harvard University Press, 1934 & 1935), 6, 33.

[114] See Roger J Sandilands, *The Life and Political Economy of Lauchlin Currie: New Dealer, Presidential Adviser, and Development Economist,* (Durham and London: Duke University Press, 1990). Frank G. Steindl, *Monetary Interpretations of the Great Depression,* (Ann Arbor: The University of Michigan Press, 1995). See Ch. 4 "The Monetary Economics of Lauchlin Currie," 61-78.

[115] One of the difficulties with a gold standard is that gold is discovered at a capricious rate – often a rate less than the growth rate that an economy is capable of. When gold availability growth rate was low, it tended to produce deflation and attendant economic downturns. During the Great Depression, nations quickest to go off the gold standard were the quickest to gain.

[116] Board of Governors of the Federal Reserve System (U.S.), *Banking and Monetary Statistics 1914-1941*, Section 1 General Statistics of All Banks In The United States, Table 9. Deposits and currency—adjusted deposits of all banks and currency outside banks, 1892-1941, first printing November 1943, from FRASER, http://fraser.stlouisfed.org/publication/?pid=38. Money Supply data in charts are based on this data.

[117] The four generations that have had the fastest GDP per capita growth in all of USA history were 1933-1959, 1934-1960, 1935-1961, and 1936-1962. Yet In the midst of this success Ayn Rand breaths fire. CBS's Mike Wallace's 1959 interview with Ayn Rand summarizes her philosophy. "Ayn Rand First Interview 1959 (Full)," http://www.youtube.com/watch?v=1ooKsv_SX4Y . You might want to consider whether you would want her or her philosophy to run your nation, or how much you might have relished your childhood had she been your mother. This comment may seem excessively personal, but so too is her individualism to the exclusion of the many human traits that I admire and find essential for human survival. Her view strikes me as intellectually impoverished and empirically bankrupt.

[118] Lauchlin Currie's memoirs, Chapter III: The New Deal, *Journal of Economic Studies,* 31 no. ¾ (2004), 207.

[119] Currie, 208.

[120] Currie, 209.

[121] Perry G. Mehrling and Roger J. Sandilands, *Money and Growth: Selected papers of Allyn Abbot Young,* (New York: Routledge, 1999), 81.

[122] "Settlement movement," Wikipedia, http://en.wikipedia.org/wiki/Settlement_house .

[123] From 1908 onward, Lewis Hine's photographs, as in Russell Freedman's book *Kids at Work,* and Google image web searches, provide an unforgettable view of child labor and how extensive it was.

[124] Downey, *The Woman Behind the New Deal: The Life of Francis Perkins*, 118.

[125] Sara Robinson, "Bring back the 40-hour workweek: 150 years of research proves that long hours at work kill profits, productivity and employees," Salon.com, Mar 14, 2012.

[126] N. Gregory Mankiw and William Scarth, *Macroeconomics Second Canadian Edition*, (New York: Worth Publishers, 2004), 316.

[127] J. S. Lawrence and R. Jewett, *The Myth of the American Superhero*, (Grand Rapids: William B. Eerdmans Publishing Company, 2002), 133.

[128] Lawrence and Jewett, 132.

[129] Jonathan Alter, *The Defining Moment: FDR's Hundred Days and the Triumph of Hope*. (New York: Simon & Schuster, 2006), 184-7.

[130] G. D. Black, *Hollywood Censored, Morality Codes, Catholics, and the Movies*, (Cambridge: Cambridge University Press, 1994), 137-144.

[131] Charles E. Bohlen, *Witness to History 1929-1969*, (New York: W. W. Norton & Company, 1973), 24.

[132] Nick Taylor, *American-Made The Enduring Legacy of the WPA: When FDR Put the Nation to Work*, (New York: Bantam Books, 2008), 41.

[133] Bob Blaisdell, *The Communist Manifesto and Other Revolutionary Writings: Marx, Marat, Paine, Mao, Gandhi, and Others*, (Mineola, New York: Dover Publications, 2003), 150.

[134] Web page: "Works of Franklin D. Roosevelt, The Forgotten Man," Radio Address, Albany, N. Y. April 7, 1932.

[135] Taylor, 153; Kim Phillips-Fein, *Invisible Hands: The Businessmen's Crusade Against the New Deal*, (New York: W. W. Norton, 2009), 10, 39.

[136] "William Graham Sumner," Wikipedia, http://en.wikipedia.org/wiki/William_Graham_Sumner . And should you want a dose of humor on the topic from America's most loquacious and amusing economist, I suggest John Kenneth Galbraith's *The Affluent Society*, which has appeared under various imprints since its 1958 first edition (the older, the better), Chapter V, section IV.

[137] A. G. Keller, *The Forgotten Man's Almanac: Rations of Common Sense from William Graham Sumner*, (New Haven: Yale University Press, 1943).

[138] Robert S. McElvaine, *The Great Depression: America, 1929-1941*, (Times Books: 1993), 38.

[139] Allyn A. Young, "Do the Statistics of the Concentration of Wealth in the United States Mean What They Are Commonly Assumed to Mean?" *American Statistical Association*, No. 117. March, 1917, 471-484.

[140] See graph-300.

[141] Based on the work of African-American author and songwriter James Weldon Johnson (1871-1938), "Dem Bones," Wikipedia, http://en.wikipedia.org/wiki/Dem_bones .

[142]Abridged and rearranged from: Jim Tankersley, "The Inequality Speech That TED Won't Show You," May 16, 2012, http://roundtable.nationaljournal.com/2012/05/the-inequality-speech-that-ted-wont-show-you.php

Nick Hanauer's TED Talk: http://www.youtube.com/watch?v=bBx2Y5Hhpll

And other of his writings: Eric Liu, Nick Hanauer, *The Gardens of Democracy: A New American Story of Citizenship, the Economy, and the Role of Government*, (Sasquatch Books, 2011).

[143] Lauchlin Currie's memoirs, Chapter III: The New Deal, *Journal of Economic Studies*, 31 no. ¾ (2004), 229. Also see above endnote 43.

[144] Years to Double= LOG(2)/LOG(1+annualized income growth rate). The section of the graph where the graph line goes off the chart is attributable to very low or negative growth rates which substantially prevent incomes from doubling.

[145] Lauchlin Currie's memoirs, Chapter III: The New Deal, *Journal of Economic Studies,* 31 no. ¾ (2004), 227-8.

[146] Interestingly with deeper analysis, this phrase was also used in a recent *Wall Street Journal* article: Dan Ariely, "Why We Lie,"(May 26-27, 2012), C1.

[147] Based on Angus Maddison's fine dataset but using methods and other data which may not reflect his intentions. Any errors are mine. Not his. Angus Maddison, "Historical Statistics of the World Economy: 1-2008 AD," http://www.ggdc.net/maddison/Historical_Statistics/horizontal-file_02-2010

[148] Mike Wallace at 18 minutes 13 seconds. See endnote #117.

[149] This can be seen on an oscilloscope. A wave form generator (a function generator) can produce waves of various shapes. Select a wave form. When a resistor and capacitor of appropriate size and configuration are applied, the wave form can be smoothed or flattened.

[150] Farad is a unit of capacitance. "Capacitance," Wikipedia, http://en.wikipedia.org/wiki/Capacitance .

[151] Nick Taylor, *American-Made The Enduring Legacy of the WPA: When FDR Put the Nation to Work,* (New York: Bantam Books, 2008).

[152] Based on Michael Darby, "Three and a Half Million U.S. Employees Have been Mislaid: Or, An Explanation of Unemployment, 1934-1941," *Journal of Political Economy*, vol. 84, no 11, (February 1975), 1-16.

[153] Darby, 1-16.

[154] "Okun's Law," Wikipedia, http://en.wikipedia.org/wiki/Okun%27s_law .

[155] *Life Magazine*, "Fortune Poll Shows That America is For Roosevelt In Spite of the New Deal," June 27,1938, 9-17

[156] Jonathan Cutler, *Labor's Time: Shorter Hours, The UAW, and the Struggle for American Unionism*, (Philadelphia: Temple University Press, 2004), 32. Also note that Cutler's book also illustrates the influence of the Communist Party in a program called "Thirty Hours' Work for Forty Hours' Pay." This is far different from the 30-hour Kellogg program, other shorter hour programs that corporations have used, or the adjustable hour program discussed in this book.

[157] "University of Michigan Consumer Sentiment Index," Wikipedia, http://en.wikipedia.org/wiki/University_of_Michigan_Consumer_Sentiment_Index .

[158] This was not altogether welcomed as implied by Ernest Haveman's article in the same year "The Emptiness of Too Much Leisure," *Life Magazine*, (Feb. 14, 1964), 76.

[159] Benjamin Hunnicutt, *Kellogg's Six-Hour Day*, (Philadelphia: Temple University Press, 1994), 13.

[160] Hunnicutt, 28.

[161] Hunnicutt, 35.

[162] Hunnicutt, 36.

[163] Hunnicutt, 63-64. Union opposition, some Kellogg management, and WWII ultimately unraveled the program, ending it in 1985. pp. 2, 91-93.

[164] Benjamin Hunnicutt, "The End of Shorter Hours," *Labor History*, XXV (Summer, 1984),373-404, http://www.uiowa.edu/~lsa/bkh/lla/eosh.htm .

[165] Note that the national maximum increase in employment will always be less than the amount indicated. The average workweek is already in the neighborhood of 33.5 hours, and about half of jobs are subject to hourly pay. The greatest effect applies primarily at the first step away from the 40-hour standard workweek.

---

[166] Taylor, 215.

[167] Lauchlin Currie's memoirs, Chapter III: The New Deal, *Journal of Economic Studies,* 31 no. ¾ (2004), 205-6

[168] Currie, 206.

[169] For more on jobs: Barbara Ehrenreich, *Nickel and Dimed: On (Not) Getting by in America*, (New York: Metropolitan Books, 2001) and Barbara Ehrenreich, *Bait and Switch: The (Futile) Pursuit of the American Dream*, (New York: Metropolitan Books, 2005).

[170] Benjamin Hunnicutt, "The End of Shorter Hours," Labor History, XXV (Summer, 1984),373-404, http://www.uiowa.edu/~lsa/bkh/lla/eosh.htm .

[171] Michael D. Yates, *Longer Hours, Fewer Jobs*, (New York: Monthly Review Press, 1994), 66.

[172] Adam Smith, *An Inquiry Into The Nature And Causes Of The Wealth Of Nations*, Book I, Chapter VIII, "Of The Wages Of Labour."

[173] "Iron law of wages," Wikipedia, http://en.wikipedia.org/wiki/The_Iron_Law_of_Wages .

[174] John D. Whidden, *Ocean Life in the Old Sailing-Ship Days*, (Boston: Little, Brown, and Company, 1916), 217. Paul Zak, *Moral Markets*. See Sarah F. Brosnan, "Fairness and Other-Regarding Preferences in Nonhuman Primates," 81. Responding to inequity may act as an insurance policy to ensure future beneficial cooperative interactions.

[175] Requiring multiple independent unbiased audits and not just being snookered by advertising ploys is a minimum standard for any self-respecting stink. The most powerful voice the consumer has is his or her pocketbook. Corporations know it.

[176] Ben S. Bernanke, *Essays on the Great Depression*, (Princeton: Princeton University Press, 2000), xii.

[177] Bernanke, 32.

[178] Bernanke, 85-86.

[179] Bernanke, 207.

[180] Bernanke, 253.

[181] "Price elasticity of demand," Wikipedia, http://en.wikipedia.org/wiki/Price_elasticity_of_demand . Paul S. Samuelson and William D. Nordhaus, *Economics*, fifteenth edition, (New York: McGraw-Hill, 1995), 82.

[182] Note "a recession may systematically wipe out the most elastic portion of demand, which further contributes towards reducing the volume gains from a price reduction (Okun, 1981; Stiglitz, 1984; Field and Pagoulatos, 1997)." from Lasse B. Lien, "Recessions Across Industries: A Survey," Working Paper No 16/10, Institute for Research in Economics and Business Administration (SNF).

[183] Lien, above.

[184] Paul Krugman, "Would cutting the minimum wage raise employment?," *New York Times*, December 16, 2009, http://krugman.blogs.nytimes.com/2009/12/16/would-cutting-the-minimum-wage-raise-employment/ .

[185] "Agriculture in the United States," Wikipedia, http://en.wikipedia.org/wiki/Agriculture_in_the_United_States .

[186] Stewart Lansley, *The Cost of Inequality: Why Economic Equality is Essential for Recovery,* Chapter 5, p. 107, Kindle locations 1751-80: As one analyst remarked: "When I talk to the corporate managers of large German and Japanese companies, they speak of products, quality, customers and costs. They assume that if they produce innovation, attractive high quality products at a competitive cost, they will do well and be profitable. With UK

and US managers, the opposite applies. Many of them seem to be a million miles away from the real [production] business." And, p. 102, locations 1672-81: "[Billionaires] have become billionaires not by the patient route of creating and building new successful companies, but, like most rich financiers, by trading in existing companies."

[187] See: Lansley, especially Chapter 3, Kindle location 1078 (p.64) onward

[188] Barry Bluestone, Bennett Harrison, *The Deindustrialization of America: Plant Closings, Community Abandonment, and the Dismantling of Basic Industry*, (New York: Basic Books, 1982), 6.

[189] Bluestone and Harrison, 8.

[190] Ferguson, *Predator Nation*, 290.

[191] Ferguson, 287.

[192] "Creative destruction," Wikipedia, http://en.wikipedia.org/wiki/Creative_destruction .

[193] Bluestone and Harrison, 20; Joseph A. Schumpeter, *Capitalism, Socialism, and Democracy*, (New York: HarperPerennial, 1976), 61.

[194] Developed from: Table 283. "Master's degrees conferred by degree-granting institutions, by field of study: Selected years, 1970-71 through 2008-09," http://nces.ed.gov/programs/digest/d10/tables/xls/tabn283.xls ; Separately, the concentration of STEM graduates (roughly analogous to Core Production, but not the same as) in the U.S. is low relative to other nations: OECD, Education at a Glance 2011, "The number of STEM graduates in relation to total employment of persons aged 25-34 is relatively low in the United States (2009)," http://www.oecd.org/dataoecd/22/33/50638736.xlsx .

[195] Brian Vastag, "U.S. pushes for more scientists, but the jobs aren't there," *The Washington Post*, July 7, 2012, http://www.washingtonpost.com/national/health-science/us-pushes-for-more-scientists-but-the-jobs-arent-there/2012/07/07/gJQAZJpQUW_story.html .

[196] "Creative accounting," Wikipedia, http://en.wikipedia.org/wiki/Creative_accounting .

[197] Ignacio de la Torre, *Creative Accounting Exposed*, (New York: Palgrave Macmillan, 2009), 139, 110-118, 17.

[198] Bluestone and Harrison, 128-9.

[199] Abraham J. Briloff, *Unaccountable Accounting*, (New York: Harper & Row, Publishers, 1972), 350.

[200] Chris Isidore, "Bernanke's bucks: Fed chair nominee lists no individual stock holdings, modest assets outside of retirement account." CNN/Money, October 26, 2005.

[201] "Shadow banking system" Wikipedia, http://en.wikipedia.org/wiki/Shadow_banking . Christopher Hayes indicated in *Twilight of the Elites*, p. 128, that at the time of the 2008 Calamity, "the shadow banking system was almost twice as large as the regulated, visible, traditional banking system."

[202] This phrase is found in the old English property law case, Vernon v Bethell (1762) 28 ER 838, according to Lord Henley LC.

[203] "Second Bill of Rights," Wikipedia, http://en.wikipedia.org/wiki/Second_bill_of_rights .

[204] Stiglitz, *The Price of Inequality*, 245. Similarly the complete chapter, "A Macroeconomic Policy By and For the 1 Percent" focuses on the disproportionate advantage granted to the rich.

[205] Stiglitz, 244.

[206] Stiglitz, 244.

[207] Following graphs based on: *Fiscal Year 2013 Historical Tables, Budget of the U.S. Government*, Office of Management and Budget, 24-25, http://www.whitehouse.gov/sites/default/files/omb/budget/fy2013/assets/hist.pdf .

[208] Lauchlin Currie, "The 'Multiplier' in Economic Literature," *Journal of Economic Studies*, Vol. 10 Iss: 3,(1983), 42-48.

[209] Paul A. Samuelson and William D. Nordhaus, *Economics*, Eighteenth Edition, (Boston: McGraw Hill,2005), 496.

[210] Note that the table uses medians, not averages. This is deliberate. The intention is to focus on the middle of the road outcome. Thus, when comparing the 1980s with FDR, look carefully at the dates and whether the comparison is based on medians or averages. On page 272 the reference is to FDR's 1933-1939 average.

[211] Note that predominantly GDP per capita (instead of GDP alone) is used here for multiplier analysis. Using this standard is desirable for analysis in a time series or between nations, where population changes can come into play.

[212] "Heart rate variability," Wikipedia, http://en.wikipedia.org/wiki/Heart_rate_variability ; "Autonomic Nervous System," Wikipedia, http://en.wikipedia.org/wiki/Autonomic_nervous_system ; "Beta blocker," Wikipedia, http://en.wikipedia.org/wiki/Beta_blocker .
To hear music based on heart rate variability listen to Zach Davids, "Heartsongs," Audio CD (Ivory Moon Records, December 1, 1995).

[213] Laura Feiveson, "Seven Questions about Income Inequality," *IMF Research Bulletin*, Volume 13, Number 2 June 2012, Figure 2: Trends in Income Inequality in OECD Countries, Mid-1980s to Mid-2000s, p.7, www.imf.org/researchbulletin , http://www.imf.org/External/Pubs/FT/irb/2012/02/index.pdf .

[214] Further, many nations are tempted to measure economic success by the number of billionaires that they produce. Yet, nations can ill afford to have many of them, because as we have seen MAJ income tends to stagnate or to move southerly when billionaires proliferate. A vastly wealthy elite also poses an often un recognized operational problem for nations. Their super rich have a propensity to move wealth "offshore" where it cannot be taxed -- taxation lost to often underfunded governments. "Offshore" activity is usually hidden and difficult to measure. In" Wealth doesn't trickle down – it just floods offshore, research reveals," guardian.co.uk, July 21, 2012, (http://www.guardian.co.uk/business/2012/jul/21/offshore-wealth-global-economy-tax-havens) , Heather Stewart reports: "The world's super-rich have taken advantage of lax tax rules to siphon off at least $21 trillion, and possibly as much as $32tn, from their home countries and hide it abroad – a sum larger than the entire American economy." Her report relies on James S. Henry, "The Price of Offshore Revisited," http://www.taxjustice.net/cms/upload/pdf/Price_of_Offshore_Revisited_120722.pdf .

[215] "America the Beautiful," Wikipedia, http://en.wikipedia.org/wiki/America_the_Beautiful .

[216] Jeffrey D. Sachs, Andrew D. Mellinger and John L. Gallup, "The Geography of Poverty and Wealth," *Scientific American*, March 2001, 73.

[217] National Oceanic and Atmospheric Administration, "Over half of the American population lives within 50 miles of the coast," http://oceanservice.noaa.gov/facts/population.html . As NOAA states, "The narrow fringe

comprising 17 percent of the contiguous U.S. land area is home to more than half of the nation's population."

[218] "Parasitic worm," Wikipedia, http://en.wikipedia.org/wiki/Parasitic_worm .

[219] A small point: The first child is not always female. Instead of a generation being defined as the mother's age at birth of first offspring, if 26 years is defined as the mother's average age at the birth of the first female child, then this example holds.

[220] "List of countries by Failed States Index" Wikipedia, http://en.wikipedia.org/wiki/List_of_countries_by_Failed_States_Index . An informative interactive map is available at: http://www.foreignpolicy.com/failed_states_index_2012_interactive .

[221] The sort key for the table double weights present population growth and single weights trend-line expected population growth rates for 2030. The objective is not to predict a particular growth rate, but to illustrate the degree of movement that could occur if recent growth patterns are perpetuated.

[222] Leslie A. White, *The Evolution of Culture: The Development of Civilization to the Fall of Rome*, (New York: McGraw-Hill, 1959), 41.

[223] "Industrial Revolution" Wikipedia, http://en.wikipedia.org/wiki/First_Industrial_Revolution ; "Steam engine" Wikipedia, http://en.wikipedia.org/wiki/Steam_engine ; "Second Industrial Revolution" Wikipedia, http://en.wikipedia.org/wiki/Second_Industrial_Revolution ; "Watermill," Wikipedia, http://en.wikipedia.org/wiki/Watermill ; "Windmill" Wikipedia, http://en.wikipedia.org/wiki/Windmill .

[224] "White's Law," Wikipedia, http://en.wikipedia.org/wiki/White%27s_Law .

[225] "Olduvai theory" Wikipedia, http://en.wikipedia.org/wiki/Olduvai_theory ; Richard C. Duncan, "Peak Oil, Total Collapse, and the Road to the Olduvai," http://www.oilcrash.com/articles/arnett05.htm .

[226] "List of apologies by Pope John Paul II," Wikipedia, http://en.wikipedia.org/wiki/Apologies_by_pope_john_paul_ii .

[227] http://www.fundforpeace.org/global/library/cfsir1210-failedstatesindex2012-06p.pdf ;

http://www.foreignpolicy.com/failed_states_index_2012_interactive ;

http://www.fundforpeace.org/global/?q=fsi-grid2012 ;

http://www.fundforpeace.org/global/library/cfsis1201-fsi-spreadsheet177-public-06a.xls ;

http://www.fundforpeace.org/global/?q=cfsir1210 .

Note that I pared the list down from 179 nations to 151 matching nations in the Modernity Timeline. The key reason that the Modernity Timeline has fewer nations is because for some nations, income distribution data was unavailable.

[228] Note the points that are raised at about 11, 15, 17, and 21 minutes into the video. "Sir David Attenborough: People and Planet," http://www.youtube.com/watch?v=1sP291B7SCw .

[229] "America the Beautiful," Wikipedia, http://en.wikipedia.org/wiki/America_the_Beautiful .

[230] Matt McGrath, "Global weight gain more damaging than rising numbers," BBC, June 17, 2012.

[231] Sarah C Walpole, David Prieto-Merino, Phil Edwards, John Cleland, Gretchen Stevens, and Ian Roberts, "The weight of nations: an estimation of adult human biomass,"

BMC Public Health 2012, 12:439 doi:10.1186/1471-2458-12-439, June 18, 2012, http://www.biomedcentral.com/1471-2458/12/439 .

[232] Based on data in Jules Janick, "New Crops and the Search for New Food Resources," http://www.hort.purdue.edu/newcrop/proceedings1999/v4-104.html .

[233] "Cotton," Wikipedia, http://en.wikipedia.org/wiki/Cotton .

[234] An American football field is 100 yards long (goal line to goal line) and 53.33 yards wide. Observe that a yard is only slightly shorter than a meter and that a hectare is 100 x 100 meters. You can convert a hectare to square American football field by multiplying hectares by 0.836132404. By way of reference, a soccer field is 100 yards long and 60 yards wide.

[235] Jared Diamond, *Collapse*, 319-24.

[236] David Montgomery, *Dirt: The Erosion of Civilizations*, (University of California Press, 2007), 174, 182.

[237] Montgomery, 23.

[238] Tim De Chant, "Income inequality, as seen from space," May 24, 2012, http://persquaremile.com/2012/05/24/income-inequality-seen-from-space/ ; P. Zhu and Y. Zhang, "Demand for urban forests in United States cities" *Landscape and Urban Planning*, 84, No. 3-4, 2008, 293-300.

[239] Montgomery, 5.

[240] Montgomery, 119.

[241] Montgomery, 138.

[242] Based on http://data.worldbank.org/indicator/AG.LND.ARBL.HA.PC .

[243] Michael Wood, Iraq: The Cradle of Civilization (DVD, 1991), starting at the 10 minute point, http://www.youtube.com/watch?feature=player_embedded&v=NXohegE-IBY&list=PLFD498432C7808DF8# ; also see Montgomery, *Dirt*, 37-39 for Uruk's history of soil salinization and degradation.

[244] "Brown Bullion - What's Your Topsoil Worth?" http://www.mo.nrcs.usda.gov/news/pubs_download/brownbullion.html .

[245] Rigoberta Menchú, Nobel Peace Prize Laureate, 2 minutes into "When the Mountains Tremble," (Skylight Pictures, DVD, 1983).

[246] Wendell Berry's essay: "Conservation and Local Economy," 1991. Also see his YouTube appearances (e.g. YouTube - Wendell Berry a rare reading session), and start at 11 minutes: http://events.tvworldwide.com/Events/NEH2012JeffersonLecture.aspx?VID=events/neh/120423_NEH_Jefferson_Lecture_KennedyCtr.flv&Cap=events/neh/120423_NEH_Jefferson_Lecture_KennedyCtr.xml .

[247] Charles A.S. Hall, "Look What's Happening to Our Earth," *Bulletin of Atomic Scientists*, March 1975, 13. Also: J. F. Parr and S. B. Hornick, "Recent Developments in Alternative Agriculture in the United States," U.S Department of Agriculture, Agricultural Research Service, Beltsville, Maryland, http://www.infrc.or.jp/english/KNF_Data_Base_Web/PDF%20KNF%20Conf%20Data/C1-4-014.pdf .

[248] Dale Allen Pfeiffer, "Eating Fossil Fuels," http://www.fromthewilderness.com/free/ww3/100303_eating_oil.html

[249] Pfeiffer, "Eating Fossil Fuels," http://www.fromthewilderness.com/free/ww3/100303_eating_oil.html ; Mario Giampietro and David Pimentel, "The Tightening Conflict: Population, Energy Use, and the

Ecology of Agriculture," (1994), http://www.dieoff.com/page69.htm ; Richard Manning, "The oil we eat: Following the food chain back to Iraq," http://www.harpers.org/archive/2004 .

[250] Montgomery, *Dirt*, 200.

[251] Michael Pollan, *Omnivore's Dilemma*, (New York, Penguin Books, 2006), 123-273.

[252] Montgomery, *Dirt*, 181.

[253] Montgomery, 41-3.

[254] Montgomery, 142-3, 242.

[255] Montgomery, 80.

[256] Montgomery, 222-3

[257] Montgomery, 179.

[258] Montgomery, 93.

[259] "Marginalism," Wikipedia, http://en.wikipedia.org/wiki/Marginalism ; "Neoclassical economics," Wikipedia, http://en.wikipedia.org/wiki/Neoclassical_economics ; "Alfred Marshall," Wikipedia, http://en.wikipedia.org/wiki/Alfred_Marshall.

[260] Yes, iniquity (not inequity) is intentional here. We are referring to wickedness, evil, injustice, et cetera.

[261] Explicitly a high marginal taxation did not prevent innovation or high income earners. David Halberstam's *The Fifties*, (New York: Villard Books, 1993), 116-179, gives a fun read of business movers and shakers.

[262] Thomas E. Mann and Norman J. Ornstein, "Let's just say it: The Republicans are the problem," *The Washington Post*, April 27, 2012, http://www.washingtonpost.com/opinions/lets-just-say-it-the-republicans-are-the-problem/2012/04/27/gIQAxCVUlT_story.html .

[263] James K. Galbraith, *Inequality and Instability: A Study of the World Economy Just Before the Great Crisis*, 147.

[264] James Madison, *The Federalist No. 10, The Utility of the Union as a Safeguard Against Domestic Faction and Insurrection (continued),* Daily Advertiser, November 22, 1787, http://www.constitution.org/fed/federa10.htm .

[265] The original story by Dietrich Fischer goes like this:

A professor of management gave a lecture on time management. He filled a mason jar with a dozen fist-sized rocks, until no more would fit. He asked his students,

"Is this jar full?" and all shouted "Yes!"

Then he took some gravel from under the desk to fill the empty spaces and asked again, "Is it full now?"

Some said, "probably not."

He filled the space between the gravel with sand, and finally poured water into the jar to the brim.

"What is the lesson of this?" he asked.

A student answered, "No matter how full your schedule is, if you try really hard, you can always fit one more thing into it."

The professor replied, "No, the main lesson is that unless you put the big rocks in first, you'll never get them in at all."

What are the "big rocks" in our life?

[266] Just as this book was going to the printer, I saw this reference that may also interest students in the field: Leonard E. Burman, Robert J. Shiller, Gregory Leiserson, Jeffrey

Rohaly, "The Rising Tide Tax System: Indexing the Tax System for Changes in Inequality." (March 8, 2007), http://newfinancialorder.com/burman-nyu-030807.pdf .

[267] Even in highly profitable times, the financial sector, under its own roof, provides few jobs and often cuts those they do have. For example, in the UK Lansley observes, "Despite its growing importance in the economy, financial services has hardly generated any net new jobs in the last thirty years. ... [Their employment] fell by 17,000 during the boom years of 2000 to 2007." Stewart Lansley, *The Cost of Inequality: Why Economic Equality is Essential for Recovery*, (Gibson Square, January 19, 2012). Chapter 3, Figure 3.5, p. 73, Kindle locations 1125-1152.

[268] Eric A. Lord, Alan Lindsay Mackay, and Srinivasa Ranganathan, *New Geometries For New Materials*, (Cambridge University Press, 2006) ("a very simple user interface ... speed and power of the underlying C++ ... runs extremely fast"); "PowerBASIC," Wikipedia, http://en.wikipedia.org/wiki/Powerbasic .

[269] Anthony B. Atkinson, Thomas Piketty, and Emmanuel Saez, "Top Incomes in the Long Run of History," *Journal of Economic Literature*, 49, No. 1 (2011), see pages 29-33 for Census CPS failure to account for Top1%, http:www.aeaweb.org/articles.php?doi=10.1257/jel.49.1.3 .

[270] "Response by Thomas Piketty and Emmanuel Saez to: The Top 1% . . . of What? By Alan Reynolds," http://elsa.berkeley.edu/~saez/answer-WSJreynolds.pdf .

[271] Table sources: 1) U.S. Census Bureau: "Table H-2. Share of Aggregate Income Received by Each Fifth and Top 5 Percent of Households, All Races: 1967 to 2010"

http://www.census.gov/hhes/www/income/data/historical/household/2010/H02AR_2010.xls

2) "U.S. Census Bureau: Table F-2. Share of Aggregate Income Received by Each Fifth and Top 5 Percent of Families, All Races: 1947 to 2010"

http://www.census.gov/hhes/www/income/data/historical/families/2010/F02AR_2010.xls ;

3) Edward N. Wolff, "Recent Trends in Household Wealth in the United States: Rising Debt and the Middle-Class Squeeze—an Update to 2007, Working Paper No. 589," March 2010, Levy Economics Institute of Bard College, based on Survey of Consumer Finances, conducted by the Federal Reserve Board (SCF), "Table 2. The Size Distribution of Wealth and Income, 1983–2007",

http://www.levyinstitute.org/pubs/wp_589.pdf ;

4) The Piketty-Saez series are based on income tax statistics.

"Table A1: Top fractiles income shares (excluding capital gains) in the United States", "Table A3: Top fractiles income shares (including capital gains) in the United States;"

http://emlab.berkeley.edu/users/saez/piketty-saezOUP04US.pdf

http://elsa.berkeley.edu/~saez/TabFig2010.xls

5) Congressional Budget Office: Pre-Tax Income Shares All Households, by Household Income Category, 1979-2006, downloadable at the links in the following endnote.

[272] The Congressional Budget Office provides a well-balanced data that all serious students of United States income distribution need to be familiar with: http://www.cbo.gov/publications/collections/tax , Table: "Pre-Tax Income Shares All Households, by Household Income Category, 1979-2006" (downloaded 10/29/2011); http://www.cbo.gov/publications/collections/tax/2009 ; http://www.cbo.gov/publications/collections/taxdistribution.cfm .

[273] Atkinson, Piketty, and Saez, "Top Incomes in the Long Run of History," 29, footnote 18.

[274] The Jeanes income distribution data prior to 1913 was created from two trajectories: the trajectories from known wealth and income Top1% starting points in 1774 to their earliest available estimates during the early 1900s. Then the proportional variations about the wealth trajectory were applied to the Top1% income distribution trajectory. These were then, in each year, matched with lookup table distributions. During this period, the distribution transitions were mainly slow. There were several estimates of wealth distribution, but few of income. Thus, the piggybacking on wealth distribution characteristics seemed to form the most reliable income distribution estimates and, for lack of a better option, was necessary. Prior to the year 1900, I relied heavily on: Jeffery G. Williamson and Peter H. Lindert, "Long-Term Trends in American Wealth Inequality," Table 1.12, p. 53, in James D. Smith, *Modeling the Distribution and Intergenerational Transmission of Wealth*, (Chicago: The University of Chicago Press, 1980).

[275] The United Nations University's WIID2C.xls, not yet updated since May 2008, http://www.wider.unu.edu/research/Database/en_GB/wiid/ .

[276] Jason Zweig, "Polishing the Dimon Principle," *The Wall Street Journal*, May 12, 2012, B1.

Perhaps the humor may not appeal to you, but when we say "Endnotes" we mean notes at the "End." The Index can be found starting at page 368.

Made in the USA
Las Vegas, NV
10 April 2026

45187182R00239